Communication in an Information Age
CCI 150

Custom Edition

University of Tennessee

Compiled for Professor Lisa Gary

SAGE

Los Angeles | London | New Delhi
Singapore | Washington DC | Melbourne

For information:

SAGE Publications, Inc.
2455 Teller Road
Thousand Oaks, California 91320
E-mail: order@sagepub.com

SAGE Publications Ltd.
1 Oliver's Yard
55 City Road
London EC1Y 1SP
United Kingdom

SAGE Publications India Pvt. Ltd.
B 1/I 1 Mohan Cooperative Industrial Area
Mathura Road, New Delhi 110 044
India

SAGE Publications Asia-Pacific Pte. Ltd.
3 Church Street
#10-04 Samsung Hub
Singapore 049483

Copyright © 2016 by SAGE Publications, Inc.

ISBN 978-1-5063-5655-6

Web pdf ISBN 978-1-5063-5656-3

DISCLAIMER: Pagination has been changed from the original book for this custom publication. Therefore, cross-references will not be accurate.

Contents

Living in a Media World

Canadian astronaut Chris Hadfield helped bring space science down to earth during his time on the International Space Station with his extensive social media presence. His most famous was a music video he recorded of David Bowie's 1969 hit "Space Oddity."

EPA/NASA/Landov

If you were asked to name an astronaut, chances are your first choice would be Neil Armstrong, the first man on the moon. Or you might go with Sally Ride, the first American woman in space. But you are not likely to come up with anyone who has flown since the early 1980s.

The only recent space traveler you might mention is retired Canadian astronaut Chris Hadfield, who showed the world what a magical place space could be and what a beautiful place Earth is spread out below his home in the International Space Station (ISS). During his five-month stay at the ISS in 2013, he demonstrated how social media can be used to bypass the traditional Big Media and communicate directly with millions of people across the globe.[1]

Even before going up to the ISS, he had an active presence on Twitter and YouTube, but following his tweets and videos from a low Earth orbit, he became a social media superstar with close to one million followers on Twitter.

While Hadfield did a great job of building a name for himself through social media during his time in space, that wasn't his real goal. Instead, he was trying to draw a whole new generation of young people into being interested in space exploration. So along with his space demonstration videos, he shared images of Earth, life in space, and the ISS itself.

Not long after he arrived at the ISS, Hadfield got started creating short videos about life in space that the Canadian Space Agency posted to YouTube. These showed Hadfield demonstrating how to use a treadmill, wash his hands, or even give a haircut. Toward the end of his stay at the ISS, Hadfield had approximately 681,000 followers on Twitter and more than 1.2 million followers across all of his social media accounts. Using the Internet from the International Space Station can be a bit of a challenge as the astronauts' connection speed is similar to what terrestrials had using dial-up Internet in the 1990s.[2]

But the thing that would really make Hadfield a global celebrity was when his son Evan convinced him to record the first music video in space—a somewhat edited cover of David Bowie's 1968 hit "Space Oddity." This video brought him to the forefront of popular culture, with nearly 21 million views as of March 2014. Hadfield does his own signing and guitar playing in the video, which was produced by Evan. This wasn't Hadfield's first foray into music, having previously recorded an Earth/space video with the Canadian band Barenaked Ladies, and while on Earth he has played with an all-astronaut rock band. Evan slightly rewrote the lyrics to include references to the space station and the Soyuz

After studying this chapter, you will be able to:

1. Identify the four levels of communication.

2. Explain the difference between mass communication and mass media.

3. Define three contemporary models of mass communication.

4. Explain the historical evolution of the media world.

5. Define what media literacy is.

6. Describe the "Seven Secrets" about the mass media.

 Video 1.1: Watch some of Commander Hadfield's social media videos.

During the moon landing era of space exploration, all public communication by astronauts like Neil Armstrong and Buzz Aldrin was carefully controlled by NASA. Now, astronauts like International Space Station Commander Chris Hadfield can talk directly to the world through social media.

space capsule that would take Hadfield home, and he also gave the song a happy ending. (The astronaut dies in Bowie's version of the song.)

The evening before Hadfield was scheduled to return to Earth, the video was posted to YouTube. Hadfield himself had to do relatively little for the project. He had shot some video, recorded his vocal track, and strummed his guitar. So before he went to sleep on his last night in space, he logged onto YouTube. "I was shocked," Hadfield writes. "There had already been close to a million hits."[3] The next day after landing on Earth, he learned that it had reached more than 7 million views.

Hadfield's success with videos and other social media was not entirely self-made. His son Evan, whose specialty is social media marketing, helped his

Timeline

1800

1812 War of 1812 breaks out.
1835 Alexis de Tocqueville publishes *Democracy in America*.
1859 Charles Darwin publishes *On the Origin of Species*.
1861 U.S. Civil War begins.
1869 Transcontinental railroad is completed.
1879 Thomas Edison invents electric light bulb.
1898 Spanish-American War breaks out.

1900

1903 Orville and Wilbur Wright fly first airplane.
1905 Albert Einstein proposes his theory of relativity.

1910

1912 *Titanic* sinks.
1914 World War I begins.
1918 Worldwide influenza epidemic strikes.

1920

1920 Nineteenth Amendment passes, giving U.S. women the right to vote.
1929 U.S. stock market crashes, leading to the Great Depression.

1930

1933 Adolf Hitler is elected chancellor of Germany.
1939 World War II breaks out in Europe.

1940

1941 United States enters World War II.
1945 United States drops two atomic bombs on Japan.
1947 Pakistan and India gain independence from Britain.
1949 Communists establish People's Republic of China.

◄ **Pre-1800s** Word of mouth and letters are the only means of transmitting messages.
◄ **1450s** The first practical printing press is developed; printed material can be mass-produced.

1814 Steam-powered printing presses speed production of books and newspapers.
1844 Samuel Morse develops the telegraph; signals can be sent at a distance.
1887–1888 Emile Berliner develops the gramophone, which plays music on mass-produced discs.
1890s Nickelodeon movie theaters become popular.

1910 Thomas Edison (right) demonstrates first talking motion picture.

AP Photo

1939 Regularly scheduled television broadcasts begin in New York City.

AP Photo

father lose his "robotic" style of Twitter writing and cross-promoted his recordings, videos, and photos using a range of social media tools.

People your author's age are children of the space age. To us, the moon landing was a highlight of our childhood, not history. But now Commander Hadfield is bringing the space program to life for a new generation using interactive media that was barely in its infancy in 1969. For my generation, it was the heroic Neil Armstrong on television and the large-format photos from *Life* magazine announcing his historic first step on the surface of a globe that wasn't Earth. For my children, it's short messages, photos, and videos downloaded to a mobile phone or tablet from a permanent habit in space.

The story of how Chris Hadfield shared the wonder of space with people around the globe tells us much about what living in a media world is like. We have a lot of new social media channels that operate outside the rules of conventional journalism, and yet our so-called Big Media continue to dominate large segments of the business. We can get news as it happens from almost anywhere in the world if we only realize that it's available, and the distinctions between media audience members and media content creators are rapidly vanishing. ∎

> **"I was shocked. There had already been close to a million hits."**
>
> —Chris Hadfield

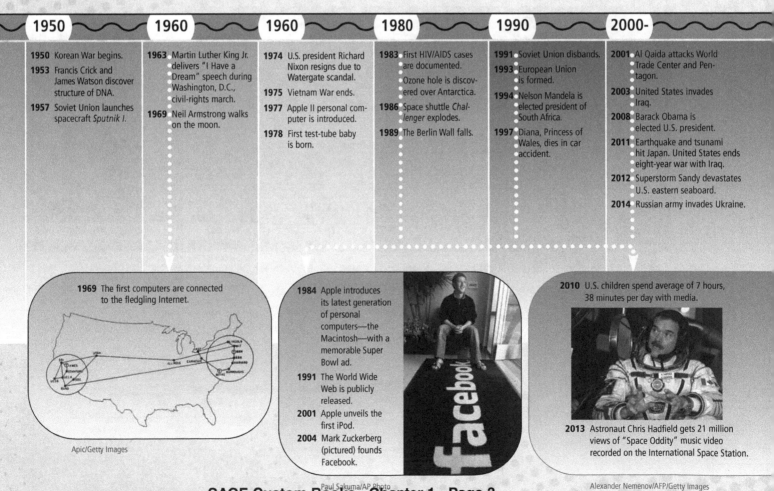

1950

1950 Korean War begins.

1953 Francis Crick and James Watson discover structure of DNA.

1957 Soviet Union launches spacecraft *Sputnik I*.

1960

1963 Martin Luther King Jr. delivers "I Have a Dream" speech during Washington, D.C., civil-rights march.

1969 Neil Armstrong walks on the moon.

1960

1974 U.S. president Richard Nixon resigns due to Watergate scandal.

1975 Vietnam War ends.

1977 Apple II personal computer is introduced.

1978 First test-tube baby is born.

1980

1983 First HIV/AIDS cases are documented.

Ozone hole is discovered over Antarctica.

1986 Space shuttle *Challenger* explodes.

1989 The Berlin Wall falls.

1990

1991 Soviet Union disbands.

1993 European Union is formed.

1994 Nelson Mandela is elected president of South Africa.

1997 Diana, Princess of Wales, dies in car accident.

2000-

2001 Al Qaida attacks World Trade Center and Pentagon.

2003 United States invades Iraq.

2008 Barack Obama is elected U.S. president.

2011 Earthquake and tsunami hit Japan. United States ends eight-year war with Iraq.

2012 Superstorm Sandy devastates U.S. eastern seaboard.

2014 Russian army invades Ukraine.

1969 The first computers are connected to the fledgling Internet.

Apic/Getty Images

1984 Apple introduces its latest generation of personal computers—the Macintosh—with a memorable Super Bowl ad.

1991 The World Wide Web is publicly released.

2001 Apple unveils the first iPod.

2004 Mark Zuckerberg (pictured) founds Facebook.

Paul Sakuma/AP Photo

2010 U.S. children spend average of 7 hours, 38 minutes per day with media.

2013 Astronaut Chris Hadfield gets 21 million views of "Space Oddity" music video recorded on the International Space Station.

Alexander Nemenov/AFP/Getty Images

Levels of Communication

As the flow of social media from Chris Hadfield on the International Space Station shows, we no longer rely just on conventional media to engage in the various levels of communication. During the Apollo era, astronauts spoke with the public through carefully controlled television, newspaper, and radio events; and while these big media are still significant, they are increasingly being supplemented by channels that allow people to engage directly with these otherworldly newsmakers.

A 2010 graduate of the University of Nebraska at Omaha, Charley Reed is now the university's media relations coordinator. As such, he communicates a lot, and that communication is often flowing through social media like Facebook, Twitter, WordPress, and Tumblr. He uses these outlets to stay in touch with friends and colleagues, keep up on the news, teach his media class, and engage in personal journal writing. "A regular day for me essentially begins and ends with some sort of social media," Charley says.

One of the first things I do when I get to work in the morning is check Facebook and Twitter to see what people are talking about. Knowing the day's trends helps me know how to pitch stories to Omaha's media outlets since many of them need help localizing national stories. I am definitely more of a Facebook user, though, since it's the closest to having a conversation. Twitter I check to see if anything new is happening that might pertain to the university because, anymore, news breaks on Twitter rather than in the paper or during the nightly news. I also use blogging sites like WordPress for the class I teach. That is where all of our class assignments are posted and where students go to find out any updates that might pertain to class. Tumblr is another site I use for personal writing that I want to share with others outside of work.[4]

When Charley is on social media, he's engaging in almost every possible level of communication, but before we try to analyze the levels of communication Charley is using, we need to define what communication is. Media scholar George Gerbner provides a simple definition: Communication is "social interaction through messages."[5] More plainly put, communication is how we interact with our entire world, whether through spoken words, written words, gestures, music, paintings, photographs, or dance. The important point is that communication is a *process*, not a static thing. Communication is an interaction that allows individuals, groups, and institutions to share ideas.

Media scholar and theorist Denis McQuail suggests that the various levels of communication can be viewed as a

---

communication: How we socially interact at a number of levels through messages.

Courtesy of Charley Reed.

University media relations coordinator Charley Reed handles his own communication with his classmates, friends, and colleagues through his Facebook page.

pyramid with a large base of intrapersonal communication where everyone is sending messages, building up to a peak of mass communication at which a relatively small number of organizations or individuals are transmitting messages (see Figure 1.1).[6]

Intrapersonal Communication

Communication at its most basic level is **intrapersonal communication**, which is really communication within the self. This is how we think and how we assign meaning to all the messages and events that surround our lives. It ranges from the simple act of smiling in response to the smell of a favorite food coming from the kitchen to the complex reaction to an unexpected proposal of marriage. Feedback, or the response from the receiver of the message, is constant because we are always reflecting on what we have done and how we will react. Intrapersonal communication is the most prevalent form of communication and is, therefore, at the base of the pyramid. When Charley debates with himself as to whether something he is posting on Facebook reflects positively on the university, he's engaging in intrapersonal communication.

Interpersonal Communication

The next level on the pyramid is **interpersonal communication**, or one-on-one communication: "The intentional or accidental transmission of information through verbal or nonverbal message systems to another human being."[7] Interpersonal communication can be a conversation with a friend or a hug that tells your mother you love her. Like communication with the self, interpersonal communication is continual when others are around because we constantly send out messages, even if those messages consist of nothing more than body language indicating that we want to be left alone.

Interpersonal communication provides many opportunities for feedback. Your friend nods, raises an eyebrow, touches you on the arm, or simply answers your question. Not all interpersonal communication is done face-to-face, however. A telephone conversation, an SMS text message, an e-mail, or even a greeting card can be interpersonal communication, though at a somewhat greater emotional distance than in a

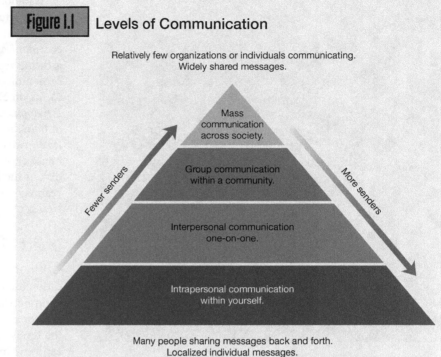

Figure 1.1 Levels of Communication

Relatively few organizations or individuals communicating. Widely shared messages.

Mass communication across society.

Group communication within a community.

Interpersonal communication one-on-one.

Intrapersonal communication within yourself.

Fewer senders

More senders

Many people sharing messages back and forth. Localized individual messages.

Source: Denis McQuail, *McQuail's Mass Communication Theory,* 6th ed. (London: SAGE Publications, 2010), 18. Reproduced by permission of Sage Publications. Copyright © Denis McQuail, 2005.

face-to-face conversation. When Charley sends a personal message over Facebook, sends an e-mail to an editor about a possible story, or talks to his roommate over breakfast, he's engaging in interpersonal communication.

Group Communication

Group communication is near the top of the pyramid and has reached a level of unequal communication in which one person is communicating with an audience of two or more people. Group communication often has a leader and is more public than interpersonal communication. In a small group—for example, a family at the dinner table or a coach with a basketball team—each individual has an opportunity to respond to the leader and is likely to do so. In a large group—such as a 350-student lecture section of a university class—each individual still has an opportunity to respond but is unlikely to do so. Other situations test the boundaries of group communication, such as a Paul McCartney concert at a baseball stadium. With the amplifiers and multiple video screens, there is a high level of communication technology but limited possibilities for audience members to provide direct feedback to the performers. However, there is still interaction between Sir Paul and the audience.

Questioning the Media

How many different ways have you engaged in interpersonal communication today? What techniques have you or your friends used to get messages (both verbal and nonverbal) across to each other? Do you prefer one technique over others? If so, why?

---

intrapersonal communication: Communication you have with yourself. How you assign meaning to the world around you.

interpersonal communication: Communication, either intentional or accidental, between two people. It can be verbal or nonverbal.

group communication: Communication in which one person is communicating with an audience of two or more people. The roles of communicator and audience can be changing constantly.

You no longer need a television set or cable/satellite account to watch video programming. Many people are turning to online streaming services like Netflix that they can view on their phone, tablet, or computer, as well as on a television set.

Charley engages in group communication when he participates in a class discussion, cheers at a hockey game, or leaves a status update on his Facebook page. For example, he once left an enthusiastic status update about the band Mastodon. His parents saw the update and bought him tickets to an upcoming Mastodon concert for his birthday.[8]

Mass Communication

Mass communication is the pinnacle of the communication pyramid; it is a society-wide communication process in which an individual or institution uses technology to send messages to a large, mixed audience, most of whose members are not known to the sender. Nationally broadcast speeches by politicians, stories about crime in the newspapers, and popular new novels are all forms of mass communication. These communications are fundamentally different from the forms described previously because the sender is separated in space, and possibly in time, from the receiver. Also, the audience is not really known to the communicator. When a communicator appears on television or writes an article for a newspaper, he or she doesn't know who will be listening or reading. What is more, the audience consists of many types of people. It might contain a young man in prison, an old woman in a nursing home, a child eating Cheerios for breakfast, or Charley as he's getting ready to go to the office. The message is communicated to all these people and to thousands or millions of others.[9]

Video 1.2: See footage from Paul McCartney's 2009 baseball stadium tour as well as the Beatles' 1965 tour.

Traditionally, mass communication has allowed only limited opportunities for feedback because the channels of communication are largely one way, but with the rise of interactive communication networks, the opportunities for feedback are growing rapidly. Charley consumes a wide range of mass communication during his day, including watching *House of Cards* on Netflix, watching the television series *Arrested Development* through Hulu, or reading DC Comics' reboot of *Batman*. You'll notice there's no traditional TV in Charley's media diet. Unless he's watching hockey at a friend's house or at a sports bar, all of his video comes to him via a disk or the Internet. "I got rid of cable and television four years ago," Charley says. "Anything I watch, I watch through Netflix or Hulu, on Amazon Prime, or on Blu-ray."[10]

A Mix of Levels

The distinctions among the various levels of communication are useful, but don't assume that every instance of communication can automatically be placed in one category or another. In reality, there are frequent crossovers in the levels of communication. Consider the Internet. You can share information with a friend via Snapchat. Through a Tumblr blog you can share your favorite images and videos. With a listserv, an employer can communicate with employees throughout the world. And through Web sites and podcasts, messages can go out to the entire world. The same is true of a newspaper, in which a classified ad can carry a proposal of marriage, a notice of a group meeting, or a political manifesto. When Charley goes out to dinner with friends, they cheer when the Stanley Cup hockey game being shown on the television gets exciting and talk about the game with each other, thus engaging in mass and group communication at the same time.

The purpose of this book is to help you better understand mass communication and the mass media. In the fifteen chapters of this book, we look at a variety of topics:

- The institutions that make up the media and how they function in and affect our society
- Who owns and controls the media business
- The media themselves, including books, magazines, newspapers, radio, recorded music, movies, television, and the Internet
- The industries that support the media, including advertising and public relations
- The laws and ethics that regulate and control the media
- The roles the media play in countries and cultures around the world

By the time you are finished, you will better understand what the media are, why they function as they do, and what roles they play in your life.

mass communication: When an individual or institution uses technology to send a message to a large, mixed audience, most of whose members are not known to the sender.

Elements of Mass Communication

Although people often use the terms *mass communication* and *mass media* interchangeably, they are significantly different concepts. Mass communication is a process, whereas the **mass media** are simply the technological tools used to transmit the messages of mass communication.[11] Earlier in this chapter we defined *mass communication* as a society-wide communication process in which an individual or institution uses technology to send messages to a large mixed audience, most of whose members are not known to the sender. Let's now take a closer look at all the players in the mass communication process and at several models that describe how these elements interact with each other.

The Players in the Mass Communication Process

There is an old way of describing mass communication known as the **Sender Message Channel Receiver (SMCR) or transmission model**. This transmission model does not do justice to the complexity of the mass communication process because it tends to portray mass communication as a largely one-directional flow of messages from the sender to the receiver, rather than as a complex interaction where senders and receivers are constantly changing places. But the model is still useful in helping to identify all the players we will be working with throughout this text.

The Sender. When critics talk about "the media" as a potent force, they are often talking about the ability of a few large corporations to control the messages that go out through the various channels of mass communication. These corporations, which are discussed in depth in Chapter 3, are the major senders in the mass communication process. They are the large, bureaucratic organizations that produce the complex messages we receive through the mass media, and they employ large numbers of people. If you look at the credits of a major movie, you'll see hundreds, if not thousands, of names listed. Even a relatively straightforward medium such as a newspaper requires a substantial staff of writers, editors, graphic artists, photographers, computer specialists, printers, truck drivers, delivery people, janitors, librarians, circulation clerks, accountants, advertising salespeople, business managers, and a publisher.

---

mass media: The technological tools, or channels, used to transmit the messages of mass communication.

Sender Message Channel Receiver (SMCR) or transmission model: A dated model that is still useful in identifying the players in the mass communication process.

bloggers: People who post their thoughts, typically with the most recent posts at the top of the page, on a regularly updated Web site.

As you may have already figured out, there are many other senders besides the major corporations. For example, although the majority of the most frequently visited Web sites are produced by large media organizations, the Internet has given rise to smaller, more intimate media without the accompanying structure and staff. For example, *Six Until Me*, one of the leading blogs for persons with diabetes, is operated by patient and diabetes advocate Kerri Morrone Sparling, assisted by one other person. *Six Until Me* started back in 2005 with a total of two readers: Kerri's mother and her then-boyfriend. By 2011, her blog was reaching more than 90,000 visitors a month.[12] You may have acted as a "sender," too, just as Charley does when he writes an occasional guest post to your textbook author's blog.

Mass communication has generally been thought of as one-on-many communication, with few senders and many receivers, in contrast to interpersonal communication, which involves roughly equal numbers of senders and receivers. Sociologist C. Wright Mills wrote that the real power of the mass media is that they can control what topics are being covered and how much attention they receive. The most significant change brought about by the media in the United States, he said, was that public communication became a matter of sending information to a large number of receivers rather than a dialogue between roughly equal numbers of senders and receivers.[13]

The balance of power between senders and receivers in the mass media has started to change in recent years, however, with the rise of bloggers as a force in the news business. **Bloggers** are people who post their thoughts on a regularly updated Web site. We got a big reminder of the importance of blogs on Thursday, June 28, 2012, when the U.S. Supreme Court ruled that the Affordable Care Act, otherwise known as Obamacare, was constitutional. Everyone in the news media knew that this story would be breaking at 10 a.m. on Thursday, June 28. The decision coming down was definitely not a surprise.

And yet . . .

Both CNN and Fox News initially got the story wrong. In their effort to be the first to break the story, both cable news networks initially reported that the court had overturned the individual mandate requirement that everyone purchase health insurance or pay a fine/tax because the court rejected the argument that this was justified by the commerce clause of the Constitution—except that Chief Justice John Roberts's opinion went on to say that the mandate could be justified under Congress's authority to levy taxes. And so . . . two of our biggest sources of breaking news got the story flat-out wrong. Meanwhile, a little blog that typically draws a few thousand readers a day, SCOTUSblog, was the authoritative news site that everyone turned to for immediate and accurate news about the decision. And on a day that several bigger Web sites had trouble staying online because of heavy

---

Web 1.1: Read why Kerri Sparling calls her blog *Six Until Me*.

broadcast ends and a new one airs the next day. Even though the message can be stored in the form of a computer file or videotape, it is generally replaced when something new comes along. The receiver's attention fades even if the physical item remains.

Production of mass communication messages is generally expensive. The average cost of producing a studio movie in 2007 was $70.8 million, and advertising it added $25.7 million, according to figures from the Motion Picture Association of America.[15] Thirty seconds of commercial time during the 2012 Super Bowl cost as much as $3.5 million. (That's $116,000 per *second*!)[16] Sponsors for the Brazilian broadcasts of the 2014 World Cup soccer tournament paid $75 million each to get their message out on Brazil's *Rede Globo*. That's roughly the same as 20 thirty-second Super Bowl spots.[17] But, again, if people do not seek to make money with their messages, they can reach a large audience through the Internet at a relatively low cost.

When news of the U.S. Supreme Court's decision on the constitutionality of the Affordable Health Act broke on June 28, 2012, competing cable news channels CNN and Fox News both got the story wrong. News consumers had to turn to the online SCOTUSblog to get an accurate report.

demand, SCOTUSblog had server capacity to spare despite drawing hundreds of times more traffic than normal.[14]

The Message. The **message** is the content being transmitted by the sender and reacted to by the receiver. Before a message can be transmitted, it must be encoded. **Encoding** requires at least two steps. First, the sender's ideas must be turned into a message: A script for a broadcast is drafted, a graphic is created, or a newspaper story is written. Then the message must be prepared for transmission: The script is taped and sent out over the air, the graphic is placed on a Web page, or the newspaper is printed.

Mass communication messages are transmitted rapidly to the receivers. Audience members can receive the message simultaneously, as they would in the case of a radio broadcast; at similar though not identical times, as in the case of a newspaper or magazine; or occasionally over an extended period, as in the case of a CD, movie, or video. In addition to being transmitted rapidly, mass communication messages are available to a wide audience. Mass communication messages also tend to be transient—here today and gone tomorrow. The newspapers and magazines are recycled, a new movie replaces the old at the theater, or a

What do all these messages mean? According to media scholar James Potter, the meaning of messages depends on who is receiving them and what kinds of media literacy skills the receivers can use to decode them. Potter writes that people with low levels of media literacy will look at the surface meanings in media content, whereas those with higher levels of media literacy can interpret messages from a wide range of perspectives with many choices of meanings.[18] For example, Jon Krakauer's book about the disaster that befell a group of Mount Everest climbers in 1996, *Into Thin Air*, can be read as a simple adventure story, an allegory of the battle between man and nature, or a study on obsession. (See box "Media Transformations: When Media Connect Us to the Most Remote Places on Earth.") Which of these interpretations is correct? Although *Into Thin Air* is most emphatically an adventure story, it also tells of Krakauer's struggle with the mountain and the weather, and it discusses why people are drawn to dangerous activities such as mountain climbing.

The Channel. The **channel** is the medium used to transmit the message. Recall that a mass medium is a technological tool. Think about a newspaper. It consists of black and colored ink printed on relatively low-quality paper. It

Web 1.2: Read how SCOTUSblog scooped both CNN and Fox News on coverage of the Obamacare Supreme Court decision.

Web 1.3: Get the latest on Super Bowl advertising and coverage.

message: The content being transmitted by the sender to the receiver.

encoding: The process of turning the sender's ideas into a message and preparing the message for transmission.

channel: The medium used to transmit the encoded message.

is portable, readily available, and cheap. An article can be clipped from the paper and placed in a pocket. A newspaper also provides local and regional news in greater depth than is possible with almost any other medium.[19]

Print media include books, magazines, newspapers, billboards, and posters. Audiovisual media include radio, sound recordings, broadcast television, cable and satellite television, and video recordings. Interactive media include the Web, social media, mobile media, and video games.

What about mobile phones, faxes, letters, and e-mail? Do they fit in as channels of mass communication? Although e-mail is not generally considered to be a mass medium, an unsolicited commercial e-mail, known as *spam,* could satisfy at least part of the definition of mass communication, since spam is distributed widely to a large, mixed, and anonymous audience. News reports and sports scores arriving via SMS text messages on the small screen on a mobile phone would also seem to qualify. But our phone calls and e-mails from friends are generally considered to be interpersonal communications unless we post them to a blog or social media site for everyone to see.

The nature of the channel used to transmit a message can change the meaning of the message. Take, for example, the daily news. On the radio, the news is something happening in the background; read in a newspaper, news is something that demands your undivided attention. But can you call information news when it is presented by comedian Jon Stewart on *The Daily Show*? A dramatic speech given by a great orator on television will likely be much more influential than a transcript of the speech that's published on the Internet the next day.

The Receiver. The receiver is the audience for the mass communication message—that is, the people who are receiving and decoding the message. Decoding is the process of translating a signal from a mass medium into a form that

German soccer fans joined the world-wide television audience for the 2014 World Cup played in Brazil. The telecasts delivered huge audiences for the tournament's advertisers.

Mehmet Kaman/Anadolu Agency/Getty Images

receiver: The audience for the mass communication message.

decoding: The process of translating a signal from a mass medium into a form that the receiver can understand and then interpreting the meaning of the message itself.

heterogeneous audience: An audience made up of a mix of people who differ in age, sex, income, education, ethnicity, race, religion, and other characteristics.

noise: Interference with the transmission of a message. This can take the form of semantic, mechanical, or environmental noise.

the receiver can understand. The term *mass* can have at least two meanings when referring to audiences. In one sense, the term refers to the mix of ordinary people who receive the message—"the masses." In the second sense, the term refers to the size of the audience. The concept of mass, or popular, taste is an old one, but the concept of a massive, or large, audience developed in the twentieth century. The mass audiences reading major newspapers, listening to the radio, watching network television, or going to the movies are much larger than the crowds of people that gather for events such as political rallies or rock concerts. They form a heterogeneous audience—an audience made up of a mix of people who differ in age, sex, income, education, ethnicity, race, religion, and other characteristics. As with size, heterogeneity is a matter of degree. A small-town radio station is likely to reach an audience whose members are more similar than those listening to a station in a major urban area.

Receivers don't always get a clear message from the sender, however. Several types of noise can interfere with the delivery of the message. There is semantic noise, when the receiver does not understand the meaning of the message, such as when you can't understand the lyrics on a Latin music channel because you don't speak Spanish; mechanical noise when the channel has trouble transmitting the message, such as when a thunderstorm produces too much static for you to hear the score of a baseball game being broadcast on an AM radio station; and environmental noise, which occurs when the action and sounds surrounding the receiver interfere with the reception

 Video 1.3: Experience the difference between watching and reading two speeches.

When Media Connect Us to the Most Remote Places on Earth

Jon Krakauer was out of his tent and on his way to the top of Mount Everest several hours before dawn on Friday, May 10, 1996. The journalist was just one of dozens of climbers trying to reach the summit at 29,028 feet. Climbing Everest had been a lifelong dream for Krakauer, and an assignment for *Outside* magazine had made it possible.

Krakauer reached the summit at 1:12 p.m., and after a brief stay at the top, he started on the long way back down. During his descent, a surprise snowstorm rolled in. At 6:45 p.m., just as it was getting dark, Krakauer stumbled back into camp and collapsed in his tent. Others in his party weren't so fortunate. By the time the storm cleared, eight of the climbers on the world's tallest mountain were dead, including guides Rob Hall and Scott Fischer.

Despite Mount Everest's remote location on the border between Nepal and Tibet, the world watched the tragedy unfold through Web sites, newspapers, television, magazines, and eventually even a major motion picture. In May of each year, Everest Base Camp becomes media central as climbers attempt to reach the summit and journalists show up to cover them, in part because of the high degree of risk involved. During a typical year, six to ten people will die on the mountain.[20]

To complete his assignment of researching and writing a story about the commercialization of Mount Everest, Krakauer climbed the peak as a paying customer of Hall. Krakauer was not the only journalist on the mountain the day of the snowstorm. Climber Sandy Hill Pittman was sending daily dispatches to NBC's Web site via satellite phone and yak courier; reporter Jane Bromet of *Outside Online,* a Web magazine, was covering the climb from Everest Base Camp; a South African newspaper was sponsoring another expedition; and an IMAX film crew was shooting a documentary about climbing the peak. The IMAX team, led by filmmaker and professional climber David Breashears, produced the movie *Everest,* which became the most successful large-format IMAX film ever and one of the top films of 1997.

Krakauer says that because of the media coverage, thousands of people around

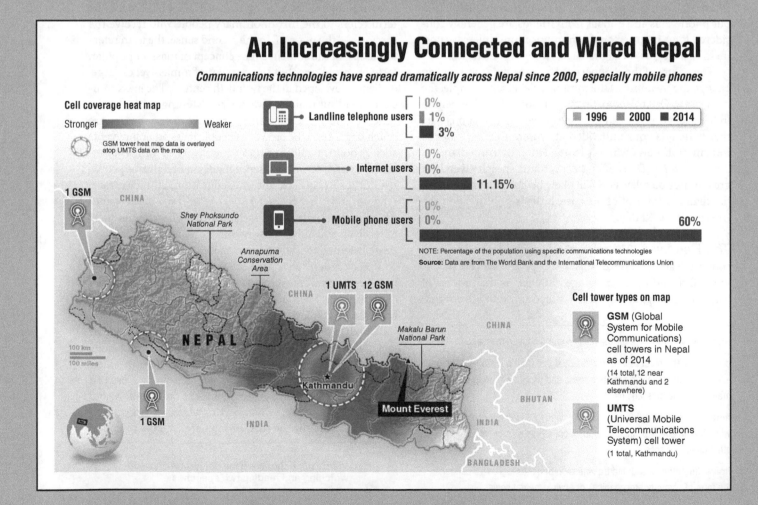

An Increasingly Connected and Wired Nepal

Communications technologies have spread dramatically across Nepal since 2000, especially mobile phones

Cell coverage heat map
Stronger ▬▬▬▬ Weaker

GSM tower heat map data is overlayed atop UMTS data on the map

| | 1996 | 2000 | 2014 |

Landline telephone users
- 0%
- 1%
- 3%

Internet users
- 0%
- 0%
- 11.15%

Mobile phone users
- 0%
- 0%
- 60%

NOTE: Percentage of the population using specific communications technologies
Source: Data are from The World Bank and the International Telecommunications Union

1 GSM
CHINA
Shey Phoksundo National Park
Annapurna Conservation Area
1 UMTS   12 GSM
Makalu Barun National Park
CHINA
NEPAL
100 km
100 miles
Kathmandu
Mount Everest
BHUTAN
1 GSM
INDIA
BANGLADESH

Cell tower types on map

GSM (Global System for Mobile Communications) cell towers in Nepal as of 2014
(14 total, 12 near Kathmandu and 2 elsewhere)

UMTS (Universal Mobile Telecommunications System) cell tower
(1 total, Kathmandu)

the world knew more about what was happening on the mountain than did the people who were climbing: "A teammate might call home on a satellite phone, for instance, and learn what the South Africans were doing at Camp Two from a spouse in New Zealand or Michigan who'd been surfing the World Wide Web."[21]

In the spring of 2014, an even worse disaster hit Everest, when a giant overhanging chunk of ice broke off and crashed down through a group of Nepalese workers climbing the Khumbu Icefall, killing 16 of them. Although there was a substantial media presence on Everest during the 1994 storm that Krakauer chronicled, climbers were even more connected to the outside world by the time of the 2014 disaster. From 2006 to 2009, famed Everest commercial guide Russell Brice had been featured in three seasons of a cable television series that documented attempts by his climbers to summit Everest. News from the 1996 disaster had to flow out via satellite phones. But by 2014, cell service, including 3G and 4G data service, was available from both base camp and the summit.[22] The Discovery Channel, which had aired Brice's Everest climbing series, had been planning to broadcast live Joby Ogwyn's attempt to summit Everest and then jump off the top of the mountain and fly down using a wing suit. But they canceled the show following the tragedy.[23] And as news of the 2014 disaster unfolded, legacy news channels such as the *Washington Post* were relying on bloggers such as climber Alan Arnette to relay the flood of news coming from the climbers, guides, and other bloggers at Everest.[24]

Media Transformations Questions

- **HOW** is a remote location like Everest changed when we have easy media access to it?

- **WHY** are people drawn to remote stories of adventure and danger from places like Everest that they are unlikely to ever visit?

- **HOW** has your life been changed by the fact that you have media around you constantly? Do you ever deliberately try to take time off from the media and communication technology?

 Web 1.4: Read more on media access to Everest climbing and disasters.

of the message, such as when your roommate's loud stereo keeps you from concentrating on your introduction to mass communication textbook.

The receivers of a mass communication message have traditionally been seen as an **anonymous audience**. This means that the sender does not personally know all, or even most, of the people receiving the message. This doesn't mean that the audience consists of isolated people who have no connection to anyone else; audience members simply don't expect the sender to know who they are. But with the increasing number of channels available for audience members to send feedback to the senders—through the Web, social media, e-mail, faxes, text messages, and phone calls—audience members typically on the receiving end are becoming senders themselves and are becoming better and better known to the original senders. Sometimes, in the case of reality TV programs such as *The Voice*, audience members become active participants by voting on who should advance to the next level of the competition.

Contemporary Models of Mass Communication

Though the transmission model (SMCR) is useful for laying out the various elements of the mass communication process, it does not explain how mass communication works in our lives. It focuses primarily on the process of transmitting messages largely from the point

---

anonymous audience: An audience the sender does not personally know. These are not anonymous, isolated people who have no connection to anyone else; they simply are anonymous in their audience status.

Reuters/Jim Bourg

Members of the IMAX expedition filming the documentary *Everest* reach the summit after abandoning their first summit attempt in order to help rescue other climbers.

Table 1.1 — Mass Communication Models

Models	Orientation of Sender	Orientation of Receiver
Transmission Model	Transfer of meaning	Cognitive processing
Ritual Model	Performance	Shared experience
Publicity Model	Competitive display	Attention-giving spectatorship
Reception Model	Preferential encoding	Differential decoding/ construction of meaning

Source: Denis McQuail, *McQuail's Mass Communication Theory*, 6th ed. (London: SAGE Publications, 2010). Reproduced by permission of SAGE Publications. Copyright © Denis McQuail, 2005.

of view of a sender trying to have an effect on the receiver. Media scholar Denis McQuail lays out three contemporary models that help us answer three different questions about the nature of mass communication[25] (see Table 1.1):

Ritual Model. Whereas the transmission model looks at how a message is sent, the ritual model puts audience members at the center of the equation. The **ritual model** looks at how and why audience members (receivers) consume media messages. This model suggests that we watch a program such as *The Voice* not so much to learn about aspiring singers or to receive advertising messages, but rather to interact in a shared ritual with family and friends. This ritual is then extended through television to other groups of people all across the United States. Media consumption thus goes beyond simply delivering messages and becomes a shared experience that brings us together as a people. For example, when news broke that Osama bin Laden had been killed on May 1, 2011, Twitter set what was then a record for sustained number of tweets being sent, with an average of 3,440 tweets per second between 10:45 p.m. and 12:30 a.m. Eastern Time. The tweeting peaked at 11 p.m. ET with 5,106 tweets per second. Audience members

Questioning the Media

Are you a media multitasker? Do you watch a single program from beginning to end, flip from channel to channel looking for something interesting, or watch two shows at once? Do you go online to chat about the show as you watch it? Could you even watch a single show from beginning to end without any other media? How does media multitasking enhance your experience?

Web 1.5: Dealing with FCC decency rules in the years since Janet Jackson's wardrobe malfunction.

were obviously not just passively watching and reading the news; they were actively responding to it.[26]

Publicity Model. Sometimes media messages are not trying to convey specific information as much as they are trying to draw attention to a particular person, group, or concept. According to the **publicity model**, the mere fact that a topic is covered by the media can make the topic important, regardless of what is said about it. For example, when Janet Jackson displayed her breast for 9/16ths of a second during the 2004 Super Bowl, there were all sorts of charges that broadcast network CBS was lowering the moral standards of America's young people. The major effect of Jackson's stunt was that the Federal Communications Commission (FCC) adopted increasingly strict rules on broadcast decency. As a result, at least twenty ABC affiliates refused to air the World War II movie *Saving Private Ryan* the following November for fear that they would be fined for all the bad language contained in the movie. Concerns about changing television standards had existed for several years prior to Jackson flashing Super Bowl viewers, but the attention Jackson brought to the issue put broadcast decency in the limelight.[27]

Reception Model. The **reception model** moves us out of the realm of social science analysis and into the world of critical theory. Instead of looking at how messages affect audiences or are used by the senders or receivers, the reception model looks at how audience members derive and create meaning out of media content. Rather than seeing content as having an intended, fixed meaning, the reception model says that each receiver decodes the message based on his or her own unique experiences, feelings, and beliefs. You can take a single news story and show it to liberal and conservative observers, and both will claim that it is biased against their point of view. In fact, a 1982 study showed the more that journalists tried to present multiple sides of an issue, the more partisans on either side of the issue viewed the story as biased.[28]

■■■■■■■■■■■■■■■■■■■■

Evolution of the Media World 🌐

Where did our media world come from? Is it just a product of the late twentieth century with its constant flow of

ritual model: A model of the mass communication process that treats media use as an interactive ritual engaged in by audience members. It looks at how and why audience members (receivers) consume media messages.

publicity model: A model of the mass communication process that looks at how media attention can make a person, concept, or thing become important, regardless of what is said about it.

reception model: A critical theory model of the mass communication process that looks at how audience members derive and create meaning out of media content as they decode the messages.

Can Television Take Anything Seriously?

In his book *Amusing Ourselves to Death,* media scholar Neil Postman argues that the primary effect of television is that it changes how people see the world; that is, with television, people start viewing everything as entertainment. Young people get their news in a comedy format, watching *The Daily Show* the same way they watch MTV. They learn about politics on the same channel that shows a professional football game.[1]

In an interview with Robert Nelson for the Civic Arts Review, Postman described the major point of *Amusing Ourselves to Death:*

Television always recreates the world to some extent in its own image by selecting parts of that world and editing those parts. So a television news show is a kind of symbolic creation and construction made by news directors and camera crews. . . .

Americans turn to television not only for their light entertainment but for their news, their weather, their politics, their religion, their history, all of which may be said to be their furious entertainment. What I'm talking about is television's preemption of our culture's most serious business. It is one thing to say that TV presents us with entertaining subject matter. It is quite another to say that on TV all subject matter is presented as entertaining and it is in that sense that TV can bring ruin to any intelligent understanding of public affairs. . . .

And stranger still is the fact that commercials may appear anywhere in a news story, before, after, or in the middle, so that all events are rendered essentially trivial, that is to say, all events are treated as a source of public entertainment. How serious can an earthquake in Mexico be or a hijacking in Beirut, if it is shown to us prefaced by a happy United Airlines commercial and summarized by a Calvin Klein jeans commercial? Indeed, TV newscasters have added to our grammar a new part of speech altogether. What may be called the

"now this" conjunction. "Now this" is a conjunction that does not connect two things but does the opposite. It disconnects. When newscasters say, "Now this," they mean to indicate that what you have just heard or seen has no relevance to what you are about to hear or see. There is no murder so brutal, no political blunder so costly, no bombing so devastating that it cannot be erased from our minds by a newscaster saying, "Now this." The newscaster means that you have thought long enough on the matter, let's say 45 seconds, that you must not be morbidly preoccupied with it, let us say for 90 seconds, and that you must now give your attention to a commercial. Such a situation in my view is not news. And in my opinion it accounts for the fact that Americans are among the most ill informed people in the Western world.[2]

WHO is the source?

Neil Postman (1931–2003), a prominent American educator, media theorist, and cultural critic, founded the media ecology program at New York University (NYU) and chaired the NYU Department of Culture and Communication. Postman wrote eighteen books and more than 200 magazine and newspaper articles for such periodicals as the *New York Times Magazine, Atlantic Monthly, Harper's,* and the *Washington Post.* He also edited the journal *ETC: A Review of General Semantics* and was on the editorial board of the *Nation.*

WHAT is he saying?

Postman argues that the primary effect of television is that it changes how people see the world; that is, with television, people start viewing everything as entertainment. In comparison, think about your own viewing habits. Do you watch the news the same way you watch MTV? Or learn about politics on the same channel that shows *Survivor?* Or see news about the war in Iraq, followed by a commercial for Domino's Pizza?

WHAT kind of evidence does the book provide?

What kind of data does Postman provide to support his arguments? What kind of evidence is needed to bolster these claims? Is there evidence that disputes his claims? How do you think Postman's background is likely to have shaped his view of television?

HOW do you or your classmates react to Postman's arguments?

What does the title *Amusing Ourselves to Death* mean to you? Do you feel that television trivializes important issues or makes them more palatable? Have you noticed similar effects in yourself as described by Postman? Do you notice differences in how news anchors make the transition from news to commercials and back again? Are the stories before and after the break any different from stories during the rest of the newscast?

DOES it all add up?

Do you believe that Postman's arguments are true today? In a study conducted in 2000, researchers found that 75 percent of television viewers under the age of thirty watched the news with the remote in their hands, ready to change channels if they got bored for a moment or two. Do you think that the data from this study support Postman's claims? Why or why not? Think back to when singer Michael Jackson died in 2009 and the cable news networks covered virtually nothing else for days on end. Do you think that Jackson's death was newsworthy enough to merit the coverage it received? Or were the cable news channels just trying to entertain their viewers?

---

[1]Neil Postman, *Amusing Ourselves to Death: Public Discourse in the Age of Show Business* (New York: Penguin Books, 1985).

[2]Robert Nelson, "Television and the Public Decline of Public Discourse," *Civic Arts Review,* vol. 3 (1990): 1. Excerpt used with permission.

 Video 1.4: Neil Postman talks about his book *Amusing Ourselves to Death.*

print and electronic messages? Not really. The world of interconnected and overlapping communication networks that surrounds us has been evolving for hundreds of years. Before the advent of the mass media, people interacted primarily face-to-face. Most of the time, they interacted only with people like themselves and had little contact with the outside world. But people gradually created communication networks that used first interpersonal channels, then print media, electronic media, and, most recently, interactive media. This section examines how various communication networks have grown over the centuries to form the media world in which we now live.

Before Print: Pre–Mass Media Communication Networks

The first major communication network in the Western world predates the mass media and was developed by the Roman Catholic Church in the twelfth, thirteenth, and fourteenth centuries. During that period, messages flowed from the Vatican in Italy through the cardinals and bishops to priests in cathedrals and villages throughout Europe and finally to congregations through sermons from the pulpit.[29]

Print: Arrival of the Book

The first major expansion in communication beyond the Church was the development of the printing press—in particular, the invention of movable type in the 1450s—and the subsequent mass production of printed materials. Mass printing made it possible for major social changes, such as the Protestant Reformation, to spread from their country of origin to the rest of Europe and the world beyond.

Although the printing press allowed for the mass production of information, printing was still relatively slow, and publications remained fairly expensive. The addition of steam power to the printing press in 1814 dramatically increased the rate at which printed material could be reproduced.

Electronic Networks: Telegraph, Gramophone, Radio, Movies, and Television

The advent of electronic communication made the media world much more complex. This type of communication began in 1844 with the opening of the first telegraph line from Baltimore, Maryland, to Washington, D.C. In 1866, telegraph cables spanned the Atlantic Ocean, overcoming a seemingly insurmountable barrier that had long hindered transoceanic communication. Instead of sending a message on a two-week journey by boat across

By the 1880s, telegraph wires criss-crossed the New York City skyline, sending messages rapidly across the city, the country, and around the world.

the ocean and waiting for a reply to come back the same way, two people on opposite sides of the ocean could carry on a dialogue via telegraph.

In the 1880s, Emile Berliner invented the gramophone, or phonograph, which played mass-produced discs containing about three minutes of music. Just as printed books made possible the storage and spread of ideas, so the gramophone allowed musical performances to be captured and reproduced.

The invention of radio in the late nineteenth century freed electronic communication from the limits imposed on it by telegraph wires. Messages could come into the home at any time and at almost no cost to the receiver. All that was needed was a radio set to receive an endless variety of cultural content, news, and other programming.

Movies were first shown at nickelodeon theaters in the late 1890s and early 1900s and were produced by an entertainment industry that distributed films worldwide. Young couples on a date in London, Ohio, and London, England, could see the same movie, copy the same styles of dress,

Web 1.6: Read more on the first transatlantic telegraph cable.

and perhaps even practice the same kisses they saw in the movie. Due to radio and the movies, the media world became a shared entertainment culture produced for profit by major media corporations.

In 1939, patrons in New York's neighborhood taverns no longer had to settle for radio broadcasts of Yankees games being played at the Polo Grounds. Instead, a small black-and-white television set located on a pedestal behind the bar showed a faint, flickering image of the game. After a series of delays caused by World War II, television surpassed radio in popularity. It also became a lightning rod for controversy as people stayed home to watch whatever images it would deliver.

The Internet: Interactive Communication

After several decades of television, people had gotten used to the idea that news, information, and entertainment could be delivered almost magically into their homes, although they could do little to control the content of this medium other than change channels. Then a new medium emerged, one that made senders and receivers readily interchangeable. The Internet became a full-fledged mass communication network in the 1990s (though many people were unaware that the first nodes of this new medium were being linked together as far back as 1969). Rather than simply making it easier for individuals and organizations to send messages to a mass audience, the new computer networks were designed for two-way communication. Audience members were becoming message providers themselves.

The Internet's interactivity was the culmination of a trend toward giving audience members new control over their media. The growth of cable and satellite television, along with the videocassette recorder (VCR), had already given viewers more choices and more control, and the remote control allowed them to choose among dozens of channels without leaving their chairs.

The implications of interactivity are significant. Whereas the commercial media have come to be controlled by a smaller and smaller number of large corporations (see Chapter 3), an important channel of mass communication is open to ordinary people in ways that were never before possible. With a trivial investment in a computer and an Internet connection, individuals can grab the spotlight with news and entertainment on the World Wide Web.

Consider the example of artist Danielle Corsetto, creator of the popular Web comic *Girls With Slingshots*. Her comic started when she was in high school under the name *Hazelnuts*, but she took it online in October 2004 when fans of her sketches asked her when she was going to start publishing her comic. Corsetto explained to the *Frederick News-Post* that *Girls With Slingshots* (or GWS) is a slice-of-life comic that tells the story of "sour, grumpy girl" Hazel and her best friend, Jamie, a "bubbly girl who is very comfortable with herself."[30] One of the fascinating things about the comic is the level of diversity within its cast. There is Melody, who is deaf; Soo Lin, who is blind; Darren, who is gay; Erin, who is asexual; and McPedro, a cactus who talks when Hazel's been drinking. Anna Palindrome, writing for *Bitch Magazine* blog, says that her favorite thing about the comic is that it looks at disability from the point of view of a disabled person. "What I like about the jokes in this strip are that they are all over the place. Some are about how clueless people can be about blindness. Some are disability-related humour as told by people with disabilities."[31]

Corsetto explains, "It's more realistic and less stereotypical. All the characters have these unusual relations, both romantic and platonic . . . that are not what you would find in, say, a sitcom, but it's written like a sitcom. I'm kind of trying to normalize these things that are taboo."

Although the strip started out small, Corsetto's Web site now typically draws about 100,000 readers a day. And since 2007, she has made her living exclusively through drawing and writing comics. In addition to *Girls With Slingshots,* Corsetto works on a variety of side projects, including writing a graphic novel in the *Adventure Time* series. Given the subject matter, alcohol use, and language in *Girls With Slingshots*, Corsetto would not be able to publish her work in a legacy newspaper or magazine. Although the strip is distributed online, Corsetto makes her drawings using pen and ink on heavyweight paper, with the coloring being electronically added. She makes

Photo courtesy of The Frederick News-Post

Web cartoonist Danielle Corsetto works on her comic *Girls With Slingshots* in her studio in Shepherdstown, West Virginia. Although her comic is online, she still does her drawing by hand.

One of the many reasons we go to the movies is to experience strong emotions such as fear, horror, surprise, or romance in a safe environment.

the majority of her income from advertising on her Web site, sales of self-published book collections of comics, and merchandise, such as a plush McPedro. She also gets income from her projects for legacy media, such as the *Adventure Time* book.[32]

Some critics would argue that the growth of cable television stations, Web sites, and magazines creates only an illusion of choice because a majority of the channels are still controlled by the same five or six companies.[33] Even so, it is a new media world, one in which audience members are choosing what media content they will consume and when they will consume it. It's a world that even media giants are being forced to adjust to.

■■■■■■■■■■■■■■■■■■■■

Understanding the Media World

Most people have ambivalent feelings about their high levels of media use. The convenience of the mobile phone is offset by the fact that it makes a person available to others at all times. The wide selection of programming on cable television is wonderful, but the content on some of those channels can be disturbing. It is liberating to be connected to the entire industrialized world through the Internet, but the risk of invasion of privacy is troubling. This section discusses the concept of media literacy and examines some common misconceptions

Questioning the Media

For as long as there have been media, there have been those who blame the media for society's ills. Others believe that critics are just trying to place the blame on a convenient target. How do you feel about this debate? Why?

about the mass media. It also examines in detail "Seven Secrets" about mass media and mass communication that are at the center of this book's look at media literacy.

Defining Media Literacy

The term **media literacy** refers to people's understanding of what the media are, how they operate, what messages they are delivering, what roles they play in society, and how audience members respond to media messages. Media scholar James Potter writes that people with high levels of media literacy have a great deal of control over the vision of the world they see through the media and can decide for themselves what the messages mean. In contrast, those with low levels of media literacy can develop exaggerated impressions of problems in society, even when those impressions conflict with their own experience. For example, media consumers who spend large amounts of time watching television often perceive society as far more dangerous and crime-ridden than it is because that's the image they see on television.[34] Potter says that too often consumers with low levels of media literacy assume that the media have large, obvious, and mostly negative effects on other people but little or no effect on themselves. Finally, those with low levels of media literacy tend to blame the media for complex social problems, such as teen pregnancy or school violence.

Potter has identified four basic dimensions of media literacy: cognitive, emotional, aesthetic, and moral.[35] Let's take a closer look at each of these dimensions.

The Cognitive Dimension. The cognitive dimension of media literacy deals with the ability to intellectually process information communicated by the media. This can involve interpreting the meaning of words on a printed page, appreciating the implications of ominous music in a movie, or understanding that a well-dressed character in a television show is wealthy. For example, the hardcover edition of Jon Krakauer's book *Into Thin Air* featured a series of ominous woodcuts at the beginning of each chapter. These illustrations may be viewed simply as decorations at the beginning of each chapter or interpreted as foreshadowing the suffering and peril to come.

The cognitive dimension also includes the skills necessary to access the media: using a computer, accessing high-definition programming on your new HDTV, or finding a book in the library. All of these are learned skills. We learn to read in school, learn the meaning of musical cues from movies we've seen, and learn how to navigate the Internet through repeated practice.

The Emotional Dimension. The emotional dimension of media literacy covers the feelings created by media

---

media literacy: Audience members' understanding of the media industry's operation, the messages delivered by the media, the roles media play in society, and how audience members respond to these media and their messages.

messages. Sometimes the emotions can be overwhelming; examples include the fear of a young child watching a scary movie or the joy of a parent watching a news story about a child in danger being rescued. People often spend time with songs, movies, books, and other media specifically to feel the emotions they generate.[36] *Titanic* became a box office champion in large part because of the young women who went to see the movie again and again to experience the emotional release it provided.[37] And it is unlikely that either the IMAX documentary *Everest* or Krakauer's *Into Thin Air* would have been such a commercial success were it not for the gut-wrenching emotions created by both the deaths and the dramatic rescues of the climbers on the mountain.

The Aesthetic Dimension. The aesthetic dimension of media literacy involves interpreting media content from an artistic or critical point of view. How well is the media artifact produced? What skills were used in producing it? How does it compare in quality to other, similar works? Understanding more than the surface dimensions of media content can require extensive learning. *Into Thin Air* was unquestionably a commercial success, and it was largely a critical success as well. But it was also controversial; several critics suggested that Krakauer had overdramatized the events that took place on Everest and unfairly portrayed one guide as a villain rather than a hero.[38] It is through such critical debate that alternative views and understandings of media content emerge.

The Moral Dimension. The moral dimension of media literacy consists of examining the values of the medium or the message. In a television situation comedy, for example, an underlying message might be that a quick wit is an important tool for dealing with problems or that a problem can be solved in a short time. In an action movie, the moral lessons may be that violence and authority are needed if one is to succeed and that the world is a mean and dangerous place. The moral message of most advertisements is that problems can be solved by purchasing something.[39] Among the many moral issues raised by *Into Thin Air* is the message that the presence of the media can change the nature of an event.

Seven Secrets About the Media "They" Don't Want You to Know

Media literacy is a tricky subject to talk about, because few people will admit that they really don't understand how the media operate and how messages, audiences, channels, and senders interact. After all, since we spend so much time with the media, we must know all about them, right? As an example, most students in an introduction to mass communication class will claim that the media and media messages tend to affect other people far more than they affect themselves. The question of media literacy can also become a political question, for which the answer depends

on whether you are a liberal or a conservative, rich or poor, young or old. But the biggest problem in the public discussion of media literacy is that certain routine issues get discussed again and again, while many big questions are left unasked.

Consider some of the things we think we know about the media: "The news media are hopelessly liberal." "Watching too much television turns children into overweight zombies, or else it makes them violent. One or the other." "Reading too many fashion magazines makes young women anorexic." "The mainstream media cover up stories they don't want us to know about." "Our media are run by giant corporations that seek world domination." How do we know these things? Well, because people in the media tell us they are so! And they wouldn't say these things if they weren't true, would they?

But there are several things we don't hear about the media. Secret things. Perhaps it's because there is no one out there who can attract an audience by saying them. Or maybe it's because the ideas are complicated, and we don't like complexity from our media. Or maybe it's because "they" (whoever "they" may be) don't want us to know them.

So here are Seven Secrets about the media that "they" don't want you to know. These key issues of media literacy—which don't get the discussion they deserve—provide a foundation for the rest of the chapters in this book. (And just who are "they"? Wait for Secret Seven.)

SECRET 1 **The Media Are Essential Components of Our Lives.** Critics often talk about the effects the media have on us as though the media were something separate and distinct from our everyday lives. But conversations with my students have convinced me otherwise. Every semester I poll my students as to what media they have used so far that day, with the day starting at midnight. I run through the list: checking Twitter, Facebook, or Pinterest; listening to the radio; checking the weather on

---

SEVEN SECRETS
"They" Don't Want You to Know About the Media

SECRET 1 The media are essential components of our lives.

SECRET 2 There are no mainstream media (MSM).

SECRET 3 Everything from the margin moves to the center.

SECRET 4 Nothing's new: Everything that happened in the past will happen again.

SECRET 5 New media are always scary.

SECRET 6 Activism and analysis are not the same thing.

SECRET 7 There is no "they."

Web 1.7: Read more on Web comics.

The meaning of yellow ribbons tied into a bow has transformed many times over the last several decades. Here nine-year-old Katie Lapp is tying ribbons on trees in front of the Pennsylvannia governor's mansion to show her support for America's troops serving overseas.

a mobile device; watching *The Colbert Report*; reading *Cosmopolitan*; reading a Nicholas Sparks novel; listening to an iPhone; and so forth. In fact, media use is likely to be the most universal experience my students will share. Surveys of my students find that more of my morning-class students have consumed media content than have eaten breakfast or showered since the day began at midnight. Are the media an important force in our lives? Absolutely! But the media are more than an outside influence on us. They are a part of our everyday lives.

Think about how we assign meanings to objects that otherwise would have no meaning at all. Take a simple yellow ribbon twisted in a stylized bow. You've seen thousands of these, and most likely you know exactly what they stand for—"Support Our Troops." But that hasn't always been the meaning of the symbol.

The yellow ribbon has a long history in American popular culture. It played a role in the rather rude World War II–era marching song "She Wore a Yellow Ribbon." The ribbon was a symbol of a young woman's love for a soldier "far, far away," and the lyrics mention that her father kept a shotgun handy to keep the soldier "far, far away." The yellow ribbon was also a symbol of love and faithfulness in the John Ford film *She Wore a Yellow Ribbon*. In the 1970s, the ribbon became a symbol of remembering

---

Web 1.8: See the actual list of my morning students' media use.

Web 1.9: Read more examples of Secret One.

the U.S. staff in the Iranian embassy that had been taken hostage. This meaning came from the song "Tie a Yellow Ribbon 'Round the Old Oak Tree," made popular by the group Tony Orlando and Dawn. The song tells about a prisoner coming home from jail hoping that his girlfriend will remember him. She can prove her love by displaying the yellow ribbon. The prisoner arrives home to find not one but 100 yellow ribbons tied to the tree. The display of yellow ribbons tied to trees became commonplace in newspaper articles and television news stories about the ongoing hostage crisis after the wife of a hostage started displaying one in her yard.

Later, during the 1990–1991 Persian Gulf War, Americans were eager to show their support for the troops fighting overseas, even if they did not necessarily support the war itself, and the stylized ribbon started to become institutionalized as a symbol of support. The yellow "Support Our Troops" ribbon was followed by the red ribbon of AIDS awareness, the pink ribbon of breast cancer awareness, and ribbons of virtually every color on other issues. And how do we know the meanings of these ribbons? We hear or see them being discussed through our media. The meaning is assigned by the creators of a ribbon, but the success of the ribbon depends on its meaning being shared through the media. So, do the media create the meanings? Not really. But could the meanings be shared nationwide without the media? Absolutely not. The media may not define our lives, but they do help transmit and disseminate shared meanings from one side of the country to the other.[40]

SECRET 2 **There Are No Mainstream Media (MSM).** We often hear charges related to perceived sins of the so-called mainstream media. But who exactly are these mainstream media? For some, the MSM are the heavyweights of journalism, especially the television broadcast networks and the major newspapers, such as the *New York Times*. For others, the MSM are the giant corporations that run many of our media outlets. New York University journalism professor and blogger Jay Rosen says that the term *MSM* is often used to refer to media we just don't like—a "them."[41] It isn't always clear who constitutes the MSM, but in general we can consider them to be the old-line legacy big-business media—newspapers, magazines, and television.

But are these old media more in the mainstream than our alternative media? Look at talk radio. Afternoon talk radio is dominated by conservative political talk show hosts, such as Rush Limbaugh and Sean Hannity. Limbaugh, in particular, is fond of complaining about how the MSM don't "get it." But how mainstream are the MSM? On a typical evening, CNN will have approximately 568,000 viewers of its evening programming; Fox News will have 1.097 million; MSNBC will have 640,000; HLN (formerly CNN Headline News) will have 395,000; and the NBC, CBS, and ABC network newscasts will have a combined total of approximately 22.4 million viewers.[42]

(The Fox broadcast network does not have a network evening news broadcast.) The Rush Limbaugh show, on the other hand, averages just shy of 15 million listeners a week, and Fox host Sean Hannity's radio show draws about 14 million listeners per week.[43] (Note that television audiences and radio audiences are measured differently.) So which is more mainstream? A popular afternoon radio show with a large daily audience or a television news program with a much smaller audience? *Daily Kos*, a leading liberal political blog—and one of the most-read blogs on the Internet—attracts more than 6 million unique visitors per month.[44] Again, these numbers are not directly comparable with television ratings, but they are substantial. The Internet video site YouTube streams approximately 4 billion videos a day. No one video gets a particularly large viewership, but the combined total is massive.[45]

Even when important news breaks, it's likely we'll hear about it first through social media. When Navy SEALs killed Osama bin Laden in Pakistan in 2011, the news first broke on Twitter with a post by Keith Urbahn, chief of staff for former secretary of defense Donald Rumsfeld. His tweet read: "So I'm told by a reputable person they have killed Osama bin Laden. Hot Damn."[46] This was followed minutes later by a tweet from CBS news producer Jill Jackson reporting: "House Intelligence Committee aide confirms that Osama bin Laden is dead. U.S. has the body."[47]

Meanwhile, the big broadcast and cable news networks were struggling to confirm the story before declaring it to be true on the air. Even CBS, Jackson's own network, waited sixteen minutes more before officially announcing bin Laden's death. As Nicholas Jackson of the *Atlantic* reported it on the night of the announcement:

> With cable news anchors afraid to confirm the news of bin Laden's death before they had multiple sources of their own—Twitter quickly backed up with more confirmations, from senior administration officials and others—newspapers quickly jumped ahead of the story. As print reporters shared notes and confidential sources over Twitter, Wolf Blitzer stood in front of a green screen on CNN (he was at home when he got the news of Obama's press conference) and teased the audience: "We have strong suspicions of what this news might be."[48]

So it is largely meaningless to describe one medium as mainstream and another as nonmainstream. They are all significant presences in our world.

Can we distinguish between old and new media? Perhaps. Can we argue that our alternative sources of news and entertainment are any less significant than the traditional ones? Absolutely not.

SECRET 3 **Everything From the Margin Moves to the Center.** The mass media, both news and entertainment, are frequently accused of trying to put forward an extremist

While President Barack Obama and his cabinet were watching the killing of Osama bin Laden unfold, news of the raid was already being reported live on Twitter.

agenda of violence, permissiveness, homosexuality, drug use, edgy fashion, and nonmainstream values.

People in the media business, be they entertainers or journalists, respond with the argument that they are just "keeping it real," portraying the world as it is by showing aspects of society that some people want to pretend don't exist. They have no agenda, the argument goes; they just want to portray reality.

Now it is true that much of what the media portray that upsets people is real. On the other hand, it is a bit disingenuous to argue that movie directors and musicians are not trying for shock value when they use offensive language or portray stylized violence combined with graphic sexuality. Think back to any of a number of recent horror movies. We all know that teenagers routinely get slashed to ribbons by a psycho killer just after having sex, right? Clearly movie producers are trying to attract an audience by providing content that is outside of the mainstream.

The problem with the argument between "keeping it real" and "extremist agenda" is that it misses what is actually happening. There can be no question that audiences go after media content that is outside of the mainstream. By the same token, the more nonmainstream content is presented, the more ordinary it seems to become. This is what is meant by Secret Three—one of the mass media's biggest effects on everyday life is to take culture from the margins of society and make it into part of the mainstream, or center. This process can move people, ideas, and even individual words from small communities into mass society.

Web 1.10: Read how news of Bin Laden's death spread.

Web 1.11: Read more examples of Secret Two.

Glee's Amber Riley played the part of Dr. Frank-N-Furter in the show's production of the gay-themed *Rocky Horror Picture Show.* The part was originally written for a man in drag.

We can see this happening in several ways. Take the popular Fox show *Glee.* Each week the members of the high school glee club perform pop songs as part of an ongoing plot in which an evil coach always tries to shut them down. For Halloween in 2010, the *Glee* kids were producing the *Rocky Horror Picture Show* as a high school musical. *Rocky Horror* tells the story of a gay male transvestite (Dr. Frank-N-Furter) who is building a boyfriend (Rocky) for himself. But the *Glee* version had actress Amber Riley playing the part of Dr. Frank-N-Furter, while the part of Rocky was still played by a male actor, Chord Overstreet. Thus, the central plotline went from being gay to straight. The *Glee* version also had Frank-N-Furter singing about being from "Sensational, Transylvania" instead of "Transsexual, Transylvania." With these changes, the *Rocky Horror Glee Show* became a perfect example of Secret Three. *Rocky Horror* started out as a camp musical in the 1970s that found enormous success in the counterculture community. But *Glee* sanitized it from a celebration of cross-dressing gay culture into a mass-market story of straight people playing with gay themes.

Glee has also made a habit of taking distinctive cover versions of popular songs that have been reimagined by independent artists and then performing them on the show without crediting the independent artist. For example, *Glee* did a version of Israel Kamakawiwoʻole's Hawaiian-styled cover of "Somewhere Over the Rainbow," and in another episode performed Jonathan Coulton's soft rock version of Sir Mix-A-Lot's rap "Baby Got Back." Even in the premiere episode of the series, the *Glee*

singers performed an a cappella version of Journey's hit "Don't Stop Believin'" that was largely based on the work of singer Petra Haden. While it seems unlikely that there was a legal requirement that the producers compensate or even credit the artists for their creative covers, it would have certainly been nice for them to have noted how they had brought the work of obscure artists into the mainstream.[49] (You can find a link to these covers on the Secret Three link.)

An alternative approach is to look at how the media accelerate the adoption of activist language into the mainstream. Take the medical term *intact dilation and extraction,* which describes a controversial type of late-term abortion. A search of the LexisNexis news database shows that newspapers used the medical term only five times over a six-month period. On the other hand, *partial-birth abortion,* the term for the procedure used by abortion opponents, was used in more than 125 stories during the same time period. Opponents even got the term used in the title of a bill passed by Congress that outlawed the procedure, thus moving the phrase into the mainstream through repeated publication of the bill's name.

This process is not a product of a liberal or conservative bias by the news media. It's simply a consequence of the repeated use of the term in the press.

SECRET 4 > Nothing's New: Everything That Happened in the Past Will Happen Again. Secret Four is a little different than the oft-repeated slogan, "Those who ignore the past are doomed to repeat it." Instead, it says that media face the same issues over and over again as technologies change and new people come into the business.

The fight between today's recording companies and file sharers has its roots in the battle between music publishers and the distributors of player piano rolls in the early 1900s. The player piano was one of the first technologies for reproducing musical performances. Piano roll publishers would buy a single copy of a piece of sheet music and hire a skilled pianist to have his or her performance recorded as a series of holes punched in a paper roll. That roll (and the performance) could then be reproduced and sold to anyone who owned a player piano without further payment to the music's original publisher.[50]

Then, in 1984, Sony successfully defended itself against a lawsuit from Universal Studios by arguing that it had a right to sell VCRs to the public because there were legitimate, legal uses for the technology. Universal had protested the sales because the video recorders could be used to duplicate its movies. Before long, the studios quit trying to ban the VCR and started selling videocassettes of movies directly to consumers at reasonable prices. All of a sudden, the studios had a major new source of revenue.[51]

©iStockphoto.com/DNY59

Web 1.12: Read more examples of Secret Three.

More recently, the recording industry has done its best to force consumers to buy its music on little plastic discs, having gotten the courts to levy large fines against consumers who "share" copyrighted music over the Internet. In the meantime, Apple sells millions of songs a week through its online iTunes music store for an average price of ninety-nine cents per song. And in the fall of 2006, Apple and Amazon started selling movie downloads through their online stores—a step that has the movie industry worried.

SECRET 5 ▶ **New Media Are Always Scary.** Concern about how new media will affect our lives is nothing new. Known as the legacy of fear, it dates back at least to the early twentieth century.

© Bettmann/CORBIS

Congressional hearings in the 1950s about horror comics, such as those pictured here, show how adults are always concerned about the possible effects of new media on children.

In the 1930s, there was fear that watching movies, especially gangster pictures, would lead to precocious sexual behavior, delinquency, lower standards and ideals, and poor physical and emotional health. The 1940s brought concern about how people would react to radio programs, particularly soap operas.[52]

Comic books came under attack in the 1950s. The notion that comic books were dangerous was popularized by a book titled *Seduction of the Innocent* by Dr. Fredric Wertham. Wertham also testified before Congress that violent and explicit comic books were a cause of teenage delinquency and sexual behavior. The industry responded to the criticism by forming the Comics Code Authority and ceasing publication of popular crime and horror comics such as *Tales From the Crypt* and *Weird Science*.

The 1980s and 1990s saw controversies over offensive rap and rock lyrics.[53] These controversies reflected widespread concern about bad language and hidden messages in songs. In 2009, pop star Britney Spears had a not-so-hidden allusion to the "*F* word" in her song "If U Seek Amy." If you speak the title aloud, it sounds like you are spelling out *F, U,* . . . well, you get the picture. Critics were, of course, shocked and dismayed at this example of a pop star lowering public taste. Of course, Spears didn't really create her naughty little lyric on her own. Aside from a host of rock and blues singers who have used similar lines, *Slate* writer Jesse Sheidlower notes that James Joyce used the same basic line in *Ulysses*, when he has a group of women sing:

If you see kay
Tell him he may
See you in tea
Tell him from me.

A careful reading of the third line will let you find a second hidden obscenity as well.[54]

Numerous media critics and scholars have argued that television and movies present a distorted view of the world, making it look like a much more violent and dangerous place than it is. More recently, mobile devices have been blamed for a range of social ills, from car accidents caused by distracted drivers to promiscuity caused by sexually explicit mobile phone text and photo messages.

The idea that new media are always scary applies as much to media companies as it does to audience members. Newspaper publishers were frightened that radio stations would

Web 1.13: Read more examples of Secret Four.

Web 1.14: Read more examples of Secret Five.

While Britney Spears attracted controversy by including not-so-subtle naughty messages in her song "If U Seek Amy," author James Joyce (wearing the eye patch) included the same trick in his 1922 novel *Ulysses*.

steal away all their readers in the 1920s and 1930s. Record companies were also afraid that radio would steal away all the customers who were paying for record albums. And as we saw earlier in this chapter, the movie industry, the television industry, and the music industry are terrified of what the Internet is doing to their business.

Why has there been such long-running concern about the possible effects of the media? Media sociologist Charles R. Wright says that people want to be able to solve social ills, and it is easier to believe that poverty, crime, and drug abuse are caused by media coverage than to acknowledge that their causes are complex and not fully understood.[55]

Writing in 1948, sociologists Robert Merton and Paul Lazarsfeld identified four major aspects of public concern about the media:

- Concern that because the media are everywhere, they might be able to control and manipulate people. This is a large part of the legacy of fear.

- Fear that those in power will use the media to reinforce the existing social structure and discourage social criticism. When critics express concern about who owns and runs the media, this is what they are worried about.
- Fear that mass entertainment will lower the tastes and standards for popular culture by trying to attract the largest possible audience. Criticism of action movies, soap operas, and wrestling as replacements for healthier entertainment, such as Shakespeare's plays, is at the heart of this concern.
- The belief that mass entertainment is a waste of time that detracts from more useful activities. When your mother told you to turn off the television set and go outside, this was her concern![56]

SECRET 6 **Activism and Analysis Are Not the Same Thing.** The five secrets we've examined so far lead us to the conclusion of Secret Six: Critics of the mass media are not necessarily interested in giving an honest analysis of how the media affect the public at large. Instead, critics may have an agenda that has nothing to do with the nature of our mass media.

When senators hold hearings on violent video games and television programming, they may well be concerned about the effects of electronic violence on children. But they may also be trying to show that they are concerned about

Children's Media Use

Teens are significant media users. According to the 2010 study *Generation M2: Media in the Lives of 8–18 Year-Olds,* a follow-up to the 2005 study *Generation M,* children in the United States spend an average of seven hours and thirty-eight minutes a day using media—more time than they spend doing anything else other than sleeping.[1] There are also a lot of stereotypes about teen media use that may or may not be supported by evidence. The study, conducted by the Kaiser Family Foundation, surveyed teens and discovered that because teens are often engaged in media multitasking, they are actually consuming ten hours and forty-five minutes of media content within those seven and a half hours. Here are some of the study's major findings:

- Teens are big users of mobile devices: 66 percent of young people aged eight to eighteen have mobile phones, and 76 percent have an iPod or other MP3 player.
- Young people spend more time consuming media (forty-nine minutes per day) than they do talking on their phones (thirty-three minutes). And the biggest mobile phone activity? Seventh to twelfth graders spent an hour and a half per day texting, which was not counted as media use in this study.
- Few young people have rules controlling how much time they spend with media. But the approximately 30 percent who do have rules limiting their media consumption spend nearly three hours less per day with media.
- Young people are spending more time consuming video than in the past (four hours and twenty-nine minutes) but less time watching

television (down by twenty-five minutes a day from 2004). How is this possible? They're watching video online and using mobile devices.

See the table for a summary of what the researchers found out about media use for children aged eight to eighteen over the last decade:

Medium	Time Spent With Medium in a Typical Day		
	2009	2004	1999
TV/Video	4:29	3:51	3:47
Music/Audio	2:31	1:44	1:48
Computer	1:29	1:02	0:27
Video Games	1:13	0:49	0:26
Print	0:38	0:43	0:18
Movies	0:25	0:25	0:18
Total Media Exposure	10:45	8:33	7:29
Multitasking Proportion	29%	26%	16%
Total Media Use	7:38	6:21	6:19

WHO is the source?

The Kaiser Family Foundation is a private, nonprofit foundation dedicated to researching and reporting on health-related issues. How do you think the Kaiser Family Foundation funded the study? How might this influence the findings and analysis? Who is the intended audience for this study?

WHAT is the report saying?

How has young people's media use changed over the last ten years? How can young people consume more than ten hours of media content in seven and a half hours?

WHAT kind of evidence does the study provide?

What kinds of data do the researchers use? Are those data sufficient to support the assumptions and thereby the recommendations?

HOW do you or your classmates react to the Generation M2 findings?

Do you think the results of the study accurately describe how you and your

friends use media? How do you think your media use differs from how your parents use media? Who or what organizations may benefit from these findings? How might they change media usage in children? What questions are left unanswered? How does your media use compare with that of the young people in the study? How much time do you spend with the various media over the course of a week?

HOW were media used in your home?

What controls over media use did you have growing up? Did you have television or Internet access in your own room? Were any limits placed on how you could use your mobile phone? If so, what were they? Do you think these limits (or the lack of them) had any effect on how you use media or your mobile device now?

---

1. Victoria J. Rideout, Ulla G. Foehr, and Donald F. Roberts, *Generation M2: Media in the Lives of 8–18 Year-Olds* (Henry J. Kaiser Family Foundation, 2010).

 Web 1.15: Read the entire *Generation M2* report.

Young people today are spending more time viewing video and less time watching television than in the past. How is this possible? They are doing more of their viewing on mobile devices like phones and tablets.

America's children, or that they are getting tough on violence, or that they want to lend support to a cause that their contributors feel strongly about. Take as an example the following excerpts from a press release supporting a bill that would limit "gratuitous and excessive" television violence:

> "Increasing fines is an important way to tell broadcasters that we are serious about taking action against indecent material," [the senator] said. "For the sake of our children, we are not going to tolerate indecency, which seems to appear at all hours of the day on more TV channels than ever. We know from numerous studies that such gratuitous and graphic programming negatively affect our children.
>
> "But it's not enough to increase fines. We need to take on this problem in a truly comprehensive and systematic way that will enable us to diminish the appetite that television producers have for producing shows full of sex and violence. Instead of merely

 Web 1.16: Read more examples of Secret Six.

 Web 1.17: Read more examples of Secret Seven.

reacting to one or two high profile incidents, we need to preempt these incidents by fundamentally transforming the culture of programming. Only then will we be able to give parents more control of what their children are watching.

"That's what . . . parents want. I hear over and over from them that they are very concerned about what their children are watching. I believe we have a moral imperative to meet this issue head on."

[The senator's] bill enjoys wide support from a variety of groups, including: Parents Television Council, Benedum Foundation, Children Now, Children's Media Policy Coalition, Kaiser Family Foundation, National Association for Family and Community Education, National Coalition for the Protection of Children and Families, and the National Institute on Family and the Media.[57]

Look through the quotes for the signs of activism: "for the sake of our children," "that's what parents want," "the bill enjoys wide support from a variety of groups." Although the senator sponsoring the bill certainly is concerned about the issue of television violence, he has also—through this criticism of media violence—managed to ally himself with parents and several significant organizations in a way that is relatively safe.

As media consumers, whenever we hear criticism of the media, we ought to ask ourselves, "What is the critic's agenda?"

SECRET 7 There Is No "They." If you listen to media criticism for long, you will hear a pair of words used over and over again: *they* and *them*. It is easy to take potshots at some anonymous bogeymen—*they*—who embody all evil. I even engaged in it at the beginning of this section with the title "Seven Secrets About the Media 'They' Don't Want You to Know."

So who are *they?* No one. Everyone. A nonspecific other we want to blame. Any time I used "they" in a news story, my high school journalism teacher would always ask who "they" were. And that's what you need to ask whenever you hear criticism of the media. It isn't that the criticism is not accurate. It very well may be. But it probably applies to a specific media outlet, a specific journalist, a certain song, or a particular movie. But we can make few generalizations about an industry so diverse that it includes everything from a giant corporation producing the $220 million *Marvel's The Avengers* movie to young people posting on Facebook. There are a lot of media out there, but no unified *them*.

Chapter SUMMARY

Communication takes place at a number of levels, including intrapersonal (within the self), interpersonal (between individuals), group (between three or more individuals), and mass (between a single sender and a large audience). Mass communication is a

communication process that covers an entire society, in which an individual or institution uses technology to send messages to a large, mixed audience, most of whose members are not known to the sender. Mass communication can be examined in terms of the process of transmission; the rituals surrounding its consumption; the attention its messages draw to persons, groups, or concepts; or how audience members create meaning out of media content.

The first communication network was developed by the Roman Catholic Church, which could send messages reliably throughout Europe as early as the twelfth century. In the mid-fifteenth century, the development of printing made it possible for books and other publications to be mass produced for the first time, leading to numerous cultural changes. Books, magazines, newspapers, and other printed media forms became readily available, although they were expensive before steam-driven printing presses became common in the nineteenth century.

The electronic media emerged in the mid-nineteenth century with the invention of the telegraph, followed by recorded music, radio, movies, and television. These media allowed popular culture to be produced commercially and to be delivered easily and inexpensively into people's homes. The first interactive digital communication network, the Internet, was developed starting in the late 1960s but wasn't available to the general public until the 1990s. The Internet added a return channel to the mass communication process, initiating a much higher level of audience feedback. The Internet also allowed individuals to disseminate their own ideas and information without the costs of a traditional mass medium.

The rapid growth of the mass media has led the public and media critics to raise questions about the effects various media might have on society and individuals. Scholars have suggested that the best way to control the impact of the media in our lives is to develop high levels of media literacy—an understanding of what the media are, how they operate, what messages they are delivering, what roles they play in society, and how audience members respond to these messages. Media literacy includes cognitive, emotional, aesthetic, and moral dimensions.

Your text suggests that the following seven principles can guide your understanding of how the media operate: (1) the media are essential components of our lives, (2) there are no mainstream media, (3) everything from the margin moves to the center, (4) nothing's new—everything that happened in the past will happen again, (5) new media are always scary, (6) activism and analysis are not the same thing, and (7) there is no "they."

 Keep up-to-date with content from the author's blog.

Take the chapter quiz.

Key TERMS

communication 4

intrapersonal
    communication 5

interpersonal
    communication 5

group communication 5

mass communication 6

mass media 7

Sender Message Channel
    Receiver (SMCR) or
    transmission model 7

bloggers 7

message 8

encoding 8

channel 8

receiver 9

decoding 9

heterogeneous audience 9

noise 9

anonymous audience 11

ritual model 12

publicity model 12

reception model 12

media literacy 16

Concept REVIEW

Levels of communication

Mass communication versus mass media

Elements of the mass communication process

Models of mass communication: transmission, ritual, publicity, and reception

Pre–mass media communication networks

Print media

Electronic networks

Interactive communication

Media literacy and its dimensions

Seven secrets about the media

Student STUDY SITE

$SAGE edge™

Sharpen your skills with SAGE edge at **edge.sagepub.com/hanson5e**

SAGE edge for Students provides a personalized approach to help you accomplish your coursework goals in an easy-to-use learning environment.

The Media Business

Consolidation, Globalization, and the Long Tail

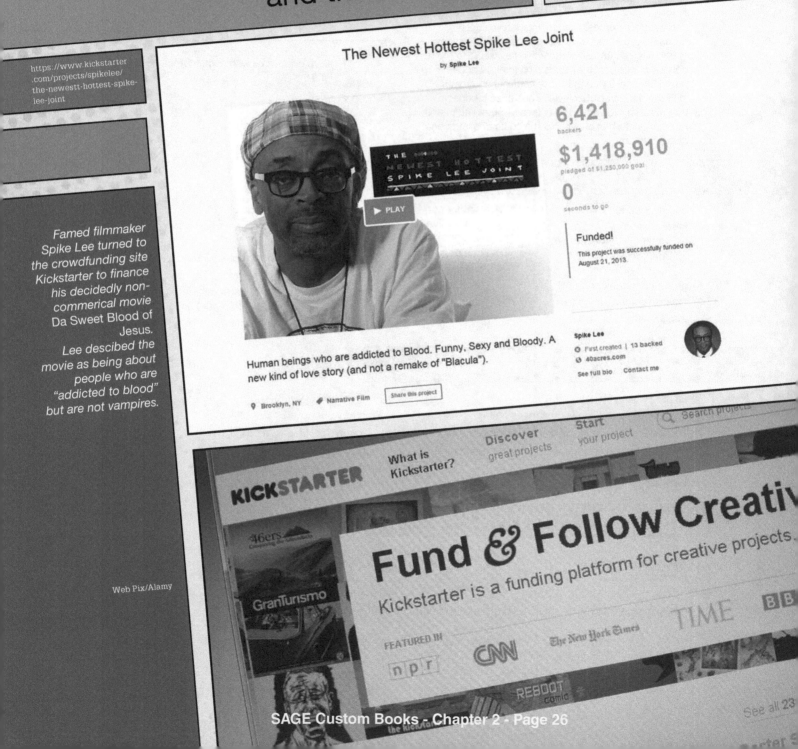

Famed filmmaker Spike Lee turned to the crowdfunding site Kickstarter to finance his decidedly non-commerical movie Da Sweet Blood of Jesus.

Lee descibed the movie as being about people who are "addicted to blood" but are not vampires.

https://www.kickstarter.com/projects/spikelee/the-newestt-hottest-spike-lee-joint

The Newest Hottest Spike Lee Joint
by **Spike Lee**

6,421
backers

$1,418,910
pledged of $1,250,000 goal

0
seconds to go

Funded!
This project was successfully funded on August 21, 2013.

Human beings who are addicted to Blood. Funny, Sexy and Bloody. A new kind of love story (and not a remake of "Blacula").

Spike Lee
First created | 13 backed
40acres.com
See full bio   Contact me

Brooklyn, NY   Narrative Film   Share this project

Web Pix/Alamy

KICKSTARTER   What is Kickstarter?   Discover great projects   Start your project   Search projects

46ers

GranTurismo

Fund & Follow Creativ

Kickstarter is a funding platform for creative projects.

FEATURED IN   CNN   The New York Times   TIME   BB

npr

REBOOT comic

See all 23

Famed African American filmmaker Spike Lee has a long record of producing independently minded films from his seminal movie *Do the Right Thing* to his biopic on Malcolm X, though he's also known for more commercial fare, like his thriller *Inside Man* starring Denzel Washington, Clive Owen, and Jodie Foster.

But during 2013 and 2014, he made an extremely low-budget, truly independent film for a little more than $1.25 million financed by more than 5,000 backers from the crowd-funding Web site Kickstarter.[1] *Da Sweet Blood of Jesus*, a movie Lee describes as a "bloody, funny, sexy movie" about people who are "addicted to blood" who are not vampires, was shot in 16 days in Brooklyn and Martha's Vineyard with a cast of unknowns.[2] Forrest Wickman, a movie reviewer for the Web site *Slate*, describes the movie as "veering wildly between pulpy exploitation . . . and art-house filmmaking," and notes that it is unlike anything that would ever get conventional funding.[3]

To get funding though Kickstarter, filmmakers (like everyone else seeking Kickstarter funding) put together a video pitch along with written details about their qualifications and the film they intend to make. Potential contributors pledge to fund projects they find interesting, but they only get charged if the project reaches the financial goal the creator set. If the project doesn't reach its funding goal, no money is exchanged.[4] Assuming the project does reach its goal and gets funded, the people who pledge do not get an investment in the movie as they might with conventional movie financing. Instead, they get the satisfaction of supporting the project and very often some kind of reward, such as a copy of the film or book produced by the project (though in the case of Spike Lee's film, the reward at the $10,000 level was getting to sit courtside with Lee at a Knicks NBA game).

At the time it was funded in August 2013, *Da Sweet Blood of Jesus* was the third largest movie project to be funded through Kickstarter (raising approximately $1.4 million), following behind a movie version of the cult TV series *Veronica Mars* ($5.7 million) and a Zach Braff film that raised $3.1 million.[5] Lee, along with Braff (a popular actor and the director of the film *Garden State*), has received criticism for funding his project through Kickstarter when he had other options available to him, with the presumption that the funding that went to him could have gone to other, more needy filmmakers.[6] The founders of Kickstarter, however, responded through their blog to defend the celebrity filmmakers:

LEARNING OBJECTIVES

After studying this chapter, you will be able to:

1 Describe how the media developed as a private industry in the United States from the colonial period to the present day.

2 Summarize how control of the media industry has changed from the 1950s to the present day.

3 Define what is meant by "media synergy" and illustrate it with at least three examples.

4 Explain why Apple, Google, and other tech companies may also be considered leading media companies.

5 Describe the concept of long-tail media and its implications for the future of the media industry.

6 Identify six groups that influence how the media behave and what content they present.

> **❝ I've been doing KICKSTARTER before there was KICKSTARTER, there was no Internet. ❞**
>
> —Spike Lee

Almost five million people have backed a project on Kickstarter, and more than a million have backed two or more projects. These repeat backers are responsible for 59% of the total money pledged to Kickstarter projects—a whopping $444 million. On average, 2,130 people a day have become new repeat backers this year. This is huge! Future creators will benefit from more and more people using Kickstarter.[7]

In his Kickstarter proposal, Lee says that using nontraditional funding to finance his films is nothing new to him:

I'm an Indie Filmmaker and I will always be an Indie Filmmaker. Indie Filmmakers are always in search of financing because their work, their vision sometimes does not coincide with Studio Pictures. But I do put my own money in my films. I self-financed RED HOOK SUMMER. My fee for MALCOLM X was put back into the budget. The truth is I've been doing KICKSTARTER before there was KICKSTARTER, there was no Internet. Social Media was writing letters, making phone calls, beating the bushes. I'm now using TECHNOLOGY with what I've been doing.[8]

(Lee is also making the point of **SECRET 4** Nothing's new: Everything that happened in the past will happen again.)

Kickstarter began in April 2009 and as of May 2014 had funded more than 60,000 projects. (Full disclosure: Your author has helped fund several music and Web comic projects through Kickstarter.)

Timeline

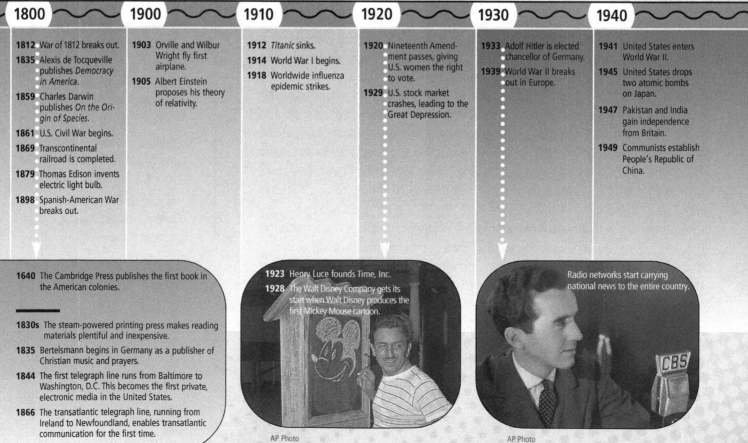

1800

1812 War of 1812 breaks out.
1835 Alexis de Tocqueville publishes *Democracy in America.*
1859 Charles Darwin publishes *On the Origin of Species.*
1861 U.S. Civil War begins.
1869 Transcontinental railroad is completed.
1879 Thomas Edison invents electric light bulb.
1898 Spanish-American War breaks out.

1640 The Cambridge Press publishes the first book in the American colonies.

1830s The steam-powered printing press makes reading materials plentiful and inexpensive.
1835 Bertelsmann begins in Germany as a publisher of Christian music and prayers.
1844 The first telegraph line runs from Baltimore to Washington, D.C. This becomes the first private, electronic media in the United States.
1866 The transatlantic telegraph line, running from Ireland to Newfoundland, enables transatlantic communication for the first time.

1900

1903 Orville and Wilbur Wright fly first airplane.
1905 Albert Einstein proposes his theory of relativity.

1910

1912 *Titanic* sinks.
1914 World War I begins.
1918 Worldwide influenza epidemic strikes.

1923 Henry Luce founds Time, Inc.
1928 The Walt Disney Company gets its start when Walt Disney produces the first Mickey Mouse cartoon.

AP Photo

1920

1920 Nineteenth Amendment passes, giving U.S. women the right to vote.
1929 U.S. stock market crashes, leading to the Great Depression.

1930

1933 Adolf Hitler is elected chancellor of Germany.
1939 World War II breaks out in Europe.

Radio networks start carrying national news to the entire country.

AP Photo

1940

1941 United States enters World War II.
1945 United States drops two atomic bombs on Japan.
1947 Pakistan and India gain independence from Britain.
1949 Communists establish People's Republic of China.

Of the more than 14,000 film and video projects that have been funded as of the summer of 2014, 70 have been screened at Sundance, and more than 100 have been screened at the SXSW festival in Austin, Texas.[9]

Beyond being a new source of funding for filmmakers, Kickstarter represents a new way of the movie industry looking at the Internet and the people who inhabit it. As *New York Times* media blogger David Carr points out, the legacy movie industry, represented through the Motion Picture Association of America and the National Association of Theatre Owners, sees the online world as a scary place where movie pirates reside, while independent filmmakers view it as an exciting source of support to make movies Hollywood isn't interested in making. And this makes Kickstarter an example of both *Secret Five*—New media are always scary—and *Secret Two*—There are no mainstream media.

In recent years, ownership of newspapers, book and magazine publishers, recording labels, movie companies, and Internet companies has become increasingly concentrated, moving from the hands of the families that started them into the hands of a small number of very large corporations. However, entrepreneurs are able to use digital technologies to create new media that can turn upside-down Big Media's focus on using traditional tools to deliver media using the same techniques they have for years. Instead of looking at "the media" as a unified whole, we look at who owns and controls the varied mass media and how new channels are emerging rapidly. ■

Video 3.1: Learn more about how even big-name filmmakers are using crowdfunding to finance their movies.

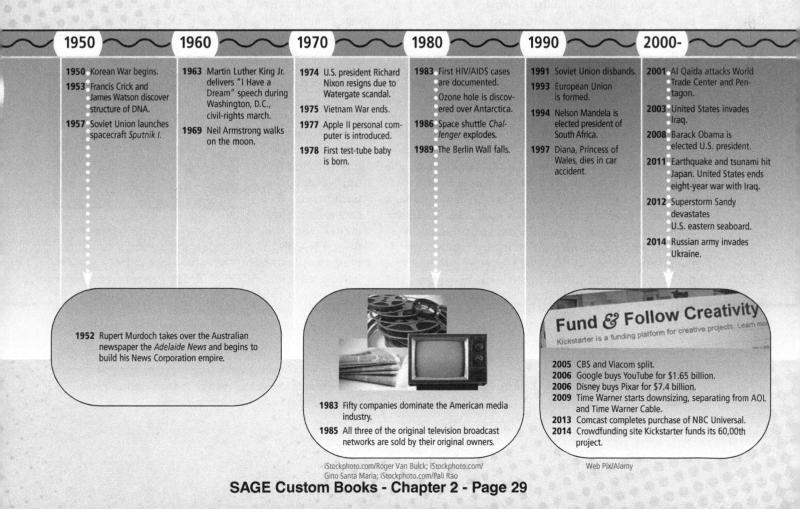

1950

1950 Korean War begins.

1953 Francis Crick and James Watson discover structure of DNA.

1957 Soviet Union launches spacecraft *Sputnik I.*

1960

1963 Martin Luther King Jr. delivers "I Have a Dream" speech during Washington, D.C., civil-rights march.

1969 Neil Armstrong walks on the moon.

1970

1974 U.S. president Richard Nixon resigns due to Watergate scandal.

1975 Vietnam War ends.

1977 Apple II personal computer is introduced.

1978 First test-tube baby is born.

1980

1983 First HIV/AIDS cases are documented.

Ozone hole is discovered over Antarctica.

1986 Space shuttle *Challenger* explodes.

1989 The Berlin Wall falls.

1990

1991 Soviet Union disbands.

1993 European Union is formed.

1994 Nelson Mandela is elected president of South Africa.

1997 Diana, Princess of Wales, dies in car accident.

2000-

2001 Al Qaida attacks World Trade Center and Pentagon.

2003 United States invades Iraq.

2008 Barack Obama is elected U.S. president.

2011 Earthquake and tsunami hit Japan. United States ends eight-year war with Iraq.

2012 Superstorm Sandy devastates U.S. eastern seaboard.

2014 Russian army invades Ukraine.

1952 Rupert Murdoch takes over the Australian newspaper the *Adelaide News* and begins to build his News Corporation empire.

1983 Fifty companies dominate the American media industry.

1985 All three of the original television broadcast networks are sold by their original owners.

Fund & Follow Creativity

Kickstarter is a funding platform for creative projects. Learn mo

2005 CBS and Viacom split.

2006 Google buys YouTube for $1.65 billion.

2006 Disney buys Pixar for $7.4 billion.

2009 Time Warner starts downsizing, separating from AOL and Time Warner Cable.

2013 Comcast completes purchase of NBC Universal.

2014 Crowdfunding site Kickstarter funds its 60,00th project.

The Development of the Media Business in the United States

The U.S. media are unique in the world in that they are almost entirely privately owned and operated for profit. Even the broadcasting industry, which in most countries is tightly controlled by the government, is run by private businesses.[10]

A Tradition of Private Ownership

The media in the United States have a long tradition of private ownership that dates back to the 1640s. The media industry was among the first in the American colonies: The first printing press came to the Massachusetts Bay Colony in 1638. It was used to establish the Cambridge press, publisher of *The Whole Booke of Psalmes*, better known as the Bay Psalm Book. This became the colonies' first best-seller and was even exported back to Great Britain and Europe. Most of the early published works consisted of religious tracts, such as sermons, and were printed under license of the colonial government.[11]

Newspapers were published throughout the colonial and revolutionary period, but they were not the large, general-appeal publications we are familiar with today. Instead, they provided commentary and gossip that would appeal to members of a particular political group. Benjamin Harris, who published the first newspaper in the colonies in 1690, also ran a coffeehouse, and the content of his paper, *Publick Occurrences Both Forreign and Domestick*, resembled the talk in his coffeehouse. Only one issue of the paper appeared, in part because Harris had failed to obtain a license to publish.

Although the newspapers of the colonial period were much smaller than those to come during the 1800s, they could nevertheless be quite profitable. Publisher and statesman Benjamin Franklin became relatively wealthy publishing his *Pennsylvania Gazette*—although his success was due at least in part to his ability, as postmaster general, to prevent competing newspapers from being distributed through the mail.[12] Franklin, along with several other successful publishers, was able to use his paper's profitability to improve his publications and thus increase his success. He was an intense competitor, vying with other publishers for the top writers and editors in the book, newspaper, and magazine businesses.[13] In many ways, he established the pattern that media moguls would follow for the next two and a half centuries.

Web 3.1: Learn more about the Bay Psalm Book.

Even though print media were widespread in America in the 1700s, subscription prices were high, and publications were subsidized by political parties. It wasn't until the development of **penny press** newspapers in the 1830s that the news industry really got started. These inexpensive, widely circulated papers were published in large numbers and were the first American newspapers to be supported primarily through advertising revenue and read by large numbers of people.[14] The same model of advertising-supported media guided the development of the magazine industry in the 1800s.

In the United States, unlike most other countries, the electronic media have always been privately owned, beginning with the telegraph line between Washington, D.C., and Baltimore, Maryland, in 1844. By 1849, the telegraph was being used to transmit news on a regular basis. Although it was replaced by newer technology in the twentieth century, the telegraph set the stage for private ownership of electronic media.[15] Today the broadcasting industry is primarily a private business in the United States, although it is regulated by the government. In contrast, while Britain has a thriving commercial broadcasting industry, the publicly funded British Broadcasting Corporation (BBC) has a much bigger presence than the U.S. Public Broadcasting Service (PBS). And while the Internet, the most recent of the electronic media, began as a partnership between the military and universities in the 1960s and 1970s, it was fully opened to business and the public in the 1990s.

The Growth of National News

Nationally circulated magazines provided news and entertainment in the nineteenth and early twentieth centuries, and radio networks carried national news from the 1930s on, but it was the growing popularity of television networks in the 1950s that gave the United States a true national media culture. For the first time, people routinely depended on nationally available media for their  news. The CBS and NBC television networks started carrying a half-hour nightly news broadcast in 1963; ABC followed suit in 1967, and CBS added its weekly newsmagazine *60 Minutes* in 1968. In 1979, ABC started running a late-night news update called *America Held Hostage* when American embassy employees in Iran were taken hostage.

penny press: Inexpensive, widely circulated papers that became popular in the nineteenth century. They were the first American media to be supported primarily through advertising revenue.

As the hostage crisis dragged on for 444 days, the update evolved into the program now known as *Nightline*.

Public affairs network C-SPAN began broadcasting on cable in 1979. It carried full coverage of the U.S. House of Representatives live and unedited; coverage of the Senate was added in 1986. CNN went on cable in 1980, promising not to go off the air until "the end of the world." CNN subsequently went worldwide with CNN International and CNN en Español.

All this means that, even though a relatively limited number of companies own the media outlets, Americans have access to a wide range of competing news sources. The absolute number of independent sources has declined, but their availability is vastly improved.[16] In addition to these giants, several slightly smaller companies are extraordinarily influential on how our media operate. While the focus in this chapter is on the media in the United States, we take a much broader look at global media in Chapter 15.

▪□▪▪▪▪□▪▪▪▪▪▪▪□▪▪▪▪▪▪▪

Big Media: The Conglomerates

Media journalist Ken Auletta notes that massive changes have taken place in the media industry during the past forty years. In 1980, the videocassette recorder (VCR) was a scarce luxury, cable television was just starting to become popular, the personal computer was for hobbyists, the Internet was available only to academics and the military, *USA Today* had yet to be published, MTV and CNN were not yet on cable, there were only three broadcast television networks, you couldn't buy a compact disc (CD), and mobile phones were connected to large boxes and used only by the wealthy and people with mobile offices.

By 2011, digital video recorders (DVRs) were in almost 40 percent of all U.S. homes with television, basic cable was in more than 52 percent of homes and was available to over 95 percent of them, direct broadcast satellite television was in 24 percent, radio was universally available, over 90 percent of American teens had access to the Internet at home, the *Wall Street Journal* sold 2.1 million copies a day, there were at least six national broadcast networks, and over 85 percent of Americans had mobile telephones.[17] In Europe, there were approximately 4,000 television channels available, and in Western Europe, approximately 86 percent of all adults had a mobile phone.[18]

Since corporations control so much of what is available to the public, it is worth examining who they are and what they control, as well as how they have had to change to react to the new media environment of the twenty-first century.

Companies that had counted on consolidation to bring in profits from synergy were likely to be disappointed as often as they were pleased. In general, the word **synergy** refers to a combination of effects that is greater than the sum of the individual effects. For example, two medications given together may do more than twice as much good as the two medicines given separately. In the media business, synergy means that a combined company can offer more value, cost savings, or strength than two companies could separately.

However, there is more to our media world than just the legacy conglomerates of Big Media. There are the newer companies that are becoming a huge part of our media landscape, such as Comcast, Google, and Apple. Then there are the companies that are more limited in the scope of their media ownership, such as Clear Channel, which has 850-plus radio stations, and Gannett, which owns approximately eighty daily newspapers (including *USA Today*), 500 nondaily publications, and twenty-three television stations.[19] So after we talk about the legacy media conglomerates, we'll look at the giant new players, along with a few other smaller, but still significant, media companies.

Disney: The Mouse That Grew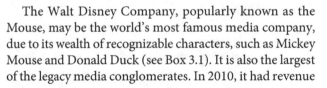

The Walt Disney Company, popularly known as the Mouse, may be the world's most famous media company, due to its wealth of recognizable characters, such as Mickey Mouse and Donald Duck (see Box 3.1). It is also the largest of the legacy media conglomerates. In 2010, it had revenue

synergy: Where the combined strength of two items is greater than the sum of their individual strengths. In the media business, synergy means that a large company can use the strengths of its various divisions to successfully market its content.

▶ Video 3.2: Search the C-SPAN archive to find a streaming copy of every program the public affairs network has ever aired.

💻 Web 3.2: Read an interview with Ben Bagdikian.

💻 Web 3.3: Take a peek at the corporate Web sites for several of the most dominant media corporations.

Book Publishing

- Hyperion Books
- Disney Publishing Worldwide

Magazine Publishing

Numerous magazines, including:

- *Biography*
- *Discover*
- *Us Weekly* (partial)
- *ESPN The Magazine*
- *Marvel Comics*

Broadcast Network

- ABC

Broadcast Television Stations

Disney owns eight ABC affiliates in major cities, including Chicago, Los Angeles, San Francisco, New York City, and Houston.

Cable Networks

Many cable networks (either partially or in full), including:

- Disney Channel (plus multiple international versions)
- ESPN Inc. (includes 15 separate properties)
- A&E Networks
- ABC Family
- Lifetime (at least three versions as part of the A&E Networks)

Movie Studios and Distributors

- Walt Disney Pictures
- Touchstone Pictures
- Buena Vista
- Pixar
- Marvel Entertainment
- Lucasfilm

Other Properties

- Theme parks in China, Japan, France, and the United States
- A cruise line business
- Disney stores
- Numerous international television broadcasting and production companies

Sources: "Who Owns What," *Columbia Journalism Review*, http://www.cjr.org/resources/?c=disney; *Hoover's Company Records—In-Depth Records: The Walt Disney Company* (Austin, Texas: Hoover's Inc., 2014).

Video 3.3: Comedian Paint gives a musical parody of what happens to several Disney princesses after the movie ends.

Web 3.4: Who owns the media you're consuming?

of $45 billion, with $34 billion coming from the United States and Canada and more than $3 billion from Asia and the Pacific.[20] (Comcast, which owns NBCUniversal, is about one-third bigger than Disney. We'll talk about that more later on.)

From Mickey Mouse to Media Giant. The Disney Company got its start in 1928 when Walt Disney started producing Mickey Mouse cartoons. The first two silent Mickey cartoons came and went with little fanfare, but the third, which featured synchronized music and sound effects, was a huge hit. Walt Disney produced more than one hundred short animated cartoons featuring Mickey and his friends. In 1937, he took animation to the next level by releasing the first feature-length cartoon, *Snow White and the Seven Dwarfs*. A major success for the studio, the film held the box-office record of $8 million until *Gone With the Wind* was released in 1939.

In the 1950s, the Disney Company started producing live-action feature films and wildlife documentaries.[21] It was also in the 1950s that Disney opened its first theme park, in California.

Walt Disney was among the first Hollywood movie producers to see the potential of television, for which he produced and hosted a weekly program for more than a decade.[22] He understood the concept of synergy very early and used his television show to promote his movies and theme park. The Disney Company has also been licensing merchandise longer than almost any other media company. In 1930, the company signed its first international licensing contract for Mickey Mouse products, and the famous Mickey Mouse watch went on sale in 1933. By 1954, the company was selling more than 3,000 Disney items, ranging from pajamas to school supplies.[23]

After Walt Disney's death in 1966, the company lost much of its direction.[24] But in 1984, Michael Eisner, formerly of ABC Television and Paramount Pictures, took over as head of the studio, a job he held until 2005. Under Eisner's leadership, the Disney Company produced a series of popular animated films; formed new movie companies, including Touchstone Pictures (which has produced films for adults, such as *Pretty Woman*); and moved into television.[25]

In addition to being a significant force in American media, the Disney Company has been developing a presence throughout Europe and Asia. As of 2013, approximately 25 percent of Disney's earnings came from outside North America, but the quest for an international audience has not always gone smoothly.[26] For example, Disneyland Paris, which opened in 1992, went through four name changes and numerous cultural changes before it became profitable. Tokyo Disneyland, which opened in 1983, started off slowly but was soon busier than the California Disneyland. But the market Disney is most interested in is China, with its 1.3 billion potential consumers.[27]

Disney had been doing business in China for several years before the communists came to power in 1949. But for the next thirty-five or so years, Disney and other Western businesses were barred from the country. By the mid-1980s, China was becoming more open to Western business and culture, so in 1985 Disney began negotiations with Chinese broadcast media to bring Mickey Mouse and Donald Duck cartoons to Chinese television.[28]

In 1996, Disney's relationship with China hit a rough period when Touchstone released the movie *Kundun*. The film, which deals with Tibet and the Dalai Lama, outraged the Chinese government. (China controls Tibet and has attempted to suppress the teachings of the Dalai Lama.) After *Kundun*'s release, Disney programming was banned briefly in China.[29]

By 2002, Disney had successfully distanced itself from *Kundun* and was airing its cartoons on *Dragon Club*, which reaches 60 million Chinese households, and by 2005 it had twenty-three programming blocks on Chinese television. The company also had more than 1,800 Disney Corners in Chinese department stores.[30]

Disney opened Hong Kong Disneyland in 2005. Despite some early problems, including overcrowding and cultural misunderstandings, the park has been growing, and Disney invested $800 million into expanding the park in 2009.[31] Since that expansion, the Hong Kong park has been moderately successful, with rising attendance and profits.[32] Chinese visitors don't seem to be bothered by the fact that the rides have English soundtracks. One Chinese guest told the *Washington Post*, "I don't expect to see many Chinese things in Disneyland. I came to see different things, fresh things."[33] Disney has continued to work on a $5.5 billion theme park in Shanghai in conjunction with a Chinese corporation. Brooks Barnes, writing for the *New York Times*, says Disney is counting on the Chinese becoming more interested in Western-style entertainment and media.[34]

Disney's reach extends far beyond its children's programming and theme park operations. Central to the Disney Company today is the ABC broadcast network and the ESPN cable networks. ABC had been an independent company until 1985, when it was bought by Capital Cities Communications. Ten years later, Disney bought Capital

The Walt Disney Company has worked extensively in recent years to expand its offerings in China, including a theme park in Shanghai.

Cities and acquired ABC as part of the deal.[35] Unlike Viacom and Time Warner, Disney is primarily a content company—a producer of programming. Although it owns ten television stations and a number of radio stations, it has not (as of this writing) invested heavily in local cable companies, theaters, or an Internet service provider. It also has invested in retail stores and theme parks.[36]

The Twenty-first Century at Disney.
Disney has had a series of ups and downs over the past several years, sometimes in the same areas of the company. These include:

- Animation—Disney's animation studio suffered a string of failures starting in 2000 with traditional, hand-drawn animation, but the company revitalized its cartoon offerings by acquiring Pixar, the studio responsible for the three *Toy Story* movies, *WALL-E*, and *Up*. In 2013 and 2014, Disney animation had its biggest hit ever (not counting the Pixar-branded movies) with *Frozen*.[37]
- Synergy at Disney—Synergy isn't just a good idea at Disney; it's a corporate passion. Two or three times a year, the company runs a "boot camp" for executives called Disney Dimensions. For eight days, executives play a costumed character at a theme park and learn how meals are cooked and beds are made, how movies are animated, how the finance and legal departments are run, and how the television networks do business.[38] While Disney still uses synergy to cross-market consumer products, theme parks,

Video 3.4: Watch a 1939 video on how Walt Disney cartoons were made.

Web 3.5: A twisted look at reimagined Disney princesses by artist Jeffrey Thomas.

Web 3.6: Read reaction to Disney's acquisition of Lucasfilm.

Australian Rupert Murdoch, shown here in 1985, heads News Corporation, which owns, among many other media properties, the *Wall Street Journal*, the *New York Post*, Fox News, and Fox Broadcasting.

and media content, the company has taken the concept much farther than that.[39]

- Media convergence at Disney—Just as Disney saw the potential for bringing together movie and television properties back in the 1950s and 1960s, in recent decades it has understood how to bring together other popular sources of media entertainment such as Marvel Entertainment (home of Iron Man and the rest of the Avengers) and Lucasfilm (home of the *Star Wars* series). The company has also moved into using online media as a partial owner of the online streaming video service Hulu and uses it to provide viewers with additional opportunities to watch shows from ABC, ABC Family, Disney Channel, and SOAPnet. Disney was also among the first of the Big Media companies to make its movies and television shows available through Apple's online iTunes store.[40]

News Corporation and 21st Century Fox: A Worldwide Giant Splits in Two

In 2013, Rupert Murdoch's worldwide news and entertainment giant News Corporation became the latest media conglomerate to break itself into two parts. News Corporation retained Murdoch's newspapers, information services, and book publishing business. It publishes the *Wall Street Journal* and the *New York Post* in the United States, along with the *Times* and the *Sun* in London. (Its biggest paper, the *News of the World*, was shut down following a phone hacking scandal in 2011. You can learn more about this in the "Test Your Media Literacy" box.) 21st Century Fox took on his cable, broadcast, film, pay television, and satellite properties. Interestingly, the entertainment-oriented 21st Century Fox owns Fox News

rather than the news-oriented News Corp. Murdoch has a worldwide presence in nine different media: newspapers, magazines, books, broadcasting, direct-broadcast satellite television, cable networks, a movie studio, home video, and the Internet. (See Boxes 3.2 and 3.3.) In fact, the only continent on which Murdoch doesn't own media properties is Antarctica.[41] In fiscal year 2012, News Corporation had sales of $8.6 billion, and 21st Century Fox had sales of $27.7 billion, for a total of $36.3 billion, making the two companies together about 25 percent smaller than Disney.[42]

From Australia to the World. Rupert Murdoch's father owned two Australian newspapers, but when the elder Murdoch died in 1952, the younger Murdoch had to sell one of the papers to cover inheritance taxes. So Murdoch's News Corporation empire grew out of a single newspaper, the *Adelaide News*, which had a circulation under 100,000.[43]

By 1964, Murdoch had put together a major newspaper chain and had begun publishing the *Australian*, a national newspaper. In 1969, he moved to Britain, taking over the Sunday tabloid *News of the World* and eventually acquiring four more tabloids. In 1977, he moved to the United States, where he acquired the *New York Post* and transformed it into a lively, politically conservative paper.

In the 1980s, Murdoch bought the 20th Century Fox movie studio and a number of U.S. television stations and used them to create the Fox television network. He also became an American citizen at this time because the United States does not permit foreign ownership of a television

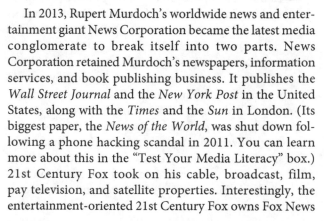

Box 3.2   **What Does News Corporation Own?**

Newspapers

More than 275 newspapers worldwide, including:

The Wall Street Journal

The *New York Post*

The *Times* (of London)

The *Sun* (London tabloid)

The *Australian* (national daily)

Magazines

All or part of four Australian magazines

Book Publishing

Multiple book publishing houses, including:

- HarperCollins Publishers (along with divisions in England, Australia, and Canada)
- Zondervan (religious publisher)

Sources: "Who Owns What," *Columbia Journalism Review,* www .cjr.org/resources/index.php; *Hoover's Company Records—In-Depth Records: News Corporation* (Austin, Texas: Hoover's Inc., 2014); *Hoover's Company Records—In-Depth Records: 21st Century Fox* (Austin, Texas: Hoover's Inc., 2014).

Broadcast Television Networks

- Fox Broadcasting
- MyNetworkTV (broadcast network launched in 2006)

Broadcast Television Stations

21st Century Fox owns at least twenty-five television stations in at least seventeen cities, including New York City; Los Angeles; Minneapolis; Washington, D.C.; and Phoenix.

Cable/Satellite Networks

Numerous cable networks, including:

- Fox News Channel
- Fox Sports Net
- Fox Sports Europe, Africa, Asia, and Latin America
- Fox Sports 1 (formerly the Speed Channel)
- FX

Global Channels

- Fox International Channels (300 channels across Latin America, Europe, Asia, and Africa, in forty-four languages)
- STAR India (network of more than thirty channels in seven languages)

Direct Broadcast Satellite Companies (all or partial ownership)

Multiple DBS services, including:

- British Sky Broadcasting (BSkyB)
- Sky Deutschland
- Sky Italia

Movie Studios

- 20th Century Fox (including at least seven spin-off studios)
- Fox Interactive

Sources: "Who Owns What," *Columbia Journalism Review,* www.cjr.org/resources/index.php; *Hoover's Company Records—In-Depth Records: News Corporation* (Austin, Texas: Hoover's Inc., 2014); *Hoover's Company Records—In-Depth Records: 21st Century Fox* (Austin, Texas: Hoover's Inc., 2014).

network. The Fox News cable network was launched in 1996 and has for years been the most popular of the cable news operations. In 2011, it had the fourth-highest ratings of any cable network (USA, ESPN, and TNT were higher) and was the top-rated cable news channel.[44] In addition to its more than twenty-five broadcast television stations, book publishing operations, and broadcast and cable networks, News Corporation is the world's dominant player

Web 3.7: Read more about the split of News Corporation here.

in the direct broadcast satellite business, owning a large portion of BSkyB (Britain), Sky Italia (Italy), and Sky Deutschland (Germany). It also owns a stake in China's state-owned telecommunications company.[45] The Murdoch family owns approximately 40 percent of both News Corporation and 21st Century Fox, and Murdoch runs his business using the same hands-on style he employed when it was a small family-owned company.

By far the biggest news surrounding News Corporation in recent years was its 2007 purchase of the *Wall Street Journal* and its parent company, Dow Jones & Company Inc. Murdoch paid a substantial premium for the paper to buy it from its longtime controlling owners, the Bancroft family. Although the *Journal* has always had a politically conservative editorial page, the paper's news coverage has generally been considered evenhanded. When Murdoch first expressed interest in the *Journal*, there were concerns in the news industry that he would apply the same partisan style to the paper that he used with the Fox News Channel. To date, that doesn't seem to have happened. Murdoch has been active in the paper's management, but he has not made substantial change in the paper's style or approach to news.[46]

The Twenty-first Century at News Corporation and 21st Century Fox. News Corporation split into two separate companies in 2013. Rupert Murdoch's media corporations seem to have figured out the rapidly changing media world of the new century. They have experienced growing revenue throughout the recent recession, rising from annual sales of $16 billion in 2002 to more than $36 billion in 2012.[47] How have his corporations managed to be so successful?

- Being willing to change to match the new media environment—News Corporation split into two separate companies in 2013 for a number of reasons, not the least of which was the toxic environment surrounding the *News of the World* phone hacking scandal. The split also allowed for the more profitable entertainment-oriented 21st Century Fox to follow a separate path from the news and publishing News Corporation.[48]
- Giving consumers what they want—Although Murdoch is known for his politically conservative newspapers and cable news channel, his companies are generally pragmatic about delivering what audiences want. Fox Broadcasting carries shows such as *The Simpsons*, *Family Guy*, and *American Dad*, which frequently make the lists of the most objectionable shows on television, and News Corporation's British tabloids can get quite racy—the London *Sun* includes a photo of a topless woman as a daily feature.
- Wise use of multiple platforms—21st Century Fox produces a wide range of content that can be distributed through multiple platforms. For example, a movie produced by 20th Century Fox can be shown in theaters, sold on a disc by 20th Century Fox Home Entertainment, aired on Fox Broadcasting, shown again on the FX cable channel, and finally used as an

TEST YOUR MEDIA LITERACY

News of the World Hacking Scandal

The *News of the World* was for many years the biggest circulating British tabloid newspaper (8.4 million copies an issue), and it long had a reputation for cutting ethical corners to report the sordid details of crimes and celebrity gossip. But it really outdid itself when reporters for the paper hacked into the phone of a murdered thirteen-year-old girl to listen to her voice mail messages. On other occasions, the paper's reporters were accused of hacking into the phones of British terrorism victims, making payoffs to members of the Scotland Yard police force, and having improper connections to prominent British politicians.

Matters got bad enough that former editors and reporters at the paper were arrested or even sent to jail over the scandals. There was even talk for a time that News Corporation officials could be prosecuted in the United States for violating the Foreign Corrupt Practices Act for bribing British officials. The scandal finally became so intense that News Corporation shut down the embattled tabloid that had been published since 1843. This was all shocking, but should it have been, given that the *NOTW*'s sister paper, the *Sun*, runs a topless pinup on page 3 of every issue?

The fact that the *News of the World* was also owned by Rupert Murdoch's News Corporation made this a big story within the press. After all, News Corporation is a major world news organization and a major media owner in the United States. It owns one of the most respected and largest-circulating newspapers in the United States, the *Wall Street Journal*.

> **SECRET 4** Through all this, it's worth remembering Secret Four—Nothing's new: Everything that happened in the past will happen again. The behavior of Mr. Murdoch's tabloids is nothing new. As you will read about in Chapter 6, if you go back to the rise of the yellow press in New York City back in the late 1800s, about the time that modern standards of journalism were being established, you will see that Joseph Pulitzer's *New York World* and William Randolph Hearst's *Evening Journal* engaged in very similar escapades. In one case, the two papers battled over covering a spectacular murder case that involved dismemberment and a love triangle. One newspaper publisher even leased the apartment where the murder took place in order to keep competing reporters away.

WHO is the source?

Rupert Murdoch has been in the newspaper business in various areas around the world since the 1950s and is one of the most powerful people in the news industry. What news outlets does he control? How do you think his background shaped how the *News of the World* behaved?

WHAT were the reporters doing?

Follow the link and read several of the supporting articles that go with the post.

What were reporters at the *News of the World* accused of doing?

WHAT have other newspapers done?

How does the behavior of the reporters at the *News of the World* compare to that at the yellow papers of the late 1800s? Would you expect reporters from contemporary American newspapers or broadcasters to behave like the reporters at the *News of the World* did? Why or why not?

HOW do you and your classmates react to the behavior of tabloid reporters?

Do you think that the press cared more about this story than the general public did? Why do you think so? Are you surprised at the behavior of the reporters at the *News of the World*? Are reporters ever justified in doing things like hacking people's voice mail accounts? Why or why not?

Sources: Nick Davies and Amelia Hill, "Missing Milly Dowler's Voicemail Was Hacked by *News of the World*," *Guardian*, July 4, 2011, www.guardian.co.uk/uk/2011/jul/04/milly-dowler-voicemail-hacked-news-of-world; Bob Garfield and Brooke Gladstone, "*News of the World* Folds: Transcript," July 8, 2011, http://www.onthemedia.org/2011/jul/08/news-world-folds/transcript/; Brooke Gladstone, "Muted U.S. Public Reaction to British Tabloid Scandal: Transcript," July 22, 2011, http://www.onthemedia.org/2011/jul/22/muted-us-public-reaction-british-tabloid-scandal/transcript/; Bob Garfield, "The Love Triangle, Murder and Missing Head That Sparked a Tabloid War: Transcript," July 22, 2011, http://www.onthemedia.org/2011/jul/22/love-triangle-murder-and-missing-head-sparked-tabloid-war/transcript/.

 Web 3.8: You can read more about the hacking scandal with this blog post.

---

afternoon or late-night program on a 21st Century Fox–owned television station.[49] This multiplatform approach then leads to global synergy.

- Global synergy at News Corporation—News Corporation's direct broadcast satellite systems currently cover much of the globe. Due to his various studios, Murdoch also owns the means to produce content to flow out over these channels. He has, in the words of media journalist Ken Auletta, both content and the pipeline. Owning every step of the process is important according to Murdoch, who says, "We'd like to be **vertically integrated** from the moment

---

vertical integration: Controlling all aspects of a media project, including production, delivery to consumers in multiple formats, and the promotion of the product through other media.

of creation through to the moment of delivery into the home."[50] Although News Corporation owns media properties around the world, Murdoch does not take a one-size-fits-all approach in providing content to these varied channels. "You would be very wrong to forget that what people want to watch in their own country is basically local programming, local language, local culture," Murdoch says. "I learned that many, many years ago in Australia, when I was loading up [News Corporation's network] with good American programs and we'd get beat with second-rate Australian ones."[51]

News of the World's final edition, published on July 10, 2011. The paper had at one time been the highest-circulating newspaper in Britain and was known for its lurid covers and headlines, but News Corporation shut down the paper following its phone hacking scandal.

Time Warner: Starting the Trend That Smaller Is Better

At one point, Time Warner was the world's largest media conglomerate; with 2008 sales of almost $47 billion, it brought in $9 billion more than Disney did that year. But in 2010, Time Warner was down to annual revenue of $26.9 billion. Why did the company have such a gigantic drop in revenue over just a two-year period? Well, hold on just a moment. It's also worth noting that in 2008 Time Warner lost $13.4 billion, but in 2010, it turned a profit of $2.6 billion. What happened? The decline in the company's size and growth of profitability came from its selling off of several assets, including Internet provider AOL in 2009 and cable TV provider Time Warner Cable. (That's right. Time Warner Cable is not owned by Time Warner. Just so that's clear. We'll talk about that a little bit further on.) Since then, Time has continued to spin off properties and grow in profitability, with 2013 revenue of $29.8 billion and a profit of $3.7 billion. Time Warner is a major player in film, television, cable TV, publishing, and online content, and it is the home to many iconic media characters, such as Scooby-Doo, Harry Potter, and Batman (see Box 3.4).[52]

Time, Warner Bros., and Turner Broadcasting.
Media giant Time Warner started out as the publisher of *Time* magazine, founded in 1922 by Henry Luce and his prep-school friend Briton Hadden. *Time* quickly prospered, and by 1930, Luce had started the business magazine *Fortune*, which was followed by the photo magazine *Life* in 1936. By the 1980s, Time Inc. had added multiple magazines, book publishers, local cable companies, and the Home Box Office (HBO) cable movie channel to its holdings. In 1989, Time merged with Warner Communications, which had grown out of the Warner

| Box 3.4 | What Does Time Warner Own? |

Cable Networks

- HBO (at least sixteen channels)
- CNN (at least six channels)
- WTBS
- TNT Drama
- truTV
- Turner Classic Movies
- Cartoon Network (at least four channels)

Broadcast Television Network

- The CW Television Network (co-owned with CBS)

Movie and TV Studios

- Warner Bros.
- DC Entertainment (Marvel's main rival for comic book–based movies)
- New Line Cinema
- Castle Rock Entertainment
- Hanna-Barbera Cartoons

Sources: "Who Owns What," *Columbia Journalism Review,* http://www.cjr.org/resources/?c=timewarner; *Hoover's Company Records—In-Depth Records: Time Warner Inc.* (Austin, Texas: Hoover's Inc., 2014).

Note: This table lists only a sample of Time Warner's holdings. The company also owns multiple television and movie production companies.

Bros. movie studio. This merger combined a major movie studio with the nation's largest magazine publisher.

Web 3.9: Visit Time Warner's corporate site.

Among Time Warner's businesses were a large number of **local cable television systems**, which delivered programming to individual homes (these have since been spun off as the separate company Time Warner Cable), and HBO, one of the first premium cable networks. In 1996, Time Warner vastly expanded its stable by purchasing cable pioneer Ted Turner's group of channels, which included the CNN networks, WTBS, TNT, Turner Classic Movies, and the Cartoon Network. Along with his cable properties, Turner also sold his Internet operations and movie studio. When Time Warner took over Turner Broadcasting System (TBS), Turner became a vice president of the new company and its largest stockholder. More significantly, the Turner networks had passed from the control of a single individual to that of a publicly owned company, in much the same way that Robert Johnson's BET would later be bought by Viacom.[53]

The Twenty-first Century at Time Warner.

Although Time Warner is the biggest of the Big Media, that bigness has been a mixed blessing for the company since 2000.

- In 2001, the big news was that AOL, then known as America Online, was merging with (some said buying) Time Warner. At the time of the merger, AOL was valued at $124 billion; when the companies separated in 2009, AOL's value was below $3 billion. The goal of the merger was to have greater synergy between AOL's online offerings and Time Warner's older legacy media. The only problem? The AOL–Time Warner synergy never really worked. The new company soon cut more than 4,000 jobs and sold off numerous properties, including its sports teams, its book division, and the Warner Music Group.[54]

- In 2014, Time Warner took its magazine publishing arm, Time Inc., and made it into its own, independent company. This means that the part of the media giant that gave Time Warner half of its name is no longer a part of the company. Time Inc. publishes more than ninety magazines and forty-five Web sites. Magazine publishing has been going through a difficult time since the Great Recession of 2007–2009, and *New York Times* reporters David Carr and Ravi Somaiya say they were not surprised to see Time Warner cutting the magazine division loose in much the same way it previously had with Time Warner Cable and AOL.[55]

Web 3.10: Visit Viacom's corporate site.

Web 3.11: Visit the CBS corporate site.

- Legacy synergy—There are examples, however, of synergy working among the longtime elements of Time Warner. Owning multiple channels allows a company to repackage media content for different audiences. Warner Bros. can first show a movie in theaters, then sell it through Time Warner Cable's pay-per-view division, then market DVDs of it through the company's home video division, air it on the HBO premium movie channel, and broadcast it on the WTBS or TNT basic cable channels.

Viacom and CBS: Two Companies, Same Management

The relationship between media conglomerate Viacom and established broadcast network CBS has been a long-term on-again, off-again one. Although they are currently two separate corporations with separate stocks, the ownership and management of the two companies heavily overlap. The companies had combined revenue for 2012 of almost $28 billion. Of that $28 billion, $13.9 billion came from Viacom and $14 billion from CBS. CBS owns the CBS broadcast network, half of the CW broadcast network, a number of television production companies, approximately thirty broadcast television stations, and the Simon & Schuster publishing group. Viacom owns the movie studio Paramount and numerous cable channels, including Comedy Central, BET, and the various MTV and Nickelodeon channels (see Box 3.5).[56]

The Child Buys/Sells the Parent.

CBS became a force in broadcasting when William S. Paley and his father bought United Independent Broadcasters and turned it into the Columbia Broadcasting System (CBS). In the mid-1980s, when all three of the original broadcast networks changed ownership, CBS was bought by investor Laurence Tisch and his Loews Corporation. Westinghouse bought Tisch's company in 1995, and by 1997 it had sold all its nonmedia businesses and was simply CBS Inc.

Then, in one of the strangest twists in media history, CBS was bought by Viacom in 1999. What made this transaction so unusual was that Viacom had begun as a small film production unit within CBS. Later, in 1971, the federal government became concerned that the broadcast networks were becoming too powerful, so it forced them to sell their content production units. As an independent company, Viacom grew into a major producer of cable television programming; its products included MTV and Nickelodeon.

In 1987, theater owner Sumner Redstone bought Viacom. Under Redstone's leadership, the company became a dominant media corporation in the 1990s. It acquired the Blockbuster video store chain, the Paramount

local cable television systems: The companies that provide cable television service directly to consumers' homes.

movie studio, and the start-up television network United Paramount Network (UPN). (In 2006, UPN was merged with the WB network to become the CW.) Finally, Viacom bought CBS, the television network that had given birth to it decades before.[57] But then in 2005, Viacom and CBS split back into two separate corporations with separate stocks being traded. So they are no longer a single Big Media company, right? Well, sort of. Sumner Redstone and his daughter Shari were, as of 2014, still top executives of both companies, though Les Moonves, who is not part of the Redstone family, was CEO of CBS.[58]

Sumner Redstone, speaking here to guests at a television studio in Istanbul, Turkey, turned the small content-production company Viacom into a media industry giant.

 Video 3.5: See what all the fuss was about with the Janet Jackson indecency case.

The Twenty-first Century at Viacom and CBS. The split of Viacom and CBS into separately traded companies was the most visible change at Redstone's companies, but other, more significant, changes have happened there as well:

- Indecency—CBS and Viacom have been at the center of the debate on broadcast indecency that came out of Janet Jackson's infamous "wardrobe malfunction" during the 2004 Super Bowl broadcast. (For more on the issue of broadcast indecency, see Chapter 13.) Radio stations owned by CBS have also drawn fire from critics and the Federal Communications Commission (FCC) for sexually explicit broadcasts by shock jocks Howard Stern and Opie and Anthony, all of whom have since left CBS. Viacom has paid more than $3.5 million in fines and promised to suspend and possibly fire anyone who makes an indecent broadcast over the company's properties.[59]
- Music videos—Viacom continues to be the dominant force in music videos, owning BET (rap and hip-hop), MTV (music appealing to teens and twenty-somethings), VH1 (music appealing to people who were teens a long time ago), and Country Music Television.
- The split was more than just finance—Common wisdom held that the split of Viacom and CBS was purely a financial move, but the two companies seem to be reacting very differently to the new media environment. While Viacom, with its cable and movie studio properties, has been vehemently opposed to video-sharing services, such as YouTube, posting Viacom-owned content to the Web without a licensing agreement, CBS, on the other hand, was able to reach an agreement with YouTube to share advertising revenue raised from clips posted from CBS-owned programs. Why this different response? Media

Unlike most of the other media giants, Bertelsmann is a privately held company—it is owned by a German foundation that mandates that the company not only earn a profit but also operate for the benefit of its employees and various social causes.[63] Bertelsmann sees book publishing as one of the key media of the twenty-first century and, having purchased the major American publisher Random House for $1.4 billion in 1998, has a much stronger presence in this area than the other media giants. It also owns the RTL Group, Europe's largest television broadcaster, and a large number of magazines through its Gruner + Jahr division.[64]

American Idol, produced by a subsidiary of German media giant Bertelsmann, is a global phenomenon with versions of the show creating new stars like Caleb Johnson on television networks all around the world.

journalist Ken Auletta has written that the most likely reason is that Viacom has always been in the business of licensing content while CBS was in the business of selling advertising time. YouTube was a good match to the CBS model and a bad match for Viacom. It may also be that Viacom is suffering more from Secret Five—New media are always scary—than is CBS.[60]

Bertelsmann: The World's Largest Publisher 🌐

Although the German media corporation Bertelsmann has historically been known for its book and music publishing and management business, it also has a major presence in magazines, newspapers, and Internet and broadcast properties (see Box 3.6). Bertelsmann is both the world's largest publisher and the largest publisher of English-language books. In 2009, it had sales of $22 billion.[61]

Books Still Matter. Bertelsmann started out in 1835 as a publisher of Christian music and prayers. It was also the original publisher of the fairy tales of the Brothers Grimm in the nineteenth century. After World War II, the company was run by Reinhard Mohn, a former German Luftwaffe officer who learned to speak English while in a prisoner-of-war camp in Kansas.[62]

 Web 3.12: Visit the Bertelsmann corporate site.

The Twenty-first Century at Bertelsmann. As a publisher and European broadcaster, Bertelsmann is not in the public eye the way Time Warner, Viacom, and Disney are. It does not have Scooby-Doo, SpongeBob, or Mickey Mouse as a mascot, but it has quietly made its presence felt by utilizing the following methods[65]:

- Returning to core strengths—Up until 2002, under the leadership of CEO Thomas Middelhoff, Bertelsmann looked like it was preparing to become a generalized media giant on the scale of Time Warner or Disney. But members of the Mohn family forced Middelhoff out and returned the company to its core business of book and magazine publishing. Ever since, the company has been gradually selling off peripheral businesses and buying back its stock.[66]

- Broadcasting in Europe—Bertelsmann is big in European television, owning 90 percent of the RTL Group, Europe's largest broadcaster. In addition to operating more than forty-five television channels in a dozen countries, it also produces the wildly popular *American Idol* and a wide range of other *Idol* versions around the world.[67]

- Adapting to the changing music business—Bertelsmann has long been in the music business, first with the Bertelsmann Music Group (BMG) and later with its partnership with Sony BMG Music Entertainment.[68] But with the massive changes that file sharing and digital downloads have brought to the music industry, Bertelsmann has taken a new approach. It sold out its interest in Sony BMG to Sony, and it's now involved with pressing CDs for other publishers and managing the song catalogs of more than 200 artists without being their publisher. So Bertelsmann has gotten out of the business of selling music and is now in the business of assisting companies that do sell it.[69]

Box 3.6 — What Does Bertelsmann Own?

Book Publishing

- Random House (including Bantam, Dell, and Ballantine)
- WaterBrook Mulnomah
- Knopf
- Fodor's Travel

Magazines

- Gruner + Jahr (publisher of numerous trade magazines)
- More than two dozen European magazines, including the German publication *Stern*
- Multiple North American magazines (partially or in full), including *National Geographic*

Broadcasting

- Numerous European television stations (partially or in full), including RTL Group, Europe's largest television company
- Multiple television production companies
- Multiple radio services throughout Europe
- FremantleMedia (multiple international versions; producer of *Idol* singing competition series)

Sources: "Who Owns What," *Columbia Journalism Review,* http://www.cjr.org/resources/?c=timewarner; *Hoover's Company Records—In-Depth Records: Time Warner Inc.* (Austin, Texas: Hoover's Inc., 2014).

Big Media: The New Players

SECRET 2 ▷ The conglomerates have long been seen as the unquestioned rulers of the American media. But trying to rank the biggest media companies has gotten to be harder and harder with the rise of new media companies. Look at Disney, generally considered to be the largest of the media conglomerates with annual income of just over $45 billion. Then compare it to cable giant Comcast, which now owns NBCUniversal (NBCU). For 2013, Comcast had annual revenue of $64.6 billion, up from $37.9 billion in 2010. Or consider search giant Google. In 2012, it had annual sales of $50.2 billion, most of which came from advertising. That would put it right between Comcast and Disney in terms of income.[70] So let us now look at the other contenders in the Big Media business. Remember Secret Two—There are no mainstream media. There is a wide range of media out there, all of which are significant.

Comcast/NBCUniversal: Cable Buys Broadcaster

NBCUniversal is one of the oldest broadcasters in the United States. It was founded in 1926 by the Radio Corporation of America (RCA), the original monopoly in the broadcast business. Initially, the federal government established RCA to consolidate all the patents required to start the radio business. RCA formed the National Broadcasting Company (NBC) to provide radio programming across the country. As is described in more detail in Chapter 7, NBC had two networks, the "Red" and the "Blue." In the 1940s, it sold the Blue network, which became ABC, now owned by Disney.[71] In the 1930s, RCA began developing television technology and was the first network with regularly scheduled television broadcasts.

In 1985, General Electric (GE) bought both NBC and RCA. The purchase was controversial from the very beginning because GE's primary business is not media but manufacturing and financial services. GE makes consumer electronics, electric generating plants, and aircraft engines. Critics questioned whether a major defense contractor ought to be allowed to own a broadcast network.[72]

Up until the fall of 2009, cable, Internet, and phone service provider Comcast wasn't on anyone's list of American media giants. Sure, it was the largest single supplier of cable television and Internet services in the United States, but it wasn't talked about in the same breath as Disney, Viacom, or Fox. But then the news started breaking that the cable giant was in negotiations to purchase 51 percent of NBCUniversal from GE, which would give the Philadelphia-based company controlling ownership of the network/movie studio. In January 2011, the FCC approved Comcast's purchase of majority ownership of NBCU.[73] The transition of complete ownership of NBCUniversal from GE to Comcast had been expected to be an extended process, with the new owner gradually acquiring the entertainment company's stock. But that changed in February 2013 with the announcement that Comcast would be completing its purchase of NBCU by the end of March of that year. Amy Chozick and Brian Stelter of the *New York Times* report a variety of reasons for the faster pace of the acquisition, including a conflict between the corporate cultures of Comcast and GE, Comcast's desire to control programming sources as well as channels for distribution, and the fact that Comcast could afford to complete the transaction.[74] Purchasing NBCUniversal made Comcast the nation's most valuable pure-media company. (Apple is often considered the world's most valuable company, depending on its stock price, but it is only partially a media company.)[75] For 2013, Comcast had revenue of $64.6 billion, making it almost a third bigger than Disney.[76]

Comcast makes the majority of its revenue by selling cable television, Internet, and phone services to its more than 17 million subscribers. Along with its media-related properties, Comcast owns an interest in professional sports teams and arenas in Philadelphia. The purchase of NBCU gave it the NBC broadcast network, the number-two Spanish-language broadcast network Telemundo, ten NBC affiliate stations, and more than twenty cable networks. These cable networks include the top-rated USA Network, along with Bravo, Syfy, and the Weather Channel. On the film side, the deal gave Comcast control of the major film studio Universal Studios and small-picture/indie studio Focus Features. And, finally, the deal included the Universal Studios theme parks in Florida and California.[77]

Although Comcast is a publicly owned corporation, one-third of the company's voting stock is controlled by CEO Brian Roberts, son of the company's founder. Comcast got its start in the cable business in Mississippi in 1963 and got its name in 1969. After acquiring cable systems in Pennsylvania, it moved to Philadelphia. Throughout the 1980s, Comcast grew by buying up local cable service throughout the United States. In the late 1980s and early 1990s, Comcast started buying up mobile phone companies as well. In 2004, Comcast made its first bid at buying a Big Media company with an offer for Disney. While that deal was not successful, it did set the stage for the cable giant making the play for NBCUniversal (see Box 3.7).

Critics of the merger were concerned that giving control of the NBCU twenty-plus major cable networks to one of the nation's leading Internet and cable providers could lead to a "walled garden" Internet, where only Comcast subscribers would have access to NBCU programing. The agreement Comcast made with the FCC on the merger requires Comcast to give up management control of the Hulu streaming video service (though it can still be an investor). Also, the FCC can require Comcast to make its shows widely available on the Internet if its competitors start doing so first.[78] Those concerns grew when in February 2014 Comcast announced that it had reached an agreement to buy Time Warner Cable for more than $45 billion in stock. This is controversial because Comcast is the nation's largest cable provider and Time Warner Cable is the nation's second largest. If the transaction is approved by the FCC and the U.S. Department of Justice, Comcast would have control of the programming going out to as many as 33 million cable subscribers. (Why is that number in doubt? There are roughly 100 million cable subscribers in the United States. If Comcast controls more than 30 percent of those subscriptions, it could run into regulatory problems. So if the merger goes through, Comcast is likely to sell off approximately 3 million subscribers to fall below that magical 30 percent figure.)

Before we go any further, let's make one thing clear. Time Warner Cable is a company that provides cable TV and Internet services to subscribers in New York, Dallas, Los Angeles, North Carolina, Maine, and Ohio. It is not the general media giant Time Warner that owns the Turner Broadcasting properties and Warner Bros. movie studio. So why the *Time Warner* in Time Warner Cable? That's easy. Time Warner the media company owned Time Warner Cable up until 2009, when it spun off the cable/Internet provider into its own company.[79]

Media reporter Ken Auletta says the purchase would give Comcast a couple of key advantages[80]:

 Box 3.7 What Does Comcast/NBC Universal Own?

Broadcast Television Networks

- NBC broadcast network
- Telemundo Spanish-language broadcast network

Broadcast Television Stations

NBCU owns twenty-eight television stations, some of which are NBC affiliates and some of which broadcast the Spanish-language Telemundo network.

Cable Networks

Numerous cable networks (partially or in full), including:

- CNBC (financial news)
- MSNBC (news)
- Bravo
- Syfy
- USA Network
- The Weather Channel

Movie Studios

- Universal Pictures
- Focus Features

Online Properties

- Weather.com
- Hulu (streaming video)

Cable/Internet/Phone Services

Comcast is a major cable/Internet/phone services provider with more than 17 million subscribers.

Sports Teams and Facilities

Comcast owns partial interest in Philadelphia-area professional sports teams and arenas.

Sources: "Who Owns What," *Columbia Journalism Review,* www.cjr.org/resources/index.php; *Hoover's Company Records—In-Depth Records: Comcast Corporation* (Austin, Texas: Hoover's Inc., 2014); *Hoover's Company Records—In-Depth Records: NBCUniversal Media, LLC* (Austin, Texas: Hoover's Inc., 2011).

- More subscribers would give Comcast more negotiating power with both television program providers and Internet program providers.
- It would give Comcast access to Time Warner Cable's powerful video-on-demand service that lets consumers have access to programming they want to see without being able to skip commercials.

One thing the deal probably won't do is make you like your cable company any better. The merger won't give customers any more choices in whom they can buy cable service from. Local service will continue to be a monopoly negotiated between a single service provider and the municipality. And consumer advocates argue that the

Web 3.13: Read more about Comcast's accelerated purchase of NBCUniversal from GE.

Web 3.14: Read more about Comcast's attempt to buy Time Warner Cable.

merger will likely lead to higher prices to consumers.[81]

Google: Making Search Mass Media

In previous editions of this book, I raised the question "Are search engines a new part of mass communication?" Certainly the Internet and the World Wide Web are a part of our mass media, and search engines, such as Google and Bing, are the tools we use to find information on the Web. They might even be considered news media. Think about Google News. It's in essence a search tool that decides what the major news stories of the day are, collects links to them on a single page, and presents them to the reader. According to Google, Google News draws stories from more than 4,500 English-language news sources from around the world. The articles are evaluated by Google's computers as to how often and on what sites the stories appear. Google claims this leads to an unbiased presentation of the news.[82]

In 2012, Google had worldwide sales of $50.2 billion, including $23.5 billion from the United States. This places Google, like Comcast, ahead of all of the legacy media conglomerates in terms of revenue. Of this income, the vast majority of it came from advertising sales. Not only is Google bringing in a lot of income; it is among the most profitable of the media companies as well. Given all this, Google has to be considered one of the major new players in the media business.[83]

Although Google was founded as a search engine, it also offers an e-mail service (Gmail), blogging (Blogger), photo sharing (Picasa), video (YouTube), and a mobile device operating system (Android). Unlike so many other media companies, Google does not try to sell its products to consumers. Instead, it sees each of these as a way of delivering highly targeted advertising to consumers whom it attracts by providing free services.

Google was founded in 1998 by two engineers who didn't even suspect they were going into the advertising business. Sergey Brin, the child of Jewish Russian immigrants, learned to program at age nine when his parents gave him a Commodore 64 computer. He partnered with Larry Page, whose father was a professor of computer science at Michigan State and whose mother was a database consultant. Brin and Page met each other while in graduate school at Stanford. One night, Page explains, he had a dream: "I was thinking: What if we could download the whole Web, and just keep the links."[84]

The two classmates created a search system based on that idea that worked by analyzing the quality of links to a

Google founders Sergey Brin and Larry Page took their company from being a search engine start-up in 1998 to being the world's leading online advertising company.

topic and then scored them according to a system known as PageRank, which stood for both Larry Page's name and the rank of the Web page itself. Google was initially launched not in a garage (though it would later move into a garage), but in graduate housing at Stanford. Google was founded without a business plan or a strategy for making money. But what the founders did have was a strategy for creating the most simple, clean search system.

While Brin and Page were quite happy to burn through investors' money without worrying about generating any, the venture capitalists who were bankrolling the company did want a return on their investments. It was in 2002 that Google finally figured out that to make money for its investors, it had to be in the advertising business. What Google's engineers came up with was the AdWords system, where advertisers bid on the rights to advertise next to search results. The advertisers buy certain keywords that they want their ads to appear next to. But Google requires that the ads that appear be relevant to the people doing the search. So, for example, advertisers can't buy the word *chocolate* and use it to put up links selling cars. But the words "helicopter parts" would be perfect for someone wanting to sell tools for repairing helicopters. Advertisers are only charged when audience members click on their ads.

Google's second big advertising product was AdSense, which places ads on blogs and Web sites that match the ads with the content of the site. Then Google splits the revenue, with about two-thirds of the money going to the owner of the Web site. This put Google in the position

Web 3.15: Visit Google's corporate site.

Who Are Our Media?

Although consumers have vastly more media choices than they did in the past, the number of companies providing those choices has declined substantially.

Media critic and Pulitzer Prize–winning journalist Ben Bagdikian wrote that in 1983 the media business was dominated by fifty corporations that controlled more than half the newspaper, magazine, television, radio, and music output in the United States. By 1987, this number had shrunk to twenty-nine companies, and as

of 2004, only five companies controlled a majority of the media output in the United States: Time Warner, Disney, Viacom, Bertelsmann, and News Corporation. A sixth company could be added to this list: General Electric, which until recently owned NBCUniversal.[85]

But that picture of six conglomerates controlling American media does not work anymore. To be sure, Disney and Bertelsmann are still single-corporation media giants. But News Corporation has now split into News Corporation and 21st

Century Fox; Time Warner has split off several divisions and is now a much smaller company than it was in 2008; and Viacom split into two corporations—Viacom and CBS—back in 2005, with CBS handling broadcasting and Viacom handling movies and cable. In the most dramatic change, cable giant Comcast acquired NBCUniversal from General Electric, so one of the original Big Three broadcast networks is now being run by a company whose major business is running local cable systems. And as this

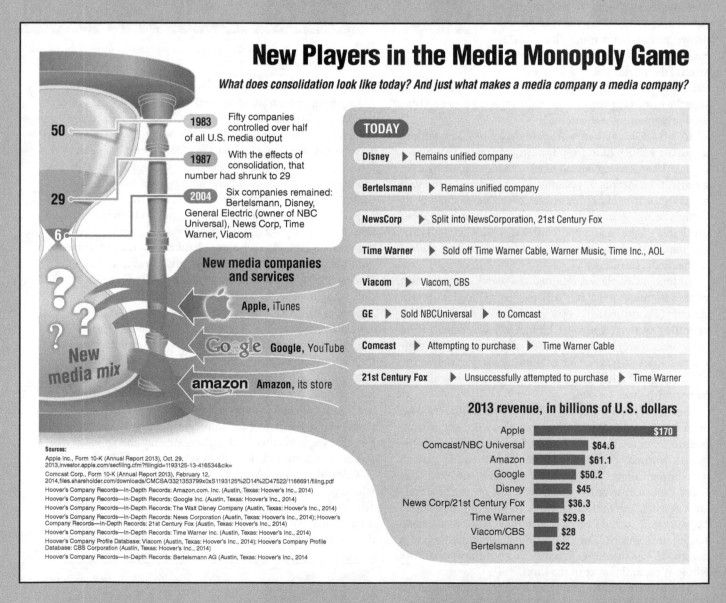

New Players in the Media Monopoly Game

What does consolidation look like today? And just what makes a media company a media company?

1983 Fifty companies controlled over half of all U.S. media output

1987 With the effects of consolidation, that number had shrunk to 29

2004 Six companies remained: Bertelsmann, Disney, General Electric (owner of NBC Universal), News Corp, Time Warner, Viacom

New media companies and services

 Apple, iTunes

Google, YouTube

amazon Amazon, its store

New media mix

TODAY

Disney ▶ Remains unified company

Bertelsmann ▶ Remains unified company

NewsCorp ▶ Split into NewsCorporation, 21st Century Fox

Time Warner ▶ Sold off Time Warner Cable, Warner Music, Time Inc., AOL

Viacom ▶ Viacom, CBS

GE ▶ Sold NBCUniversal ▶ to Comcast

Comcast ▶ Attempting to purchase ▶ Time Warner Cable

21st Century Fox ▶ Unsuccessfully attempted to purchase ▶ Time Warner

2013 revenue, in billions of U.S. dollars

Company	Revenue
Apple	$170
Comcast/NBC Universal	$64.6
Amazon	$61.1
Google	$50.2
Disney	$45
News Corp/21st Century Fox	$36.3
Time Warner	$29.8
Viacom/CBS	$28
Bertelsmann	$22

Sources:
Apple Inc., Form 10-K (Annual Report 2013), Oct. 29, 2013,investor.apple.com/secfiling.cfm?filingid=1193125-13-416534&cik=

Comcast Corp., Form 10-K (Annual Report 2013), February 12, 2014,files.shareholder.com/downloads/CMCSA/3321353799x0xS1193125%2D14%2D47522/1166691/filing.pdf

Hoover's Company Records—In-Depth Records: Amazon.com. Inc. (Austin, Texas: Hoover's Inc., 2014)

Hoover's Company Records—In-Depth Records: Google Inc. (Austin, Texas: Hoover's Inc., 2014)

Hoover's Company Records—In-Depth Records: The Walt Disney Company (Austin, Texas: Hoover's Inc., 2014)

Hoover's Company Records—In-Depth Records: News Corporation (Austin, Texas: Hoover's Inc., 2014); Hoover's Company Records—In-Depth Records: 21st Century Fox (Austin, Texas: Hoover's Inc., 2014)

Hoover's Company Records—In-Depth Records: Time Warner Inc. (Austin, Texas: Hoover's Inc., 2014)

Hoover's Company Profile Database: Viacom (Austin, Texas: Hoover's Inc., 2014); Hoover's Company Profile Database: CBS Corporation (Austin, Texas: Hoover's Inc., 2014)

Hoover's Company Records—In-Depth Records: Bertelsmann AG (Austin, Texas: Hoover's Inc., 2014

is being written, Comcast is now attempting to purchase Time Warner Cable, which is the second largest cable provider in the country.

Perhaps the biggest changes of all have been with new media companies coming to the forefront. Search giant Google, which draws 96 percent of its revenue from advertising, makes more money than Disney, the biggest of the old media companies. In addition to being in the search business, Google also distributes an almost unimaginable amount of video through YouTube. And how does one even attempt to classify a company like Apple? While it clearly generates most of its income selling hardware, much of that hardware is related to media consumption and production. Apple is also the largest music retailer in the United States. It's no accident that Apple dropped *Computer* out of its corporate name back in 2007.[86]

All this brings us back to Secret Two: There are no mainstream media. We have lots of different media out there, ranging from the legacy corporations, to new media giants, to individuals sharing their work through services like YouTube. And they are all our media.

Media Transformations Questions

- **DO** you think of Apple as a media company? Why or why not?
- **SHOULD** we be concerned that one company might control cable access for one-third of all subscribers in the United States?
- **WHICH** companies do you think of as major media? Do you think much about where you get your media?
- **DO** you worry about who controls the media you consume?

of collaborating with a lot of smaller, independent sites and being seen as a benefactor. This not only made Google quite profitable; it allowed lots of small sites to make money as well.

While in retrospect using search as an advertising medium seems really obvious, Google was founded on the idea of making the best possible search engine, not making money. The founders figured that if they built a great product, they would eventually come up with a good source of revenue.

SECRET 5 ▷ Secret Five says new media are always scary, and we should remember that the scariness is oftentimes bigger for the media industry than it is for consumers. This is why Google's approach to the media business is so different from that of legacy media. At a time when the music and movie industries are terrified of their fans/users/customers and are taking them to court for being "pirates," Google is trying to figure out how to better serve them. Google co-founder Larry Page told media journalist Ken Auletta, "[Thinking that] your customers or users are always right, and your goal is to build systems that work for them in a natural way is a good attitude to have. You can replace the system. You can't replace the user."[87]

Apple: Reinventing the Media

Although Apple is best known as a technology company, it has done as much as any corporation to change the media business in the twenty-first century. A quick check of Apple's balance sheet shows that in 2013 the California company sold $91 billion worth of iPhone products; $32 billion worth of iPads; $21 billion worth of more conventional computer equipment; $16 billion worth of iTunes, software, and other services; $4.4 billion worth of iPods; and $5.7 billion worth of accessories. Apple also has gone through incredible levels of growth. Apple had $66 billion in revenue for 2010, which grew to $170 billion in 2013. That's close to tripling its income over three years.[88]

And if you look carefully at the numbers, computers are only a small part of the company's business. That's why these days the company's name is Apple, not Apple Computer.

Steve Jobs co-founded Apple back in 1976 with his friend Steve Wozniak. "Woz" was the inventor, and Jobs was the businessman and visionary. Wozniak left the company in 1983, and Jobs was forced out by Apple's board of directors in 1985.[89] After leaving Apple, Jobs founded NeXT Inc., which built an innovative UNIX-based computer that was used by Tim Berners-Lee to create the World Wide Web.[90] (You can read more about Berners-Lee in Chapter 10.)

Then in 1997 Apple had a change of heart, bought out NeXT Inc., and brought Jobs back as its interim CEO. The NeXTSTEP software morphed into OS X, Apple's radical and successful remake of its computer operating system. By 2001, Jobs had dropped *interim* from his title and started Apple on the path to its current success, in which the Mac is not just a computer, but rather a "digital hub" for all types of media and entertainment content. It was also in 2001 that Apple introduced its iconic media player, the iPod.[91]

With the iPod, and its accompanying iTunes software, Jobs solidified his company as a player in the new media business. Jobs did numerous things people told him he couldn't do. He persuaded the major recording labels to offer their music through Apple's iTunes store. He persuaded the major broadcast and cable networks to sell their television shows through the iTunes store. He persuaded major movie studios to sell and rent their movies through . . . oh, you get the picture.[92]

In addition to running Apple, Jobs took Pixar, a computer graphics company he bought for $10 million from *Star Wars* director George Lucas, and turned it into America's leading animation studio, valued in excess of $7 billion when he sold it to Disney in 2006.[93] Upon the sale of Pixar, Jobs became Disney's biggest stockholder and a member of the company's board of directors, thus cementing an already strong relationship between Apple and Disney.[94] Disney CEO Robert Iger depended on Jobs for

AP Photo/Noah Berger

Apple CEO Tim Cook introduces the iPad Air and a new version of the iPad Mini at one of the company's highly anticipated media events. While Apple is primarily in the hardware business, they've transformed how people consume media in the 21st century.

guidance on how his company could avoid the problems the music industry faced in dealing with the Internet. Iger's response was to license his studio's content to Apple's iTunes store so that customers could legally buy and watch Disney entertainment on their computers and mobile devices.[95]

When Jobs lost his long battle with pancreatic cancer in 2011, the response from fans and the news media—from Facebook to cable news—was at a level you might have expected from the death of Joan Rivers or Robin Williams, not from the head of one of the world's most valuable corporations. But then few companies inspire the level of intense loyalty that Apple does, and few companies have been more associated with the personality and identity of its founder.[96] Tim Cook took over as Apple's CEO in 2011 after Jobs stepped down due to his illness, and Apple has continued its rapid growth under Cook's leadership. Although some question whether Apple can continue to thrive without Jobs at the helm, Cook has overseen Apple's expansion into the Chinese market, as well as the purchase of Dr. Dre's headphone and music company Beats Electronics for $3.2 billion.[97]

Web 3.16: Read a remembrance of Apple co-founder Steve Jobs.

Other Major Players

Although they do not challenge any of the cross-media giants for size and scope, there are at least fifty more major players in the American media market. A complete list of these companies can be found on the "Who Owns What" page at *Columbia Journalism Review*'s Web site (www.cjr .org/resources/index.php).

Let's take a brief look at two of these companies that illustrate the strong concentration of ownership in individual media.

Gannett Co. Inc. Gannett is the biggest newspaper publisher in the United States, owning approximately eighty daily newspapers and the second-largest single paper, *USA Today*. Gannett also owns the Army Times Publishing Company, British newspaper publisher Newsquest, television stations in sixteen U.S. states, nine printing plants, and a direct marketing division.

USA Today has a daily circulation of 1.7 million, and the rest of Gannett's approximately eighty American daily papers deliver a total of 5 million copies a day. In addition, Gannett owns approximately 500 nondaily publications in the United States and 200 papers in the United Kingdom.[98] Gannett started out in 1906 with a single newspaper, the *Elmira Star-Gazette* in New York. Gannett then bought out the competing paper in town, the *Evening Star*, and merged it in with the *Gazette*, thus eliminating the competition. The company repeated this pattern—buying up the competition and shutting it down—across the country.[99] The Gannett newspaper chain grew steadily through the 1970s and early 1980s, but it gained the most attention in 1982 when it launched *USA Today* as a national newspaper. Starting a new national paper was an expensive, long-term project; the paper didn't turn a profit until 1993.

There is widespread concern that the newspaper industry as a whole is in a major circulation and advertising sales decline, and Gannett is no exception. For 2013, Gannett had earnings of $5.2 billion and turned a 7.5 percent profit.[100]

Clear Channel Communications, Inc./iHeart-Media. No company illustrates better the rapid move to consolidation of ownership than Clear Channel Communications. Up until 1996, Clear Channel was a significant, though not large, player in the radio business, owning thirty-five radio stations and nine television stations. But in 1996 the FCC lifted most of the restrictions on the number of stations a single company could own. By 2005, Clear Channel owned, operated, or programmed more than 1,200 radio stations in the United States. After reaching that peak, the owners took the company private and sold off a number of stations so that, as of 2014, Clear Channel owned approximately 860 stations reaching more than 239 million people.[101] The company also owns more than 840,000 outdoor advertising billboards. Although it is by far the dominant radio company in the United States, it does face substantial competition from the new satellite

Google's Core Principles

Google has long been known as the company with the unofficial slogan of "Don't be evil." While that was really intended to be more of a rule for working with colleagues than a business philosophy, the company does have a statement of ten core principles that are supposed to guide its actions.[1] They are:

1. Focus on the user and all else will follow.
2. It's best to do one thing really, really well.
3. Fast is better than slow.
4. Democracy on the Web works.
5. You don't need to be at your desk to need an answer.
6. You can make money without doing evil.
7. There's always more information out there.
8. The need for information crosses all borders.
9. You can be serious without a suit.
10. Great just isn't good enough.

You can see the full explanation of these principles at http://www.google.com/about/company/philosophy/.

In addition to its "Don't be evil" culture of excellence, Google is also famous for its worker-friendly environment. It has masseuses on staff not just for executives, but for the engineers who write code. It has free meals served out of a kitchen that is supervised by the Grateful Dead's former chef. An employee can get his or her hair cut or car washed, visit the dentist, go for a workout, or receive child care, all without leaving the Google campus.

Are all these benefits to be nice to employees? Or are they just a way of getting more productivity out of them?

Douglas Edwards, who was the fifty-ninth employee hired by Google back in 1999, wrote in his book *I'm Feeling Lucky* about how the free food that the company offered cut the time people spent eating:

> Like most googlers, I spent less than half an hour at lunch. . . . Without the café, I would have lost twenty minutes getting to a restaurant, half an hour eating, and another twenty minutes getting back. I would have stopped thinking about Google as I cleared the front door.[2]

WHO is the source?

Who are the founders of Google? How do they differ from the founders of other media companies? How does Google differ from other Big Media companies?

WHAT are they saying?

Google's founders brought a distinct philosophy to their business. How would you describe it from what you've read? How does it differ from other major companies? (Feel free to follow the link above to get more details.)

WHAT is the lasting impact?

Has Google's approach to doing business affected its success? Is Google trying to be supportive of its employees, or is it just trying to keep them at work longer by offering lots of services at the office? Does Google live up to its principles? Why or why not?

HOW do you and your classmates react to Google's approach to doing business?

Do you and your classmates think that Google truly tries to avoid being evil? Can a company succeed in a world market when it tries to uphold American values of freedom of information and speech? Would you want to work for Google? Why or why not?

---

[1] Google, "Our Philosophy," September 2009, http://www.google.com/about/company/philosophy/.
[2] Douglas Edwards, *I'm Feeling Lucky: The Confessions of Google Employee Number 59* (New York: Houghton Mifflin, 2011).

 CQ Researcher 3.1: Read a report on Google's success and dominance.

Video 3.6: Douglas Edwards talks about his time with Google.

---

radio services.[102] In September 2014, Clear Channel Communications changed its name to iHeartMedia to better reflect the fact that the company does business as a streaming audio provider in addition to being an owner of hundreds of radio stations.[103]

Media Economics and the Long Tail

Lists of major media companies generally include companies such as cable television company Comcast, magazine publisher Meredith, or the movie and music divisions of Sony. What don't show up as often are the independent artists, writers, and videographers whose works appeal to a relatively small group of consumers. But when those many small groups are added together, they become an audience big enough to rival those being attracted by Big Media.

The world of Big Media is the world of blockbusters—selling a lot of copies of a limited number of products. Blockbusters include the big summer movies that cost more than $100 million to produce and require the sale of millions of tickets to be a financial success. They are novels by Nicholas Sparks and Stephenie Meyer. They are albums by Jay-Z, Taylor Swift, and the Black Eyed Peas. They are the common media products, the common culture we all share.

Despite the consolidation of the media business and the ever-growing emphasis on the importance of blockbusters to Big Media, a strange phenomenon has been taking place. The annual box office has been falling for movies, broadcast television has lost one-third of its audience, and sales of CDs are plummeting, yet people seem to be consuming more media content than ever.

The Short Head Versus the Long Tail

Chris Anderson, in his book *The Long Tail*, argues that we are leaving the era of mass culture and entering one that is vastly more individualistic and much less mass oriented. He writes that, when he was growing up, the only alternatives to Big Media were the library and the comic book store. But today there are vastly more choices at both the commercial and noncommercial levels. Take Apple's iTunes music and video store. Through it, you can buy current blockbuster songs, movies, and television shows, but you can also find rather obscure materials, such as the songs of indie music duo Pomplamoose (*pamplemousse* means "grapefruit" in French), who have built a following through videos on YouTube. Or an EP by the Arizona-based band Calexico. Or the crowd-sourced dance film *Girl Walk // All Day* that was posted serially online over a month and a half. Or you could take a look the gross-out horror film *The Human Centipede* from mail-order DVD rental/streaming video company Netflix.

This is how Anderson describes the shift that has taken place as consumers turn from the mass content produced by broadcasters and publishers to the more focused content provided by broadband connections to the Internet:

The great thing about broadcast is that it can bring one show to millions of people with unmatchable efficiency. But it can't do the opposite—bring a million shows to one person each. Yet that is exactly what the Internet does so well. The economics of the broadcast era required hit shows—big buckets—to catch huge audiences. The economics of the broadband era are reversed. Serving the same stream to millions of people at the same time is hugely expensive and wasteful for a distribution network optimized for point-to-point communication.[104]

In short, our mass communication is becoming less mass, and we have new media companies that specialize in providing narrowly focused content. Anderson uses the statistical term the **long tail** to refer to this phenomenon.

Figure 3.1 depicts this phenomenon as a distribution curve showing that a relatively limited number of media products—books, songs, DVDs—sell the most copies. This area of a limited number of products and high sales on the left—the **short head**—is where Big Media companies like to live. When a movie comes to a local theater, it needs to attract about 1,500 people over a two-week period for the run to be a success. That means that you won't see a lot of the more obscure movies in your local theater. A CD has to sell at least four copies a year to justify the shelf space it takes up—that is, to pay the rent on its shelf space. Even if it sells 5,000 copies nationwide, if it can't sell four copies in your local store, your local store can't pay the rent on the half-inch of shelf space the CD takes up. So Big Media are all about finding the limited number of hits that will appeal to the most people. As Anderson observes, that's what they have to do to survive.[105]

To see the short-head portion of the demand curve, look at Walmart, the United States' biggest music retailer. The discount giant carries about 4,500 different CDs in its stores. Of those, 200 CDs account for more than 90 percent of their sales. But what about the remaining thousands and thousands of songs that a limited number of people are

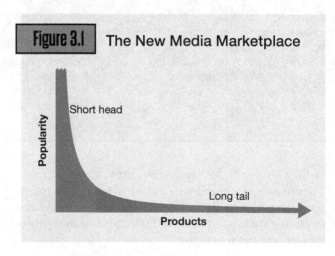

Figure 3.1 **The New Media Marketplace**

long tail: The portion of a distribution curve where a limited number of people are interested in buying a lot of different products.

short head: The portion of a distribution curve where a large number of people are interested in buying a limited number of products.

interested in buying? They constitute the long-tail portion of the graph that extends off to the right. This is where a limited number of people are interested in buying a lot of different products (as opposed to the short head, where a lot of people are interested in buying a limited number of products).

In contrast to Walmart, Anderson uses online music service Rhapsody as an illustration of the long-tail portion of the demand curve. As of 2011, Rhapsody offered approximately 13 million different music tracks to download. Not surprisingly, the big hits sell a lot of copies. But if you move beyond the big hits—the top 25,000 tracks—you find that Rhapsody still sells a lot of music. From the 25,000 best-selling tracks to the 100,000th best-selling track, sales of each song are at least 250 copies a month and make up nearly a quarter of Rhapsody's downloads. From the 100,000th to the 800,000th most popular songs—and that's a long way down the popularity chart—Rhapsody is still selling enough to make up 16 percent of its business. How can Rhapsody afford to do this? Two factors come into play: (1) Its cost of inventory is minimal—it just has to store the songs on a big array of hard drives; it doesn't have to physically stock the music, and (2) it does business over the entire country with a single store, so it doesn't need a lot of consumers in a single location who want to buy something. If they live anywhere in the United States, that's good enough.[106]

Characteristics of the Long Tail

Anderson writes that the biggest players in the long tail include Rhapsody, which lets subscribers download songs; Apple, the largest seller of legal music downloads; Netflix, which offers hundreds of thousands of different movies by DVDs sent through the mail or through online streaming; and Amazon, the dominant online seller of books, movies, and CDs. These companies can offer selection far beyond the current hits. Anderson argues that there are six principles that drive the success of the long-tail portion of the media marketplace:

- High number of goods—There are far more niche goods than hits. This means that if you can sell enough different niche goods, you can get as many sales as if you were selling a limited number of hits.
- Low cost of reaching markets—The cost of reaching niche markets is falling dramatically, thanks to the ease of access provided by the Internet and the ability to—in many cases—sell a digital download rather than a physical product.
- Ease of finding niche products—Consumers need to be able to find these niche products. This means there need to be tools—Anderson calls them filters—that allow consumers to search through a huge selection of media content to find the particular material they are looking for. This is something Internet movie rental store Netflix excels at. Netflix has consumers rate a series of movies and then provides recommendations based on those ratings.

- Flattening of the demand curve for mainstream hits—Once consumers can find their niche products, the demand curve tends to flatten. Now that consumers can find the full range of products available, there will be relatively less demand for the hits and more demand for the niche products. This will make the long tail longer and lower the demand for the hits.
- Size of collective market—There are so many niche products that they collectively can have as big a market as the hits do. In other words, you can sell as much focusing on the long tail as on the short head if you can offer enough choices.
- Tailoring to personal tastes—Once niche products become available, findable, and affordable, consumers will choose to go with media content that fits their personal wants and needs rather than consuming the hits that hold a mild appeal to so many. Media hits will become less important because consumers can get what they want rather than what happens to be available locally.[107]

Consequences of the Long Tail

Anderson says that a number of consequences arise out of a shift to the long tail from traditional mass media:

- Democratization of the means of production—It used to be that to record a CD you needed a big, expensive recording studio. Now anyone with a laptop computer and some inexpensive software can put together a multitrack recording or edit a short video. You can publish a professional-looking book without the benefit of a major publisher using a laser printer and a local copy shop. The development of the powerful home computer has made it possible for anyone to be a media producer.
- Democratization of the means of distribution—Through the Internet and sites such as eBay and Amazon, anyone can open a national, or even international, sales channel. YouTube gives ordinary people a place to distribute their home-produced videos. I even run a tiny media-oriented bookstore using an Amazon partnership. As Anderson puts it, "The PC made everyone a producer or publisher, but it was the Internet that made everyone a distributor."[108]
- Greatly reduced cost of connecting suppliers and consumers—Sellers and consumers can now find each other through tools such as Google search, iTunes, YouTube, and blogs.

Our twenty-first-century media world has room for a wide range of distribution channels. For the hits, there is nothing like Big Media for distribution. Movie theaters, book stores, big-box retailers (such as Walmart), broadcast network television, and magazines do a great job of selling or distributing media content that appeals to a large group of people. Second are the hybrid retailers—companies such as Amazon and Netflix that have no brick-and-mortar retail stores but have to send out a physical product, such as books, CDs, or DVDs. The hybrid retailers can have national distribution and serve niches, but they still deliver a physical product. Finally, the digital retailers, such as Apple iTunes and Rhapsody, sell downloads with no physical product. Any store that sells a virtual rather than a physical product handles the farthest end of the long tail.[109]

One of the most successful providers of long-tail content has been Google's video service YouTube. While YouTube started as a way to make video easy to share, it quickly grew into a major alternative source of video entertainment. "We are providing a stage where everyone can be seen. We see ourselves as a combination of *America's Funniest Home Videos* and *Entertainment Tonight*," cofounder Chad Hurley told Associated Press reporter Michael Liedtke.[110]

Unlike the infamous site Napster, which used to share music files, YouTube has not been confrontational with Big Media. It has always promptly removed any content at the request of corporate copyright owners, but it has also pursued extensive revenue-sharing projects with those same companies. It also limits clips by users to ten minutes, which helps prevent large-scale copyright infringement from users posting entire movies or television shows.[111] (YouTube has entered into contracts with Big Media companies to stream longer videos of professionally produced content.)[112]

As of July 2014, YouTube reported showing 6 billion hours of video per month. (Yes, that's *billion* with a "b.") The company also reported 100 hours of new videos being uploaded to the site per minute.[113]

SECRET 1 With 128.4 million unique viewers in the United States per month, YouTube has a bigger audience than most cable channels.[114] But YouTube differs significantly from cable television. A television channel decides to put up a limited amount of programming each day and hopes that an audience will look at it, whereas YouTube puts up lots of content produced by both professionals and amateurs and then sees what the audience decides to look at. Unlike traditional television, YouTube is capable of delivering programming that reaches audiences that range in size from dozens to millions. "We accept everyone that uploads video to our site, and it's the community that decides what's entertaining," Hurley says.[115] YouTube's expansive approach is a prime example of Secret One—The media are essential components of our lives. YouTube combines the roles of creator, program manager, and viewer into a single person. YouTube is an expression of the audience's interests with almost unlimited levels of choice.

Questioning the Media

What kinds of long-tail media content do you consume on a regular basis? Are there any long-tail artists/authors you like better than short-head/mainstream media? How did you discover them?

AP Photo/Noah Berger

Steven Chen (left) and Chad Hurley launched the video-sharing Web site YouTube in 2004. It has since become one of the top locations on the Internet for user-generated video.

Diane Mermigas of the *Hollywood Reporter* sees the merger of Google and YouTube as "the first viable new-media successor to broadcast and cable television."[116] She says the combination provides the tools needed to post, view, find, and place advertising on both amateur and professional video programming over broadband channels. She sees the pair leading the charge to have the "eyeballs, ad dollars and creative content that have sustained traditional television" move over to Internet video.[117] This is also why the late Steve Jobs succeeded in making Apple a success in the online media world. Apple understood that consumers needed an easy way to find and then use digital content, providing both the online iTunes music store and the various iPods and iPhones to play back the downloads. Using Apple's products, a consumer can download, transport, and access content anywhere and at any time.[118] The new media companies that are becoming significant and growing players understand the nature of the long tail and will deliver what consumers want.

Who Controls the Media?

Despite the growing presence of the long tail, the news and entertainment business is still dominated by a small number of highly profitable big businesses. This is clearly a source of concern for those who worry that only a limited number of interests control what is being presented to the public at large. But media scholar Michael Schudson argues that, even though the media are run by profit-seeking capitalists, the media do a good job of providing responsible journalism. The *New York Times* still views its primary responsibility as providing readers with an accurate reporting of the day's news. Furthermore, the media present a variety of viewpoints, even if they tend to focus on the middle ground rather than the extreme left or right.[119]

SECRET 7 It is easy to view the media giants as powerful forces (the "they" of Secret Seven—There is no "they") that control the lives of their audiences. While it is true that there is no "they," reality is far more complex than that. Numerous pressures on the media influence what they deliver—pressures that come from owners, stockholders, advertisers, or even the audiences. Companies seek profits, but they must also seek credibility, largely because their credibility gives value to the product they are selling. As long as a wide range of audiences exists, the media will strive to carry a diversity of content.

Bob Herbold of Microsoft told *Advertising Age* that the media landscape is being changed radically by the rise of **broadband networks**, which are high-speed channels for sending data and video into the home via cable or wireless connections. No longer can the networks dictate what people will view. As Herbold puts it, "One of the things that will be dramatically different than the past is that your ability to capture the individual for a period of time and almost force them to watch something will be greatly diminished."[120]

Consumers now have the option of going to traditional Big Media companies or viewing events directly. Those with the time and inclination can watch the actions of the U.S. government on three separate C-SPAN networks. Anyone who can afford a high-speed Internet connection can receive virtually an unlimited array of media choices.

SECRET 1 Critics often ask whether Big Media control society. This is a worthy question, but it is overly simplistic because it assumes that a single force runs these powerful institutions. The media-literate consumer will remember Secret One—The media are essential components of our lives—and ask a somewhat different question: "Who controls the media and their content?" It's not an easy question to answer. The influence of media owners is limited. If people don't want to watch a certain movie, no amount of promotion can get them to go see it. If a television show is offensive, few major companies will want to advertise on it. So the list of those who control the media needs to include advertisers, governments, pressure groups, news sources, and audience members themselves.

---

broadband networks: High-speed channels for transmitting multimedia content into the home via cable or wireless connections.

Owners

Owners of the media have ultimate control over the content their newspapers, Web sites, or television stations carry. Critics charge that corporate owners may attempt to control the news that is reported by the news organizations they own. There is rarely a direct order from headquarters to kill a story, but that doesn't mean the owners don't exercise control over content, either directly or indirectly. In the late nineteenth and early twentieth centuries, financiers such as J. P. Morgan and the Rockefeller family bought controlling ownership of magazines that had been harassing them, such as *Harper's*, *Scribner's*, and *Century*, and simply stopped the unflattering exposés. It wasn't so much censorship as new owners taking the magazines in safer directions.[121]

Perhaps the biggest issue is how news organizations cover stories involving their owners. In the case of ABC News, that owner is the Walt Disney Company. Disney's tight control of all aspects of its properties is legendary. For example, in 2011 Johnny Depp's contract for *Pirates of the Caribbean 4* prohibited ABC affiliates from interviewing or videotaping the actor at the premiere of his non-Disney movie *The Rum Diary*.[122] Former Disney president Michael Eisner told National Public Radio, "I would prefer ABC not to cover Disney. . . . I think it's inappropriate for Disney to be covered by Disney. . . . ABC News knows that I would prefer them not to cover [Disney]."[123]

But the potential for conflicts of interest may be more hypothetical than real. General Electric, former owner of the NBC broadcast network, was frequently cited as an example of a company that might try to control how its news operation would cover its parent company. In a story about consumer boycotts, NBC made no mention of boycotts against its parent company, GE. Nor did it mention GE in a story about defective bolts in nuclear reactors. But media critic Todd Gitlin writes that since 1990 NBC News has "routinely" covered scandals involving General Electric.[124]

Advertisers

With the exception of books, CDs, and movies, American commercial media are supported largely by advertising revenue. As a result, advertisers have a major influence on the types of news and entertainment presented in the media. They can threaten to withdraw their advertising if they don't like a story; they might even suggest that a particular topic should be covered or not covered. Some companies simply don't want to have their ads associated with controversial material, whereas others may be trying to stop the media from running stories that would be directly damaging to the company.[125] Tobacco companies have long punished magazines that run antismoking stories by withholding ads from those publications. But the influence of advertisers can be subtler. For a period during the 1990s, automaker Chrysler asked magazines to alert the company if controversial articles would be appearing near its ads.[126]

There is no question that television programming is produced to attract the specific audiences that advertisers

This image of a man standing up to the tanks in Tiananmen Square came to symbolize to the world the protesters against the Chinese government. A Google search of images from the Tiananmen Square protests will bring up this photo most anywhere in the world other than China.

While the United States has a relatively unregulated media marketplace, the government still places numerous controls on the broadcast industry. These are discussed in depth in Chapter 13.

Special Interest Groups

Special interest groups often put pressure on the media either to avoid dealing with particular topics in what they consider to be an offensive manner or to stay away from certain topics altogether. For example, when the *Philadelphia Inquirer* made the decision to reprint controversial Danish cartoons that portrayed the prophet Muhammad in an offensive way, Muslims in the Philadelphia area responded by picketing the paper. The cartoons also ran in the University of Illinois student paper, the *Daily Illini*. Publishing the cartoons sparked a debate about the issue on campus, prompted peace protests, and started a public dispute by the staff of the paper as to whether the cartoons should have run.[131] For more on the Danish cartoons, see Chapter 15.

News Sources

Among the strongest influences on the news media are the people who provide stories. Those who are available to provide information or be interviewed will determine what kinds of stories are reported. In general, the views that are most likely to be reported come from people who are in positions of authority or have institutional connections. These people are often government officials, business executives, or experts in a specialized field. They can choose with whom they will speak, and they are able to negotiate ground rules for interviews.

In contrast, ordinary people, poor people, and the disadvantaged typically have little influence on the media or how stories are covered.[132] For example, in 1992 Zoë Baird was nominated to be attorney general of the United States. It soon became known, however, that she had hired two Hispanic domestic workers to take care of her children and had not paid Social Security taxes for them. Baird eventually had to withdraw her name from nomination. The story received extensive coverage both because of the political implications and because of the likelihood that other professional women would run into similar problems. But most of the news media ignored the plight of Latino domestic workers who weren't receiving Social Security benefits. Because they were not in positions of power, domestic workers such as those Baird had employed weren't seen as sources and hence had no influence. The one exception was the Spanish-language television network Univision, which reported the story from the point of view of low-paid immigrant workers.[133]

want to reach. A group of advertisers has even established a fund to promote the development of "family-friendly" television programs—that is, programs designed to attract the kind of audience the advertisers want to target.[127] For further discussion on this, see Chapter 11.

Government 🌐

Governments around the world influence how media companies operate. When Comcast made its bid for NBCUniversal, it had to go through more than a year of governmental review before it was allowed to complete the deal, and when AOL and Time Warner merged, they faced eleven months of review by the U.S. Federal Trade Commission.[128] The companies had to deal with a similar review by government regulators in Europe as well.

Rupert Murdoch's News Corporation and 21st Century Fox, whose satellite services provide television to much of Europe and Asia, have had to make compromises in the content they provide. For example, objections by the Chinese government led Murdoch to drop the BBC from his Star satellite system in China. Although he wasn't happy with the decision, he says it was the only way he could sell television services in China.[129] Similarly, Google has faced extensive criticism for censoring its search results on the Chinese version of its search and news sites. For example, a search for pictures of Tiananmen Square on Google in London will produce the iconic photo of a man in a white shirt blocking the path of a tank headed toward the protesters. The same search in China produces a photo "of happy smiley tourists."[130]

When a magazine is planning to run a story about a major celebrity, it must negotiate who the photographer will be, who the writer will be, and how much control the source will have over photo selection and article content. The negotiations involve not just the particular story being run, but also whether the celebrity will be available for future articles for that magazine and other publications handled by the same company. Since many magazines depend on newsstand sales, and having a top celebrity on the cover can make the difference in an issue's success, the magazines are often willing to negotiate. Not all magazine editors are satisfied with the practice, however. Bob Guccione Jr., founder of *Spin*, says, "Access to stars today is so controlled. In the '60s and '70s, there was a fresh reporting that was honest and frank. Today, readers can sense this is propaganda, just a stage in a marketing campaign."[134]

In 2007, the magazine *GQ* killed a lengthy, unflattering story about the Hillary Clinton presidential primary campaign. At about the same time, the magazine was also working on a story about the charitable work being done by former president Bill Clinton—a story that was scheduled to run on the cover. According to the Washington, D.C., news Web site Politico, the Clinton campaign "pulled a page from the book of Hollywood publicists and offered *GQ* a stark choice: Kill the piece, or lose access to . . . Bill Clinton."[135] Why would the magazine agree to do this? Primarily because the former president's face "is viewed within the magazine industry as one that can move product."[136] *GQ* editor Jim Nelson denies that there was a connection between the killing of one story and the former president's willingness to pose for the magazine's cover.

Audiences

The power of audiences comes primarily from their willingness to read a particular book, watch a particular movie, or listen to a particular CD. Nothing can make audience members pay attention to media content. If the audience is not there, the media are not likely to carry the programming.

In an attempt to gauge their audiences' interests, the major media companies conduct continual research. *Sports Illustrated* used a Facebook poll to have fans from around the world pick the cover for the 2011 end-of-the-year issue. This was the first time that the cover was picked by fans rather than by *SI* editors. (In case you were wondering, the cover featured injured Rutgers football player Eric LeGrand returning to the field in a motorized wheelchair.)[137]

Movie producers and directors routinely make changes in their films on the basis of test audience research. The 2006 independent film *Little Miss Sunshine* grossed eight times its cost of production after incorporating edits to the movie based on the results of a small test screening. Audience members had liked the movie but had been confused about where the family was traveling in the road trip at the center of the film.[138]

Focus group research sometimes affirms what the director already wanted to do. When Warner Bros. questioned whether young people would sit still for a two-and-a-half-hour version of the movie *Harry Potter and the Sorcerer's Stone*, producers showed it to a children's focus group. Members of the test audience reported that the length was not a problem; in fact, they wanted to see more details from the book in the film.[139]

Questioning the Media

Who do you believe controls the media? What evidence do you have of their influence? Has this chapter changed your understanding of who runs the media?

Chapter SUMMARY

The American media industry, the largest in the world, is run by private business with only minor government control. Having gotten its start in the 1640s, it was among the first industries in the American colonies. However, media business did not become big until the 1830s, when high levels of literacy and the development of the steam-powered printing press allowed for the mass production of newspapers, books, and magazines. The growth of the electronic media in the second half of the twentieth century helped create a national media culture, as the same content became available simultaneously throughout the country.

For many years, six large media conglomerates dominated the American and much of the global media. They own the major television networks, broadcast stations, cable channels and providers, newspapers, magazines, record labels, movie studios, and Internet services. These companies tend to be vertically integrated—producing, promoting, and delivering content to the consuming audience. But there are a number of new players in the media business who are also significant. They provide cable television and Internet services, online search and content, and integrated media content and hardware. Among the biggest media companies operating in the United States are Time Warner, Disney, News Corporation, 21st Century Fox, Viacom/CBS, Bertelsmann, Comcast/NBCUniversal, Google, and Apple.

Widespread access to the Internet has brought about the rise of smaller-scale new media companies that specialize in providing a wide range of media content that appeals to relatively small numbers of consumers. When combined, these niche markets, known as the long tail of media, can rival the size of the markets for blockbuster media content.

While the media industry is dominated by a limited number of companies, these companies have to please a wide range of groups in order to operate successfully. Those groups include the companies' owners, advertisers, government, special interest groups, news sources, and audience members.

 Keep up-to-date with content from the author's blog.

 Take the chapter quiz.

Key TERMS

penny press   54

synergy   55

vertical integration   60

local cable television systems   62

long tail   72

short head   72

broadband networks   75

Concept REVIEW

American tradition of private ownership of media

Growth of Big Media

Revenue sources for the media

Media synergy

Long-tail media

Forces that control the mass media (owners, advertisers, government,

special interest groups, news sources, and audiences)

Student STUDY SITE

$SAGE edge™

Sharpen your skills with SAGE edge at **edge.sagepub.com/hanson5e**

SAGE edge for Students provides a personalized approach to help you accomplish your coursework goals in an easy-to-use learning environment.

Mass Communication Effects

How Society and Media Interact

Former National Security Agency contractor Edward Snowden shocked the world in 2013 by releasing thousands of documents to journalist Glenn Greenwald that he had smuggled out using a small flash drive. Prior to the digital age, taking that many documents out of an office would have required a busy photocopy machine and dozens of boxes.

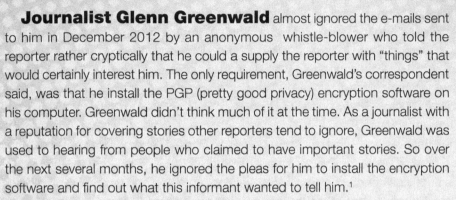

Journalist Glenn Greenwald almost ignored the e-mails sent to him in December 2012 by an anonymous whistle-blower who told the reporter rather cryptically that he could a supply the reporter with "things" that would certainly interest him. The only requirement, Greenwald's correspondent said, was that he install the PGP (pretty good privacy) encryption software on his computer. Greenwald didn't think much of it at the time. As a journalist with a reputation for covering stories other reporters tend to ignore, Greenwald was used to hearing from people who claimed to have important stories. So over the next several months, he ignored the pleas for him to install the encryption software and find out what this informant wanted to tell him.[1]

But six months after that first e-mail, Greenwald was convinced by documentary filmmaker Laura Poitras to install the software and exchange e-mail with the informant, who turned out to be former National Security Agency contract worker (and high school dropout) Edward Snowden.

Greenwald travelled to Hong Kong to meet with Snowden in May 2013 along with Poitras and another reporter from London's *Guardian* newspaper. Snowden, who was 29 years old at the time, had put together a huge collection of electronic copies of meticulously categorized top-secret documents that he believed would show the overreach of the NSA without endangering lives.[2]

Snowden told Greenwald that he wanted to see traditional journalism be done with the documents rather than just turn them loose on the world the way that Julian Assange did a couple of years earlier with the WikiLeaks Web site. "If I wanted the documents just put on the Internet en masse, I could have done that myself," Snowden said. "I want you [Greenwald] to make sure these stories are done, one by one, so that people can understand what they should know."[3]

The stories, written by Greenwald and others using the documents Snowden released, ended up telling Americans just what the NSA was doing with all the information it was collecting from the public. Snowden discovered that the NSA could:

- Track who is talking on a phone call, where the person is calling from, and to whom, when, and for how long
- Read text messages
- Know what you are watching on YouTube
- Know what you like on Facebook, as soon as you click on it
- Read your e-mail
- Recognize who is in your online photos
- Record your phone calls[4]

Snowden has been charged by the U.S. government "with theft of government property, unauthorized communication of national defense information and willful communication of classified communications intelligence." Each of

LEARNING OBJECTIVES

After studying this chapter, you will be able to:

1 Discuss the history and development of our understanding of media effects.

2 Name four types of effects the mass media can have.

3 Explain eight major communication theories and their uses.

4 Describe two ways in which political campaigns affect voters.

5 Identify Herbert Gans's eight basic journalistic values when reading a news story.

Web 2.1: Read more about Glenn Greenwald's reporting on Edward Snowden.

these charges carries a possible 10-year prison sentence.[5] He initially went to Hong Kong, where he met with journalists, and then moved on to Russia, which promised him asylum for a year. It was unknown as of this writing where he would move to once that year of asylum expired.

More than a year after Snowden handed over copies of secret NSA documents to the *Guardian* and the *Washington Post*, stories continue to emerge from the treasure trove of information. In July 2014, the *Post* reported that 90 percent of the people who had their communications collected by the NSA were ordinary Internet users from the United States and around the world who were not actual surveillance targets. Among the information retained by the NSA are "stories of love and heart-break, illicit sexual liaisons, mental-health crises, political and religious conversions, financial anxieties and disappointed hopes." The *Post*'s reporting was based on approximately 160,000 e-mail and instant-message conversations collected by the NSA and handed over by Snowden.[6] Reporters from the *Guardian* and the *Washington Post* won the public service Pulitzer Prize in 2014 for their reporting based on Snowden's documents.

The Snowden case illustrates how much has changed since Daniel Ellsberg gave copies of many of the volumes of the so-called Pentagon Papers to reporters back in 1971. Ellsberg had to physically photocopy pages at a time when photocopy machines were not common and typically locked down after hours. (You can read more about the Pentagon Papers case and Ellsberg in Chapter 13.) Snowden had to know how to bypass computer security, but beyond that, all he had to do was download the files to a flash drive. Ellsberg had to smuggle hundreds of physical pages out of the Pentagon.[7]

A blogger writing for the newsweekly the *Economist* says that whether you view people who leak top-secret electronic documents as heroes or traitors really doesn't matter. The writer argues that

Timeline

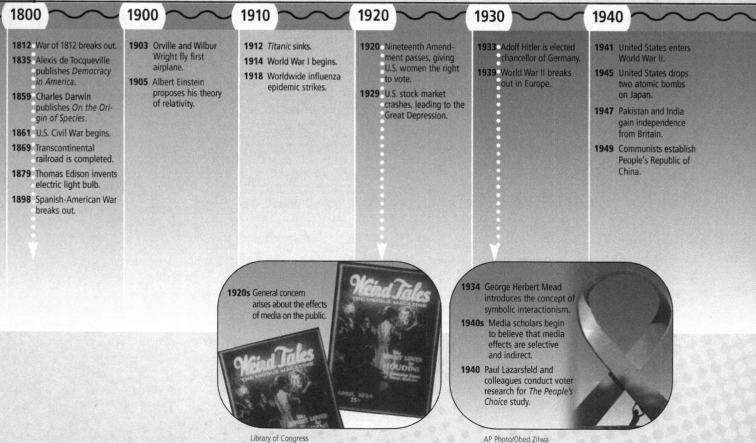

1800

1812 War of 1812 breaks out.

1835 Alexis de Tocqueville publishes *Democracy in America*.

1859 Charles Darwin publishes *On the Origin of Species*.

1861 U.S. Civil War begins.

1869 Transcontinental railroad is completed.

1879 Thomas Edison invents electric light bulb.

1898 Spanish-American War breaks out.

1900

1903 Orville and Wilbur Wright fly first airplane.

1905 Albert Einstein proposes his theory of relativity.

1910

1912 *Titanic* sinks.

1914 World War I begins.

1918 Worldwide influenza epidemic strikes.

1920

1920 Nineteenth Amendment passes, giving U.S. women the right to vote.

1929 U.S. stock market crashes, leading to the Great Depression.

1930

1933 Adolf Hitler is elected chancellor of Germany.

1939 World War II breaks out in Europe.

1940

1941 United States enters World War II.

1945 United States drops two atomic bombs on Japan.

1947 Pakistan and India gain independence from Britain.

1949 Communists establish People's Republic of China.

1920s General concern arises about the effects of media on the public.

1934 George Herbert Mead introduces the concept of symbolic interactionism.

1940s Media scholars begin to believe that media effects are selective and indirect.

1940 Paul Lazarsfeld and colleagues conduct voter research for *The People's Choice* study.

Library of Congress

AP Photo/Obed Zilwa

we are undergoing a major shift from a world with paper documents that are heavy and tied to a place to electronic documents that can be moved around the globe with the click of a mouse, and no amount of prosecuting cyberleakers will change that. The writer is not defending those who release electronic documents; rather, he's explaining the long-term impact that this change of media means. The blogger is essentially bringing to the forefront the ideas of Canadian economist Harold Innis, who believed that any given medium has a bias of lasting a long time or of being easy to distribute. Paper documents, which we are more used to, are heavy and hard to move. Electronic documents, on the other hand, don't have a physical form and thus can be moved about with incredible ease. As you will read later in this chapter, Innis was the scholar who inspired media theorist Marshall McLuhan's popular concept of "the medium is the message."[8]

As we think about Snowden and the transformations that electronic documents have brought to our society, remember that it is a key example of **SECRET 5** New media are always scary. In this chapter, we look at how our understanding of media and their effects have evolved over the past century and consider several approaches to studying these effects. Finally, we look at how media effects can be analyzed within the realm of politics. ∎

> **❝I want you [Greenwald] to make sure these stories are done, one by one, so that people can understand what they should know.❞**
> — Edward Snowden

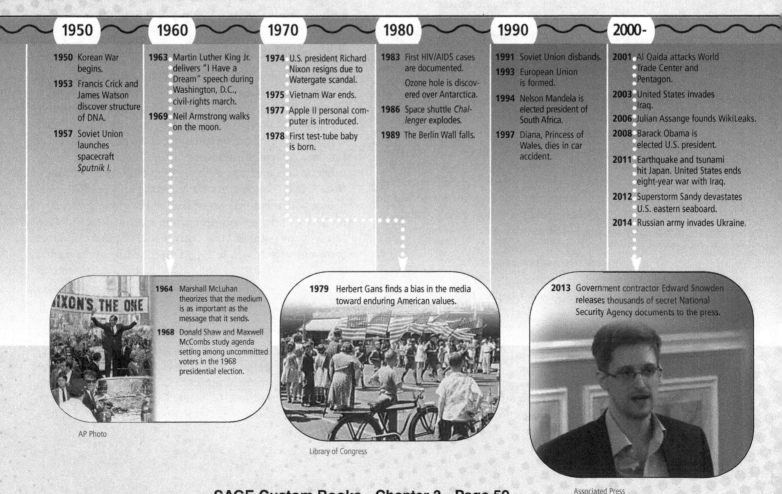

1950

- **1950** Korean War begins.
- **1953** Francis Crick and James Watson discover structure of DNA.
- **1957** Soviet Union launches spacecraft *Sputnik I.*

1960

- **1963** Martin Luther King Jr. delivers "I Have a Dream" speech during Washington, D.C., civil-rights march.
- **1969** Neil Armstrong walks on the moon.

1970

- **1974** U.S. president Richard Nixon resigns due to Watergate scandal.
- **1975** Vietnam War ends.
- **1977** Apple II personal computer is introduced.
- **1978** First test-tube baby is born.

1980

- **1983** First HIV/AIDS cases are documented.
  Ozone hole is discovered over Antarctica.
- **1986** Space shuttle *Challenger* explodes.
- **1989** The Berlin Wall falls.

1990

- **1991** Soviet Union disbands.
- **1993** European Union is formed.
- **1994** Nelson Mandela is elected president of South Africa.
- **1997** Diana, Princess of Wales, dies in car accident.

2000–

- **2001** Al Qaida attacks World Trade Center and Pentagon.
- **2003** United States invades Iraq.
- **2006** Julian Assange founds WikiLeaks.
- **2008** Barack Obama is elected U.S. president.
- **2011** Earthquake and tsunami hit Japan. United States ends eight-year war with Iraq.
- **2012** Superstorm Sandy devastates U.S. eastern seaboard.
- **2014** Russian army invades Ukraine.

1964 Marshall McLuhan theorizes that the medium is as important as the message that it sends.

1968 Donald Shaw and Maxwell McCombs study agenda setting among uncommitted voters in the 1968 presidential election.

AP Photo

1979 Herbert Gans finds a bias in the media toward enduring American values.

Library of Congress

2013 Government contractor Edward Snowden releases thousands of secret National Security Agency documents to the press.

Associated Press

History of Media Effects Research

As we discussed in Chapter 1 in the section on media literacy, media consumers often assume that the media have large, obvious, and generally negative effects on people, and they look to blame the media for complex social problems.[9] In this section, we look at how our understanding of media effects has evolved and changed over the past 200 years.

Rise of Mass Society

Prior to the 1800s, most people in Europe and North America lived in rural communities where their neighbors were likely to be similar in ethnic, racial, and religious background. People knew their neighbors, and their neighbors knew them. There were only limited opportunities for people to change their station in life or to learn much about the outside world. But with the rise of the Industrial Revolution in the nineteenth century, we started to see massive migration from the rural areas into the cities and from various countries to the United States. As people moved into the cities, they started working for wages in factories with people who were quite different from them. With industrialization, people went from small, close-knit communities where they knew everyone to a mass society where they learned about the world from mass media sources, such as the new inexpensive newspapers, magazines, and paperback novels.[10]

SECRET 7 At the end of the nineteenth century, people came to believe that the traditional ties of church, community, and family were breaking down and losing their power to influence people. The comfortable local community was being replaced by something impersonal, complex, and removed from the traditions that had previously held people together. Concerned observers noted that people seemed to be alienated, isolated, and interchangeable members of a faceless mass audience, separated by the decline of the family and the growth of technology. So what held this new mass society together?[11] The increasingly frequent answer was that the mass media were replacing the church, family, and community in shaping public opinion.[12]

(For additional discussion of the growth of the mass media from its origins in the 1400s to the present day, see Chapter 1.)

Propaganda and the Direct Effects Model

Fears that media messages would have strong, direct effects on audience members grew out of propaganda efforts by all combatants during World War I and by Nazi Germany and Fascist Italy in the 1930s. Critics worried that mass media messages would overwhelm people in the absence of the influences of family and community. With traditional social forces in decline, it was inevitable, critics feared, that the media would become the most powerful force within society.

This argument viewed audience members as passive targets who would be hit or injected with the message, which, like a vaccine, would affect most people in similar ways. But research looking for powerful, direct effects leading to opinion and behavioral changes generally came up short. In fact, in the 1940s and 1950s, researchers sometimes doubted whether media messages had any effect on individuals at all.[13] Although most scholars now focus on the media's indirect effects on society rather than their direct effects on individuals, they remain concerned about how the media influence individuals.

The big problem is that the direct effects approach viewed media messages as a stimulus that would lead to a predictable attitudinal or behavioral response with nothing intervening between sender and audience. But although people have a shared biological heritage, they have different backgrounds, needs, attitudes, and values. In short, everyone has been socialized differently. The indirect effects approach still looks at the effects that messages have on individuals, but it accounts for the fact that audience members perceive and interpret these messages selectively according to individual differences. Because people's perceptions are selective, their responses to the messages vary as well. A person who is preparing to buy a car, a person who just bought a car, and a person who doesn't drive will each react differently to an automobile commercial.

Voter Studies and the Limited Effects Model

During the 1920s and 1930s, the decades when the Nazis, Italian Fascists, and Soviets were using propaganda, many critics worried that the media might be responsible for powerful direct effects on the public. Their general worries about the media extended to the possible effects of political campaign messages. Critics, considering recent urbanization and the decline of traditional institutions, feared that political media campaigns would "inject" people with ideas that would lead to the message creator's desired actions, such as supporting a particular candidate, ideology, or point of view. This model of powerful direct campaign effects was largely discredited by voter studies in the 1940s and 1950s, but it remains important because many people still believe that it is accurate.[14]

©iStockphoto.com/jamesbin

The People's Choice. One of the first large-scale social-scientific studies of campaign influences was *The People's Choice* study of the 1940 U.S. presidential election contest between Democrat Franklin D. Roosevelt and Republican Wendell Willkie.

A team of researchers led by Paul Lazarsfeld looked at how voters in Erie County, Ohio, decided which candidate to vote for. Lazarsfeld's team found that people who were highly interested in the campaign and paid the most attention to media coverage of it were the least likely to be influenced by the campaign. Why? Because they had decided whom they supported before the campaign had even begun.[15]

In contrast, voters who decided at the last minute usually turned to friends or neighbors, rather than the media, for information about the campaign. In general, they turned to people who followed the campaign closely, the ones whom Lazarsfeld called opinion leaders.

Opinion leaders are influential community members—friends, family members, and coworkers—who spend significant time with the media. Lazarsfeld suggested that information flows from the media to opinion leaders, and then from opinion leaders to the rest of the public. Keep in mind that the opinion leaders are ordinary people who are simply very interested and involved in a topic. Although this finding was not expected, it should not be terribly surprising that interpersonal influence is more important than the media. The idea here is fairly simple: People in groups tend to share opinions with one another, and when they want reliable information, they go to the people they know. With the lengthy campaigns today, people find it easier to turn to interpersonal sources than the wealth of media information. Yet this trend is nothing new. Although many people believe that our election campaigns are starting earlier and earlier every election cycle, presidential candidate William Jennings Bryan started his campaign for the 1900 election one month after the election of 1896![16] Even as early as the 1830s, when the penny press was just getting started, presidential campaigns could run as long as two years.

The People's Choice study, as well as other early voter studies, found that campaigns typically reinforced existing political predispositions and that few people changed their minds about whom they were going to support. There are several reasons for this:

- The voters who start off with strong opinions are unlikely to change them.
- The voters who pay the most attention to a campaign are those with the strongest political views; thus, they are the least likely to change their opinions.
- The most persuadable voters (those who are least informed) are not likely to pay attention to political communication and therefore are not strongly influenced by media coverage of the campaign.[17]

---

opinion leaders: Influential community members who invest substantial amounts of time learning about their own area of expertise, such as politics. Less well-informed friends and family members frequently turn to them for advice about the topic.

Allied propaganda posters designed to build support for World War I weren't afraid to make use of strong negative stereotypes of the Germans.

The Importance of Meaning and the Critical/Cultural Model

Up through the 1940s, most of the research on the mass media focused on direct and indirect effects of media messages on the behaviors of groups and individuals. But another school of thought looks at how people use media to construct their view of the world rather than looking at how media change people's behaviors. Instead of using

Questioning the Media

Can you come up with a recent example of someone publicly making the argument that "the media" have powerful direct effects on people? How would you respond to his or her arguments?

Audio 2.1: Learn about the long presidential campaigns of the 1800s.

National Archives

Minnesota Department of Transportation

Are you surprised to see car sharing as a subject of propaganda? What's your reaction to each poster? How does looking at these images as propaganda, rather than as advertisements or marketing material, influence your view of their message? Would the message promoting car sharing have more influence on you if you were already considering doing it?

The Messages in Propaganda

There's an Internet meme known as Godwin's Law of Nazi Analogies that states: "As an online discussion grows longer, the probability of a comparison involving Nazis or Hitler approaches one."[1]

With the common use of Nazi name-calling these days, it's hard sometimes to remember that during World War II when people talked about Hitler and the Nazis, they were talking about actual Nazis. Hitler was a popular figure used by American and European government propagandists, as can be seen in the poster on the left promoting car sharing. Although it doesn't invoke Hitler, the Minnesota Department of Transportation also wants to get people carpooling with its Greater Minnesota Commuter Challenge and is promoting the cause using propaganda posters as well.[2]

WHAT are these posters saying?

What message is the World War II poster on the left trying to convey? What is the message of the poster on the right from the Minnesota Department of Transportation trying to say?

WHY are they sending the message?

Why are these two groups sending these messages? What is their goal in trying to persuade you to carpool?

HOW do you and your classmates interpret these messages?

How do you react to messages like these? How do arguments today comparing someone to Hitler differ from those made during the World War II era? How do the arguments for carpooling during World War II differ from arguments today? Do you think one is more persuasive than the other? Why?

---

[1]Mike Godwin, "Meme, Counter-Meme," *Wired*, October 1994, www.wired.com/wired/archive/2.10/godwin.if .html.

[2]Minnesota Department of Transportation, "The Greater Minnesota Commuter Challenge," 2012, www.dot.state .mn.us/transit/commuter/commute.html.

 Web 2.2: Read more on Godwin's law.

the quantitative data analysis of the voter studies, the critical/cultural approach takes a more qualitative examination of the social structure in which communication takes place. It considers how meaning is created within society, who controls the media systems, and the roles the media play in our lives. Instead of looking at how messages affect people, it looks at how people use and construct messages.[18]

Under the critical/cultural approach, ordinary people are seen as moving from being information providers to information receivers, with only limited opportunities to answer back to the ideas being provided by the people in power. Thus the mass media become a tool for controlling the flow of information and the topics that can be discussed.[19] As we discuss in Chapter 3, with increasing media consolidation, more and more of our media are owned by fewer and fewer companies, so that there is an increasing level of control of what topics can be discussed and debated. Critical theorists would argue that the subjects that get covered are those in the best interests of the advertisers who support the media and the companies that own them.[20]

An example of the critical/cultural approach is the charge, leveled by many critics, that the crime stories that deal with attractive, wealthy, white women and girls attract much more media attention than do disappearances of women of color or those who are poor. Consider the story of Casey Anthony. The attractive, young, white mother was accused of murdering her two-year-old daughter. During her trial in 2011, the news media, especially cable television, was obsessed with the case. When Anthony was found not guilty, Facebook, Twitter, and other social media sites were filled with outraged comments about the verdict. In addition, talk shows hosts such as Nancy Grace seemed to be obsessed with the case. Six months after the court acquitted Anthony, Google News still featured more than 1,500 links to news stories about the case. On the other hand, a Google search for Jahessye Shockley, a five-year-old African American girl from Arizona who disappeared in 2011, only turned up four news stories.[21]

A similar media silence characterized the 2004 disappearance of twenty-four-year-old Tamika Huston, an African American woman from Spartanburg, South Carolina. Her case received one or two mentions on Fox News, but it was noted mostly in stories about how disappearing black women are ignored while stories about white women and girls, such as the "runaway bride" and missing teenager Natalee Holloway, get story counts in the hundreds or thousands. Keith Woods, an expert on diversity issues at the Poynter Institute, a journalism think tank, says stories about minority women tend to receive less attention because reporters are more likely to report about people they see as being like themselves. And since most newsrooms tend to be disproportionately white and middle class,

© Phelan Ebenhack/ZUMA Press/Corbis

When Casey Anthony was acquitted of charges of murdering her daughter in 2011, cable news channels and social media devoted massive coverage to the verdict. Critics charge that when cases such as this don't involve an attractive white woman or girl, they get very little media attention.

the disappearance of a white woman is seen as a bigger story. This control over which stories are reported means that the public at large is not aware that African American women are disproportionately more likely to disappear than white women.[22]

Effects of the Media in Our Lives

Media scholars throughout the twentieth century who studied the effects of the mass media on individuals and society questioned several aspects of the media, including the messages being sent, the media sending them, the owners of the media, and the audience members themselves.[23]

Message Effects

Not surprisingly, the earliest concerns about the effects of mass communication focused on how messages might change people's behaviors, attitudes, or beliefs. These message effects can take a variety of forms.

Cognitive Effects. The most common and observable message effect is on the short-term learning of information. This can be as significant as learning about a new medical treatment or as trivial as remembering the lyrics to a popular song. The amount of learning that takes place from media content depends largely on the motivation

Web 2.3: Read stories about media coverage on missing white women.

level of the person consuming the media. Political scientist Doris Graber found that people who want to be able to talk intelligently with others about media content (whether it be the news, a sporting event, or an entertainment program) learn much more from the media than people who are simply seeking entertainment. Research also shows that people learn more from people they identify with and pay more attention to political commentators they agree with than ones they dislike.[24] Hence the most popular political radio talk shows, such as those hosted by conservatives Rush Limbaugh and Sean Hannity, argue a single and consistent point of view rather than providing a range of views.[25]

Attitudinal Effects.

People can develop feelings about a product, an individual, or an idea on the basis of media content. Viewers might decide that they like a new product, political candidate, or hairstyle because of what they have seen in a television commercial, a news broadcast, or a sitcom. Typically it is much easier to get people to form new opinions than to get them to change existing ones.[26] For example, political advertising generally tries to change the opinions of uncommitted voters rather than those of voters who already have strong political loyalties. In the 2008 presidential campaign, the Obama campaign frequently targeted young voters who had less established political loyalties with ads found on Comedy Central, VH1, or Xbox Live video games.[27] (For more on advertising in video games, see Chapter 10.)

©iStockphoto.com/mstay

Behavioral Effects.

Behavioral effects include actions such as clipping a coupon from a newspaper, buying a product, making a phone call, or voting for a candidate. They might also include imitating attractive behaviors (for example, dressing a certain way). Behavioral effects are in many ways the most difficult to achieve because people are reluctant to change their behavior. Sometimes, however, people go to the media deliberately looking for behavior to copy, as when a child watches an episode of *Batman* and then imitates it in play, or when a teenager watches a movie to learn how to behave on a date.[28]

Psychological Effects.

Media content can inspire fear, joy, revulsion, happiness, or amusement, among other feelings.[29] A major psychological effect of media content, especially violent or erotic material, is arousal. Symptoms of arousal can include a rise in heart rate, adrenaline levels, or sexual response. Seeking a psychological response is a common reason for spending time with the media, whether the response sought is relaxation, excitement, or emotional release. Arousal can come from content (action, violence, sexuality, loud music or sound) and from style (motion, use of color, the rate and speed at which new images appear). Notice that music videos, which often offer little in terms of learning, provide many of these elements.[30] Contemporary composer John Adams talked about how his Pulitzer Prize–winning composition about the September 11, 2001, attacks, "On the Transmigration of Souls," makes people feel:

> Modern people have learned all too well how to keep our emotions in check, and we know how to mask them with humor or irony. Music has a singular capacity to unlock those controls and bring us face to face with our raw, uncensored, and unattenuated feelings. That is why during times when we are grieving or in need of being in touch with the core of our beings we seek out those pieces which speak to us with that sense of gravitas and serenity.[31]

Medium Effects

As mass media consumption grew in the 1950s, scholars also started paying more attention to the particular medium being used to transmit messages. Until the 1950s, most media effects research focused on the interactions among the sender, the message, and the receiver, ignoring the influence of the medium itself. But the medium used to communicate is crucial. Canadian communication researcher Marshall McLuhan argued that the medium used for transmission can be as important as the message itself, if not more so. McLuhan is best known for his statement "The medium is the message," by which he meant that the method of message transmittal is a central part of

AP Photo/Frank Franklin II

Politicians like former U.S. Secretary of State Hillary Rodham Clinton often go on Comedy Central's *Daily Show* with host Jon Stewart as a way of reaching out to younger voters who would be hard to reach through more traditional news channels.

the message. For example, television does an excellent job of transmitting emotional messages because it includes both visual (explosions, luxury interiors) and audio (laugh tracks, scary music) cues along with words. And consider technology that enhances the sound of movies: Surround sound systems are designed to create a realistic experience by surrounding viewers with five distinct sound channels, as well as shaking them with a deep bass channel. The goal is not to transmit the message better, but to create a more overwhelming experience. (Think of how the impact of a summer blockbuster film would be diminished if the sound were turned down.) The same is true of large-screen high-definition television sets. Books and newspapers, in contrast, are much better at transmitting complex rational information because these media allow us to review the information and consider its meaning at our own pace.[32] The Web excels at providing obscure materials that appeal to a limited, widely dispersed audience, and it makes it easy for receivers to respond to what they've seen or heard.

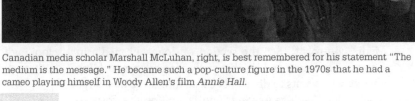

©MGM/UA

Canadian media scholar Marshall McLuhan, right, is best remembered for his statement "The medium is the message." He became such a pop-culture figure in the 1970s that he had a cameo playing himself in Woody Allen's film *Annie Hall*.

SECRET 1 Media scholars now recognize that communication technology is a fundamental element of society and that new technologies can lead to social change.[33] (As Secret One points out, the media are essential components of our lives.) Media sociologist Joshua Meyrowitz, for example, argues that the existence and development of various media can lead to radical changes in society.

He writes that the development of publishing and books in the sixteenth century made it easy for new ideas to spread beyond the person who originated them and that this tended to undermine the control of ideas by both the monarchy and the Roman Catholic Church.[34] As can be seen by the Edward Snowden story discussed at the beginning of the chapter, the existence of digital documents, encrypted e-mail, and high-capacity thumb drives now allows a small group of technically skilled individuals to spread news and documents around the world, with governments powerless to stop them. Meyrowitz also identifies some social effects of particular media. In *No Sense of Place*, he argues that the major effect of print as a medium is to segregate audiences according to education, age, class, and gender. For example, a teenager needs to be able to read at a certain level to understand the content of a magazine targeted at young women or young men—content that a young child would be unable to comprehend. In contrast, electronic media such as television tend to cross the demographic boundaries. A child too young to read a magazine or book can still understand at least some of the information in a television program targeted at adults.[35]

This is why parent groups and childhood educators push to have early-evening programming on television contain more "family-friendly" programs and why parents seek to restrict certain Internet sites on a family computer.

The importance of the particular medium used to convey a message applies at every level of communication, from intrapersonal (how is an audio journal different from a written one?) to interpersonal (how is a phone call different from an e-mail?) to mass (how is a book different from a movie?).

Ownership Effects 🌐

Instead of looking at the effects of media and their messages, some scholars examine the influence of those who own and control the media.[36] These critical scholars are concerned because owners of media determine which ideas will be produced and distributed by those media.

In the United States, the majority of media outlets are owned by a small number of giant multinational conglomerates and new media companies: Disney, News Corporation/21st Century Fox, Time Warner, Viacom/CBS, Bertelsmann, Comcast/NBCUniversal, and Google. Some

🔊 Audio 2.2: Listen to an interview with, and to the music of, John Adams.

▶ Video 2.1: Watch clips of McLuhan speaking.

observers, such as German academic and sociologist Jürgen Habermas, fear that these corporations are becoming a sort of ruling class, controlling which books are published, which programs are aired, which movies are produced, and which news stories are written.[37] As we discuss in Chapter 3, Disney, News Corporation, and Google have all had to compromise at times with the Chinese government in order to keep doing business there. For example, Google had to agree to censor its search results about sensitive topics in China for the company to be allowed to operate there.[38]

Media critic and former newspaper editor Ben Bagdikian suggests that the influence of media owners can be seen in how the news media select stories to be covered. He argues that large media organizations will kill news stories and entertainment programs that don't reflect well on the corporation. The roots of this tendency go back to when captains of industry such as J. P. Morgan and the Rockefellers bought out magazines that criticized them in order to silence that criticism. What we end up with, Bagdikian says, is not the feared bogeyman of government censorship, but rather "a new Private Ministry of Information and Culture" that gives corporations control over what we will see, hear, or read.[39] Increasingly, however, the new alternative media are providing channels that allow consumers to bypass Big Media controls.[40] (See the section on long-tail media in Chapter 3 for more on how these new channels are enabling anyone who wants to distribute content to do so on a large scale.) Blogs such as *RedState* and *Daily Kos* give voice to issues from a partisan point of view with no controls at all other than those the authors choose to employ.

Active Audience Effects

Some of the early fears about the effects of the media on audience members arose from the belief that the audience truly was a faceless, undifferentiated mass—that the characteristics of the audience en masse also applied to the audience's individual members. Early critics viewed modern people as alienated and isolated individuals who, separated by the decline of the family and the growth of a technological society, didn't communicate with one another. After World War II, the concept of the mass audience began to change

Questioning the Media

Does the medium you use for mass communication change how you perceive the message? How does watching a movie at an IMAX theater differ from watching it on your television set? How does listening to a speech on the radio or on television differ from reading a copy of the speech online or in a newspaper? Are you more comfortable reading something disturbing than seeing a video about the same subject?

Web 2.4: Check out the corporate sites of media giants.

Video 2.2: Watch commercials targeting different audiences.

as scholars came to realize that the audience was made up of unique members who responded as individuals, not as undifferentiated members of a mass.[41]

Today, communicators, marketers, and scholars realize that individuals seek and respond to different messages at different times and for different reasons. Therefore, they divide audiences on the basis of **geographics**, or where people live; **demographics**, or their gender, race, ethnic background, income, education, age, educational attainment, and the like; or **psychographics**, a combination of demographics, lifestyle characteristics, and product usage. Hence a young woman buying a small SUV to take her mountain bike out into the mountains will respond to a very different kind of advertising message than a mother seeking a small SUV so that she can safely drive her child to school during rush hour in the winter.

Audiences can also be classified by the amount of time they spend using media or by the purposes for which they use media. Each segment of the media audience will behave differently. Take television viewing as an example. Some people tune in daily to watch their favorite soap opera or talk show and won't change the channel for the entire hour. This is known as appointment viewing. Others surf through a number of channels using the remote control, looking for something that will capture their interest. Still others switch back and forth between two channels.

SECRET 7 With regard to television, the concept of a mass audience consuming the same content at the same time existed to some extent from the 1950s to the 1970s, when the vast majority of viewers had access to only three broadcast networks, but that concept broke down completely with the advent of cable, satellite, multiple broadcast networks, TiVo, DVDs, and VCRs. (This is an example of Secret Seven—There is no "they.")

Media scholar James Potter suggests that the media audience resembles a pyramid. (Remember the pyramid figure in Chapter 1?) At the peak of the pyramid we are all consuming the same messages, such as the horrifying reports of the September 11, 2001, terrorist attacks. At the base of the pyramid we are all different, consuming what interests us personally, such as when we surf the Internet. In between the narrow top and the wide base are the various audience segments that the media and advertisers are trying to reach.[42]

In addition to recognizing that different people use the media in different ways, scholars have realized that mass com-

---

geographics: The study of where people live; a method typically used to analyze potential markets for products and programs.

demographics: The study of audience members' gender, race, ethnic background, income, education, age, educational attainment, and the like; a method typically used to analyze potential markets for products and programs.

psychographics: A combination of demographics, lifestyle characteristics, and product usage; a method typically used to analyze potential markets for products and programs.

munication messages are generally mediated through other levels of communication. One reason this book discusses intrapersonal, interpersonal, and group communication in addition to mass communication is that these levels all come into play in how mass communication operates. People discuss political news with one another, cheer together for their favorite teams while watching a hockey game on television, and think about how stock market information is going to affect their investment plans. A young man's reaction to a love scene in a movie will differ depending on if he watches it with a group of friends, with his sweetie, or with his parents.[43]

Theories of Media and Society

There is a scene in *Star Wars Episode V: The Empire Strikes Back* in which Luke Skywalker is nervous about entering a cave beneath a tree in the Dagobah jungle. He asks Master Yoda, "What's in there?" Yoda replies, "Only what you take with you." And so it is with mass communication. What we find with mass communication research depends in large part on the theory base we take with us and the questions the theories suggest we pose. It's not so much that different approaches to research give us different answers—it's more that they take us to different questions. In this section, we look at several of the theoretical approaches to mass communication and the types of questions they raise.

Functional Analysis

The effects of the media are not limited to those on individuals or groups. Some of the media's most significant effects reach society as a whole.

According to media scholar Harold Lasswell, the mass media are simply an extension of basic functions that society has always needed. Earlier societies had priests, town criers, storytellers, bards who sang ballads, and travelers who brought news from distant lands.[44] Communication can be functional or dysfunctional, but in either case it operates within the social system.[45] For example, some people respond inappropriately to the news of approaching danger. Instead of going to the basement during a tornado warning, a functional response, they go outside with their video cameras to get footage of the storm, a dysfunctional response. In both cases, they are responding to the news of the storm.

Lasswell wrote that the media perform three major social functions[46]:

1. Surveillance of the environment, looking for both threats and opportunities

2. Correlation of different elements of society, allowing segments of society to work together

3. Transmission of culture from one generation to the next

To these three, media sociologist Charles Wright adds the function of entertainment.[47] Let's look more closely at each of these functions.

Surveillance of the Environment. Much of what we know about the world we learn from the media through the process of **surveillance**. The media show us what is happening not only within our own culture, but in other societies as well. Our only other sources of knowledge about the world are our own direct experiences and the direct experiences that others share with us. For example, much of what we learned about the Arab Spring rebellions of 2011 came from social media, such as Facebook or Twitter. (We will discuss this in much more depth in Chapter 15, which focuses on global media.)

The constant flow of information from the media allows us to survey our surroundings. It can give us warnings of approaching danger—everything from changes in the weather to earthquakes to violence in the streets. This flow of information is essential for the everyday operation of society. The stock markets depend on the business news, travelers depend on weather forecasts, and grocery shoppers depend on knowing what's on special this week.

Surveillance can also serve to undermine society. For example, when people in poor nations see media images of what life is like in the United States and other industrialized Western nations, they may become dissatisfied with the conditions of their own lives, and this may lead to social unrest and violence. News about violence may also make people more fearful for their own safety.

Surveillance is not just for the masses. Government and industry leaders worldwide watch CNN or C-SPAN or read the *New York Times* or the *Financial Times* to know what other government leaders are saying and thinking.

News can also give status to individuals. Because media coverage exposes them to large audiences, they seem important. This process is known as **status conferral**. Thus, the U.S. president's press spokesperson becomes famous and important simply because he or she is speaking with

©iStockphoto.com/Nlshop

---

surveillance: How the media help us extend our senses to perceive more of the world surrounding us.

status conferral: The process by which media coverage makes an individual gain prominence in the eyes of the public.

Web 2.5: View tweets on the 2011 Egyptian revolution.

Web 2.6: Can social media move faster than an earthquake?

Web 2.7: Read about media coverage of big trial verdicts.

Members of the Roberston family (Si, left; Willie, center; and Phil, right) became famous through the process of status conferral when they and their duck call company Duck Commander started being featured on the A&E Television Network show *Duck Dynasty*.

teaser on the magazine cover promoting the story?

Although many people say that they would prefer just the facts, virtually the only news outlet that provides no interpretation of events is the public affairs network C-SPAN, which has rigid rules governing how every event is covered. Far more viewers choose to go to the broadcast networks or cable news channels, which provide some interpretation, rather than watch the relatively dry, "just the facts" C-SPAN.[51]

It is often difficult to distinguish between communication that is informative and communication that is persuasive. Editorial judgments are always being made as to which stories should be covered and which should be omitted, which picture of a politician should be published, or what kind of headline should be written. Thus, it is useful to view surveillance and correlation as two functions that can be shared by a particular message.

the media.[48] Think about the level of coverage the Casey Anthony not-guilty verdict (mentioned earlier in this chapter) received in the summer of 2011. According to the Project for Excellence in Journalism's news coverage index, during the week of the verdict the story filled 38 percent of the time on cable news channels. CNN's HLN channel, which is credited with bringing the trial to national attention through the efforts of talk show host Nancy Grace, had its ratings increase by 1,700 percent on the afternoon the verdict was announced.[49] No other trial since 2007 has even come close to this level of coverage. For example, the verdict in the murder trial for Dr. Conrad Murray, who was found guilty of involuntary manslaughter in the death of singer Michael Jackson, commanded only 8 percent of the cable news coverage that week.[50]

Correlation of Different Elements of Society.
Correlation is the selection, evaluation, and interpretation of events to impose structure on the news. Correlation is accomplished by persuasive communication through editorials, commentary, advertising, and propaganda. Through media-supplied correlation, we make sense out of what we learn through surveillance. It puts news into categories and provides cues that indicate the importance of each news item. Does it appear on the front page of the newspaper? Is it the first item on the broadcast? Is there a

 Video 2.3: Watch C-SPAN coverage.

Socialization and Transmission of Culture.
Socialization is the process of integrating people within society through the transmission of values, social norms, and knowledge to new members of the group.

SECRET 1 It is through the media, as well as through our friends, family, school, and church, that we learn the values of our society. Socialization is important not only to young people as they are growing up, but also to immigrants learning about and assimilating into their new country, high school students heading off to college, and new graduates going to work.[52] (Another example of Secret One—The media are essential components of our lives.)

The media provide socialization in a variety of ways:

- Through role models in entertainment programming
- Through goals and desires as presented in media content

---

correlation: The process of selecting, evaluating, and interpreting events to give structure to the news. The media assist the process of correlation by persuasive communication through editorials, commentary, advertising, and propaganda and by providing cues that indicate the importance of each news item.

socialization: The process of educating young people and new members about the values, social norms, and knowledge of a group or society.

- Through the citizenship values portrayed in the news
- Through advertisements for products that may be useful to us in different stages of our lives

Entertainment. Entertainment is communication designed primarily to amuse, even if it serves other functions as well, which it almost always does. A television medical drama would be considered entertainment, even though it might educate a person about life in a hospital or the symptoms of a major illness. In fact, a major characteristic of all television programming, including entertainment programming, is to let people know what life outside their own world is like.[53]

Agenda Setting

Although explanations of powerful direct effects did not hold up under research scrutiny, people still had a hard time accepting that the news media and political campaigns had little or no effect on the public. **Agenda-setting theory** provides an alternative explanation that does not minimize the influence of the media on society.[54] This theory holds that issues that are portrayed as important in the news media become important to the public—that is, that the media set the agenda for public debate. If the media are not able to tell people what to think, as the direct effects model proposed, perhaps they can tell people what to think *about*. Agenda-setting theorists seek to determine whether the issues that are important to the media are also important to the public.[55] For example, the 2012 presidential election, and the Iowa caucuses in particular, received widespread discussion and attention in the United States following extensive coverage of campaigns and debates in 2012 and late 2011. The Project for Excellence in Journalism found that during the week of the Iowa first-in-the-nation caucuses, the election got 52 percent of all news space, overwhelming discussion of the economy and the ongoing conflict with Iran.[56]

The initial study of agenda setting was conducted in Chapel Hill, North Carolina, by Donald Shaw and Maxwell McCombs. The researchers found, among uncommitted voters in the 1968 presidential election, a strong relationship between the issues the press considered important and the issues the voters considered important. Since these voters had not already made up their minds about the upcoming election, their most likely source of cues, the researchers concluded, was the mass media. The study compared the content of the press and the attitudes of voters and found a strong correlation. Even though the researchers did not find evidence that the press persuaded people to change their opinions, they did find that the issues featured in the campaign and in the press were also the issues that voters felt were important.[57]

There are, however, some limits on the usefulness of the agenda-setting concept. If a story does not resonate with the public, neither the media nor the candidates will be able to make people care. For example, reports that Ronald and Nancy Reagan had conceived a child before they were married did not seem to do any damage to Reagan's image; nor was the Rev. Pat Robertson's campaign damaged by reports that the candidate and his wife had lied about the date of their wedding anniversary to hide the fact that their first child was conceived premaritally.

Uses and Gratifications Theory

Uses and gratifications theory turns the traditional way of looking at media effects on its head. Instead of looking at the audience as a sheep-like mass of receivers of messages, uses and gratifications theory views audience members as active receivers of information of their own choosing. Uses and gratifications theory is based on the following assumptions:

- Audience members are active receivers who have wants and needs. They then make decisions about media use based on those wants and needs. For example, in this approach, television doesn't *do things* to children, children *make use* of television.
- Media compete with many sources of gratification. I might watch television in the evening to relax. Television would be competing with reading a magazine, going for a walk, and playing with my son as alternative ways of relaxing.
- Audience members are aware of these choices and make them consciously.
- Our judgments about the value of various media uses must come from the audience's perspective.[58]

The idea behind uses and gratification theory is that individuals are constantly seeking gratifications, and the media compete to provide them. Media scholar Arthur Asa

Questioning the Media

Can you name a story that has become an important issue primarily because it has received extensive coverage from the news media? What's an important issue that's been ignored or not covered enough by the news media? Considering both stories, why was one covered more extensively than the other?

---

entertainment: Media communication intended primarily to amuse the audience.

agenda-setting theory: A theory of media effects that says that the media tell the public not what to think but rather what to think *about*—thus the terms of public discourse are set by what is covered in the media.

uses and gratifications theory: An approach to studying mass communication that looks at the reasons why audience members choose to spend time with the media in terms of the wants and needs of the audience members that are being fulfilled.

Berger says that among the gratifications that audience members might seek are to be amused, to experience the beautiful, to have shared experiences with others, to find models to imitate, and to believe in romantic love.[59] So someone who doesn't care about football might still watch a game on television and enjoy it because he wants to spend time with friends. Although he is consuming media, that's not the real point of his interaction with the television set.

Social Learning

At some point in your life, you've been told that experience is the best teacher. While experience may be a good teacher, it is also a harsh one, forcing us to suffer from our mistakes. Fortunately, we don't have to make all these mistakes ourselves, according to social psychologist Albert Bandura's social learning theory. Bandura writes, "If knowledge and skills could be acquired only by direct experience, the process of human development would be greatly retarded, not to mention exceedingly tedious and hazardous."[60] Instead, he says that we are able to learn by observing what others do and the consequences they face. Bandura says humans go through three steps to engage in social learning:

- We extract key information from situations we observe.
- We integrate these observations to create rules about how the world operates.
- We put these rules into practice to regulate our own behavior and predict the behaviors of others.

The media, by widening the information about the world that we are exposed to, play an important role in social learning. Think about a small boy who watches Batman defeat evil bad guys (EBGs) by physically fighting with them. Fighting with the EBGs proves to be a successful strategy and generally earns the superhero praise and the keys to Gotham City. Thus, while watching the animated show may not lead directly to the child engaging in violence, it could teach him that fighting is an effective way of solving problems and leads to social approval. He may then try out the practice by fighting with his sister, at which point he discovers it does not lead to social approval from his parents, and he stops the behavior. Or he might try it out by fighting with his friends and discover that it leads to his receiving respect. From this simplistic example, we can see how social learning theory can be applied to analyzing media. The content of the media can provide a large-scale source of content from which social learning can take place.[61] If the behavior being modeled is successful in achieving the person's goals, it may continue to be used. Think of the *Batman*-watching child who gains respect among his friends by fighting. If the behavior is unsuccessful in achieving results, the person may try other strategies. Think of the *Batman*-watching child who earns parental disapproval by fighting with his sister. He may instead sharpen his verbal or negotiating skills to gain the upper hand in conflicts with his sister.

Symbolic Interactionism

George Herbert Mead wrote back in 1934 that what holds us together as a culture is our common creation of society through our interactions based on language, or **symbolic interactionism**. We engage in symbolic interactions in which we continually attempt to arouse in others the feeling we have in ourselves by telling others how we feel.

SECRET 1 If our language is understood, we are able to communicate; if, on the other hand, we do not share common meanings, we will not be understood.[62] The mass media are by far the biggest source of shared meanings in our world. (Secret One—The media are essential components of our lives.)

If you think back to our discussion of the meaning of the yellow ribbon in Chapter 1, you can see how this works. We start with an arbitrary symbol: the yellow ribbon. We assign it meaning and then propagate that meaning through portrayal through the media. Eventually nearly everyone comes to have the same shared meaning of the looped ribbon, and the ribbon becomes a universal symbol of support—support for the troops, for disease sufferers, and for all kinds of social causes.

Sociologist W. I. Thomas provides us with one of the most quoted and understandable statements of symbolic interactionism: "If men define situations as real, they are real in their consequences."[63] If we ignore the outdated gender bias of the quote, there's a lot to analyze there. What Thomas is saying is that if people view a problem as being real, and behave as though a problem is real, it will have real consequences, even if the problem does not truly exist. Back in 1938, Orson Welles narrated a famous radio adaptation of H. G. Wells's *War of the Worlds*. The radio play was misinterpreted by some to be an actual news story, and there were many accounts at the time of people panicking and even committing suicide out of fear of the Martians invading New Jersey. Ever since then, broadcasters have been very careful to run extensive disclaimers on the air every time they run a *War of the Worlds*–style story, to make sure they don't panic their audience. There is also a widespread fear of powerful effects that the mass media can have on susceptible audience members. The only problem is that the research conducted at the time on the *War of the Worlds* panic was seriously flawed, and criticism of the research, which dates back to the 1940s, has largely been ignored, in part because the belief in the *War of the Worlds* effect is so strong. The truth is that there was far more perception of panic than

---

social learning theory: The process by which individuals learn by observing the behaviors of others and the consequences of those behaviors.

symbolic interactionism: The process by which individuals produce meaning through interaction based on socially agreed-upon symbols.

Audio 2.3: Listen to Orson Welles's *War of the Worlds* broadcast.

actual panic at the time. In summary, it doesn't matter much now whether the panic actually took place. What matters is that people believe that it did.[64]

Spiral of Silence

German media scholar Elisabeth Noelle-Neumann, with her **spiral of silence**, has raised the question of why people become unwilling to express what they perceive to be a minority opinion. Noelle-Neumann became interested in this question in part from trying to find out why the Germans supported political positions that led to national defeat, humiliation, and ruin in the 1930s and 1940s, or why the French under German occupation were seemingly complacent as Jewish friends and neighbors were sent to concentration camps. Noelle-Neumann says that societies function on the basis of perceived consensus. We want to view ourselves as part of a majority and as holding the consensus opinion. Thus people will refrain from expressing opinions that they think will be at odds with those of their friends and neighbors, even though their neighbors might actually agree with them.[65]

So how do people receive the cues that indicate what popular public opinion is, so that they might agree with it? The media are important public institutions because they are often our best source of public opinion. Central to Noelle-Neumann's argument is that when people believe they are in the minority with their opinion, they will tend to stay quiet on the topic, thus feeding the sense that a particular opinion is held by a minority. Thus it becomes a death spiral of diversity of ideas, as more and more people come to believe that they hold a minority opinion.[66]

While the spiral of silence is a fascinating explanation of how public opinion functions, it is difficult to independently verify and prove whether it, in fact, works that way. Radicals will oftentimes speak up with unpopular opinions precisely because they are unpopular. And people who care deeply about an issue will speak out simply because they feel they are correct. As an example, think about the willingness of the country crossover group the Dixie Chicks to put themselves and their careers at risk by criticizing President George W. Bush in the early days of the Iraq war, at a time when they knew their views would be unpopular.[67] But a recent study from the Pew Research Internet Project found support for the spiral of silence when it comes to discussing controversial issues on social media. The researchers were attempting to find out whether social media such as Facebook or Twitter might make people more willing to express their opinions on political issues. The Pew study looked at how willing people were to express an opinion about Edward Snowden's release of classified documents as discussed in the opening vignette for this chapter. Not surprisingly, the study showed that Americans were split as to whether Snowden's leaks were a good idea and whether the surveillance policy was a good idea. But the study went on to show the following:

- People were less willing to discuss the Snowden case on social media than they were in person.
- People were more likely to share their opinions about Snowden if they thought their audience agreed with their point of view. This was true both in person and online.
- People who wouldn't share their opinion on Snowden in a face-to-face conversation were even less likely to share their opinion on social media.

Overall, the Pew study found a strong spiral of silence effect for controversial issues on social media.[68]

Media Logic

Media logic is an approach to analyzing the effects of mass media that was developed by David Altheide and Robert Snow. They argue that we live in a media world in which the dominant cultural forms are those defined by the media.[69] The media provide major types of content—news, sports, action, drama, comedy, and advertising—that follow standardized formats. When we turn on a television set, long before we can say what specific program is on, we can use format cues to tell what type of program it is, even if we've never seen it before. These standard formats become a lens through which we view our everyday life. For example, we may use the format of a sports broadcast to describe our presidential races and apply soap opera formats to describe ongoing political scandals. We also use these formats to shape our behaviors, especially when we want to get media attention. So when an organization has something important happening, its officials plan the event around the needs and schedules of the media they want to cover it.[70] Thus the event that the media covers is constructed especially to facilitate its being covered. Think about a group of protesters protesting the construction of a new power plant on a cold, rainy day. They huddle under their shelters with their signs until a news crew from a local television station shows up. Then the protesters come to life, marching and chanting for the benefit of the cameras. The mere fact that the cameras are there changes what's happening.

Cultivation Analysis

George Gerbner (1919–2005), the best-known researcher of television violence, did not believe televised violence has direct effects on people's behavior, but he was deeply concerned about its effect on society as a whole.[71] Gerbner

---

spiral of silence: A theory that suggests that people want to see themselves as holding a majority opinion and will therefore remain silent if they perceive that they hold a minority opinion. This tends to make the minority opinion appear to be less prevalent than it is.

media logic: An approach to studying the mass media that says the forms the media use to present the world become the forms we use to perceive the world and to create media messages.

 Web 2.8: Read more about the Pew report on social media and the spiral of silence.

Filmmaker Eli Roth, left, with Marilyn Manson, has drawn extensive criticism for the extreme torture violence in his *Hostel* horror film series.

developed an alternative to traditional message effects research called **cultivation analysis**. His argument was that watching large amounts of television cultivates a distinct view of the world that is sharply at odds with reality.[72]

Over the years, Gerbner and his colleagues analyzed thousands of network television programs for the themes they presented and the level of violence they included. In a series of studies beginning in 1967, Gerbner's team found high levels of violence on television. They defined violence as "the overt expression of force intended to hurt or kill."[73]

Network officials have been openly critical of Gerbner, saying that his studies weren't representative of television as a whole and that his definition of violence is not useful because it does not discriminate between the fantasy violence of a Road Runner cartoon and the more graphic gore of a *Saw* or *Hostel* movie.

Gerbner compared the rate of violence on television to the rate of it occurring in the real world. He concluded that television cultivates a view of the world that is much more violent than the world we live in. The nature of the violence is different as well, with most television violence occurring between strangers rather than between family members, as does real-life violence. Gerbner said that, because of this,

 Video 2.4: Watch ads from a variety of recent political campaigns.

people who watch a great deal of television perceive the world differently than do light viewers. Heavy television viewing cultivates a response that Gerbner calls the **mean world syndrome**. In an appearance before Congress, Gerbner testified:

> The most general and prevalent association with television viewing is a heightened sense of living in a "mean world" of violence and danger. Fearful people are more dependent, more easily manipulated and controlled, more susceptible to deceptively simple, strong, tough measures and hard-line postures. . . . They may accept and even welcome repression if it promises to relieve their insecurities. That is the deeper problem of violence-laden television.[74]

The effect of violent television, Gerbner argued, is not that it will program children to be violent; instead, the real harm is more complex:

- Violent programming pushes aside other ways of portraying conflict.
- Violent programming deprives viewers of other choices.
- Violent programming facilitates the victim mentality.
- Violent programming discourages production of alternative programming.[75]

Media, Politics, and Society

Our understanding of the media and the campaign process has evolved over the past hundred years. In the early decades of the twentieth century, scholars and critics worried that voters might be manipulated and controlled by campaign messages sent through the media, especially those that might be sent subliminally. This understanding changed in the 1940s and 1950s as scholars came to suspect that media effects might in fact be selective and indirect. Currently it is believed that an interactional relationship exists among politicians, the press, and the public in which each influences the others.

How Do Political Campaigns Affect Voters?

If, as *The People's Choice* study indicates, campaigns do not have strong direct effects on voters, what are candidates trying to accomplish with their campaigns? They may be trying to directly persuade voters with the content of the messages, but more likely they are trying to shape the campaign

cultivation analysis: An approach to analyzing the effects of television viewing that argues that watching significant amounts of television alters the way an individual views the nature of the surrounding world.

mean world syndrome: The perception of many heavy television watchers of violent programs that the world is a more dangerous and violent place than facts and statistics bear out.

Cultivation Theory

By and large, most people who aren't media scholars would be hard pressed to name a single media theorist who isn't Marshall McLuhan. But the one possible exception would be George Gerbner because of his cultivation theory. Dr. Gerbner testified before Congress about televised violence in October 1981, and his cultivation theory is one of the top three cited theoretical approaches in communication research.

As you read in the section on cultivation analysis, one of the biggest areas of concern about media effects is how violence on television affects viewers, especially children. George Gerbner was one of the nation's leading researchers on televised violence.

Gerbner explained what he considered to be major misconceptions about the effects of televised violence and what his research suggested the real effects were. He argued that watching large amounts of television cultivates a distinct view of the world that is at odds with reality.

Gerbner argued that, because of televised violence, heavy television viewers are more likely to

- overestimate their chances of experiencing violence,
- believe that their neighborhoods are unsafe,
- state that fear of crime is a very serious personal problem, and
- assume that the crime rate is rising, regardless of the actual crime rate.[76]

While Gerbner's developmental work on cultivation theory was done in the 1960s, '70s, and '80s back when most people had access to only three or four broadcast cable channels, it has continued to interest both audience members and scholars into the era of high definition and hundreds of cable channels.

Dr. Patrick E. Jamieson and Dr. Dan Romer at the University of Pennsylvania took a fresh look in 2014 at Gerbner's work to see how it would hold up to an examination of twenty-five years of data

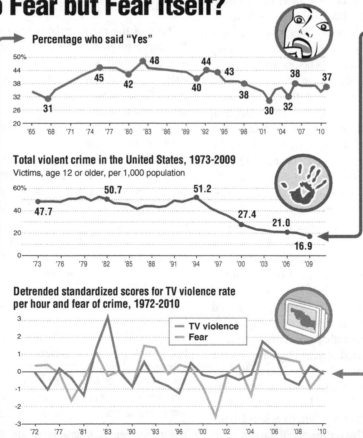

Nothing To Fear but Fear Itself?

- **As a way of measuring** the American public's perception of the threat of violence, in 1965 **Gallup** began asking Americans:

"Is there any area near where you live—that is, within a mile—where you would be afraid to walk alone at night?"

Responses show that the fear of violence increased over time until 1982. Perceptions then decreased to 30% in 2001, but have since gone back up to 37%.

Sources: Patrick E. Jamieson and Daniel Romer, "Violence in Popular U.S. Prime Time TV Dramas and the Cultivation of Fear: A Time Series Analysis," Media and Communication (2014) 2.2: 31-41. http://repository.upenn.edu/cgi/viewcontent.cgi?article=1365&context=asc_papers; Gallup, http://www.gallup.com/poll/144272/nearly-americans-fear-walking-alone-night.aspx

Percentage who said "Yes"

50% 44 38 32 26 20
31 45 42 48 40 44 43 38 30 32 38 37
'65 '68 '71 '74 '77 '80 '83 '86 '89 '92 '95 '98 '01 '04 '07 '10

Total violent crime in the United States, 1973-2009
Victims, age 12 or older, per 1,000 population

60% 40 20 0
47.7 50.7 51.2 27.4 21.0 16.9
'73 '76 '79 '82 '85 '88 '91 '94 '97 '00 '03 '06 '09

Detrended standardized scores for TV violence rate per hour and fear of crime, 1972-2010

3 2 1 0 -1 -2 -3
— TV violence
— Fear
'72 '77 '81 '83 '90 '93 '96 '00 '02 '04 '06 '08 '10

- **Yet over roughly the same period**, the actual rate of violent crime has dropped dramatically, falling from a high in 1994 of 51.2 victims per 1,000 to just 16.9 in 2009.

What explains the fact that the fear of violence doesn't rise and fall with the actual rate of violence?

- **Jamieson and Romer's** study measured the number of violent sequences per TV hour over roughly the same time frame, and their findings show that while the amount of violent content on television did not affect people's estimations of how dangerous the world around them was, it did make people more afraid of violence. The bottom graph here shows how instances of TV violence correlate to fear, using standardized scores that reflect how far above or below the overall average the scores are.

Jamieson and Romer give a more nuanced understanding of how cultivation may work. In their conclusion, they go back to one of Gerbner's chief concerns: that increasing amounts of televised violence could lead to increased fear, which could lead to people being supportive of authoritarian governance.

(Continued)

about televised violence and people's fear of crime. Jamieson and Romer looked at 475 hours of television programming and Gallup interviews with more than 27,000 people. In their study, they found that while increased violent content on television did not change people's estimations of how dangerous the world around them was, it did make people more afraid of violence.[77]

Alyssa Rosenberg, writing for the Act Four blog at the *Washington Post*, says that shows like NBC's *Law & Order: Special Victims Unit* "create intense emotional bonds between viewers and on-screen characters," and Dr. Romer told her that shows like this might have

distinctive effects: "Women report more fear of crime on surveys and the source of discrepancy is not clear. . . . Men are more likely to be victims of murder but women are more likely to be victims in domestic disputes and of course in rapes. So, these sorts of situations may loom larger in women's minds. Gerbner argued that movies and TV tend to show women as victims more than men, and this may also play a role."[78]

Media Transformations Questions

- **WHAT** is cultivation theory, and why has it remained so popular over the years?

- According to Gerbner, **WHAT** are the effects of television violence?

- **HOW** has the media world changed since Gerbner developed cultivation theory?

- **HOW** did reading about Gerbner's research and the follow-up to it by Jamieson and Romer change your understanding of the effects of media violence?

 Web 2.9: Revisiting Dr. Gerbner and TV violence.

---

in more subtle ways. These are interactional models that say that the interaction among voters, the media, and the campaigns that are triggered by the ads are more important than any direct persuasion of voters. Here are two examples:

The **resonance model** says that the candidate's success depends in part on how well his or her basic message resonates with voters' preexisting political feelings. Thus, the candidate who does the best job of sending out messages that connect with target voters is the one most likely to win. The communication goal for the campaign is not so much to get people to change their minds as it is to get voters to believe that they share viewpoints with the candidate.[79] The resonance model was clearly used in the 2008 campaign in ads by both Democratic candidate Barack Obama and Republican candidate John McCain. Obama got strong resonance out of a commercial that claimed McCain was out of touch with ordinary people because he didn't know how many houses he owned. McCain got a similar resonance by charging Obama with being more of a celebrity than a serious politician.

The **competitive model** looks at the campaign not in isolation but as a competition between two or more candidates for the hearts and minds of voters. Hence the success of a campaign message, such as a speech that criticizes the candidate's opponent, depends as much on the opponent's reaction as it does on the message itself. Voter response can also depend on how the media react to the message. If the message attracts media attention, it may be played repeatedly on news broadcasts, as well as on political talk shows.[80] During the 2008 Democratic presidential primary, candidate Hillary Clinton leveled charges against Obama that he had lifted political rhetoric from Massachusetts governor Deval Patrick. Similar charges that Sen. Joe Biden had lifted a speech from the British Labor Party leader helped sink his campaign for the presidency back in 1988.[81]

But Obama did not suffer the same sort of damage that Biden did. Why not? First, Obama and Governor Patrick are friends, they share the same political adviser, and they

have long shared a similar message. Second, Patrick did not object to the use of his words. Finally, Obama did not react particularly defensively to the charges of plagiarism. So, according to the competitive model, the public's direct reaction to the charges didn't matter as much as how the public reacted to Obama's reaction to the charges.

Media and Political Bias

One of the main reasons the direct effects model still has some support is that many critics believe the media affect the public's political opinions by presenting reports that are biased toward a particular candidate or political party. But, as we discuss in Chapter 6, in holding up detached, factual, objective journalism as an ideal for reporting, the press was making a commercial decision, not a moral one. During the penny press era of the 1830s to the 1860s, newspapers tried to appeal to the broadest possible audience. The best way to attract a large number of people, publishers felt, was not to take an identifiable political point of view, as had newspapers of the colonial era. The alternative to this supposedly objective style is a more opinionated form of reporting that takes on an explicit point of view, such as that found in *Time*, *Newsweek*, and many British or European newspapers, such as London's liberal *Guardian* or conservative (Tory) *Telegraph*. These publications have a clearly understood political viewpoint that is designed to appeal to a specific audience.[82]

This opinionated style has also been adopted by the brash cable channel Fox News, which rejects the traditional

---

resonance model: A model of political campaign effects that attributes a candidate's success to how well his or her basic message resonates with and reinforces voters' preexisting political feelings.

competitive model: A model of the effects of a political campaign that looks at the campaign as a competition for the hearts and minds of voters.

neutral style of CNN and the major broadcast networks.[83] Fox News commentator Bill O'Reilly says that part of his network's popularity comes from its willingness to think about what audience members want. "Unless your package is meaningful to the viewer, they're gone," he says. "The networks—and I include CNN in this—haven't figured that one out yet."[84] Erik Sorenson, former president of the MSNBC cable news channel, suggests that there is nothing wrong with taking a particular point of view. "I think a lot of people are beginning to ask, 'Is there something phony about pretending to be objective and reading off a teleprompter in the twenty-first century?'"[85] There can be no question that airing partisan news and commentary is a successful business strategy. Since 2002, Fox News has been the top-rated twenty-four-hour news network with its conservative point of view, attracting approximately 1.5 million prime-time viewers during the second quarter of 2014. MSNBC has had the second-largest audience, an average of 570,000 prime-time viewers, with its slate of liberal/progressive hosts. CNN, which takes a more neutral stand, is in third place with an average of 459,000 prime-time viewers. The audiences for all three of the major cable news networks have declined since the presidential election year of 2008, falling by an average of 13 to 16 percent, depending on the measure used.[86]

During the 2012 Republican presidential primary campaign, candidates (left to right) Ron Paul, Rick Santorum, Mitt Romney, and Newt Gingrich debated in Mesa, Arizona. The goal of the series of debates was not so much for the candidates to explain their viewpoints as it was an opportunity for them to show how they could interact and score points off each other and the moderators.

Liberal Versus Conservative Bias.

Leaving aside the news media that take an explicit political viewpoint, is there a predictable bias in the American news media? Critics on both the right and the left maintain that there is either a liberal or a conservative bias in the media's coverage of the news. Journalist and author Richard Reeves notes that for each example of a bias in one direction, there is an example of bias in the opposite direction. For instance, Cokie Roberts at ABC News is the daughter of two Democratic members of Congress, but Diane Sawyer, anchor of ABC's *World News*, was on Republican president Richard Nixon's staff.[87] Although individuals and individual programs in the media clearly hold differing views about the news, does the argument of an overall bias within the news media hold up to scrutiny?

Liberals and conservatives trade arguments about media bias. Conservatives point out that there are disproportionate numbers of liberals working as reporters. Liberals argue that large corporations own the media and that they slant the news in favor of industry and business. The argument that there is a liberal bias in the news media often focuses on charges that reporters are more liberal than the public at large. According to the study *The American Journalist in the 21st Century*, which surveyed more than 1,150 journalists, 40 percent of journalists described themselves as having views from the left, or liberal, side of the political spectrum; 33 percent described themselves as "middle of the roaders"; and 25 percent described themselves as having views from the right, or conservative, side.[88] The study concluded that journalists were more likely to hold a range of liberal views than the public at large, especially on social issues.

The explanation for this finding may be that people who go into journalism tend to be concerned about injustices within society, a personality type that could tend toward liberal or progressive political views. Some observers argue that journalists have a "liberal and cosmopolitan" approach to the world, and this shapes journalistic views of good and bad.[89] A widely reported study in 2007 said that journalists who made political contributions were more likely to give to Democrats than Republicans. What wasn't reported nearly as often was that very few journalists made political contributions. In fact, the study found that less than two-tenths of 1 percent of all journalists made political contributions.[90] On the other hand, if one looks at the editorial pages of the major newspapers, a somewhat different bias might appear.

SECRET 6 Between 1948 and 1990, 78 percent of newspaper presidential endorsements were for Republicans, but Republican candidates for president received 51 percent of the popular vote, which would tend to suggest that the editorial pages of newspapers are somewhat more conservative than the public at large.[91] So when you hear charges of media bias being thrown about, remember Secret Six—Activism and analysis are not the same thing.

TEST YOUR MEDIA LITERACY

Bias in the News

No matter what the news media do, they are likely to be charged with being biased. How do critics know this bias exists? They just have to look at the news. It's perfectly obvious, "they" say. But a pair of research studies found that if you examine a news story about a partisan issue, readers or viewers from both sides will claim that it is biased against their point of view. The studies showed that as long as the story tried to present a nuanced view that presented multiple sides of an issue—that is, what journalists would call an unbiased view—partisans on either side of the issue viewed the story as hopelessly biased. On the other hand, if the story had a strong point of view—that is, it *was* biased—people tended to perceive it as less biased.[1]

WHO **are the sources?**

Who conducted the two studies written about in the story? Where do they work? What are their fields of study?

WHAT **are they saying?**

How do partisans react to stories that are supposedly neutral (or unbiased)? How do neutral observers react? How do members of the two groups react to stories that have an explicit point of view? How would you categorize this research in terms of being message, medium, ownership, or audience based? Can you categorize the type of theory base the researchers were using?

WHAT **evidence exists?**

How did the two researchers reach their conclusions? How did they conduct their research?

WHAT **do you and your classmates think about media bias?**

What stories do you or your classmates see as being biased? Do you ever think that stories are biased in your favor? How do you feel when a story is trying to be balanced by presenting information you disagree with? In light of these studies, how do you think the news media should respond to charges of being biased? Do you prefer neutral-style reporting or news with an explicit point of view? Why?

---

1. Shankar Vedantam, "Two Views of the Same News Find Opposite Biases," *Washington Post*, July 24, 2006, A02.

 Web 2.10: Read the linked research study on bias in the news.

In a speech to college students, Karl Rove, former top adviser to President George W. Bush and a major Republican strategist, summed up the issue by saying that while he thinks the press is generally liberal,

> I think it's less liberal than it is oppositional. . . . Reporters now see their role less as discovering facts and fair-mindedly reporting the truth and more as being put on earth to afflict the comfortable, to be a constant thorn of those in power, whether they are Republican or Democrat.[92]

Gans's Basic Journalistic Values. There is more to the bias argument than the liberal-versus-conservative issue. For example, some observers charge that the media have a bias toward attractiveness or charisma. There can also be a bias toward making money or attracting an audience. Political scientist and media scholar Doris Graber argues that when it comes to selecting stories for coverage, the strongest bias is for those that will have the greatest appeal to the publication's or program's audience.[93]

Rather than looking for examples of bias in the news, media sociologist Herbert Gans set out to find the actual values exhibited within the stories themselves. He asked what the values—the biases—of journalism

were. To find the answer, he studied the content of the CBS and NBC news programs, *Time* magazine, and *Newsweek*.

Gans found eight enduring values in the stories he studied: ethnocentrism, altruistic democracy, responsible capitalism, small-town pastoralism, individualism, moderatism, social order, and leadership. These values were not stated explicitly; rather, they emerged from what was presented as being good and normal and what was presented as bad.[94] Let's look briefly at each of Gans's values:

1. *Ethnocentrism* is the idea that your own country and culture are better than all others. This shows up in the U.S. media in stories that compare other countries' values to American values. To the degree that other countries live up to American ideals, they are good; if they are different, they are bad. Therefore, enemies of the United States are presented as evil because they don't conform to our values. Stories can be critical of the United States, but they are criticizing deviance from basic American values, not those values themselves.

2. *Altruistic democracy* is the idea that politicians should serve the public good, not their own interests. This leads to stories that are critical of corrupt politicians. By the

same token, citizens, as voters, have the same obligation to work for the public good and not for selfish interests. Special interest groups and lobbyists are suspect because they are not working for the common good. This was perhaps best illustrated by the Watergate hearings in the 1970s, which revealed the corrupt behavior that occurred in the White House so that President Richard Nixon could stay in power. President Bill Clinton was criticized for his affair with Monica Lewinsky in part because he was serving his own interests rather than working for the good of the American public.

3. *Responsible capitalism* is the idea that open competition among businesses will create a better, more prosperous world for everyone. But by the same token, businesses must be responsible and not seek excess profits. The same is true of labor unions. Hence the news media tend to be harsh in their coverage of greed and deception by big businesses, yet they still tend to praise people who develop and grow companies. This is why there has been so much negative coverage of banking and investment companies following the stock market crash and recession in the late 2000s.

4. *Small-town pastoralism* is nostalgia for the old-fashioned, rural community. The agricultural community is where all goodness is rooted, while big cities are dangerous places that suffer from numerous social problems. Suburbs, where many people live, tend to be overlooked entirely.

5. *Individualism* is the constant quest to identify the one person who makes a difference. People like the notion that one person can make a difference, that we are not all cogs in a giant machine. Reporters like to use a single person as a symbol. That explains in part why journalists focused on the murder of Neda Agha-Soltan during protests about the contested 2009 Iranian elections. Instead of trying to talk about the wide range of people involved in the protests, they used Agha-Soltan as a symbol to represent all the protesters.[95]

6. *Moderatism* is the value of moderation in all things. Extremists on both the left and the right are criticized. Although the media attempt to present a balance of opinions, they tend to report on views that are mildly to the left and right of center. One of the strongest criticisms the media can make is referring to an individual as an extremist.

New York University journalism professor Dr. Jay Rosen argues that journalists could do a better job of reporting the news if they worked at covering multiple sides of issues rather than "both" sides. His arguments build on those of Dr. Herbert Gans on the values of the news media. The link below is to a conversation between Drs. Rosen and Gans.

7. The value of *social order* is seen primarily in the coverage of disorder. When journalists cover stories that involve disorder, such as protests, floods, disasters, or riots, the focus of the story tends to be on the restoration of order. This was one of the biggest issues in the media's coverage of the floods following Hurricane Katrina. The social order was in question for months following the storm, and the press focused heavily on how that order might be restored.[96]

8. Finally, the media value *leadership*. The media tend to look at the actions of leaders, whereas the actions of lower-level bureaucrats—which may well be more important—are ignored. This is in some ways an extension of the bias toward individualism, the difference one person can make.

Questioning the Media

Take a look at a recent news story from a major American news outlet. How many of Gans's news values can you find illustrated in it? Do you think Gans's eight news values still apply to what is being covered by American media? Why or why not?

Web 2.11: Read an interview with Herbert Gans.

Overall, Gans argues that there is reformist bias to the media, which tend to advocate "honest, meritocratic, and anti-bureaucratic government."[97] Journalists like to argue that since both sides criticize the press, they must be doing a good, balanced job.[98] Perhaps a better explanation for why both conservatives and liberals charge the media with bias is that the eight values Gans found within the media reflect a combination of both liberal and conservative values—again illustrating why people holding a particular viewpoint will see bias in the media's attempt to be neutral and balanced.

Center-right media commentator David Frum resigned from the American Public Media business radio show *Marketplace* because he felt he could no longer reliably represent the views of mainstream conservatives. In general, the commentators in American media try to represent the mainstream liberal or conservative point of view. Very few represent an intermediate viewpoint. You can read more about why Frum resigned at www .ralphehanson.com/2011/10/12/david-frum-the-problem-with-balanced-commentary/.

Chapter SUMMARY

With the rise of mass society and the rapid growth of the mass media starting in the nineteenth century, the public, media critics, and scholars have raised questions about the effects various media might have on society and individuals. These effects were viewed initially as being strong, direct, and relatively uniform on the population as a whole. After World War I, critics were concerned that media-oriented political campaigns could have powerful direct effects on voters. This view, though still widespread, was largely discredited by voter studies conducted in the 1940s and 1950s. These studies found that the voters with the strongest political opinions were those most likely to pay attention to a campaign and hence were least likely to be affected by it. More recently, research has expanded to move beyond looking just at the effects that media and media content have on individuals and society to examinations of how living in a world with all-pervasive media changes the nature of our interactions and culture.

Understanding the effects of media on individuals and society requires that we examine the messages being sent, the medium transmitting these messages, the owners of the media, and the audience members themselves. The effects can be cognitive, attitudinal, behavioral, or psychological.

Media effects can also be examined in terms of a number of theoretical approaches, including functional analysis, agenda setting, uses and gratifications, social learning, symbolic interactionism, spiral of silence, media logic, and cultivation analysis.

Our understanding of the relationship among politicians, the press, and the public has evolved over the past half century. Recent studies have supported interactional approaches to understanding campaign effects, including the resonance and competitive models.

Many people claim that the media are biased toward one political view or another. Conservative critics argue that there is a liberal bias arising from the tendency of reporters to be more liberal than the public at large. The liberals' counterargument is that the press has a conservative bias because most media outlets are owned by giant corporations that hold pro-business views. Finally, some critics argue that the media hold a combination of values that straddle the boundary between slightly left and slightly right of center. The press in the United States began as partisan during the colonial period but adopted a detached, factual, objective style in the 1830s to appeal to a broader audience.

 Keep up-to-date with content from the author's blog.

Take the chapter quiz.

Key TERMS

Concept REVIEW

Rise of mass society and mass communication

Message effects

Medium effects

Ownership effects

Active audience effects

Conceptions of media bias

Student STUDY SITE

$SAGE edge™

Sharpen your skills with SAGE edge at **edge.sagepub.com/hanson5e**

SAGE edge for Students provides a personalized approach to help you accomplish your coursework goals in an easy-to-use learning environment.

Public Relations
Interactions, Relationships, and the News

Kraft turned a small shortage of Velveeta into an opportunity to promote the popularity of the cheese product for making queso dip during the football playoffs season.

AP Photo/Paul Sakuma, File

The news broke the first week of January 2014. Football fans in the heat of the NFL playoffs were facing potential disaster. It wasn't a potential strike of NFL players or a lockout by management. And it wasn't a dispute between a cable company and the network broadcasting the big game, threatening a blackout of the Super Bowl over a major urban area. No, this was something really serious, the Cheesepocalypse—a shortage of Velveeta with which to make queso dip for Super Bowl and playoff watch parties.

It started when *Advertising Age* magazine contacted Kraft Foods after news reports surfaced of shortages at East Coast grocery stores. Kraft spokeswoman Jody Moore told *Ad Age*, "Given the incredible popularity of Velveeta this time of year, it is possible consumers may not be able to find their favorite product on store shelves over the next couple of weeks."[1]

And with that, Kraft had a minor crisis on its hands. In some ways, it was a good problem to have—consumers wanted more of its iconic product than the company could supply, which demonstrated that its marketing efforts promoting making salsa and cheese dip were successful. But how would the company respond to its customers and stores? How would they interact with their publics?

There were charges that the Velveeta shortage was some kind of a marketing ploy, but Kraft spokespeople insist that the shortage was real, caused by a combination of some "minor manufacturing challenges" and heavy seasonal demands.[2]

As word of the shortage spread, Twitter users started lamenting it. Among the early tweets collected by *People* magazine's Great Ideas blog were these[3]:

> **oldwaver** ✓
> @oldwaver　　　　　　　　　　　▼ Follow
>
> just bought a half eaten block of velveeta on ebay for 80 bucks. 10 chip per guest rationing in effect for super bowl party. no double dips.
>
> 11:52 AM - 8 Jan 2014
>
> 3 FAVORITES

https://twitter.com/oldwaver, accessed on 08/11/2014.

> **Dragon**
> @LittlePegAMcKay　　　　　　　▼ Follow
>
> Velveeta is the first thing they took away from all the Districts in Hunger Games. Don't ignore the warning signs. #Velveetashortage
>
> 7:53 PM - 7 Jan 2014
>
> 4 RETWEETS 2 FAVORITES

https://twitter.com/LittlePegAMcKay, accessed on 08/11/2014.

Fans of Velveeta got online to talk about the spot shortages of the product using hashtags on Twitter. One of the most popular ones was #Velveetashortage.

Kraft built on this social media response in a number of ways. The company promoted the use of the #cheesepocalype hashtag, and built a Cheesepocalpyse Web site that mapped out reports of Velveeta shortages using Twitter reports from across the country. The company also used its Tumblr blog, which normally suggested humorous uses for Velveeta, to officially announce the shortage.[4]

So what did Kraft and Velveeta get out of the Cheesepocalypse social media campaign? According to *Ad Age*'s Jack Neff, the brand got a huge amount of free publicity—publicity that was likely out of proportion to the "crisis." (The shortage was only of one packaging size.) But Kraft marketing executive Cannon Koo points out the #cheesepocalypse hashtag helped the company identify its so-called "super-consumers," the people who consume the most of the brand. Super-consumers are the folks who make up about 10 percent of the buyers for any brand, but account for anywhere from 30 to 70 percent of the brand's sales. Information about how these super-consumers use Velveeta has let the company increase its sales.[5]

Greg Gallagher, marketing director at Kraft, told the *Harvard Business Review*, "The previous thinking was that the quickest, easiest path to growth was to identify light users or lapsed users. But when we waked to super-consumers, we learned that in fact they wanted to use Velveeta more—they were starving for it."[6] Another benefit of the Cheespocalypse publicity was that a recall of a limited number of Velveeta products for being mislabeled went almost completely unnoticed—not because Kraft engaged in any kind of cover-up, but rather because the press and consumers were more engaged in a more compelling story line.[7]

Beyond the social media content itself, the active discussion drew a large amount of news media and blog coverage of Velveeta. Web sites from Michigan to Alabama wrote about the Cheesepocalypse. The publicity generated was not always positive, with the aforementioned Alabama news blog mocking the Kraft Velveeta shortage map, saying, "Hopefully folks in severe areas of Alabama and across the country will learn to function without Velveeta. If they use it to make dips, mac and cheese casseroles, melt on burgers etc., maybe they will rethink those recipes and substitute a healthier, real food option."[8]

But given that this was about Super Bowl food, I doubt too many people were worried about the health bit . . .

Timeline

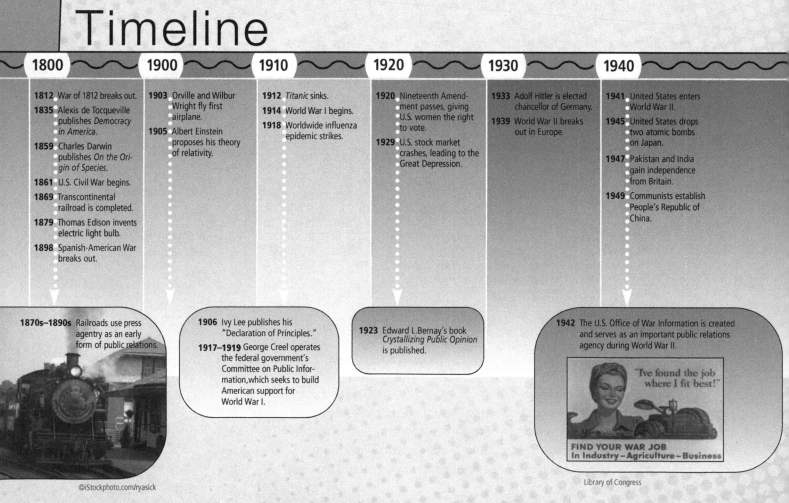

1800	1900	1910	1920	1930	1940
1812 War of 1812 breaks out. **1835** Alexis de Tocqueville publishes *Democracy in America*. **1859** Charles Darwin publishes *On the Origin of Species*. **1861** U.S. Civil War begins. **1869** Transcontinental railroad is completed. **1879** Thomas Edison invents electric light bulb. **1898** Spanish-American War breaks out.	**1903** Orville and Wilbur Wright fly first airplane. **1905** Albert Einstein proposes his theory of relativity.	**1912** *Titanic* sinks. **1914** World War I begins. **1918** Worldwide influenza epidemic strikes.	**1920** Nineteenth Amendment passes, giving U.S. women the right to vote. **1929** U.S. stock market crashes, leading to the Great Depression.	**1933** Adolf Hitler is elected chancellor of Germany. **1939** World War II breaks out in Europe.	**1941** United States enters World War II. **1945** United States drops two atomic bombs on Japan. **1947** Pakistan and India gain independence from Britain. **1949** Communists establish People's Republic of China.

1870s–1890s Railroads use press agentry as an early form of public relations.

©iStockphoto.com/ryasick

1906 Ivy Lee publishes his "Declaration of Principles."

1917–1919 George Creel operates the federal government's Committee on Public Information, which seeks to build American support for World War I.

1923 Edward L. Bernay's book *Crystallizing Public Opinion* is published.

1942 The U.S. Office of War Information is created and serves as an important public relations agency during World War II.

"I've found the job where I fit best!"

FIND YOUR WAR JOB
In Industry – Agriculture – Business

Library of Congress

Kraft's promotion of the Cheesepocalypse is at the core of how social media can be effectively used in public relations. Social media are not just new ways to push marking information; they are a great tool for interacting with and getting to know the people who love a product best. In the case of Velveeta, Kraft got to know the product's super-consumers better and helped them share recipes and new ways to use the soft cheese product. (Kraft's effective use of social media to interact with its consumers and turn what could have been a problem into a big plus for the brand is a great example of Secret Two—There are no mainstream media. In this case, interactive social media were far more important to Kraft than legacy media were.) The Cheesepocalypse highlights many of the key issues we look at in this chapter. In addition to examining the development of the public relations industry, we discuss how the public relations process works, the various publics that organizations need to work with, and how public relations professionals have used public relations to protect and advance their employers' interests. ■

> **❝The previous thinking was that the quickest, easiest path to growth was to identify light users or lapsed users. But when we waked to the super-consumers, we learned that in fact they wanted to use Velveeta more—they were starving for it.❞**
>
> —Greg Gallager, Kraft Foods

 Web 12.1: Get the whole story on the Cheesepocalypse.

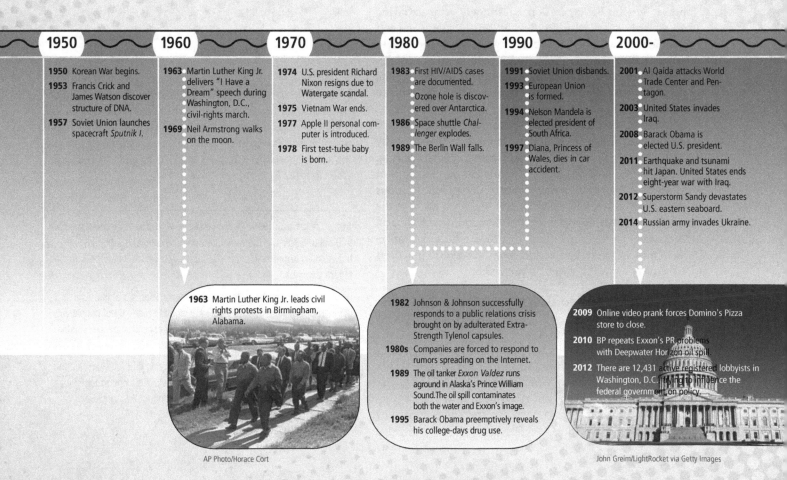

1950

1950 Korean War begins.

1953 Francis Crick and James Watson discover structure of DNA.

1957 Soviet Union launches spacecraft *Sputnik I.*

1960

1963 Martin Luther King Jr. delivers "I Have a Dream" speech during Washington, D.C., civil-rights march.

1969 Neil Armstrong walks on the moon.

1970

1974 U.S. president Richard Nixon resigns due to Watergate scandal.

1975 Vietnam War ends.

1977 Apple II personal computer is introduced.

1978 First test-tube baby is born.

1980

1983 First HIV/AIDS cases are documented.

Ozone hole is discovered over Antarctica.

1986 Space shuttle *Challenger* explodes.

1989 The Berlin Wall falls.

1990

1991 Soviet Union disbands.

1993 European Union is formed.

1994 Nelson Mandela is elected president of South Africa.

1997 Diana, Princess of Wales, dies in car accident.

2000-

2001 Al Qaida attacks World Trade Center and Pentagon.

2003 United States invades Iraq.

2008 Barack Obama is elected U.S. president.

2011 Earthquake and tsunami hit Japan. United States ends eight-year war with Iraq.

2012 Superstorm Sandy devastates U.S. eastern seaboard.

2014 Russian army invades Ukraine.

1963 Martin Luther King Jr. leads civil rights protests in Birmingham, Alabama.

AP Photo/Horace Cort

1982 Johnson & Johnson successfully responds to a public relations crisis brought on by adulterated Extra-Strength Tylenol capsules.

1980s Companies are forced to respond to rumors spreading on the Internet.

1989 The oil tanker *Exxon Valdez* runs aground in Alaska's Prince William Sound. The oil spill contaminates both the water and Exxon's image.

1995 Barack Obama preemptively reveals his college-days drug use.

2009 Online video prank forces Domino's Pizza store to close.

2010 BP repeats Exxon's PR problems with Deepwater Horizon oil spill.

2012 There are 12,431 active registered lobbyists in Washington, D.C. trying to influence the federal government on policy.

John Greim/LightRocket via Getty Images

From Press Agentry to Professionalism

The field of **public relations** (also called **PR**) has had an uneven image in the United States. (The term *public relations* is discussed more extensively later in this chapter.) In his book on corporate public relations, Marvin Olasky noted that practitioners have been called "high-paid errand boys and buffers for management."[9] Other names have been less flattering. Despite such criticisms, public relations is critical to industry, government, and nonprofit organizations. These organizations need to deal with the people who work for them, invest in them, are served by them, contribute to them, regulate them, or buy from them. They need to interact with the world. Ultimately, that's what public relations is all about—relating with a wide range of publics. A **public** is a group of people who share a common set of interests. An *internal public* is made up of people within the organization. An *external public* is made up of people outside the organization.

The Origins of Public Relations

The origins of public relations go back as far as the American Revolution, with pamphlets like Thomas Paine's *Common Sense*, which built up the case for the colonies' break with England. In the early 1800s, author Washington Irving used publicity to build excitement for his latest book. But the PR profession is generally seen as having grown out of the Industrial Revolution. As companies and their accompanying bureaucracies grew, so did the need to manage their image.[10] Advances in communications also made publicity campaigns more feasible. It wasn't until the penny press of the 1830s and 1840s produced widespread newspaper circulation that publicity began to be particularly effective. Circus entrepreneur P. T. Barnum raised publicity to a fine art, building interest in his shows by writing letters to the editor under fake names and accusing himself of fraud. Thus, this early publicity process, known as **press agentry**, was a one-way form of public relations that involved sending material from the press agent to the media with little opportunity for interaction and feedback. Press agentry was used to support causes such as temperance with speakers, books, and songs. It was also practiced effectively by the abolitionist movement.

One-Way Communication. As noted in the preceding section, press agentry consisted of one-way communication. For the most part, press agents before the 1920s worked at building publicity for their clients rather than managing or creating a specific image. Standard Oil's efforts in the 1890s were typical of the time. The oil giant's advertising agency sent out news articles as paid advertisements, but the agency paid for the ads only if they

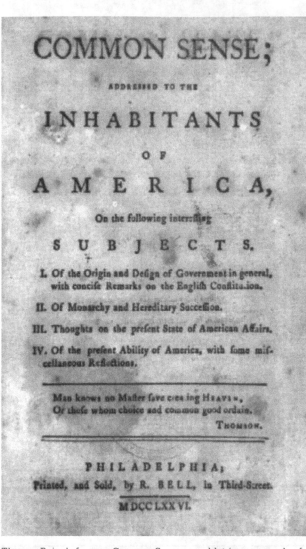

Library of Congress

Thomas Paine's famous *Common Sense* pamphlet is an example of an early PR effort. It was used to build the case for the American Revolution.

looked like articles or editorials.[11] In the early years of the twentieth century, however, companies started realizing that they needed to respond to criticism from various populist and progressive political groups and to muckraking investigative reports by magazines such as *McClure's* (see Chapter 5).

---

public relations (PR): Public relations is "the management function that establishes and maintains mutually beneficial relationships between an organization and the publics on whom its success or failure depends."

public: Any group of people who share a common set of interests and goals. These include *internal publics*, which are made up of people within the organization, and *external publics*, which consist of people outside the organization.

press agentry: An early form of public relations that involved sending material from the press agent to the media with little opportunity for interaction and feedback. It often involved conduct that would be considered deceptive and unethical today.

The Beginnings of Image Management. The first major users of public relations were railroads, which had numerous reasons for working on their images.[12] In the 1870s, many railroads wanted to divide freight traffic among themselves according to predetermined percentages so as to avoid competition. The railroads did not want criticism of their monopolistic practices in the press, so they bribed reporters and editors, either by making cash payoffs or, more subtly, by giving free passes for travel on the railroad to cooperative members of the press. The Illinois Central Railroad realized that praise of the railroads coming from academics would do more good and be more persuasive than puffery coming from the industry itself, so it funded university research on the railroads, the findings of which could then be quoted by the press.

Like the railroads, the utility and telephone industries saw the value of public relations. Chicago Edison argued to both the government and the public that providing electricity was a "natural monopoly" and should not be open to competition. In the early 1900s, AT&T required newspapers in which it advertised to run positive articles about its actions. Both the utilities and the phone company used publicity firms to write articles and editorials promoting the companies' points of view that were placed in newspapers around the country.

Ivy Lee. Ivy Lee, one of the two key founders of modern public relations, brought to the business a strong understanding of both economics and psychology. Lee recognized that the public often reacted more strongly to symbols and phrases than to rational arguments, and he built his campaigns around the importance of symbolism.[13] He also saw that it was important to put a human face on corporations.[14]

Lee was the first PR professional to deal with crisis management, and although *spin control* did not become a popular term until the 1980s, he was practicing it as early as 1910. Lee wanted to do much more for his clients than just send out favorable publicity; he wanted to manipulate public opinion in favor of his clients. That meant actively working with the press.

Among the problems faced by the railroads was reporting on accidents. The accepted practice of the industry in the late 1800s was either to cover up accidents or to bribe reporters not to write about them. Lee suggested that it might be in the railroads' best interests to deal with the press openly. When his client, the Pennsylvania Railroad, had a wreck, Lee invited reporters to visit the scene of the accident at the company's expense. After they arrived, he helped them report on the story. Company officials were amazed to see that the publicity they received when they cooperated with the press was a vast improvement over what they received when they fought with it.[15]

Lee also recognized the importance of telling the truth. Although the arguments he presented clearly supported his clients' viewpoints, Lee was always careful to be accurate in any factual claims. This was not so much because telling the

Library of Congress

Circus promoter P. T. Barnum built publicity for his shows through posters such as this one, as well as by staging protests and complaints about his circus.

truth was right or moral as because doing so was effective.[16] Lee once told oil giant John D. Rockefeller Jr., "Tell the truth because sooner or later the public will find it out anyway. And if the public doesn't like what you are doing, change your policies and bring them into line with what the people want."[17]

In 1902, American coal mine operators were facing a strike. The mine owners ignored the press, but the unionized miners worked with reporters to their advantage, and due to this the public strongly supported the workers. When the mine owners faced another strike in

The Committee on Public Information had 75,000 "Four-Minute Men" who gave brief speeches about the war to churches and civic groups across the United States.

propagandist because he had worked for the German Dye Trust. The damage to his reputation from this association came at least in part from the many enemies he had made over the course of his career.[20]

Edward L. Bernays. Along with Ivy Lee, the other founder of public relations was Edward L. Bernays, who was the first person to apply social-scientific research techniques to the field. Bernays, a nephew of Sigmund Freud, promoted the use of psychology to manipulate public opinion, a technique that he called "**engineering consent**":

> This phrase means, quite simply, the use of an engineering approach—that is, action based only on thorough knowledge of the situation and on the application of scientific principles and tried practices in the task of getting people to support ideas and programs. Any person or organization depends ultimately on public approval and is therefore faced with the problem of engineering the public's consent to a program or goal.[21]

In addition to promoting his clients, Bernays actively promoted the concept of public relations as a profession. To that end, he wrote the first books on the practice, *Crystallizing Public Opinion* (1923) and *Propaganda* (1928). In 1923, Bernays taught the first course in public relations, which he offered at New York University.

Like Lee, Bernays recognized the importance of the crowd in modern life. He found that the best way to influence the public was to arrange for messages to be delivered by credible sources. "If you can influence the leaders, either with or without their conscious cooperation, you automatically influence the group which they sway," he commented.[22] While the guaranteed influence of leaders over groups may be a bit of an overstatement, the use of credible or admired individuals to speak on behalf of a company is certainly central to public relations.

To Bernays, the chief characteristic distinguishing public relations from the press agentry of the past was that public relations was a two-way interaction between individuals or organizations—communication that involved listening as well as speaking. Bernays wrote that by the 1920s it had became clear to practitioners that words alone did not constitute public relations; there had to be actions to go with the words.

World War I: The Federal Government Starts Using Public Relations

The years 1914–1918 were a period of major growth for public relations. According to Bernays, during this time governments figured out how important persuasive

1906, they hired Lee's publicity firm, Parker and Lee.[18] Lee convinced the mine operators that they could no longer ignore public opinion. A former business reporter, he started giving newspapers all the information they asked for. Supplied with clear and accurate statements from the mine owners, reporters started writing stories that were considerably less antagonistic to the mine owners.

At about this time, Lee developed his "Declaration of Principles," which outlined how he thought public relations ought to be carried out. These principles can be summarized quite simply: Openly and honestly supply accurate and timely news to the press.[19]

Lee himself suffered from bad public relations late in his career: In the 1930s, he was accused of being a Nazi

▶ Video 12.1: Learn more about Edward L. Bernays.

engineering consent: The application of the principles of psychology and motivation to influencing public opinion and creating public support for a particular position.

False Reports Garner Publicity

Back in 1939, a young actress by the name of Rita Hayworth was trying to become a household name, and her press agent, the legendary Henry Rogers, was willing to do whatever it took to make her a Hollywood star. One of these efforts was putting out a made-up press release naming Hayworth the winner of a nonexistent "best-dressed off-screen actress" contest held by a nonexistent group. That story landed Hayworth a big photo story in *Look* magazine (a competitor of *Life*) and launched the buxom actress's career.[1]

Why do we care? Because it's happened again.

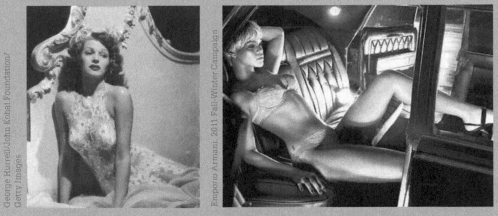

George Hurrell/John Kobal Foundation/Getty Images

Emporio Armani, 2011 Fall-Winter Campaign

Truthfulness is not always the first priority when it comes to entertainment publicity. Actress Rita Hayworth in the 1930s and singer Rihanna in the 2010s had their publicity agents pull similar stunts and claim that the performers had won imaginary awards for their appearances.

SECRET 7 More recently, the British newspaper the *Daily Mail* ran a story proclaiming that singer Rihanna's ad campaign for Armani undies had won an award from *Advertising Age* magazine for being the sexiest of the year. It even quoted *Ad Age* as saying: "It's Rihanna at her sexiest. She's never looked this good." They also added: "She's in amazing shape and the pictures are stunning."[2] (As a side note, the "they" in the attribution should have been a tip-off that there was not really a source behind the story. Remember Secret Seven—There is no "they.")

Even Rihanna tweeted about the award.

The only problem? As press blogger Jim Romenesko points out, *Ad Age* didn't actually give out an award for the sexiest ad. That's why none of the stories about it (including those from the *Huffington Post,* the *Hindustan Times*, the *Global Grind*, and others) had links back to *Ad Age*.[3]

The actual source of the story? A company called TNI Press Ltd. that writes stories for British tabloids and is the source for a number of recent stories extolling Rihanna's sexiness. In his *New York Times* obituary, Henry Rogers was quoted as saying in 1987, "If I did now what I did then, I'd be barred from every news media outlet."[4]

Hmmm . . . maybe not. Think about **SECRET 4** Nothing's new: Everything that happened in the past will happen again.

As a side note, at the time this story was spreading, your author ran a Google search on Rihanna's Armani ad and found twenty-four media stories about it but only one link to the actual correction. When it comes to celebrity gossip—gossip likely put forward by the celebrity himself or herself—do we really care whether it's true?

WHO are the sources?

What is the *Daily Mail*? What kind of stories does it run? Who was Henry Rogers?

WHAT are they saying?

What did Henry Rogers do for Rita Hayworth? What did the *Daily Mail* do for Rihanna? What connection is there between Henry Rogers and the Rihanna story?

WHAT evidence is there?

What evidence did the *Daily Mail* have that the Rihanna story was true? How about the news sites that reprinted the story? What could these publications have done to check the story before they published it?

WHAT do you and your classmates think about fabricated celebrity stories?

Why do you think that the *Daily Mail* ran the story with photos about Rihanna? Do you think that it cared whether or not the story was true? Was there any difference between what the *Daily Mail* did for Rihanna and what Henry Rogers did for Rita Hayworth? Do you and your friends have any faith in the truth of tabloid stories about celebrities?

[1] Robert McG. Thomas Jr., "Henry Rogers, 82, Press Agent Who Built Hollywood Stars," *New York Times*, May 1, 1995, www.nytimes.com/1995/05/01/obituaries/henry-rogers-82-press-agent-who-built-hollywood-stars.html?src=pm.

[2] Deborah Arthurs, "Rihanna's Steamy Armani Adverts Voted the Sexiest of 2011 (and Let's Not Forget Miranda Kerr's and Kate Moss Too)," *Daily Mail*, December 28, 2011, www.dailymail.co.uk/femail/article-2079455/Rihannas-steamy-Armani-adverts-voted-sexiest-2011.html.

[3] Jim Romenesko, "Ad Age *Did Not* Name Rihanna's Armani Ad Year's Sexiest," December 30, 2011, jimromenesko.com/2011/12/30/ad-age-did-not-name-rihannas-armani-ad-years-sexiest/.

[4] Thomas Jr., "Henry Rogers, 82, Press Agent Who Built Hollywood Stars."

 Web 12.2: Read the original story about Rita Hayworth and Rihanna.

communication could be to mobilize popular support for a major war: "Ideas and their dissemination became weapons and words became bullets."[23] The U.S. government used public relations extensively during World War I. Within a week of the U.S. entry into the war, President Woodrow Wilson established the Committee on Public Information (CPI) under the direction of George Creel, the former editor of the *Rocky Mountain News*. The committee operated from April 6, 1917, until June 30, 1919, building American support for the war. Although the committee lacked many of the modern tools of mass communication—radio was still in its infancy, and the movie industry was just taking its first steps—it was still able to use advertising, billboards, and posters, as well as newspaper opinion pieces, articles, and pamphlets.

The committee also used interpersonal channels. It enlisted 75,000 "Four-Minute Men" who took the committee's messages to churches and civic groups by delivering four-minute speeches. Research conducted in the 1940s later proved the effectiveness of this technique by confirming that people often turn to individuals they know and trust when they are looking for guidance about an important topic. So if an organization wants to influence a particular public, the best way may be to use influential local individuals, along with the mass media.[24] Bernays referred to this process as **opinion leadership**—using "journalists, politicians, businessmen, scientists, professional men, authors, society leaders, teachers, actors, women of fashion and so on" to deliver influential messages to the public.[25]

Woodrow Wilson's use of public relations was not limited to the war effort. He was the first president to hold regular television screenpress conferences, and under Wilson the Federal Trade Commission used publicity to force the food industry to adopt more sanitary practices.

The federal government turned to public relations once again during World War II. The Office of War Information served much the same purpose that the CPI had during World War I. The main difference was that the new group was able to use talking films and radio to supplement the print and interpersonal communications used by the CPI.

Public Relations Becomes a Profession

During the 1940s and 1950s, public relations continued to grow as a profession, and colleges and universities began offering degrees in the field. Advances in polling made it easier to measure public opinion, and clients began to realize that PR firms could help shape how people felt about companies and issues. Clients were also looking for help in making use of the emerging medium of television.

Throughout the 1960s, the media became more critical of both business and government as the United States became caught up in the Vietnam War, the civil rights movement, the student and women's movements, environmentalism, and consumerism (for example, groups such as Ralph Nader's consumer activist organization). This trend continued into the 1970s with the rise of Watergate-inspired investigative reporting. It was a time when institutions had to actively manage their images, and they realized the importance of communicating with individuals, businesses, governments, and social organizations.[26]

■■■■■■■■■■■■■■■■■■■

The Business of Public Relations

There is a popular misconception among students that public relations primarily involves talking and meeting with people. Although it certainly includes these elements, there is much more to the profession. Public relations involves managing an organization's image through planning, research, communication, and assessment.

What Is Public Relations?

Edward Bernays described three major functions of public relations[27]:

1. Informing—Sending out information to a variety of publics, ranging from the people who work in a company's office to its customers on the other side of the world. An example of information would be a press release announcing a new product line to stores that sell the company's products.

2. Persuading—Attempting to induce members of various publics to change their attitudes or actions toward an idea, product, or institution. An example of persuasion would be a lobbying campaign to persuade the government to remove a tax on the company's product.

3. Integrating—Attempting to bring publics and institutions together with a shared set of goals, actions, and attitudes. An example of an integrative event would be a charity auction designed to raise funds for a park in the city where the company has its offices as the company works to become a vital part of the community.

Bernays saw public relations as a public good, necessary for the proper functioning of society. He argued that society was moving too fast and becoming too complex for the average person to cope with and that the only hope for a functional society was to merge public and private interests through public relations.

This two-way model of interaction between the institution and its publics is the central notion of modern public relations, which can be defined as "the management function that establishes and maintains mutually beneficial

---

opinion leadership: A two-step process of persuasion that uses respected and influential individuals to deliver messages with the hope of influencing members of a community, rather than just relying on the mass media to deliver the message.

relationships between an organization and the publics on whom its success or failure depends."[28]

This definition has three basic segments:

1. Public relations is a *management function.* This means that it is central to the running of a company or organization and not merely a tool of the marketing department.

2. Public relations establishes *mutually beneficial relationships.* This means that public relations is an interaction that should benefit both sides—the organization and the public(s).

3. Companies depend on *various publics* to succeed. One of the primary reasons PR campaigns fail is that they neglect these relationships and consider only the company's point of view.

One mistake companies must avoid is to assume that glib communication can be a substitute for real action when solving a public problem. This can be seen clearly in the case of the film industry in the 1920s and 1930s. As discussed in Chapter 8, during that period movies were being criticized for their immorality. Industry leaders responded by hiring former U.S. postmaster Will Hays to supervise the moral content of movies. Throughout the 1920s, Hays preached a message of corporate responsibility to the press, but the industry made no significant changes in response to criticism of the portrayal of sex, violence, and drug use in the movies.[29]

By 1934, critics had had enough of soothing words without action, and the Catholic Legion of Decency started a movie boycott. With the threat of government censorship growing, the movie industry finally adopted a production code that put strict limits on what directors could portray. Public relations historian Marvin Olasky argues that if the movie industry had dealt with its critics in a meaningful way in the 1920s, it might have avoided the restrictions forced on it in the 1930s.[30]

The Public Relations Process

Although there are a number of different ways of looking at the PR process, we are going to look at it using a model known as ROPES: research, objectives, programming, evaluation, and stewardship.[31]

1. Research—Researching the opportunities, problems, or issues the organization is facing.

2. Objectives—Setting specific and measurable objectives for the PR campaign.

3. Programming—Planning and implementing the activities necessary to carry out the objectives.

4. Evaluation—Testing the messages and techniques before using them, monitoring the programming while it's being delivered, and measuring the results of the programming.

5. Stewardship—Maintaining the relationships created through the previous steps.

Central to the ROPES process is the notion that public relations is concerned primarily with creating, developing, and nurturing relationships between an organization and its key publics.[32] To see how this process is carried out, let's look at how Breathe Right used public relations both to build awareness of its nasal strips and to promote alternative uses of the product.

Research. CNS, the original parent company of Breathe Right, was looking to broaden the market for its nasal strips, and through research it found that customers were using the product in new ways. Breathe Right strips were initially designed to hold people's nostrils  open while they slept to help prevent snoring. But athletes, especially professional football players, soon began using the nasal strips to get more air into their lungs during competitions. At the 1995 Super Bowl, players wearing Breathe Right strips scored eight of the game's ten touchdowns.[33] CNS wanted to capitalize on this positive publicity, so the company commissioned research to measure various publics' initial perceptions of its product. Such research can include the following elements:

- Public opinion research—Finding out how the public views the company or product, its actions, and its image.
- Content analysis—Analyzing what is being written or said about the company in the media.
- Focus groups—Bringing together members of a particular public to talk about how they perceive an organization, a product, or an issue.[34]

Through consumer research, Breathe Right's manufacturer found that the visibility of the strips during the 1995 Super Bowl had helped build public awareness of the product. According to marketing manager Kirk Hodgdon, "After the game, three out of every four adults had heard of Breathe Right, compared to one in four a year earlier."[35]

Objectives. A successful PR campaign depends on a clear definition of what the client wants to accomplish.

Web 12.3: The Public Relations Society of America defines public relations.

to highlight the product so that fans would be likely to notice the players wearing the strips.[36] The media relations campaign emphasized the players who wore the strips and publicized the company's status as one of the smallest Super Bowl advertisers.

Evaluation. Evaluation of the campaign happened at every stage of the process. Campaign materials were tested during development, while they were being delivered, and at the conclusion of the campaign. This involved seeing how well the campaign met the objectives that had been set earlier in the campaign.

Breathe Right's evaluation showed that CNS had gained a great deal from its 1996 Super Bowl campaign. Not only did it reap the advertising benefit of reaching the big game's massive audience, but it also generated a significant amount of good publicity for the company. Breathe Right received coverage on the front page of *USA Today*'s money section, which mentioned it as one of the smallest companies to advertise during the Super Bowl.[37] The product also received unpaid endorsements from athletes who said that the product improved their performance by giving them more oxygen, a claim the company itself did not make.

Stewardship. Breathe Right's communication campaign based on working with professional football players and football fans has continued. In 2001, Breathe Right created limited edition colored nasal strips honoring Super Bowl competitors Green Bay Packers and Dallas Cowboys.[38] And, in 2010, Breathe Right had a partnership with the New York Giants. Breathe Right produced Giants-themed nasal strips and had an interactive Web page where fans could post their "game face" wearing the strip.[39] (By this point, Breathe Right's parent company CNS had been acquired by pharmaceutical giant GlaxoSmithKline.)

As a side note, in 2014, nasal strips for horses, produced by a former subsidiary of CNS, brought the perceived performance benefits of nasal strips back to national attention when a controversy emerged over whether star horse California Chrome would be allowed to wear the strips in the Belmont Stakes race in his attempt to be only the twelfth horse ever to win the Triple Crown in thoroughbred racing. And along with the news about California Chrome came the inevitable mention that many NFL athletes have found success using the Breathe Right strips.[40]

Matthew Stockman/Getty Images

Breathe Right nasal strips have long depended on unpaid endorsements from professional athletes to promote their product. But they got an unexpected boost from racehorse California Chrome when its owner refused to enter him in one of the Triple Crown races if he couldn't have the horse wear nasal strips to help him breathe.

This depends on having clearly measurable objectives for the campaign. In the case of Breathe Right, CNS wanted to build awareness of the product and identify it with athletic performance. Among the objectives CNS set was raising the percentage of the target public that was aware of the Breathe Right brand and raising the percentage of the audience that knew athletes used the strips to improve athletic performance.

Programming. The company decided to build on its campaign of working with NFL trainers. In 1996, it advertised during the Super Bowl, gave strips to everyone attending the game, and publicized its advertising and promotion. CNS combined advertising, promotion, and media relations to build awareness of its product. The promotion involved building relationships directly with football fans by distributing the Breathe Right strips at the game. The company also advertised during the game

Who Are the Publics?

The term *public relations* seems to imply that there is a single monolithic group of people—"the public"—with whom the client needs to communicate. But, in reality,

 Web 12.4: Get the rest of the story on California Chrome and the nasal strips.

there are many such groups, since a public is any group of people who share a common set of interests.[41] These could include a company's employees, customers, stockholders, government regulators, or even people who live in the community where a new factory is to be built. In general, however, these publics can be divided into two main groups: internal publics and external publics, as mentioned earlier.

Internal Publics.

An important audience for companies, and one that is easy to forget, is the internal public—the people who work for the company. Not only are good relations with employees important for morale and responsiveness, but employees are also an important informal source of news about the company. Through e-mail, chat rooms, phone calls, and media contacts, employees are a central part of a company's communication environment.[42] When Cannon Koo at Kraft makes plans to communicate with his internal publics, he first looks at the food giant's marketing staff.

Corporations use a variety of media to communicate with their internal publics. In the case of employees and managers, this communication can be done through something as simple as a weekly e-mail or as elaborate as a four-color company newspaper. But internal communication is not limited to simple written materials. Web video, closed-circuit television, and even satellite conferences can be used to bring important news to employees. When the Three Mile Island nuclear plant suffered a major accident in 1979, a neighboring utility used videotaped programs to help its employees learn more about nuclear power. This form of education decreased the likelihood that the employees would spread misleading information when they talked with friends and family members.[43]

Many organizations have started **intranets**, which are computer networks that are open only to members of that organization. Such a network can be used as an internal news source, a collection of corporate documents, or even an interactive communication channel. Canadian public relations agency Thornley Fallis uses an intranet-based video chat service to help employees avoid the flood of e-mails. CEO Joseph Thornley writes, "For us, video is the best communications channel. Unlike e-mail and text, it

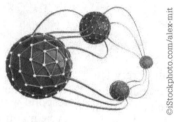

©iStockphoto.com/alex-mit

enables us to read facial expressions, posture, and all the physical clues that add nuance to communications."[44]

Intranets can also go beyond being a channel for important internal communications to serve as a hub for social interaction within the company or organization. These functions could include photo albums, an online swap meet, or even a store featuring company-branded products.[45]

External Publics.

Whereas internal publics are well known to an organization, the range of external publics is far larger and relatively less well known. The press is one of the most important external publics because it is through the press that organizations communicate to many of their publics. Building a good relationship with the press is critical. Public relations practitioners as early as Ivy Lee and Edward Bernays found that working with the press during good times would lead to better relations during bad times.[46] Ian Monk, a British journalist turned PR practitioner, says that the relationships he built up as a reporter help him immensely in the PR business: "I deal with former colleagues and protégés all the time, and the relationships I have already built with them are invaluable."[47] For Kraft, external publics would include Velveeta buyers, super-consumers, and anyone who eats macaroni and cheese.

Media relations can be defined as two-way interactions with members of the press. Typically, media relations involve the placement of unpaid messages within the standard programming or news content of the medium. Good media relations, ultimately, are good relations with the public at large. A positive image with the press will often become a positive image with the general public. And a company that the public likes to begin with tends to weather a crisis much better than one that is disliked. According to PR practitioner Susanne Courtney, "Corporate PR is about building up an 'equity' account with groups like the investment community, customers, media, employees and others that a company may need to draw on in a time of need."[48]

Presenting a company to the press is the most visible part of public relations. Press conferences, feature stories for the trade press, photographs, news releases, and streaming video are all tools that PR practitioners use to help manage the messages they send out to various publics through the media. Sometimes the press activities of an agency may be subtler. A PR firm may encourage a prominent leader to write an opinion piece favorable to its client's point of view for publication on the editorial page of a major newspaper. Or it may arrange for a reporter to interview a company president. Or it may simply provide useful background material to reporters.

For Kraft, communication with the professional media is an ongoing relationship. In addition to holding press events, Kraft spokesperson Jody Moore communicated with the advertising trade press through e-mail to make sure that *Ad Age* fully understood the company's Cheespocalypse campaign.[49]

---

intranets: Computer networks designed to communicate with people within an organization. They are used to improve two-way internal communication and contain tools that allow for direct feedback. They are a tool for communicating with internal publics.

media relations: Two-way interactions between PR professionals and members of the press. These can involve press conferences, press releases, video news releases, or interviews. Typically, media relations involve the placement of unpaid messages within the standard programming or news content of the medium.

These unpaid messages gain credibility because they come through the press rather than directly from the corporation. When a company wants to directly control the message it sends to the public, it uses advertising as a part of its PR plan.

Crisis Communication

Nothing tests an organization's PR ability more than a **crisis**, an event perceived by the public as being damaging to the organization's reputation or image. Al Tortorella, an executive with the PR firm Burson-Marsteller, claims, "A crisis is what the media says it is."[50] What he means is that a problem can be defined as a crisis when it becomes public and begins to be perceived as a crisis. This means that it is possible to prevent a problem from becoming a crisis, but companies should never count on problems being kept secret; they need to have a plan for handling them if they turn into crises.

For example, in 1994, computer programmers discovered that the Pentium computer chip designed by Intel could, in certain rare cases, compute a wrong answer. The flaw in the chip was a minor problem affecting only a very few scientists, but no one wanted to have a computer that "made mistakes." Public relations consultant Susan Thomas says that the flurry of negative publicity about the flaw created a crisis for the company:

> What Intel learned from the original Pentium crisis is [that] the difference between the perceived size and actual size of a problem is irrelevant. Just because the chance of the miscalculation happening was slim, it didn't matter. Customers were upset. They wanted responsiveness and answers.... When Intel said "only a very small percentage would be affected," it sounded like the company was saying "this isn't worth bothering about."[51]

Intel eventually resolved the crisis by offering all of its customers a "no-questions-asked" replacement chip.

Principles of Crisis Communication. What should a company do when it faces a crisis? In general, it should communicate promptly and honestly with all its publics. More specifically, there are five principles of crisis communication[52]:

1. Be prepared—The most important principle is to have a crisis plan. For every company there are certain things that are unlikely to happen but would be enormously damaging if they did. Such events could, if serious enough,

put the existence of the company at risk by damaging its most important assets: its credibility and reputation.[53] Airlines should have a plan in the event of a plane crash; universities should have plans in the event of an academic or athletic scandal; a factory should be prepared for a chemical spill. These events might be unlikely to occur, but they can and should be prepared for.

2. Be honest—One of the problems with lying is that liars are often caught. Cover-ups almost always end up being exposed, and the cover-up looks worse than the original problem. Instead, get the story out and over with quickly. President Richard Nixon's lies about the break-in at the Democratic Party's headquarters in the Watergate building created far more problems for him than did the actual burglary itself. For President Bill Clinton lying about his relationship with Monica Lewinsky was infinitely more damaging to his reputation than was the affair itself.[54] Public relations consultant Bob Wilkerson says, "The truth is going to get out. I want it out of my lips. It's bad enough I've had an incident. It's even worse if it looks like I was trying to cover up."[55]

3. Apologize, and mean it—The company should respond with real action, not just words. In 2006, motorcycle manufacturer Yamaha got caught claiming that its new middleweight sport bike had an engine that would rev up to 17,500 RPM. This was significantly higher than any competing motorcycle. It turned out that both the tachometer and the marketing department were a little optimistic because the motorcycle's true redline was 16,200 RPM. In real life, this discrepancy probably doesn't matter much. But when complaints about the overstated redline started surfacing on the Internet, Yamaha made a simple decision to completely neutralize the crisis. The company sent a letter to everyone who had bought the motorcycle, apologized for the discrepancy, and offered to buy back the bike—including tax, setup, and interest—no questions asked.[56] In addition to having done the right thing, Yamaha squelched the crisis immediately and kept it from damaging the company's otherwise good reputation with motorcyclists.

4. Move quickly—Public relations critics say that how a company reacts in the first few hours after a crisis occurs will determine how the crisis is perceived from that point on. "All crises have a window of opportunity to gain control of 45 minutes to 12 hours," says crisis communication expert Paul Shrivastava.[57] Beyond that point, people will have already decided what they think about the crisis, and once they have made up their minds, they are reluctant to

Web 12.5: How Yamaha effectively handled its public relations problem.

---

crisis: Any situation that is perceived by the public as being damaging to the reputation or image of an organization. Not all problems develop into crises, but once a situation develops into a crisis, it can be damaging to an organization's reputation even if information

change them. In the past, companies could build their response around the time the morning newspapers were published or the nightly news was broadcast, but cable news channels and newspaper Web sites can publish news at any time, and social media will spread unfounded and unverified speculations that traditional news outlets might avoid. Bad news can also spread rapidly over the Internet.[58] Even when things move quickly, the company still needs to act carefully. Crisis management decisions are much more difficult to make than conventional decisions because they deal with things that have important consequences. They also need to be made quickly, while the whole world watches.[59]

5. Communicate with the press and other constituencies—These include the company's own employees and management, stockholders, government regulators, and customers, as well as the press. It was immediate communication with all publics that helped minimize Yamaha's problems with its advertising misinformation.

The application of these principles can be seen in two examples of crisis communication that are discussed in the following subsections. In the first, the company handled both the physical response and the communication response almost perfectly and emerged from the crisis with a good market position and a stronger image than it started with. In the second, mishandled communications led to a blot on the company's reputation that has endured for more than twenty years.

AP Photo/Marty Lederhandler

When President Bill Clinton was accused of having an affair with intern Monica Lewinsky, he initially denied that it had taken place. Months later, he finally admitted that he had lied about the affair. In the long run, critics say Clinton was damaged more by his denials than by the news of the affair itself.

The Tylenol Scare. In September 1982, the consumer products giant Johnson & Johnson faced a crisis that could have destroyed one of its most important brands, Tylenol. Seven people in the Chicago area died after taking cyanide-laced Extra Strength Tylenol capsules. The deaths set off what the *New York Times* called "the biggest consumer product scare in history."[60] (The perpetrator was never caught.) But Johnson & Johnson, with the help of PR agency Burson-Marsteller, managed to preserve the brand and the company's reputation with a combination of appropriate ethical action and good public relations.

The first thing the company did right was to be entirely honest with the media and public. The praise it subsequently received for its openness improved its image.[61]

The next thing the company did right was to take immediate action in response to the tampering. As soon as Johnson & Johnson learned of the problem, it immediately stopped advertising the product and took it off the market in Chicago.[62]

Throughout the crisis, Burson-Marsteller conducted nightly telephone surveys to measure public opinion. When those polls showed that the public feared that other Tylenol capsules might be tampered with, Johnson &

Johnson took the product off the market nationwide.[63] The company was perceived as acting responsibly, and in fact it *was* acting responsibly.

Johnson & Johnson had clearly won the first PR battle and was being perceived as a responsible company that had been the victim of a vicious attack. The second battle was the campaign to rebuild trust in the Tylenol brand.

In November 1982, Johnson & Johnson announced the relaunch of Extra Strength Tylenol with the news that the product would now be sold in a triple-sealed container. Along with the expected marketing support, Johnson & Johnson engaged in an extensive PR campaign that utilized educational advertising, media appearances, and personal contacts.

The company sent out more than 2,000 sales representatives to meet with major retailers and doctors. An advertising campaign informed people about the new tamper-resistant packaging, and Johnson & Johnson announced the relaunch of the brand in a thirty-city

 Web 12.6: In the fall of 2014, the NFL had a crisis with star players committing violence against women.

Johnson & Johnson had to handle the recall of millions of containers of Tylenol in 1982 after tainted capsules led to the deaths of seven people in the Chicago area.

teleconference delivered via satellite. Simultaneously, it held a press conference that was attended by nearly 600 journalists. Finally, Johnson & Johnson's CEO, James Burke, appeared on both *60 Minutes* and the daytime talk program *The Phil Donahue Show*.

The campaign was a success. Before the crisis, Tylenol had had a 37 percent share of the pain reliever market; this number dropped to 7 percent during the tampering scare. But within a month of the relaunch Tylenol was back to 28 percent of the market, and it eventually regained its status as the industry leader.[64]

Johnson & Johnson succeeded in protecting its brand and reputation for a number of reasons. First, few people blamed the company for the tampering; the fault appeared to lay with an individual beyond the span of the company's control. Second, the company acted quickly and responsibly in the interests of consumers. It was also open with its various publics, freely admitting what it did and didn't know. Finally, the company actively worked through the difficult situation and engaged the press by viewing it as an ally instead of as an adversary.

The Exxon Valdez *and BP Oil Spills.*

On March 24, 1989, the oil tanker *Exxon Valdez* ran aground in Alaska's

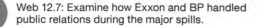

Web 12.7: Examine how Exxon and BP handled public relations during the major spills.

Prince William Sound, spilling 240,000 barrels of crude oil into the ocean. This oil soon washed up on shore, coating beaches, birds, and sea life in an environmentally sensitive area. Exxon spent more than $2 billion on the cleanup of the oil spill, but it still ended up with a tarnished image. Former reporter and network news president William Small notes that no company ever spent as much as Exxon did following the oil spill and still came out looking so bad.[65]

Exxon's post-spill image problem had numerous causes that illustrate the difference between Johnson & Johnson's response to a crisis and Exxon's:

- Perception of fault—Unlike the Tylenol tampering case, Exxon was considered at fault for the oil spill. Exxon's first problem was that it was the company's tanker that had run aground. It is difficult from a PR point of view to defend a company that has done something wrong.[66]
- Lack of effective crisis plan—Exxon never developed a crisis plan for dealing with such a serious oil spill. Although Exxon shared responsibility with the Coast Guard for the lack of proper facilities, the fact that it did not have cleanup equipment in Alaska forced it to shoulder the blame after the spill.[67]
- Failure to take immediate control—Exxon did not take immediate control of the flow of information. Not until a week after the spill did Exxon's CEO, Lawrence Rawl, make public comments. Meanwhile, numerous heartbreaking images of fouled wildlife started coming from the area. Almost all the press coverage of the spill was negative. In fact, Exxon made it actively difficult for reporters to get the company's point of view. The company's initial response was reportedly handled by a one-person PR office in Houston that had trouble coping with all the requests for information. Moreover, Exxon held all its news briefings for reporters in Valdez, Alaska, which had limited communication channels, instead of in a more accessible location, such as New York.[68]
- Failure to accept responsibility immediately—Exxon didn't initially accept ethical responsibility for the spill and apologize. The company started off by trying to spread the blame, claiming that the Coast Guard, Alaska environmental officials, and the weather were also responsible. Whether or not these claims were valid, the press and the public saw Exxon as responsible. As one Alaska official put it, "I would suggest it's Exxon's tanker that ran up on the rocks."[69]

The final blow to Exxon's image came in the fall after the oil spill, when a memo from a company official was leaked to the press. The memo said that Exxon would end the cleanup effort whenever it chose to, that it would do nothing in the winter, and that it did not promise to return in the spring. The memo made the company look arrogant and uncaring.[70] Exxon eventually accepted responsibility for the oil spill and the cleanup, but by then the company's image was damaged irrevocably.

SECRET 4 Even twenty-five years after the accident, the *Exxon Valdez* remained the standard to which environmental disasters were compared. When the Deepwater Horizon oil rig that was drilling for the London-based BP PLC exploded and sank in the Gulf of Mexico during the summer of 2010, triggering the world's largest oil spill, people immediately began comparing it to the Exxon spill. Critics contrasted BP's cleanup efforts to Exxon's, but they also compared public relations responses. Of course, the current media world full of online social media, blogs, and multiple 24/7 cable channels that faced BP was very different from the one Exxon had to deal with. Yet the issues facing the two oil companies remained similar: Both tried to focus on technological issues rather than the effects on people, and both companies tried to shift blame away from themselves and onto others. But most of all, it appears that neither company had a plan to deal with a major oil spill. Communications professor Kathleen Fearn-Banks told the *New York Times* blog *Greenwire*, "BP never had a plan in place for the worst-case scenario or they would have put it in place. I don't think it's a question of money . . . They absolutely don't know what to do at all."[71] (This is a prime example of Secret Four—Nothing's new: Everything that happened in the past will happen again.)

AP Photo/Dave Martin

Despite the lessons learned after the catastrophic *Exxon Valdez* oil spill that had occurred twenty-one years earlier, the BP oil company seemed ill prepared to deal with its wide range of publics following the 2010 Deepwater Horizon spill in the Gulf of Mexico.

Public Relations and the Internet

In the late 1980s and early 1990s, the PR industry acquired a new friend and enemy—the Internet. The Internet gave PR practitioners a new way to research and to distribute information, but it also provided a powerful new channel for the spreading of rumors that had the potential to develop into crises.

A New Information Channel. Among many other things, the Internet has given the PR industry a new tool. Now companies can distribute press releases, background information, and photos to the media through e-mail and Web sites. If a company's Web site or social media feed has a good reputation, it can become the first place reporters go to for information. Since reporters often start by going online to research articles, placing statistics and facts on a Web site can affect the way a company is covered.

The Internet has also given companies a means of bypassing the traditional media and communicating directly with various publics. Customers, stockholders, and even critics may go to a company's Web site in search of information. A Web site also ensures that a company's point of view is being presented the way the company intends it to be. Along with having a good Web site, companies need to make sure that their site will show up at the top of the list of search results for their company. It can be embarrassing if a company's critics appear above the company itself in a Web search.[72]

The Internet also allows companies to find out what people are saying about them. Many organizations monitor Web sites and social media to see what complaints and kudos are coming their way. Public relations practitioners may join chats and discussion groups to help shape what is being said about their clients. Of course, with millions of Web sites and social media accounts in existence, just finding out what is being said about a company can be a massive undertaking.[73]

Crisis management consultant Jonathan Bernstein says that online media create significant new PR challenges. He writes that organizations need to consider the following:

SECRET 5 The Internet gives critics access to the world without the checks and balances of traditional journalism. Prior to the Internet, the only way to reach a broad, general audience was through the professional media, which might not always be a fan of your company but would probably treat you fairly. Many Internet sites can be biased or don't engage in editorial oversight or fact-checking.

- Once a crisis hits the Internet, it can't be contained. It used to be that a local news story would stay local. Now, once a story is posted to a newspaper's or television station's Web site, it's gone national.
- The Internet makes it easy for critics to leak confidential information. This can include not just reports of confidential information, but also images of original documents or recordings of phone calls.
- In the absence of good information, rumors will flourish on the Internet. Of course, this problem isn't unique to the Internet. Anytime an organization

Workers fired for Domino's prank video

Screenshot: The Today Show 04/16/2009

FAST FOOD SHOCKER
DOMINO'S WORKERS FIRED FOR PRANK

0:43 / 2:24   HQ

Domino's Pizza faced an enormous image crisis in 2009 when two employees at a North Carolina store posted a prank video of themselves tampering with pizzas and subs.

doesn't provide creditable information, rumors and gossip will fill the gap.[74] But the Internet can accelerate the process by which rumors travel.

- These considerations illustrate perfectly the importance of Secret Five—New media are always scary.

Coming to Terms With Social Media. One of the great challenges that online media bring to the public relations business is that they are a continually moving target. Just when PR professionals think they have blogs and the Web figured out, along comes the rise of social media such as Facebook, Twitter, Pinterest, and Instagram. Social media expert Pamela Seiple has written that PR professionals need to realize that social media are an opportunity for interactions with various publics, not just a channel to send out information. She notes that, through social media, stories about your company's brand can spread and mutate at a much faster rate than in the past. According to her, "If your company is not participating in social media today, it's missing an opportunity to spread its message and missing valuable—and even damaging—conversations that could be taking place about your brand." One of the most important uses for social media, according to Seiple, is building ongoing relationships with publics, including customers, vendors, opinion makers, and the press.[75]

UCB is a pharmaceutical company that makes drugs to treat epilepsy. Trish Nettleship, as its director of social media, wanted to work with a social media service that could help epilepsy patients have a reliable source of

information and connect with other people suffering from the same problems. So she had UCB partner with a medical social media site called PatientsLikeMe. In addition, UCB continued to develop Epilepsy Advocate, its presence on Facebook. But these social media sites wouldn't help UCB communicate back and forth with patients if its social media managers had to go through a lengthy approval process before posting anything to the sites. In the past, every social media post from the company had to go through a two-week-long approval process with visits to the medical, legal, and regulatory departments. But by the time the response had been approved, the original poster would have lost interest. So UCB trained its in-house managers on what they could or couldn't post online, and then gave them the authority to respond immediately. As Leigh Householder reported for *Health Care Communication News,* "the team was able to refocus . . . on actively supporting patients and increasing the general amount of discussion (online and in the exam room) about partial-onset seizures."[76] This gets at the heart of what companies need to do as they move into interacting with publics through social media. The old rules simply won't keep up with the new tools.

Domino's: Fighting Back Against Social Media. It used to be that the worst media a company had to worry about was a scathing story by an investigative journalist on a program such as *60 Minutes.* But today a corporation's worst PR nightmare can come from amateur-produced video posted on video-sharing sites, such as YouTube, and then publicized through social media sites, such as Twitter and YouTube. That's what Domino's Pizza discovered in April 2009 when two employees in Conover, North Carolina, posted a video showing one of them putting cheese up his nose and then placing it on a sandwich, blowing his nose on a sandwich, and farting on a sandwich. The other employee narrated the video with comments:

> In about five minutes it'll be sent out on delivery where somebody will be eating these, yes, eating them, and little did they know that cheese was in his nose and that there was some lethal gas that ended up on their salami.[77]

Once the video was posted on YouTube, word about it spread rapidly online through Twitter and other social media, and the video quickly racked up more than 1 million views.

The Domino's Pizza chain attempted to respond quickly and responsibly, but it may have spoken out too late in the rapidly changing environment of the Internet. The company responded publicly to the video within forty-eight hours of finding out about it, delaying its response reportedly to keep from drawing further attention to the video. Domino's eventual response included a YouTube video

---

Video 12.2: Find out how Domino's and Pizza Hut reacted to ugly videos created by rogue employees.

Web 12.8: Read the backstory on UCB and social media.

featuring company president Patrick Doyle, a complete cleaning of the store where the video was shot, and a revision of the company's hiring practices. The company also started a Twitter account with which to respond to customers.[78]

Richard Levick of the PR firm Levick Strategic Communications told *Advertising Age* that Domino's handled the crisis well after its initial delay in responding: "After the first 24 hours, they were largely textbook. They started a Twitter account, separated themselves from the villains, shut down the store, apologized, went to their demographic, went to YouTube—I think all of that is great."[79]

Levick said that companies need to do several things to prepare for online crisis communication:

- Identify your crisis team—This includes PR professionals, lawyers, and digital communication specialists.
- Imagine your nightmare scenarios—Make sure that you have the online resources so that when a crisis hits and people start searching for information, they come to your Web site first.
- Track the blogosphere and other social media—Make sure you know what people are saying about you, and be responsive to the people who are talking about your company.
- Don't wait—You have a very limited time to respond.[80]

SECRET 2 Following the posting of the video, the two employees were identified by bloggers, arrested, and charged with distributing prohibited foods. Although the Domino's Pizza chain has largely recovered from the crisis created by the video, the North Carolina store where the video was shot has not. After closing briefly for cleaning following the posting of the video, the store closed for good five months later.[81] Note that while this story was covered by legacy media, it really moved through social media, thus illustrating Secret Two—There are no mainstream media. The Domino's story is also an illustration of **SECRET 4** Nothing's new: Everything that happened in the past will happen again. How so? In February 2014, a Pizza Hut in Kermit, West Virginia, had to explain why a security video had surfaced of one of its district managers urinating in a dish-washing sink at the restaurant. The video was subsequently posted to YouTube where it accumulated more than 600,000 views in three months. The video, and subsequent news coverage of it, resulted in the manager being fired, the restaurant being first temporarily and then permanently closed, and the parent company apologizing and pointing out to the news media that it doesn't tolerate the sort of behavior depicted in the video.[82]

Rumors on the Internet. Controlling the spread of rumors has always been a problem for the PR industry, but the growth of the Internet has allowed rumors to spread faster and more frequently than ever before.

Seattle-based coffee giant Starbucks faced an Internet rumor that the company did not support the war in Iraq or anyone who was fighting in it. According to the *Seattle Times*, the rumor got started when a Marine sergeant sent an e-mail to friends. In the e-mail, he claimed that Starbucks had written a letter saying the company did not support the troops or the war in response to another Marine who had asked for free coffee. The e-mail then circulated extensively on the Internet. Several months later, the sergeant sent out an e-mail apologizing for the incorrect statement, but the apology didn't get nearly the amount of attention that the initial accusation did. Starbucks responded to the rumor through a rumor-control page on its Web site and through an entry on Snopes.com, the urban legend debunking site. Despite the company's active response, the rumor continued to circulate for more than two years after it got started. As a precautionary measure, Starbucks monitors blog and Web coverage of the company, but it doesn't respond to every rumor.[83]

Questioning the Media

How do social media change the public relations process? Can you think of an example of how social media content has helped or hurt an organization? Why do you think this happened?

Public Relations and Society

This chapter has so far looked at public relations largely from the point of view of either PR firms or their clients. But it is also useful to look at it from the public's perspective. Public relations shapes the news we receive through newspapers, magazines, television, radio, and even the Internet. In the form of "spin control," it attempts to shape our view of politicians and public policy, and it is also a central component of social movements.

Public Relations Supports the News Business

Public relations plays a significant role in what is presented as news in the media. Sociologists David Altheide and Robert Snow argue that public relations is an integral part of the news business because most of the events—including crime and disaster reporting—covered by the media were created by PR practitioners to obtain coverage for their clients.[84] Just how much of the news originates with public relations?

Depending on how it is measured, anywhere from 40 to 90 percent of all news starts out as public relations. The *Columbia Journalism Review* (*CJR*) tried to narrow this down by studying an issue of the *Wall Street Journal*. The researchers selected 111 stories from the paper. The companies mentioned in the stories were then contacted and asked to send a copy of their original press releases. *CJR* found that 72 percent of the stories they were able to analyze were based almost exclusively on material from a press release. The

Press secretary Josh Earnest is responsible for making sure that President Barack Obama gets his message out to reporters in a way that portrays the administration in the best possible light.

their government relations departments, PR firms represent their clients before the federal government, federal agencies, state legislatures, and even municipal bodies. As businesses face increasing government regulation, they have increased their efforts to work with government to shape legislation and regulations that are favorable to their interests.[87] Government relations includes lobbying for laws that will best meet the needs of the organization, as well as simply building goodwill with legislators and regulatory bodies. The Center for Responsive Politics, a non-partisan research group that studies the influence of money on elections and public policy, estimates that, in 2012, there were 12,431 active, registered lobbyists in Washington who spent approximately $3.23 billion trying to influence the federal government on policy issues.[88] But that figure, as big as it is, only tells part of the story. Work by the Sunlight Foundation, another nonprofit focused on open government, found that for every dollar spent on reported lobbying, another dollar was spent on influencing activities that didn't meet the narrow legal definition of lobbying that was required to be reported. Thus, they estimate the total amount spent on "government relations" in 2012 to be $6.7 billion.[89]

The government itself is a major practitioner of public relations. All elected federal officials have a press secretary, and many have a communications director. The various agencies themselves have PR offices. The role of the political press secretary is a challenging one, as the spokesperson has to serve his or her boss while still dealing honestly with the press and the public. Sometimes this involves being evasive. As one congressional press secretary told the Washington, D.C., paper the *Hill*,

> It is a matter of practice and experience and being able to steer a conversation toward issues you are looking to advance . . . The golden rule is you don't answer the question you are asked, you answer the question you want to answer.[90]

Lanny Davis, who advised President Bill Clinton on damage control, says that when the press and the public are interested in an issue, the spokesperson only has one option: "Tell the truth, tell it all, tell it early, tell it yourself."[91] During the Monica Lewinsky sex scandal, President Clinton ignored the "tell the truth" rule, and the scandal stuck with him throughout the remainder of his second term in office. Had he acknowledged the affair when the story first broke rather than denying it, the story might well have blown over quickly. That's what happened when President Barack Obama

---

Questioning the Media

What do spin doctors do? Do our news media pay too much attention to spin doctors? Why or why not? Whom do spin doctors help?

study estimated that 45 percent of all the stories in the *Wall Street Journal* that day had been based on press releases, and that 27 percent of the actual news space was devoted to press releases.[85] The newspaper's executive editor estimated that 90 percent of the stories in the paper started with a company's announcement.

How does this happen? Think about a typical news day. Most news coming from Washington, D.C., involves a press conference, a speech, a press release, or an event created specifically to be covered by the media. A scientific report on an environmental issue is published, and both environmentalists and industry groups hold press conferences to provide background information. A bank robber is arrested, and the police hold a media briefing. Even a basketball game will be reported using statistics provided by the sports information office and quotes from an official postgame interview session hosted for the media.

Although a lot of news may originate in PR efforts, executives and other individuals covered by the media sometimes have an exaggerated sense of what public relations can accomplish. One movie studio boss reportedly told an applicant for a PR position, "Your responsibility will be, if I step out of my limousine and my pants fall down, you make sure that no one gets a photo to the press."[86] That's a guarantee no PR practitioner can make.

Public Relations and the Government

Along with the general public and media, the various levels of government are major external publics. Through

revealed his college-days drug use in his 1995 memoir, *Dreams From My Father.* The book allowed him to time the revelation of his drug use early in his political career and kept others from using it against him.[92]

The U.S. military has been actively involved in public relations since World War I. Although the military's initial PR efforts were intended to recruit volunteers, they were also interacting with the press. Today the Armed Forces Radio and Television Service provides internal public relations in the form of radio and television broadcasts for service people overseas. There are also public information activities and community relations for the areas surrounding military bases.[93]

Spin Control: A More Personal Form of Public Relations

A new kind of public relations, known as spin control, has risen to the forefront since the 1970s. Rather than simply providing press releases, events, and background information, so-called spin doctors attempt to influence how a story will be portrayed and discussed. Newspaper columnist and former speechwriter William Safire suggests that the word *spin* came from the idea of spinning a yarn—that is, telling a story. It may also have a sports connotation, as in putting a spin on a tennis or billiard ball.[94]

John Scanlon, a New York City publicist, is often cited as a top spin doctor. He is acquainted with many members of the national press corps and will call them when he considers a story unbalanced—or at least contrary to his client's interests. He also sends out frequent mailings to influential people in which he presents his point of view regarding events in the news. Scanlon's goal is not so much to give information to the press as to influence how stories are interpreted—that is, to control the spin put on them.

Here are some of the things spin doctors do:

- Selectively leak information in advance, hoping that reporters will pay more attention to it than to information received later.
- Contact members of the press immediately after an event in an effort to get them to adopt the desired spin or interpretation of the event.
- Push the idea that there are always two sides to every story. As Scanlon notes, "What seems to be true is not necessarily the case when we look at it and we dissect it and we take it apart, and we turn it around and we look at it from a different perspective."[95]

Public Relations and Political Activism

Not all public relations is practiced by professionals working for large agencies. As numerous political activists have shown, public relations can be an effective tool for social change as well. In 2005, the farm labor group Coalition of Immokalee Workers won a battle with Yum Brands, the parent company of Taco Bell, over rights and pay for migrant workers. The laborers engaged in a work boycott against Taco Bell's produce farmers, held an extended hunger strike to draw attention to their cause, carried out a 230-mile protest walk, and organized a consumer boycott against Taco Bell. Despite the fact that migrant farmworkers are typically seen as a relatively powerless group, the workers were able to force a change in the fast-food business.[96]

Public Relations and the Civil Rights Movement

Civil rights leader Martin Luther King Jr. displayed a brilliant understanding of public relations throughout the campaign to integrate the South in the 1950s and 1960s. King knew that it would take a combination of action, words, and visibility in the media to eliminate segregation laws and integrate lunch counters, restrooms, water fountains, and businesses. He practiced public relations in churches, hotel rooms, and even jail.

In 1963, King and the Southern Christian Leadership Conference, a civil rights group, wanted to do something highly visible that would let the entire nation see the evils of segregation. The goal of the campaign was to hold nonviolent demonstrations and acts of resistance that would force segregated stores and businesses to be opened to African Americans.

King and his colleagues picked Birmingham, Alabama, as one of their targets, in part because the city's police commissioner was Eugene "Bull" Connor. Connor was a

Web 12.9: Learn how Dr. King demonstrated his understanding of public relations.

Old and New Tools for Integrated Marketing Communication

When West Virginia University wants to reach out to its many publics, it needs to use a wide range of tools, ranging from old-school techniques like newsletters and press releases all the way to interactions through social media.

The biggest challenge WVU's integrated marketing communication (IMC) staff faces is the wide range of publics with which it needs to communicate and build relationships. WVU is a big institution, with approximately 10,000 employees across all of its campuses, 5,000 employees at its hospital and in its health

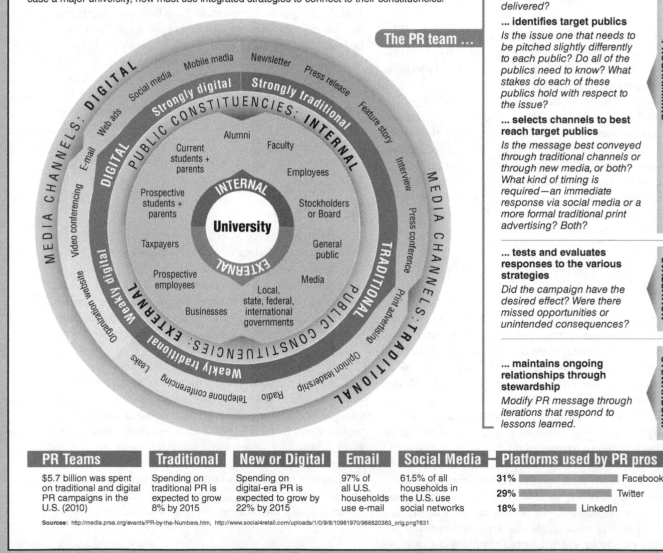

A University's Integrated Communication Strategy for the Digital Age

Various media channels available to public relations teams have changed. Organizations, in this case a major university, now must use integrated strategies to connect to their constituencies.

The PR team ...

... researches, analyzes need, crafts message
Is there a problem or crisis to respond to, or some kind of special message or information that needs to be delivered?

... identifies target publics
Is the issue one that needs to be pitched slightly differently to each public? Do all of the publics need to know? What stakes do each of these publics hold with respect to the issue?

... selects channels to best reach target publics
Is the message best conveyed through traditional channels or through new media, or both? What kind of timing is required—an immediate response via social media or a more formal traditional print advertising? Both?

PROGRAMMING

... tests and evaluates responses to the various strategies
Did the campaign have the desired effect? Were there missed opportunities or unintended consequences?

EVALUATION

... maintains ongoing relationships through stewardship
Modify PR message through iterations that respond to lessons learned.

STEWARDSHIP

PR Teams	Traditional	New or Digital	Email	Social Media	Platforms used by PR pros	
$5.7 billion was spent on traditional and digital PR campaigns in the U.S. (2010)	Spending on traditional PR is expected to grow 8% by 2015	Spending on digital-era PR is expected to grow by 22% by 2015	97% of all U.S. households use e-mail	61.5% of all households in the U.S. use social networks	31%	Facebook
					29%	Twitter
					18%	LinkedIn

Sources: http://media.prsa.org/events/PR-by-the-Numbers.htm, http://www.social4retail.com/uploads/1/0/9/8/10981970/968620383_orig.png?831

sciences program, and nearly 30,000 undergraduate and graduate students. And that's just the beginning of university's list of publics. There are the parents for these students and more than 160,000 alumni supporters, not to mention prospective students and opinion leaders throughout the state.[97]

The central goal for the IMC office is telling the story of the university to that long list of publics. "The exciting part of this job is that as a public university we are at ground zero of telling the story of the American dream for many people," according to Chris Martin, the former vice president for university relations at WVU. "We are a nexus of journalism, multimedia storytelling, and traditional communication."

The IMC staff at West Virginia University is filled with people who have journalistic talent who understand storytelling and content marketing and who have communication strategy skills and technical skills. "WVU needs people who can tell stories on various platforms," Martin says, pointing out that it's no longer enough to send out press releases to legacy media and hope the stories get broadcast or published.

Increasingly, WVU is communicating directly with its publics. This means it has to establish a relationship of trust with its wide-ranging audiences. It means the university has to be willing to talk openly and honestly about the bad news as well as the good. One issue Martin had to deal with while at WVU was when a crew for the *I'm Shmacked* college-partying documentary showed up in Morgantown on a sunny and warm St. Patrick's Day to shoot video of WVU students drinking more than their recommended share of alcohol. When the video hit YouTube, there was a lot of chatter about it on social media sites such as Twitter and Facebook.

"We were prepared to deal with occasions where students will have an alcohol-fueled situation," Martin said. "But this one caught us somewhat by surprise because of the good weather." So while WVU's IMC office did have to deal with some fallout from the video, Martin says people have to keep things in perspective. "Look at what people were calling viral video. It initially had about 200,000 hits, but a viral video of the WVU marching band on Veterans Day had more than 2 million views."

Martin says her greater concern at the time was a story she missed getting out:

The day after the *I'm Shmacked* video went online, I went to a presentation by a Nobel Prize winning physicist that had 400 people trying to get into a 350 seat theater. And I thought, "Shame on us for not getting press here for this story." We have all these students packed in here for a lecture on the origins of the universe. Why didn't we anticipate this? Why didn't we have a crew here?

That's really where you have to be vigilant. Stereotypes exist because the total volume of narrative is so thin. So you need to tell a bigger story. And that's how you really have to handle an issue like *I'm Shmacked*.

Media Transformations Questions

- **WHAT** tools does a university IMC office use to communicate with its various publics?

- **HOW** should an IMC office respond to negative material showing up on social media? Is it too late to respond when the material actually shows up?

- **CAN** an IMC office just get rid of old tools in the era of social media?

 Video 12.3: Watch how WVU communicates with its publics.

racist who could be counted on to attack peaceful marchers. King's campaign was called Project C, for confrontation, and it included press conferences, leaflets, and demonstrations in front of hundreds of reporters and photographers. Starting in April 1963, African American volunteers marched in the streets, held sit-ins at segregated lunch counters, and boycotted local businesses. As the protests started, so did the arrests. The story was covered by the *New York Times* and the *Washington Post.* King and his colleagues knew that all the protests in the world would be ineffective if they were not covered by the press and that being beaten up by police would accomplish little if no photographers were present to document the event.

David Halberstam, who was a newspaper reporter in the South at the time, commented on the civil rights leaders' understanding of public relations:

The key was to lure the beast of segregation out in the open. Casting was critical: King and his aides were learning that they needed to find the right venue, a place where the resistance was likely to be fierce, and the right local official to play the villain. Neither was a problem: King had no trouble finding men like . . . Bull Connor, who were in their own way looking for him, just as he was looking for them.[98]

On Good Friday, King and Ralph Abernathy joined in the marching so that they would be arrested. While King was in jail, he wrote the "Letter from Birmingham Jail," which was smuggled out and published as a brochure. His eloquent words, given added force by having been written in jail, were reprinted across the country.

After King was released, he and his followers raised the stakes. Adults would no longer march and be arrested;

In 1963 Americans were shocked by images, such as this one from photographer Bill Hudson, of police attacking civil rights marchers with dogs, fire hoses, and clubs.

instead, children became the vanguard of the movement. The images, which appeared in print media throughout the world, were riveting. In his biography of King, Stephen Oates wrote, "Millions of readers in America—and millions overseas—stared at pictures of police dogs lunging at young marchers, of firemen raking them with jet streams, of club-wielding cops pinning a Negro woman to the ground."[99]

King faced criticism for allowing young people to face the dangers of marching in Birmingham. But he responded promptly by criticizing the white press, asking the reporters where they had been "during the centuries when our segregated social system had been misusing and abusing Negro children."[100]

Although there was rioting in Birmingham and King's brother's house was bombed, the campaign was ultimately successful. Business owners took down the "WHITE" and "COLORED" signs from drinking fountains and bathrooms, and African Americans were allowed to eat at the lunch counters and sit on the buses. The successful protest in Birmingham set the stage for the march on Washington in August 1963, during which King gave his famous "I Have a Dream" speech.[101]

Chapter SUMMARY

Public relations (PR) developed out of the press agentry of the late 1800s. Publicity firms used one-way communication, deceptive techniques, and bribery. By the beginning of the twentieth century, large corporations such as railroads and utilities realized that they needed to develop more sophisticated relationships with the press if they hoped to control their images.

Ivy Lee and Edward L. Bernays are generally considered to be the founders of public relations as a profession. Lee was among the first press agents to recognize that dealing with the press promptly and truthfully was the best way to obtain positive coverage for his clients. In 1906, he codified this approach in his "Declaration of Principles." Bernays wrote the first book about public relations and taught the first college course on the subject.

During World War I, the federal government realized the value of public relations and used a variety of techniques to build support for U.S. participation in the war. Public relations continued to grow as a profession as businesses became increasingly regulated and the public began to distrust both businesses and the government.

Public relations can be seen as performing three main functions: informing, persuading, and integrating (bringing together) publics, both internal and external. Among the most important publics are the media. Effective public relations generally includes both communication and action. The PR process consists of four steps: (1) defining the problem, (2) planning, (3) communicating, and (4) evaluating. Successful companies work at communicating with their publics during both good times and times of crisis. The rise of the Internet and instantaneous communication not controlled by major media has forced the public relations industry to speed up its rate of response to problems and to deal with a wider range of problems. Public relations is used by a wide range of organizations, including corporations, the government, and activist groups.

Keep up-to-date with content from the author's blog.

Take the chapter quiz.

Key TERMS

Concept REVIEW

One-way versus two-way communication

The professionalization of public relations

The public relations process

Managing a public relations crisis

The impact of the Internet on public relations

The relationship between public relations and the news business

The uses of public relations by the government and government officials

The uses of public relations by advocacy groups

Student STUDY SITE

$SAGE edge™

Sharpen your skills with SAGE edge at **edge.sagepub.com/hanson5e**

SAGE edge for Students provides a personalized approach to help you accomplish your coursework goals in an easy-to-use learning environment.

Advertising

Selling a Message

THE POWER OF
HABIT

WHY WE DO WHAT WE DO
IN LIFE AND BUSINESS

Charles Duhigg

Earl Wilson/The New York Times/Redux

Charles Duhigg, author of The Power of Habit: Why We Do What We Do in Life and Business.

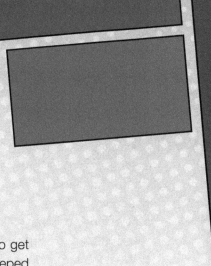

In the age of online shopping and digital information, it's easy to get paranoid about how much vendors know about us. You want to get creeped out? Start paying attention to the recommendations that Amazon makes to you based on what you've previously looked at and purchased.

But taking all your shopping to a brick-and-mortar department store won't help preserve your privacy. Exhibit number one? Target figured out that a high school girl was pregnant and started sending her direct-mail coupons for maternity products before her father knew anything was going on.[1]

How did Target know the young woman was preggers? It seems that pregnant women have very predictable buying patterns. Sometime during the second trimester, four to six months into the pregnancy, pregnant women start buying things such as prenatal vitamins and maternity clothing. Once a woman starts buying these products, she's likely to be giving birth in three to six months.

According Charles Duhigg, author of the book *The Power of Habit: Why We Do What We Do in Life and Business,* Target tracks every consumer who comes to its stores with a unique number tied to his or her credit/debit card. Using this number, Target knows what pattern of products every consumer buys. This information is then paired with data about the consumer that is purchased by the store, says Target statistician Andrew Pole. Before long, the store knows a lot of information about a customer, including preferred purchases, address, income, race, and even estimated earnings.[2]

So our high school student was buying the right combination of cocoa butter lotions, soaps, and mineral supplements that told Target there was an 86 percent likelihood she was pregnant. So Target started sending her coupons for the products people expecting babies are likely to buy.

When these coupons showed up in the mail, the young woman's father got upset and called the manager of his local Target to complain. "My daughter got this in the mail!" the father told the manager. "She's still in high school, and you're sending her coupons for baby clothes and cribs? Are you trying to encourage her to get pregnant?"

The manager apologized repeatedly to the father. Then the father had an interesting discussion with his daughter and called Target back to apologize. His daughter *was* pregnant, but she hadn't told him.

Obviously, Pole's system of evaluating the young woman's purchases worked as intended. But how were he and his employer going to deal with the backlash from consumers who just figured out how much the company knew about them?

"If we send someone a catalog and say, 'Congratulations on your first child!' and they've never told us they're pregnant, that's going to make some people uncomfortable," Pole told Duhigg. This led Target to work on figuring out how to get its ads delivered to pregnant women without the women knowing they were being targeted. As Duhigg puts it, "How do you take advantage of someone's habits without letting them know you're studying their lives?"

The solution ended up being fairly simple. Target mails out coupon books to consumers based on their purchasing history all the time. Usually, those coupons don't upset people. So the secret, according to a Target executive, was to mix the pregnancy product coupons in with a collection of other innocuous coupons that hid the fact that Target knew the woman was pregnant.

"We found out that as long as a pregnant woman thinks she hasn't been spied on, she'll use the coupons," the executive said. "As long as we don't spook her, it works."

What the Target department store is doing in this example is not so different from what every major U.S. advertiser is trying to do: figure out who its prime audience members are and what motivates them and then reach those members with a persuasive message at the time they are ready to buy or make up their mind about a purchase. As we will see later in this chapter, that's why Godiva chocolates target upscale adult women, Miller Lite hires celebrity spokespeople with whom beer drinkers would like to sit down at a bar, and a Minnesota medical center targeted people who were interested in and could afford cosmetic surgery.

Communication professor Joseph Turow told NPR's *On the Media* that this kind of targeting raises all sorts of ethical questions for the companies doing it. "So I think the issue here is how much do people know about what's going on, and do they have any control over it?" he said.

Timeline

1800
- **1812** War of 1812 breaks out.
- **1835** Alexis de Tocqueville publishes *Democracy in America*.
- **1859** Charles Darwin publishes *On the Origin of Species*.
- **1861** U.S. Civil War begins.
- **1869** Transcontinental railroad is completed.
- **1879** Thomas Edison invents electric light bulb.
- **1898** Spanish-American War breaks out.

1900
- **1903** Orville and Wilbur Wright fly first airplane.
- **1905** Albert Einstein proposes his theory of relativity.

1910
- **1912** *Titanic* sinks.
- **1914** World War I begins.
- **1918** Worldwide influenza epidemic strikes.

1920
- **1920** Nineteenth Amendment passes, giving U.S. women the right to vote.
- **1929** U.S. stock market crashes, leading to the Great Depression.

1930
- **1933** Adolf Hitler is elected chancellor of Germany.
- **1939** World War II breaks out in Europe.

1940
- **1941** United States enters World War II.
- **1945** United States drops two atomic bombs on Japan.
- **1947** Pakistan and India gain independence from Britain.
- **1949** Communists establish People's Republic of China.

1704 The *Boston News-Letter* carries the first American newspaper advertisement.

1830s The penny press becomes the first advertising-supported medium.

1841 Volney Palmer opens the first advertising agency in Boston to sell space in newspapers for paid advertisers.

1848 An Irish immigrant, Alexander Turney Stewart, opens the Marble Dry-Goods Palace, the first department store in New York, a business that would make heavy use of advertising.

1869 N. W. Ayer, the first full-service advertising agency, is opened in Philadelphia and creates some of the most memorable slogans, such as "When it rains, it pours," for Morton Salt.

1887 The magazine *Ladies Home Journal* is designed as a medium for consumer advertising.

1927 William S. Paley acquires what would become CBS Radio, one of the first radio networks supported almost wholly by advertisers.

Library of Congress

So, for example if you get an ad, say from NewYorkTimes.com and it's tailored to you, it would be great if there were a way that you could know, a) that it's tailored for you, b) where did they get those data from, c) how does it fit into a larger picture of you that advertiser or that periodical has? And can you do anything about it?[3]

It's worth noting here that Turow made these comments nearly three years before the Target pregnancy advertising case came to light. Later on in the chapter, we'll continue looking at how data targeting can go wrong when companies make incorrect assumptions about their customers' pregnancies.

Although advertising has been a part of American media since the 1700s, the challenge today is to get consumers to pay attention to the messages that pay for so much of the media we receive. In this chapter, we look at the development of the advertising industry in the United States, the major players in the advertising process, and the influence advertising has had on contemporary culture. ■

> **❝How do you take advantage of someone's habits without letting them know you're studying their lives?❞**
>
> —Charles Duhigg

Web 11.1: Read more about Target's targeting.

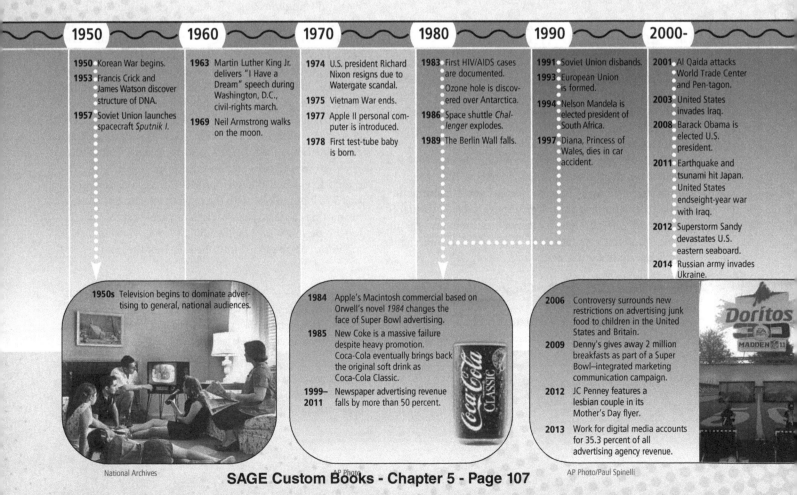

1950	1960	1970	1980	1990	2000-
1950 Korean War begins.	**1963** Martin Luther King Jr. delivers "I Have a Dream" speech during Washington, D.C., civil-rights march.	**1974** U.S. president Richard Nixon resigns due to Watergate scandal.	**1983** First HIV/AIDS cases are documented.	**1991** Soviet Union disbands.	**2001** Al Qaida attacks World Trade Center and Pen-tagon.
1953 Francis Crick and James Watson discover structure of DNA.	**1969** Neil Armstrong walks on the moon.	**1975** Vietnam War ends.	Ozone hole is discovered over Antarctica.	**1993** European Union is formed.	**2003** United States invades Iraq.
1957 Soviet Union launches spacecraft *Sputnik I*.		**1977** Apple II personal computer is introduced.	**1986** Space shuttle *Challenger* explodes.	**1994** Nelson Mandela is elected president of South Africa.	**2008** Barack Obama is elected U.S. president.
		1978 First test-tube baby is born.	**1989** The Berlin Wall falls.	**1997** Diana, Princess of Wales, dies in car accident.	**2011** Earthquake and tsunami hit Japan. United States endseight-year war with Iraq.
					2012 Superstorm Sandy devastates U.S. eastern seaboard.
					2014 Russian army invades Ukraine.

1950s Television begins to dominate advertising to general, national audiences.

1984 Apple's Macintosh commercial based on Orwell's novel *1984* changes the face of Super Bowl advertising.

1985 New Coke is a massive failure despite heavy promotion. Coca-Cola eventually brings back the original soft drink as Coca-Cola Classic.

1999–2011 Newspaper advertising revenue falls by more than 50 percent.

2006 Controversy surrounds new restrictions on advertising junk food to children in the United States and Britain.

2009 Denny's gives away 2 million breakfasts as part of a Super Bowl–integrated marketing communication campaign.

2012 JC Penney features a lesbian couple in its Mother's Day flyer.

2013 Work for digital media accounts for 35.3 percent of all advertising agency revenue.

National Archives

AP Photo

AP Photo/Paul Spinelli

The Development of the Advertising Industry

One element of the media that is almost inescapable is advertising. The American Marketing Association defines **advertising** as "any paid form of nonpersonal communication about an organization, product, service, or idea by an identified sponsor."[4] Advertisements are the commercial messages that pay for an article about cardiovascular health in *Prevention*, an editorial about foreign policy in the *New York Times*, and the block of Rolling Stones hits on the local classic rock radio station.

SECRET 1 ▶ Advertising makes possible the vast array of inexpensive media available worldwide. But there is more to advertising than just cheap media. Advertising drives the size and diversity of the world's economy by telling consumers the multimedia functions they can perform by using a new computer, the image they will project by wearing a brand of clothing or driving a particular car, or the eating pleasure and health benefits they will experience by sampling a new variety of breakfast cereal. Advertising has been a key element of the American economy and culture of consumption and acquisition for more than one hundred years and has existed since before the United States was a nation. With the pervasiveness and importance of advertising in our society, we see once again Secret One—The media are essential components of our lives.

The Birth of Consumer Culture

The earliest American advertising was published in newspapers and was targeted at a narrow, elite audience, just as the papers themselves were. Advertising was not a major source of income for the early papers, but it was still important. The *Boston News-Letter*, one of the first successful colonial newspapers, solicited advertising as early as 1704. Most ads were simple announcements of what a merchant or shop had for sale. There was little point in promoting particular products because most manufacturers produced similar goods. Consumers judged the quality of the goods they bought by inspecting them and taking into account the reputation of the individual merchant. There were no brand names.[5]

Industrialization and the Growth of Advertising.
Major societal changes had to occur before advertising could become a significant social force. The most important of these changes was the Industrial Revolution. The 1800s

Due to the advent of transcontinental railroads in the late nineteenth century, products such as beer went from being predominantly locally produced to being national brands produced for a larger market.

were a period of rapid **industrialization**, in which work done by hand using muscle or water power in small shops was replaced by mass production of goods in large factories that used steam power or, later, electricity. Industrialization brought about the mass production of low-cost, standardized products that had never been available before. Due to advances in transportation, these goods could be manufactured in a single location and then distributed over a wide area. Personal conversations between shop owners and their customers began to be replaced by sales messages placed in newspapers and magazines or posted on signs. Standardized goods were sold using standardized messages—advertisements. In essence, the mass production of consumer goods was developing along with the mass production of messages promoting those goods. Advertising grew explosively during this period as the responsibility for transmitting marketing information passed into the hands of the media.[6]

---

advertising: Defined by the American Marketing Association as "any paid form of nonpersonal communication about an organization, product, service, or idea by an identified sponsor."

industrialization: The movement from work done by hand using muscle or water power in small shops to mass production of goods in factories that used energy sources such as steam power or electricity. It was part of the modernization process.

Web 11.2: Check out vintage ads from the 1700s through the early 2000s.

Modernization: Satisfying Needs Through Shopping. Along with industrialization, the nineteenth century was characterized by **modernization**, the social process by which people go from being born with an identity and a role in life to being able to decide who they want to be, where they want to live, what they want to do, and how they want to present themselves to the world.

As more products became available, advertising was used to promote them and what they stood for. People could now adopt a certain style and purchase the items necessary to portray that style to others—the clothes they wore, the food they served, the soap they washed with, and so forth. Each of these goods was associated with an image that was supposed to rub off on its user. How did people learn about these meanings? Through the advertising that gave meaning to the products.[7]

Media historian Michael Schudson has written that in modern societies people believe they can satisfy their social needs by buying and using mass-produced goods.[8] The late 1800s brought department stores that received new merchandise frequently and then sold it quickly, in contrast to the older dry-goods and clothing stores, which might receive new goods twice a year. As people moved into new communities where their old family identities had little meaning, they could create a new identity for themselves through the products they chose. For example, in the 1920s, people started to buy more ready-made clothes rather than sewing clothes for themselves. This ready-made clothing, which they learned about through advertisements, allowed them to be fashionable and "modern" and to "put on" the identity that went with the clothes.

The Growth of Brand Names

With the growth of industry allowing more production and the construction of transcontinental railroads and steamships making possible better distribution, more and more prepackaged consumer goods came on the market, ready to be promoted through advertising. Among the first were patent medicines—manufactured remedies that often consisted primarily of alcohol and laudanum (opium). Instead of being shipped to stores in large containers and bottled at the point of sale, these products

Library of Congress

Manufacturers of patent medicines promising cures for almost anything—internal ailments, weight gain or weight loss, debility, the common cold—were among the biggest of the early national advertisers.

modernization: The process of change from a society in which people's identities and roles are fixed at birth to a society where people can decide who they want to be, where they want to live, what they want to do, and how they want to present themselves to the world.

economy of abundance: An economy in which there are as many or more goods available as there are people who want to or have the means to buy them.

brand name: A word or phrase attached to prepackaged consumer goods so that they can be better promoted to the general public through advertising and so that consumers can distinguish a given product from the competition.

arrived bottled and ready to be sold to the consumer. These were the first products of the **economy of abundance**, in which there are as many or more goods available as there are people who want to buy them.[9]

Brand-name goods became popular at the end of the nineteenth century. A **brand name** is a word or phrase attached to prepackaged consumer goods so that they can be better promoted

Questioning the Media

With modernization, we can try on new personas by using products that are marketed to help us create our identities. What are some advertised products you use because they say something about who you are? How are these products advertised? What do they tell others about you?

Pears' Soap.

You Dirty Boy!

ALL THE LEADING DRUGGISTS SELL PEARS' SOAP.

Pears' Soap was one of the earliest national brands. Pears' ads encouraged consumers to ask not for soap, but for Pears'.

to the general public through advertising. In a highly mobile society, these standardized, branded products became a source of stability for consumers. The idea of stability coming from a brand-name product has persisted into the twenty-first century. For example, wherever they are, weary travelers are likely to stop for a meal at a familiar and comfortable landmark such as a McDonald's or a Pizza Hut.[10]

The development of brand-name goods was a driving force behind the growth of advertising. Brands were necessary to distinguish the new mass-produced products from one another. The names made it possible for people to ask for goods produced by a specific manufacturer,

Web 11.3: See "Larry" and ads for Quaker Oats.

Video 11.1: Check out commercials with a list of famous advertising catchphrases.

and advertising let people know what these brands were and what they stood for.

Quaker Oats, which was among the first prepackaged cereals, was typical of early brand-name products. It was sold in a multicolored box illustrated with the trademarked "man in Quaker garb." The cereal was a product of consistently high quality that was manufactured in Cedar Rapids, Iowa, and distributed to the entire country. Wherever you purchased the product, it would be the same. Quaker Oats promoted its trademark everywhere, including "on billboards, streetcars, newspapers, calendars, magazines, blotters, cookbooks, Sunday church bulletins, metal signs on rural fences, company-sponsored cooking schools, free samples given away house-to-house, booths at county fairs and expositions."[11]

Thomas J. Barratt developed the first branded soap. "Any fool can make soap," he commented. "It takes a clever man to sell it."[12] Barratt created the Pears' Soap brand and promoted it with outdoor and newsprint ads asking, "Have you had your Pears' today?" Other versions included "How do you spell soap? Why, P-E-A-R-S', of course," and "GOOD MORNING! Have you used Pears' Soap?" Pears' became one of the most talked-about brands of its era and was even mentioned by prominent writers such as Mark Twain. The Pears' Soap catchphrases were the "Where's the beef," "Keeps on going and going," or "Just do it" of their day.

Advertising-Supported Media

The growth of products that needed advertising to succeed brought about a similar growth in advertising-supported media. Beginning in the 1830s, newspapers became much easier and cheaper to produce due to the availability of inexpensive wood-pulp paper and the steam-powered rotary press. The new penny papers (see Chapter 6) were sold to large numbers of people. These large audiences appealed to advertisers, so newspapers moved from depending on subscription revenue to advertising revenue as their primary form of support. The change was dramatic. Instead of merely tolerating advertising, newspapers began to encourage it and even created special advertising sections to seek it out.

Magazines also started out with an uneasy relationship with advertising. In the 1800s, publications such as *Harper's* ran only limited advertising in an attempt to preserve their elite image. Another reason early magazines carried little advertising was that their circulation was national, whereas most advertising was done in local publications. Because there were few national brands at the time, few companies wanted or needed to reach a national audience.

Once manufacturers needed to reach the magazines' national audiences, the economics of magazine publishing changed. No longer were publishers selling magazines to subscribers; instead, they were selling subscribers to advertisers. The *Ladies' Home Journal*, which published from 1887 to 2014, was designed specifically as a medium for consumer advertising.[13] Publisher Cyrus H. K. Curtis put it this way in a speech to advertisers:

> Do you know why we publish the *Ladies' Home Journal*? The editor thinks it is for the benefit of American women. That is an illusion, but a very proper one for him to have. But I will tell you; the real reason, the publisher's reason, is to give you people who manufacture things that American women want and buy a chance to tell them about your products.[14]

Curtis also used advertising to promote his magazine and build its circulation. When *Ladies' Home Journal* closed in 2014, it was not for lack of circulation—it still had more than 3 million subscribers—but the fact that advertisers had lost interest in the magazine's somewhat older readership.

Although the radio industry flirted with revenue options such as taxes and profits from selling radios, it soon became clear that the only way to make enough money to pay for top-notch entertainers and make a profit was to sell advertising. William Paley founded the CBS radio network after he saw how successful radio advertising was for his family's cigar company (see Chapter 7). Paley understood that good programming could attract a large audience that advertisers would want to reach. Sponsors frequently bought not just advertising time, but the entire program. This gave rise to shows such as the *Maxwell House Coffee Time*, the *Lucky Strike Dance Orchestra*, and the *General Motors Family Party*.

There was never any debate about whether television would be driven by advertising. Television grew quickly in the 1950s, and advertisers recognized its potential as a powerful tool for reaching all Americans. By 1960, 90 percent of all homes had television sets.[15] As with the rest of the media, television's "product" is the audience watching its programs. Thus, the primary purpose of the Super Bowl, from television's point of view, is not to choose a

©iStockphoto.com/CurvaBezier

professional football champion but rather to deliver 45 percent of the American audience to advertisers for one evening each year. Robert Niles, a network marketing executive, echoed Cyrus Curtis's promise to deliver an audience to American manufacturers almost a century earlier when Niles stated, "We're in the business of selling audiences to advertisers. [The sponsors] come to us asking for women 18 to 49 and adults 25 to 54 and we try to deliver."[16]

Consumer Advertising. **Local advertising** attempts to induce people to go to a local store or business to buy a product or service, whether it be a new Toyota truck, a gallon of milk, or a travel agent's services. These ads announce the product or service and its price and tell consumers where they can buy it. The local ad is also looking for immediate, direct action. Thus, a **direct action message** is designed to get consumers to purchase a product or engage in a behavior. For example: "Hurry down, these prices won't last, buy today!"

National advertising is designed to build demand for a nationally available product or service, but it does not send consumers out to a particular store to buy a can of Pepsi, a movie video, or a bag of cat food. National advertising assumes that the consumer knows where to buy the product or service or can be told in a local ad where and how to do so. The national advertiser is also more patient and can wait for consumers to take action. Thus, an **indirect action message** is designed to build the image of and demand for a product. Perhaps a consumer won't buy a new washing machine this week, but he will eventually, and that's when he should buy a Maytag.

Advocacy Advertising. **Advocacy ads** are intended to promote a particular point of view rather than a product. In 1993, for example, the state of California ran a $28 million antismoking campaign financed through a cigarette tax. U.S. unions and businesses have fought foreign competition with advocacy ads. Companies express their concerns directly to the public through advocacy ads, bypassing traditional news channels. Such advertising has a long history in the United States, dating back to 1908, when AT&T ran a campaign arguing that it was natural that the phone company should be a monopoly.

Public Service Advertising. Some of the most iconic advertising in the United States comes not from

---

local advertising: Advertising designed to get people to patronize local stores, businesses, or service providers.

direct action message: An advertising message designed to get consumers to go to a particular place to do something specific, such as purchasing a product, obtaining a service, or engaging in a behavior.

national advertising: Advertising designed to build demand for a nationally available product or service and that is not directing the consumer to local retail or service outlets.

indirect action message: An advertising message designed to build the image of and demand for a product, without specifically urging that a particular action be taken at a particular time and place.

advocacy ads: Advertising designed to promote a particular point of view rather than a product or service. Can be sponsored by a government, corporation, trade association, or nonprofit organization.

▶ Video 11.2: See a collection of national ads.

▶ Video 11.3: View examples of the classic ads.

WHY?

remember—
only you can PREVENT FOREST FIRES!

Smokey Bear has been getting the word out about fire safety for more than sixty-five years. This poster dates from the 1960s. One change is that he is now working to prevent "wildfires" instead of "forest fires."

business, but from long series of **public service ads** created by the Advertising Council. The Ad Council got its start as the War Advertising Council back in 1942 with such memorable messages as the Rosie the Riveter "We Can Do It" campaign, which was designed to promote women working in factories producing goods for the war effort. The best-known creation of the Ad Council is likely Smokey Bear, who has stayed on message for more than sixty-five years, telling members of the public that only they can prevent forest fires. He is the second-most-recognized image in the United States, falling just behind Santa Claus. What is more, generations of children have taken great joy in delivering his basic message of fire prevention to their parents and other adults. Other prominent Ad Council campaigns include the 1971 "Crying Indian" antipollution campaign, support for the United Negro College Fund, and McGruff the Crime Dog taking "a bite out of crime."[17]

The editorial and opinion pages of the prestigious national newspapers are popular spots for placing advocacy ads. This is partly due to the credibility associated with appearing on those pages and partly because it's a

good place to reach the target audience of influential decision makers. These ads might, for example, support or oppose a piece of legislation. Sometimes the target of an advocacy ad in the *Washington Post* might be senators or representatives who are being reminded of the support they have received in the past from a given company or industry.[18]

Trade Advertising. **Business-to-business (trade) ads** promote products directly to other businesses rather than to the consumer market. Business-to-business advertising is a critical part of the advertising industry. Consider the fact that General Electric earns 80 percent of its revenue from nonconsumer business.[19] Business customers can be reached through trade magazines, such as *Electronic Engineering Times*; business-oriented cable news channels, such as CNBC; or local weekly business newspapers.

The Advertising Business

Advertising is a multifaceted business that involves four major groups. First, there's the *client*, the person or company that has a product or an idea to promote. Then there's the *advertising agency or department* that researches the market, creates the advertising, and places it in the media. Next, there's the *medium*, be it television, the Internet, a newspaper, a magazine, or some other medium, that carries the advertisement. Finally, there's the *audience*, the people who see or hear the advertisement, whom the client hopes to influence.[20]

For a product to be successful in the marketplace, all four of these groups must work together successfully. There must be a good product backed by advertisements that have a strong sales message delivered through well-chosen media to an appropriate audience. If any part of this process is flawed or seriously miscalculated, the product is likely to fail.

The Client

The first component of advertising is the client, the company with something to sell. The client may want to increase awareness of a new product, encourage people to use an existing product more often, build a positive image of a product, convince users of competitors' products to

---

public service ads: Advertising designed to promote the messages of nonprofit institutions and government agencies. The messages are typically produced and run without charge by advertising professionals and the media. Many of these ads are produced by the Ad Council.

business-to-business (trade) ads: Advertising that promotes products and services directly to other businesses rather than to the general consumer market.

switch brands, promote a benefit of a product, or demonstrate some new use for a product. The 3M Company increased sales of its Scotch brand cellophane tape by suggesting other uses for the product beyond repairing torn paper. Arm & Hammer baking soda's original purpose was to make cakes rise, but the company also increased sales by promoting the product as a cleaner and deodorizer. One of Arm & Hammer's best ads tells consumers to buy a box of baking soda and pour it down the drain to clean and deodorize the sink. In essence, the company was suggesting that people buy its product to throw it away! Arm & Hammer's research showed that people used baking soda to freshen laundry and to brush their teeth, so the company introduced detergent and toothpaste enhanced with baking soda.[21] Begun in 1993 on behalf of the California Milk Processor Board, the "Got Milk?" advertising campaign succeeded at boosting milk sales and has become one of America's longest-running and most celebrated ad series. The "Got Milk" ads ran both in California and nationally until 2014, when the national milk promotion board decided to focus on milk's protein content in its advertising. But the campaign does still live on in California more than twenty years after it started.[22]

For details on America's top advertisers, take a look at Table 11.1.

For a product to be successful, it needs more than a good advertising campaign. It also needs to be a good product at the right price and has to be available for consumers to buy. When Sony launched its PlayStation 2 video game system, it did relatively little initial advertising and held off releasing popular games because it couldn't manufacture enough of the consoles to satisfy public demand. Customers were ready and willing to buy, but the product simply was not available.[23] Once there was a sufficient quantity of the product, Sony started advertising.

SECRET 4 No amount of advertising can save a product that the public just doesn't want to buy, as Coca-Cola discovered when it launched New Coke in 1985. Coca-Cola spent $4 million on research that seemed to indicate that consumers would like the new formula better than the original recipe. But consumers reacted to the change with anger and frustration, and Coca-Cola eventually had to bring back the old drink under the name Coca-Cola Classic.[24] The research may have shown what people liked best in blind taste tests, but it didn't take into account how people felt about the product, what meaning they assigned to it, and the fond memories they associated with it.[25] What the research missed was "the abiding emotional attachment" Coke drinkers had for the product in its familiar form. One Coke executive told *Advertising Age* magazine, "We obviously tried to do psychological research, but it wasn't adequate."[26]

Casual-wear retailer Gap experienced a similar reaction in 2010 when it rolled out a new logo to replace its two-decades-old iconic blue square with white capital letters without testing it with customers first. The response on the

Rank	Brand	2012 U.S. Ad Spending (in millions)
1	AT&T	$1,586
2	Verizon	$1,427
3	Chevrolet	$958
4	McDonald's	$957
5	Geico	$921
6	Toyota	$879
7	Ford	$857
8	T-Mobile	$772
9	Macy's	$762
10	Walmart	$690
40	Apple*	$662

Table 11.1 Top Advertisers in the United States, by Brand

*For comparison, Apple is the world's highest-valued corporation. It is ranked number twelve in terms of advertising spending.

Source: Data from the *Advertising Age Top 200 Megabrands.* Reprinted with permission from *Advertising Age/American Demographics.* Copyright, Crain Communications Inc., 2014.

Internet was instant and negative. In a matter of days, Gap management brought back the old logo and issued a statement that said, "O.K. We've heard loud and clear that you don't like the new logo." A second statement, this one from company president Marka Hansen, went on to say, "We've learned a lot in this process. And we are clear that we did not go about this in the right way. We recognize that we missed the opportunity to engage with the online community."[27] (This is also an example of Secret Four—Nothing's new: Everything that happened in the past will happen again.)

The Agency

The advertising profession originated in the 1840s when agents started selling ad space to clients in the new

---

Web 11.4: Find out more about how milk is being promoted.

Singer Beyoncé has been featured in the long-running "Got Milk?" campaign aimed at promoting the consumption of a wide range of milk and dairy products.

advertising-supported newspapers. At first, the advertising agents worked directly for the newspapers, but before long, they became more like brokers dealing in advertising space for multiple publications. George Rowell, the leading advertising agent of the 1860s and 1870s, was the first agent to buy large amounts of newspaper advertising space wholesale and sell it to his customers as they needed it. Rowell was also the first to publish a directory of newspaper circulation numbers, thus providing clients with an independent source of this vital information. Before Rowell's innovation, newspapers could, and did, lie about the size of their circulation.

The early agents earned a 15 percent commission on the space they sold for the newspapers. This is why advertising agencies were traditionally paid by commission on the media space and time they sold; initially, that was all they were selling.[28]

Before long, advertising agents moved beyond just selling space in the media. Their clients wanted help developing the ads for the space they were purchasing. In 1868, twenty-one-year-old Francis W. Ayer opened N. W. Ayer and Son (giving his father a 50 percent share in the company and the lead name), one of the first agencies to write copy, put together the artwork for an ad, and plan campaigns. The agency recognized that providing the associated services

that would make advertising easier for clients would help the agency sell more space for the media.

Gradually, ad agencies came to represent their clients rather than the media in which they sold advertising space. This shift resulted from the **open contract**, which enabled the agency to provide advertising space in any publication (and eventually on broadcast outlets as well) rather than only a few. The agent was now handling the advertising services for the client, not selling space for the media.[29]

In the 1920s and 1930s, advertisers increasingly recognized that there were different market segments and that ads should be tailored to those segments. Agencies also realized that they needed to use a different mix of media for each of their target audiences. Eventually, they began offering clients three major services: research, creative activity, and media planning.

Research and Planning. Agencies typically use research throughout the entire advertising campaign. The initial research activity is aimed at identifying the characteristics of the target audience and what those people are looking for in a product. Ads are then tested to see how well members of the target audience respond to them. After the campaign, the agency will evaluate its success. How many people remembered seeing the ad? How many people clipped the coupon or called the phone number? How much did sales go up or down?

The process starts with objectives. What does the client want to accomplish with the ads? These objectives could be increasing sales, increasing awareness, or getting people to clip a coupon or make a phone call. The agency may also study characteristics of the product's target audience, a process that is discussed later in the chapter.

Finally, the agency may test the ads itself, either as a pretest before the ads are run or as a recall test after the campaign. One problem advertising researchers face is that the people they want to reach may be unwilling to participate in the research. And the people who are willing to participate may be trying to give the agency the answers they are looking for. Although advertising research continues to be a powerful tool for reducing uncertainty, it is still a difficult process at best.[30]

Creative Activity. There is more to marketing a product than advertising, but advertising is the most visible aspect of marketing, and it has to provide what legendary advertising executive David Ogilvy called **the big idea**—an advertising concept that will grab people's attention, make them take notice, make them remember, and—most important—make them take action. Leo Burnett, founder of one of the nation's biggest agencies, agrees with Ogilvy:

---

open contract: An arrangement that allows advertising agencies to sell space in any publication (and eventually on broadcast outlets as well) rather than just a limited few.

the big idea: The goal of every advertising campaign—an advertising concept that will grab people's attention and make them take notice, remember, and take action.

The word "idea" is loosely used in our business to cover anything from a headline to a TV technique. [But] I feel that a real idea has a power of its own and a life of its own. It goes beyond ads and campaigns. Properly employed, it is often the secret of capturing the imagination of great masses of people and winning "the battle for the uncommitted mind," which is what our business really is about.[31]

In advertising, a tension often exists between creativity and salesmanship. An ad may do a great job of grabbing people's attention and generating talk, but if the ad doesn't have a solid sales message, consumers will not remember the product or give serious thought to buying it. There have been a number of ads that have done a great job of grabbing the public's attention. But have they done a good job of promoting the product? Have they built the value of the brand?

Consider Anheuser-Busch back in 2009. Its brand Bud Light (the most popular beer in the United States) was launching its Bud Light Lime beer in cans. (Previously it had only been available in bottles.) Anheuser-Busch promoted the launch with an online ad that had people talking about "getting it in the can"—as in a suburban housewife confessing, "I never thought I'd enjoy getting it in the can as much as I do." The crude sex joke attracted a lot of talk and attention from the advertising press. But it's not clear what the message did to promote the brand or increase sales.[32]

American Apparel has long been known for producing explicit ads for its line of young adult clothing that have featured nudity and provocative poses. One recent campaign promoted its knitwear, bodysuits, and stockings with poses that made women appear "vulnerable and overtly sexual," according to Britain's Advertising Standards Authority. American Apparel executives defended their ads, saying they had tried to create "authentic, honest and memorable images relevant to their customer base."[33] There can be no question that American Apparel has been successful with its shock-style ads. The problem comes in figuring out what the company can do next to grab attention.

Irish brewer Guinness, on the other hand, has been successful in grabbing attention, generating talk, and building its

AP Photo/Keith Srakocic

Young adult clothing manufacturer and marketer American Apparel has long used provocative and controversial ads to promote their clothes.

brand image with an ad that features a group of men playing wheelchair basketball in a gym. As the ad comes to an end, all but one of the men stand up and then join their one wheelchair-bound friend in a bar for a round of Guinness. The ad has all the standard elements of a beer ad—guys playing sports and then going out to drink beer together afterward. But it adds the unexpected twist that gives it a huge dose of heart.[34]

Adman Hank Seiden puts it this way: "All good advertising consists of both idea and execution. All bad advertising consists of just execution."[35]

Ogilvy believed that all advertising should be created to sell a product or promote a message. It does not exist to be innovative, exciting, creative, or entertaining. Good ads may be all of those things, but the central principle is that they must achieve the client's goals:

A good advertisement is one which sells the product *without drawing attention to itself*. It should rivet the reader's attention on the product. Instead of saying, "What a clever advertisement," the reader says, "I never knew *that* before. I must try this product."[36]

For products that are similar, the **brand image** attached to them is often critical. This image gives a brand and the

---

brand image: The image attached to a brand and the associated product that gives the product a personality or identity that makes it stand out from similar products and stick in the mind of the consumer.

associated product a personality or identity and helps it stand out from the pack. Ogilvy once headed a campaign to give Hathaway shirts a personality when the company's competitor, Arrow, was spending almost a hundred times more on advertising than Hathaway, a smaller company, could. Ogilvy's solution was to buy a black eye patch in a drugstore for $1.50. A model wearing the eye patch was shown conducting an orchestra, driving a tractor, and sailing a boat. This simple bit of brand identity boosted Hathaway out of 116 years of obscurity and turned it into a leading brand.

Ogilvy argues that at the heart of all advertising is an appeal based on facts that are of interest to consumers. As he wrote in the early 1960s, "The consumer isn't a moron. . . . You insult her intelligence if you assume that a mere slogan and a few vapid adjectives will persuade her to buy anything. She wants all the information you can give her."[37]

For print ads, the most important element is the headline, because five times as many people read the headline as read the rest of the copy. This means that 80 percent of the ad's effectiveness comes from the headline. The headline must tell readers whom the ad is for, what the product is, what the product does for the consumer, and why he or she should buy it. That's a lot of responsibility for eight to fifteen words. Ogilvy says that the most powerful headline words are *free* and *new*. Other words favored by Ogilvy are

> how to, suddenly, now, announcing, introducing, it's here, just arrived, important development, improvement, amazing, sensational, remarkable, revolutionary, startling, miracle, magic, offer, quick, easy, wanted, challenge, advice to, the truth about, compare, bargain, hurry, *[and]* last chance.[38]

Although these phrases are overused, they do work. Look at what Ogilvy considered to be the greatest headline he ever wrote: "At Sixty Miles an Hour the Loudest Noise in the New Rolls-Royce Comes from the Electric Clock." It uses the word *new*, it contains a fact that also sells a benefit, and it is true.

Media Planning. **Media planning** involves figuring out which media to use, buying the media at the best rates, and then evaluating how effective the purchase was. It is the least glamorous part of the advertising business, but it is central to a successful campaign. No matter how brilliant the idea or how beautiful the execution, if the ad doesn't reach the target audience, it can't accomplish anything. Typically, advertisers try to pick a mix of media that will deliver the highest percentage of the target audience at the lowest cost per thousand views, or **CPM**. (M is the Roman numeral for 1,000.) Selecting the right media involves identifying the audience for the ad and knowing which media they use.[39]

Agency Size and Income. Advertising agencies have grown immensely since their modest start selling newspaper advertising space. According to *Advertising Age*'s 2014 advertising agency report, the 900-plus agencies studied had their income grow in 2013 by 3.7 percent from the previous year to reach a total of $39.1 billion. (That figure included advertising, media, digital marketing services, health care communication, and public relations.) Work for digital media now dominates the business, accounting for 35.3 percent of all advertising agency revenue in 2013.[40] Keep in mind that this is just the portion of the income that goes to the agency. This figure doesn't include the amount that goes to pay the media for advertising time and space. According to *Advertising Age*'s 2014 annual report, advertisers in 2014 were on track to spend $167.3 billion on advertising in the United States using media for which the size of the audience is measured. (This does not include, for example, direct-mail advertising.) Of that, television accounted for the largest share with 38.3 percent, followed by online with 24.6 percent, newspapers with 12.1 percent, radio with 10 percent, magazines with 9.8 percent, and outdoor and cinema with 5.2 percent. Overall, advertising spending among the hundred top national advertisers increased by 2.8 percent in 2012 for a total of $104.5 billion, a number still below that of the 2009 recession.[41]

Several major trends have emerged in the agency business since the 1980s. One trend is toward the purchase of independent agencies and small groups of agencies by larger holding companies. The biggest of these are WPP, Omnicom Group, Publicis Groupe, and Interpublic Group of Companies.[42] A second trend is a shift toward greater specialization of agency functions. One agency may do research and creative work, whereas another agency (known as a media buyer) develops the media plan and buys the time and space. Because of this specialization, agencies are moving from the commission structure to charging fees for their services. After all, if an agency is just doing creative work, it can't charge a commission on media space that it isn't buying.[43]

The Media

The third group in the advertising business is made up of the media that carry advertisements. These include newspapers, magazines, radio, television, outdoor sites such as billboards and metro buses, and digital. The two media that do not receive large amounts of advertising revenue are movies and books, although movies are increasingly using paid product placements and theaters run advertisements before showing movies. Books initially did not carry ads because advertising was not common when books were first published. In the nineteenth century,

 Web 11.5: Find out more about these advertising agencies.

media planning: The process central to a successful ad campaign of figuring out which media to use, buying the media at the best rates, and then evaluating how effective the purchase was.

CPM: Cost per thousand exposures to the target audience—a figure used in media planning evaluation.

when advertising became popular, there were other, cheaper media in which to advertise. Postal regulations also pose a barrier to advertising in books: Materials containing advertising can't be shipped using the post office's inexpensive book rate. But advertising scholar James Twitchell suggests that as delivery options expand through companies such as FedEx and UPS, advertising in books may become commonplace, especially in expensive academic books.[44] This textbook doesn't yet contain advertisements in its pages, but you probably found a few advertising pieces for credit cards or magazine subscriptions in the bag the bookstore clerk gave you. In Table 11.2, you can see the relative importance of different media to the top hundred leading national advertisers in the United States.

PSL Images/Alamy

Digital billboards with changing messages, such as these in New York City's Times Square, have revitalized the outdoor advertising business.

Newspapers.

Newspapers were the original advertising medium, but they have been suffering major declines in advertising revenue. Between 1999 and 2011, ad revenue declined by more than 50 percent, with classified advertising falling off by 75 percent. Some of this was due to the recent recession, but advertising analyst Ken Doctor says that much of it is coming from newspapers failing to make the digital transformation: "Despite uneven digital ad results reported by newspaper and magazine companies, it's not that the money isn't there—they just haven't transitioned their businesses enough to compete for it."[45] According to the Newspaper Association of America, newspaper print advertising fell 8.6 percent from 2012 to 2013, but newspaper digital advertising increased by 1.5 percent.[46]

Nevertheless, newspapers remain an advertising medium, carrying a majority of local advertising and a significant amount of national advertising. They allow advertisers to present detailed information (such as grocery prices) that would be confusing on radio or television, and they give audience members plenty of time to interpret the information. Newspaper ads make it easy to include coupons, Web addresses, and 800 numbers that readers can clip and save. They also allow advertisers to target not only specific cities, but also specific areas of the city (this is known as **zoned coverage**). Cities typically have only one or two newspapers, so advertisers can cover the entire market with a single purchase. Finally, newspapers allow advertisers to buy space at the last minute.[47]

---

zoned coverage: When a newspaper targets news coverage or advertisements to a specific region of a city or market.

Magazines.

Magazines are an excellent medium for reaching a specific niche audience. Before the 1950s, general-interest magazines were the best way to reach a mass, national audience. Since the 1960s, however, that role has fallen to television. The response of magazines has been to seek ever narrower audiences—there are magazines for motorcyclists, computer users, young women, retired people, knitters, and video game players. Whatever audience an advertiser wants to reach, it is likely to find a magazine to help it do so. For business advertisers, magazines may be the only alternative to direct mail for reaching their target audiences. Magazines offer higher print quality than newspapers do but have a much longer lead time, so magazine advertising requires careful planning. The advertising market for magazines has been changing over the last decade. While the number of ad pages sold has been falling, the revenue from digital sources, such as Web sites and mobile apps, has been growing.[48] Go back to the chapter on magazines (Chapter 5) and reread the section about the *Atlantic* and its "digital-first" strategy as a reminder.

Outdoor Advertising.

Outdoor ads (also known as "out of home advertising") catch people in a captive environment—such as in a car surrounded by slow-moving traffic on the way to work—but they are limited to short, simple messages. The biggest change to have happened to outdoor advertising is the advent of the digital billboard. Essentially giant video screens, digital billboards display a static image that stays up for six to eight seconds before shifting to a new image. Digital billboards can include changing information, such as time or temperature, or even the day's television schedule for a local station.[49] In major cities, there are transit

Table 11.2	U.S. Ad Spending Totals by 100 Leading National Advertisers in Measured Media[50]	
Medium		**2012 spending Medium (in millions)**
Network TV		$27,434
Cable TV network		$24,373
Magazines (consumer, Sunday, B-to-B, local)		$23,825
Newspapers (national to local, inserts)		$18,878
Spot TV		$17,091
Internet display		$10,279
Radio (network, national spot, local)		$8,361
National syndicated TV		$5,133
Outdoor		$4,221

signs—posters on bus-stop shelters, on subway platforms, and on the buses and in the subway cars themselves. Ads have also been placed in the bottom of golf holes so that you see them when you pick up your ball. Overall, $6.38 billion was spent on outdoor advertising in 2011, with billboards accounting for 65 percent of the spending, transit signs making up 17 percent, street furniture 6 percent, and alternative outdoor advertising 12 percent.[51] New York City's Times Square is one of the most valuable places in the United States for outdoor advertisements because of the large number of people who pass through it each day, its frequent coverage on television, and the nearly constant presence of tourists who are photographing the area.[52]

Radio. Radio enables advertisers to broadcast their message repeatedly and to target a narrow audience. Advertisers can choose stations with programming aimed at teens, women ages twenty-five to fifty-four, young adult males, Spanish speakers, or almost any other demographic group. Like outdoor advertising, radio ads can be very effective in big cities where advertisers can reach a captive audience in their cars during the morning and afternoon commutes, which are known as **drive time**. Radio also offers a short lead time and relatively low costs.

Television. Although the most popular television shows remain an appealing place to advertise to a general, national audience, the remote control, the mute button, and the proliferation of cable channels have made it difficult to get viewers to pay attention to commercials. The audience for broadcast television has been declining, but the Big Four networks (see Chapter 9) can still reach a mass audience quickly and effectively. Television offers sound, motion, and visuals. A drawback, however, is that many of the best advertising time slots on the networks, such as those during the Super Bowl, are sold nearly a year in advance. There is also the problem of viewers channel surfing during commercial breaks or skipping commercials using the fast-forward button on their digital video recorders (DVRs).

The new television environment allows targeted advertising, such as ads aimed at the youth market on MTV or CW, the Hispanic market on Univision, or the African American market on BET. For local television advertising, there are independent stations along with the network affiliates. In many communities, local advertisers can buy time on a range of cable stations with local commercial breaks as well. The biggest problem facing television advertisers is that of clutter, which is discussed later in this chapter.

Digital. Digital advertising has been the fastest-growing segment of the advertising market, increasing by double-digit percentages for several years. During the recession in 2009, online advertising saw its first decline since the dot-com bubble burst in 2002 and sent numerous Web properties into bankruptcy.[53] But since then, online advertising has resumed its rapid growth. A study by eMarketer found that in 2013 American consumers spent more time with digital media than with television for the first time. The study estimated that they would spend an average of four hours and twenty-eight minutes a day with television, but that they spent five hours and forty-six minutes with all digital media combined. eMarketer defines digital media as all online, mobile, and streaming services. The growth of use of digital media comes almost exclusively from the growth of mobile devices, with their daily amount of use growing by 23 percent between 2013 and 2014.[54] eMarketer is reporting that mobile advertising spending is growing between 50 and 100 percent per year while desktop ad spending is growing by just single digits.[55]

Digital advertising has the advantage of being able to closely target consumers. As an example, when your author visits Web sites that contain advertising, ads for

Web 11.6: Check out the selection of outdoor ads.

drive time: The morning and afternoon commutes in urban areas; the captive audience makes this a popular time to advertise on radio.

motorcycle accessories often appear because the cookies in his browser history tell the ad server that he's interested in motorcycles. And we all expect that kind of behavior with online ads. But sometimes, as marketing professional David Berkowitz points out, that level of knowledge about us seems a little creepy. Berkowitz asks you to suppose you are searching for a camera using the Web browser on your smartphone. You bring up an ad from Target for a camera you're interested in. The ad can tell that you already have the Target shopping app on your phone, so it automatically sends you the appropriate page on the app to view the camera you are searching for. The question then becomes: Are you creeped out by the fact that an ad on a Web page knows what apps you have installed on your phone? Or do you like the fact that the ad is smart enough to redirect you to an app you already have on your phone?[56] (For more on digital advertising, look ahead to the section of the chapter on long-tail advertising.)

The Audience

As we talked about in the opening vignette of this chapter, the audience is made up of the people advertisers want to reach with their messages. The audience is also the central "product" that media sell to advertisers. In yet another example of **targeting**, advertisers try to make a particular product appeal to a narrowly defined group. Ads for Starburst candies, for example, target the teen and preteen audiences, whereas ads for Godiva chocolates target upscale adult women. The people appearing in an ad are chosen carefully to make members of the target audience say, "This is a product made for someone like me." Advertising executive Robert Meury notes that his agency carefully selects the celebrities who appear in Miller Lite ads: "We make sure our stars are guys you'd enjoy having a beer with. And the locations we film in are always real bars."[57]

As with other types of media, such as radio and television, audience members for advertising are often defined by the "graphics": demographics, geographics, and psychographics. As you may recall from Chapter 2, demographics are the measurable characteristics of the audience, such as age, income, sex, and marital status, whereas geographics involve measurements of where people live. Psychographics combine demographics with measurements of psychological characteristics, such as attitudes, opinions, and interests.

Psychographics and VALS®. In advertising, it's not enough to know the demographics of the client's target audience (age, income, sex, etc.). Advertisers also want to know what the target audience dreams about, aspires to,

When the lights went out on the New Orleans Super Bowl in 2013, the big television advertisers like Coke and Pepsi didn't like having their carefully planned series of ads disrupted. On the other hand, Oreo's agency quickly put together a social media ad that they delivered almost immediately. Oreo's spur of the moment social media ad got the company more attention than they could have gotten out of elaborate computer preparations. (The ad quickly picked up more than 15,000 retweets and 5,400 favorites.)

and feels. These are the topics covered by psychographic research.

The term *psychographics* was first used in the 1960s to refer to a measure of consumer psychology. Depending on the project, researchers may look at a person's lifestyle, relationship to the product, and personality traits.[58]

Emanuel Demby, one of the first users of the term, defines *psychographics* as the use of psychological, sociological, and anthropological data to segment a market into relevant groupings. The way the income variable is conceived is more sophisticated than just grouping markets by income levels. Demby argues that it is just as important to know whether someone's income is increasing, decreasing, or remaining stable as it is to know the person's actual income. Why? Because how things are going in people's lives will say something about how they see

Questioning the Media

Can you name several advertisers who are targeting people like you? Who are they? How can you tell they are targeting you? How do you feel about this?

---

targeting: The process of trying to make a particular product or service appeal to a narrowly defined group. Groups are often targeted using demographics, geographics, and psychographics.

Figure 11.1   The VALS Types

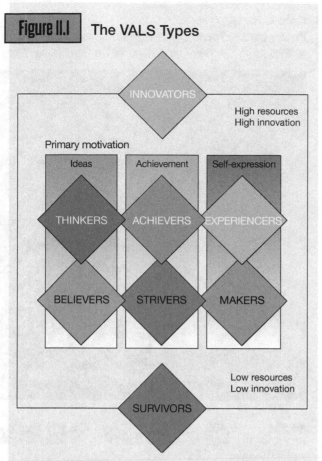

To Receive an Accurate VALS Type:
By design, the questions are for use by people whose first language is American English. If you are not a citizen of the United States or Canada, residency should be for enough time to know the culture and its idioms. **If you do not meet these conditions, your VALS type will not be valid.**

Source: Strategic Business Insights (SBI), www.strategicbusinessinsights.com/vals. Reprinted by permission.

themselves. If advertisers understand how members of the target audience see themselves, they can craft ads that will more readily appeal to the target.[59]

The best-known psychographic system, VALS™, was developed by SRI International and is currently owned and operated by Strategic Business Insights. VALS places people in one of eight consumer groups according to their primary motivation and level of resources (see Figure 11.1). Resources are the tangible and intangible things that people have to draw on as they seek success: their education, income, health, and self-confidence, among other factors. Primary motivation is the person's approach to life. Ideals-motivated consumers ("Thinkers" and "Believers") are guided by knowledge and principles; achievement-motivated consumers ("Achievers" and "Strivers") look for products that will

Web 11.7: Want to know your own VALS category? Take the survey!

Web 11.8: Here are several ads from mainstream companies supporting gay marriage.

demonstrate their status and success to others; and Self-Expression-motivated consumers ("Experiencers" and "Makers") seek action, variety, and risk.

At the top of the VALS framework are the innovators, described as being "successful, sophisticated, take-charge people with high self-esteem." These are people who have established careers and value the image of a product as "an expression of their taste, independence, and personality." At the bottom of the VALS framework are the survivors, who have few resources and believe "the world is changing too quickly." VALS describes them as cautious consumers with little to spend but with high brand loyalty.[60]

How might a company use psychographics and these personality types to target its advertising? As an example, a Minnesota medical center used VALS to identify and understand consumers who were interested in and able to afford cosmetic surgery. The resulting ad campaign targeted to these individuals was purportedly so successful that the clinic was fully booked.[61]

To see targeting in action, we can look at some real-world examples. The first example discusses the targeting of a product (Mountain Dew); the second, a particular audience (gays and lesbians); and the third, some instances of targeting failures.

Targeting a Product: Mountain Dew.

Advertising soft drinks can be a particular challenge because all the drinks are basically the same thing—sweetened carbonated water and a small amount of flavoring—with just a few variations, such as regular or diet, caffeinated or caffeine free. Since the products are so similar, the key to promoting the brand is selling not just a drink but an entire attitude and approach to life, thus making the product appeal to a particular audience. Television scholar Joshua Meyrowitz describes the basic message of a diet soda commercial as "Drink this and you'll be beautiful and have beautiful friends to play volleyball with on the beach."[62]

Mountain Dew has existed as a product since the 1940s and has always projected a rebellious and irreverent image, according to Scott Moffitt, who was director of marketing:

> We have a great unity of message and purpose that has been consistent over time about what we are and what we aren't. The brand is all about exhilaration and energy, and you see that in all that we do, from advertising and community to grassroots programs and our sports-minded focus. We have a very crystal clear, vivid positioning.[63]

In keeping with its young, energetic image, Mountain Dew sponsors events such as ESPN's X Games because they project the same image the soft drink does. It also goes after heavy consumers who drink three or more cans of Mountain Dew a day.

Mountain Dew now holds a coveted spot among the top four or five soft drinks, behind Coke, Pepsi, and Diet Coke, but it started out as a bar mix consisting of lemon-lime juice, orange juice, low carbonation, and caffeine. It cultivated a hillbilly image and logo and was billed as "zero-proof hillbilly moonshine." In the 1960s, Pepsi bought the brand and started giving it more of a hip image. Following a period of confused advertising images in the 1980s, Mountain Dew came into its own in 1992. Bill Bruce, who was the creative director on the Mountain Dew account, describes Mountain Dew's coming-of-age process:

> Seattle grunge music was happening at the time. Extreme sports were happening. So there was this subculture that we wanted to tap into. The idea was to show the most extreme things. We created these four characters, the Dew Dudes, who represented what was happening at the time musically and culturally.[64]

This approach was first used with Diet Mountain Dew, but given its success, it eventually became the central theme of the entire campaign.

The ongoing challenge to Mountain Dew as it grows in popularity is to maintain its edginess and youth appeal so that it can maintain both its sales and its image. Most recently, Mountain Dew has been trying to engage young urban consumers. (In marketing speak, urban marketing means reaching out to African American and Latino consumers. We'll talk more about that in a bit.) The company's goal is to go beyond the rural markets where Mountain Dew has been enormously successful into the cities where it has traditionally sold less well. Mountain Dew is doing this by featuring hip-hop performers Lil Wayne; Tyler, The Creator; and Rick Ross. (It should be noted that some of the ads to come out of this campaign have backfired for the soft drink maker by offending virtually everyone with racist and misogynistic storylines.[65])

Targeting an Audience: Advertising to the Gay Market.

One audience that advertisers are increasingly targeting is the gay and lesbian market. Gays are desirable as a market to advertisers because they are perceived to be relatively upscale and highly educated.[66] "Because they primarily don't have children and there is one income for each person in the household, you are talking about a population with large sums of disposable income that non-gay families with children wouldn't have," says Rick Dean of the research firm Overlooked Opinions.[67] Media company Rivendell Media estimates that the gay and lesbian market has an annual buying power of $641 billion.[68]

As early as 1994, vodka producer Absolut was among the first major companies to place ads in gay publications, including *Out* and the *Advocate*.[69] In addition to advertising in gay publications, companies are using gay couples in ads. Some advertisers have gone further, experimenting with gay-specific ads. Hyatt Hotels and Resorts has targeted the gay and lesbian market since the late 1990s and has depicted same-sex couples in its messages.[70] Advertising to the gay community carries the risk of antigay groups organizing boycotts of companies that do so, but the effectiveness of such boycotts has been limited.[71]

SECRET 3 The gay advertising market has grown considerably in the twenty-first century, due in part to the

Photo by Casey Rodgers/Invision for Mountain Dew/AP Photo

Mountain Dew has reached out to young, active people by using spokesmen such as professional snowboarder Danny Davis.

launch of at least three gay-themed cable television channels, including Viacom's Logo TV. These join 145 separate gay and lesbian publications, including both newspapers and magazines.[72] Advertising targeted at gay audiences is also showing up increasingly outside of gay media. Bud Light, the most popular beer in the United States, re-created the red equal sign (signifying support for same-sex marriage equality) using a red background and two cans for Bud Light) as a social media avatar. And travel site Expedia has a three-minute online ad that tells the story of a father overcoming his attitudes and traveling to his daughter's same-sex wedding. The ad is unique in being told completely from the questioning father's point of view.[73] This continued growth of advertising in gay publications and of gay-themed ads is another example of Secret Three—Everything from the margin moves to the center.

Web 11.9: See how Mountain Dew's add featuring Felicia the Goat went terribly wrong.

TEST YOUR MEDIA LITERACY

Advertising to Targeted Markets

It's pretty obvious, given demographic trends, that major corporations are going to need to target racial and ethnic communities if they want to stay relevant in today's market. The census estimates that approximately 65 percent of Americans identify themselves as "white only." The exact figures get a bit confusing, given that Hispanic is an ethnic category, not a racial category. But that means if companies make their advertising primarily relevant to white people, they're leaving 35 percent of the market out there on the table.

As companies try to market to Hispanic, African American, and Asian American audiences, they need to appeal to their target and avoid offensive and dated stereotypes. McDonald's, for example, has targeted the African American market though efforts often called "urban marketing." One ad that has attracted both positive and negative attention for the fast-food chain is an ad called "McNuggets Love," which features an R&B singer crooning about his lady sneaking out at night to meet with her true love—a ten-piece box of Chicken McNuggets. The campaign was a major success for McDonald's, increasing McNuggets sales by 20 percent.[1] But some consumers found the ad offensive or annoying, with one saying, "It's sad that this is how the marketing execs at the McDonald's corporate office think they can attract the urban consumer."[2] In 2012, McDonald's featured African American actress Teyonah Parris from the AMC show *Mad Men* in a more traditionally themed urban-targeted ad. McDonald's spokesperson Danya Proud had this to say about the company's urban marketing efforts:

> We have a responsibility to all of our customers to effectively reach them. We certainly take pride in all of our advertising and try to make it relevant and appealing.
>
> We work with a dedicated African-American advertising agency that works with us to develop relevant, contemporary creative for our brand, that will resonate with this demographic. Again, as with all our advertising, these commercials reflect a light-hearted, fun approach to our brand, our menu, and our customers' experience with our brand.[3]

WHO are the sources?

What kind of a company is McDonald's? Who is it trying to reach with its urban marketing campaign?

WHAT are they saying?

How is McDonald's attempting to reach the urban audience? What does McDonald's mean by "urban marketing"?

WHAT evidence is there?

Why is McDonald's trying to target ethnic and racial minority groups? What can it gain? What can it lose? Do ads targeting specific minority groups appeal to the wider population as a whole?

WHAT do you and your classmates think?

How do you and your friends feel about companies advertising to targeted audiences? Watch the "McNuggets Love" ad online. Do you find it appealing? Insulting? Offensive? Funny? Why or why not? Do you think this ad appeals to a broad or narrow audience? How does it compare with the Teyonah Parris ad?

---

[1]Laurel Wentz, "'McNuggets Love' a Multicultural Ad Winner," *Chicago Business*, October 6, 2009.
[2]Geoffrey Bennett, "McDonald's Going Too Far to Market Their McNuggets?" *NPR*, December 3, 2008, www.npr.org/blogs/newsandviews/2008/12/mcdonalds_going_too_far_to_mar.html.
[3]Ibid.

 Video 11.6: View several urban McDonald's ads.

Failures of Targeted Advertising. Efforts to target specific audiences are not always successful. When Hornell Brewing launched its western-themed Crazy Horse malt liquor, the company thought it had a product to complement its Dakota Hills Black Sunday brand. The beer was targeted not at Native American groups, but rather at people on the East Coast who were interested in western culture. But Native American groups expressed outrage at the use of the venerated chief's name to sell alcohol.[74] Crazy Horse, a leader of the Oglala Sioux in the nineteenth century, was opposed to drinking.[75] Objections by the Native American community eventually led the U.S. Commerce Department to refuse Hornell a trademark on the product; in addition, the beer was banned in Minnesota and Washington, and its sale was discouraged in Nebraska.[76]

As we saw with the opening vignette about Target reaching out with coupons to women who are pregnant, people expecting a child are highly valued by marketers. What gets people to spend more money than having a baby? Photo-sharing site Shutterfly thought it had a sure winner with a campaign that sent out an e-mail to people it thought had new babies, based on the photos they had posted. But unfortunately for Shutterfly, not everyone it reached out to had actually had a baby, and some of the recipients had had a miscarriage, had a child die, or were dealing with infertility. Following the social media

 Web 11.10: See how Shutterfly missed with their campaign targeting new parents.

backlash, Shutterfly sent out a sincere apology for its mistake, which helped the company some with the folks who had received the e-mail in error. But that wasn't the end of the problem. Some of the Shutterfly customers who were properly targeted because they had had new babies were freaked out by the fact the company knew they had a baby. The lesson here? Always be careful when you target people to talk about their babies![77]

Richard Milnes/Demotix/Corbis

Coca Cola has embraced marketing its soft drink to the gay community with their display of the rainbow flag at their store in Sydney, Australia.

Advertising in Contemporary Culture

Advertising is much more than a part of the marketing and media business; it is a central element of American culture. Children sing advertising jingles the way they once sang nursery rhymes. In the 1970s, the music from a Coca-Cola commercial even became a hit single, "I'd Like to Teach the World to Sing."

Critics argue that advertising places a burden on society by raising the cost of merchandise and inducing people to buy things they don't need. The American Association of Advertising Agencies has defended the ad business, claiming that there are four common misconceptions about the industry[78]:

1. Advertising makes you buy things you don't want—The industry responds by saying that no one can make you buy things you don't want. People are free to do as they please.

2. Advertising makes things cost more—Advertisers claim that advertising builds demand for products, which can then be manufactured in larger quantities, more efficiently, and at a lower cost. (This defense ignores the idea of the prestige brand, however. Advertising does not make a bar of Clinique soap cost more to produce, but the premium image attached to the soap allows the company to charge more for it. Consumers apparently want to be able to buy better, more expensive products.)

3. Advertising helps sell bad products—The industry responds that a good ad may lead people to buy a product once, but it won't sustain demand for a product they don't like. In fact, the industry argues that good advertising for a bad product will kill the product faster than if it hadn't had a good campaign behind it. M. Night Shyamalan, director of the movies *The Sixth*

Sense and *Signs*, says that with enough advertising studios can buy a good opening weekend for a movie, but only good word-of-mouth reports by fans will make the movie a long-term success.[79]

4. Advertising is a waste of money—The ad industry counters that advertising strengthens the economy by helping to move products through the marketplace and supporting the mass media.

SECRET 6 Throughout this section of the chapter, you will see numerous examples of Secret Six—Activism and analysis are not the same thing. In many of the following cases, you will see activism and analysis continually intertwined. See if you can sort out the two from each other.

The Problem of Clutter

When critics complain that there are too many ads on television, few would be quicker to agree than advertising agencies and their clients. They are very concerned about the huge number of commercials and other messages—collectively referred to as clutter—that compete for consumer attention between programs.

Advertisers dislike clutter because the more ads and nonprogram messages there are on television, the less attention viewers will pay to any given message. A study conducted by the Cabletelevision Advertising Bureau found that viewers are much more likely to remember the first ad in a group (called a *pod*) than the fourth or fifth.[80]

---

clutter: The large number of commercials, advertising, and other nonprogramming messages and interruptions that compete for consumer attention on radio, television, and now the Internet.

 Video 11.7 Watch Coca-Cola's famous vintage commercial (and a new one from the 2014 Super Bowl).

Movie director M. Night Shyamalan argues that while movie studios can spend enough on advertising to buy themselves a good opening weekend, only good word-of-mouth can bring a movie long-term box-office success.

The clutter problem is not limited to television; each day the average American adult is exposed to 150 advertisements in one form or another.

According to a study commissioned by advertising agencies and their clients, clutter is reaching record levels. In 2005, U.S. network television averaged about fifteen minutes of advertising and promotional clutter per hour during prime time.[81] Cable television rates were even higher, with MTV averaging sixteen minutes and thirteen seconds of clutter per hour. In 2010, cable channel Spike may have set a record for clutter with a single commercial pod running ten minutes during an episode of *Entourage*.[82]

Clutter is generally defined as anything that is not part of the program itself: ads, public service announcements, network promotions, and other gaps between programs. In the spring of 2009, Fox Broadcasting experimented with

 Web 11.11: Check out claims of subliminal advertising.

what the network called "Remote-Free TV," in which the network cut the commercial load during shows such as *Fringe* and *Dollhouse* to only ten minutes as a way of keeping viewers from channel surfing or fast-forwarding through the breaks. The network charged advertisers a 40 to 50 percent premium for spots that ran during Remote-Free TV. The experiment proved to be a mixed success for Fox. Both sponsors and viewers liked the reduced commercial load. So what made the response mixed? Fox earned less money and so abandoned the experiment at the end of the 2009 spring television season.[83]

Despite the problems of higher clutter, lower-rated network programs, and increasing CPM rates, networks continue to sell advertising time, and advertising experts say that clutter won't disappear until clients stop buying time from the networks.

Advertising clutter in the United Kingdom has also grown dramatically over the past several years, though it's still nowhere near the level seen in the United States. In 2001, the average Briton saw 258 television commercials per week. By 2005, that total had risen to 311. But this was still dramatically lower than the 789 ads per week seen by typical U.S. viewers. Ad clutter in the United Kingdom is lower partly because of legal restrictions on the number of minutes of commercials per hour and because the BBC, a state-supported media entity, doesn't carry ads.[84]

Breaking through the clutter is a continuing challenge for advertisers, who have come up with a variety of solutions to the problem. Tire company Goodyear breaks through the clutter by putting its message on the Goodyear Blimp, which flies over sporting and other entertainment events that draw large audiences.[85] Drug companies fight clutter by using celebrities in their advertisements. Former senator and presidential candidate Bob Dole served as an early spokesman for the impotence drug Viagra; NBA star Alonzo Mourning talked about the anemia drug Procrit, which is used to treat a kidney disorder that almost ended his career; and actress Lorraine Bracco, who played a psychiatrist on *The Sopranos*, discussed depression in ads for drugs manufactured by Pfizer Inc.[86]

Debunking Subliminal Advertising

With all the concern about advertising clutter, it is ironic that there is substantial public concern about **subliminal advertising**—messages that are allegedly embedded so deeply in an ad that they cannot be perceived consciously. The concept has been popularized by several writers, but no research has ever been done to demonstrate that advertising audiences can be influenced by messages they don't perceive consciously.

SECRET 3 > Although there is no evidence that it works and little evidence that any advertisers try to create ads with

subliminal advertising: Messages that are allegedly embedded so deeply in an ad that they cannot be perceived consciously. There is no evidence that subliminal advertising is effective.

hidden messages, much of the public believes that subliminal advertising is used and is effective. A survey published in 1993 found that among people who were familiar with the concept of subliminal advertising, 72 percent thought it was effective.[87] The concept of subliminal advertising came to public attention in 1957, when Jim Vicary, a market researcher, claimed to have exposed movie audiences to the commands "*drink Coca-Cola*" and "*eat popcorn*" flashed on the screen so quickly (less than .03 of a second) that they could not be perceived consciously. Vicary claimed that popcorn sales increased by an average of 57.5 percent and Coke sales went up 18.1 percent. Vicary claimed that people could be influenced strongly by things they didn't see. It turned out, however, that Vicary had not conducted the tests but had simply made up the statistics on increased sales of popcorn and Coke. Throughout 1957 and early 1958, Vicary collected more than $4 million in consulting fees; in June 1958, he disappeared.

In 1970, Wilson Bryan Key, a university professor in Canada, revived the idea of subliminal advertising. While looking at a photo in an article in *Esquire,* he thought he saw an image of a phallus. Key has since been arguing that Madison Avenue hides images of death, fear, and sex in advertisements to increase sales.[88] It is unclear how these hidden images are supposed to influence viewers, who presumably are ignoring the clutter of overt advertising.

When Advertisements Are More Important Than the Program

Sometimes television ads are as interesting as the programs during which they appear. Commentators have even argued that people sometimes stay tuned to a boring Super Bowl broadcast just to see the commercials. Ridley Scott, best known as the director of blockbuster movies such as *Gladiator, Hannibal,* and *Black Hawk Down,* made a name for himself by directing the 1984 Super Bowl commercial that introduced Apple's Macintosh computer. Scott's commercial, known as "1984," changed the world of advertising. Not only was it one of the most talked-about commercials of all time, but it also showed that good commercials can be more memorable than the shows they accompany.[89]

The commercial, created by the Chiat/Day agency, was a success on a number of levels. It portrayed a dramatic image of a young woman athlete rebelling against an Orwellian "Big Brother" situation. It generated talk among the 100 million viewers who saw it, and it transmitted the central message that Apple wanted to get across: that there was an alternative to what was perceived at the time as the all-encompassing power of IBM (a role that has since been taken over by Microsoft).[90]

The commercial aired once on network television during the third quarter of the Super Bowl. After the Super Bowl,

the commercial was broadcast free on the Big Three network news shows, and the trade magazine *Advertising Age* named it the commercial of the decade. Steve Hayden, who wrote the spot while employed at Chiat/Day, says that the agency wanted to sum up the whole philosophy of the computer in one commercial: "We thought of it as an ideology, a value set. It was a way of letting the whole world access the power of computing and letting them talk to one another."[91]

Ironically, the commercial almost didn't run at all. When it was previewed for Apple's board of directors, several members were horrified by it and wanted the spot scrapped. John O'Toole, former president of the American Association of Advertising Agencies, explained the significance of the ad as follows:

> What "1984" as a commercial for Apple really signified was the first time somebody could put a great deal of production money into a single commercial and run it only once and get tremendous benefit from running it only once. It took great coordination with PR. It was really event marketing, with sales promotion and PR built in. That was the beginning of the new era of integrated marketing communications.[92]

Advertising to Children

Few aspects of advertising raise more concerns than commercials targeted at children. Yet children (and through them, their parents) are a highly desirable audience and market for advertisers. If your parents tell you that there weren't as many commercials targeted at children when they were young, they're right. In 1983, companies were spending $100 million a year to reach children. But by 2008, spending on advertising directed at children had grown to $17 billion a year. That means that marketers are spending 170 times more today to reach children than they were a generation ago.[93]

Television Advertising to Children. A U.S. Federal Trade Commission study published in 1978 under the title "Television Advertising to Children" found that children between the ages of two and eleven see approximately 20,000 television commercials a

©iStockphoto.com/iqoncept

Questioning the Media

Do you watch the Super Bowl every year for the ads? What are your favorite Super Bowl ads? What makes you like them?

Web 11.12: See the latest on Super Bowl advertising.

Video 11.8: Apple's "1984" Super Bowl commercial.

year—that's the equivalent of about three hours a week, or slightly less than half an hour per day. The study was highly controversial at the time because it called for bans (never implemented) on all advertising in programs for which a "significant" portion of the audience was under the age of eight and on television ads for sugary foods targeted at children ages eight to eleven.[94]

Marketing to children in the twenty-first century goes far beyond the traditional print and thirty-second television ads. Companies are instead pouring money into product placement, in-school programs, mobile phone ads, and video games.[95] In 2006, the advertising industry revised its guidelines for advertising to children for the first time in thirty-two years. The new guidelines require companies to distinguish between advertising and programming content, show mealtime foods as part of a single balanced meal rather than as part of a larger balanced diet, and identify when online games contain advertising.[96]

Food Ads Directed at Children. In recent years, the biggest criticism of advertising directed at children has moved from cigarettes to junk food. The U.S. federally chartered Institute of Medicine says that there is "strong evidence that exposure to television advertising" is connected with obesity, which can lead to numerous illnesses, including diabetes.[97] The institute goes on to say that ads for junk food targeted at children under age eight can help establish a lifetime of poor eating patterns.[98] Of course, what constitutes healthy food is subject to some debate. Would a high-fiber granola bar with significant levels of sugar qualify as health food or junk?

Richard Martin, a spokesman for the Grocery Manufacturers Association, said at a U.S. Federal Trade Commission hearing that the association does not believe there are bad foods: "Any food can be responsibly consumed by everyone, including kids."[99]

The advertising industry has been critical of the report's recommendations to regulate food ads targeted at children. Daniel L. Jaffe, an executive with the Association of National Advertisers, told the *Washington Post* that

the government stepping in and saying what should be in messages on TV is a very radical proposal. . . . If you do it for food, there's no reason it can't be done for other controversial product categories. People are already trying to restrict the advertising for prescription drugs.[100]

In response to the report and other criticism from activist groups, the U.S. advertising and food industries say they are working to limit the advertising of junk food to children. A group of ten of the largest food and beverage companies—including Kraft, Coca-Cola, PepsiCo, and Hershey's—has pledged to use at least half of its ads directed at children under age twelve to promote healthier foods or encourage healthy lifestyles. It will also take junk food promotions out of online interactive games.[101]

Televised advertising of junk food to children has been a major issue in the United Kingdom as well, with the government putting in place strong new regulations of the practice. The new restrictions limit the promotion of high-fat, high-sugar, and high-salt foods to children under age sixteen to certain hours of the day. The ban has been controversial in Britain because these food ads provide funding for popular children's programming, such as *Bob the Builder* and *My Parents Are Aliens*. Producers argue that without the revenue from food ads, the commercial broadcast networks will stop producing high-quality children's content.[102] Critics of the ban say that this would leave British children with the choice of commercial-free BBC programming or imported satellite programming from companies such as Disney.[103] Anne Wood, creator of the popular *Teletubbies* series, told the *Guardian*,

I am horrified and, believe me, it's not from a personal or self-interested position. . . . The health lobby seems to have won the day, but what about the other cultural side, protecting the rights of children to have television made for them, as adults do?[104]

Because the restrictions include ads targeted at children under sixteen, the ban will also affect MTV, costing the network as much as 8.8 percent of its income.

■ ■ ■ ■ ■ ■ ■ ■ ■ ■ ■ ■ ■ ■ ■ ■ ■

The Future of Advertising

With the rise of new advertising media, including computers connected to the Internet, mobile phone screens, and video games, the older media, such as television, newspapers, and magazines, are going to be facing substantial challenges.

Integrated Marketing Communication

One response to the rapidly changing marketing environment advertisers are facing is **integrated marketing communication**, or IMC. The idea is that there should be an overall communication strategy for reaching key audiences and that this strategy can be carried out using advertising, public relations, sales promotion, and interactive media. Dating back to the 1980s and 1990s, IMC is a long-term approach to building the value of a brand or an organization.[105]

We can see how IMC gets used to build a brand by looking at how Denny's worked to "re-introduce" the restaurant to America and to bring "light and lapsed" Denny's customers back into the fold in the winter of 2009.[106] At the center of the IMC campaign was a creative ad that ran during the Super Bowl featuring a group of "wise guy" gangsters planning a hit while a waitress delivers clown-faced pancakes. The message? Serious people deserve a serious breakfast. The ad then closed out with the announcement

---

integrated marketing communication: An overall communication strategy for reaching key audiences using advertising, public relations, sales promotion, and interactive media.

Limits on Advertising Food to Children

Advertising to children in general has been controversial for years, but as of late the criticism has become more focused on children's food ads. As mentioned earlier in this chapter, the controversy is a great example of Secret Six—Activism and analysis are not the same thing. In a nutshell, a recent research study conducted by the Institute of Medicine found the following, in respect to food preferences and diets:

- There is strong evidence that television advertising influences the food and beverage preferences of children aged two to eleven years. There is insufficient evidence about its influence on the preferences of teens aged twelve to eighteen years.

- There is moderate evidence that television advertising influences the food and beverage beliefs of children aged two to eleven years. There is insufficient evidence about its influence on the beliefs of teens aged twelve to eighteen years.

- There is strong evidence that television advertising influences the short-term consumption of children aged two to eleven years. There is insufficient evidence about its influence on the short-term consumption of teens aged twelve to eighteen years.

- There is moderate evidence that television advertising influences the usual dietary intake of younger children aged two to five years and weak evidence that it influences the usual dietary intake of older children aged six to eleven years. There is also weak evidence that it influences the usual dietary intake of teens aged twelve to eighteen years.[1]

WHO are the sources?

You have read about groups in the United States and the United Kingdom that have both advocated for and opposed advertising food products to children. Who are these groups?

WHAT are they saying?

Why do critics oppose food advertisements targeted at children? What types of food ads do they object to? How have supporters of this advertising responded? How have the responses in the United Kingdom and the United States differed?

WHAT evidence is there?

What evidence has been presented that food advertising directed at children is harmful? What evidence has been presented that it is benign or even helpful? Who is sponsoring and funding the studies?

WHAT do you and your classmates think about food advertisements directed at children?

What kinds of effects do you think food advertisements have on children? Do you think that the arguments that advocates and opponents are presenting are sincere? Or are the advocates just trying to advance their own agendas?

[1] J. Michael McGinnis, Jennifer Appleton Gootman, and Vivica I. Kraak, *Food Marketing to Children and Youth: Threat or Opportunity?* (Washington, D.C.: Institute of Medicine of the National Academies, 2005), books.nap.edu/openbook.php?record_id=11514&page=1.

Web 11.13: Read the Institute of Medicine report on advertising food to children.

---

that the chain was giving away a free breakfast to everyone who came to Denny's on the following Tuesday between 6 a.m. and 2 p.m.[107]

The result? Roughly 2 million people came in for their free Grand Slam breakfast of two eggs, two strips of bacon, two sausages, and two pancakes. That's an effective message. Especially when you consider that most of the people who took advantage of the free food also paid for a drink that came close to covering the cost of the meal.[108]

Brian Quinton, an editor at large for *Promo* magazine, sees the Denny's campaign as a mixed success from an IMC point of view. Denny's had a clever ad that ran twice during the Super Bowl, a full-page ad that ran in *USA Today*, an e-mail sent out to Denny's customers, and a compelling promotional offer. Denny's also sent out press kits about the promotion, placed signs within the stores, and highlighted the promotion on the company Web site. The campaign was discussed on NBC's *Today Show*, and it received extensive media attention elsewhere.[109] But while the Denny's

campaign was a success, the integration of it was not as well done as it could have been. The biggest problem was that the company did not have enough capacity on its Web site to handle the sudden 1,700 percent increase in viewership during the game. The Web site crashed as soon as the first ad ran and stayed down throughout the game. The company also didn't include its Web address in the commercials.[110]

Despite these difficulties, Denny's IMC campaign would have to be considered a success from a results point of view. Denny's estimated that the promotion, including the ads and food, cost $5 million and claimed it generated $50 million in publicity, though it did not elaborate on how that was measured.[111] The Super Bowl ads were seen by 98 million viewers, and millions more saw local news stories generated by

---

Video 11.9: Watch the Denny's IMC ads and read more about the campaign.

From Advertorials to Native Advertising

Back in 1950, legendary adman David Ogilvy created one of the best examples of an ad trying to masquerade as magazine editorial content. "The Guinness Guide to Oysters" gave readers a delicious look at Atlantic oysters and suggested that a Guinness Extra Stout would go great with them. As Brian Clark wrote in his advertising column at the Web site *Say Daily,* "I don't even like oysters, and this sounds amazing right now."[112] Ogilvy's Guinness and oysters ad is oftentimes held up as the real start of the advertorial—a paid message where the advertisement blends in with the surrounding materials in the magazine, newspaper, or Web site. While advertorials have been around for more than sixty years, a new version known as *native*

advertising has emerged. Native ads are essentially a more sophisticated form of sponsored content that "matches a publication's editorial standards while meeting the audience's expectations."[113] (They are also an example of Secret Four—Nothing's new: Everything that happened in the past will happen again.) Lots of prestige media companies—including the *Atlantic,* the *Washington Post,* and the *New York Times*—are making use of native ads, especially on their Web sites.[114]

While ads designed to look like editorial content are nothing new, having the publication's editorial staff producing articles appearing as sponsored content is breaking down the old barrier between "church and state"—the blurred line between the business side and the content

side of a publication.[115] The big challenge to both the advertiser and the publication is that the content of native ads needs to really match the style and standards of the hosting publication. This called for a fair amount of bravery for Southwest Airlines when it partnered with the news parody Web site *The Onion*. The airline's basic message is that it offers great fares and is loyal to its customers. The message in its native ad video on *The Onion* gets that message across, but in the sarcastic and crude *Onion* style. Microsoft used an *Onion* video to get across the message

---

advertorial: Advertising materials in magazines designed to look like editorial content rather than paid advertising.

The Anatomy of a Native Advertisement

Native ads work best when they match both the style of the publication they appear in and the tastes of the target audience. Case in point: the Onion Lab's successful minute and a half long video ad campaign called "Loyalty Goes Both Ways" for Southwest Airlines.

the ONION

• Presented as a fake news report on ONN, the video parodies Southwest's loyalty program and captures the brand's well-known sense of humor, but with the Onion's legendary satirical "fake news" bite.

• The reporter introducing the story says:

"For years Southwest Airlines has boasted having the most loyal customers in the industry; now the low-cost airline is calling on its most frequent customers to finally do something in return for the airline, after years of selflessly offering inexpensive flights ..."

And a member of Southwest's ground crew is shown saying,

"You said you wanted free checked bags, and we listened. *Now you listen to us."*

Parody of marketing message banners from airport

Typical b-roll (or background action) footage for news story about airlines

Authentic-looking show title

Recreation of the news ticker used by news channels

Parody of the CNN logo

Sources:
http://labs.the onion.com
http://www.cmo.com/articles/2013/10/21/15 Stats_Native_Advertising.html
http://www.sharethrough.com/portfolio-item/native-advertising-research-study-from-nielsen-and-sharethrough-shows-how-native-video-ads-beat-preroll
http://25h4pl1p8r9f2fc6of24zpt71dz2.wpengine.netdna-cdn.com/wp-content/uploads/2014/04/Native_Advertising_Infographic_Sharethrough_Nielsen.pdf

Why native advertising works

101,463 Number of YouTube views of Southwest "Loyalty Goes Both Ways" advertisement, 5 months since posting.

90% Percentage of U.S. publishers who have offered native ads or who plan to offer native ads on their websites.

38.9% Percent of all paid social advertising on social media sites that is spent on native ads.

32% The likelihood that a consumer will share a native ad with others.

19% The likelihood that a consumer will share a conventional banner ad with others.

2.1% Percentage of "brand lift" generated by viewers toward a brand after watching pre-roll ad.

82% Percentage of "brand lift" generated by viewers toward a brand after watching native ad.

85% **Percentage of consumers who have never heard of native ads.**

that Internet Explorer, "the web browser you love to hate, just got better."[116]

Native ads can go horribly wrong, however, when the content of the article/ad doesn't match the standards of the hosting publication. One of the most notorious examples came from 2013 when the *Atlantic* ran a sponsored article on its Web site extolling the opening of twelve new Scientology churches. Along with the article, which seemed to be at odds with content from the *Atlantic,* the comments section following the article appeared to have nothing but positive comments about Scientology. Comments on most articles at the site are both positive and negative. After the article

was up less than twelve hours, it was pulled from the Web site, and the next day an apology was posted that began:

We screwed up. It shouldn't have taken a wave of constructive criticism—but it has—to alert us that we've made a mistake, possibly several mistakes. We now realize that as we explored new forms of digital advertising, we failed to update the policies that must govern the decisions we make along the way.[117]

The *Atlantic* followed up that apology two weeks later with new guideless for how it would handle sponsored content in the future.[118]

Media Transformations Questions:

- **DO** you think that native advertising or sponsored content lowers the reputation of publications that sell it?

- **HOW** do you feel about reading articles that are sponsored by the people being written about? Would you find them as interesting as articles that were not sponsored? Why or why not?

Video 11.10: Take a look at some of the native ads discussed above.

---

the promotion on the two days following the ads.[119] What's more, it appears Denny's did a good job of hitting its target audience of light and lapsed customers, as follow-up research showed that approximately 60 percent of the customers for the Tuesday promotion fell into that group.[120]

Is Anyone Watching Television Ads?

There is only a fixed amount of money available for advertising and marketing products. And as companies move their advertising dollars to new media—online for ads and streaming content and to mobile phone screens—there will be less money for older media, such as television. If that were not enough, television is grappling with declining audience sizes and new technologies, such as DVRs, which allow viewers to skip watching commercials altogether. As of 2011, DVRs were in nearly 40 percent of American households.[121]

The broadcast networks are responding to this threat in various ways. CBS is selling Web ads as a package with broadcast ads. These aren't the simple banner ads of the 1990s; they are video ads that come before streaming Web content. Sneaker manufacturer Converse used its broadcast ads to get consumers to generate short videos featuring Converse sneakers, and the company then featured the videos on its Web site.[122]

Mobile Advertising. Mobile devices like smartphones and tablets have become the latest frontier for advertising, with their bright color screens and their ubiquitous use among the notoriously hard-to-reach population of adults aged eighteen to thirty-four. Although many companies are simply using banner ads to go with wireless Web content, others are creating interactive apps to promote their products.

Despite having small screens, cell phones have several key advantages to advertisers. They are always on, they are

always with the person who owns them, and the phone belongs to an identifiable individual. This lets advertisers send out highly targeted messages that can contain time-sensitive offers. Another popular use of mobile phone advertising is to get consumers to participate in activities such as voting for contestants on reality shows.[123]

Advertising consultant Kathryn Koegel said she learned a lot about mobile advertising being done around the world when she served as a judge of the GSMA Global Mobile Awards. What did she discover? That folks are doing much more interesting and creative things globally using simpler tools than marketers are in the United States.[124]

The problem, Koegel claims, is that in the United States advertisers are obsessed with fancy iPhone apps that really don't do much to promote the brand. What Koegel found globally was that companies promoted involvement using simple SMS text messages and creative approaches that led to publicly visible activity.

She points to a Japanese campaign that uses the GPS and motion sensor in the iPhone to lead people to try to catch virtual butterflies by waving their phones about in public areas. "Catching" the butterflies leads to delivery of coupons to participants. So not only are the participants collecting coupons using the app, they're doing it in a way that's bound to get the people around them talking about it.

As a second example, she discusses the winning mobile campaign from the competition—one that sells Cornetto ice cream in Turkey through the use of a video game projected on the wall of a building in Taskim, Turkey's answer to Times Square. People compete by controlling game characters on the side of the building using text messages from their phones. If they complete the task, they win free ice cream that is collected on the spot.

The lesson from Koegel isn't that there is anything wrong with mobile apps, you just want to make sure that

Denny's used a complete IMC campaign to bring in light and lapsed customers that included Super Bowl advertising, a free breakfast giveaway promotion, and extensive contacts with the press around the country.

ing consumers are increasingly ignoring television ads by skipping past them on the DVR, surfing other channels during commercial breaks, or leaving the room to get a snack.[126]

The biggest challenge to product placement is making it seem natural rather than intrusive, as intrusive placement tends to put off consumers, according to *New York Times* advertising columnist Stuart Elliott. That may be why so much of the product placement is in reality shows, where the use of products as rewards and prizes makes them fit in better.

There seem to be no limits now to which products can get placed in prime-time programs. Pregnancy was an unmentionable topic on television in the 1950s, but pregnancy tests are showing up frequently in product placements in shows ranging from *Gossip Girl* to *Sex and the City*.[127]

you have clear goals for what you are trying to accomplish with them.

What kind of mobile marketing could you think up?

Product Placement

Product placement has long been with us. When Paul Newman drank a beer in the 1981 movie *Absence of Malice*, it was a Budweiser. And when Steve McQueen played cop Frank Bullitt back in 1968, he chased criminals through San Francisco in a Ford Mustang GT. But in recent years, product placement has gotten considerably more sophisticated, rising occasionally to the level known as plot placement, branded entertainment, or **product integration**, in which the product or service being promoted is not only seen, but is central to the story.[125]

One of the forces driving the growth of this expanded form of product placement is that multitask-

Questioning the Media

How do you feel about television programs featuring sponsored products within the shows? Do you find product placement more annoying in scripted programs than in reality shows? Why or why not?

Television and movie writers have rebelled against product integration, complaining that it interferes with their creative integrity; they've also called for getting a cut of the placement income if they're going to be writing the placements into the stories. Patric Verrone, president of a movie and broadcast writers' union, explained why writers are concerned about product integration: "Product placement is simply putting a branded box of cereal on the kitchen table in a show. Product integration is having the characters talk about the crunchy deliciousness of the cereal."[128]

The Long Tail of Advertising

For all the talk about the importance of Internet advertising, it remains a relatively small part of advertising spending, accounting for only 6.9 percent of all advertising spending in the United States. Despite recent declines in spending, online advertising is expected to resume growth and should be more and more important in the years to come.[129]

Among the best known of the long-tail advertising tools are Google's AdWords and AdSense programs. Rather than buying a particular Web site, advertisers instead buy certain keywords, which place their ads next to particular content. Under AdWords, when surfers do a Google search that includes the keyword, the ad appears next to the search result. With AdSense, Web sites have a code on them that searches the content of the site and puts ads relevant to the subject matter next to the content

Video 11.11: Take a look at Kathryn Koegel's analysis of successful mobile advertising efforts, including the iButterfly campaign.

Video 11.12: Check out examples of both punk polka and techno polka.

product integration: The paid integration of a product or service into the central theme of media content. This is most common in television programming or movies, but it can be found in books, magazine articles, Web pages, or even songs.

posted there. So if I had AdSense on my site and wrote about DVDs in a blog entry, ads for retailers that sold DVD players would start coming up. The advertisers pay for each person who clicks on the served-up ad, with a portion of the money going to the owner of the site where the ad appeared.[130] Although this tool can be used to market any product, it is especially useful for advertising long-tail media. If I were trying to sell punk polka CDs, for example, I would try to maximize the return on my advertising money by reaching only people who were already reading about punk polka bands. Google also supports its Android mobile device operating system software with advertising sales.[131]

One of the big problems with Internet advertising is documenting how many people have actually clicked on the ad. Major advertisers have complained that "click fraud" drives up their cost of online advertising. The owner of a Web site with online ads may pay friends to click on the ads repeatedly to generate more page views and hence more income.[132] Or competitors of a particular advertiser will click on that advertiser's ad to run up his bill.[133] There are even automated programs known as clickbots or hitbots that will click away twenty-four hours a day, running up the bill for advertisers.

In an interesting move, in 2006, Google started selling advertising space in newspapers using the same program the company uses to sell advertising on its search engine and on Web pages.[134] As discussed in Chapter 3, Google is rapidly moving into becoming more and more of a general purpose media company, once more illustrating Secret Three—Everything from the margin moves to the center.

The iButterfly mobile advertising campaign in Japan had consumers waving their smartphones around in the air to catch virtual butterflies and receive electronic coupons.

Mario Perez/CBS via Getty Images

Microsoft has used product integration in the crime series *Hawaii Five-0* to feature the company's Surface tablet computer.

Chapter SUMMARY

Advertisements are paid messages about an organization, a product, a service, or an idea that appear in the mass media. Advertising provides numerous benefits to society, including making media less expensive and contributing to a large and diverse economy. While advertising has existed in the United States since colonial times, it was industrialization, urbanization, and the growth of national transportation networks in the nineteenth century that allowed it to become a major industry. Advertising transformed the media industry from one supported primarily by subscribers to one supported by advertising revenues. Publishers (and later broadcasters) were no longer sellers of content to audience members; they were now sellers of audiences to advertisers.

Advertising can be broken down into consumer advertising, advocacy advertising, and trade (business-to-business) advertising, according to the audience the client is attempting to reach and the idea or product it is trying to sell. The advertising industry encompasses four main groups: the client who has something to advertise, the advertising agency or department that creates the advertising, the media that carry the ads, and the audiences targeted by the advertisements.

Advertisers use a variety of strategies to reach their audiences. They may attempt to understand the needs, wants, and motivations of audience members through psychographic research. They also target products to specific demographic groups.

Critics argue that advertising raises the cost of merchandise, that many ads are tasteless, and that ads can exploit young people and other vulnerable audiences. Advertisers join the critics in complaining that there are too many advertisements in the media, creating the problem referred to as clutter. Although there have been complaints of advertisers embedding subliminal messages in ads, there is no evidence that such messages have been used or that they are effective.

Advertising is going through a period of significant change as new technology emerges that allows consumers to bypass viewing commercials on television. But technology is also providing numerous new venues for advertising, including the Internet and mobile phones. Companies are increasingly making use of integrated marketing communication strategies that bring together multiple forms of marketing communication to promote their brands. Advertisers are also looking at promoting their products through elaborately developed product placement schemes.

 Keep up-to-date with content from the author's blog.

 Take the chapter quiz.

Key TERMS

advertising 276

industrialization 276

modernization 277

economy of
   abundance 277

brand name 277

local advertising 279

direct action
   message 279

national advertising 279

indirect action
   message 279

advocacy ads 279

public service ads 280

business-to-business
   (trade) ads 280

open contract 282

the big idea 282

brand image 283

media planning 284

CPM 284

zoned coverage 285

drive time 286

targeting 287

clutter 291

subliminal
   advertising 292

integrated marketing
   communication 294

advertorial 296

product integration 298

Concept REVIEW

Industrialization, modernization, and the growth of consumer advertising

The importance of brands

Advertising-supported media

Types of advertising

The players in advertising: clients, agencies, media, and audiences

Advantages and dangers of targeted advertising

The use of demographics and psychographics in targeting markets

The challenge of advertising in a cluttered market

The growth of integrated marketing communication

Student STUDY SITE

$SAGE edge™

Sharpen your skills with SAGE edge at **edge.sagepub.com/hanson5e**

SAGE edge for Students provides a personalized approach to help you accomplish your coursework goals in an easy-to-use learning environment.

Magazines

The Power of Words and Images

Photo by Evan Agostini/
Invision/AP, file

Lena Dunham—the creator, executive producer, and actress in the HBO series Girls—is no stranger to controversy; and her cover story from the February 2014 issue of Vogue was no exception. Critics were concerned that the images by famed photographer Annie Leibovitz had been excessively Photoshopped.

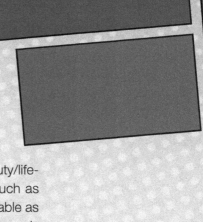

The level of Photoshopping going on at fashion/beauty/lifestyle magazines has been an ongoing controversy, with performers such as Adele, Kelly Clarkson, and Kate Winslet being made almost unrecognizable as photographers and photo editors try to make the curvy stars' bodies comply with fashion magazine standards of beauty.

So it should come as no surprise that when Lena Dunham, the unconventional star of the HBO series *Girls*, posed for famed photographer Annie Leibovitz for the cover of *Vogue* magazine that questions would start being raised as to how authentic her images were. Dunham, in case you've missed the story, is famous for being naked in *Girls*—a lot—and her tattooed, un-toned body is both celebrated and criticized for being an alternative to conventional standards of Hollywood beauty.

When the Dunham issue of *Vogue* came out, the blog *Jezebel*—which tends to be very critical of Photoshopped images of women—offered $10,000 to anyone who would supply it with the original, unedited images of the photos *Vogue* published. It didn't take long for someone to provide *Jezebel* with the photos. As it turns out, the photos themselves were highly manipulated: New backgrounds were added, locations were changed, and a bird was placed on Dunham's head. But surprisingly little was done to Dunham herself. On the cover photo, for example, her neck was made thinner, her head was made smaller (which makes her eyes look bigger), and her jawline was made narrower. The bigger manipulations included taking a studio image of Dunham, adding a pigeon to her head, and then placing her on a street in Brooklyn.[1]

Dunham told *Slate* following *Jezebel's* publication of the unedited images that she had no problem with how Leibovitz had digitally altered her, and that she understands and appreciates the difference between reality and what is published in a fashion magazine:

> A fashion magazine is like a beautiful fantasy. *Vogue* isn't the place that we go to look at realistic women, *Vogue* is the place that we go to look at beautiful clothes and fancy places and escapism and so I feel like if the story reflects me and I happen to be wearing a beautiful Prada dress and surrounded by beautiful men and dogs, what's the problem? If they want to see what I really look like go watch the show that I make every single week.[2]

Dunham goes on to say that she didn't feel like anyone pressured her into doing anything that she didn't want to do. "I never felt bullied into anything," she said. "I felt happy because they dressed me and styled me in a way that really reflects who I am. And I felt that was very lucky and that all the editors understood my persona, my creativity and who I am. . . . I know some people have been very angry about the cover and that confuses me a little. I don't understand why, Photoshop or no, having a woman who is different from the typical *Vogue* cover girl could be a bad thing."[3]

LEARNING OBJECTIVES

After studying this chapter, you will be able to:

1 Explain the importance of the *Saturday Evening Post* in the development of the mass media in the United States.

2 Describe the key characteristics of trade, literary, and consumer magazines.

3 Illustrate how magazines have given a voice to different groups of people.

4 Discuss the role that magazines and magazine ads play in defining people's body image.

5 Describe what is meant by "native advertising" and why it is controversial.

6 Discuss the major trends in twenty-first-century magazine publishing.

Web 5.1: Links to some of the controversial images of Lena Dunham.

The controversy surrounding Leibovitz's cover featuring Dunham is nothing new. The photographer has long been known for her controversial magazine covers and images. From her 1981 *Rolling Stone* cover featuring a nude John Lennon taken the day he was murdered, to the 1991 *Vanity Fair* cover featuring a nude and very pregnant Demi Moore, to her 2008 implied-topless photo of a then-underage Miley Cyrus, Leibovitz's work has always been able to get people talking.

Leibovitz started out wanting to be a painter, but she submitted a photo she had taken of beat poet Allen Ginsberg to *Rolling Stone* magazine. Her photo was accepted, and she went to work for the publication full-time at age twenty. The photo that put her on the map was a cover portrait for *Rolling Stone* of a naked John Lennon clinging to Yoko Ono. The photo was taken just hours before Lennon was murdered.[4]

It was during her time at *Rolling Stone* that Leibovitz learned the practical details of shooting successful magazine covers: The subject of the photo has to be recognizable, there has to be something worthy of notice in the picture, and there has to be room for the magazine's name and a few lines of type.

Leibovitz went on to shoot for *Vanity Fair*, creating many of its best-known covers, including the infamous one that featured a nude Demi Moore, who was eight months pregnant at the time. The Moore cover sold an extra 500,000 copies of the magazine, and former editor Tina Brown notes that *Vanity Fair* picked up about 75,000 new subscriptions as a result.

Ad man and designer George Lois, who produced many of the most memorable covers of *Esquire* magazine back in the 1960s, says that whatever else it was, the Moore photo was a great magazine cover.

"A truly great magazine cover surprises, even shocks, and connects in a nanosecond," Lois wrote in *Vanity Fair*.

Timeline

1800	1900	1910	1920	1930	1940
1812 War of 1812 breaks out.	**1903** Orville and Wilbur Wright fly first airplane.	**1912** *Titanic* sinks.	**1920** Nineteenth Amendment passes, giving U.S. women the right to vote.	**1933** Adolf Hitler is elected chancellor of Germany.	**1941** United States enters World War II.
1835 Alexis de Tocqueville publishes *Democracy in America*.	**1905** Albert Einstein proposes his theory of relativity.	**1914** World War I begins.	**1929** U.S. stock market crashes, leading to the Great Depression.	**1939** World War II breaks out in Europe.	**1945** United States drops two atomic bombs on Japan.
1859 Charles Darwin publishes *On the Origin of Species*.		**1918** Worldwide influenza epidemic strikes.			**1947** Pakistan and India gain independence from Britain.
1861 U.S. Civil War begins.					**1949** Communists establish People's Republic of China.
1869 Transcontinental railroad is completed.					
1879 Thomas Edison invents electric light bulb.					
1898 Spanish-American War breaks out.					

◀ **1704** Daniel Defoe founds the Review, the first magazine in England.

1821 The Saturday Evening Post, the first truly national magazine in the United States, starts publication.

1828 The Spectator, the oldest continuously published magazine in the English language, publishes its first issue in England.

1837 Sarah Josepha Hale becomes the editor of Godey's Lady's Book and creates the modern women's magazine.

1840 Mathew Brady gains reknown as a portrait photographer and later becomes famous for his Civil War photos.

1910 W. E. B. DuBois founds the Crisis as the NAACP's official magazine.

Library of Congress

1920s Harold Ross founds the New Yorker, which becomes a home for highbrow magazine writing.

1923 Henry Luce founds Time magazine, the eventual centerpiece of the Time Warner media empire.

AP Photo

A glance at the image . . . depicting a famous movie star beautifully bursting with life and proudly flaunting her body, was an instant culture buster—and damn the expected primal screams of those constipated critics, cranky subscribers, and fidgety newsstand buyers, who the editors and publishers surely knew would regard a pregnant female body as "grotesque and obscene."[5]

SECRET 3 Looking at Leibovitz's long career in magazine journalism, you can see a prime example of Secret Three—Everything from the margin moves to the center. Leibovitz started shooting counterculture figures for the upstart magazine *Rolling Stone* and progressed to shooting A-list celebrities for *Vanity Fair* and *Vogue* in the 1990s, 2000s, and 2010s.[6] In fact, over the last five decades, you would be hard pressed to not find a year where one or more of the most talked-about magazine covers was shot by Leibovitz.

Provocative covers by photographers such as Annie Leibovitz help draw readers into magazines that cover every imaginable topic, from fashion to sports to news. In this chapter, we look at how the magazine industry grew from a general national medium into one that serves a wide range of narrow interests. We look at the types of magazines published today, some controversies that surround magazine articles and advertisements, how the magazine industry operates, and what the future of the magazine industry holds. ∎

> **"A truly great magazine cover surprises, even shocks, and connects in a nanosecond."**
>
> —George Lois

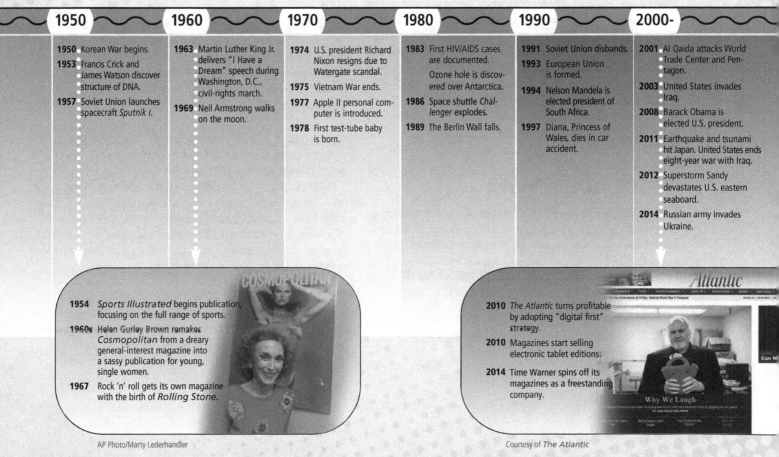

1950

1950 Korean War begins.

1953 Francis Crick and James Watson discover structure of DNA.

1957 Soviet Union launches spacecraft *Sputnik I*.

1960

1963 Martin Luther King Jr. delivers "I Have a Dream" speech during Washington, D.C., civil-rights march.

1969 Neil Armstrong walks on the moon.

1970

1974 U.S. president Richard Nixon resigns due to Watergate scandal.

1975 Vietnam War ends.

1977 Apple II personal computer is introduced.

1978 First test-tube baby is born.

1980

1983 First HIV/AIDS cases are documented. Ozone hole is discovered over Antarctica.

1986 Space shuttle *Challenger* explodes.

1989 The Berlin Wall falls.

1990

1991 Soviet Union disbands.

1993 European Union is formed.

1994 Nelson Mandela is elected president of South Africa.

1997 Diana, Princess of Wales, dies in car accident.

2000-

2001 Al Qaida attacks World Trade Center and Pentagon.

2003 United States invades Iraq.

2008 Barack Obama is elected U.S. president.

2011 Earthquake and tsunami hit Japan. United States ends eight-year war with Iraq.

2012 Superstorm Sandy devastates U.S. eastern seaboard.

2014 Russian army invades Ukraine.

1954 *Sports Illustrated* begins publication, focusing on the full range of sports.

1960s Helen Gurley Brown remakes *Cosmopolitan* from a dreary general-interest magazine into a sassy publication for young, single women.

1967 Rock 'n' roll gets its own magazine with the birth of *Rolling Stone*.

2010 *The Atlantic* turns profitable by adopting "digital first" strategy.

2010 Magazines start selling electronic tablet editions.

2014 Time Warner spins off its magazines as a freestanding company.

AP Photo/Marty Lederhandler

Courtesy of *The Atlantic*

The Development of a National Culture

Before radio and television, magazines were people's primary source for in-depth news, ideas, and pictures. In 1704, Daniel Defoe, later famous for writing *Robinson Crusoe*, founded the first real magazine in England—a weekly periodical called the *Review*. Physically, the *Review* looked just like the newspapers of the era. But newspapers focused exclusively on news, whereas Defoe's magazine covered public policy, literature, and morals. Edward Cave's *Gentleman's Magazine* was the first publication to use the word *magazine*, which was derived from the original meaning of the word as a place where goods or supplies are stored.[7]

What is a **magazine**? It is a periodical that contains articles of lasting interest. Typically, magazines are targeted at a specific audience and derive income from advertising, subscriptions, and newsstand sales. Magazines are also intended for a broader geographic area than newspapers, and in the nineteenth century, they increased in both number and circulation as the demand for nationwide advertising grew. (For more about the connection between the growth of advertising and magazines, see Chapter 11.)

Early Magazines

In 1740, Benjamin Franklin announced his plan to publish the *General Magazine*, with lawyer John Webbe as editor. But in a story that could rival any of today's headlines, Webbe was stolen away by publisher Andrew Bradford to edit his *American Magazine*. As a result, Bradford's magazine was published three days before Franklin's. The magazine industry in the New World was less than a week old, and it had already had its first battle.[8]

The hundred magazines published prior to 1800 contained many reprints from newspapers around the colonies, as well as items from British magazines. Magazines were free to reprint whatever they wanted because at the time there were no copyright laws or copyright protections.

The *Saturday Evening Post*

Just as television and the Internet do today, the magazines of the eighteenth and nineteenth centuries provided news, education, and entertainment. Their collections of humor, verse, and stories were designed for the small amounts of leisure time people had in the early 1800s. Because libraries were in short supply, magazines

 Web 5.2: Read what the *Saturday Evening Post* is like today.

For more than a century, the Saturday Evening Post *was one of the dominant magazines in the United States.*

The Granger Collection, New York

often were the only regular source of high-quality written entertainment.

The most significant of the early magazines was the *Saturday Evening Post*, first published on August 4, 1821. It looked like a four-page newspaper, and a year's subscription cost two dollars, half payable in advance.[9] It featured essays, poetry, obituaries, stories, and a column called "The Ladies' Friend." It contained advertising, and by the 1830s, it was illustrated as well.

SECRET 1 The *Post* was in many ways the first truly national medium—unlike the newspapers that covered a single city, it was read in every American state from Maine to Florida. For at least forty years, the *Post* was *the* voice of the United States. It published the writings of Edgar Allan Poe, Harriet Beecher Stowe, James Fenimore Cooper, and Nathaniel Hawthorne. The *Post* appealed to a broad, general audience rather than the more exclusive audience of literary magazines. By 1848, it was the leading weekly in

magazine: A periodical that contains articles of lasting interest. Typically, magazines are targeted at a specific audience and derive income from advertising, subscriptions, and newsstand sales.

War photography hasn't changed that much since its beginnings during the American Civil War. This image of the Battle of Gettysburg (left) was taken in 1863 by photographer Timothy H. O'Sullivan, who initially trained under Mathew Brady. The photo on the right was taken in August 2009 in Kabul by Massoud Hossaini and is of three gunmen killed by Afghan security forces after they attacked a bank building in the Afghan capital.

the United States, and even as late as 1937, it had a circulation of more than 3 million.

In 1928, Leon Chipple described the *Post* as follows:

This is a magic mirror; it not only reflects, it creates us. What the [*Saturday Evening Post*] is we are. Its advertising helps standardize our physical life; its text stencils patterns on our minds. It is a main factor in raising the luxury-level by teaching us new wants. . . . But it does more than whet our hunger; by blunt or subtle devices it molds our ideas on crime, prohibition, Russia, oil, preparedness, immigration, the World Court. . . . This bulky nickel's worth of print and pictures is a kind of social and emotional common denominator of American life.[10]

This is an early statement, though not a unique one, that speaks to Secret One—The media are essential components of our lives. It does not imply that magazines are the creators of our world. Rather, it claims that the magazine is an integral, inseparable part of who we are in the media world.

With the coming of television, the *Post* found its preeminent position in American culture fading. The world was changing, but the *Post* did not change with it. It was stuck in the middle-class America of the pre–World War II era that it depicted in its Norman Rockwell covers. Following a series of editorial and advertising missteps, the *Post* gradually became a monthly publication, and as of 2001, it was being published only bimonthly as a nostalgia and health magazine. The coming of television also forced magazines in general to change from appealing to broad audiences to focusing on narrower, more specific ones.

Questioning the Media

In the 1800s, magazines were our major national-level medium. Which media serve that role today? Are magazines still a "magic mirror" of our culture? If not, what's replaced them? Is this new medium a more interactive mirror? Why or why not?

The Birth of Photojournalism

In addition to providing the first national source of news and commentary, magazines were the first source of **photojournalism**—the use of photographs to portray the news in print. At first, pictures were printed in periodicals by using hand-engraved plates copied from photographs. Then in the 1880s came the invention of the **halftone**, an image produced by a process in which photographs are broken down into a series of dots that appear in shades of gray on the printed page. The halftone allowed the photograph to be reproduced directly in the publication rather than being copied into a drawing.

photojournalism: The use of photographs to portray the news in print.

halftone: An image produced by a process in which photographs are broken down into a series of dots that appear in shades of gray on the printed page.

 Web 5.3: View the Library of Congress's collection of Civil War era photos.

Photographer Mathew Brady is often credited with inventing photojournalism in the mid-nineteenth century. In 1845, Brady began to become famous for his portraits of noted Americans. He attempted to sell printed reproductions of his photographs, and though the effort failed because the costs were too high, he set the stage for later celebrity photographers, such as Annie Leibovitz. Brady also realized that much of the value of his photographic portraits came from their being reproduced as engravings, woodcuts, lithographs, and the like. The original was valuable, but so were the reproductions. Today Brady is best remembered for his pictures of the American Civil War, the first war to be photographed from beginning to end.

During the war, Brady was as much a studio operator as a photographer. He supervised the work of a number of talented photographers, and he made sure that the photos found their way into magazines and newspapers. By 1863, *Harper's Weekly* was reproducing Brady's Civil War photos, which horrified American audiences. The photographers followed the Union Army in wagons filled with their equipment and portable darkrooms. Many of the photos credited to Brady, whose eyesight was failing, were likely shot by his assistants. Photographers working for Brady often got extremely close to the line of fire. Thomas C. Roche, who often worked for Brady, got so close that he was seen shaking dirt off himself and his camera after shells hit nearby. In fact, some of Brady's best photographers left his employ so that they might get the credit they thought they deserved for taking pictures under such dangerous conditions. Brady's greatest contribution was not so much the individual war photographs that he may or may not have taken, but what evolved from the photographs: the idea that photographs are published documents preserving history.[11]

███ █ ███████ ██ ███ █ ███

The Magazine Business

After the American Civil War, the number of magazines and their circulation grew rapidly. This growth was fueled by a number of factors, such as the emergence of a new middle class, whose members had learned to read in public schools and were now starting to read magazines. Also, a growing number of national advertisers saw the magazine as an efficient means by which to reach their target audiences. Magazine distribution was aided by the **Postal Act of 1879**, which allowed periodicals to be mailed across the

nation easily and inexpensively. Improvements in printing, typesetting, and illustration engraving also contributed to the growth of magazines.

The Economics of Magazine Publishing

The post–Civil War era saw the introduction of several magazines, including *Popular Science*, *Good Housekeeping*, *National Geographic*, *Vogue*, and *Outdoor Life*, that are still in existence. From the start, these magazines provided news, ideas, advice for the home, and entertainment. They are all examples of **consumer magazines**—publications targeting an audience of like-minded consumers. As of 2012, there were approximately 7,390 consumer magazines.[12] Of those, 231 were new magazines launched in 2012.

Consumer magazines cover a wide range of topics, but if it seems to you that the most popular subject is celebrities, you aren't far off. An analysis of the content of top consumer magazines found that the largest number of pages (14.6 percent) were devoted to entertainment and celebrity coverage. This was followed by apparel and accessories with 13.1 percent of the pages and food and nutrition with 8.5 percent of the pages. You can see the full analysis in Table 5.1.[13]

Deriving their revenue from subscriptions, newsstand sales, and advertising, consumer magazines tend to be the most visible and profitable segment of the industry. Their continued success is due to their focus on specific audiences; they stand in contrast to the many general-interest magazines that have failed as new media took their places. Top magazine advertisers include toiletries and cosmetics, food and food products, pharmaceuticals, apparel and accessories, retail, and media and advertising.

Trade Magazines

The second major category of periodicals consists of **trade magazines** (also known as business-to-business magazines), which are published for people who work in a particular industry or business. Trade magazines tend to be smaller, less colorful, and more specialized than consumer

Web 5.4: Read the latest on magazine statistics.

Postal Act of 1879: Legislation that allowed magazines to be mailed nationally at a low cost. It was a key factor in the growth of magazine circulation in the late nineteenth century.

consumer magazines: Publications targeting an audience of like-minded consumers.

trade magazines: Magazines published for people who work in a particular industry or business.

magazines. While there are about twice as many trade magazines as consumer magazines, they account for only about 17 percent of the industry's revenue.[14] Trade magazines vary radically in circulation, scope, and the degree to which people outside of the industry know about them. For example, *Women's Wear Daily* is routinely quoted in the mainstream press and talked about by anyone interested in fashion. On the other hand, *Practical Accountant*, which covers all aspects of public accounting, is unlikely to be heard of outside of its very specialized field. The biggest topics for trade magazines are the computer industry, agriculture, medicine, and manufacturing.[15] Whereas some trade magazines are available by subscription, many have *controlled* circulation, meaning that people have to qualify in order to subscribe. For example, the grocery trade magazine *Refrigerated & Frozen Foods* is sent free of charge to people who work as frozen food producers, processors, and marketers. Subscribers have to fill out a survey form once or twice a year to continue qualifying for their free subscription. Advertisers know that most of the people who receive the magazine actually buy the products being advertised.[16] Trade magazines have suffered during the recent recession, with ad revenues down more than 30 percent in 2009.[17]

Literary and Commentary Magazines

Although today in the United States there are relatively few **literary magazines**—publications that focus on serious essays and short fiction—they were part and parcel of the magazine market of the 1800s. Two that still survive are *Harper's* (not to be confused with *Harper's Bazaar*) and the *Atlantic*.

The literary magazines helped to establish authors such as American writers Edgar Allan Poe and Mark Twain, as well as British writers such as Joseph Conrad and Thomas Hardy. *Harper's* magazine was founded in 1850 and was known for its illustrations, especially during the American Civil War. By 1863, *Harper's Weekly* was reproducing Mathew Brady's portraits and Civil War photos. *Harper's* continues today as an influential publication, best known for its monthly "Index" of loosely connected facts and statistics.

In recent years, the *Atlantic* (known in the past as *Atlantic Monthly*) has gained a reputation for publishing provocative nonfiction by authors such as Tracy Kidder, and it still occasionally publishes poetry and short fiction. (Take a look back at Table 5.1 to see how small a role fiction plays in magazine content these days.) Despite the overall trend toward specialization, the *Atlantic* has been doing

---

literary magazines: Publications that focus on serious essays and short fiction.

| Table 5.1 | Top Magazine Topics by Page Count, 2013 |

Type of content	Pages	Percent
Entertainment/Celebrity	18,724	14.6%
Wearing apparel/Accessories	16,902	13.1%
Food and nutrition	10,913	8.5%
Business and industry	9,079	7.1%
Home furnishings/Management	8,765	6.8%
Culture	7,464	5.8%
Travel/Transportation	6,975	5.4%
Miscellaneous	6,258	4.9%
Beauty and grooming	6,233	4.8%
Sports/Recreation/Hobby	5,738	4.5%
National affairs	4,919	3.8%
General interest	4,502	3.5%
Health/Medical science	4,134	3.2%
Self-help/Relationships	3,921	3.0%
Personal finance	2,996	2.3%
Fitness/Beauty	2,455	1.9%
Building	2,380	1.9%
Global/Foreign affairs	2,132	1.7%
Gardening and farming	1,415	1.1%
Children	1,246	1.0%
Consumer electronics	1,098	0.9%
Fiction	403	0.3%

Sean Gearhart/Getty Images

Source: Adapted by the author from *Magazine Media Factbook* 2013/2014 (New York: Association of Magazine Media, 2013).

well in the twenty-first century. It cut back from twelve to ten issues a year in 2007 but has had a steady increase in circulation, and in 2010, it turned its first profit in decades, based in large part on its increase in revenue from digital editions.[18] This trend continued through 2012, with the *Atlantic* seeing modest growth in magazine circulation and much larger growth with its online properties.[19] (You can read more about how the *Atlantic* turned profitable through its digital strategy in the section on the future of magazines at the end of the chapter.)

Political journals also flourished in the late nineteenth and early twentieth centuries. The *Nation* and the *New Republic* are examples of progressive political opinion still being published today. The *Nation*, founded in 1865, discussed current affairs, improving the lot of the working class, and civil rights. The *New Republic*, founded in 1914, promoted labor, civil rights, and antifascism. Both magazines featured letters from readers as an interactive forum for discussion. More than just filler, these letters were central to the magazines' content. The idea of reader feedback as a central component of a publication has reached its full potential on Internet magazines that feature elaborate discussion boards.

The *Nation* and the *New Republic* depend on subsidies from the capitalist system they often criticize. Although the *Nation* claims to be the oldest continuously published American weekly, it loses money every year.[20] According to publisher Victor Navasky, the magazine's poor financial showing is due to a combination of factors, including small circulation and the fact that the magazine is not "advertiser friendly":

> At *The Nation*, we're in the business of attacking the companies that more financially successful magazines are in the business of soliciting for advertising, most notably tobacco. But these titles of opinion are at the core of what journalism should be about, and at their best, they can set the standard for the profession.[21]

William F. Buckley's *National Review* was founded in 1955 as a conservative response to these magazines. In terms of circulation, it is the largest of the three discussed here (more than 178,000 copies per month). Although it is technically a for-profit venture, which means it can endorse candidates and legislation, its leading source of income remains donations from readers. As is typical for opinion magazines, the conservative *National Review* gains readership when Democrats are in power and loses readership when Republicans win elections. (That pattern is reversed for the liberal *New Republic* and *Nation*, which lose circulation when Democrats win elections.[22]) Founder Buckley died in 2008, and his son Christopher left the board of directors of the magazine after endorsing Barack Obama for president.

The Crisis: *Giving African Americans a Voice.*

One of the most important functions of a magazine of ideas is to offer a voice to those who otherwise would be kept silent. That was the purpose of W. E. B. Du Bois's journal, the *Crisis*. Du Bois, a Harvard-educated civil rights leader, started the *Crisis* as the official voice of the National Association for the Advancement of Colored

People (NAACP) in 1910. At first, the magazine had only 1,000 subscribers, but by 1920, it had a monthly circulation of 100,000. The *Crisis* became as successful as other political journals, such as the *Nation* and the *New Republic*, with almost as many white readers as black readers.

At its inception, the journal was one of a very few outlets for black writers. "Up until [1910] there were only five black writers who'd been published. The NAACP saw a need for art and literature," said Manie Barron, who edited an anthology of writings from the *Crisis*.[23] The *Crisis* was the leading voice against segregation in the South. It published debates between Du Bois and African American educator and leader Booker T. Washington over the proper role of black education and featured the first appearance of many of Langston Hughes's poems.[24]

Du Bois edited the *Crisis* until 1934. After he stepped down, the journal gradually became more of an African American consumer magazine than an independent journal of black intellectual writing. To address the problem, the NAACP suspended publication of the magazine for

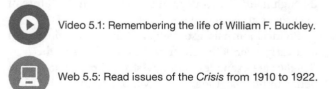

Video 5.1: Remembering the life of William F. Buckley.

Web 5.5: Read issues of the *Crisis* from 1910 to 1922.

William F. Buckley Jr. founded the *National Review* as a conservative response to magazines such as the *New Republic* and the *Nation*.

AP Photo/ The Journal Gazette, Ed Breen

about a year in the mid-1990s to work on giving it a new focus. According to civil rights leader Julian Bond, who oversaw the remake of the magazine, "[The *Crisis*] was once the place where you read about race, and the new board wanted to make it that again." In 2008, the magazine moved from being a monthly publication to quarterly in order to control costs, and in 2010, the *Crisis* celebrated its hundredth anniversary.[25]

The Muckrakers. Investigative reporting was made famous by the Watergate political scandal of the early 1970s, but it began in the late 1800s at several newspapers and magazines. The most lasting examples came from the so-called muckraking magazines. The term **muckrakers** was coined by President Theodore Roosevelt to describe socially activist investigative journalists publishing in progressive-minded magazines in the early years of the twentieth century. Although Roosevelt favored the social and political reforms that the exposés clearly indicated were necessary, he suggested that the investigative reporters who published such stories were "muckraking"—that is, they were digging up dirt without stopping to see the good things in the world.

The most famous of the muckrakers was Samuel S. McClure, who led the fight at the beginning of the twentieth century for "business, social, and political reform."[26] Although McClure was a reformer, he also sought to make a profit through the investigative articles he published in his magazine, *McClure's*. Although the writing in *McClure's* was sensationalistic, it was based on fact. Circulation skyrocketed, and it was hard to find copies of the magazine on newsstands. Advertisers liked the magazine for the attention it attracted and its high readership.

McClure's took on the insurance industry, the railroads, and urban problems. Two of the most prominent writers at *McClure's* were Lincoln Steffens and Ida Tarbell. Steffens started work at *McClure's* in 1902 and was quickly sent out into the field to report on municipal government corruption. Over the next two years, his reporting on the misdeeds of officials in St. Louis, Minneapolis, Pittsburgh, Philadelphia, Chicago, and New York led to indictments and reform. The resulting six articles were eventually collected in the classic book *The Shame of the Cities*.[27] But the magazine's most famous target was Standard Oil. Tarbell had been assigned to write a series of stories that would showcase the oil giant's achievements. Working with the full cooperation of company officials, Tarbell spent five years writing the fifteen-article series, which revealed that the company had achieved its incredible success through the use of bribes, fraud, and violence.[28]

By 1908, the muckraking movement had played itself out. The original talented and committed muckrakers had moved on to other pursuits, and they were replaced by people who were more concerned with sensationalism than with accuracy.

Newsmagazines

Henry Luce, through the now-enormous Time Warner media empire, has probably done more to shape the American media environment than virtually anyone else. Luce was born in China, the son of a Christian missionary, and he graduated from Yale in 1920. He conceived the idea of *Time* magazine while in prep school with his friend Briton Hadden.

The two founded the magazine in 1923 as a reaction against the journalism of the time. They wanted a magazine that would keep readers up-to-date on current events in a single weekly magazine. Organized around news departments, *Time* was written in a style that put the news in context and told the reader how to think about the issues—a style that the magazine maintains to this day. While *Time* presents multiple sides of a story, it also indicates which side the magazine thinks is correct, rejecting the notion of objectivity as impossible.

Luce later took on the world of business with *Fortune*, a glossy magazine featuring the photography of Margaret Bourke-White. The magazine's purpose was to "reflect industrial life as faithfully in ink and paper and word as the finest skyscraper reflects it in stone, steel, and architecture."[29] Luce also was convinced that Americans wanted to get their news through pictures, so he started *Life* magazine in 1936. A success from the start, *Life* had 230,000 subscribers for its first issue and a print order for 466,000 copies. Within four months, the print order was for more than 1 million copies.[30]

When *Life* was launched, the big star at the magazine was neither the editor nor a writer; it was photographer Margaret Bourke-White. Bourke-White was more than just a photographer—she became a cultural icon. Bourke-White's greatest love was industrial photography. Smokestacks, trains, steam pipes, bursts of flame—these were the subjects she most wanted to shoot. In 1929, Henry Luce, the founder of *Time*, saw Bourke-White's photos of the Otis Steel mill and foundry and decided that she was the photographer he wanted to take pictures for his new magazine, *Fortune*. Bourke-White shot photos using such daring methods as hanging off the stone gargoyles at the tops of skyscrapers. She also photographed in Russia at a time when most foreigners were not allowed to take pictures of Soviet industry.[31]

---

muckrakers: Progressive investigative journalists typically publishing in magazines in the early years of the twentieth century.

 Web 5.6: See famous images from *Life* magazine.

on a lifeboat in the middle of the night, Bourke-White's biggest frustration was that the darkness prevented her from taking photographs:

> I could think of nothing but the magnificent pictures unfolding before me, which I longed to take and could not. I suppose for all photographers their greatest pictures are their untaken ones, and I am no exception. For me the indelible untaken photograph is the picture of our sinking ship viewed from our dangling lifeboat.[33]

Margaret Bourke-White rests her camera on a steel gargoyle at the top of New York's Chrysler Building in 1934.

In 1936, Bourke-White journeyed across the South with writer Erskine Caldwell, who had written the controversial novels *God's Little Acre* and *Tobacco Road*. At the time, Caldwell was America's most banned writer because of his sexually explicit (for the time) descriptions of relationships between men and women. Together Caldwell and Bourke-White documented the poverty of the South in the book *Have You Seen Their Faces?*

Following Bourke-White's work at *Fortune*, Luce put her to work on *Life* two months before it started publication. Her first assignment for the new magazine was photographing the dams of the Columbia River basin. But she also shot pictures of people living in Montana—the taxi dancers in the bars, the prostitutes, the customers bowling. The cover photo was typical of Bourke-White's industrial photography: the monumental Fort Peck Dam with a couple of tiny figures included to indicate scale. But her photo essay about the people in the bar, which included a picture of a four-year-old who sat there at night while her mother waited tables, created an uproar among *Life*'s readers and brought the magazine a tremendous amount of attention.[32]

During World War II, Bourke-White became the first woman photographer accredited by the U.S. Army. The army even designed a uniform for her that became the model for those worn by all women correspondents. During the war, she was on an American ship in the Mediterranean Sea that was torpedoed by a German U-boat. As she left the ship

Luce went on to create *Sports Illustrated*, which debuted on August 12, 1954. Critics suggested that the magazine would face an early demise because no one would be interested in it. After all, football fans wouldn't want to read about basketball or hockey. But by 1968, *Sports Illustrated* had a circulation of 1.5 million, and it currently sells more than 3.1 million copies a week.[34]

As of this writing in the spring of 2014, Time Warner was preparing to spin off its magazine properties, including *Time*, *Sports Illustrated,* and *People,* as a freestanding company.[35] (See Chapter 3 for more on this change.)

Women's Magazines

One of the biggest categories of consumer magazines is those targeted at women. Women's magazines got their start in 1830, when Louis Godey began publishing *Godey's Lady's Book*. Edited by Sarah Josepha Hale from 1837 to 1877, *Godey's* was one of the most influential magazines dealing with American life, even though it was much more lowbrow than *Harper's* or *Atlantic Monthly*. According to magazine historian James Wood,

> Godey's became an American institution in the nineteenth century. It affected the manners, morals, tastes, fashions in the clothes, homes, and diet of generations of American readers. It did much to form the American woman's idea of what she was like, how she should act, and how she should insist that she be treated.[36]

Godey's also was a place where women writers could be published alongside established male authors. Hale took

---

Web 5.7: See the complete text and picture plates of *Godey's* January 1851 issue.

responsibility for openly promoting women writers. Previously, women writers had to use initials or male pseudonyms, or they had to publish in unsigned columns. Hale, however, boldly printed the names of women authors. In the same way that the *Crisis* gave voice to African American writers, *Godey's* gave women a forum. (Black women's magazines existed then as well. For example, *Ringwood's Afro-American Journal of Fashion* was being published in Cleveland in the 1890s.)

Hale also campaigned for education and exercise for women, so it isn't surprising that illustrations in *Godey's* frequently showed women carrying books, magazines, and letters. Hale argued that women needed to receive an education for their own sakes, not just to make them better wives and mothers. The fiction Hale published in *Godey's* even portrayed single women leading satisfying lives.

Hale wrote a column for fourteen years, and her last editorial appeared in *Godey's* in December 1877. She was eighty-nine years old. Hale died in 1879, and though the magazine lived on without her for a while, it was never the same.

Why does Hale still matter to us today? It is because women's magazines continue to follow in her footsteps. They provide a place for women to come together apart from men and provide material that is of specific interest to women, such as articles about women's health. They also celebrate women artists and writers.[37]

The "Seven Sisters." Following in the tradition of *Godey's Lady's Book* were the mainstream women's **service magazines**—magazines that primarily contain articles about how to do things in a better way. These articles cover such topics as health advice, cooking tips, employment help, and fashion guides. The top service magazines were once known as the "seven sisters": *Good Housekeeping, McCall's, Redbook, Ladies' Home Journal, Woman's Day, Better Homes and Gardens,* and *Family Circle.* Each is distinctive, but they all deal with a concern for home, family, and quality of life from a traditional woman's perspective.

Cyrus H. K. Curtis founded the *Ladies' Home Journal* in 1883, and in many ways, it was essentially the same magazine then that it was when it shut down in 2014. It promoted a traditional view of a woman's role in the home; it told her how to dress, what to cook, how to raise children, and how to decorate the house. But it also dealt with issues that were controversial at the time, such as venereal disease and premarital sex. In 1906, the magazine argued against the so-called double standard, in which young men were allowed to sow their wild oats while women were expected to remain virgins. Women and children were paying the

service magazines: Magazines that primarily contain articles about how to do things in a better way. These articles cover such topics as health advice, cooking tips, employment help, and fashion guides.

Godey's Lady's Book, under editor Sarah Josepha Hale, featured hand-colored fashion plates of the latest styles from Europe, such as those pictured here from 1842.

price, the magazine argued, because parents would not discuss the implications of sexual promiscuity with their sons, and the young men who were most promiscuous and likely to carry disease were those most likely to appeal to women. Similar concerns about AIDS and other sexually transmitted diseases appear in magazines today.[38]

The "seven sisters" were reduced to six in 2001 when *McCall's*, founded in 1876, ceased publication. It was reformulated and renamed *Rosie*, after television talk show host and movie star Rosie O'Donnell. The new magazine was successful, experiencing growing circulation and ad pages, until O'Donnell quit her talk show and publicly came out as a lesbian, at which point she started having trouble with her publisher. The feud over editorial direction and the choice of editor led to the magazine's folding in December 2002. *Rosie* was the first major women's service magazine to cease publication since 1957.[39]

Anna Wintour shows off the style she promotes as editor of *Vogue*—the fashion bible.

Then, in the summer of 2014, *Ladies' Home Journal* ceased publication as a monthly, moving to being a "quarterly, newsstand-only publication with 'a robust digital presence.'" According to reporting from industry publication *Ad Age*, though the *Journal* had held onto its circulation well with 3.2 million subscribers, it had had serious declines in advertising revenue. A spokesperson for Meredith, the *Journal's* publisher, told *Ad Age,* "You've got a women's lifestyle field that has expanded from the original Seven Sisters to a much broader field competing for limited ad dollars."[40]

Fashion/Beauty/Lifestyle Magazines.
The fashion/beauty/lifestyle (FBL) magazines are read by about 40 million women every month. This number includes the

Web 5.8: Take a look back at *Ladies Home Journal* over the years.

Video 5.2: Get to know famed women's magazine editor Bonnie Fuller.

readers of women's service magazines, as well as those who read the more youth-oriented magazines, such as *Glamour* and *Cosmopolitan.*

Compared to service magazines, the fashion books (magazines are often called books in the trade) focus more on clothes and style and less on lifestyle. Prominent among them are *Vogue* and *Harper's Bazaar. Vogue,* which we discussed in the opening vignette, was established in 1892 and has long been the leading fashion magazine. Edna Woolman Chase started working for *Vogue* in the 1890s, became its editor in 1914, and remained there until 1952, thus becoming one of the longest-tenured voices in fashion. *Vogue* has some editorial content about people, culture, and ideas, but it is devoted primarily to fashion, both in its editorial content and in its advertising. *Vogue* has long been an international presence, with Paris, Milan, and London editions, and it started publishing a Russian edition in 1998.

Each of the FBLs claims that it has a unique editorial focus. Such protestations aside, the magazines may be more alike than they are different. Paula Span of the *Washington Post,* a former freelance writer for *Glamour,* says,

> [These magazines] take a remarkably narrow view of women's interests. The proverbial visitor from space would conclude that earthling women in their twenties and thirties care only about their bodies and what to put in them and on them, their relationships with men and, to a far lesser extent, their jobs; the rest of the world is largely absent.[41]

Cosmopolitan. If the "seven sisters" were the most venerable members of the women's magazine family, *Cosmopolitan* is the naughty cousin. Until 1996, *Cosmo* spoke with the voice of its longtime editor, Helen Gurley Brown. Brown took over at *Cosmo* in 1965 and turned the "insipid, faintly intellectual" magazine into *the* magazine for young women, with a peak circulation of 3 million in 1985. (As of 2013, *Cosmo* had a monthly circulation of just over 3 million.[42]) Brown coined the term *mouseburger* to describe the quiet, introverted "girl" *Cosmo* was out to help. Under Brown, readers were "*Cosmo* girls," though more recently the magazine has updated its image to "fun, fearless, and female."

Cosmo has always focused on practical advice about relationships, work, fashion, health, beauty, and sex. But when acclaimed women's magazine editor Bonnie Fuller took over the helm, the magazine started dealing with issues such as AIDS and sexual harassment. Fuller told the *New York Times,* "I wanted to make it more seductive, not so much in a sexual sense, but in a sense that the reader just couldn't wait to get it and then just couldn't possibly put it down."[43] Fuller also eliminated the occasional male pinups that have appeared in *Cosmo* over the years. (The most famous pinup was the one of Burt Reynolds published in 1972. His nude photo in *Cosmo* may have cost him the Oscar for the movie *Deliverance.*)

Cosmopolitan has a presence that extends far beyond the United States, with fifty-six international editions published in locations such as Britain, Thailand, Poland, Indonesia, and Malaysia. Its British edition has a circulation in excess of 400,000 copies a month. Critics charge that *Cosmo* is exporting American culture and values to the rest of the world. Helen Gurley Brown, who remained as editor of the international editions after stepping down as editor of the U.S. edition, had this to say to the *South China Morning Post*:

People have very flatteringly said that *Cosmo* is like Coca-Cola or McDonald's, and I say "Glory Hallelujah!" There is nothing bad about Coca-Cola—unless you drink too much of it—and McDonald's makes delicious hamburgers. We are exporting what people want. . . . We're not trying to change Asian culture. . . . It's a magazine for women who love men, who love children and motherhood, and who have a choice of doing work. Now, that doesn't sound so heinous or reprehensible, does it?[44]

Kevin Foy/Alamy

This collection of women's magazines for sale in China illustrates the incredible diversity in the magazine market. Among them are a Chinese edition of the American magazine *Fitness*, a Japanese manga, and several Chinese magazines.

Men's Magazines

Many men's magazines, such as *Field & Stream* and *Motor Trend*, appeal to men through their hobbies. Women might read them, but the target audience is male. There are also men's magazines featuring provocative photos of women, such as *Playboy* and (originally) *Esquire*. The most recent trend in men's magazines is toward lifestyle magazines that resemble women's magazines but are intended for men; these include *Maxim* and *Men's Health*.

Esquire: *A Morale Booster for the Troops.*
Esquire was founded in 1933, and though it published original work by writers such as Ernest Hemingway and F. Scott Fitzgerald, it was also known for its risqué pinups by artists Alberto Vargas and George Petty. These airbrushed drawings of impossibly perfect women frequently got the magazine into legal trouble for violating obscenity laws, but the pictures would be considered extremely mild by today's standards. (The University of Kansas houses the *Esquire* archives of pinup art, some of which is quite valuable. The collection's estimated value is between $10 and $20 million.) *Esquire*, due in no small part to its pinups, was considered an important morale booster during World War II and the Korean conflict, with comedian Bob Hope quoted as saying, "Our American troops are ready to fight at the drop of an *Esquire*."[45]

In recent years, *Esquire* has suffered from an identity crisis and experienced declining circulation and advertising revenue. It has changed ownership at least twice in recent decades, and it has changed its look and formula several times. Despite its problems, *Esquire* always has room for fine writing. Jim Harrison's *Legends of the Fall* first appeared there, as did many of Tom Wolfe's most influential nonfiction articles in the 1960s. In the early 2000s, *Esquire* returned to its roots and started placing greater emphasis on good writing and, as a result, picked up advertisers who want to reach a more upscale audience and more subscribers.[46]

Playboy: *A Magazine and a Lifestyle.*
Playboy first appeared in 1953 as a competitor to *Esquire*, and it made no pretense about what it was really about—pictures of nude women—though, like *Esquire*, it publishes articles by many noted writers. But in addition to the photos and the articles, *Playboy* promoted a lifestyle: the sexually free good life.

Founder Hugh Hefner started out doing circulation promotion for *Esquire* at $60 a week. He wanted to create a magazine that would appeal to young urban males much like himself. He started by paying $200 for color printing plates and the rights to publish a nude photo of Marilyn Monroe. He obtained permission to reprint stories and articles by well-known writers, as well as cartoons and dirty jokes. After collecting subscriptions from around the country, he started *Playboy* for less than $7,000.[47] Hefner says that he would like to be remembered for changing attitudes toward sex: "I would like to be remembered as someone who has had a significant impact in changing sexual values, in changing the repressive attitudes toward sexuality."[48]

Although *Playboy* still goes out to 1.3 million readers every month (it sold 7 million copies a month at its peak of popularity in 1972 and was down to 2.6 million readers in 2008), it gets very little attention compared to newcomers such as *Maxim*. In September 2002, *Playboy* hired away

Maxim's executive editor in an attempt to bring a more modern attitude to the aging magazine.[49]

Maxim: *The Rebirth of Men's Magazines.*

The top men's magazine is *Maxim*, which offers a blend of sex, sports, and humor. Launched in April 1997 as a spin-off of the British version, it has been highly influential, and *Details*, *GQ*, and *Esquire* have all mimicked its style. As of 2013, *Maxim* had a monthly circulation of 2 million copies, enough to make it the thirty-first-largest circulation magazine in the United States (see Table 5.2 for a list of the top ten magazines). As recently as 1998, it wasn't even in the top 200. (For comparison, *Men's Health* is the number-two men's magazine, coming in at thirty-fifth on the circulation list.) If you measure magazine success by number of ad pages, however, the more fashion- and current events–oriented *GQ* is at the top.[50]

Questioning the Media

How do magazines appealing to men and women differ from each other? What do the articles in each tell you about the audiences? Are these magazines getting more alike or more different over time? What accounts for the change, or lack of it, in a magazine's content over the years?

Table 5.2 What Are the Top Ten Magazines?

Magazine	Circulation***
1. *AARP The Magazine*	21,931,184*
2. *Game Informer*	7,829,179**
3. *Better Homes and Gardens*	7,624,505
4. *Reader's Digest*	5,241,484
5. *Good Housekeeping*	4,396,795
6. *Family Circle*	4,014,881
7. *National Geographic*	4,001,937
8. *People*	3,542,185
9. *Woman's Day*	3,394754
10. *Time*	3,301,056

Source: "Magazines by Circulation for Six Months, Ended June 30, 2013." *Advertising Age*, adage.com/datacenter/datapopup.php?article_id=244466. Reprinted with permission from Advertising Age/American Demographics. © Crain Communications Inc., 2014.

AARP The Magazine may be a bit of a surprise as the top magazine in the country, but as the magazine of AARP, it goes out to every member.

**Game Informer* was the number-eleven magazine in 2008, with a circulation of 3,517,598.

***Sports Illustrated* comes in at thirteen (3.1 million), *Cosmopolitan* at fourteen (3 million), *O, The Oprah Magazine* at eighteen (2.4 million), *Maxim* at thirty-one (2 million), *Rolling Stone* at fifty (1.5 million), and *Playboy* at fifty-nine (1.3 million).

Web 5.9: Read more about magazines, media, and body image.

Former editor Mark Golin, one of the few men to have been on the staff at *Cosmopolitan*, says that *Maxim* stands out among men's magazines because it is not about a single topic, such as cars, clothes, or computers. Instead, it tries to meet the needs of the "inner guy." "There's a guy inside all men," Golin told the *New York Times*, "and whether you're pumping gas in Iowa or you're working on Wall Street, you can't ignore your inner guy."[51]

The *Times* has referred to *Maxim* as "the *Playboy* of the 1990s," and its cleavage-laden covers and sexy humor would seem to support that label. Why the adolescent focus on women? Golin explained it this way: "I think if you are going to have a general-interest magazine for men, well—surprise, surprise, one of men's general interests is women."[52]

One reason magazines such as *Maxim* are so profitable is that they attract a great deal of fashion and gadget advertising. They feature scantily clad women, reviews of electronics, entertainment, fashion, and humor. Moreover, they tend to feature "quick tidbits" of information rather than full-fledged articles.[53]

In Britain, *Maxim* and competitors *FHM* and *Loaded* have seen sharp declines in circulation in recent years, as have the weekly magazines for men, *Zoo* and *Nuts*. The weeklies feature the same raunchy sexual content but have more up-to-date humor and sports gossip.[54] What has taken their place as the most popular men's magazine? *Men's Health*, which features articles on improving your diet, drinking less, and exercising more.[55]

Adventuring is another important area for men's magazines. Some men like to go looking for danger, and magazine articles give readers a chance to do so—but safely. For example, an issue of *Men's Journal* contained an article titled "Climb Mount Rainier: A Serious Mountaineering Challenge With Minimal Risk of Headline-Making Deaths. Call It Everest for Everyman."[56]

The magazine industry has recently tapped men as a major new audience for service magazines such as *Men's Health* and *Men's Journal*. The editors of these magazines have been featured in gossip columns and are getting the kind of high-profile media attention that was formerly limited to the editors of leading women's magazines such as *Vogue* and *Harper's Bazaar*.[57]

Magazines and Modern Society

Magazines may not hold the dominant place in the media market today that they did in the late nineteenth and early twentieth centuries, but they are still a critical component of our culture. One reason magazines remain important is that they are able to reach narrow, specific communities with a slickly produced message. Among the major controversies surrounding magazines today are the images of women they present, the blurring of editorial and advertising content, the level of reality in editorial content, and the appropriateness of material aimed at teenagers.

Magazines and Body Image

It's no secret that a significant number of girls and young women suffer from eating disorders as a result of their quest to find beauty through thinness. The trend toward excessive thinness as a standard of beauty has become more prominent in recent decades. In 1972, 23 percent of U.S. women said that they were dissatisfied with their overall appearance. By 1996, that figure had grown to 48 percent. Critics frequently charge that the thin models in fashion magazines (both in ads and in editorial content) are at least partially responsible for promoting extreme thinness as attractive. In 1953, when Marilyn Monroe was featured in the debut issue of *Playboy*, she was a size twelve with measurements close to the then-ideal of 36-22-35, which by today's standard would make her a **plus-sized model**. Today, the much-photographed Jennifer Aniston is an impossible (for most women) size zero.[58]

British Calvin Klein model Kate Moss was known in the 1990s for her waif-like look that was dubbed "heroin chic" because of her resemblance to an emaciated heroin addict. After Moss admitted she had been drunk on the job for ten years, Calvin Klein ended his long-running contract with the super-thin model, though the designer claimed the separation had nothing to do with her confession.[59] The controversy surrounding Moss went beyond her drinking, alleged drug usage, heroin-chic look, and posing nude in slick magazine advertisements for jeans and underwear. The big source of criticism was that she presented an unrealistic and unobtainable image of what an attractive woman should look like. A teenage girl who ran track, weighed ninety-five pounds, and was five feet tall told *People* magazine,

> I'm not happy if I think I look fat in what I'm wearing. Kate Moss looks so cool in a bathing suit. I don't know if I'm conditioned [to think this way] or if it's just me, but I don't think anything could make me abandon my desire to be thin.[60]

SECRET 3 ▶ Advertisers of products other than clothing have become concerned about the thin image being presented in fashion magazines. When photos of model Trish Goff appeared in the British edition of *Vogue* in 1996, Omega Watches pulled its ads from the magazine, saying that the magazine was portraying skeletal, anorexic-looking models.[61]

By 2006, criticism of overly thin models was coming from no less than former Victoria's Secret model Frederique van der Wal. The Fashion Week shows that year in Madrid, Spain, banned models whose body mass index was too low.[62] In 2007, Madrid's Fashion Week shows again banned super-thin models, as did the Milan shows.

A model walks the runway at the British Plus Size Fashion Weekend show during London Fashion Week. Plus size models are becoming more common in magazines as the publications try to feature a full range of size in their fashion spreads.

Remember Secret Three—Everything from the margin moves to the center? It's possible that the willingness of women's magazines to use models of differing sizes is becoming more commonplace than it was several years ago.

It all started back in 2005 with the Dove Campaign for Real Beauty and its so-called Lumpy Ladies. That ad campaign, featuring attractive women of a variety of sizes posing in their underwear for photographer Annie Leibovitz, helped open up a dialogue about size, beauty, and magazine content. Were we going to see more images of "realistic-looking" women in magazine features and advertisements?[63] (That, of course, begs the question as to what constitutes "real women." Are size-two women not real? Or is it more that average-sized women are ignored by the media?)

The campaign paved the way for differently sized models (although they are still the exception rather than the rule, as can be seen in several examples from 2011). The cover of the June 2011 issue of Italian *Vogue* featured scantily clad plus-sized models Tara Lynn, Candice Huffine, and Robyn Lawley sitting around a table set with bowls of pasta as part of an effort to fight anorexia among fans of fashion magazines. The inside photos went considerably further, featuring sexually charged images shot by photographer Steven Meisel, who became famous for shooting singer Madonna's book *Sex*.[64]

---

plus-sized model: A female fashion model who wears an average or larger clothing size.

Presenting a Broader Range of Beauty

Walter Chin/Trunk Archive

How do you react to this *"unconventional"* photo of a model showing a belly pooch? Do you think it's unattractive, a great realistic image, or no big deal? Why do you think you have this instinctive reaction?

Glamour magazine set off something of an Internet uproar with a small photo it ran in its September 2009 issue. It was a nearly nude image of model Lizzie Miller sitting on a bench with a big smile on her face. As FBL magazine photos go, it's not a shocker. Certainly other photos in the magazine, either editorial or advertising, showed more skin. So why did this photo garner so much attention? Because Ms. Miller has a small belly pooch.

Glamour editor-in-chief Cindi Leive wrote on her blog:

It's a photo that measures all of three by three inches in our September issue, but the letters about it started to flood my inbox literally the day *Glamour* hit newsstands. . . . "I am gasping with delight . . . I love the woman on p 194!" said one . . . then another, and another, and another and another and another. So . . . who is she? And what on earth is so special about her?

Here's the deal: The picture wasn't of a celebrity. It wasn't of a supermodel. It was of a woman sitting in her underwear with a smile on her face and a belly that looks . . . wait for it . . . *normal*.[1]

The photo went with a story by Akiba Solomon about women feeling comfortable in their own skin. The photo had no caption, no mention of who the model was, no mention of the fact that she wore a size twelve or fourteen and weighed 180 pounds.

The response to this small photo was big. In less than two weeks, more than 770 comments about the photo were posted to Leive's blog, not to mention the many e-mails. Most of the comments were laudatory. One woman called it "the most amazing photograph I've ever seen in any women's magazine," while another wrote, "Thank you Lizzie, for showing us your beauty and confidence, and giving women a chance to hopefully recognize a little of their own also."[2]

Not everyone loved the photo and what it stood for, however. One commenter wrote, "I must say I have to agree that the normalization of obesity is a disturbing trend today." Another commented, "We have enough problems with obesity in the US and don't need your magazine promoting anymore of it. Shame on *Glamour* for thinking this was sexy!"[3]

Mary Pipher, author of *Reviving Ophelia*, a book about teen girls and body image, says the new emphasis on diverse images of beauty in fashion magazines is a

good, if limited, step. "Presenting a broader range of beauty, even if it's under the guise of selling cosmetics, gives girls more permission to think they too are attractive."[4]

Miller told journalist Lydia Slater of London's *Daily Mail* that she initially felt embarrassed when the photo was published because it showed her stretch marks and a tummy roll. "I said to myself: 'OK, It's not the best picture, but it's not a big deal. And anyway, nobody's going to see it.'"[5] But more than a year after the photo was published, Miller had become a superstar of the modeling world and says she has become much more accepting of her own size. "We need to be celebrating skinny girls, curvy girls, tall girls, short girls, black girls, Asian girls, and all nationalities," Miller said. "I think that would make women feel a lot better about themselves. We have a long way to go until a girl who's curvy can be in a magazine without a lot of attention being drawn to her."[6]

___

WHO is the source?

Who is Lizzie Miller? What does she do?

WHAT makes her photo from *Glamour* magazine stand out?

Look at the Lizzie Miller photo from *Glamour* magazine. What makes it differ from the typical photo in fashion/beauty/lifestyle magazines for women? What makes it differ from photos in special "size" issues of magazines?

WHAT do people say about the photo?

How does Miller describe her feelings about the photo? What did it do for her career? How did *Glamour*'s readers react to the photo? What did critics of the photo have to say?

HOW do you and your classmates react to the Miller photo?

What do you and your friends think about the Miller photo? Why do you think the photo drew such strong reactions? Is it important for fashion magazines to publish photos of models of different sizes? Will plus-sized models find a place in fashion spreads that aren't devoted to "curvy" models?

___

Web 5.10: Find out about model Lizzie Miller and "the photo."

[1]Cindi Leive, "On the C.L.: The Picture You Can't Stop Talking About: Meet 'The Woman on p. 194,'" *Glamour*, August 17, 2009, www.glamour.com/health-fitness/blogs/vitamin-g/2009/08/on-the-cl-the-picture-you-cant.html.
[2]Ibid.
[3]Ibid.
[4]Associated Press, "Fashion Magazines Showing More Body Types," *USA Today*, August 9, 2005.
[5]Lydia Slater, "The Spare Tyre That Started a Revolution: Model Lizzie Miller on the 'Embarrassing' Picture That Made Her a Star," *The Daily Mail*, September 20, 2010, www.dailymail.co.uk/femail/article-1313462/Plus-size-model-Lizzie-Miller-embarrassing-picture-star.html.
[6]Ibid.

The contrast between plus-sized models and more conventionally sized magazine models was highlighted with a story in *PLUS Model Magazine* (an online magazine at http://plus-model-mag.com/) that had relatively tame naked photos of plus-sized model Katya Zharkova next to an unnamed "straight-sized" model. *PLUS Model* editor in chief Madeline Figueroa-Jones explained the magazine's photo spread thusly:

The answer to the question is this, there is nothing wrong with our bodies. We are bombarded with weight-loss ads every single day, multiple times a day because it's a multi-billion dollar industry that preys on the fear of being fat. Not everyone is meant to be skinny, our bodies are beautiful and we are not talking about health here because not every skinny person is healthy.

What we desire is equality to shop and have fashion options just like smaller women. Small women cannot be marketed to with pictures of plus-size women, why are we expected to respond to pictures of small size 6 and 8 women? We don't! When the plus size modeling industry began, the models ranged in size from 14 to 18/20, and as customers we long for those days when we identify with the models and feel happy about shopping.[65]

Figueroa-Jones worked as a plus-sized model and now runs a photo agency in addition to editing *PLUS Model Magazine*. Although the article makes a number of unsupported claims about the average weight of women and models, there can be little doubt that models are significantly smaller than typical women.[66] The popular blog *Jezebel* notes that there are growing numbers of plus-sized models being featured in magazines, and not just in "the usual 'Love Your Body' special issues."[67]

Typical of the "Love Your Body" features that *Jezebel* was referring to is one from *V* magazine from its "size" issue, in which one story compared a "straight-sized" model with a plus-sized model, while a second story featured several plus-sized models, including Tara Lynn, in varying states of dress. Lynn also had the cover of the "curvy" issue of *Elle* France. But this may be starting to change, at least a little. In March 2014, as we discussed in the opening vignette, unconventional actress Lena Dunham was on the cover of *Vogue* as a celebrity, not as a part of a "special" issue.

Who's in Control? Advertising Versus Editorial

One of the biggest conflicts in the magazine business is the separation between the editorial and advertising departments. Articles attract readers, but advertisements pay many of the bills. So a continual struggle exists between editors and advertisers to keep content separate from advertisements, to please advertisers, and to make money for the publishers.

Synergy and Magazines.

We're used to seeing massive synergy in the movie and television business due to product placement and product-themed shows. But *Shape* magazine seems to have hit a new high—or low—with the practice. The September 2005 issue of the women's fitness magazine featured the cover line, "Win Liz Hurley's Cover Look." Hurley is on the cover wearing a bikini from her own line of clothing, and she's wearing makeup credited to Estée Lauder, for whom Hurley is a paid endorser. This all goes with a two-page ad inside the cover from the cosmetic maker. So Hurley is promoting her clothing line and the cosmetics she endorses, and *Shape* is getting a major ad from the cosmetics manufacturer. Hurley and *Shape* magazine said that there is no connection between the ad and the editorial feature. Magazine expert Samir A. Husni told the *New York Times* that what *Shape* did was nothing new. "It's more a reflection of the entire industry."[68]

Fashion/beauty/lifestyle magazine *W* is working to extend synergy to its social media channels as well. The magazine's 2014 spring fashion issue was built around an "Instaglam" theme, playing off the name of the photo-sharing Instagram social media site. Lucy Kriz, publisher of *W* magazine, told *Luxury Daily*, "As March was our social media issue, we wanted to highlight the synergy between magazine, digital and social content. From coordinating tweets, Instagrams and Facebook posts with those feature in the issue . . . we drove the biggest traffic spike on the site since its relaunch, delivering click-through rates above industry average to our brand partners."[69]

What does she mean with that "marketing speak"?

W coordinated its social media posts to go with the articles in the magazine and the social media of its advertisers with the goal of increasing the number of readers visiting both *W*'s Web site and the advertisers' sites.

The Blurring of Advertising and Editorial Content.

The often strong connection between advertisers and editorial content at fashion magazines does not necessarily carry over to other periodicals, but that doesn't mean that advertisers don't try to make their ads look like magazine articles. This used to be known as "advertorial content"—combining the words *advertising* and *editorial*—but has now

Questioning the Media

Do popular consumer magazines pander too much to advertisers? Do you have trouble telling the difference between advertisements and articles? Or does it matter as long as the advertising is interesting?

Web 5.11: Check out controversial magazine covers.

Web 5.12: Learn more about the *studies* of race and magazine covers.

Around the Web

Buy a link here

- Nominees/Winners | Television Academy - Emmy
- Emmys 2014: Complete list of nominees | NJ.com
- 2014 Emmys: Will Orange is the New Black laugh last? - Arts ... - Cbc
- [PHOTOS] Emmys 2014: Best Actress in a Drama Series — Our 6 ...
- Who Will Win the Drama Emmys? Category Breakdowns - Indiewire
- Emmys 2014: The News' predictions on who will (and should) take ...
- Here's who will win, might win, and should win at the Emmys - Vox
- Emmys 2014: 'Breaking Bad' dominates drama awards; Robin Williams gets ...
- Emmys' Best Actress in Drama Goes To Julianna Margulies

Conversations

These links to stories about the 2014 Emmy Awards look like standard links that appear following a Huffington Post story, but they are there as paid "native ads" designed to look like regular editorial content. Note the link at the upper right corner that says "Buy a link here."

come to be known as **native advertising**. This is where paid content is created by the staff of the publication on behalf of paid clients. This content often looks just like the "real" articles on the pages with only minimal labeling.[70] One women's magazine featured a "senior merchandising editor" wearing a beautiful new coat in a feature called "Hot Shot of the Month." However, the "editor" was really an advertising staffer, and the "hot shot" was really a free promotion for a favored advertiser.[71] Such **native ads** are nothing new, but they have generally been accompanied by a disclaimer saying that the item is an advertisement or a special advertising section.

The *Atlantic*, which now considers itself as much an online publication as a magazine, frequently posts native ads to its various Web sites. In fact, native ads were responsible for 59 percent of the company's online revenue in 2012.[72]

The Importance of Magazine Covers

As Annie Leibovitz has demonstrated time and again, what (and who) appears on a magazine's cover can make or break its newsstand sales. With the steady fall of

magazine circulation since 2008, publishers have been eager to find ways to make their publications stand out from the crowd.[73] For example, *Family Circle* magazine decided that it would try to stand out in the displays near supermarket checkout lines by using soothing, homey images rather than celebrity covers.

Dick Stolley, one of the founding editors of *People* magazine, established the following rules for covers:

- Young is better than old.
- Pretty is better than ugly.
- Rich is better than poor.
- Music is better than movies.
- Movies are better than television.
- Nothing is better than a dead celebrity.[74]

Janet Chan, who has served as editorial director of parenting publications for Time Inc., says,

You'll follow a lot of rules and you could say that's the science, but I think a lot of it is gut. For me, thinking of designing a cover is looking for the image that says, "You want to take this puppy home."[75]

Covers and Race. The fear of losing sales can make editors reluctant to take chances, and one result of this editorial caution is that relatively few nonwhites appear on the covers of men's, women's, teen, and entertainment magazines. *New York Times* reporter David Carr notes that in 2002 less than 20 percent of American magazine covers featured people of color and five years earlier only 12.7 percent of people appearing on magazine covers were nonwhite.[76] (This survey did not include fashion magazines, such as *Vogue*.)

Since then, things have not changed much. A survey of magazines that typically feature women on the cover found that between September 2012 and September 2013, 18 percent of the covers featured women of color, while 82 percent featured white women. Of the 16 magazines analyzed, *Teen Vogue* was the most diverse, featuring a 50/50 split with four white women and four women of color. On the other hand, the men's magazine *Maxim* was the least diverse, featuring 12 covers with white women and none with women of color.[77] If you compare those figures to the most recent census data, women of color make up 36.3 percent of the United States' female population.[78]

One of the clearest examples of the segregation of magazine covers can be seen with the ever-controversial *Sports*

PRNewsFoto/David's Bridal/AP Photo

One magazine that always has an African American model on the cover is *O, The Oprah Magazine*. The publication always features Oprah Winfrey on the cover—in this case she's wearing a Vera Wang gown that extends across two aditional pages.

native advertising: Advertising materials mixed in with articles and written by staff writers designed to look like editorial content rather than paid advertising.

Illustrated swimsuit issue. Over its first fifty years, the swimsuit issue featured only two women of color on the cover—Tyra Banks in 1996 and 1997, and Beyoncé in 2007. Even in 2006, when the cover featured eight models wearing swimsuit bottoms, all of them were white, and most were blond. (It is worth noting that *Sports Illustrated* has had at least five Hispanic cover models over the years.[79]) On a television special celebrating the fiftieth anniversary of the *Sports Illustrated* swimsuit issue, Banks thanked the magazine for putting her on the cover, saying, "I want to thank *Sports Illustrated* . . . for being daring and for making every little black girl that year that saw that issue go 'oh my God, mama, I think I'm pretty because a black girl's on the cover just like me.'"

According to Carr, editors at the top consumer magazines believe that, all things being equal, covers with white models sell better than those with a minority model. However, *O*, which always features Oprah Winfrey on the cover, has a largely white readership. And singer-actress Jennifer Lopez, golfer Tiger Woods, and tennis-playing sisters Venus and Serena Williams have increasingly appeared on magazine covers. Teen magazines, which often focus on the multiracial music business, are also quite likely to show people of color on their covers. Of course, since Barack Obama was elected president, first lady Michelle Obama has been on numerous magazine covers, including *Vogue, O, Us Weekly, People,* and *Glamour.*

Cover Lines. Along with the cover image, cover lines have to draw readers into the publication. **Cover lines** are teaser headlines used to shock, intrigue, or titillate potential buyers. Keep in mind that it is important for cover lines to interest subscribers, as well as drive newsstand sales. If a subscriber is going to renew a magazine, he or she must want to read it, preferably as soon as it arrives. The goal is for cover lines to appeal to as many readers of the magazine as possible. "I would say 85 percent of your cover has to appeal to 100 percent of the audience," says magazine editor Susan Kane.[80] Numbers are often used in cover lines because they suggest value ("79 beat-stress ideas. Rush less, work smarter, find happiness and balance now!")—in other words, they imply that a great deal of good material is to be found inside the magazine.[81]

One thing that makes FBL magazines stand out in the checkout line is their distinctive cover lines. The first issue of *Glamour* under editor Bonnie Fuller had the cover line "Doing it! . . . 100 women's secret sexual agendas—Who wants what, how bad and how often." The same month, *Cosmopolitan* had the cover line "Sex Rules! 10 Make-Him-Throb Moves So Hot You'll Need a Fire Hose to Cool Down the Bed." Even *Redbook*, a service magazine targeted at mothers approaching middle age, proclaims "Sex every night: can it deepen your love? Yes! Yes! Yes!" "Put 'orgasm' on the cover and it will sell," says former *Glamour* editor Ruth Whitney.[82] Of course, some of these covers are *too* hot

There is a magazine for almost every imaginable group. There's even *Backyard Poultry* for people who raise chickens, ducks, or geese in their yards in urban settings. This family raises chickens in the backyard of their Takoma Park, Maryland, home.

for grocery stores, which may place blinders over them to avoid offending their customers.[83]

■□■■■■■■■■■■■■■■■■■■■

The Future of Magazines

SECRET 4 ▶ Although the magazine industry has gone through massive changes, in many ways it is still the same as it was when it was founded in 1741 (providing another example of Secret Four—Nothing's new: Everything that happened in the past will happen again).

Magazines for the Twenty-first Century

According to media scholar Leara D. Rhodes, the American magazine industry has been a series of "launches and failures, new magazines, and revitalization of old ones."[84]

Rhodes says that successful magazines have traditionally shared a number of characteristics, including the following:

Questioning the Media

What magazines (if any) do you read regularly? Which of the characteristics noted by Rhodes do they share? How have the magazines you read changed over time, and why do you think those changes were made? Did they lead to a better magazine?

- Building a relationship between the magazine and its readers
- Providing information readers can't easily find other places

cover lines: Teaser headlines on magazine covers used to shock, intrigue, or titillate potential buyers.

Going From Paper to Digital

When the iPad was first released in 2010, it was clear that this new tablet computer had the potential to be a successful delivery system for electronic editions of magazines. The big question that remained was whether traditional magazine publishers would be willing to put out the effort to create tablet versions of their magazines that were easy to use and that provided readers with something of value.

The *New Yorker*, the magazine your author reads as a tablet edition, is available through Apple's App Store for the iPad, the Amazon Appstore for Android for the Kindle Fire, and Next Issue Media for the Galaxy Tab. There is also an edition for the regular e-ink Kindle and a stripped-down version for the iPhone.

The *New Yorker*'s tablet edition went live for the iPad in October 2010, and debuted on the Kindle Fire a little over a year later. The magazine also offers a complete archive online. The *New Yorker* has been somewhat of a pioneer in electronic offerings, as it initially sold its electronic archive as an engraved portable hard drive.[85]

The *New Yorker* has done particularly well in the transition to a tablet era. The Pew foundation reports that the magazine has successfully raised its basic subscription price and has many subscribers paying for both the print and the tablet versions of the magazine. It's also brought in new online humor content that isn't behind the paywall to help draw people in to the magazine's Web site. "We decided that this was a serious

The *New Yorker* offers their magazine in a variety of tablet formats, including Apple's iPad and Amazon's Kindle.

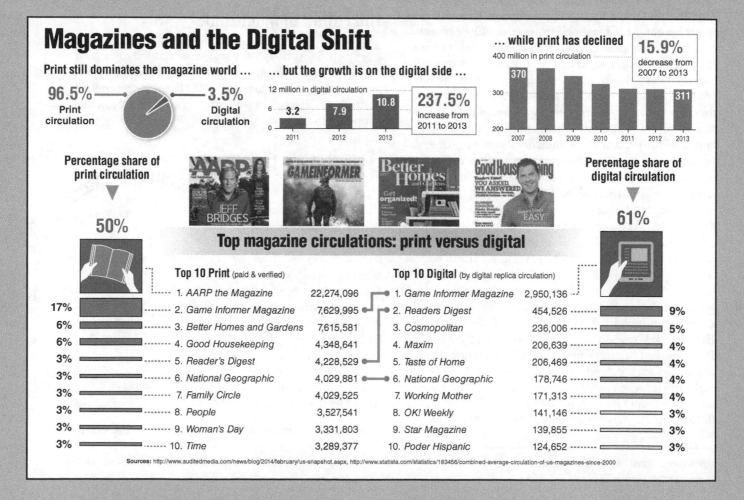

Magazines and the Digital Shift

Print still dominates the magazine world ...

96.5% — Print circulation

3.5% — Digital circulation

... but the growth is on the digital side ...

12 million in digital circulation

2011	2012	2013
3.2	7.9	10.8

237.5% increase from 2011 to 2013

... while print has declined

400 million in print circulation

15.9% decrease from 2007 to 2013

2007	2008	2009	2010	2011	2012	2013
370						311

Percentage share of print circulation ▼ **50%**

Percentage share of digital circulation ▼ **61%**

Top magazine circulations: print versus digital

	Top 10 Print (paid & verified)		Top 10 Digital (by digital replica circulation)		
	1. AARP the Magazine	22,274,096	1. Game Informer Magazine	2,950,136	
17%	2. Game Informer Magazine	7,629,995	2. Readers Digest	454,526	9%
6%	3. Better Homes and Gardens	7,615,581	3. Cosmopolitan	236,006	5%
6%	4. Good Housekeeping	4,348,641	4. Maxim	206,639	4%
3%	5. Reader's Digest	4,228,529	5. Taste of Home	206,469	4%
3%	6. National Geographic	4,029,881	6. National Geographic	178,746	4%
3%	7. Family Circle	4,029,525	7. Working Mother	171,313	4%
3%	8. People	3,527,541	8. OK! Weekly	141,146	3%
3%	9. Woman's Day	3,331,803	9. Star Magazine	139,855	3%
3%	10. Time	3,289,377	10. Poder Hispanic	124,652	3%

Sources: http://www.auditedmedia.com/news/blog/2014/february/us-snapshot.aspx, http://www.statista.com/statistics/183456/combined-average-circulation-of-us-magazines-since-2000

business for us," *New Yorker* publisher Lisa Hughes told the Pew Research Center. "It was the moment to invest in NewYorker.com; to build it out and make it a real game changer."[86]

Hearst, which publishes a range of popular magazines, has taken to selling "continuous-service" electronic subscriptions that cost $1.99 a month, billed to a credit card. This results in an annual subscription rate of about $24 a year, more than the publisher typically gets for a paper subscription. Hearst, like many other publishers, is finding that electronic editions are a great way to sell back issues of the magazine. In fact, Hearst reports that 40 percent of its single-copy electronic sales are made after the paper copy is off the newsstand.[87]

Owners of tablets are not abandoning print, however, and a study from consumer research group GfK MRI showed that tablet owners were 66 percent more likely than the average U.S. adult to be heavy users of printed magazines. (In case you were wondering, the study defined a heavy magazine user as someone who read thirteen or more magazines, on average, per month.[88])

When Apple's iPad first was released, magazines were trying to sell electronic single issues for the same (high) price as newsstand copies. Then, in 2011, Apple started selling online subscriptions, but took its usual cut of 30 percent on each sale. More problematic to magazine publishers, Apple also kept all of the information about who the subscribers were—information potentially as valuable as the subscription revenue itself.[89]

Magazines have responded to this by selling combined subscriptions that include both the print and digital versions. These digital versions may include a PDF version that will display on any device or a platform-specific app version that will run on an Apple or Google Android device.

Media Transformations Questions

- **WHY** is the switch to digital publishing, and especially "digital first" (discussed later in this chapter), so scary for magazines? (Remember Secret Five— New media are always scary—applies especially to media companies!) Why would the *New Yorker* be willing to take the chance?

- **WHAT** makes offering tablet editions of magazines along with print editions difficult for publishers?

- **HOW** have magazines benefited by adopting digital-first and tablet-publishing strategies? What problems have they had to accept?

- Adapting to social changes
- Being supported by advertisers
- Adjusting to economic changes and limitations
- Shaping public discourse by defining the major issues of society[90]

Just as *McClure's* led to reform of the oil industry at the turn of the previous century, Seymour Hersh's *New Yorker* articles about the abuses at Abu Ghraib prison in Iraq led to investigations of the way prisoners were being treated.

The total circulation of magazines in the United States has risen as the population's overall level of education has increased, thus raising the level of literacy. From 1970 to 2005, the annual paid circulation of all magazines measured by the Audit Bureau of Circulation grew by 67 percent. (The Audit Bureau of Circulation certifies to advertisers how many copies of the largest consumer magazines are actually sold.[91]) Rhodes says that, as educational availability and literacy rise in Asia and Latin America, it seems likely that they will also see a substantial growth in magazine circulation. While overall circulation for magazines dipped starting with the recession of 2008, that decline appears to have leveled out by 2013. Keep in mind, however, that magazines can boost their circulation by offering deeply discounted subscriptions.[92]

We can identify several current trends in magazine publishing:

Atlantic Media/Richard A. Bloom

The *Atlantic*, a literary/political magazine that dates back to the 1800s, has been successful at adopting a "digital-first" strategy that has helped it start turning a profit for the first time in years.

- Magazines are targeting narrower audiences—Unlike the general-interest magazines of the nineteenth century and first half of the twentieth century, contemporary magazines are targeted at specific audiences. While *Maxim* has successfully targeted young men, a group the magazine industry ignored previously, the niches can be much smaller. For example,

Backyard Poultry targets readers interested in raising chickens and other poultry on a small scale. It publishes six times a year and has 60,000 subscribers along with 35,000 copies distributed on newsstands. *All About Beer* (which is all about beer) has been in print for more than thirty years, publishes eight times per year, and distributes about 35,000 copies per issue.[93] Says magazine executive Kevin Coyne, "It's the Me Generation saying, 'I have tastes and preferences, and now I can seek them out in various forms.' It's all about the consumer exercising his choices."[94]

- Presentation is important—The layout and graphics of magazines are critical in determining how people will respond to them. Journalist Michael Scherer writes that magazines today "are filled with color, oversized headlines, graphics, photos, and pull quotes."[95]
- Articles are short—Magazines such as *Maxim*, *InStyle*, and *Us Weekly* have replaced many of their full-fledged articles with text boxes that look like extended captions. According to Keith Blanchard of *Maxim*,

If you are trying to reach cranky retirees, maybe six-thousand-word rants are appropriate. [*Maxim*] readers are busier today than they will ever be in their lives; they have shorter attention spans than any previous generation; they are chronically over-stimulated and easily bored.[96]

Magazines in the Digital Age

The twenty-first century has been challenging for the magazine industry, to say the least. The economic collapse in 2008 and 2009 led to a 25 percent drop in ad pages sold in 2009 accompanied by a 2.2 percent drop in circulation.

The field of newsmagazines in particular has been suffering, with *U.S. News & World Report* going totally online and discontinuing its print version. *Newsweek*, formerly owned by the Washington Post Company, sold for $1. In 2013, the new owners suspended publication of the paper edition to go totally online, but they then resumed paper publication in March 2014. As recently as 2007, *Newsweek* had had more than 3 million subscribers, but that number fell off the cliff that year, declining by half as of 2010, with the number of ad pages declining by a similar amount.[97]

Time magazine has had declines both in readership and in advertising pages. *Time*'s circulation dropped to 3.3 million copies in 2012, down 1.7 percent from the year before, and suffered a 12 percent drop in advertising pages.[98]

One magazine that has done relatively well during this period of transition is the *Atlantic*. The Pew Research Center's "State of the News Media" report estimated the *Atlantic*'s 2010 profits at $1.8 million. This is from a company that had long been financially marginal and had been losing money for at least a decade. (At its lowest point in 2005, the magazine was losing close to $7 million a year.) What made the difference? Jeremy Peters, writing for the *New York Times,* said the magazine "needed to kill itself to survive."[99] According to Justin Smith, president of the *Atlantic*'s parent company, "[We] brainstormed the question, 'What would we do if the goal was to aggressively cannibalize ourselves?'"[100]

Instead of fighting the Internet and all the changes it has wrought, the *Atlantic* adopted a **digital-first strategy**, in which online and electronic editions are the first priority, not preserving the print edition. In October 2011, the magazine's digital revenues topped its print revenues, but not because the print revenues fell. In fact, in that same month the print edition had one of its best ad sales months in years.[101]

The *Atlantic* had a number of advantages that aided its move to a digital-first strategy. It's a small organization, which makes change simpler. It also targets an upscale, well-educated audience, which also facilitated the change. Overall, the *Atlantic* gets about half of its revenue from advertising, and 40 percent of that revenue comes from digital advertising. Advertising representatives working for the company were told not to worry about the platform they sold for. Digital ads and print ads were of equal importance.

 Web 5.13: Read magazine reports for the last several years.

digital-first strategy: An approach to magazine publishing where online and electronic editions are more important than preserving circulation and revenue from print editions.

Chapter SUMMARY

Magazines were the first media to become national in scope rather than appealing to a limited geographic area. They also contained articles designed to be of lasting appeal. Although there were magazines available during the colonial period, the first significant American magazine was the *Saturday Evening Post*. Espousing conservative, middle-class values, the *Post* was seen as a reflection of American society. Literary and commentary magazines flourished in the nineteenth century, and several of them survive today. These magazines provided a forum for important authors and were among the first to feature the work of pioneering photojournalists such as Mathew Brady.

W. E. B. Du Bois expanded the range of commentary magazines with the founding of the *Crisis* as the official magazine of the NAACP. The *Crisis* became the first magazine to provide a forum for black writers. The early twentieth century saw a trend in investigative magazine reporting known as muckraking. The work of the muckrakers set the stage for much of the investigative reporting done today by newspapers and television news.

Henry Luce founded *Time* magazine in 1923, creating what would become one of the nation's largest media companies—Time Warner. Luce's publishing empire grew to include not just the news in *Time*, but also photojournalism in *Life*, sports journalism in *Sports Illustrated*, and personality and celebrity journalism in *People*.

Women's magazines got their start with *Godey's Lady's Book* under the editorship of Sarah Josepha Hale. In addition to editing the magazine, Hale established many of the principles of modern magazines: copyrighting the stories, running original material, and paying authors for their work. The "seven sisters" women's service magazines followed in much the same tradition as *Godey*'s and were concerned mainly with the home, family, and quality of life. An alternative to the traditional values of service magazines is offered by the more youth-oriented fashion/beauty/lifestyle magazines, such as *Glamour* and *Cosmopolitan*.

Many magazines targeted at men appeal to them through their hobbies, but the two most influential men's magazines are *Esquire* and *Playboy*. Although *Playboy* was initially more explicit with its pinup photography, both it and *Esquire* now feature men's fashion, lifestyle coverage, and articles by well-known writers. In recent years, a new type of men's magazine focusing on adventure, fashion, health, and sex has appeared; the most popular of these magazines is *Maxim*.

Trade publications are magazines that cover a particular industry rather than being designed for consumers. Although they often are more serious and feature less photography and color than the consumer magazines, they make up a substantial portion of the magazine market.

Fashion magazines have been criticized in recent years for featuring extremely thin models in both ads and editorial content. Critics argue that the unrealistic image promoted by these models can contribute to the development of eating disorders in young women. Several magazines and advertisers have bucked this trend and featured plus-sized models and even ordinary people. Other conflicts in the magazine industry can involve the blurring of editorial content and advertising, as well as the photos and headlines used on covers.

Magazines in the twenty-first century are continuing many of the trends that made them successful throughout their history, including building relationships with readers, adapting to change, being supported by advertisers, and defining major issues in society. Magazines continue to be successful in their print formats but are expanding their content with tablet versions and other digital offerings.

Keep up-to-date with content from the author's blog.

Take the chapter quiz.

Key TERMS

Concept REVIEW

Development of the magazine industry

The influence of magazines on national culture

The development of photojournalism

The difference between consumer and trade magazines

The role magazines play in giving voice to groups

The controversy over the influence of magazine content on body image

The battle between advertising and editorial content

Function and controversy of magazine covers and cover lines

Relationship between magazines and their readers

The growth of digital publishing

Student STUDY SITE

$SAGE edge™

Sharpen your skills with SAGE edge at **edge.sagepub.com/hanson5e**

SAGE edge for Students provides a personalized approach to help you accomplish your coursework goals in an easy-to-use learning environment.

Newspapers and the News

Reflection of a Democratic Society

Amazon founder and CEO Jeff Bezos announced his plans to buy The Washington Post for $250 million in August of 2013.

The news started breaking on Twitter on the afternoon of August 6, 2013, that there was a big meeting scheduled at the *Washington Post*. Not long after, word came that Amazon founder and space memorabilia collector Jeff Bezos had purchased the paper for $250 million from the Graham family, who had run the paper for four generations. Although Bezos founded and is the largest stockholder in book sales and media giant Amazon.com, he bought the paper out of his own personal fortune (and with a fortune estimated at $26 billion, the *Post* cost less than 1 percent of his net worth). When Bezos does things, he doesn't do them in a small way. As an example, not long before buying the *Washington Post*, he funded and led an expedition to recover two of the massive F-1 Saturn V moon rocket engines from the bottom of the Atlantic Ocean.[1]

The fact that this is a personal purchase is important. *Washington Post* reporter Paul Farhi pointed out at the time of the purchase that under Bezos the paper will be privately owned, so he will not be accountable to shareholders or other investors. He'll be allowed to take a long-term approach, something he has a track record of doing. Although the *Post* reported being profitable at the time of the sale, it has been suffering a steady decline in revenue over the past several years and has had declining print circulation as well.[2]

At a time when the common wisdom says that newspapers are a dying medium from the last century, why would one of the wealthiest men in the world purchase a paper that has had declining revenue for six years? Bezos told the *Post*'s Farhi that he does not see any magic answer to the problems metropolitan newspapers are facing:

> The *Post* is famous for its investigative journalism.. . . It pours energy and investment and sweat and dollars into uncovering important stories. And then a bunch of Web sites summarize that [work] in about four minutes and readers can access that news for free. One question is, how do you make a living in that kind of environment? If you can't it's difficult to put the right resources behind it.[3]

When the Graham family decided to sell the *Washington Post*, they were looking for an investor who could pay the $250 million asking price and not demand an immediate return on the investment. And that's when CEO Don Graham thought about his friend Bezos. Despite dealing with cutting-edge

LEARNING OBJECTIVES

After studying this chapter, you will be able to:

1 Discuss the development of the colonial and early American press.

2 Explain how tabloid newspapers differ from broadsheet newspapers.

3 Describe the four major types of newspapers today, with examples.

4 Name six basic news values used by journalists.

5 Discuss the risks that reporters take to cover the news.

6 Explain how the Internet and mobile technology have changed the news and newspaper business.

technology, Bezos has a reputation for taking the long-range view of business.[4] Back in 2011 in an interview with longtime tech journalist Steven Levy, Bezos talked about the fact that his companies have always taken a long view. Bezos says:

> Our first shareholder letter, in 1997, was entitled, "It's all about the long term." If everything you do needs to work on a three-year time horizon, then you're competing against a lot of people. But if you're willing to invest on a seven-year time horizon, you're now competing against a fraction of those people because very few people are willing to do that. Just by lengthening the time horizon, you can engage in endeavors that you could never otherwise pursue.[5]

One of Bezos's first innovations after buying the paper was providing subscribers to other metropolitan papers, including the *Dallas Morning News*, the *Honolulu Star-Advertiser*, and the *Minneapolis Star-Tribune*, unlimited free access to the *Post*'s Web site and mobile apps. Normally, people who want to view more than a limited number of articles at the *Post* have to pay a monthly subscription fee (your author among them). The goal of Bezos's plan is to bring people in to the site who are outside of the paper's print circulation area and who are unlikely to be good candidates for being paying customers, but who still have a documented interest in news. Bezos might also look at bundling access to the *Post* with other online subscription services, such as Amazon Prime or Spotify.[6] In another action, the *Post* actually has been hiring people, adding fifty new staffers during the first half of 2014. This is in sharp contrast to the years of buyouts of senior employees that had cut the size of the newsroom over previous years.[7]

Timeline

1800	1900	1910	1920	1930	1940

1812 War of 1812 breaks out.
1835 Alexis de Tocqueville publishes *Democracy in America*.
1859 Charles Darwin publishes *On the Origin of Species*.
1861 U.S. Civil War begins.
1869 Transcontinental railroad is completed.
1879 Thomas Edison invents electric light bulb.
1898 Spanish-American War breaks out.

1903 Orville and Wilbur Wright fly first airplane.
1905 Albert Einstein proposes his theory of relativity.

1912 *Titanic* sinks.
1914 World War I begins.
1918 Worldwide influenza epidemic strikes.

1920 Nineteenth Amendment passes, giving U.S. women the right to vote.
1929 U.S. stock market crashes, leading to the Great Depression.

1933 Adolf Hitler is elected chancellor of Germany.
1939 World War II breaks out in Europe.

1941 United States enters World War II.
1945 United States drops two atomic bombs on Japan.
1947 Pakistan and India gain independence from Britain.
1949 Communists establish People's Republic of China.

1618 *Curanto*, the first English-language newspaper, is published in Amsterdam.
1690 *Publick Occurrences* is the first newspaper published in the American colonies.
1785 The *Times* begins publishing in London.

1833 The *New York Sun* starts publication as the first of the penny press newspapers.
1883 Joseph Pulitzer buys the *New York World*, ushering in the era of yellow journalism.
1896 Adolf Ochs buys the failing *New York Times* and turns it into the most respected newspaper in the country.

1905 The *Chicago Defender*, one of the most successful and profitable African American newspapers, is founded.
1917 The first Pulitzer Prizes for excellence in journalism, endowed by Joseph Pulitzer in his will, are handed out. The awards are now an annual event.
1920s Tabloids—smaller-format newspapers—with their blaring headlines and scandalous stories become popular especially with urban commuters.

Library of Congress

Although Bezos has said he hasn't figured out how to make a major metropolitan paper into a growing, profitable media outlet, he does know that the paper's readers have to be at the company's core. "I'm skeptical of any mission that has advertisers at its centerpiece. Whatever the mission is, it has news at its heart."[8]

Some media observers have questioned whether newspapers, the oldest of news media, have any future. They have suggested that words and pictures on paper will be replaced by news and images flowing out over digital channels. The newspaper industry is clearly going through an intense period of change, but it is far from dying. In this chapter, we look at how journalism and the press developed in the United States, how newspapers operate today, whom newspapers large and small are now serving (that is, their audiences), and how newspapers are being transformed in the digital age. ■

Web 6.1: Read more about Jeff Bezos and the businesses he owns.

> **"** The *Post* is famous for its investigative journalism… It pours energy and investment and sweat and dollars into uncovering important stories. And then a bunch of Web sites summarize that [work] in about four minutes and readers can access that news for free. **"**
>
> —Jeff Bezos

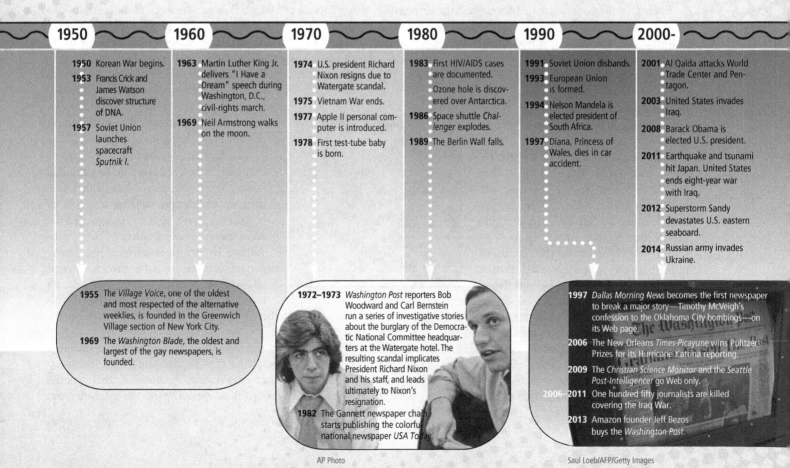

1950

1950 Korean War begins.
1953 Francis Crick and James Watson discover structure of DNA.
1957 Soviet Union launches spacecraft *Sputnik I.*

1960

1963 Martin Luther King Jr. delivers "I Have a Dream" speech during Washington, D.C., civil-rights march.
1969 Neil Armstrong walks on the moon.

1970

1974 U.S. president Richard Nixon resigns due to Watergate scandal.
1975 Vietnam War ends.
1977 Apple II personal computer is introduced.
1978 First test-tube baby is born.

1980

1983 First HIV/AIDS cases are documented.
Ozone hole is discovered over Antarctica.
1986 Space shuttle *Challenger* explodes.
1989 The Berlin Wall falls.

1990

1991 Soviet Union disbands.
1993 European Union is formed.
1994 Nelson Mandela is elected president of South Africa.
1997 Diana, Princess of Wales, dies in car accident.

2000-

2001 Al Qaida attacks World Trade Center and Pentagon.
2003 United States invades Iraq.
2008 Barack Obama is elected U.S. president.
2011 Earthquake and tsunami hit Japan. United States ends eight-year war with Iraq.
2012 Superstorm Sandy devastates U.S. eastern seaboard.
2014 Russian army invades Ukraine.

1955 The *Village Voice*, one of the oldest and most respected of the alternative weeklies, is founded in the Greenwich Village section of New York City.
1969 The *Washington Blade*, the oldest and largest of the gay newspapers, is founded.

1972–1973 *Washington Post* reporters Bob Woodward and Carl Bernstein run a series of investigative stories about the burglary of the Democratic National Committee headquarters at the Watergate hotel. The resulting scandal implicates President Richard Nixon and his staff, and leads ultimately to Nixon's resignation.
1982 The Gannett newspaper chain starts publishing the colorful national newspaper *USA Today.*

1997 *Dallas Morning News* becomes the first newspaper to break a major story—Timothy McVeigh's confession to the Oklahoma City bombings—on its Web page.
2006 The New Orleans *Times-Picayune* wins Pulitzer Prizes for its Hurricane Katrina reporting.
2009 The *Christian Science Monitor* and the *Seattle Post-Intelligencer* go Web only.
2006–2011 One hundred fifty journalists are killed covering the Iraq War.
2013 Amazon founder Jeff Bezos buys the *Washington Post.*

AP Photo

Saul Loeb/AFP/Getty Images

cartoon, the oft-reprinted "Join, or Die" cartoon, and he introduced the weather report as a regular feature.[11]

Inventing the Modern Press 🌐

Newspapers first appeared soon after Johannes Gutenberg's invention of movable type. The first English-language newspaper was *Curanto,* which was published in Amsterdam in June 1618. This was not a newspaper as we would recognize it today, but rather a single broadsheet filled with both British and foreign news. By 1622, similar papers (or newsbooks, as they were called) were being published in Britain. The government attempted to control these papers, which were empowering the new capitalist class at the expense of the aristocracy, but the papers were still distributed through places such as coffeehouses.[9]

SECRET 4 ➤ If you look ahead to the 1960s and 1970s in the United States, this is not all that different from how the early gay and alternative newspapers were distributed, thus illustrating Secret Four—Nothing's new: Everything that happened in the past will happen again.

Among those publishing broadsheets were church reformers Martin Luther and John Calvin, and their religious writings also helped bring about some of the earliest attempts at censorship.[10]

Colonial Publishing: A Tradition of Independence

Publick Occurrences is frequently cited as the first newspaper in the American colonies; its first and only issue was published in 1690. As happened with many papers of the era, the government promptly shut it down. In this case, the government objected to the paper's disparaging remarks about the king of France. The first paper to publish multiple issues was the *Boston News-Letter,* which was founded in 1704.

Benjamin and James Franklin.
Just as media dynasties exist today, they existed in the American colonies, with Benjamin and James Franklin having their hands in just about every medium available at the time. Starting in 1721, James, the elder of the two brothers, published the *New-England Courant,* the first newspaper to be published without the explicit approval of the British Crown. When James was thrown into prison for irritating the authorities, sixteen-year-old Benjamin, who had been working as a printer's apprentice, took over the paper. By 1729, he had purchased the *Pennsylvania Gazette* and began turning it into the most influential paper in the colonies. Franklin published the colonies' first political

©iStockphoto.com/joecicak

The Penny Press: Newspapers for the People

The newspapers of the American colonies had little in common with newspapers today. Before the 1830s, daily papers contained shipping news and political essays. Designed primarily for the wealthy elite, these papers were often underwritten by political parties, and their content was determined by the editors' opinions. Although we might consider this biased coverage, these early papers made no pretense of objectivity. Why should they? Each political party had its own paper, and the small number of subscribers (2,000 at most) tended to share similar viewpoints. Battles between rival newspapers could get quite heated, even extending to physical violence.

Colonial newspapers were quite expensive, costing as much as six cents a day at a time when a worker might make eighty-five cents a day. Papers were typically available only by annual subscription, which had to be paid in advance. These papers showed their business bias with names like the *Advertiser* or the *Commercial.* They typically consisted of four pages, with the front and back filled primarily with advertising and the inside pages with news and editorial content.[12]

Benjamin Day and the New York Sun.
In the 1830s, Benjamin Day conceived a new type of newspaper, one that would sell large numbers of copies to the emerging literate public. On September 3, 1833, he started publishing the *New York Sun.* The paper's motto was "It shines for all." The newly developed steam engine made the *Sun* possible. Hand-powered presses, which hadn't changed much since Gutenberg's time, could print no more than 350 pages a day, but a steam-powered rotary press could print as many as 16,000 sections (not just pages) in the same amount of time (see Chapter 4).[13]

The *Sun* emphasized facts over opinion. Papers that followed in its wake had names like *Critic, Herald,* or *Star.* These inexpensive papers sold for a penny or two on the street, so they soon earned the name penny press. Instead of being subsidized by political parties, the penny papers were supported by circulation and advertising revenues. They also didn't have to worry about subscribers who wouldn't pay their bills, since they were all sold on the street for cash.[14]

Now that publishers could economically print large numbers of papers, they could command a big enough circulation to attract advertising. As a result, their profits came primarily from advertising revenues, not from subscriptions or subsidies. The makers of patent medicines, which often consisted largely of alcohol or narcotics, were the biggest advertisers. Want ads (today's classifieds) also became a prominent feature of the papers.

Penny papers were typically independent rather than being the voice of a particular political party. In fact, they tended to ignore politics altogether because their readers weren't interested in political issues. As an example, one day the *Sun*'s congressional news column reported: "The proceedings of Congress thus far, would not interest our readers."[15]

The concept of "news" was invented by the penny press: These papers emphasized news—the newest developments from the police, courts, and the streets. The traditional papers called the penny papers sensationalistic, not because they ran big headlines or photos—neither existed at the time—but because they were printing "news" instead of political arguments or debates. The penny press also moved toward egalitarianism in the press. The affairs of ordinary people were as much news as accounts of rich aristocrats.[16]

The British press went through a similar period of change, moving from the highly partisan press of the 1700s to a more "objective" focus on news by the end of the nineteenth century—again a change largely in response to the rise of a literate working class and the desire to reach a large audience for the paper's advertising.[17]

Library of Congress

Newsboys sold newspapers on the streets of New York and other major cities for one or two cents a copy during the penny press era of the nineteenth century.

A Modern Democratic Society. The 1830s were a period of intense growth for the United States—in industry, in the economy, and in political participation. The penny newspaper was a vital part of this growth, providing the information the public needed to make democracy work. In 1830 there were 650 weeklies and sixty-five dailies in the United States, but in just ten years those numbers had doubled: to 1,241 weeklies and 138 dailies.[18] It was a period when more people were working for wages outside the home and were starting to use consumer goods purchased with cash. The penny press provided a means for advertising these goods, which in turn expanded the market for them.

The United States was being transformed from a rural community to an urban society, from an agricultural nation to an industrial one, from self-sufficient families to a market-based economy. Michael Schudson argues that the penny papers were a strong force in this change:

These papers, whatever their political preferences, were spokesmen for egalitarian ideals in politics, economic life, and social life through their organization of sales,

their solicitation of advertising, their emphasis on news, their catering to large audiences, their decreasing concern with the editorial.

The penny papers expressed and built the culture of a democratic market society, a culture which had no place for social or intellectual deference.[19]

SECRET 1 During the Civil War era, the press continued its move toward being independent from political parties. The press provided people with news about the war and whether the nation would continue to exist. Following the war, newspapers continued to grow and began to be an important part of people's everyday lives. This was the establishment of Secret One—The media are essential components of our lives. Hazel Dicken-Garcia, in her history of the nineteenth-century press, wrote,

The press became a "habit" as Americans, perhaps for the first time, recognized a vital need for it and established it as [a] part of their lives in a way that was unprecedented. Families sought news of relatives fighting in the war, and national leaders needed information about events as a basis for making decisions and forming policies for conducting the war. . . . Since everyone had a stake in the war and thus a driving need to know about events, the newspaper became primary reading material as never before.[20]

The Granger Collection, New York

Pioneering woman journalist Nellie Bly created a sensation in the late 1800s with her "stunt journalism" written for Joseph Pulitzer's *New York World*.

Pulitzer, Hearst, and the Battle for New York City

If the penny papers of the first half of the nineteenth century gave birth to modern journalism, the battles between New York publishers Joseph Pulitzer and William Randolph Hearst in the 1880s and 1890s provided journalism's turbulent adolescence.

Pulitzer and the New York World. Joseph Pulitzer came to the United States from Austria in 1864 at the age

---

Video 6.1: Watch an interview with Paul Weaver.

Web 6.2: Read about Nellie Bly's visit to an insane asylum.

---

of seventeen to fight in the Civil War. He survived the war, studied law, and went on to become a reporter for a German-language newspaper. In 1878, he bought the *St. Louis Post and Dispatch* and became its publisher, editor, and business manager.

In 1883, Pulitzer bought the failing *New York World*, and in just three years, he boosted its circulation from 15,000 to more than 250,000. High circulation was critical because large readership numbers attracted advertisers who were willing to pay premium prices. Twelve years after Pulitzer bought the paper, it had a daily circulation of 540,000.[21]

Pulitzer changed the appearance of the paper's front page, replacing dense type with huge multicolumn pictures and big headlines. He brought to journalism a sense of drama and style that appealed immensely to his turn-of-the-century audience. Author and press critic Paul Weaver credits Pulitzer with the invention of the modern newspaper's front page. Before Pulitzer, the front page was no different from any other page in the paper. Pulitzer started the practice of giving the most important story the biggest and widest headline and running that story above the fold of the paper, where it would be immediately visible to anyone looking at the paper on a newsstand. Thus, **above the fold** came to refer to a prominent story.

Pulitzer made many other innovations. He changed headlines so that they said something more specific about the story. For example, a pre-Pulitzer New York paper ran the story about President Lincoln's assassination under the headline "Awful Event." Pulitzer required his editors to use headlines containing a subject and an active verb, so that the Lincoln assassination might have run under the headline "Lincoln Shot." Pre-Pulitzer stories told readers what they needed to know in a formal, structured way. Pulitzer presented the news as a story that people wanted to read; journalists went from just being reporters to being storytellers as well.[22]

New Readers: Immigrants and Women. The New York City of the 1880s and 1890s was a city of immigrants—people who wanted to learn to speak and read English—and the city's newspapers were important teachers. Pulitzer's *New York World* used big headlines, easy words, and many illustrations, all of which helped the paper appeal to the immigrant community. This was also the period when the modern Sunday paper got its start. In 1889, half of all New Yorkers bought Sunday papers. To make his Sunday editions more appealing, Pulitzer started trying out illustrations, comic strips, and color Sunday comics.

Pulitzer also tailored his newspaper to women readers by publishing women's pages and romantic fiction. He had a difficult time balancing the interests of women against those of male readers. He didn't want to offend working-class male

---

above the fold: A term used to refer to a prominent story; it comes from placement of a news story in a broadsheet newspaper above the fold in the middle of the front page.

readers by making the paper too feminist in content, but he couldn't ignore the independent women who were now reading papers. Women were the primary purchasers of household items, and advertisers wanted to reach them. So the newspaper needed to tailor its content to reach these "new women" while still appealing to its working-class male readers.

No one epitomized the journalism of Pulitzer's *New York World* better than "stunt journalist" Nellie Bly, who proved that women could go to the same extremes as men when trying to get a story. From her first act at the *World* (pretending to be insane in order to get an insider's report on a women's lunatic asylum) to her most famous stunt (traveling around the world in under eighty days), she always did things more extravagantly than anyone else.[23]

Bly, who lived from 1864 to 1922, authored hundreds of newspaper articles, which were generally long and written in the first person, for the *Pittsburg Dispatch*, the *New York World*, and the *New York Evening Journal*. She was born Elizabeth Jane Cochran but went by the nickname Pink (probably for the pink dresses she wore). It was at the *Dispatch* that she started using the pen name Nellie Bly. In addition to covering women's stories for the *Dispatch*, Bly wrote a travelogue of a journey to Mexico under the headline "NELLIE IN MEXICO." She also made a name for herself covering the plight of young women working in factories.

In 1887, Bly moved to New York in the hope of finding a job at one of the city's vibrant daily papers. First on her list was Pulitzer's *New York World*. She eventually was able to see John Cockerill, managing editor of the *World*. It was Cockerill who suggested that Bly go undercover to write a story about the women's lunatic asylum. If her story was good, he told her, she would get the job.

The asylum had been charged with abusing inmates, but none of the stories written about it had the power of Bly's insider account. To gain access, Bly moved into a rooming house and proceeded to act erratically so as to be committed to the asylum. Once inside, she wrote articles describing patients being fed rotten food and being choked and beaten by nurses. After ten days, an attorney for Pulitzer came to rescue her. The series of stories she produced was a masterpiece.

With this series, Bly proved that a woman could find success in sensationalistic journalism and that she could tell a great story under dangerous circumstances. Today many people would consider it unethical for reporters to pretend to be someone they aren't, and many major papers would reject their work. But in the New York of Hearst and Pulitzer, Bly's stunts were wildly successful and were imitated by other reporters.[24]

The Era of Yellow Journalism.
William Randolph Hearst came from a wealthy family and began his newspaper

AP Photo

"The Yellow Kid" was such a popular early comic strip character that both the *New York Journal* and the *New York World* had separate versions of the feature drawn by two different artists.

career as editor of the *San Francisco Examiner*, which was owned by his father. Having dominated the San Francisco newspaper market, Hearst followed Pulitzer into the New York market by purchasing the *New York Journal*. Soon he was using Pulitzer's own techniques to compete against him. Hearst and Pulitzer became fierce rivals, each trying to outdo the other with outlandish stories and stunts. This style of shocking, sensationalistic reporting came to be known as **yellow journalism**. Why yellow? At one point, the two papers fought over which one would publish the popular comic strip "The Yellow Kid," which featured a smart-aleck character and could be considered the "Doonesbury" of its day. Eventually, both papers featured their own "Yellow Kid" drawn by different artists.

---

yellow journalism: A style of sensationalistic journalism that grew out of the newspaper circulation battle between Joseph Pulitzer and William Randolph Hearst.

Web 6.3: Learn more about "The Yellow Kid."

DAILY ■ NEWS **EXTRA** EDITION

New York's PICTURE NEWSPAPER

Vol. 9. No. 178 66 Pages   New York, Friday, January 13, 1928.   2 Cents

DEAD!

Story on page 3

RUTH SNYDER'S DEATH PICTURED!—This is perhaps the most remarkable exclusive picture in the history of criminology. It shows the actual scene in the Sing Sing death house as the lethal current surged through Ruth Snyder's body at 11:06 last night. Her helmeted head is stiffened in death, her face masked and an electrode strapped to her bare right leg. The autopsy table on which her body was removed is beside her. Judd Gray, mumbling a prayer, followed her down the narrow corridor at 11:14. "Father, forgive them, for they don't know what they are doing!" were Ruth's last words. The picture is the first Sing Sing execution picture and the first of a woman's electrocution. *Story p. 3/ other pics. p. 28 and back page.*

Tom Howard/NY Daily News Archive via Getty Images

One of the most shocking and sensationalistic tabloid covers of all time ran when the *New York Daily News* snuck a photographer into the execution of murderer Ruth Snyder in 1928.

Nowhere was yellow journalism more exaggerated than in the *World*'s and *Journal*'s attempts to drum up fury over the events taking place in Cuba that led to the Spanish-American War. War, then as now, sold a lot of newspapers, and Hearst did his best to sensationalize the conflict in Cuba. He sent reporter Richard Harding Davis and artist Frederic Remington to Havana, Cuba, to cover the possible hostilities between the Spaniards and the Cubans. But there was little to report, and Davis and Remington were kept away from the fighting. According to a popular story, Remington became so discouraged that he telegraphed Hearst asking permission to return to New York: "Everything is quiet. There is no trouble here. There will be no war. Wish to return." Hearst's supposed reply? "Please remain. You furnish the pictures and I'll furnish the war."[25] It's uncertain whether this story is true, but there is no doubt that Hearst used the power of the press to sway public opinion.

 Web 6.4: Read more on the New York *Daily News*'s "DEAD!" cover.

Pulitzer eventually repented for his excesses during the era of yellow journalism by endowing a school of journalism at Columbia University. He also endowed the Pulitzer Prizes that every year honor the best reporting, photography, and commentary in journalism.

The Tabloids

Reading newspapers isn't the sort of thing people ever feel a need to apologize for—unless they are reading one of the tabloids. These include not only weekly supermarket tabloids, such as the *Star* and the *National Enquirer*, but also a substantial number of daily tabloids, such as the *New York Daily News* and the *Chicago Sun-Times,* that present the news in a lively style that makes people want to read them.

The **New York Daily News.** Tabloids first became popular during the 1920s. **Tabloid newspapers** are printed in a half-page (11- by 14-inch) format and usually have a cover rather than a traditional front page. They stand in contrast to **broadsheet newspapers**, which are the standard size of 17 by 22 inches. Riding a resurgence of sensationalism that hadn't been seen since the yellow journalism days of Hearst and Pulitzer, the papers of the 1920s became known for a lively, illustrated style known as **jazz journalism**.

One of the great early tabloids was the *New York Daily News*, which is still popular today.[26] The paper features big photos, huge headlines, and sensationalistic stories. Its most famous cover ran on January 13, 1928. Ruth Snyder had been convicted of murdering her husband and had been sentenced to electrocution. Then, as now, executions of women were rare. Although photographers were excluded from the execution, the *Daily News* sent in a Chicago photographer (because he wouldn't be recognized by anyone present) who had strapped a camera to his ankle. At the moment of the execution, he pulled up his pant leg and took the picture. The photo ran the next day under the headline "DEAD!"[27]

Today's tabloids are no less cutthroat and competitive than Hearst's and Pulitzer's papers in the late 1800s or the tabloids in the 1920s. The *Daily News* continues to do battle on the streets of New York with its rival, the *New York Post.* They compete not only to be the primary paper of working-class New Yorkers, but also to be the tabloid that readers of the more serious *New York Times* pick up for their gossip stories, sometimes referred to as "twinkies."[28]

How fierce is the competition between these two papers? On one occasion the *New York Post* ran an

---

tabloid newspapers: Newspapers with a half-page (11- by 14-inch) format that usually have a cover rather than a traditional front page like the larger broadsheet papers.

broadsheet newspapers: Standard-sized newspapers, which are generally 17 by 22 inches.

jazz journalism: A lively, illustrated style of newspapering popularized by the tabloid papers in the 1920s.

Associated Press photo of a girl competing in a spelling bee. But because she was sponsored by the *Daily News*, the *Post*'s biggest rival, the *Post* used a computer to edit out the *Daily News* logo from the sign she was wearing.[29] Of course, competition among the American tabloids is nothing compared to that of the British working-class papers. Those tabloids, such as the *Sun* and the *Daily Mirror*, are intensely sensationalistic, and the *Sun* even features a daily topless pinup on its page three. The tabs substantially outsell the more responsible papers.

Broadcast News 🌐

In the 1920s, newspapers started facing competition from new outlets. Broadcast media began to provide up-to-the-minute news delivered with a speed and immediacy that newspapers could not match.

Radio News. **SECRET 4** ▷ News was a part of radio programming from the very start. KDKA demonstrated the power of radio news with its 1920 nighttime broadcast of the Harding-Cox presidential election results—before the newspaper stories appeared the next morning. The newspapers, understandably, were upset by radio's apparent poaching on their territory. In fact, in the 1930s, they threatened to cut off radio stations' access to Associated Press news and even threatened to stop running radio program listings. The newspapers insisted that unless the news was of "transcendent importance," radio shouldn't broadcast it until the newspapers were available. Not surprisingly, the radio networks didn't think much of this idea. Although various restrictions were tested for a short while, in the end, radio news could not be stopped. As we will see again and again, old media usually try unsuccessfully to hold back the development of new media, providing yet another example of Secret Four—Nothing's new: Everything that happened in the past will happen again. Yet the old media do not go away. Instead, after a period of resistance, they change and adapt to the new environment.[30] Radio eliminated the extra editions of newspapers that used to be published whenever dramatic news occurred, but newspapers as a whole suffered only a slight decline in circulation.[31]

One place where radio held clear superiority over newspapers was in the realm of live news. Radio could, for the first time, bring news from around the world to people "as it happened." At no time was this more apparent than during World War II. When Adolf Hitler's army marched into Austria in 1938, CBS was on the air from Europe with immediate news and up-to-the-minute commentary. No radio correspondent of the era stood out more than CBS's European director, Edward R. Murrow. When Germany declared war on England in 1939, Murrow reported it from London in a voice that became familiar to all Americans. During the bombing of London, Americans listened to his live reports, which contained not just the news but also the sounds of everyday life: the air raid sirens, the anti-aircraft guns, and the explosions of bombs. Murrow spoke directly to listeners from London rooftops and made them feel as if they were there with him.[32]

Television News Goes 24/7. Television news started with brief coverage of the 1940 Republican national convention on an experimental NBC television station in New York City. By 1948, both the Democratic and Republican conventions were covered extensively for the still-tiny television audience. Documentary programs, such as *See It Now*, which was hosted by former CBS radio newsman Edward R. Murrow, took on lightweight topics, as well as intensely controversial issues, such as Wisconsin senator Joseph McCarthy, who had accused numerous people of being communists. The program also aired notable segments on the Korean War. In 1947, NBC started TV's longest-running news and commentary program, *Meet the Press*, which is still on today.

In August 1948, the *CBS-TV News* started airing for fifteen minutes every weeknight, setting the standard length for network news until the 1960s. When the ocean liner *Andrea Doria* sank in 1956, a CBS camera crew on a seaplane got footage of the ship going down, which was broadcast promptly. Journalist and broadcast professor Edward Bliss Jr. noted that with the film of the *Andrea Doria*, "Television had demonstrated that it could take the public to the scene of a major story more effectively than any other news medium."[33]

Television started playing a major role in presidential elections starting in 1960 with the famous Kennedy-Nixon debates.

In 1963, CBS expanded its nightly news show to half an hour, with Walter Cronkite at the anchor desk. Along with the news, the program featured commentary from veteran newsman Eric Sevareid. NBC soon followed the new format, joined four years later by ABC. During this time, videotape, satellite communication, and color started coming into common use, giving television news more immediacy and impact than ever before. With correspondents bringing into American homes graphic news from the war in Vietnam, as well as spectacular coverage of the moon landing in 1969, television news rose in importance as the way to see what was happening in the world.

On November 3, 1979, the staff of the American Embassy in Tehran was taken hostage by Iranian militants, and ABC started a nightly news update at 11:30 p.m. Eastern Time.

Questioning the Media

How do you get your news? Do you read a newspaper, go to a legacy media site online, watch television, or listen to the radio? What advantages do you experience from using this news source? What is the downside of relying on that source?

🔊 Audio 6.1: Listen to one of Edward R. Murrow's broadcasts.

That news update eventually turned into *Nightline* with anchor Ted Koppel, and it became one of the most respected news shows on television. The following year, Ted Turner's CNN went on the air with news twenty-four hours a day and the promise that the station would not sign off until the end of the world.[34] By the time the Gulf War began in January 1991, viewers were turning to CNN, not the networks, for news.[35] But CNN's dominance was not to last. By 2003 and the war in Iraq, CNN was facing competition in the twenty-four-hour news business from Fox News and, to a lesser extent, MSNBC. As early as 2002, the year after the September 11 terrorist attacks, Fox News was getting consistently higher ratings than the more established CNN. Fox did a number of things to distinguish itself from its rival. Most significantly, it was willing to take a point of view. While CNN and the broadcast networks followed the traditional objective, or neutral, style of reporting, Fox took an opinionated view in the manner of the major newsmagazines and European newspapers.[36] According to the Nielsen ratings, Fox News has fewer unique viewers than does CNN, but they watch the channel for a longer period of time.[37]

■□■■■■□■■■■■■□■■■□■■■

The News Business

The newspapers during the era of yellow journalism were the primary source of news at the time. They faced

Ted Koppel anchored a nightly news update on ABC about the American Embassy staff taken hostage in Iran in 1979. That news update eventually became the long-running late-night news show *Nightline*.

© American Broadcasting Companies, Inc.

▶ Video 6.2: Watch excerpts from the early days of *Nightline*.

competition from magazines, but heavyweights such as *Time* and *Newsweek* had yet to weigh in. Radio news was a decade or two away, television news would have to wait half a century, and CNN was nearly a hundred years in the future. Although newspapers today owe a huge debt to the great papers of the past, they are operating in a substantially different media environment, one that is saturated with fast, up-to-the-minute competition.

Newspaper Conglomerates— Consolidation and Profitability

Unlike those of Hearst and Pulitzer, today's newspapers typically face little competition from other newspapers. There are 1,382 daily newspapers currently being published, down about 25 percent from one hundred years ago. This doesn't mean that cities are going without newspapers, however; it means only that there are relatively few cities (less than 1 percent) that have competing papers.[38] Also, most newspapers today are owned by large **chains**, corporations that control a significant number of newspapers or other media outlets. Former journalist Ben Bagdikian notes in his book *The Media Monopoly* that before World War II more than 80 percent of all American newspapers were independently owned. Today that picture has reversed, with chains owning more than 80 percent of all papers. The British press has had a longer tradition of concentration of ownership, with three lords owning 67 percent of the daily circulation as early as 1910.[39]

Why is the consolidation in the publishing business taking place? Sometimes family owners just want to get out of the newspaper business. In many cases, inheritance laws virtually force the sale of family-owned papers after they have been passed down through three generations. The chain with the largest circulation is Gannett, the publisher of *USA Today*, which owns approximately eighty-five daily newspapers that have a combined circulation of more than 6.5 million.[40] In addition to Gannett, other major publishers include Thomson Newspapers, Cox Media Group, the New York Times Company, Advance Publications (formerly Newhouse), the Tribune Company, and Dow Jones & Company. In Britain, the largest single owner of newspapers is Rupert Murdoch's News Corporation, which publishes the tabloid the *Sun* as well as the more respected broadsheets the *Times* and the *Sunday Times*. News Corporation publishes more than 175 newspapers in five countries and is the largest publisher of English-language newspapers.

Until recently, newspaper publishing was one of the most profitable businesses in the United States. The Gannett newspaper chain had earnings as high as 30 to 40 percent profits from its papers.[41] The average profit for

---

chains: Corporations that control a significant number of newspapers and other media outlets.

publicly owned newspaper chains in 2005 was nearly 20 percent, noticeably higher than that for companies in the Fortune 500.[42] But all that changed in the late 2000s. Annual newspaper advertising revenue fell by 58 percent from its peak in 2000 until 2013.[43] The drops in income were the worst at metropolitan dailies, whereas the national newspaper the *Wall Street Journal* performed relatively well. While the stock prices of newspaper companies have stabilized somewhat since 2010, overall they are down anywhere "between a half and a tenth of their value" from the mid-2000s, according to the Pew 2010 "State of the Media" report.[44] For more on what these economic changes mean to the newspaper industry, see the section titled "The Future of Newspapers" at the end of this chapter.

National Newspapers

Until 2009, the United States had three national newspapers: *USA Today,* the *Wall Street Journal,* and the much smaller *Christian Science Monitor.* But in April 2009, the *Monitor* suspended its daily publication as a newspaper and became an all-electronic, Web-based news channel.[45] Both *USA Today* and the *Journal* rely on satellite distribution of newspaper pages to printing plants across the country. In other respects, the two papers could not be more different: The *Journal* has the look of an old-fashioned nineteenth-century paper, and *USA Today* originated the multicolored format. The *New York Times,* although it is a major metropolitan newspaper, is also generally considered to be a national newspaper.

The Wall Street Journal. The nation's premier newspaper for business and financial news has been doing well recently and experiencing increases in both its print circulation and digital revenues. At a time when other papers have been cutting newsroom staff size and budgets, the *Journal* has been hiring staff and producing new features. The *Journal* stands out in contrast with its major competition, *USA Today.* The *Journal* was the last major paper to start using color, and it has still not fully embraced photography. Instead, it uses pen-and-ink drawings for the "mug shots" that accompany its stories. The *Journal* has cultivated a traditional look that deliberately evokes the newspaper layouts of the pre-Pulitzer era.[46] It did undergo a substantial redesign in 2006, primarily to make the paper narrower so that it didn't use as much newsprint, and it has continued a slow movement toward a more modern look. The *Journal*'s circulation is the largest of any American newspaper, with a combined print/digital circulation of 2.38 million.[47] It is the definitive source of financial news, it is highly regarded for its national and international news from reporters such as the late Daniel Pearl, and its editorial page is one of the nation's leading conservative voices. As was discussed in Chapter 3, the *Wall Street Journal,* along with its parent Dow Jones & Company Inc., was acquired by Rupert Murdoch's News Corporation. To date, this has not resulted in substantial changes to the paper.[48]

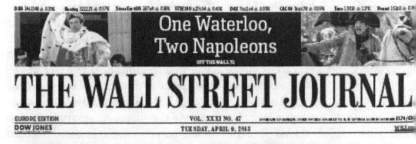

The *Wall Street Journal* is the United States' biggest circulation newspaper with a mix of business, national and international news, along with a conservative editorial focus.

USA Today: *News McNuggets.* When the Gannett newspaper chain founded *USA Today,* journalists made fun of the new national paper, calling it McPaper. They claimed that the brightly colored paper full of short stories was serving up "news McNuggets" to an audience raised on television news. John Quinn, a former editor of the paper, once joked that *USA Today* was "the newspaper that brought new depth to the meaning of the word shallow."[49] Critics of the paper warned that starting a national newspaper was a good way for Gannett to lose a lot of money in a hurry, and the critics were right. In its first decade, *USA Today* reportedly lost more than $800 million, but by 1993, the

Web 6.5: Links to the top ten U.S. newspapers.

paper started turning a profit. Coming out of the recession, *USA Today* had declining circulation, and it had fewer "sponsored" copies being bought in bulk by hotels; in 2013, it had an average daily combined print/digital circulation of 1.67 million.[50] The Pew Foundation's "State of the Media" report for 2011 speculated that some of the decline for the national paper could be in part because travelers are now getting their news via their laptops, smartphones, or tablets.[51] We'll have more on that topic in the "Future of Newspapers" section at the end of the chapter.

The paper now has strengthened its national news section, increased its international news section, and begun running in-depth stories. The paper also tries to get stories other papers don't have rather than just providing an easy-to-understand product. In addition, it has beefed up its foreign staff and hired outside reporters from prestigious newspapers and magazines.

One reason *USA Today* has become more influential is that it is found everywhere. A traveler is much more likely to find *USA Today* in a hotel than the *Washington Post* or the *New York Times*. Even the critics have started coming around in recent years. Ben Bagdikian, who once described the paper as "a mediocre piece of journalism," recently said, "It has become a much more serious newspaper. They have abandoned the idea that every person who picks up the paper has an attention span of 30 seconds. . . . I don't think it's a joke anymore."[52]

What influence has *USA Today* had on the newspaper industry as a whole? First and foremost, *USA Today* changed the look of newspapers. It drove color onto the front page and made black-and-white papers look drab in comparison. Second, it was organized clearly by section, thus initiating a trend in which papers began imposing more structure on the news. Finally, and most controversially, *USA Today* has led the trend toward shorter stories.[53]

The most important effect of *USA Today* is that it has forced industry professionals to reconsider what business they are in. The publication's Web site describes *USA Today* as a "multi-platform news and information media company . . . Through its unique visual storytelling, USA TODAY delivers high-quality and engaging content across print, digital, social and video platforms."[54]

English-Language International Newspapers.
There are three major English-language international newspapers. The best known of these is the *International New York Times* (formerly the *International Herald Tribune)*, which is published in Paris and distributed in 180 countries. Formerly owned in partnership by the *Washington Post* and the *New York Times*, it is now owned exclusively by the *New York Times*.[55] The paper was founded in 1887 as a European edition of the now-defunct *New York Herald*. Traditionally, the *Tribune* reprinted

articles from a variety of papers, but it is now based more directly on the *New York Times* content.[56]

Financial Times, owned by British media conglomerate Pearson, is primarily a business newspaper. Its one-time editor Gordon Willoughby told *Ad Age Global* magazine, "We see ourselves as an international window on the business world. There is a global business engine, and it is becoming increasingly outward looking, and that plays to what we're good at."[57]

Although the *Wall Street Journal* is thought of primarily as a U.S. paper, it also publishes European and Asian editions. "We aspired to be the global newspaper of business and the newspaper of business globally. We don't aspire to overtake local newspapers in the U.K., Germany, or Japan," says Richard Tofel of the *Journal*.[58]

None of these papers has a large circulation, with the *Tribune* selling approximately 217,000 copies a day, the international editions of the *Journal* selling 156,000, and the *Financial Times* 319,000.[59]

The Metropolitan Press

The metropolitan newspapers are the big-city papers that most people think of when they talk about the power of the press.

***The* New York Times.** If there has been a debate over whether *USA Today* or the *Wall Street Journal* is the nation's biggest paper, there is no question about which paper is most influential. When people in the United States refer to the *Times* without naming a city, they are almost certainly referring to the *New York Times*. According to at least one definition, news is what is "printed on the front page of the *New York Times*." News stories in the United States often don't become significant until they have been covered in the *New York Times*. The front page of the *New York Times* has as much news on it as is contained in an entire half-hour network newscast. The Sunday *New York Times* is huge: In September 1998, the paper published an Arts and Leisure section with 124 pages, a record for the *New York Times*—and that was just one section![60]

According to *Time* magazine,

A *Times* morning-after analysis of a presidential debate can set the agenda for days of campaign coverage and punditry. Its decision to feature, say, a murder in Texas on Page One can prompt hordes of reporters to hop a plane south. Its critics can make or break a Broadway play or turn an obscure foreign film into tomorrow's hot ticket.[61]

While the company's longtime motto is "All the News That's Fit to Print," the Hoover's business report suggests that a better choice would be "All the News That's Fit to

Print and Post Online."[62] While the *Times* is classified here as a metropolitan paper, it has as much in common with the major national papers as with the city papers. More than one-third of its readership is located outside New York City. For a list of the top ten newspapers in the United States, see Table 6.1.

The *New York Times* has been a respected newspaper ever since Adolph Ochs bought the failing penny press paper in 1896 and gave it an emphasis on serious national and international news. Its stodgy look, with long columns of type, earned it the nickname "Gray Lady." However, on October 16, 1997, the *Times* started running color photos on its front page, joining virtually every other paper in the country in this practice. Yet even with color the paper doesn't look like *USA Today.* As the *American Journalism Review* put it, "Don't expect the Gray Lady to step out in any gauche dress just to show off."[63] The *Times* is basically a black-and-white paper with color used as accents, according to newspaper design expert Mario Garcia.[64]

The Washington Post. The *New York Times* set the standard for newspaper journalism in the twentieth century and continues to do so today, but in the 1970s, the *Washington Post* inspired a generation of young journalists with its coverage of the **Watergate scandal**, the subsequent cover-up, and the downfall of President Richard Nixon. Watergate was a story that shook the nation and transformed the *Post* from a big-city paper to one with a national reputation.

The scandal started with a "third-rate burglary" of the Democratic National Committee headquarters in the Watergate office and apartment complex on June 16, 1972. When the five Spanish-speaking burglars were arrested, one was found carrying an address book that contained the number for a phone located in the White House.

Among those assigned to cover the story were two young reporters, Bob Woodward and Carl Bernstein. They soon realized that this was no ordinary burglary. As weeks and then months went by, their painstaking reporting connected the burglars to the White House and eventually to the president himself. They further discovered that the White House had been systematically sabotaging the Democratic presidential candidates and attempting to cover up these actions.

During the summer of 1973, Americans were spellbound by the Senate hearings into the Watergate scandal. Finally, with impeachment seeming a certainty, Nixon resigned as president on August 8, 1974.[65] Watergate was no doubt a high point for the *Washington Post*, but the Janet Cooke story was likely one of its lowest. Cooke was hired by

---

Watergate scandal: A burglary of the Democratic National Committee headquarters in the Watergate office and apartment building that was authorized by rogue White House staffers. Its subsequent cover-up led to the resignation of President Richard Nixon in 1974. Bob Woodward and Carl Bernstein, two reporters from the *Washington Post*, covered the Watergate scandal.

Bob Woodward (left) and Carl Bernstein helped bring the *Washington Post* to national prominence in the 1970s with their coverage of the Watergate break-in and the subsequent cover-up.

the *Post* to improve its coverage of the African American community. She was a young African American woman who claimed to have a degree from Vassar, and she was a fantastic writer. On Sunday, September 28, 1980, Cooke delivered just the kind of story she had been hired to write—a compelling account of an eight-year-old boy named Jimmy who was a heroin addict being shot up by his mother's boyfriend. Although the story was compelling, it wasn't

TABLE 6.1 Top Ten Daily Newspapers in Terms of Average Weekday Circulation, March 2013

Paper	Print	Digital	Total
1. *Wall Street Journal*	1,480,725	898,102	2,378,827
2. *New York Times*	731,395	1,133,923	1,865,318
3. *USA Today*	1,424,406	249,900	1,674,306
4. *Los Angeles Times*	432,873	177,720	610,593
5. *New York Post*	299,950	200,571	500,521
6. *Washington Post*	431,149	42,313	473,462
7. *Chicago Sun-Times*	184,801	77,660	262,461
8. *Denver Post*	213,830	192,805	406,635
9. *Chicago Tribune*	368,145	46,785	414,930
10. *Dallas Morning News*	190,613	65,912	256,525

Source: Average Circulation at the Top 25 U.S. Daily Newspapers, Alliance for Audited Media, March 2013, www.auditedmedia.com/news/research-and-data/top-25-us-newspapers-for-march-2013.aspx.

Truth-Telling as a Journalistic Priority

In January 2012, *New York Times* public editor Arthur Brisbane set off a disturbance on the Internet and Twitterverse when he asked, apparently seriously, whether reporters ought to be calling out sources for claiming things as "facts" that are demonstrably not true. (The public editor at the *Times* is a position some papers call the reader representative or the ombudsman. Brisbane is a longtime print journalist who has worked for the *Kansas City Times*, the *Washington Post*, and the *Kansas City Star*.) The column appeared under the headline "Should *The Times* Be a Truth Vigilante?"

The column began, "I'm looking for reader input on whether and when *New York Times* news reporters should challenge 'facts' that are asserted by newsmakers they write about."[1] In other words, he was asking, "Should reporters call out sources for lying?"

He went on to write that there is no question that columnists on the opinion pages of newspapers can point out lies, but should reporters do this?

Brisbane was prompted to write the column based on a message he got from a reader:

> My question is what role the paper's hard-news coverage should play with regard to false statements—by candidates or by others. In general, the *Times* sets its documentation of falsehoods in articles apart from its primary coverage. If the newspaper's overarching goal is truth, oughtn't the truth be embedded in its principal stories? In other words, if a candidate repeatedly utters an outright falsehood . . . shouldn't the *Times* coverage nail it right at the point where the article quotes it?[2]

Brisbane's online column drew a huge range of comments, many of which could be paraphrased as, "Well, duh!"

A commenter from Pennsylvania gave a typical response: "If you genuinely do not know whether or not the paper of record should act as a stenographer for liars, then count me among the rest of the commenters who is incredulous that you had to ask."[3]

Another commenter, this one from Seattle, posted sarcastically, "I'm a pharmacist. Do you think it is absolutely imperative that the next time you come to me for medication I actually give you what your doctor ordered or will just any old medication be just fine? . . . This whole article is about the dumbest thing I have ever read in ANY newspaper."[4]

Among the hundreds of comments were accusations that the paper was printing lies from President Obama, the government of Israel, or the Bush administration during the lead-up to the war in Iraq.

But the answer to Brisbane's question is not necessarily so simple. Greg Sargent, writer of the *Washington Post*'s political blog *Plum Line*, says that trying to fact-check everything before it gets printed would be difficult. On the other hand, Sargent points out that the *Times* prints misleading statements from candidates repeatedly, to the point that a reasonable person reading the paper would think those claims were true.[5]

Journalists, of course, always want to be reporting "the truth," but knowing what is true, what is false, and what is opinion can be challenging. One response to this has been the so-called fact-checking movement in journalism. The Annenberg Public Policy Center's FactCheck.org, begun in 2003, was the first project to address the issue. It monitors the accuracy of articles and ads about political figures. The *Washington Post* has its own version of this system called "The Fact Checker," which rates claims by politicians on a scale of one to four Pinocchios. PolitiFact.com, sponsored by the *Tampa Bay Times*, has sometimes caused controversy with its "Truth-O-Meter," which rates political claims from "true" to "pants-on-fire false." All of these Web sites publish fact-checking stories online as freestanding stories.

Rem Rieder, editor of *American Journalism Review*, writes that incorporating fact-checking into regular news stories would be a big improvement. He says, "Allowing a politician to get away with nonsense day after day lets false statements seep into the public consciousness. Once that happens, it can be hard to dislodge them."[6] He writes that journalists need to be sure to hold all politicians to account,

---

true—something that was not discovered until the story was awarded the Pulitzer Prize in 1981. Days after Cooke won the award, reporters learned that her college credentials had been fabricated, and soon she confessed that Jimmy's story had been made up as well.[66]

Cooke obviously had not behaved ethically in fabricating the story and her credentials. But Bob Woodward, who was one of Cooke's editors, also accepted responsibility for

 Web 6.6 Read more about the fact-checking controversy.

printing the story. Woodward explained the journalistic and moral lapse in an interview with *Washingtonian* magazine:

> When we found [the story] was a fraud, we exposed it ourselves, putting all the information, very painfully, in the paper. We acknowledged a lapse of journalism.
>
> It took me a while to understand the moral lapse, which was the more unforgivable one. I should have tried to save the kid and then do the story. . . . If it happened now, I'd say, "Okay, where's this kid who's being tortured to death?"

regardless of political party, without falling into the trap of false equivalency: "If Democrats are prevaricating more than Republicans, or vice versa, don't succumb to the temptation to be equally tough on both sides."[7]

Jill Abramson, the now former executive editor for the *New York Times,* responded to Brisbane's column by arguing that the paper does "rigorous fact-checking and truth-testing" on a daily basis in a variety of ways, including in-depth stories, commentaries, and blogs. "Can we do more?" she asks. "Yes, always. And we will."[8]

One of the strongest reactions to Brisbane's column came from New York University journalism professor Dr. Jay Rosen. Rosen, who has been an outspoken critic of the approach mainstream journalists take to objectivity, says that the need to ask Brisbane's question comes out of an increasing desire for journalists to seem "unbiased." He wrote on his blog *Press Think*,

> Something happened in our press over the last 40 years or so that never got acknowledged and to this day would be denied by a majority of newsroom professionals. *Somewhere along the way, truthtelling was surpassed by other priorities the mainstream press felt a stronger duty to.* These include such things as "maintaining objectivity," "not

imposing a judgment," or "refusing to take sides" . . . Journalists felt better, safer, on firmer professional ground—more like pros—when they stopped short of reporting substantially untrue statements as false.[9]

WHO are the sources?

Arthur Brisbane is the former public editor for the *New York Times* (August 2010–August 2012), and Jay Rosen is a professor of journalism for New York University. How do you think their backgrounds shaped their responses to the question about real-time fact-checking? Does it make a difference that one is a professional journalist and the other a professional academic?

WHAT are they saying?

Go online and read what Brisbane and Rosen have to say on the issue of real-time fact-checking. What are their central arguments? What do they disagree about? What do they agree on?

WHAT do others say about their reporting?

Read some of the comments from readers on Brisbane's posts. What are they saying? What kinds of criticism are they leveling against the *Times*? Are they criticizing Brisbane's question or the way the *Times* covers issues? Is anyone supportive of his question?

HOW do you and your classmates react to the issues Brisbane and Rosen raise?

Do you and your classmates think that reporters need to call out sources, especially politicians, when they say things that aren't true? Do you think that it's possible to do so? Will calling out sources for lying make reporters appear to be biased? Is it bad if you know what point of view a reporter holds about a topic?

---

[1]Arthur Brisbane, "Should *The Times* Be a Truth Vigilante?" January 12, 2012, *New York Times*, publiceditor.blogs.nytimes.com/2012/01/12/should-the-times-be-a-truth-vigilante/.

[2]Ibid.

[3]Ibid.

[4]Ibid.

[5]Greg Sargent, "What Are Newspapers For?" *Washington Post*, January 12, 2012, www.washingtonpost.com/blogs/plum-line/post/what-are-newspapers-for/2012/01/12/gIQAuUCqtP_blog.html.

[6]Rem Rieder, "Real Time Fact-Checking," *American Journalism Review*, February 2012, ajr.org/Article.asp?id=5237.

[7]Ibid.

[8]Arthur Brisbane, "Update to My Previous Post on Truth Vigilantes," *New York Times*, January 12, 2012, publiceditor.blogs.nytimes.com/2012/01/12/update-to-my-previous-post-on-truth-vigilantes/.

[9]Jay Rosen, "So Whaddaya Think: Should We Put Truthtelling Back Up There at Number One?" January 12, 2012, pressthink.org/2012/01/so-whaddaya-think-should-we-put-truthtelling-back-up-there-at-number-one/.

My journalistic failure was immense, but the moral failure was worse. And if I had worried about the kid, I would have learned that the story was a fraud. There would have been no journalistic failure.[67]

Fourteen years after Cooke's story was written, retired *Post* editor Ben Bradlee was still haunted by the story and by the blow it delivered to the paper's credibility: "That was a terrible blot on our reputation. I'd give anything to wipe that one off."[68]

In more recent years, as discussed in the opening vignette, the *Washington Post* has become known for its national

presence through its online presence and for the fact that it was recently purchased by Amazon founder Jeff Bezos.

The Los Angeles Times. When people talk about the press in general, they are usually speaking of the major East Coast papers such as the *Washington Post* and the *New York Times*. In the early 2000s, the *Los Angeles Times* established a national presence as well. While it may not have "push[ed] the *New York Times* off its perch,"[69] it has been one of the most respected papers on the West Coast, winning three Pulitzer Prizes in 2003, five in 2004, two in 2005, and one each in 2007 and 2009.

Lately, however, the *Los Angeles Times* has been in the news more often for the controversy surrounding cost-cutting by its owner, the Tribune Company, which also owns the *Chicago Tribune* and superstation WGN.

Since 2003, the paper has cut more than 500 people from its newsroom, reducing the number of journalists working for it from more than 1,100 to approximately 550. In addition, the paper's last four respected editors and a publisher either quit or were fired over disputes about the newsroom cuts.[70]

As of this writing in the summer of 2014, Tribune Company was in the process of spinning off the newspaper publishing wing of the company into its own new company—Tribune Publishing. The new company would own the Tribune Company's publishing assets, including the *Chicago Tribune* and the *Los Angeles Times*.[71]

The paper had previously attracted controversy over its requirement in the late 1990s that reporters attempt to include quotes from women and minorities in their stories. This wasn't so much political correctness as it was marketing correctness. Just as the penny papers started running less politically biased stories to attract the largest possible audience, so the *Los Angeles Times* is now quoting more women and Latinos to boost that segment of the paper's readership.[72] Publisher Mark Willes, who ran the paper from 1995 to 2000, set goals for increasing the number of quotes from women and minorities and made those goals a factor in determining editors' raises.[73]

Reporters at the paper have raised several questions about the new requirement: (1) Should they always identify people by race and/or sex to make sure each source gets counted as a woman or minority? What if the race or sex of a person isn't relevant to the story? (2) What if the reporter is interviewing someone over the phone and doesn't know the race of the interviewee? Does he or she have to ask? (3) What categories constitute diversity? Women, blacks, Native Americans, gays and lesbians, Hispanics? Certainly. But what about a Russian immigrant, a Jew, or a Muslim? (4) Does interviewing one African American guarantee that all black viewpoints have been covered? Some reporters have questioned whether specific minority groups even have a unified point of view.[74]

Editors refer to building diversity by quoting minorities and women in stories that aren't about minority issues as **mainstreaming**. Mainstreaming has extended far

Questioning the Media

Should news outlets identify a source quoted in a story as being female or a minority even if the source's race or sex has no bearing on the story? Why or why not? Does having women and minority sources improve the quality of the news?

Web 6.7: Learn more about community newspapers.

beyond the *Los Angeles Times*. The *San Jose Mercury News* uses the process in its food section to include material on Eastern Europeans, Southeast Asians, and African Americans and how they are cooking. Keith Woods, former diversity coordinator for the Poynter Institute, writes that mainstreaming is a problem when "people with little expertise and less to say have been forced into stories simply because they fit a demographic quota."[75] Yet when the process brings in a wider range of sources and allows journalists to learn more about their community, then it is successful. Quotas for mainstreaming by quotes are currently in a decline, but the principle—making newspapers more inclusive—is still very much alive.[76]

Community and Suburban Papers

The **community press** consists of weekly and daily newspapers serving individual communities or suburbs instead of an entire metropolitan area. These papers make extensive use of the Web. While there are more than 1,400 daily newspapers being published in the United States, there are also more than 7,000 nondaily community newspapers, according to the National Newspaper Association.[77]

One of the reasons community papers are important is that they publish news that readers can't get anywhere else. Journalism professor Eric K. Meyer points out that community newspapers "have the most loyal audiences and the news that you can't get elsewhere. A local newspaper won't get scooped by CNN."[78]

Readers often go to a local newspaper, either in the paper format or on the Web, when they feel that the national press isn't covering a story in enough detail. According to the Pew Research Center's Project for Excellence in Journalism, for the past twenty years about 90 percent of newspaper readers have gone to the local paper for news about where they live. During Hurricane Katrina, the New Orleans *Times-Picayune* went from 80,000 page hits a day to 30 million as people around the world tried to find out what was happening in the Crescent City. While the *Times-Picayune* is generally considered a metropolitan paper, in the days, weeks, and months following Hurricane Katrina, it was functioning very much as a community paper.[79]

News and Society

What is news? Ask ten different journalists, and you'll come up with ten different definitions. One way of defining news is to list its characteristics, the values

---

mainstreaming: The effort by newspapers such as the *Los Angeles Times* to include quotations by minorities and women in stories that aren't about minority issues.

community press: Weekly and daily newspapers serving individual communities or suburbs instead of an entire metropolitan area.

journalists use when they select which stories to report. These include the following:

- Timeliness—An earthquake that happened last night is more newsworthy than one that happened two months ago.
- Proximity—An auto accident in your town in which two people are injured is more likely to make it into the paper than an auto accident 300 miles away in which two people are killed.
- Prominence—When two movie stars have lunch together, it's news. When you have lunch with your mother, it's not.
- Consequence—A $50 billion tax cut is more newsworthy than a $5,000 one.
- Rarity—The birth of an albino tiger is news.
- Human interest—Events that touch our hearts, such as the birth of octuplets, often make the news.

AP Photo/Ivor Prickett Sunday Times

Sunday Times reporter Marie Colvin, shown here in Egypt's Tahrir Square during the Arab Spring protests, covered the world's most dangerous places for more than two decades before she was killed in 2012 while covering the fighting in Syria.

Another way to define news is to look at the wide range of ways newspaper editors think of it. Charles Dana, editor of the New York *Sun* in the late 1800s, defined news as "anything that will make people talk."[80] John B. Bogart, a city editor of the *Sun*, gave us a classic definition: "When a dog bites a man, that is not news. But when a man bites a dog, that *is* news." As mentioned earlier in the chapter, news is often defined as "that which is printed on the front page of the *New York Times*."[81] Noted journalist Walter Lippmann defined news as a "picture of reality on which men can act."[82] And there are cynics who say that the perfect news story is one that deals with "pets, tits, or tots."[83]

Sources, Advertisers, and Readers—Whom Do You Please?

Traditionally, newspapers have maintained a figurative wall between the business department and the newsroom, sometimes jokingly called the "separation of church and state." Reporters and editors are supposed to be concerned not with profits, but rather with reporting the news as best they can. But the barrier is coming down, and editors are increasingly looking at their newspaper as a product that should appeal to advertisers as well as readers.

John Oppedahl, who has served as editor and publisher of the *Arizona Republic*, as well as publisher of the *San*

Francisco Examiner, says that editors must be concerned about the business health of their papers:

Editors have to become more interested and more involved in how their enterprises make money.... If you take the view that editors really have been marketers all along, and maybe never wanted to say it, now I think they need to admit that they are.[84]

However, sometimes publishers go from printing news that *readers* want to publishing news that *advertisers* want. For example, many newspapers now publish advice and news about personal investing in addition to the traditional stock reports. While these features are undoubtedly popular with readers, they are even more popular with advertisers, who want their ads for financial services surrounded by stories telling readers that they ought to be investing.

The Project for Excellence in Journalism annual report for 2006 stated the situation fairly baldly: "At many old-media companies, though not all, the decades-long battle at the top between idealists and accountants is now over. The idealists have lost."[85]

Patriotism and the Press—Reporters Risk Their Lives to Report the News 🌐

Covering the news, especially from a war zone, can be a dangerous occupation. Journalist deaths in Iraq peaked in 2006 and 2007, with thirty-two journalists dying each of those years. Between March 2003, when the United States invaded Iraq, and December 2011, when the war ended, 150 journalists were killed covering the conflict. According to statistics compiled by the Committee to Protect Journalists, more than 60 percent of the journalists who died during the Iraq war were deliberately murdered as opposed to dying in battles or on dangerous assignments. In addition, fifty-four media workers were killed, including translators, drivers, guards, fixers, and administrative workers.[86]

"The deaths in Iraq reflect the utter deterioration in reporters' traditional status as neutral observers in wartime," said Committee to Protect Journalists executive director Joel Simon. "When this conflict began . . . , most journalists died in combat-related incidents. Now, insurgents routinely target journalists."[87] This continues a trend that started with the murder of popular *Wall Street Journal* reporter Daniel Pearl back in 2002. A videotape discovered on February 25, 2002, showed Pearl being stabbed to death and then decapitated. Pearl had been kidnapped in Pakistan on January 23 while attempting to reach a radical Islamic cleric for an interview.[88] The story he was chasing, however, was apparently a trap designed by a group calling itself the National Movement for the Restoration of Pakistani Sovereignty.[89] Four men were eventually captured and convicted in Pakistani courts for his kidnapping and murder. Pearl and his wife, Mariane, a freelance broadcast journalist, had arrived in Pakistan shortly after the September 11, 2001, attacks. He was covering the country as part of his job as the *Journal*'s South Asia bureau chief.

©iStockphoto.com/Anutik

Mariane Pearl says that her husband's kidnapping was not a typical one, in which the goal is ransom or exchange. "My feeling is that the killing of Danny was more of a declaration of war."[90] Why Pearl was murdered is not clear. His widow speculates that it could have been for a story he had written or something he was working on. He may have simply been seen as a symbol of the West.

In 2013, at least seventy journalists were killed around the world in direct connection to their work, according to the Committee to Protect Journalists. Of those deaths, twenty-eight came from reporters covering the civil war in Syria. The Committee to Protect Journalists reports that deteriorating security conditions have "made it virtually impossible for foreign journalists to work in Syria." Among the dozens of journalists who have been kidnapped, there was NBC's chief foreign correspondent Richard Engel and his crew. The journalists were captured by a Syrian militia group while traveling with a group of Syrian rebels. Although Engel and his team were not physically harmed, they were subject to repeated mock executions. The news team was finally freed when the militia members holding them got into a fire fight at a rebel checkpoint. Iraq was the number-two country for journalism fatalities in 2013 with ten, Egypt with six, Pakistan with five, and Somalia with four.[91]

Terry Anderson, an Associated Press reporter who was kidnapped in Lebanon in 1985 and held hostage for seven years, asks, "Why would anyone undertake this kind of work?" He finds the answer within Pearl's life. At the time of his kidnapping, Pearl was determined to try to understand why a man would pack his shoes with explosives before boarding an airplane. Anderson says that correspondents like Pearl put themselves at risk because they believe in reporting the truth:

They believe it is better for you to know that such things happen than not to know. They believe it is better for you to see the faces of the victims, almost always innocent children and women, and to hear their voices than to let them die ignored and unrecognized. They believe that if they can just make you pay attention, your horror and anger and outrage will match theirs, and you will demand that such things stop. And sometimes, they are right.[92]

The Alternative Press

Throughout this chapter we have emphasized mainstream, corporate-run, big-city newspapers. But there are also a wide range of **alternative papers** that serve specialized audiences such as racial and ethnic minorities, gays and lesbians, and young people.

Contemporary Minority/Ethnic Papers. The African American press has had a significant presence in the United States since at least 1827. Nearly 4,000 black newspapers have been published in the United States at one time or another.[93]

Freedom's Journal was among the first black newspapers; it was founded in 1827 to show all readers, white and black, that "black citizens were humans who were being treated unjustly."[94] Many black editors of the era faced great danger when they printed articles that contained fact-based accusations against whites. Mobs would destroy the newspaper's

---

Video 6.2: Learn about the career of Associated Press war correspondent George Esper.

Video 6.3: Watch an interview with NBC reporter Richard Engel and his crew about being kidnapped in Syria.

Web 6.8: Read more on the risks journalists face.

---

alternative papers: Weekly newspapers that serve specialized audiences such as racial minorities, gays and lesbians, and young people.

offices, and editors who had not left town might be murdered.

Editors of black papers faced further difficulties because much of the intended audience for the papers was illiterate. Moreover, because the majority of the audience was poor, relatively little advertising was available. These editors put their lives and livelihoods at risk publishing a paper that few might read and that probably would lose money.

A variety of emancipation papers followed in the footsteps of *Freedom's Journal*, but none had as great an impact as the *North Star*, which published its first issue in Rochester, New York, on December 3, 1847. Its editor, Frederick Douglass, was known as a gifted writer, and his new paper let readers know that it would be fighting for an end to slavery and the recognition of the rights of blacks. The *North Star* was read and noticed, but it faced the same problems as earlier black papers, including antiblack violence, a shortage of qualified staff, and a chronic lack of money. What it did have was a clear mission and a distinctive journalistic style. The *North Star* was published from 1847 until 1860.[95]

Another important African American paper is the *Chicago Defender*. Founded in 1905, the *Defender* was considerably less serious than the *North Star*, modeling its style on the yellow journalism of William Randolph Hearst. It was designed to be a black paper with a mass following rather than a publication for black intellectuals and white elites. It was also designed to appeal to advertisers and even make money for its publisher.

Clearly, the *Defender*'s goals included profit as well as advocacy. The paper was sensational, with large red headlines trumpeting stories of crime. By 1920, the *Defender* had a circulation of more than 280,000, a spectacular number at the time. It reached far beyond Chicago, with two-thirds of its readers located outside the city.[96]

The *Defender* encouraged southern blacks to move north to find jobs in Chicago and, not coincidentally, become loyal subscribers to the paper. In retaliation, it was banned throughout the South, and at least two of the paper's distributors were murdered. *Defender* editor Robert Abbott fought for civil rights and an end to lynchings. Abbott, born in 1868, has been credited with founding "the modern Negro press."[97] He demonstrated that black papers could be profit-making institutions, as well as activist publications.

In the 1950s, the *Defender* became a daily tabloid. For a while it provided extensive, day-by-day coverage of the civil rights movement. In 2003, following the death of

Library of Congress

John Sengstacke, part owner and manager of the *Chicago Defender*, a leading African American newspaper with a national circulation in the middle of the twentieth century, reviews layouts with an assistant.

longtime publisher and editor John H. Sengstacke in 1997, the *Defender* and three other papers owned by relatives of Abbott were sold to Real Times Media. In 2011, the *Defender* laid off its executive editor, news editor, and several staffers in an attempt to cut costs.[98]

What makes a black paper authentically black? In his book *The Black Press, U.S.A.*, Roland Wolseley suggests several qualifications: The paper must be owned and managed by blacks, it must be intended for black readers, and it must be an activist for the black community.[99]

Spanish-language newspapers are also doing well. While their circulation is declining—as is the case with newspapers across the board—their advertising revenue is growing, most of which comes from local advertising.[100] *El Nuevo Herald*, published as a companion to the *Miami Herald*, is the United States' largest Spanish-language paper, with a circulation in excess of 80,000. But the two papers differ in many more ways than just the language. Journalist Dan Grech, speaking on the NPR radio show *On the Media*, said, "The *Miami Herald*, like most U.S. newspapers, prizes objectivity. *El Nuevo Herald* is more like papers in Latin America and Europe that push for social change."[101]

Web 6.9: Check out several alternative papers.

From Newspapers to News Brands

Newspapers may not be selling as many sheets of newsprint as they did in the past, but they are certainly not going away as a place that people turn to for news. Consider the *New York Times*. Over the past several years, *New York Times* owner and publisher Arthur Sulzberger has been talking about how the paper will be changing. He set off a storm of controversy in spring 2007 with a comment at the World Economic Forum in Switzerland: "I really don't know whether we'll be printing the *Times* in five years, and you know what? I don't care

either . . . The Internet is a wonderful place to be, and we're leading there."[102]

This statement generated comments on almost every major press blog, but what few people noticed was that Sulzberger had been saying the same thing for at least eight years. When he was part of an *Advertising Age* roundtable in 1999, Sulzberger was asked about the future of the *Times*. He answered,

> I don't care how they get it 100 years from now. And the key is not

caring. It goes back to knowing the audience, and being, not ambivalent, but agnostic, rather. Agnostic about the methods of distribution. Because we can't afford to be tied to any production process . . . There will still be communities of interest. There will still be a need, both socially and politically, for common and shared experiences.[103]

Now there is a big difference between "I don't care how they get it 100 years from now" and "I really don't know if we'll be

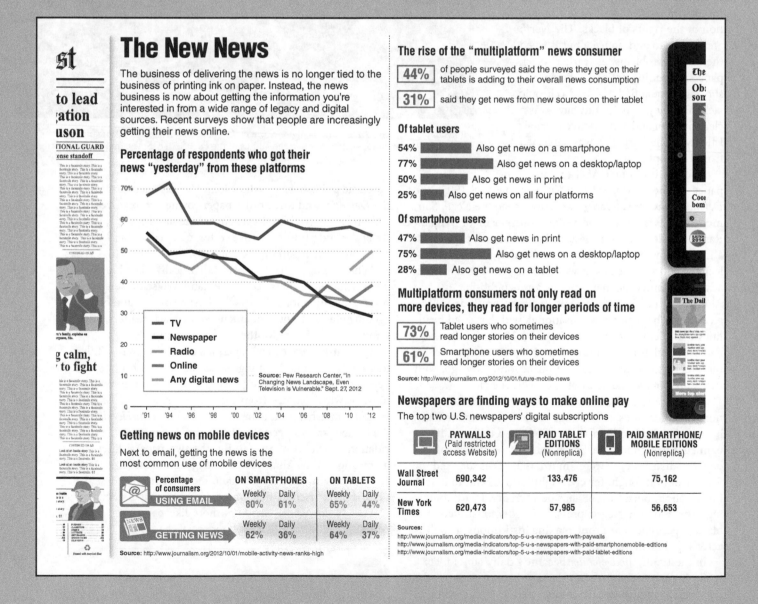

The New News

The business of delivering the news is no longer tied to the business of printing ink on paper. Instead, the news business is now about getting the information you're interested in from a wide range of legacy and digital sources. Recent surveys show that people are increasingly getting their news online.

Percentage of respondents who got their news "yesterday" from these platforms

Legend:
- TV
- Newspaper
- Radio
- Online
- Any digital news

Source: Pew Research Center, "In Changing News Landscape, Even Television is Vulnerable." Sept. 27, 2012

Getting news on mobile devices

Next to email, getting the news is the most common use of mobile devices

Percentage of consumers	ON SMARTPHONES		ON TABLETS	
	Weekly	Daily	Weekly	Daily
USING EMAIL	80%	61%	65%	44%
GETTING NEWS	62%	36%	64%	37%

Source: http://www.journalism.org/2012/10/01/mobile-activity-news-ranks-high

The rise of the "multiplatform" news consumer

44% of people surveyed said the news they get on their tablets is adding to their overall news consumption

31% said they get news from new sources on their tablet

Of tablet users

- 54% Also get news on a smartphone
- 77% Also get news on a desktop/laptop
- 50% Also get news in print
- 25% Also get news on all four platforms

Of smartphone users

- 47% Also get news in print
- 75% Also get news on a desktop/laptop
- 28% Also get news on a tablet

Multiplatform consumers not only read on more devices, they read for longer periods of time

73% Tablet users who sometimes read longer stories on their devices

61% Smartphone users who sometimes read longer stories on their devices

Source: http://www.journalism.org/2012/10/01/future-mobile-news

Newspapers are finding ways to make online pay

The top two U.S. newspapers' digital subscriptions

	PAYWALLS (Paid restricted access Website)	PAID TABLET EDITIONS (Nonreplica)	PAID SMARTPHONE/MOBILE EDITIONS (Nonreplica)
Wall Street Journal	690,342	133,476	75,162
New York Times	620,473	57,985	56,653

Sources:
http://www.journalism.org/media-indicators/top-5-u-s-newspapers-with-paywalls
http://www.journalism.org/media-indicators/top-5-u-s-newspapers-with-paid-smartphonemobile-editions
http://www.journalism.org/media-indicators/top-5-u-s-newspapers-with-paid-tablet-editions

printing the *Times* five years from now." But the basic thought, the real point of his comments, is the same—the *New York Times* is no longer in the business of putting black ink on white paper. Instead, the *Times* is in the news business and the ad sales business, and it is going to be delivering news and advertising in whatever forms will turn a profit.

Under its new ownership by Amazon founder Jeff Bezos, the *Washington Post* is now moving from a strategy of being "for and about Washington" to building a national and international readership, where its targeted audience is the English-speaking world. As *Columbia Journalism Review*'s Michael Meyer wrote in June 2014, Bezos's main objective for the *Washington Post* is "reaching the maximum number of customers by putting the *Post*'s journalism in a package (a tablet, a mobile site) that will draw the greatest number of readers. As it has been with Amazon, his obsession at the *Post* is finding a way to integrate product into millions of people's lives in a way they haven't yet experienced."[104]

The world that Sulzberger and Bezos are talking about is already well on its way to being a reality. Data from the Pew Research Journalism Project shows that while a majority of readers still consume their newspaper news exclusively as ink on paper, many others do at least some of their consumption in digital formats as well. For a complete look, see Table 6.2.

 TABLE 6.2 Newspaper Audience by Platform

Platofrm	Percentage of Circulation
Print	55 percent
Print/web	15 percent
Print/web/mobile	10 percent
Web-only	7 percent
Web/mobile	5 percent
Print/mobile	4 percent
Mobile only	3 percent

Source: Newspaper Audience by Platform, Pew Research Journalism Project, March 26, 2014, www.journalism.org/media-indicators/newspaper-audience-by-platform.

Media Transformations Questions

- **IS** a newspaper still a newspaper if a majority of its readers access it online or with a mobile device? If so, what makes it a newspaper?

- **DO** metropolitan papers (or even local newspapers) become national media like cable news networks if the adopt a digital first strategy?

- **DOES** it matter to you whether your favorite news source exists in a form other than digital? (That is, do you care whether there is a newspaper, magazine, or broadcast operation connected with it?)

The Gay Press. The question of authenticity is a difficult one for the entire alternative press, not just for ethnic papers. How can a paper represent the interests and concerns of a particular group yet still operate as a profitable commercial venture? This question has been particularly problematic for the gay press.

The *Washington Blade* was the oldest and biggest gay weekly paper in the country.[105] It was started in 1969 as a one-page mimeograph that was distributed in several gay bars at a time when such establishments were routinely raided by police. More recently, a typical edition of the *Blade* ran to more than a hundred pages and included news about health, as well as legal and political issues. In the early 1990s, one of the key features of the *Blade* was the large number of obituaries of men who had died of AIDS; these have become much less numerous in recent years. The *Blade* became such a success that it expanded outside the District of Columbia in 1997 with the *New York Blade*.

But in 2009, the recession hit the media industry hard, including the lesbian/gay/bisexual/transgender (LGBT) press. The most prominent of the gay papers to be affected was the *Washington Blade*. Just weeks after the *Blade*'s fortieth anniversary party, the paper's parent company, Window Media, shut down after investors were unable to meet financial requirements from their Small Business Administration financing. With the closing of Window Media, a number of gay papers across the country were shuttered along with the *Blade*. The *New York Blade* also ceased publication in 2009, when its parent company, HX Media, closed.[106] While many of these papers stayed closed, the *Washington Blade* did manage a revival under new management in April 2010, and as of 2012 was back to publishing both on paper and online on a regular basis.[107]

Although the *Washington Blade* has revived itself, it is the exception rather than the rule. Why did these previously successful publications fail? There are several likely reasons:

- Like many media companies in the late 2000s, the owners of LGBT newspapers were facing severe financial problems. Even though the *Washington Blade* was reportedly turning a profit up until the time it closed, its parent company was not.
- The audiences for LGBT media were early adopters of online social media and Web-based publications.

SECRET 3 Gay culture has moved into the mainstream. Remember Secret Three—Everything from the margin moves to the center. When gay and lesbian papers were founded in the 1960s and 1970s, reporters at the papers

National newspaper *USA Today* is known as much for its online and mobile content as for its print edition. The paper optimizes its sites for display on phones, tablets, and computers.

feared for their personal safety. Reporter Lou Chibbaro Jr., an employee of the *Blade* since 1976, told the *Washington Post* that, over the course of his career there, he had gone from writing under an assumed name in the 1970s to sitting in the front row at a presidential press conference in 2009. With gay and lesbian issues increasingly being covered by Big Media, there may not be the same demand for gay-specific newspapers now.[108]

The trend of gay publications moving to the mainstream has been an ongoing one. In the 2000s, there was an extensive debate in New York over whether straight-owned papers could adequately cover the LGBT community. In a 1997 interview with *Editor & Publisher* magazine, Troy Masters, the former publisher of a gay-owned New York newspaper, laid out the issue clearly in a way that could apply equally well to culture- or community-specific alternative papers outside the gay community:

> There needs to be a hard look at whether or not a publication that serves a specific group of people—whether they're of a certain race, nationality, sexual orientation, or whatever—can be owned and run by people who are not from that place. Do they truly understand the culture they're getting involved with, to treat the business the way it needs to be treated and to be sensitive to those they're trying to reach? It's very important, I think, for those kinds of publications to be treated first as a culture, and lastly as a marketplace.[109]

"Underground Papers." A third kind of alternative paper is the so-called alternative weekly. When these papers got started in the 1960s and 1970s, they were known first as underground newspapers, then as alternative weeklies. Today some prefer to be called just weeklies.[110] Among the popular weeklies now are the Chicago *Reader*, the Boston *Phoenix*, and the New Times chain.

Alternative weeklies present a stark contrast to the traditional urban newspapers in that they continue to grow in circulation. Among the Association of Alternative Newsmedia, average circulation reached 7.64 million in 2005.[111]

Although much of the content of these papers is relatively mainstream, the advertising often includes personals and ads for phone sex lines and massage parlors. Many of these papers, which depend solely on ad revenues, are distributed for free. They attract young people who have left behind daily newspapers and network news in favor of CNN, MSNBC, Fox News, and the Internet.

Just as mainstream newspapers are bought up by corporate newspaper chains, so are alternative papers being consolidated in alternative chains. This trend raises the question of whether these feisty papers will retain their independence and unique voice after becoming part of corporate America, or whether they will lose the qualities that made them popular in the first place. For example, in some cases, new owners have blocked potentially offensive cartoons and April Fools' Day editions. However, advertisers like the young, affluent readership these weekly papers can deliver, and they have expressed concern that watered-down content will lead to reduced reader interest.[112]

Questioning the Media

What makes an alternative paper authentic? Does a gay newspaper need to have a gay publisher or editor? Can a newspaper serving the African American community be owned by a white newspaper chain?

TEST YOUR MEDIA LITERACY

Can Journalists Be on Social Media?

Everyone needs to be careful about revealing too much personal information through social media such as Twitter or Facebook, but journalists see this as a particularly difficult issue because of fears of alienating sources and readers.

Wall Street Journal reporters are not supposed to post about how a story was reported. The paper's code of conduct says: "Let our coverage speak for itself, and don't detail how an article was reported, written, or edited." Reporters are also required to get their editor's permission before friending a confidential source.[1]

The BBC has fairly elaborate guidelines on using social media, especially in cases when its workers identify themselves as BBC employees. One rule suggests that BBC employees should not include a political identification online, even if they don't indicate that they work for the BBC.[2]

The *Toronto Star* also has a reasonably extensive social media policy that, among other things, bans reporters from offering opinions about the stories the paper covers. It also tells reporters and editors that they can't respond to reader comments: "As well, journalists should refrain from debating issues within the *Star*'s online comments forum to avoid any suggestion that they may be biased in their reporting."[3]

Mathew Ingram, writing for the blog *Gigaom*, says that this policy, which keeps reporters from engaging with the public, completely misses the point of social media. He writes,

> [The] main point being missed is that social media is powerful precisely *because it is* personal. . . . The best way to make social media work is to allow reporters and editors to be themselves, to be human, and to engage with readers through Twitter and Facebook and comments and blogs.[4]

Even tweets intended for a limited, private audience can be problematic. Raju Narisetti, one of two managing editors for the *Washington Post*, discontinued his personal Twitter account after questions about his tweets were raised by *Post* staff members. One of the tweets in question read, "We can incur all sorts of federal deficits for wars and what not, but we have to promise not to increase it by $1 for healthcare reform? Sad."[5] Another read, "Sen Byrd (91) in hospital after he falls from 'standing up too quickly.' How about term limits. Or retirement age. Or commonsense to prevail."[6]

The *Washington Post* issued guidelines in fall 2009 about what editorial employees ought to be posting online. The guidelines read, in part:

> When using [social networks], nothing we do must call into question the impartiality of our news judgment. We never abandon the guidelines that govern the separation of news from opinion, the importance of fact and objectivity, the appropriate use of language and tone, and other hallmarks of our brand of journalism.
>
> What you do on social networks should be presumed to be publicly available to anyone, even if you have created a private account. It is possible to use privacy controls online to limit access to sensitive information. But such controls are only a deterrent, not an absolute insulator. Reality is simple: If you don't want something to be found online, don't put it there.
>
> *Post* journalists must refrain from writing, tweeting, or posting anything—including photographs or video—that could be perceived as reflecting political, racial, sexist, religious, or other bias or favoritism that could be used to tarnish our journalistic credibility.[7]

WHO are the sources?

You have looked at codes of conduct for journalists using social media at several major news organizations from around the world. What are these news organizations? How do they differ from each other?

WHAT are they saying?

These codes of conduct tell reporters under what circumstances they can make posts on social media such as Twitter and Facebook. What kinds of rules do they expect reporters to follow? What happens to journalists who violate these standards?

WHAT kind of evidence indicates that journalists misuse social media?

What examples do the news organizations give to illustrate the problem of journalists misusing social media? What harm do they say this will bring to the news organization?

HOW do you and your classmates react to journalists using social media?

Do you or your classmates follow the social media feeds of any journalists? What do you discover about them from their tweets or Facebook posts? Do you think that journalists risk appearing biased by what they post to their social media feeds? Do you think it is right for news organizations to restrict how journalists use their social media accounts?

---

[1]Diane Brady, "What's the Right Corporate Policy for Twitter, Facebook and Blogs?" *Businessweek*, May 14, 2009, www .businessweek.com/careers/managementiq/ archives/2009/05/whats_the_right.html.
[2]BBC, "Editorial Guidelines," www.bbc.co.uk/ guidelines/editorialguidelines/advice/ personalweb.
[3]Mathew Ingram, "Newspapers and Social Media: Still Not Really Getting It," April 5, 2011, gigaom.com/2011/04/05/newspapers-and-social-media-still-not-really-getting-it/.
[4]Ibid.
[5]Andrew Alexander, "*Post* Editor Ends Tweets as New Guidelines Are Issued," *Washington Post*, September 25, 2009, voices .washingtonpost.com/ombudsman-blog/2009/09/post_editor_ends_tweets_as_ new.html?wprss=ombudsman-blog.
[6]Ibid.
[7]Ibid.

Questioning the Media

What do you think is the future for newspapers? Do you or your parents read newspapers? If newspapers die off in the "dead tree" format, what will replace them?

When the first edition of this book came out, there were two major alternative chains: New Times, which is based in Phoenix, Arizona, and publishes at least ten papers, and Stern Publishing of New York. Stern, which produces the most established alternative newspaper, the *Village Voice*, publishes at least seven papers. The *Village Voice*, founded in 1955, has a weekly circulation of 247,502, by far the largest of all the alternative weeklies in the country. *Phoenix New Times*, established in 1970, has a weekly circulation of 132,000. In 2005, New Times merged with the *Village Voice* chain. The new combined company controls about 14 percent of the circulation of alternative weekly papers.[113]

The Future of Newspapers

SECRET 2 Trying to make sense of what is happening to the newspaper business is difficult, in part because of Secret Two—There are no mainstream media. Some of the most visible segments of the newspaper business are facing major challenges, which critics are fond of pointing out. But other portions of the business, especially the more rural community papers, are thriving. So to understand the changing newspaper market we have to look at it as several media, not just one.

Are Newspapers a Dying Medium?

There can be no doubt that the business of the major urban newspapers is changing. Newspapers have been among the slowest media to recover from the 2008 recession. While things are not getting better for newspapers, they have been getting worse at a much slower pace recently. Advertising dollars and circulation numbers are continuing to decline, but at radically slower rates than in the previous couple of years. And Pew's 2011 "State of the News Media" report says that newspapers are still profitable. As was mentioned earlier in the chapter, the difference is that they are now averaging a profit of about 5 percent a year, as opposed to the 20 to 25 percent that was the norm in the 1990s. Keep in mind that in the not-so-distant past, newspapers were among the most profitable businesses in America.[114]

On the other hand, the newspapers that can be seen as national in scope (the *Wall Street Journal* and the *New York Times* in particular) are holding tight in terms of paid circulation and readership. And smaller newspapers in more rural areas are also doing well. The big problem is with the major urban papers.

The afternoon dailies were the first to feel the effects of the changing media landscape. Afternoon papers, especially the giant papers published by Hearst and Pulitzer, were enormously popular in the early 1900s. These papers were bought by factory workers who started their jobs too early to read a paper in the morning and preferred to buy papers on their way home. Today, however, afternoon papers don't fit neatly into most people's schedules. Morning papers are still convenient and valued, but afternoon papers have to compete with the evening television news. Also, it is easier for morning papers to provide up-to-date coverage. Not much happens overnight as the morning paper is being put together, but the afternoon paper's news is already old. Distribution is also difficult because of heavy traffic during the day, something that morning papers, which go out between midnight and four in the morning, don't have to worry about.[115]

Most of the job losses have been at the major urban papers. According to the 2006 Project for Excellence in Journalism report, the top three newspapers lost no circulation, and the loss at the smaller newspapers was "modest." The big-city papers that have to cover a large metro area and a host of suburbs are the ones in trouble. And with the loss of staff, it becomes harder for these big papers to serve "as watchdogs over state, regional, and urban institutions, to identify trends, and to define the larger community public square."[116] A good example of a paper undertaking this watchdog function is the *Washington Post*'s stories about the substandard conditions and care for injured Iraq war veterans at Walter Reed military hospital. In addition to being an important national story, it was also an important local story for the Washington, D.C., area.

A few of these papers have suspended their print editions and become exclusively digital publications. Among the most prominent of these was the *Christian Science Monitor*, which went all digital in April 2009.[117] Another paper to go digital-only was the *Seattle Post-Intelligencer*, which stopped publication in March 2009 but retained an online presence dominated by commentary.[118]

The change at the *Monitor* to all-electronic distribution is not as radical as some observers are claiming. Although the *Monitor* has had a substantial online presence for some time, its daily circulation of approximately 50,000 copies was relatively small compared to either *USA Today* or the *Wall Street Journal*, both of whom measure their circulation with the word *million* attached. The *Monitor*'s importance comes not from its size, but rather from its overall reputation as one of the country's best papers. Its Web site attracts about 1.5 million page views per month.[119]

🔊 Audio 6.2: Learn more about *Bloomberg News*.

Chapter SUMMARY

The first newspapers were published in Europe in the seventeenth century. Numerous papers were published in the American colonies, but they faced extensive censorship from the British government. Newspapers printed before the nineteenth century tended to be partisan publications that were supported through high subscription fees and political subsidies. This changed with the rise of the penny press in the 1830s. The penny papers were mass produced on steam-powered printing presses and contained news of interest to ordinary people. The papers cost one or two cents and were supported by advertisers who wanted to reach the papers' large numbers of readers.

The late nineteenth and early twentieth centuries were characterized by the yellow journalism of the New York newspapers published by Joseph Pulitzer and William Randolph Hearst. The two publishers tried to attract circulation and attention by running comic strips, advice columns, and sensational stories about sex, crime, and scandal. This was also the time when newspapers started running extensive headlines and illustrations.

The major classes of newspapers today include

- national papers that attempt to cover issues of interest to the entire country, such as *USA Today* and the *Wall Street Journal*;
- metropolitan papers that cover a particular city, such as the *New York Times* and the *Washington Post*;
- community papers that serve a particular town or suburb and provide news that readers cannot get elsewhere; and
- alternative newspapers that serve specialized populations rather than a broad, general audience. These can serve ethnic populations within a community, groups such as gays and lesbians, or even young people that are not interested in traditional newspapers.

Evolving technology has brought changes to the newspaper business. The rise of television news resulted in a decline in the number of afternoon newspapers, and changes in news-consumption patterns have drawn audiences and advertisers away from both newspapers and broadcast television news. Digital media have given newspapers new opportunities to update the news rapidly and fresh ways to deliver the news. Whatever the method of delivery, reporters struggle with the issue of objectivity, especially when the story is close to home and when they are risking their lives to report the news.

 Keep up-to-date with content from the author's blog.

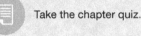 Take the chapter quiz.

Key TERMS

above the fold   138

yellow journalism   139

tabloid
    newspapers   140

broadsheet
    newspapers   140

jazz journalism   140

chains   142

Watergate scandal   145

mainstreaming   148

community press   148

alternative papers   150

Concept REVIEW

Reporter objectivity and detachment

Tradition of journalistic independence

Advertising-supported media

Changing newspaper market

Consequences of corporate ownership of newspapers

Determining the proper role for the alternative press

Balancing serving investors, advertisers, and readers

Risks of reporting from a war zone

New media versus old sources of news

Student STUDY SITE

$SAGE edge™

Sharpen your skills with SAGE edge at **edge.sagepub.com/hanson5e**

SAGE edge for Students provides a personalized approach to help you accomplish your coursework goals in an easy-to-use learning environment.

Audio

Music and Talk Across Media

Film Magic/ Getty Images

Mash-up Artist Gregg Gillis of Girl Talk performs in San Francisco during the 2011 Outside Lands Music and Arts Festival. Gillis is known for mixing together hundreds of music clips to create a sonic collage.

Anne Marsen dances the part of "The Girl" in the feature-length Girl Walk // All Day video interpretation of the Girl Talk mash-up album All Day. The video was filmed in New York City and features a small cast of dancers and passers-by that the dancers interact with.

Jacob Krupnick Productions

Trying to explain what Gregg Gillis, a.k.a. Girl Talk, does to someone who grew up in the days of the Doors or the Ramones can be a bit challenging. He's a disc jockey who plays clips from multiple songs at the same time. Put more elegantly, Gillis is a mash-up artist—someone who combines two or more pieces of music to create something new.[1]

As an example, one of the most famous mash-ups is DJ Danger Mouse's *Grey Album*, a combination of the vocals from rapper Jay-Z's *Black Album* and samples from the Beatles' 1968 album *The Beatles* (better known as the *White Album*). While Jay-Z had created the a cappella version of his album specifically for mash-up use, Beatles publisher EMI was not amused and attempted to get the *Grey Album* suppressed.[2]

As great as the work by people such as Danger Mouse may be, nothing really compares to the level of mash-ups done by Pittsburgh's Gillis. Gillis has a degree in biomedical engineering, but several years ago he quit his day job to create the incredible mixes that have gone into his five albums. His 2010 album *All Day* reportedly contains 400 different samples—typically some kind of rapping combined with samples of pop, rock, or soul music from the last forty or fifty years. The artists he uses include the Doors and the Ramones.

Both Danger Mouse and Girl Talk have given away their albums online, and none of the samples have been licensed or paid for use. Capitol/EMI, the Beatles' publisher, sent out a cease-and-desist letter telling Danger Mouse and the Web sites hosting his work to take down the album because it infringed on the Beatles' copyright. But when the album remained online, nothing happened to those distributing the content. And so far no one has sued Girl Talk's Gillis for his massive sampling.

Were he to attempt to license the music, Gillis estimates that it would cost several million dollars and that many of the songs wouldn't be available at any price. According to Duke law professor James Boyle, speaking on NPR's *On the Media*, there may be a range of reasons no one has gone after Gillis:

> There is the story that the labels learned from DJ Danger Mouse and don't want to risk creating the Che Guevara of the digital sampling age, the lost hero to which all of us will offer reverence and thus make him even more popular.
>
> Another story is, they're going, hmm, this is really interesting. Let's let him run a bit, and when we finally see how things are playing out then we'll figure out a way of getting a revenue stream out of this. A third story is they realize it's actually fair use and they don't want a bad precedent brought against them. And then a fourth one is that they are gibbering in terror and are so scared by this new phenomena, they're incapable of rational action of any kind and so are caught in a kind of fugue state, as the digital music scene develops.[3]

▶ Video 7.1: See or download Girl Talk's albums.

▶ Video 7.2: Learn more about *Girl Walk // All Day*.

Gillis told *Wired* that artists are still coming to terms with the implications of remix and collage culture. "Sharing ideas and being influenced by those who come before you has always been the foundation of progress in art and music," he said. "I think it's become a lot more obvious in the internet age, though. People are more directly interactive with what they consume. . . . It's commonplace now for people to take pre-existing media, recontextualize it and show it to the world."[4]

There's also an argument to be made that sampling can even help the career of artists who have had their music "recontextualized." As an example, in 2000 rapper Eminem sampled trip-hop artist Dido's song "Thank You" in his single "Stan." "Stan" became a hit for Eminem and led to Dido becoming an international star. (To be fair, Dido was credited on the album and was featured in the video that went with "Stan.")[5]

The most impressive outgrowth of Girl Talk's *All Day*, however, is a full-length dance film called *Girl Walk // All Day* directed by indie filmmaker Jacob Krupnick. Krupnick, working with a cast of three principal dancers (The Girl, The Gentleman, and The Creep), tells the story of a young woman's day in Manhattan as she rebels against the restrictions of her dance class and attempts to get everyone else in the city moving with her. Since the film is based around an album that uses hundreds of unlicensed music samples, it's being distributed for free using streaming media online. It is also being shown as part of a multimedia dance party experience held in a range of venues, including a church in Manhattan, an upscale restaurant in Seattle, and the SXSW festival in Austin, Texas. The movie itself was funded through Kickstarter, an online service that raises start-up capital from the public.

Gillis released *All Day* using a Creative Commons license that said other people could make use of his work as long as they attribute it back to him, so Krupnick tells *Wired* he figured he was allowed to freely use the music. (You can read more about Creative Commons in Chapter 13, "Media Law.") He says, "I just heard this album that you have to download immediately. Wouldn't it be wild if we danced all over New York and made a music video to the whole thing?"[6]

Timeline

1800	1900	1910	1920	1930	1940

1812 War of 1812 breaks out.
1835 Alexis de Tocqueville publishes *Democracy in America*.
1859 Charles Darwin publishes *On the Origin of Species*.
1861 U.S. Civil War begins.
1869 Transcontinental railroad is completed.
1879 Thomas Edison invents electric light bulb.
1898 Spanish-American War breaks out.

1903 Orville and Wilbur Wright fly first airplane.
1905 Albert Einstein proposes his theory of relativity.

1912 *Titanic* sinks.
1914 World War I begins.
1918 Worldwide influenza epidemic strikes.

1920 Nineteenth Amendment passes, giving U.S. women the right to vote.
1929 U.S. stock market crashes, leading to the Great Depression.

1933 Adolf Hitler is elected chancellor of Germany.
1939 World War II breaks out in Europe.

1941 United States enters World War II.
1945 United States drops two atomic bombs on Japan.
1947 Pakistan and India gain independence from Britain.
1949 Communists establish People's Republic of China.

1844 Samuel Morse develops the telegraph; electronic signals can be sent over long distances.
1897 Guglielmo Marconi develops ship-to-shore radio.

1912 The sinking *Titanic* sends distress call by radio.
1916 David Sarnoff writes the Radio Music Box memo.
1920 KDKA, broadcasting out of Pittsburgh, Pennsylvania, becomes the first commercial radio station.
1922 The BBC is created as a public broadcasting service in England.

1938 Orson Welles's 60-minute live radio broadcast of the H. G. Wells novel *War of the Worlds* creates a panic among listeners who believed that Martians attacked the United States.
1949 Dewey Phillips's program, *Red, Hot, & Blue*, becomes one of the first rock 'n' roll and R&B music shows on the air.

Looking at all this creativity and the attention that Girl Talk and *Girl Walk // All Day* have attracted, we see a couple of the Seven Secrets coming into play:

SECRET 2 ▶ There are no mainstream media. Neither Girl Talk's album *All Day* nor the *Girl Walk // All Day* film were released through traditional "mainstream" media operations. Yet both have been highly acclaimed and consumed by people across the country.

SECRET 5 ▶ New media are always scary. Both the album and the film are upsetting to the existing media industry. At a time when major media companies and advocacy groups are making a big noise about file sharing and piracy, two separate artists are working at putting together completely different models for economic success. As you will see later on in this chapter, there are accusations that the audio industry is dying, while others respond that it is merely changing. Either way, change and new media are always scary.

In this chapter, we look at how the recording industry and radio developed together as our first electronic media. We then examine how society has changed, how cultures have grown and merged, and how audience members have responded to the production of shared music and talk. Finally, we look at where the industries are headed in the twenty-first century. ■

> **"** People are more directly interactive with what they consume. . . . It's commonplace now for people to take pre-existing media, recontextualize it and show it to the world. **"**
>
> —Gregg Gillis, a.k.a. Girl Talk

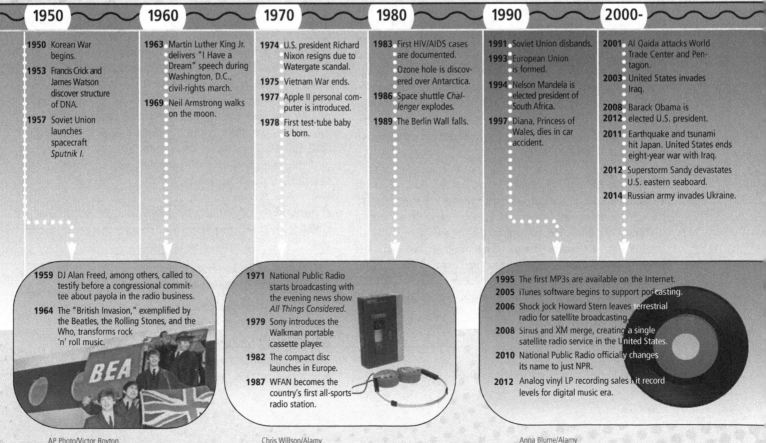

1950

1950 Korean War begins.

1953 Francis Crick and James Watson discover structure of DNA.

1957 Soviet Union launches spacecraft *Sputnik I.*

1960

1963 Martin Luther King Jr. delivers "I Have a Dream" speech during Washington, D.C., civil-rights march.

1969 Neil Armstrong walks on the moon.

1970

1974 U.S. president Richard Nixon resigns due to Watergate scandal.

1975 Vietnam War ends.

1977 Apple II personal computer is introduced.

1978 First test-tube baby is born.

1980

1983 First HIV/AIDS cases are documented.

Ozone hole is discovered over Antarctica.

1986 Space shuttle *Challenger* explodes.

1989 The Berlin Wall falls.

1990

1991 Soviet Union disbands.

1993 European Union is formed.

1994 Nelson Mandela is elected president of South Africa.

1997 Diana, Princess of Wales, dies in car accident.

2000-

2001 Al Qaida attacks World Trade Center and Pentagon.

2003 United States invades Iraq.

2008 Barack Obama is
2012 elected U.S. president.

2011 Earthquake and tsunami hit Japan. United States ends eight-year war with Iraq.

2012 Superstorm Sandy devastates U.S. eastern seaboard.

2014 Russian army invades Ukraine.

1959 DJ Alan Freed, among others, called to testify before a congressional committee about payola in the radio business.

1964 The "British Invasion," exemplified by the Beatles, the Rolling Stones, and the Who, transforms rock 'n' roll music.

1971 National Public Radio starts broadcasting with the evening news show *All Things Considered.*

1979 Sony introduces the Walkman portable cassette player.

1982 The compact disc launches in Europe.

1987 WFAN becomes the country's first all-sports radio station.

1995 The first MP3s are available on the Internet.

2005 iTunes software begins to support podcasting.

2006 Shock jock Howard Stern leaves terrestrial radio for satellite broadcasting.

2008 Sirius and XM merge, creating a single satellite radio service in the United States.

2010 National Public Radio officially changes its name to just NPR.

2012 Analog vinyl LP recording sales hit record levels for digital music era.

AP Photo/Victor Boyton

Chris Willson/Alamy

Anna Blume/Alamy

History of Sound Recording and Transmission

Before there could be mass consumption of popular music, there had to be a means of recording and distributing it. Those means evolved through the decades via Thomas Edison's early efforts with the phonograph, the development of the gramophone, and the creation of the LP and the compact disc. The recording industry changed the way people consumed music. Before the phonograph and gramophone, the only way to experience music was to perform it yourself or go to a concert. The invention of the record meant that recordings of professional musicians became the standard way to listen to music.

Storing Musical Performances: The Development of the Recording Industry

A variety of stories have been told about Thomas Edison and his invention of an early sound-recording machine, the **phonograph**, in 1877. One version has Edison giving a sketch of the phonograph to employee John Kruesi with the instruction, "the machine must talk."[7] Another has Edison sketching the phonograph, with a note at the bottom telling his assistant to "build this."[8]

Edison's First Recordings. These stories do not do justice to Edison's true genius or to the difficulties of creating a machine that could record and play back the voice. Running through these myths is the mistaken notion that Edison came up with an idea for sound recording that worked perfectly the first time it was tried. In reality, Edison and his assistants probably worked as long as ten months on the problem of the phonograph before they finally succeeded in recording Sarah Josepha Hale's children's rhyme, "Mary Had a Little Lamb." This famous first recording lasted no more than ten seconds.[9]

Emile Berliner: Mass-Produced Music. As with so many media inventions, no one was quite sure what to do with Edison's phonograph. Edison envisioned it as a dictation machine. Reproducing music was only the fourth on his list of possible uses.[10] The biggest flaw with his invention was that Edison's foil cylinders did not hold up to repeated playing and could not be reproduced. It took the work of a young German immigrant to make the phonograph a truly practical device.

 Web 7.1: More on Thomas Edison.

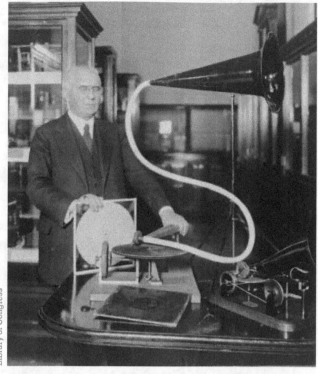

Library of Congress

Emile Berliner was able to turn Thomas Edison's idea for a phonograph into a commercially viable product that lasted in one form or another for more than one hundred years.

Emile Berliner arrived in the United States in 1870 at the age of nineteen. By 1888, he had developed a method for recording sound on flat discs rather than on cylinders. Berliner's disc recordings (or records) were louder and more lifelike than the cylinder recordings of Edison or Bell. Berliner called his device the **gramophone**. Eventually, however, all record players were called phonographs.

Berliner also helped develop the idea of the recording industry. With Edison's phonograph, every recording was an original. Berliner viewed his invention not as a business dictating machine, but as an entertainment device. His discs could be reproduced from the original etched-zinc master, allowing publishers to mass produce high-quality—at least for the time—musical recordings almost as easily as printers could reproduce books. Because of this, Berliner saw that "prominent singers, speakers, or performers may derive an income from royalties on the sale of their phonautograms."[11]

A New Way of Publishing Music. By 1935, the term **high fidelity (hi-fi)** was being used to refer to a combination

---

phonograph: An early sound-recording machine invented by Thomas Edison; the recorded material was played back on a cylinder.

gramophone: A machine invented by Emile Berliner that could play prerecorded sound on flat discs rather than cylinders.

high fidelity (hi-fi): A combination of technologies that allowed recordings to reproduce music more accurately, with higher high notes and deeper bass, than was possible with previous recording technologies.

of technologies that allowed recordings that reproduced music more accurately, with higher high notes and deeper bass, than previous forms of recording had allowed. One of the developments that helped pave the way for hi-fi was the electric phonograph (along with the amplifier and loudspeakers), which began replacing the all-mechanical gramophone. By 1949, magnetic tape recorders were commonplace in recording studios. Musicians no longer had to record directly onto discs.

The phonograph changed the face of music. Previously, there were only two ways to store music. The first, and oldest, was for parents to teach their children the traditional songs of their culture. The alternative was written music, or musical scores, that contained symbols for the musical notes to be played. The phonograph provided a revolutionary way of storing the actual music, not just the symbols written down by the composer. It also made possible the storage of non-notated music, such as folk songs or jazz solos, which did not necessarily exist in written form. Music scholar Charles Hamm has compared the phonograph to a musical time machine that allows listeners to go back and hear the actual sounds.[12]

Transmitting Music and Talk: The Birth of Radio 🌐

Around the time the recording industry was getting started, radio was under development as one of the first media to break through the barrier of space. With print media such as books, magazines, and newspapers, the message being transmitted was always on a piece of paper that had to be carried from one place to another. Thus, the fastest form of transportation at the time was also the fastest channel of communication. This meant that it could take weeks for a message to cross the Atlantic or Pacific Ocean, or even to get from New York to California or from London to Moscow. But in the nineteenth century, several inventions separated communication and transportation, starting with the wired media of the telegraph and telephone and moving on to the wireless technology of radio.

Samuel Morse's invention of the telegraph in 1844 allowed messages to be sent electrically, so that they didn't have to be carried from place to place. No longer did transportation set

limits on communication. Messages could travel at the same speed as electrons traveling along a wire.[13] By 1866, a telegraph cable extended across the Atlantic Ocean, so that even that giant barrier had been conquered.

But the wire itself was a serious limitation. Telegraph wires could break (or be cut, as they frequently were during the American Civil War). To communicate with ships at sea, a *wireless* telegraph was necessary.

In 1888, German physicist Heinrich Hertz found that he could detect the signal created by an electrical spark on one side of a room with a small loop antenna on the other side. What he had created was essentially the simplest possible radio transmitter and receiver. In 1894, Guglielmo Marconi read about Hertz's work and concluded that he could create a wireless telegraph, a point-to-point communication tool that used radio waves to transmit messages. Over a period of several years, he developed a system to send and receive radio signals, with the distance traveled by his signals expanding from the length of his attic to the width of the Atlantic Ocean.[14]

Radio as Mass Communication. In 1901, physicist Reginald Fessenden started sending voice signals over a radio in his laboratory. On Christmas Eve in 1905, he broadcast poetry and Christmas carols. Since his continuously modulated voice signals could be received by the same equipment that received Morse code, wireless operators up and down the Atlantic coast heard Fessenden's amazing broadcast. Though it would be years before regularly scheduled commercial broadcasts would begin, Fessenden had set the stage for broadcasting something more than just Morse code.

Up until 1905, it was the scientists who were driving the radio business with their new technologies, but it was a young American Marconi employee who saw that radio could be much more than just a way to send messages from one person to another. David Sarnoff, born in 1891, was a good student, but the need to help support his Russian-immigrant family led him to leave school after the eighth grade to work full-time. In a story that seems almost too good to be true, the fifteen-year-old Sarnoff went to the *New York Herald* to try to get a job as a journalist. As luck would have it, the first person he met at the *Herald* building worked for a telegraph company. Sarnoff went to work for the Commercial Cable Company, and from that point on, he never left electronic media.[15]

The Radio Music Box Memo. In 1915, Sarnoff addressed to the director of American Marconi a document that he considered the most important of his career. The so-called Radio Music Box memo outlined radio's

---

non-notated music: Music such as a folk song or jazz solo that does not exist in written form.

telegraph: The first system for using wires to send messages at a distance; invented by Samuel Morse in 1844.

wireless telegraph: Guglielmo Marconi's name for his point-to-point communication tool that used radio waves to transmit messages.

Radio Music Box memo: David Sarnoff's 1915 plan that outlined how radio could be used as a popular mass medium.

 Web 7.2: Learn more about Guglielmo Marconi.

Listening to music over headphones is nothing new, but in the 1920s, this farmer needed a wheelbarrow to move the radio set (left) from place to place.

Library of Congress

potential as a popular mass medium. While Sarnoff did not invent the technology of radio and was not the first person to send out entertainment over the radio, he did summarize what radio could, and indeed did, become. Sarnoff's insight was that radio could be more than a point-to-point medium, a one-on-one form of communication. As Sarnoff saw it, what was then perceived as the great disadvantage of radio as a telegraph tool—that everyone who listened could hear the message—could be turned into an enormous advantage if one wanted to send out messages that everyone was *supposed* to listen to. In his memo, Sarnoff wrote,

> I have in mind a plan of development which would make radio a household utility in the same sense as the piano or phonograph. The idea is to bring music into the houses by wireless.
>
> While this has been tried in the past by wires, it has been a failure because wires do not lend themselves to this scheme. With radio, however, it would be entirely feasible. For example, a radio telephone transmitter having a range of, say, 25 to 50 miles can be installed at a fixed point where instrumental or vocal music or both are produced. . . . The receiver can be designed in the form of a simple "Radio Music Box" and arranged for several different wave

Web 7.3: Read and see more about broadcasting pioneer David Sarnoff.

lengths, which should be changeable with the throwing of a single switch or pressing of a single button.[16]

With this memo, Sarnoff essentially invented radio as a social institution. But this new medium would have to wait, because on the eve of U.S. involvement in World War I, the navy was buying all of Marconi's transmitters. Although American Marconi did not act on Sarnoff's memo, the young immigrant did not forget the ideas for radio's potential that he had laid out so clearly.

More Receivers Than Transmitters.
One of the biggest surprises of the radio business was that so many more receivers were sold than transmitters. Manufacturers had assumed at the start that there would be almost as many people sending as receiving messages.[17] In reality, however, electronic communication was following in the footsteps of print. The earliest books had been copied by hand and passed from one person to another. But just as the printing press provided books, magazines, and newspapers to the masses, radio was now becoming a mass medium.

The RCA Radio Monopoly.
During World War I, the navy had taken control of all radio technology, including the patents, and it wanted to maintain control after the war. But civilian government officials in the United States, in keeping with the U.S. tradition of independent media, rejected the idea of all-government control. In an attempt to avoid anarchy in the new medium, the navy advocated creating a private monopoly to control radio development.

The Radio Corporation of America (RCA) was formed as a consortium of four major companies: General Electric, AT&T, Westinghouse, and United Fruit Company. General Electric was included because it made radio transmitters and owned what had formerly been American Marconi. AT&T was the world leader in wired communication, and Westinghouse owned many critical patents. But why was United Fruit Company a part of RCA? United Fruit had used radios to connect its boats to banana plantations in South America and while doing so had developed improved technology that the monopoly needed. These four companies brought together the 2,000 or so patents that were needed to make the radio business work. RCA not only became a major producer of radio equipment, but it also founded NBC, the first of the major broadcasting networks.[18]

Westinghouse employee and self-educated engineer Frank Conrad started making Sarnoff's dream of the Radio Music Box come true. In 1920, with Westinghouse's support, Conrad started broadcasting music on Sunday afternoons. Westinghouse then built Conrad a more powerful transmitter and put together a broadcast schedule.

Pittsburgh's radio station KDKA was licensed for broadcast on October 27, 1920. Others soon followed. Over in Britain, the British Broadcasting Company was created in 1922. It was initially a privately run company owned by the manufacturers of broadcasting equipment, and its first station was licensed in 1923. In 1927, the company became the British Broadcasting Corporation, a public, noncommercial monopoly for broadcasting in the United Kingdom.[19]

Radio Advertising.

Although KDKA was the first commercial radio station, it was not the first station to run a commercial. KDKA existed to provide programming with the goal of getting people to buy radio sets. But WEAF, broadcasting in New York City, was the first station to sell airtime to advertisers. The modest success of these commercials soon led to radio advertising by oil companies, department stores, and American Express.

©iStockphoto .com/robas

The radio industry considered several possibilities for making money. One possibility was to support radio broadcasting with a "tithe" (a specified percentage) of revenues from sales of radios by all manufacturers. Another possibility was to support it with a substantial public endowment. The problem was that neither of these schemes would provide enough money to pay for the high-priced entertainers that listeners wanted to hear. This meant that radio stations were going to need advertising revenue. Ultimately, the rest of the media industry would accept advertising as the main source of income for broadcasting. In Britain, by contrast, the original BBC was supported by revenue from selling radio receivers and radio-receiving licenses, and it was prohibited from selling commercials.[20]

Radio Networks.

By 1923, more than 600 radio transmitters were broadcasting in the United States. These stations were limited to the programming they could produce locally. How did these stations fill their broadcast day? In big cities, this was no problem because there were plenty of concerts, lectures, and sporting events to put on the air, but rural areas or small towns were limited in their selection of locally produced culture and entertainment. In another of his famous memos, Sarnoff suggested that RCA form a new company, a **network**, to provide programming to a large group of broadcast stations, thus making a wider selection of programming available to smaller stations.

RCA established the National Broadcasting Company (NBC) on July 22, 1926. It was the United States' first major broadcasting network, and it survives today in the form of the NBC television network. NBC was actually two networks, the "Red" and the "Blue." (See Figure 7.1.) (Due to an antitrust ruling, RCA was eventually forced to sell the Blue network, which then became ABC.)

William Paley and the Power of Radio Advertising.

With the growing demand for radio programming, the two NBC networks soon faced new competition, none more significant than William Paley's Columbia Broadcasting System (CBS). Although Paley was born in the United States, his parents were Russian immigrants. He grew up in a wealthy household, and his family owned a successful cigar company. William Paley's father, Sam, had been approached about advertising his cigars on the fledgling United Independent Broadcasters (UIB) network. Sam Paley was not interested, but William was.

William Paley bought his first radio ads while his father was away on business, and although Sam initially chastised his son for wasting money, he soon heard people talking about the wonderful show his company sponsored. That was enough to convince him. William then developed a program called *La Palina Smoker* that featured an orchestra, a singer, and a comedian. It also resulted in increased cigar sales. Before long William, who was not quite twenty-seven years old, had the opportunity to buy UIB, which he did with help from his father. Once he became president of the network, he promptly renamed it the Columbia Broadcasting System.[21]

Paley understood better than anyone else that broadcasting was a business that had to make a profit on its own. NBC believed that its mission was to develop programs for the benefit of its listeners, but CBS realized that its real clients were the advertisers who sponsored the programs. Its programs were designed and produced specifically to attract the kind of audience a particular advertiser was looking for. For CBS, the "product" was the audience its programs attracted.

From the Golden Age to the Television Age 🌐

The 1920s, 1930s, and 1940s came to be known as the **golden age of radio**, an era in which radio played the same role that television does today. Radio was the mass medium that served as the primary form of entertainment in the household. This was a big change. It meant that people were getting most of their entertainment from outside the home rather than from within. Instead of being entertained by Aunt Martha's and Cousin Sue's piano duets, they were listening to Bing Crosby's crooning or Bob Hope's comedy on the radio.

---

network: A company that provides common programming to a large group of broadcast stations.

golden age of radio: A period from the late 1920s until the 1940s, during which radio was the dominant medium for home entertainment.

🔊 Audio 7.1: Check out the KDKA all-news station.

Figure 7.1 The Early Red and Blue NBC Radio Networks

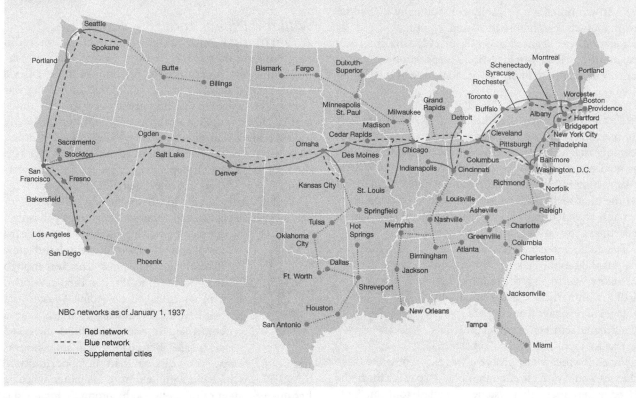

NBC networks as of January 1, 1937

——— Red network
- - - - Blue network
············· Supplemental cities

Source: Library of Congress.

Golden Age Radio Programming.

Golden Age Radio Programming. A wide range of programming was available on the radio during the golden age. Live music, both popular and classical, was a staple. NBC even had its own orchestra that performed on a regular basis. There were also dramas and action programs, including *Little Orphan Annie*, *The Lone Ranger*, and *The Shadow*.

Some radio programs from the golden age survive today as television programs, most notably **soap operas**. The soaps, as they are called for short, are daytime dramas targeted primarily at women; they got their name from the commercials for soap and other cleaning products that ran during the shows. For better or worse, soaps were the first programs targeted specifically at women, a key audience for advertisers. It wasn't until the advent of television in the 1950s that soaps ceased to be a major part of radio programming.[22] CBS's *Guiding Light* started on the radio in 1937, moved over to television in 1952, and finished its seventy-two-year run on September 18, 2009.

Amos 'n' Andy. Despite the popularity of soap operas, no radio show attracted a bigger audience than *Amos 'n' Andy*, the first nationally broadcast daily drama.[23] *Amos 'n' Andy* began in January 1926 on Chicago radio station WGN as *Sam 'n' Henry*. The show was a fixture on the radio, in one form or another, for nearly thirty-five years. Starring on the show were two white actors—Charles Correll and Freeman Gosden—who played the roles of two African Americans, Sam and Henry, who owned the Fresh Air Taxi Company. Correll and Gosden wrote all the scripts themselves and furnished the voices for the title characters and the members of their fraternal lodge, the Mystic Knights of the Sea. Their names were later changed to Amos and Andy when Correll and Gosden syndicated the show nationally, since WGN owned the characters of Sam and Henry. At the peak of its popularity, *Amos 'n' Andy* was played in restaurants and in movie theaters between shows so that people wouldn't have to stay home to listen.

For the history of radio news, see Chapter 6, "Newspapers and the News."

The BBC: Voice of the Old Empire.

The BBC: Voice of the Old Empire. Although in the United States radio is generally seen as an entertainment medium, the British Broadcasting Corporation (BBC) has been broadcasting news and culture worldwide for more than seventy years.

 Audio 7.2: Listen to the BBC World Service.

soap operas: Serialized daytime dramas targeted primarily at women.

When Is a Radio Show Racist?

Amos 'n' Andy has been both praised and criticized. It was condemned as racist by many groups, including the National Association for the Advancement of Colored People (NAACP), that saw the humor in the show as demeaning and the characters as uneducated and ignorant of city life. The most lasting criticism of the show, however, was that it was produced by whites predominantly for the entertainment of whites. One of my African American students summed up the issue clearly: "So what you are telling me is that the most popular show in the country was about white people making fun of black people?" Clearly a show created under these parameters wouldn't be acceptable today.

But Amos 'n' Andy may not have been as racist as it seemed. Freeman Gosden and Charles Correll were guests of honor at an annual picnic hosted by the Defender, Chicago's leading weekly black newspaper in 1931. In addition, several members of the black press had good things to say about the show in its early days. It was also one of the few programs that showed African Americans (even if played by whites) in everyday life. The supporting characters in the fictional lodge were middle-class blacks, a social phenomenon many whites at that time didn't even know existed.[1]

WHO is the source?

Who wrote, acted in, and produced the show? Who were the critics of the program?

WHAT are they saying?

What are the central criticisms of the program? What are the arguments in support of it?

WHAT kind of evidence is provided?

What evidence is provided that the show had support in the African American community at the time it was aired? What is the evidence that the program was racist? How did these views change over time?

HOW do you and your classmates react to Amos 'n' Andy?

Was it the fact that the stars were white and the characters were black that made the show racist? If you say yes, why do you think this is so? Is it possible for a program to make jokes about racial issues without being racist? How could it do this?

One of the most popular, and controversial, programs of the golden age of radio was *Amos 'n' Andy*, which featured white performers Freeman Gosden (l) and Charles Correll playing the part of two African Americans.

[1]Melvin Patrick Ely, *The Adventures of Amos 'n' Andy* (New York: Free Press, 1991).

 Audio 7.3: Listen to excerpts from *Amos 'n' Andy*.

As mentioned earlier, the BBC was created as a public service in the 1920s. In the 1930s, it started broadcasting on the shortwave radio band, which allowed its signals to extend around the world. During World War II, the BBC was the international voice of opposition to the Nazis, broadcasting in more than forty languages, including French, Danish, and Hindi.[24] Listening to BBC broadcasts in Nazi-occupied Europe was a punishable offense.

Today the BBC's World Service radio network has an audience of approximately 150 million people. According to the BBC's Caroline Thomson, the goal of the World Service is to reach approximately 95 percent of the world's population.[25] The logistics of doing this become complicated when the BBC is broadcasting in a dozen or more different time zones. When do you broadcast a morning show on a network heard around the world?

BBC's international reach can be seen with the program *Focus on Africa*. For a continent that depends on radio as its primary medium of mass communication (for more on media in Africa, see Chapter 15), the BBC provides a reliable source of news that is not censored by local governments. To avoid charges of being a colonial voice of white Britain in black Africa, most of the reporting on the show is done by African journalists. *Focus on Africa* is such an important source of news that it is often rebroadcast on local African stations, sometimes just by taking a shortwave radio and holding it up to the station's microphone.[26]

While the BBC has long been known for its shortwave broadcasts, it has been changing in recent years. It still broadcasts by shortwave in Asia and Africa, but it now relies on webcasting, FM stations, and satellite services to reach the United States, Canada, Australia, New Zealand, and the Pacific Islands.[27] Also, since the collapse of communism in Eastern Europe and the rising conflict in the Middle East, the BBC has closed a number of its Eastern European–language radio services and has been working on launching an Arabic-language television service.[28]

Becoming a Companion Medium.

As television began claiming more and more of the broadcast audience, radio was forced to change. No longer were people sitting down in their living rooms to listen to programs on the radio. Instead, they turned on the radio while they did other things: working, washing dishes, driving. Yet radio did not fade away; instead, it reinvented itself as companion radio, a medium that would always be there to keep listeners company. Radio host Julius Lester put it this way:

> Radio is so integral a part of us now that we do not consciously notice its presence; it is a member of the family, a companion, and the voices issuing through its speakers are those not of strangers but of friends.[29]

Changing the Musical Experience: From Social Music to Personal Soundtracks

Being able to store and transmit musical performances was extremely important, but that may not have been the biggest change brought about by the invention of the phonograph and radio. Rock historian James Miller writes that the phonograph (and eventually radio) represented a vast expansion of people's access to music: "Symphonies that a person living in the nineteenth century would have been lucky to hear once were available for repeated listening on home phonographs."[30] Before the invention of the phonograph or radio, people had to go to a concert hall, theater, or club to hear music if they didn't play it themselves.

Questioning the Media

How do personal music players, such as smartphones, iPods, and Walkmans, change how we interact with people? Does walking around with headphones on isolate us from each other? Do you use your headphones or earbuds to keep people at a distance?

The Death of "Social Music."

The phonograph and radio brought a wider range of music into the household, but this led to the loss of so-called social music, or music that people play and sing for one another in the home or in other social settings. Prior to the new technology, people had to play an instrument or sing to have music in the home. Sheet music was a popular feature in magazines like *Godey's Lady's Book*, along with recipes and sewing patterns. For most people, there was little social distance between the performer and the audience, and musical instruction played a greater role in the education of the upper and middle classes. With advances in technology over the years, however, the social connections available through a shared musical experience changed profoundly.

Akio Morita's "Personal Soundtrack."

Akio Morita is not a household name, but the Japanese engineer who invented the Sony Walkman has influenced how people listen to music as much as anyone since Thomas Edison and Emile Berliner.

When the Walkman was introduced in 1979, it was available in two versions—either as a tiny tape player or as a stereo FM radio. They were relatively expensive, with the tape player version costing upwards of $200, but they allowed each person to live in his or her own "personal musical cocoon."[31]

Until 1979, the only way to take music away from home was with either a poor-quality pocket AM radio or a giant boom box. Writer RiShawn Biddle points out that the Walkman was more than just a way to protect your fellow bus passengers from your choice of music: "It's also been a coach, concert hall, and personal reader for millions of workout warriors, housewives, and retirees. For travelers, it is a trusty companion, something to ward off talkative salesmen and grandmothers loaded with wallet-size photos."[32]

Media scholar Michael Marsden notes that the Walkman gives people privacy in public areas: "It's your personal space that you've created, in a world in which we don't have a lot of personal space. It's a totally private world."[33]

Not everyone is so enthralled with the effects of the Walkman, however. Critic John Zerzan argues that the Walkman is one of a number of technologies that lead to a "sort of withdrawal from social connections."[34] One thing the Walkman has clearly done, however, is contribute greatly to the trend of personalized media use characterized by iPods, MP3 players, music downloads, and podcasts.

Music, Youth Culture, and Society

Though recorded music was on the market long before there was **rock 'n' roll**, rock 'n' roll was born alongside modern recording technology and flourished on the radio. It was amplified from the start, featured new instruments such as the solid-body electric guitar, and brought together a host of traditions from white hillbilly music to black

---

social music: Music that people play and sing for one another in the home or other social settings. In the absence of radio, recordings, and, later, television, this was the means of hearing music most readily available to the largest number of people.

rock 'n' roll: A style of music popularized on radio that combined elements of white hillbilly music and black rhythm and blues.

rhythm and blues. World War II spurred the development of rock 'n' roll as a cross-cultural phenomenon because blacks and whites mixed socially during the war more often than they had before and because the Armed Forces Radio played a range of white and black musical styles.

"Rock 'n' Roll" and the Integration of Music

Before 1948, recordings by popular black musicians were referred to as **race records** and included everything from blues to gospel to jazz. But in 1949, the editors of *Billboard* magazine, which ranks sales of all types of records, started calling the genre rhythm and blues (R&B).[35] It was at the same time that "folk" records began to be called "country and western."[36]

Why did R&B emerge when it did? There are a number of reasons. One is that the big bands that played jazz and swing (popular in the 1930s and 1940s) were expensive because there were so many musicians. An amplified blues band with a singer, an electric guitar, an electric bass, and a drummer could make a lot of sound, and great dance music could be built around the strong bass beat.[37] Also, African American musicians gained respect when white artists recorded cover versions of black songs.[38]

On December 28, 1947, a black R&B singer named Wynonie Harris recorded "Good Rockin' Tonight" in a studio in Cincinnati, Ohio. The song would become a big hit on black jukeboxes and radio stations. Was this the first rock 'n' roll song? Entire books have been devoted to answering that question, but "Good Rockin'" is as likely a candidate as any. It was a jukebox hit for Harris, and later became a radio hit when **covered** by young Elvis Presley. It certainly helped give this new kind of music its name. The following year brought a series of songs with the word *rock* in the title, including "We're Gonna Rock, We're Gonna Roll," "Rockin' at Midnight," "Rock the Joint," and "Rock and Roll."

By and large, these songs were not played on white radio stations. The problem wasn't the color of the musicians; it was the meaning of the word *rock*. As record promoter Henry Glover put it,

> We were restricted with our possibilities of promoting this song because it was considered filth.... They had a definition in those days of the word "rock," meaning the sex act, rather than having it known as "a good time," as they did later.[39]

---

race records: A term used by the recording industry prior to 1949 to refer to recordings by popular black artists. It was later replaced by more racially neutral terms such as *R&B*, *soul*, and *urban contemporary*.

covers: Songs recorded (or covered) by someone other than the original artist. In the 1950s, it was common for white musicians to cover songs originally played by black artists, but now artists commonly cover all genres of music.

Rhythm and blues records produced by African American artists were more likely to be played on jukeboxes in clubs than on the radio in the 1940s.

Elvis Presley and Chuck Berry: Blending Black and White Musical Traditions. While Harris and numerous other R&B singers were performing rock 'n' roll in the late 1940s and early 1950s, two stars—one white, the other black—would put rock 'n' roll on the national and international map. Elvis Presley and Chuck Berry demonstrated what could be done with the blending of hillbilly (or country) and R&B.[40]

Elvis Presley made his first recording in 1953, although no one knows the exact date. Marion Keisker, the woman behind the desk at Memphis Recording Service, remembered a young man who recorded a couple of songs on a ten-inch acetate disc for his mother. When she asked Presley whom he sounded like, his response was "I don't sound like nobody."[41] Keisker had the good sense to make an extra copy of Presley's recording and file it under the heading "good ballad singer." "The reason I taped Elvis," she explained, "was this: Over and over I remember Sam [Phillips, Keisker's boss] saying, 'If I could find a white

---

Web 7.4: Learn more about the history of rock 'n' roll.

Video 7.3: Watch Swedish dance music star Robyn and American folk singer Lucy Wainwright Roche preform very different versions of "Call Your Girlfriend."

Keystone Pictures USA/Alamy

Elvis Presley became the "king" of rock 'n' roll by combining elements of hillbilly and R&B music.

man who had the Negro sound and the Negro feel, I could make a billion dollars,' this is what I heard in Elvis."[42]

The man who would become known as "the king" soon started performing hillbilly music in Memphis and recording for Phillips, starting with "Good Rockin' Tonight." To Presley, performing was almost a religious experience: "It's like your whole body gets goose bumps," Presley said. "It's like a surge of electricity going through you. It's almost like making love, but it's even stronger than that."[43]

Just as hillbilly singer Elvis Presley borrowed from R&B, so blues guitarist Chuck Berry borrowed from the white hillbilly singers. The song "Maybellene" was based on an old fiddle tune called "Ida Red" and supposedly got its name from a mascara box. Others claim that Maybellene was the name of a cow in a third-grade reading book. Either way, the song combined a hot guitar, a hot car, and a hot woman.

Berry wanted to break out of some of the restrictions of traditional blues. While his audience at the clubs wouldn't stand for any change in the basic blues style, they had no problem with Berry's original rendition of an old white fiddle tune. Berry's unconventional style made people sit up and take notice. Berry recalls people talking about his music at an African American club:

Some of the clubgoers started whispering, "Who is that black hillbilly at the Cosmo?" After they laughed at me a few times, they began requesting the hillbilly

stuff and enjoyed trying to dance to it. If you ever want to see something that is far out, watch a crowd of colored folk, half high, wholeheartedly doing the hoedown barefooted.[44]

Presley started playing "Maybellene" in Louisiana while Berry was playing it in New York. This illustrates a key feature of the birth of rock 'n' roll: Two previously segregated types of music were coming together and becoming a new musical form—one that teens couldn't get enough of.

Rock Radio. Another reason for rock 'n' roll's growing popularity was that disc jockeys such as Alan Freed and Dewey Phillips were playing rock 'n' roll and R&B records on their radio shows.

On October 29, 1949, Dewey Phillips started a show on WHBQ in Memphis called *Red, Hot & Blue* that played R&B records. The show became an instant hit and quickly went from forty-five minutes in length to three hours. WHBQ's program director remembered it this way: "He got something like seven requests his first night. Well, the next night, I don't know the exact amount, but it was more like seventy requests. Then, even more incredible, the next night, it was closer to seven hundred."[45] Although Phillips was white, he played music by black artists and had a substantial audience of black radio listeners in Memphis. This

Michael Ochs Archives/Getty Images

Chuck Berry's music, played on rock 'n' roll stations in the 1950s and early 1960s, appealed to African American and white listeners alike.

was unusual at a time when most stations appealed either to the white or the black community, but not to both.

The Changing Face of Popular Music

The 1950s were a period of transition for popular music, with tastes shifting from the Tin Pan Alley songs of an Irving Berlin or Cole Porter to the songs of a Chuck Berry or Buddy Holly that were rooted in R&B. Already firmly established through concerts and radio airplay, rock 'n' roll now took center stage with records produced by artists ranging from **girl groups** to the Rolling Stones.

Motown: The Sound of Young America. No record label was more important in bringing R&B to the masses than Detroit's Motown Records. Motown, founded by Berry Gordy Jr., was the most successful of the independent record labels and one of the most successful black-owned businesses.

Michael Ochs Archive/Getty Images

Motown Records put together a number of African American girl groups, including the Supremes (pictured) and Martha and the Vandellas.

SECRET 3 Popular culture scholar Gerald Early says that the real importance of Motown was that it took black music and sensibilities and made them important for the public at large. He also credits Motown with establishing a black popular culture at a time when jazz—especially the improvisational work of Miles Davis and John Coltrane—was becoming highbrow culture. One of the big accomplishments of Motown was that it no longer published songs by black artists for white artists to cover, as was common practice in the 1950s and early 1960s. Instead, the African American Motown artists themselves turned out the hits. Motown moved black music into the mainstream and out of the world of race records, thus illustrating Secret Three—Everything from the margin moves to the center.[46]

The move of African American music and artists into the mainstream mirrored larger changes in society. In May 1961, African American Freedom Riders staged sit-ins to desegregate restrooms and lunch counters in bus stations in the South. In October 1962, the Motown Revue was doing its part to promote desegregation with such established acts as the Marvelettes, Marvin Gaye, and the Supremes. While

the Motown artists were not Freedom Riders, they broke some of the same ground on their tour. Mary Wilson of the Supremes put it this way:

Our tours made breakthroughs and helped weaken racial barriers. When it came to music, segregation didn't mean a thing in some of those towns, and if it did, black and white fans would ignore the local customs to attend the shows. To see crowds that were integrated—sometimes for the first time in a community—made me realize that Motown truly was the sound of young America.[47]

Motown's years as an independent company came to an end in 1988 when Gordy sold the label to Boston Ventures for $61 million. Motown was subsequently sold to PolyGram in 1993 for $301 million. It still exists, but it is now a small unit within media giant Universal Music Group.

The lasting effect of Motown artists can be seen with the huge outpouring of affection for Michael Jackson following his death in 2009.

The British Invasion: A Rougher Rock. In the 1960s, rock underwent a number of changes. The most significant of these were brought about by groups that came to the United States from England. The so-called **British invasion** began in 1964 and brought a rougher edge to white rock 'n' roll with the music of the Beatles, Dusty

---

girl groups: A musical group composed of several women singers who harmonize together. Groups such as the Shirelles, the Ronettes, and the Shangri-Las, featuring female harmonies and high production values, were especially popular in the late 1950s and early 1960s.

British invasion: The British take on classic American rock 'n' roll, blues, and R&B transformed rock 'n' roll and became internationally popular in the 1960s with groups such as the Beatles and, later, the Rolling Stones and the Who.

Video 7.4: Take a video walk through rock 'n' roll history from Elvis to hip-hop.

Audio 7.4: Use Spotify to listen to this playlist of one hundred great Motown songs.

STEREO

The Beatles' album *Sgt. Pepper's Lonely Hearts Club Band*, along with The Beach Boys' *Pet Sounds* and Frank Zappa's *Freak Out*, was among the first rock concept albums that brought together a set of songs on a common theme.

Interpretations of the songs on this album have varied. Some claim that "Lucy in the Sky With Diamonds" is about the drug LSD. Lennon said that the song was based on a picture his son Julian drew when he was four years old. Others say that McCartney's song "Fixing a Hole" is about injecting himself with heroin, though McCartney's own account claimed that it was about renovating an old farmhouse he had recently purchased. In 2004, McCartney acknowledged publicly that there are, indeed, drug references in many Beatles songs, including in "Lucy in the Sky With Diamonds."[52] Part of what makes *Sgt. Pepper* so successful, however, is that it doesn't matter which interpretation the listener supplies. They all work. The members of the band were more concerned about how the songs sounded than what they meant.

Sgt. Pepper gave rise to albums that were designed to be played from beginning to end, though these two-sided vinyl records had to be turned over at the twenty-three-minute mark. The seamless presentation of seventy minutes of music would have to wait for the 1980s and the advent of the CD.

Sgt. Pepper highlights a change that was starting to take place in the music business: The long-playing record (LP) was replacing the single as rock music's main format. Moore notes that in 1967 bands still relied primarily on singles to promote themselves and albums were of secondary importance. But that was changing with groups such as Cream and Led Zeppelin focusing on albums. Led Zeppelin's greatest hit, "Stairway to Heaven," was never released as a single, probably because it wouldn't fit the short format of the 45.[53]

Springfield, the Hollies, the Who, and, of course, the Rolling Stones. To appreciate the influence of these British bands, one need only look at the charts. In 1963, only one British band made it onto *Billboard*'s charts; in 1964, thirty-four did so.[48]

Traditionally, recorded music by popular groups was a means of promoting their live shows. But by 1966, it had become almost impossible for the Beatles to perform live because their screaming fans drowned them out. In fact, Beatles scholar Allan Moore notes that by 1966 the band had ceased touring because they couldn't hear themselves play. Instead, they became a studio band whose music was heard primarily on records and the radio.[49] In 1967, the Beatles recorded an album, *Sgt. Pepper's Lonely Hearts Club Band,* that transformed rock in a number of ways: It was one of rock's first **concept albums**—an album that brought together a group of related songs on common themes. It was also one of the first rock albums that was more than a collection of hit singles and their flip sides.[50]

What exactly is the concept of this album? Many of the songs have autobiographical themes derived from John Lennon's and Paul McCartney's childhood memories of Liverpool, England. Also, the songs are supposedly being played by the fictional band of the title.[51]

The Growing Importance of Producers. As popular music increasingly became a studio creation, the albums' **producers** became as important as the artists themselves. The main job of a producer is to put together the right songs, songwriters, technicians, and performers in the creation of an album.

Rock historian Charlie Gillett argues that the producer is the person who is responsible for making hit records. Producer Rick Rubin revitalized Johnny Cash's career near

---

concept album: An album by a solo artist or group that contains related songs on a common theme or even a story, rather than a collection of unrelated hits or covers.

producer: The person who puts together the right mix of songs, songwriters, technicians, and performers to create an album; some observers argue that the producer is the key catalyst for a hit album.

 Web 7.5: An in-depth look at super-producer Rick Rubin.

the end of his life with a series of albums that included songs by U2, Nine Inch Nails, and Tom Petty, among others. Producer Kenneth "Babyface" Edmonds has created or revived the careers of such artists as Aretha Franklin, Toni Braxton, Whitney Houston, Boyz II Men, and TLC. Unlike the producers and writers of the Motown era, Edmonds occasionally goes into the studio himself. Although he has produced at least fifty-seven top hits, Edmonds is quick to give praise to the artists who perform his songs.[54]

With rock, the producer shapes the sound and becomes an integral part of the musical process. Few albums demonstrate this as clearly as Pink Floyd's *Dark Side of the Moon*. Starting in 1973, *Dark Side of the Moon* spent 741 weeks on the *Billboard* Top 200 album chart, far longer than any competitor (though other albums have sold more copies). Alan Parsons produced the album, released in 1973, which paints a bleak picture of "alienation, paranoia, schizophrenia." But more than any message of the songs, *Dark Side of the Moon* presents an incredible sonic picture. It uses stereo to its fullest extent, sending sounds swirling around the listener's head. Parsons recorded a wide variety of voices talking, laughing, and screaming, which were mixed in at various times and speeds.[55] Pink Floyd continued the direction of the Beatles' *Sgt. Pepper* album, in which rock was music made to be recorded and constructed as much as performed.

The role of the producer continued to grow throughout the 1970s with the advent of **disco** and a range of heavily produced club music, including rap, house, and techno. Disco was primarily a means of getting people to dance. It came out of the gay male subculture in New York City and was popularized in the 1977 hit movie *Saturday Night Fever*. Disco was in many ways the ultimate producer music, in which the beat and the overall sound created by the producer mattered more than the vocals or talents of the instrumentalists.

Why does disco matter today? First and foremost, it was an entire genre of music that depended on technology and the producer, building on trends started by bands such as Pink Floyd and the Beatles. It also made black and Latino music more important commercially and led the movement toward the splintering of pop music into a range of genres.[56]

Hip-Hop Brings Together DJing, Dancing, Rapping, and Art.
While the terms *hip-hop* and *rap* are often used interchangeably, rapping is really just a

© AMR ABDALLAH DALSH/Reuters/Corbis

Mohamed El Deeb, a 28-year-old North African hip hop singer, poses in front of a wall decorated with graffiti near Tahrir Square in Cairo, Egypt, during pro-democracy protests in the summer of 2012. El Deeb writes and performs songs inspired by the protests in Egypt.

single facet of the larger world of hip-hop. According to English professor Mickey Hess, the hip-hop sound got started in the 1970s, when DJs began name-checking where they were from, including their cities, streets, or even neighborhoods. Although the music went national, it was still local in its orientation and was a statement of pride about the rapper's home. As Mr. Cheeks from the Lost Boyz put it, "It's only right to represent where I'm from."[57]

Where did hip-hop begin? Many sources point to a block party in the Bronx, New York, on August 11, 1973, at which DJ Kool Herc is credited with inventing the breakbeat, "using two turntables and two copies of the same record to loop the same instrumental break over and over."[58] But Hess argues that it wasn't so neat and clear-cut of a start. He claims instead that credit goes to a series of DJs working in Harlem nightclubs using similar techniques along with doing "call-and-response" from the audience. Hess lists four main elements of **hip-hop** culture:

- MCing—The spoken word or rapping over recorded music
- DJing—Playing recorded music from multiple sources, oftentimes overlapping
- B-boying—Physical movement, a style of hip-hop dancing, often referred to as breakdancing
- Graffiti art—The visual images of the culture

These separate elements show how hip-hop evolved from a variety of areas of the country, with DJing coming out of New York, graffiti art growing out of styles popularized in Philadelphia, and the dancing coming from both New York and Los Angeles. The MCing, or rhyming, is credited as coming from the work of a variety of rhyming

---

disco: The name of the heavily produced techno club dance music of the 1970s, which grew out of the urban gay male subculture, with significant black and Latino influences. In many ways, disco defined the look and feel of 1970s pop culture, fashion, and film.

hip-hop: A cultural movement that originated in the 1970s and 1980s that features four main elements: MCing, or rapping over music; DJing, or playing recorded music from multiple sources; B-boying, a style of dancing; and graffiti art.

radio hosts in cities such as Detroit, Philadelphia, New Orleans, and Austin.

SECRET 3 ▷ Rap music started to spread out of the Bronx via cassettes that were passed from person to person. Remember, however, that these were analog recordings that couldn't be copied repeatedly like digital recordings can today. There was also a high level of borrowing/stealing/remixing going on even at the very beginning. Sugar Hill Gang's "Rapper's Delight," which introduced rap and hip-hop into the mainstream, used lyrics from a Bronx MC who hadn't released a record. Blondie's rap hit "Rapture," which came out in 1980, was among the first rap songs to receive radio airplay on stations that appealed to white audiences[59] (thus showing us another example of Secret Three—Everything from the margin moves to the center).

Understanding the importance of a rapper's roots and locale is key to understanding how hip-hop has spread around the world. Global rappers give shout-outs to homes as varied as Norway, Japan, Egypt, and Korea. Linguistics professor Marina Terkourafi talks about how hip-hop has followed in the footsteps of rock and jazz in moving out of the United States and then blending with traditional and regional musical styles from around the world.[60] She writes that while the central themes of hip-hop in the United States have typically centered on race and gender, globally it has been used to protest against the status quo and raise awareness of local issues.

Libyan exile Abdulla Darrat told NPR's *On the Media* how North African hip-hop was used to fuel rebellion against oppressive political leaders such as former Libyan strongman Moammar Gadhafi during the Arab Spring movement of 2011. Given that these artists could not perform openly, their videos got distributed through social media such as Facebook or YouTube. Darrat says that these songs give voice to protesters who otherwise would not be heard: "What the world really needs to understand about the struggle in these regions is there is a youth that has hope. They have optimism about the future, but they see lots of obstacles in their way."[61]

Fernando Salazar/Wichita Eagle/MCT via Getty Images

Country singer George Strait has had more hit records over more years than anyone else in the music business.

Country: Pop Music for Adults

Country music was born in the late nineteenth century, evolving out of a range of musical forms that included Irish and Scottish folk music, Mississippi blues, and Christian gospel music.[62] It was originally called "old-timey" or hillbilly music. Country grew in the 1950s and 1960s with the so-called Nashville sound that was popularized by musicians such as Jim Reeves, Eddy Arnold, and Patsy Cline. It was at about this time that Elvis Presley took the hillbilly sound in another direction with early rock 'n' roll, but country never disappeared.

In 1980, many Americans rediscovered country music due to the hit film *Urban Cowboy*, starring John Travolta, and the 1990s and 2000s saw the further growth of country music thanks to songs from artists such as Rascal Flatts, the late Johnny Cash, and Carrie Underwood, as well as the soundtracks of movies such as *O Brother, Where Art Thou?* and *Walk the Line*.[63] According to research done by *Billboard* magazine prior to its 2011 Country Music Summit, the top five country acts from 1985 to 2011 were:

5. Tim McGraw, who had twelve number-one albums;

4. Alan Jackson, who had twenty-six number-one hits;

Questioning the Media

Do you listen to hip-hop or other sampled music? Do you think hip-hop artists are stealing from the musicians who created the sampled music? Why or why not? Is music created with samples something original?

🔊 Audio 7.5: Learn about the role of hip-hop in the Arab Spring revolts of 2011.

▶ Video 7.5: See *Billboard*'s complete Top 25 Country Artist List.

rap music: This genre arose out of the hip-hop culture in New York City in the 1970s and 1980s. It emerged from clubs where DJs played and remixed different records and sounds and then spoke (or rapped) over the top.

country music: Originally referred to as hillbilly or "old-timey" music, this genre evolved out of Irish and Scottish folk music, Mississippi blues, and Christian gospel music and grew in the 1950s and 1960s with the so-called Nashville sound.

3. Reba McEntire, the only woman on the list to have number-one country singles in four consecutive decades;

2. Garth Brooks, who has been the top-selling country album artist;

and, in the number-one spot,

1. George Strait, the legendary country singer who is the only artist in Billboard history to have a top-ten single every year for thirty-one consecutive years.[64]

Why does country music continue to be so popular? "Country music is about lyric-oriented songs with adult themes," according to Lon Helton, a music journalist. "You've probably got to be 24 or 25 to even understand a country song. Life has to slap you around a little bit, and then you go, 'Now I get what they're singing about.'"[65] Unlike the sex and drugs of rock 'n' roll, country deals with suburban issues like "love, heartache, family ties, and middle-aged renewal."[66]

Concerns About Effects of Music on Young People

Some of the biggest controversies surrounding rock have involved not the music but the words—from 1950s lyrics dealing with "rocking and rolling" to references to drugs in the 1970s to derogatory comments about women in contemporary rap.

It is difficult to know what the influence of a song's words will be. Adults often read metaphorical meanings into a song while young people see only the literal meaning of the lyrics. Understanding music also goes beyond the content of the lyrics. Listeners pay as much attention to the melody, rhythm, and style of music as they do to the lyrics. Finally, songs are often as much about feelings as they are about rational thought. They set a mood rather than transmit a specific message.[67]

SECRET 5 > Since rock's inception, parents and other concerned adults have wondered about the effects of its lyrics on impressionable listeners, thus illustrating Secret Five—New media are always scary. This questioning has led to product liability trials, congressional hearings, and movements to label and/or ban certain albums for objectionable content.

Few music formats have engendered as much controversy as rap and hip-hop. Rap can be partially understood as an outgrowth of several trends, dating back to the Beatles' *Sgt. Pepper* and Pink Floyd's *Dark Side of the Moon*. With the advent of multitrack recording, producers were adding layers of talk and ambient sound to the music created by band members. Rap simply extended this process, making the DJ

part of the music and sampling from a range of already completed musical recordings. There was no longer a single "correct" mix of the various tracks; instead, the final version was constructed by whoever wanted to work with it.

Among the controversies surrounding rap is the complaint that it is misogynistic and violent. Rappers defend the violence in their recordings by noting that we live in a violent world; the violence in the recordings is simply "keeping it real." Michael Fuchs, a former executive of media giant Time Warner, says that he sees some of the criticism of rap as racist:

It's a fact that white kids are buying black music and are being influenced by it, and that frightens their parents. It's not very different than the feeling my parents had thirty years ago when rock and roll came out—about the influence of black music.[68]

The Importance of Pop Music. Popular music today goes well beyond just the composition; it is an entire social statement. Besides the music, there are the photos on the cover of the CD, the text within the booklet inside the CD, the music video, the interviews on *Entertainment Tonight*, the posters, the Web site, and the fashion. It is through popular music that young people often have their first contact with much of our culture. It provides young people not just with music, but with an entire identity.[69] Our identification with the music of our youth is something that sticks with us throughout adulthood. Alternative rocker Liz Phair points out:

There's something that happens to people as they reach adulthood. They spend a lot of time trying to figure out what first hit them about rock 'n' roll. It's like the first time you took a drug. You want that first time back.[70]

■ ■ ■ ■ ■ ■ ■ ■ ■ ■ ■ ■ ■ ■ ■ ■ ■ ■ ■

From Singles to Digital Downloads: Making Money in the Recording Industry

For as long as there have been methods for recording and playing back sounds, there have been debates over how to make money selling music. Berliner's 78-rpm discs were fragile, held only three and a half minutes of music, and had only marginal sound quality by today's standards. So while there was no question that 78s needed to be replaced, there was no consensus on what the new format should be.

LPs Versus 45s

The **long-playing record (LP)** was developed by Columbia Records and introduced in 1948. The discs were labeled unbreakable; this was not quite true, but the vinyl LPs were much less delicate than the 78-rpm discs. More importantly, an LP could reproduce twenty-three minutes of high-quality music on each side. CBS demonstrated the

---

long-playing record (LP): A record format introduced by Columbia Records in 1948. The more durable LP could reproduce twenty-three minutes of high-quality music on each of two sides and was a technological improvement over the 78-rpm.

Vinyl records have had a resurgence in sales in recent years as listeners, such as these at Rough Trade East in London, rediscover the sound and artwork on the larger format discs.

system to RCA president David Sarnoff and offered to let RCA, its competitor, use the system. But RCA declined the offer and put out its own format, the **45-rpm disc**. It had high-quality sound, but the 45 could play only about four minutes of music at a time.[71] Eventually, record players were sold that could play both 45s and LPs, and both formats existed side by side, with the LP used for longer compositions and the 45 for single popular songs.

Vinyl LPs have staged a resurgence in recent years, as both artists and consumers have latched onto the twelve-inch discs containing analog music. Sales of vinyl recordings grew by 19 percent in 2012, according to a *Billboard* report, while digital download sales increased by only 14 percent. CD sales, in contrast, fell by 13 percent for the year. That's not to say that vinyl sales are a big part of the market, making up only 2.3 percent of all physical sales of music for the year. Why are LPs regaining their popularity? Part of it is their size. The discs come with big covers that have plenty of room for dramatic art and liner notes. Recording artists, from big names like Justin Timberlake and Pink to obscure indie acts, like the prestige and "specialness" that a vinyl release brings. And consumers often get a code for a free digital download with the premium-priced analog recording so they can still listen to the music on their computer, phone, or iPod.[72]

Compact Discs and Digital Recording

Work on the **compact disc (CD)** was started by Philips Electronics physicist Klaas Compaan as early as 1969. Compaan had the idea of photographically recording music or video on discs that could be read with a laser. Not wanting to get into the kind of format war that raged between the 45 and the LP in the 1940s, Philips joined with Sony to create a standard for the compact disc. The CD was launched in Europe in 1982 and in the United States in 1983.

SECRET 5 While we have generally talked about new media being scary to consumers (Secret Five), **digital recording** (a method of recording sound that involves storing it as a series of numbers) has been the scariest of the new media to people in the music industry. With **analog recording** (the original method of recording that involved cutting a groove on a record or placing a magnetic signal on a tape that was an image of the sound wave being recorded), copies were not as good as the originals, and copies of copies showed further degradation in quality. Thus, the prospect of home digital recordings, which are exactly the same as the originals without loss of quality, upset companies whose livelihood depended on the sales of original recordings.

For several years, home digital copying was held up by the recording industry, which wanted CD players to include security chips that would stop people from making copies. Of course, as soon as the industry came up with a way to stop people from copying digital music, hackers responded with ways of breaking the system. Ultimately, home CD copying emerged from the computer industry rather than the music industry. People wanted to be able to "burn" CDs with their own data, programs, and music.[73]

Music on the Internet

The most recent format for music is a compressed music file known as an **MP3** (short for Moving Picture Experts Group audio layer 3). MP3s can be played on a computer or on a portable MP3 player, such as an iPod, or they can be burned onto a recordable CD. The files can be easily shared over the Internet by e-mail, on Web sites, or through music-sharing services.

SECRET 2 Aside from allowing people to share music files, one of the biggest effects of this new distribution channel has been to allow new groups to publicize their

---

45-rpm disc: This record format was developed in the late 1940s by RCA. It had high-quality sound but held only about four minutes of music per side. It was the ideal format for marketing popular hit songs to teenagers, though.

compact disc (CD): A digital recording medium that came into common use in the early 1980s. CDs can hold approximately seventy minutes of digitally recorded music.

digital recording: A method of recording sound—for example, that used to create CDs—that involves storing music in a computer-readable format known as binary information.

analog recording: An electromechanical method of recording in which a sound is translated into analogous electrical signals that are then applied to a recording medium. Analog recording media included acetate or vinyl discs and magnetic tape.

MP3: Short for Moving Picture Experts Group audio layer 3; a standard for compressing music from CDs or other digital recordings into computer files that can be easily exchanged on the Internet.

Who Is Being Hurt by Declining Sales of Recorded Music?

SECRET 6 The recording industry has had more than a decade of declining sales. In 2000, American music fans bought 785.1 million albums. By 2006, that number had dropped to 588.2 million (including both CDs and digital downloads). And in 2008, that number had reached 428.4 million.[1] That's a 45 percent drop in sales over eight years. The industry has blamed consumers for the decline because of file sharing, piracy, and easy home duplication of CDs. What the industry has not done is come up with a coherent response to the massive change that's taking place in the music business, whether it likes it or not. But as you think about this, remember Secret Six—Activism and analysis are not the same thing.

The decline in the sales of prerecorded music is not imaginary. Take a look at Figure 7.2 on page 179, a graph put together by tech writer Michael DeGusta based on sales data from the Recording Industry Association of America (RIAA). The graph shows the sales in inflation-adjusted dollars of recorded music in the United States from 1973 to 2009. As DeGusta points out in his explanation of the graph, U.S. recorded music sales in 2009 were down 64 percent from their peak in 1999 and down 45 percent from where they were in 1973. Why have these sales declined so much? Common wisdom suggests that it's illegal sharing/copying (commonly called piracy) and a general lack of interest in buying complete albums. Some of it also may be that in the 1990s people were re-buying music on CDs that they had bought years earlier on vinyl. People converting from CDs to digital players such as iPods simply had to scan in their CDs to convert them to the new format.[2]

There have even been suggestions made that the music industry as a whole is dying. But as journalist-blogger Matthew Yglesias explains, it's really the recording industry that's dying, not the music business. He writes in his blog, "People still listen to music. People still play music. People who play music even still earn money. But the business of *selling recordings of music* is shrinking."[3]

Take, for example, the eclectic country singer-songwriter Lyle Lovett. Lovett tells *Billboard* that while he has sold 4.6 million albums over the last twenty years, he's made all of his money from performing and touring. "I've never made a dime from a record sale in the history of my record deal," he said. "I've been very happy with my sales, and certainly my audience has been very supportive. I make a living going out and playing shows."[4] So why does Lovett still record and sell albums? "Records are very powerful promotional tools to go out and be able to play on the road." (Note from your author—if you get the chance to see Lovett in concert, do so. He puts on a great show!)

WHO is the source?

Who is Lyle Lovett? What has he done in the music industry?

WHAT is he saying?

How much money has Lovett made selling albums? Is he worried about the problem of file sharing or "record piracy"? Why does he record albums?

WHAT kind of evidence is there?

According to tech writer Michael DeGusta, what does the evidence say has happened to recorded music sales since 1973? How does he explain the changes? What are the causes?

HOW do you and your classmates feel about the music industry?

How often do you and your friends pay for music compared to "sharing" it over the Internet? Why do you pay for or not pay for music? What could record labels do that would make you more willing to buy CDs or legal downloads? Do you think declining sales of record music have hurt artists such as Lyle Lovett?

---

[1]James Callan, "U.S. Album Sales Decline 14% While Online Track Sales Surge," Bloomberg.com, January 1, 2009, www.bloomberg.com/apps/news?pid=20601103&sid=aC7ekniUw9Fs&refer=us; Brian Hiatt and Evan Serpick, "The Record Industry's Decline," *Rolling Stone*, June 28, 2007.
[2]Michael DeGusta, "The REAL Death of the Music Industry," *Business Insider*, February 18, 2011, www.businessinsider.com/these-charts-explain-the-real-death-of-the-music-industry-2011-2.
[3]Matthew Yglesias, "The Death of the Recordings-Sale Industry," February 19, 2011, thinkprogress.org/yglesias/2011/02/19/199969/the-death-of-the-recordings-sale-industry/.
[4]Reuters/Billboard, "Lyle Lovett Sells Millions, Earns Nothing," July 10, 2008, www.reuters.com/article/2008/07/10/us-lovett-idUSN1030835920080710.

Web 7.6: Check out Jon Bon Jovi's claim against Apple and its co-founder Steve Jobs.

Web 7.7: Read more about what Michael DeGusta has to say about the decline of music sales.

Video 7.6: Watch Lyle Lovett in concert.

© Everett Collection Inc / Alamy

Singer Katrina Leskanich was the namesake of the '80s band Katrina and the Waves, but these days she's performing on her own and releasing her music independently using long-tail tools.

the 1980s aren't going to get a lot of attention from the music industry twenty-five years later. Her latest album, *Walking on Sunshine*, was released independently in February 2009. It's received little, if any, radio airplay, but it was featured on the popular podcast *Coverville*. You won't find a copy of the CD at your local music retailer, but you can find it on Amazon.com as either a download or a burn-to-order CD, or you can buy a download from iTunes.[74] An alternative version of the album was released through CD Baby, which sells music through its own Web site, as well as other online channels.

What has happened is that Leskanich has made the move from the short head to the long tail of the music industry, as we talked about back in Chapter 3.

Some independent or maverick musicians and bands might applaud the increased exposure they get from the Internet, but the music industry is intensely concerned about music file "sharing," preferring to call it theft, piracy, or copyright violation. What worries publishers is that no one is paying for these files.[75] Publishers have tried various copy protection schemes to stop consumers from making digital copies, some going so far as to put software on their CDs that spies on consumers and reports back to the publisher how the music is being used.[76] And, as is discussed in Chapter 10, the recording industry for the past several years has been filing suit against consumers who have been downloading unlicensed copies of music from the Internet.[77]

music by delivering it directly to the consumer through the Internet, either through their own Web site or social networking sites, thus illustrating Secret Two—There are no mainstream media.

Questioning the Media

Do you listen to independent artists or big recording stars? If you listen to independent artists, who are they? How did you find out about them? How did you find their music? What makes independent artists more interesting to you? Do you think long-tail distribution of indie artists makes it harder to find their work? Why or why not?

Take the example of Katrina Leskanich. If you lived through the 1980s, you likely remember the Katrina and the Waves summer anthem "Walking on Sunshine." And even those too young to have noticed it the first time around have probably heard it in movie soundtracks and on TV shows. The band had several other modest hits in the United States and the United Kingdom. But now Ms. Leskanich, the band's lead singer, is fifty-plus years old, and fresh-faced stars of

The Business of Radio

With the coming of television, radio was forced to change and no longer tried to be all things to all people. Instead, each station now appeals to a particular audience. Teenagers don't have to listen to the same programs as store clerks; stockbrokers don't have to listen to the same programs as college students. Want rock 'n' roll? There's a station for it. Oldies? Another choice or two. News? Talk? Classical music? Soul? If you live in an urban area, chances are you can find stations providing all these different radio formats. Over the past decade, radio has continued to change, undergoing a massive change of ownership and seeing the growth of numerous new competitors.

Finding a Niche: Popular Radio Formats

The most popular radio format in 2012 in the United States was country and new country, with 14.2 percent of stations carrying it (see Table 7.1), followed closely by news/talk, which commands 11.4 percent of the national audience. Pop Contemporary Hits **format radio** is what used

Web 7.8: Wondering what all those different radio formats are? Wonder no more.

format radio: A style of radio programming designed to appeal to a narrow, specific audience. Popular formats include country, contemporary hits, all talk, all sports, and oldies.

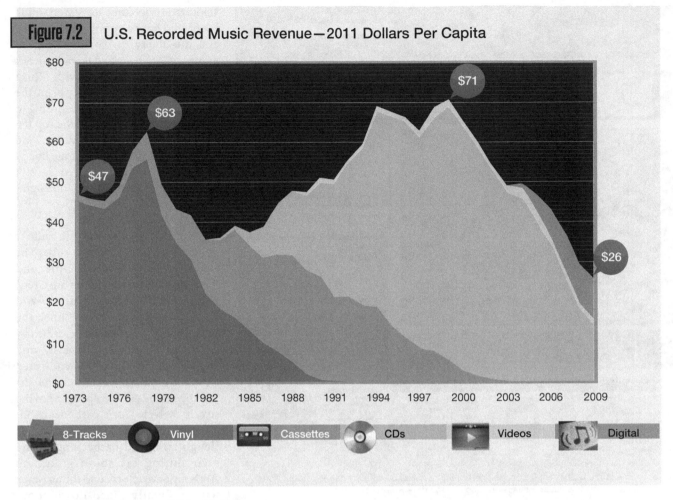

Figure 7.2 U.S. Recorded Music Revenue—2011 Dollars Per Capita

$47 $63 $71 $26

8-Tracks   Vinyl   Cassettes   CDs   Videos   Digital

Source: Reprinted with permission of Michael DeGusta.

to be known as Top 40 and is made up of a range of current hits; while it would seem to be primarily a teen format, more than half of its audience is older than twenty-five. It draws 8.2 percent of the radio audience. Adult Contemporary and Soft AC consist of light and soft rock and are designed to appeal to listeners aged twenty-five to forty, especially women; it draws about 8.1 percent of the audience. While audience members might call lots of what they listen to oldies, the radio business breaks it down into a variety of categories, including Classic Hits (5.2 percent), Classic Rock (5.2 percent), and Oldies (1.2 percent). Rhythmic CHR was a format developed to appeal to the United States' changing ethnic makeup, with listeners spread fairly evenly among black, Hispanic, and "other."[78]

Spanish-Language Broadcasting. As the Hispanic population in the United States, especially in the Southwest and Florida, continues its rapid growth, Spanish-language stations are increasing in popularity and drawing high ratings. As of fall 2009, more than 1,300 Spanish-language stations were broadcasting in a variety of formats.[79] This is a huge growth from the 533 that were broadcasting in 1998. Spanish-language formats include multiple styles of music, news/talk/information, and religious programming.[80] The top-rated stations in Los Angeles

frequently broadcast in Spanish and play either Mexican or adult contemporary music. The Los Angeles Dodgers baseball team has two sets of play-by-play announcers, one for English broadcasts, and the other for the team's Spanish-language network. And ESPN has a Spanish-language, all-sports radio network based out of Miami that focuses heavily on soccer games and news.[81]

Spanish-language stations are getting strong support from advertisers who want to reach the Hispanic community, and evidence indicates that Spanish-speaking consumers respond better to advertisements in their own language than to those in English.[82]

Talk Radio: Politics, News, Shock Jocks, and Sports

As mentioned earlier, news/talk is one of the top radio formats. Talk radio has exploded during the past twenty-five years. In 1985, only 200 stations carried the format; by 1995, that number had grown to more than 1,000. Marvin Kalb, formerly with CBS News, credits talk radio with providing a sense of community that people don't find anywhere else: "If we still gathered at town meetings, if our churches were still community centers, we wouldn't need talk radio. People feel

http://www.espndeportes.com/espndeportesradio/

ESPN Deportes is a popular Spanish-language sports radio network headquartered in Miami. Not surprisingly, ESPN Deportes's major focus is on soccer, or as they would say, "futbol."

stations are looking for entertaining hosts who have a strong point of view and the ability to "connect with an audience."[87] Overall, talk radio leans strongly conservative, with Rush Limbaugh and Sean Hannity being the two most popular hosts. According to *Talkers* magazine, eight of the top ten talk show hosts are conservative. And the listenership of the top four liberal talk show hosts combined is still smaller than that of Rush Limbaugh's show alone.[88]

Shock Jocks. Not all talk radio is political; some is just plain rude. The **shock jocks**, including Opie and Anthony (whose real names are Gregg Hughes and Anthony Cumia) and Todd Clemm (known as "Bubba the Love Sponge"), have been described by critics as "disgusting," "racist," and "repulsive."[89] Nationally syndicated Opie and Anthony were fired after airing the sounds of two people having sex in a New York cathedral, but Clemm was kept on the air after slaughtering and barbecuing a wild boar during his show. Opie and Anthony have returned to the airwaves with a slightly toned-down show. Howard Stern, the most controversial of the shock jocks, left terrestrial radio in 2006 for satellite broadcasting, where he has a multiyear contract worth $500 million.[90]

increasingly disconnected, and talk radio gives them a sense of connection."[83] Talk radio is also important to the radio industry as more and more young people turn away from broadcasting to digital sources of music.[84]

Political Talk. Talk radio is a major source of political information for 44 percent of Americans, and the political information they are getting from talk radio is largely conservative.[85] Although journalism generally values balanced coverage, New York radio host Brian Lehrer notes that such coverage doesn't mesh well with the nature of talk radio:

> Some people's views don't fit neatly into traditional conservative or liberal labels. But that's not what's wanted in the media these days, especially in talk radio. They want you to be 100 percent confident that you have the truth and 100 percent predictable in your views.[86]

Carl Anderson, senior vice president for programming and distribution for ABC Radio Networks, says that radio

All-Sports Radio. Sports programming occupies a growing segment of the talk format. The cable television network ESPN now provides sports radio programming and even has its own station in Chicago.[91] Some stations have gone so far as to adopt what has been called a "guy" radio format. "This isn't sports radio, it's guy radio," says forty-something radio host Glenn Ordway of Boston's WEEI. "It's what guys our age talk about in bars and on golf courses. . . . This is not broadcasting we're doing, it's narrowcasting."[92]

Although it's a narrow segment of the radio-listening public, the dedicated, loyal, and fanatic fans are very attractive to advertisers. "What separates sports radio from other radio is the passion of its listeners, and that makes it fertile hunting ground for us," says one major guy radio advertiser. "These are men who scream at their radios instead of punching the dial looking for the next cool song."[93]

 Web 7.9: Check out the latest on Rush Limbaugh.

shock jocks: Radio personalities, such as Howard Stern, who attract listeners by making outrageous and offensive comments on the air.

Radio Consolidates and Goes High Tech

Prior to 1985, broadcast owners were restricted nationally to seven AM radio, seven FM radio, and seven television stations.[94] During the 1980s, with the growth of cable and satellite television, the **Federal Communications Commission (FCC)** relaxed some ownership rules, which resulted in greater consolidation of ownership through media mergers. The trend toward broadcast deregulation was accelerated greatly with the Telecommunications Act of 1996. Although most of the law dealt with the cable television and telephone industries, the law lifted the restrictions on overall broadcast ownership. A single company could now own unlimited numbers of radio stations, with up to eight stations in a single market.[95]

The impact on radio was almost immediate. Within a year and a half, radio ownership had become far more concentrated and far less diverse. By 2003, the number of radio stations on the air had grown by 5.9 percent, but the number of station owners had fallen by 35 percent.[96] Clear Channel used the rule change to buy up $30 billion worth of radio stations nationwide, going from owning forty-two stations in 1995 to more than 1,200 stations by 2003.[97] As of 2014, Clear Channel was still the largest station owner in the United States, with 860 stations reaching more than 239 million listeners. In addition to owning all those stations, Clear Channel also provides syndicated programming for more than 5,000 stations through its Premiere Networks. It also sells advertising spots for about 4,000 radio stations (and 600 television stations) through Katz Media.[98] As an amazing side note, in 2014 Clear Channel changed its name to iHeartMedia to highlight the company's streaming audio business along with its legacy radio stations.[99]

Many stations now operate with virtually no staff other than a few people to sell and produce advertising. The music, news, weather, and talk all come from either a satellite service or a computer hard drive, with automation software serving up the local commercials, announcements, and programming. If it sounds like programming on the radio is the same from one side of the country to the other, it could be because the stations you are listening to all get their programs from the same centralized source.[100]

Public Radio

With approximately 11,000 commercial stations, radio is a big business in the United States. But for all the power and reach of the commercial radio business, public radio provides a significant alternative.

NPR. Public radio was authorized by the 1967 Public Broadcasting Act, which was designed primarily to create educational television. The act allocated stations at the lower end of the FM dial for noncommercial broadcasting,

Federal Communications Commission (FCC): The federal agency charged with regulating telecommunications, including radio and television broadcasting.

Table 7.1 — Popular Radio Formats

Although the ratings of various radio formats vary from month to month, here is an overall picture of the audience percentage of the various top formats. Note that the report of number of stations includes FM, AM, HD, and Internet streaming.

FORMAT	AUDIENCE PORTION	# OF STATIONS
Country + New Country	14.2%	2,893
News/Talk/Information	11.4%	3,984
Pop Contemporary Hit Radio (Top 40)	8.2%	1,012
Adult Contemporary + Soft AC	8.1%	1,390
Classic Hits	5.2%	883
Classic Rock	5.2%	944
Hot Adult Contemporary	4.7%	810
Urban Adult Contemporary	4.1%	336
Rhythmic Contemporary Hit Radio	3.4%	370
All Sport	3.1%	1,274
Urban Contemporary	3.0%	274
Contemporary Christian	2.9%	1,691
Mexican Regional	2.9%	550
Adult Hits + 80's Hits	2.2%	395
Active Rock	2.1%	356
AOR + Mainstream Rock	2.0%	336

Source: "Radio Today 2013: How America Listens to Radio" (Arbitron, Fall 2012 survey period).

Note: Among the other formats are Alternative, Oldies, Spanish Contemporary, All News, Classical, Religious, Album Adult Alternative, Classic Country, Spanish Adult Hits, Gospel, Contemporary Inspirational, Spanish Religious, and Tejano. *Audience Portion* is of 12+ persons. *# of Stations* includes AM, FM, HD radio, and streamed stations.

and most of the station licenses went to colleges and universities. In 1971, National Public Radio (NPR) went on the air with its first program, the evening newsmagazine *All Things Considered.*[101]

One thing *All Things Considered* can do that other news shows can't is present the news in depth. Eight-minute-long stories are not unusual, and twenty-minute stories are broadcast when the topic

Questioning the Media

Do you listen to any shock jocks? If so, who? Should shock jocks such as Opie and Anthony be allowed on broadcast radio, or should they be forced onto alternative audio channels such as satellite broadcasting or the Internet? Why or why not?

News commentator Juan Williams was fired by NPR in 2010 over controversial comments he made on Fox News.

merits the length. This occurs in a medium in which thirty seconds is considered a long story.

The public radio network remained relatively small until two major developments occurred. The first was the growth of the satellite delivery of network programming. Satellite allows good signals go out to all stations no matter how remote they are. The second development was the installation of FM radios in most private cars. Since public radio was almost exclusively on the FM band, the advent of FM car radios made it possible to reach interested people with enough time to pay attention. Not surprisingly, NPR's biggest audiences are in cities whose workers have long commutes.[102] By 2013, there were 835 NPR member stations reaching a monthly audience of 27.3 million.[103]

NPR launched the two-hour news program *Morning Edition* in 1979, and since then it has become the most-listened-to morning news show in the country, with 7.6 million listeners tuning in daily. This is about one-third

Web 7.10: The many ways to consume NPR using mobile technology.

Audio 7.6: Find out more about *Mountain Stage* and listen to podcasts.

larger than the *Today* show's audience and 60 percent higher than that of ABC's *Good Morning America*.[104] Of course, this isn't a completely fair comparison because *Morning Edition* is on radio and the other two shows are on television. Americans also view NPR as being a particularly credible source of news, with people rating the radio network as having a higher level of believability than CBS, NBC, ABC, MSNBC, and Fox News.[105]

Although NPR is widely respected for the depth and quality of its reporting, it has become embroiled in a series of partisan controversies. In 2010, the network fired contributor Juan Williams over comments he made on Fox News about some people feeling anxiety when they see Muslims on airplanes. NPR president Vivian Schiller later said that Williams was fired for a long series of comments that violated NPR guidelines. The firing, and the way it was handled, led to extensive criticism of NPR by conservative media hosts and politicians. This led to calls in Congress to discontinue all federal funding of the network. Eventually Schiller resigned over the controversy, as did NPR's vice president for news.[106]

One of the major challenges facing public radio is funding. For 2014, NPR had expected revenue of $178.1 million and projected expenses of $183 million, leading to a deficit of $6.1 million.[107] Of that money, approximately 25 percent came from sponsorship, which allows corporations, organizations, and individuals to run short messages during programs. While most of these underwriting announcements promote the companies themselves as institutions, there are also announcements promoting particular books or television programs. NPR's news division had a yearly budget of about $70.7 million and a staff of about 365 people in 2012, not counting the reporters working for all the affiliated stations. The largest sources of revenue for NPR are programming fees paid by local member stations (37 percent of the budget) and the above-mentioned sponsorship fees (25 percent). While NPR gets relatively little money directly from the federal government, it does get funds from it indirectly through the programming fees paid its member stations, which do get federal funds.[108]

You may have noticed that this section of the chapter was headed as "NPR" and not "National Public Radio." That's because in 2010 the network changed its name from National Public Radio to just NPR to reflect the fact that much of its programming is delivered over the Web or via apps for mobile devices and tablets. So to understand the full reach of NPR, it should be noted that in addition to its 27.3 million radio listeners, it has 28.6 million podcast programs downloaded per month and 20.8 million unique visitors to its Web site, NPR.org. As NPR's new chief executive said in a tweet, "We need to reach audience in ways convenient and accessible to them in emerging and traditional platforms."[109]

Live Music on the Radio. Not all music broadcast on the radio today is prerecorded on CDs. One of public radio's most popular shows is Garrison Keillor's *Prairie Home Companion*, which features a range of live music, skits,

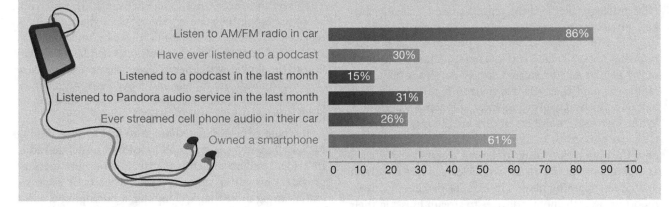

Table 7.2 Digital Audio Audiences, 2014

According to Triton Digital and Edison Research, consumers get audio programming from a wide range of sources. Here are a few examples.

Source	Percent
Listen to AM/FM radio in car	86%
Have ever listened to a podcast	30%
Listened to a podcast in the last month	15%
Listened to Pandora audio service in the last month	31%
Ever streamed cell phone audio in their car	26%
Owned a smartphone	61%

Source: "The Infinite Dial 2014: Navigating Digital Platforms" (Triton Digital, Edison Research, 2014), www.edisonresearch.com/home/archives/2014/03/the-infinite-dial-2014.php.

guests, and the centerpiece of the show, Keillor's monologue delivery of the news from Lake Wobegon, a mythical town in Minnesota that represents the stereotypical small Midwestern town "where the women are strong, the men are good looking, and all the children are above average." *Mountain Stage,* produced by West Virginia Public Radio, has been broadcasting live performances by a variety of artists since 1984. In addition to country, bluegrass, and folk artists, the show has featured performers such as Crash Test Dummies, Sheryl Crow, Sarah McLachlan, Counting Crows, and They Might Be Giants. Although *Mountain Stage* does not generally carry stadium show headliners, R.E.M. did do an acoustic segment on the show.[110]

Former producer Andy Ridenour told *Billboard* magazine that the show's greatest strength is that it exposes audience members to different artists and types of music: "One of the most common complaints we hear is that people don't get to hear anything new on the radio. Here, they get a chance to hear an artist they like and maybe two artists they never heard of."[111]

The Future of Sound

For the past hundred years or so, the recording industry has been making money off the sale of little packages, either discs or cartridges of some sort. The coming of radio created the first blip in the market, leaving sellers wondering why people would buy records when they could get the music for free on the radio. The record companies soon learned that they could earn revenue from licensing the music to the radio stations and from promoting their records by having them played on the radio. Then came computers and the Internet, which allowed people to burn copies of CDs on blank media or transmit them to other people as MP3 files.

Now radio—the recording industry's old nemesis—is facing new competition and transformations of its own. Radio started with AM broadcasting as the primary medium for news and entertainment. Then, in the late 1940s and early 1950s, television displaced radio and transformed it into a companion medium that people listened to in the background rather than something that dominated their attention. A third round of change came when FM broadcasting became popular in the 1970s, bringing stereo and high fidelity to broadcasting. FM eventually surpassed AM in popularity, especially in the realm of music, leaving AM radio to be dominated by sports, talk, and news—formats that don't suffer from low fidelity and the lack of stereo.[112]

People used to listen to radio predominantly in their cars and at home. Now people are listening in the office using radio stations' Web streams. They also download audio podcasts or go to pay satellite services. Despite the new options, analog broadcasting remains by far the most popular choice—93 percent of Americans age twelve or older still listen to **terrestrial radio** every week. But traditional radio is facing stiff competition. According to the Pew Foundation's "State of the News Media 2012" report, up to 38 percent of Americans listen to audio on digital devices every week.[113] (See Table 7.2.)

There is no question of whether the entire sound industry is going through a massive change. The only real question is what will emerge.

---

terrestrial radio: AM and FM broadcast radio stations.

Radio's New Look: HD and Satellite

Among the digital technologies closest to terrestrial radio are HD radio and satellite radio.

HD Radio. Terrestrial radio isn't just sitting still as digital technology takes over the sound business. In many markets, **HD radio** provides listeners with CD-quality sound and the choice of multiple channels of programming. But HD radio has not really taken off as a new medium. As of 2010, only 7 percent of Americans expressed a strong interest in HD radio, and that was down from 8 percent the year before. So instead of growing, interest is actually declining. While increasing numbers of cars are offering HD radios either as options or as standard equipment, buyers now have the option of adding streaming Internet audio, such as Pandora or Spotify, to their vehicles. And even without dedicated streaming players in cars, 11 percent of drivers report using their mobile devices to stream music in their vehicles.[114]

Satellite Radio. In 2008, the two competing **satellite radio** services, Sirius and XM, merged to become SiriusXM. The two services still offer separate programming but have overlap between them. They've also united their efforts to promote the idea of subscription radio. Sirius XM ended 2013 with more than 24 million subscribers.[115] Neither of the two companies turned a profit as independents, and the newly merged company came close to filing for bankruptcy in February 2009, saved only by an infusion of cash provided by Liberty Media, the owner of major pay TV services.[116]

The biggest name on satellite radio is former broadcast shock jock Howard Stern, who moved over to Sirius after his protracted and very public battle with Viacom, which syndicated him, and the FCC, which fined his stations more than $2.5 million over a ten-year period.[117] Stern seems to be thriving on satellite radio with no corporate or FCC censors to put limits on him. In an interview with the *New York Times,* Stern said, "We're talking about the stuff you can't talk about. The show on terrestrial radio in the last ten years had been so watered down."[118]

Satellite radio also provides news and public affairs channels, such as CNN, Fox News, BBC World Service, and NPR. One advantage of satellite radio over regular radio is that travelers are able to tune in to a channel in New York and listen to it all the way to California. The disadvantage, other than the cost, is that these services provide no local content, such as traffic reports, local news, or weather forecasts—the staples of car radio.[119]

Web 7.11: Look at recent audio industry reports.

Audio 7.7: Listen to the University of Nebraska at Kearney's student radio station KLPR.

Music and the Long Tail: Alternatives to Broadcasting

Terrestrial radio is also facing competition from the new audio media that are redefining how we view radio. The Project for Excellence in Journalism (PEJ), which has been discussing the state of American media since 2005, replaced its chapter on "radio" with one on "audio" in 2009. PEJ said at the time that radio can handle the transition to the digital world better than other media because "voice and music are mobile and move easily among new platforms. And audio has done better as a medium of holding its audience than some other sectors."[120]

It would be a mistake, though, to just look at the Big Media alternatives such as HD radio and satellite radio. Individual audience members can now become message providers by setting up their own Webcasts or podcasts with nothing more than a computer, a microphone, and a connection to the Internet. With these technologies, even programming that extends deep into the long tail of media content can be distributed easily.

Streaming Audio. The original online alternative to radio was **streaming audio**, also known as webcasting, or Internet radio. This can take a wide range of forms. Some content is tied to a terrestrial station; others are Internet only, such as Pandora or Spotify. Pandora, for example, was started in 2005, and as of 2014, 31 percent of Americans age 12 or older listen to Pandora at least monthly, and 50 percent of all smartphone owners have downloaded the Pandora app.[121] In essence, smartphones and other mobile devices are becoming the new portable radio, as well as being players for your personal collection of recorded music.

Streaming audio also greatly extends the reach of stations, especially small ones with low-powered transmitters. A 3,800-watt student station that can barely cover fifteen miles over the air can reach an entire city, not to mention the world, through streaming. In essence, streaming can do for a small radio station what cable did for Ted Turner's local Atlanta television station, WTBS—turn it into a radio superstation that anyone in the world can receive.

The Infinite Dial 2014 study from Triton Digital and Edison Research found that an estimated 124 million

HD radio: Sometimes also referred to as high-definition radio, this technology provides listeners with CD-quality sound and the choice of multiple channels of programming, but it is not yet commonly available in mass-market outlets or as standard equipment in cars.

satellite radio: The radio service provided by digital signal broadcast from a communications satellite. Supported by subscribers, this service covers a wider area than terrestrial radio and offers programming that is different from corporate-owned terrestrial stations. However, it is costly and doesn't provide local coverage, such as traffic and weather reports.

streaming audio: Audio programming transmitted over the Internet.

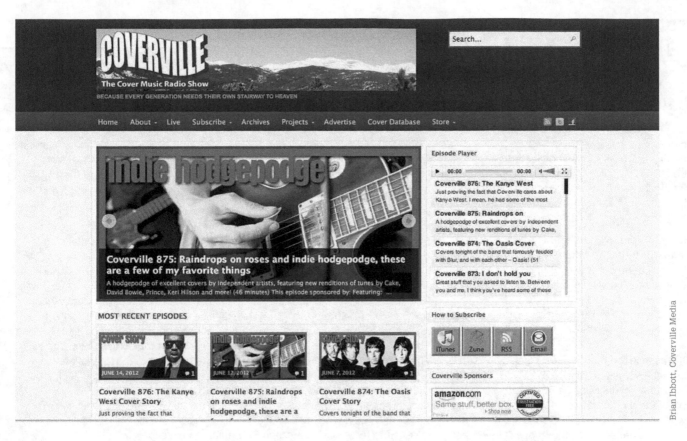

Brian Ibbott's *Coverville* podcast generally airs three times a week and can feature such unusual songs as the Norwegian version of "Time Warp" from *The Rocky Horror Picture Show.*

Americans listen to an online radio station or other streaming audio service on a monthly basis.[122]

Podcasting. A long-tail alternative to terrestrial radio and prerecorded music is the **podcast**. Podcasts are audio programs distributed over the Internet as MP3 compressed music files that can be listened to online or downloaded to a computer or an MP3 player. They open up distribution of audio programming to anyone with a basic computer and an online connection.

It is difficult to say exactly when podcasting got started, but summer 2004 is the commonly held period because that's when RSS 2.0, which could handle enclosures (essentially attachments) along with straight text, was released. It's also when former MTV VJ Adam Curry and software developer Dave Winer wrote the program iPodder. It was one of the first programs available that could download a podcast off the Internet and transfer it to an iPod. It's much easier to say when podcasting became widely known—February 9, 2005, when *USA Today* ran two articles about the new medium and phenomenon in the paper.[123]

podcast: An audio program produced as an MP3 compressed music file that can be listened to online at the listener's convenience or downloaded to a computer or an MP3 player. Podcasts sometimes contain video content as well.

In May 2005, podcasting became easier when Apple's iTunes software started supporting subscriptions to podcasts. You don't need an iPod to listen to a podcast (any computer or MP3 player will do), but iPods have a huge portion of the market, and iTunes support means that even those with low levels of technical sophistication are able to listen to podcasts.[124]

That's not to say that podcasting is anywhere nearly as popular as radio. As of 2011, 45 percent of Americans said they were aware of podcasts, up only marginally from the 43 percent who were aware of them in 2009. Twenty-five percent of all Americans have listened to an audio podcast, and 12 percent (approximately 35 million) listen to them on a monthly basis. But podcasts have a long way to go to come even close to terrestrial broadcasting in popularity, as 93 percent of Americans aged twelve and older report using AM/FM radio at least once a week.[125]

Questioning the Media

How do you listen to audio programs? Do you listen to terrestrial radio? Satellite radio? Podcasts? Streaming services such as Spotify or Pandora? Why do you use these sources?

Audio 7.8: Listen to several classic episodes of *Coverville.*

Creating a Radio Show Without a Radio Station

Colorado podcaster Brian Ibbott says that he's always known he wanted to be a DJ. The only question was what kind of music he would play. Back in 2007, he told me:

> I knew if I did my own show, I wanted it to have something unique and not just a sampling of my favorite music. I wanted it to be something that had a theme to it. And one of the types of music I collect are cover songs.[126]

Ibbott was inspired by a program that aired several years ago on the XM satellite radio channel Special X. "And every day for two hours they had a show that was all covers with no announcing. It was just cover, after cover, after cover,"

he said. Then Special X got canceled, and Ibbott started dreaming about creating his own show.

The only problem was that Ibbott didn't have a radio station to use to broadcast his program. But then he heard about former MTV VJ Adam Curry's work on software to distribute audio files over the Internet—essentially some of the earliest podcasting software. "I said, I could do this," Ibbott said. "So I just jumped in with both feet." So in September 2004, Ibbott posted his first twenty-six-minute episode of *Coverville* that opened with Jellyfish performing their take on Argent's "Hold Your Head Up." Now, more than ten years later, Ibbott has moved from producing an average of three half-hour shows a week to a single hour-and-a-half to two-hour show each

week that has even more of the feel of a conventional radio show. As of this writing, he has posted more than 1,025 episodes, each of which averages about 10,000 downloads.

Coverville is notable for being one of the first podcasts to play music that's been licensed by the **American Society of Composers, Authors and Publishers (ASCAP)** and Broadcast Music Inc. (BMI), the two major organizations that collect royalties for songwriters every time a published song is performed. But reaching the agreement took some doing because no one had ever tried to negotiate the rights for a podcast before. In fact, Ibbott had to explain to the ASCAP representative what a podcast was. They finally set up an agreement similar to that for streaming audio.

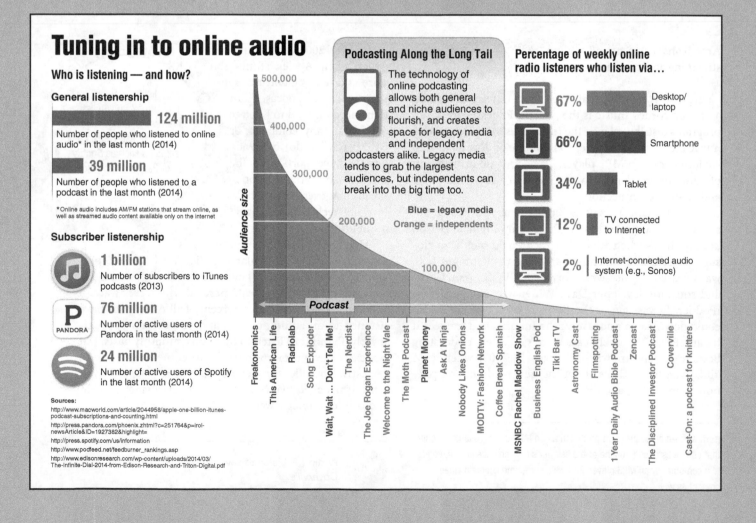

After producing so many episodes, Ibbott has a good handle on what makes for a great cover song:

> It has to be unique. It has to sound like the band covering it and not try to be a note-by-note reproduction f the original. It has to be a good song. It has to stand on its own even if it weren't a cover. It doesn't have to be recognized, but it helps.[127]

Ibbott plays some highly unusual covers, such as William Shatner's version of Pulp's "Common People," but he does have limits. He has a few that he sets aside for a worst-cover-ever show and others that he just won't play. "I stay away from covers done by current pop stars who get enough airplay. There's nothing clever about the cover. It's like their agent said, 'I really like this song. Why don't you do a cover of this?'"[128]

Just as podcasts grew out of combining radio-style programing with Internet distribution of shows that can be listened to on an MP3 player or smartphone, Ibbott's alternative broadcasting efforts continue to grow. Ibbott now has his own twenty-four-hour streaming Coverville Radio that plays covers all day and night with a Web page that tells what songs are going out; he's produced 292 episodes of his *Lyrics Undercover*

podcast that gives the story behind popular songs; he co-hosts a four-day-a-week show called *The Morning Stream*; and he has his own record label, Coverville Records.

Media Transformations Questions

- **HOW** have podcasts and streaming media transformed who can create radio-style programming?

- **HOW** do podcasts and streaming media programming differ from what you can get on radio? Think about both content and how you listen.

New Economic Models for the Music Industry

SECRET 5 There can be no question that the many sectors of the sound industry are currently facing a heavy dose of Secret Five—New media are always scary. The issues of file sharing, user-generated content, and music videos (topics also covered in Chapter 9 and Chapter 10) are forcing changes in how radio and the recording industries can make money.

Computer technology has made it easy to manufacture pirate editions of CDs that can be sold on the street at a deep discount. (For that matter, it has made it easy for consumers to "burn" copies of their CDs for their friends for free.) The industry charges that this is stealing from artists and that the new media for distributing music are going to destroy the recording industry. These new technologies are certainly changing the music business, but they probably aren't destroying it.

USA Today's technology writer Kevin Maney points to the example of China, where the music business is thriving even in the face of

rampant piracy. Maney argues that in China, most CDs on the market are pirate editions, so artists have no choice but to make an income through live performances, sale of merchandise, and commercial endorsements.[129]

It can be argued that piracy and file sharing hurt the record labels more than they do the musicians. File sharing may even help musicians. Roger McGuinn, former front man of the 1960s band the Byrds, says that he received only a fraction of a cent per record on the early Byrds albums and never saw any royalties at all on a solo album that sold 500,000 copies. How did he make his money? Touring. Now McGuinn gives away tracks on his Web site and sells

American Society of Composers, Authors and Publishers (ASCAP): The original organization that collected royalties on musical recordings, performances, publications, and airplay.

Nine Inch Nails' Trent Reznor, left, and Robin Finck perform during the Bonnaroo Arts and Music Festival in Manchester, Tenn. Reznor offers his recordings as everything from free downloads to autographed deluxe $300 packages.

CDs that he's recorded at a home studio straight to fans at concerts and online. He tells *USA Today* that these home-produced CDs are the only ones that have made him money.[130] Classical and jazz banjo player Béla Fleck, of Béla Fleck and the Flecktones, makes the majority of his income touring across the United States in the summer. Fleck says his band makes 70 percent of its income from concerts, 20 percent from album sales, and 10 percent from merchandise. The CDs are mostly made to help fans discover his music.[131] Trent Reznor of Nine Inch Nails offers his recordings as free downloads online to save his fans from having to go to file sharing sites. He also helps them share fan videos through his Web site. But according to Techdirt's Mike Masnick, Reznor also offers his music for sale in a variety of packages. With his album *Ghosts I-IV,* fans wanting to pay for the music could buy everything from a pair of CDs for $10 to an autographed "Ultra-Deluxe Limited Edition Package." The $300 edition sold out in thirty hours. Now, granted, Reznor is not a typical musician, but he does illustrate how by interacting with fans in a meaningful way he can make them want to pay him for his music.[132]

Media technology journalist Mark Glaser writes that record labels and artists don't have a "god-given right" to sell CDs for $13 to $18 apiece. He outlines the wide range of choices consumers have now:

As music lovers, we now have many more choices for how we can get our music fix. We can listen to the radio, to satellite radio, to Internet radio, or hear new music on TV shows like American Idol or on commercials. We can download free music from file-sharing networks [though that can be illegal]. We can hear music straight from the websites of artists, and even get their tracks from MySpace pages. We can buy physical albums from the dwindling number of retail music stores or Wal-Mart and Target, or buy digital tracks or albums from iTunes or other online outlets.[133]

Chapter SUMMARY

The ability to record sounds began in 1877 with Thomas Edison's invention of the phonograph. Though Edison's machine could record and play back sound, it was relatively fragile, and the foil-covered cylinders could not be reproduced and did not stand up to repeated playing. Emile Berliner's gramophone, however, played music on flat discs that were stronger than Edison's cylinders and could be mass produced. This technology allowed musical performances to be stored and replayed. As prerecorded music became widely available, the nature of music consumption changed. People's major contact with music became recordings by professional musicians rather than live performances by amateurs.

Radio was an outgrowth of work done on the telegraph by Samuel Morse. Physicists such as Heinrich Hertz conducted early experiments on the detection of radio waves, but it was Guglielmo Marconi who developed the commercially viable wireless telegraph.

Radio was used initially as a tool for sending messages from one person to another. David Sarnoff was among the first to see radio's potential as a tool for mass communication; CBS founder William Paley saw its potential as an advertising medium that incidentally provided entertainment. KDKA, the first commercial radio station, went on the air in 1920, ushering in the golden age of radio, in which radio was the dominant medium for home entertainment. Radio was also a major source of news, offering an intimacy and immediacy that newspapers couldn't match.

The organizations ASCAP and BMI were established to ensure that musicians and composers would be paid for the music they wrote and performed on stage, on records, and on the radio, as well as for songs they published in written form.

A wide range of recording formats has been used over the years, including the 78-rpm disc, the 45-rpm single, the LP, the compact disc, and the MP3 computer file. Each has given rise to concerns about changes in the purchasing and use of music.

Rock 'n' roll was a hybrid style of music that grew out of white hillbilly music and black rhythm and blues in the late 1940s and early 1950s. Because rock 'n' roll crossed racial lines, it became part of the integration of American society in the 1950s and 1960s. Rock 'n' roll became popular largely through recordings sold in record stores and played on the radio rather than through live performances. It evolved into an art form that existed primarily for recorded playback rather than live performance.

In the 1960s and 1970s, rock music became more heavily produced, and there was a shift from hit singles to albums. Music by groups such as the Beatles and Pink Floyd brought the role of the producer to the forefront, a move that accelerated with the development of disco and rap. Hip-hop culture brought together playing music, talking over the songs, dancing, and a distinctive graffiti art style.

Parents and other adults have expressed concern about lyrics that include profanity, references to suicide and violence, and sentiments that are derogatory toward women.

As television displaced radio as the dominant broadcast medium, radio was transformed into a companion medium with a wide range of formats designed to appeal to narrow, specific audiences. These formats include many types of music, Spanish-language broadcasting, talk, news, and sports.

FM has gradually replaced AM as the dominant radio band. Although FM has a shorter broadcast range, it has much higher-quality sound (higher fidelity).

Although the majority of radio stations are commercial, public radio—a staple of FM radio programming—provides an important alternative. Terrestrial radio is still the dominant sound medium; however, it faces growing competition from digital alternatives such as HD radio, satellite radio, streaming audio, and podcasting.

Keep up-to-date with content from the author's blog.

Take the chapter quiz.

Key TERMS

phonograph   162

gramophone   162

high fidelity (hi-fi)   162

non-notated music   163

telegraph   163

wireless telegraph   163

Radio Music Box memo   163

network   165

golden age of radio   165

soap operas   166

social music   168

rock 'n' roll   168

race records   169

covers   169

girl groups   171

British invasion   171

concept album   172

producer   172

disco   173

hip-hop   173

rap music   174

country music   174

long-playing record (LP)   175

45-rpm disc   176

compact disc (CD)   176

digital recording   176

analog recording   176

MP3   176

format radio   178

shock jocks   180

Federal Communications Commission (FCC)   181

terrestrial radio   183

HD radio   184

satellite radio   184

streaming audio   184

podcast   185

American Society of Composers, Authors and Publishers (ASCAP)   187

Concept REVIEW

Creation of recording industry

Changing ways of experiencing music

Popular music and social change

Role of music producers

Technology and the transformation of the music business

Radio and the transformation of the news business

The changing role of radio

Student STUDY SITE

$SAGE edge™

Sharpen your skills with SAGE edge at **edge.sagepub.com/hanson5e**

SAGE edge for Students provides a personalized approach to help you accomplish your coursework goals in an easy-to-use learning environment.

Television

Broadcast and Beyond

AP Photo/Alan Diaz

Jorge Ramos moved to the United States from Mexico in 1973, and he's now the anchor of one of the most watched television news shows in Spanish in the United States.

Jorge Ramos came to the United States from Mexico in 1973 on a student visa. He had left his job as a reporter at Mexico City TV when his supervisors complained about a story he was doing that was critical of the Mexican government. Before long, Ramos was working at KMEX-TV, a Spanish-language station in Los Angeles. Now, more than thirty years later, he's the evening news anchor at Univision, the nation's fifth-largest broadcast network. *Noticiero Univision*, the show he co-hosts with María Elena Salinas, draws more than 2 million viewers nightly. To put that in context, that's three times the size of the audience for CNN's *Situation Room With Wolf Blitzer*.[1]

While he has been compared to the legendary CBS news anchor Walter Cronkite, who in the 1960s established the basic format for evening network news, he actually follows a very different model—one that has more in common with the clear point of view of Latin American and European journalism than that of the more detached objective American reporting.

Ramos has been criticized for engaging in advocacy journalism by the conservative media watchdog group Media Research Center, and he's been accused of being a "Democratic pundit," but Ramos defends himself, saying that he is a tireless advocate for Latino and immigrant groups.

"Our position is clearly pro-Latino or pro-immigrant. We are simply being the voice for those who don't have a voice," Ramos told the *Los Angeles Times*.[2] When he interviewed President Barack Obama during his 2012 reelection campaign, Ramos confronted he president on his policies that have led to the deportation of more than 1.4 million undocumented immigrants. And he did that confrontation in English so clips from it could be easily replayed on English-language stations. "I am emotionally linked to this issue," Ramos told the *LA Times*. "Because once you are an immigrant, you never forget that you are one."[3]

Ramos argues that it is vital for the Spanish-language media to speak up on issues like immigration because Hispanics don't have many other advocates. In an interview on NPR's *On the Media*, he said,

> The big difference is that without looking for that we are representing a group of people who have no political representation. We are 17% of the population, but we only have three senators, only three. Where are the other 14 senators that we need to represent the Hispanic community? And that, historically, has been—relied on Univision and Spanish-language journalists.[4]

In addition to his shows in Spanish on Univision, he appears on Univision's English-language *Fusion* network done in partnership with ABC. Although he now speaks excellent English, Ramos says that when he first came the United States to study journalism at work at the Los Angeles station KMEX-TV, his English skills were poor. "My English was—I couldn't even understand myself."

To Ramos, broadcasting in English is becoming increasingly important because that's how he connects with people who are in power in the United States. He tells *New York* magazine that he likes broadcasting in English on the Fusion network. "What I really like is that for the first time, I don't need translation. And without translation, there's an immediate impact. And definitely the language of power is English."[5]

Ramos told NPR's Brooke Gladstone that there can be a big difference between reporting in English and reporting in Spanish because the audience for his English-language programs skews much younger than that for his Spanish-language programs. "So, yeah, doing a story about gays and abortion in English, I would go straightforward and just explain the facts. When I'm doing the same story in Spanish, I will always have the point of view of the Catholic Church, the point of view of very conservative groups, even some people on the street criticizing what we are doing, because those are their values."[6]

Ramos, who anchors the news out of Univision studios in Miami, Florida, is one of the most well-known Hispanic media figures in the United States. In fact, a recent Pew Research Center survey of Latinos found that Ramos was the second most known Hispanic leader in the United States, following only Supreme Court justice Sonia Sotomayor.[7]

He has been called the "Mexican Anderson Cooper," referring to his silver-haired resemblance to the CNN anchor. Ramos is also part of a transition from neutral reporting, or a "view from nowhere," to an anchor with a knowable point of view.

Frank Sesno, a former CNN journalist and director of the George Washington University School of Media and Public Affairs, told Politico.com, "What we would or would not have accepted years ago has changed as more broadcast personalities and bloggers especially have assumed more opinionated/ lead roles in the conversations. The candidates will know that, but they'll still want Jorge—as last time— to reach the powerful demographic of Hispanic voters, which may be the key to success or failure for both parties in 2016."[8]

Timeline

1800

1812 War of 1812 breaks out.

1835 Alexis de Tocqueville publishes *Democracy in America*.

1859 Charles Darwin publishes *On the Origin of Species*.

1861 U.S. Civil War begins.

1869 Transcontinental railroad is completed.

1879 Thomas Edison invents electric light bulb.

1898 Spanish-American War breaks out.

1900

1903 Orville and Wilbur Wright fly first airplane.

1905 Albert Einstein proposes his theory of relativity.

1910

1912 *Titanic* sinks.

1914 World War I begins.

1918 Worldwide influenza epidemic strikes.

1920

1920 Nineteenth Amendment passes, giving U.S. women the right to vote.

1929 U.S. stock market crashes, leading to the Great Depression.

1930

1933 Adolf Hitler is elected chancellor of Germany.

1939 World War II breaks out in Europe.

1940

1941 United States enters World War II.

1945 United States drops two atomic bombs on Japan.

1947 Pakistan and India gain independence from Britain.

1949 Communists establish People's Republic of China.

1927 Inventor Philo T. Farnsworth demonstrates his all-electronic television system.

AP Photo

1939 NBC starts regular television broadcasts from New York City; these are suspended with the advent of World War II.

1948 Milton Berle (right) and Ed Sullivan go on the air with variety shows, initiating the golden age of television; the first community antenna television (CATV) systems are established.

AP Photo

One thing that politicians of all stripes have learned is that Ramos never stops asking pointed questions and never pulls his punches. And this has earned Ramos respect. Matt Drudge, who runs the essential conservative news Web site *Drudge Report*, has called Ramos "the last journalist standing." In a tweet, Drudge wrote, "Warning to politicians. If you see him . . RUN!"[9]

The television environment today has radically changed from the time when CBS news anchor Walter Cronkite was the most respected broadcaster in America. We've gone from three nationwide broadcast networks to at least six, gone from no cable-only stations to hundreds, and gained multiple formats for viewing prerecorded movies and shows at home. In this chapter, we look at how this new television world came about and how it has influenced society. We start with the development of broadcast television and then cable/satellite television. We then consider who controls the television industry, how the world portrayed on television compares to the "real" world, and how television is becoming more interactive. We look at the roles television plays within society as a major recreational activity, a view of the world, and an influence on young people. And, finally, we look at where television is headed. ■

> **"**Our position is clearly pro-Latino or pro-immigrant. We are simply being the voice for those who don't have a voice.**"**
>
> —Jorge Ramos

Audio 9.1: Listen to *On The Media's* Brooke Gladstone interview Univision anchor Jorge Ramos.

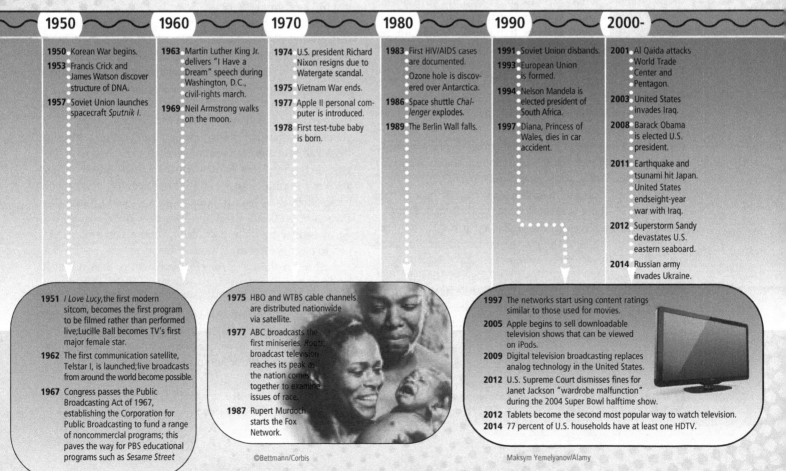

1950	1960	1970	1980	1990	2000-
1950 Korean War begins.	**1963** Martin Luther King Jr. delivers "I Have a Dream" speech during Washington, D.C., civil-rights march.	**1974** U.S. president Richard Nixon resigns due to Watergate scandal.	**1983** First HIV/AIDS cases are documented.	**1991** Soviet Union disbands.	**2001** Al Qaida attacks World Trade Center and Pentagon.
1953 Francis Crick and James Watson discover structure of DNA.	**1969** Neil Armstrong walks on the moon.	**1975** Vietnam War ends.	Ozone hole is discovered over Antarctica.	**1993** European Union is formed.	**2003** United States invades Iraq.
1957 Soviet Union launches spacecraft *Sputnik I*.		**1977** Apple II personal computer is introduced.	**1986** Space shuttle *Challenger* explodes.	**1994** Nelson Mandela is elected president of South Africa.	**2008** Barack Obama is elected U.S. president.
		1978 First test-tube baby is born.	**1989** The Berlin Wall falls.	**1997** Diana, Princess of Wales, dies in car accident.	**2011** Earthquake and tsunami hit Japan. United States endseight-year war with Iraq.
					2012 Superstorm Sandy devastates U.S. eastern seaboard.
					2014 Russian army invades Ukraine.

1951 *I Love Lucy*, the first modern sitcom, becomes the first program to be filmed rather than performed live; Lucille Ball becomes TV's first major female star.	**1975** HBO and WTBS cable channels are distributed nationwide via satellite.	**1997** The networks start using content ratings similar to those used for movies.
1962 The first communication satellite, Telstar I, is launched; live broadcasts from around the world become possible.	**1977** ABC broadcasts the first miniseries, *Roots*; broadcast television reaches its peak as the nation comes together to examine issues of race.	**2005** Apple begins to sell downloadable television shows that can be viewed on iPods.
1967 Congress passes the Public Broadcasting Act of 1967, establishing the Corporation for Public Broadcasting to fund a range of noncommercial programs; this paves the way for PBS educational programs such as *Sesame Street*	**1987** Rupert Murdoch starts the Fox Network.	**2009** Digital television broadcasting replaces analog technology in the United States.
		2012 U.S. Supreme Court dismisses fines for Janet Jackson "wardrobe malfunction" during the 2004 Super Bowl halftime show.
		2012 Tablets become the second most popular way to watch television.
		2014 77 percent of U.S. households have at least one HDTV.

©Bettmann/Corbis

Maksym Yemelyanov/Alamy

Television: Broadcast and Cable/Satellite

Television has gone through massive changes since its birth in the 1930s. Initially, it provided a limited number of options that were broadcast at no cost to viewers. Viewers could watch only the programs offered by the major networks, and only at the times when those programs were being broadcast. But in the 1980s, the balance of power between audience and broadcasters began to change. Not only did videocassette recorders (VCRs) allow viewers to choose when they would watch programs, but a range of broadcast, cable, and satellite channels allowed viewers a wider choice of what programs to watch. Television has in effect become two media: broadcast and cable/satellite.

Broadcast Television

Broadcast television in the United States is based on the idea that programming should be available to all viewers and should be paid for through advertising. Although today broadcast television is just one part of our TV diet, for many years it was the only item on the menu.

The Invention of Television. The story of Philo T. Farnsworth, the man who invented electronic television, is almost too good to be true. He was born in a log cabin, he rode a horse to school, and he developed the central concepts of television at the age of fourteen. Unlike Edison or even Samuel Morse, Farnsworth did not become a household name, yet he invented one of the most significant devices of the twentieth century.

Farnsworth was born in Utah in 1906. When he was twelve, his family settled in Idaho, and in their new house were magazines about radio and science, which fueled Farnsworth's creativity and imagination.[10] Farnsworth's heroes were Edison and Bell, but he wanted to do them one better. He wanted to send out moving pictures as well as sound, and he wanted to do it all electronically, without any moving parts.

Farnsworth came up with the idea of breaking a picture into lines of light and dark that would scan across a phosphor-coated screen like words on a page. The electrons that would paint the picture on the screen would be manipulated by an electromagnetic field. According to television scholar Neil Postman, legend has it that Farnsworth's great idea came to him "while he was tilling a potato field back and forth with a horse-drawn harrow and realized that an electron beam could scan images the same way, line by line, just as you read a book."[11]

 Video 9.1: Watch a conversation between Daniel Stashower, a Farnsworth biographer, and Brian Lamb on C-SPAN.

Philo T. Farnsworth developed the central principles of television broadcasting at age fourteen, and by the age of twenty-one he had produced a working television transmission system.

By age twenty-one, Farnsworth had developed an all-electronic system for transmitting an image using radio waves. On September 7, 1927, he successfully transmitted an image of a straight line. "There you are, electronic television," he commented.[12]

Farnsworth, however, was not the only person working on the concept of television. Vladimir Zworykin, a Russian immigrant with a doctorate in engineering, was trying to develop television for David Sarnoff at RCA. Although he had made progress on electronic television and had filed for a patent on it in 1923, the U.S. Patent Office eventually ruled that Farnsworth had been the first to make a working television transmitter. The ruling was based in part on testimony from Farnsworth's high school chemistry teacher, who presented drawings that Farnsworth had made when he was sixteen showing almost exactly how to build a television transmitter. RCA kept fighting Farnsworth and promoting Zworykin and Sarnoff as the inventors of television, but Farnsworth eventually prevailed. For the first time, RCA had to pay royalties to an outside inventor.[13]

Just when all looked rosy for Farnsworth, World War II broke out, and for four years nothing was done with commercial television. Farnsworth's patents expired in 1947, right before television took off. Yet it was not missing out on the chance to cash in on his invention that Farnsworth came to regret. Farnsworth's son Kent later noted that his father was rather bitter about his invention in general:

I suppose you could say that he felt he had created kind of a monster, a way for people to waste a lot of their lives. Throughout my childhood his reaction to television was "There's nothing on it worthwhile, and we're not going to watch it in this household, and I don't want it in your intellectual diet."[14]

The Beginning of Broadcasting. The first significant television broadcasts using all-electronic systems occurred in 1939, when NBC started sending out television broadcasts from the New York World's Fair. But American involvement in World War II halted the manufacture of television sets in 1942, and most stations went off the air. Peace came in 1945, and by 1946 RCA had television sets back on the market.

From 1948 to 1952, the licensing of new television stations was frozen to give the Federal Communications Commission (FCC) and television producers time to figure out how the technology should be used and controlled. Because of the freeze, only some cities had television. The television cities saw drastic drops in attendance at movies and sporting events. Restaurant owners hated the popular variety program *Your Show of Shows*, which aired on Saturday nights, because customers rushed home to watch television instead of staying out to eat and drink.[15] During the same period, the Supreme Court issued its ruling in *United States v. Paramount* that broke the studios' control over the movie industry (see Chapter 8). Television was ready to take over the entertainment industry.

A number of shows characterized this early period of television. Milton Berle, host of the *Texaco Star Theatre*, came to be called "Mr. Television" and was known for his funny costumes and physical humor. The *Ed Sullivan Show* (originally called *Toast of the Town*) became the place to see new and innovative talent. In later years, Sullivan would feature the Beatles and Elvis Presley. The 1950s also saw a number of anthology dramas, essentially short plays or movies, with a new cast and story each week. One show that made a successful leap from radio to television was Edward R. Murrow's CBS news documentary series *Hear It Now*, which became *See It Now* on the new visual medium.

Lucy, Desi, and the End of Live Television. No other entertainment program of the 1950s would have a longer, more lasting impact than one produced by a brash redheaded actress and her Cuban American husband.

When Lucille Ball and Desi Arnaz created their groundbreaking sitcom *I Love Lucy* in 1951, they had to overcome two major obstacles. The first was persuading CBS to let Arnaz play Lucy's television husband. At that time, this was controversial because Ball was white and Arnaz Hispanic. The second challenge was that most television shows at the time were being broadcast live from New York City studios, but Lucy and Desi wanted to continue to live in California. Their solution was to film the show before a studio audience, edit the program like a movie, and ship it to New York to be broadcast. Within a year, *I Love Lucy* was the most popular show on television.

Lucille Ball and her husband, Desi Arnaz, created the modern situation comedy in 1951 with their show *I Love Lucy*, which was filmed rather than performed live.

Being filmed rather than performed live meant that there were high-quality copies of *I Love Lucy* that could be shown again and again. Arnaz held the rerun rights to the show, which gave the couple the money to build their own television production company, Desilu Studios. More than fifty years after *Lucy* first went on the air, audiences are still laughing at the show.

The format Ball and Arnaz created, a half-hour comedy filmed with three cameras before a live studio audience, became a mainstay of television programming. Today, the situation comedy remains one of the most popular program formats.[16]

The Arrival of Color Television. The networks started experimenting with color television as early as 1954, but by 1959, only three shows were regularly being shown in color. (The familiar NBC peacock logo was initially created to show black-and-white viewers that they were missing programs in color.) It wasn't until 1965 that all three of the original television networks were broadcasting in color. One reason for the slow acceptance of color was the price of the television sets. The *Boston Globe* notes that in 1965 color televisions cost the equivalent of what a midline HDTV set cost in 2000 (between \$2,500 and \$5,000).[17] The switch to color was not completed until the early 1970s.[18]

Cable and Satellite Television 🌐

Today, cable and satellite television constitutes almost a separate medium from broadcast television, but initially

---

 Video 9.2: Watch classic *I Love Lucy* episodes online.

Local cable television companies offer a variety of programming choices via satellite.

AP Photo/Saurabh Das

Home Box Office (HBO) was the first service to make the leap from merely providing access to providing programming. In 1975, it requested permission from the FCC to start sending out its programming nationwide via satellite. Surprisingly, not one of the **Big Three networks** (NBC, CBS, and ABC) objected to the upstart service as it gained access to their viewers across the country. After all, HBO was just an office, some videotape machines, and a satellite uplink. It had no affiliates, had no stations, and could reach only people who were on cable, a small fraction of the viewing market. But the satellite system had a key advantage. Five hundred cable systems could obtain the programming as cheaply as one. They just had to put up a dish to bring in the signal.

Although HBO was the first to go nationwide, no one has done more than Ted Turner to create modern cable television. After his father's suicide in 1963, the twenty-four-year-old Turner inherited a billboard company that was in financial trouble.[22] Turner was not content with running one of the nation's largest billboard companies, so in 1970, he bought Channel 17 in Atlanta. The UHF station was in serious financial trouble, largely because it was located on a part of the broadcast band that many television sets couldn't receive and many people didn't bother to look at. Turner promptly renamed the station WTCG, which stood for Turner Communication Group.

Turner's next big step was buying the last-place Atlanta Braves baseball team and the Atlanta Hawks basketball franchise, thus guaranteeing him exclusive rights to a pair of shows (the teams' games) that would run more than 200 episodes a year. It was also programming that would motivate Atlantans to make the effort to find Channel 17.

When RCA launched a television satellite in 1976, Turner saw his next big opportunity. He realized that he could use the satellite to send his station nationwide and provide programming to the growing number of cable systems. On December 27, 1976, WTCG became Superstation WTBS (Turner Broadcasting System). With that step, Turner became one of the first of a new breed of television entrepreneurs who were turning local stations into national powerhouses.

At this point, Turner made the riskiest move of his career: He created Cable News Network (CNN), the first

cable was designed as nothing more than a delivery system for broadcast channels.

Community Antenna Television. In the early days of television, people in remote areas or in communities sheltered by mountains frequently could not receive the new signals. Among these was Mrs. L. E. Parsons of Astoria, Oregon. Parsons wanted to have television, but the nearest station was 125 miles away. Her husband solved the problem by placing an antenna on top of a local hotel and running a cable into their apartment. Once word got out that the Parsons family had television, the hotel, local bars, and even the neighbors started asking for connections to their antenna. This early form of cable television, which simply retransmitted broadcast channels, came to be known as **community antenna television (CATV)**.[19]

Connecting to these early cable systems was expensive; the cost ranged from $100 to $200. Although there were isolated experiments with subscription channels, for the most part cable remained a way to serve areas with poor reception, and the FCC devised restrictive rules to keep it that way. Until the 1970s, cable was primarily a way to get a good TV signal, not additional programming.[20]

Satellite Distribution and the Rebirth of Cable. By 1975, the face of cable television was beginning to change. The FCC began loosening the rules on cable companies, and new channels were being distributed via satellite.[21]

 Video 9.3: Watch Ken Auletta talk about Ted Turner's career.

community antenna television (CATV): An early form of cable television used to distribute broadcast channels in communities with poor television reception.

Big Three networks: The original television broadcast networks: NBC, CBS, and ABC.

twenty-four-hour news channel. In its early years, CNN had many technical problems and no reputation to speak of. Critics, in fact, referred to CNN as the "Chicken Noodle Network" because it paid its employees poorly and was run amateurishly.[23] Despite the network's problems, however, viewers soon discovered that if they wanted breaking news, they could find it immediately on CNN. Unlike ABC, NBC, and CBS, CNN did not have to interrupt soap operas or sitcoms to put news on the air.

When ABC and Westinghouse tried to start a competing cable news service in 1982, Turner launched his second news network, CNN Headline News, which featured round-the-clock, half-hour newscasts. Since then, CNN has expanded to provide CNN Radio, CNN International, CNN Airport Network, and CNN en Español.

Turner took his idea of repackaging material a step further by buying up the MGM movie library and the Hanna-Barbera cartoon library, which gave him control of the Flintstones, the Jetsons, and Scooby-Doo. He used these pop-culture figures, along with additional sports broadcasting rights he acquired, to program WTBS, along with Turner Network Television (TNT), the Cartoon Network, and Turner Classic Movies.

In 1996, Turner Broadcasting was acquired by media giant Time Warner, and although Turner lost direct control of his networks, he did get access to the Warner Bros. library of movies and classic cartoons. When *Time* magazine's editors declared Turner their "Man of the Year" in 1991, they wrote that he had fulfilled Marshall McLuhan's ideal of the global village. CNN has not made all people brothers and sisters, but *Time* said that the network has given people a window on the world:

> In 1991, one of the most eventful years of this century, the world witnessed the dramatic and transforming impact of those events of live television by satellite. The very definition of news was rewritten—from something that *has happened* to something that is *happening* at the very moment you are hearing of it. A war involving the fiercest air bombardment in history unfolded in real time—before the cameras.[24]

Before long, numerous channels were available to cable companies via satellite, including Black Entertainment Television (BET) and the children's network Nickelodeon. In 1978, amid much ridicule, the Entertainment and Sports Programming Network (ESPN) was launched as a twenty-four-hour-a-day sports channel carrying such little-known sports as Australian-rules football and curling. But ESPN quickly grew into one of the most popular channels on cable.[25]

During this period, nine out of ten viewers were watching prime-time programs on the networks, which were still controlled by the people who had started the first radio networks: William Paley at CBS, David Sarnoff at NBC, and Leonard Goldenson at ABC.[26]

Cable television pioneer and CNN founder Ted Turner created a media empire with global reach that goes a long way to fulfilling the ideal of the global village.

However, the 1980s saw the growth of a new kind of cable—a service that brought new channels into the household along with the original networks. Cable television viewers now have access to a wide range of programming, most of which can be grouped into a few major categories:

Questioning the Media

In the home where you grew up, did you have cable/satellite television or just broadcast television? If you had cable/satellite, do you know how much your bill for it was per month? If you had to give up one, which would it be, and why?

- Affiliates of the Big Four broadcast networks (ABC, NBC, CBS, and Fox)
- Independent stations and smaller network affiliates
- Superstations—Local independent stations that broadcast nationwide via satellite (WTBS, WGN, etc.)
- Local-access channels—Channels offering local government programming and community-produced shows
- Cable networks—Advertiser-supported networks that may also receive small fees for each subscriber on a particular cable system (MTV, CNN, BET, etc.)
- Premium channels—Extra-cost channels that don't carry advertising (HBO, Showtime, etc.)

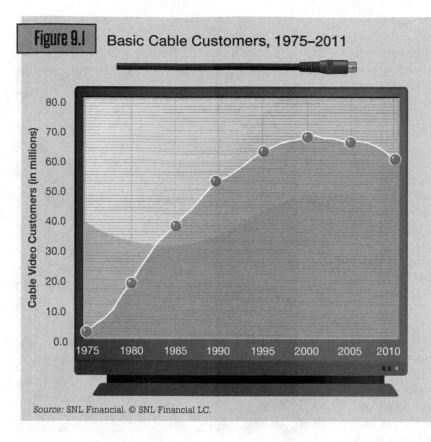

Figure 9.1 Basic Cable Customers, 1975–2011

Cable Video Customers (in millions)

Source: SNL Financial. © SNL Financial LC.

Consumers loved the fact that they could record programs and watch them later, but movie and television producers were upset that people were recording—and keeping—programs without paying for them. They were also concerned that movies and programs would be duplicated and resold around the world. Universal and Disney sued Sony over its promotion of the VCR for recording movies, but in 1984, the U.S. Supreme Court ruled that television viewers had the right to record copyrighted programs for their own personal use. Piracy of the programming was clearly illegal, but this was not the fault of the equipment manufacturers.[30]

Direct Broadcast Satellites. Satellite programming providers have been competing with cable since the 1980s, but their success was limited initially because of the rapid growth of cable, the large dish antennas required, and the limited number of channels consumers could receive. All this changed in the 1990s with the advent of the low-earth-orbit **direct broadcast satellite (DBS)**. Several DBSs were launched to deliver programming through a new kind of antenna about the size of a pizza.

As of December 2011, approximately 29 percent of U.S. households had satellite television. Satellite service in the United States grew rapidly from the mid-1990s until about 2007, when adoption of the new delivery system stabilized at current levels.[31] In Europe, which has less of a tradition of cable television than the United States, DBS services are very popular. 21st Century Fox's Sky Italia has almost 5 million subscribers in Italy, offering approximately 190 channels of programming through satellite and mobile delivery.[32]

DBS is now competing head-to-head with cable. A problem the satellite services face in this competition is that their subscribers still have to put up an old-fashioned antenna to get local broadcast stations. To address this drawback, in major markets DBS companies provide local stations via satellite as well.[33]

Digital Television

Just as sound recording has moved to digital formats with CDs and MP3 files (see Chapter 7), so is television

- Pay-per-view channels—Channels showing special events, concerts, and movies that subscribers pay for on an individual basis
- Audio services—High-quality music services[27]

Cable services offered massive competition to the broadcasters and created a new television landscape. Approximately 50 percent of all American households (about 58 million) subscribe to cable service. And 48 million of those subscribers also get the extended digital video service.[28] By way of comparison, in the United Kingdom, cable was in 13.1 percent of all homes by the end of 2011. (Direct broadcast satellite service is much more popular in the UK than cable, reaching roughly 39 percent of TV viewers there.[29]) (See Figure 9.1.)

Hollywood and the VCR. Although videotape has been used in television studios since the 1950s, it was not until the late 1970s that the **videocassette recorder (VCR)** became a household appliance that allowed viewers to make permanent copies of television shows. VCRs took time to catch on. Initially, there were two incompatible formats (VHS and Beta), and the machines themselves were expensive, costing $800 or more. In 1985, only two out of ten U.S. homes had VCRs, but by 1991, they could be found in seven out of ten homes.

 Web 9.1: Get the scoop on HDTV presence in U.S. homes.

videocassette recorder (VCR): A home videotape machine that allows viewers to make permanent copies of television shows and, thus, choose when they want to watch programs.

direct broadcast satellite (DBS): A low-earth-orbit satellite that provides television programming via a small, pizza-sized satellite antenna; DBS is a competitor to cable TV.

shifting from the analog technology of Farnsworth and Zworykin to computerized digital technology. All television broadcasting in the United States was scheduled to be digital by February 17, 2009, but in January 2009, the federal government decided that people weren't ready for the transition, despite several years of warnings that the change would be taking place. Critics of the move to digital broadcasting pointed out that many of the households that rely on broadcast signals for television have incomes under $30,000 and may have trouble affording the set-top box that converts digital broadcast signals into analog signals that old-fashioned television sets can display. To help solve this problem, the government issued coupons to help poor families buy the converters. In fact, a shortage of the coupons was among the reasons that the conversion was delayed.

SECRET 4 VCR ownership peaked in 1999, with nearly 89 percent of households owning a VCR. By the end of 2006, that proportion had fallen ten points to 79 percent. VCRs were replaced predominantly by DVD players, which are now in 79 percent of all homes.[34] VCRs are also facing competition from the new digital video recorders (DVRs), such as TiVo, that record television programs on a computer hard disk. The DVR lets a viewer jump in to start watching a recorded show fifteen minutes after it comes on the air. The viewer can then fast-forward through the commercials, and by the time the show is over, the viewer has caught up with the "live" broadcast. DVRs are seen as easier to use than VCRs but typically require a monthly subscription fee to use. As of December 2013, DVRs were in 47 percent of American households, up from 40 percent in 2010 and 23 percent in 2007.[35] (This gives us another example of Secret Four—Nothing's new: Everything that happened in the past will happen again.)

As you may have noticed from those figures, the rate of growth of DVR adoption has slowed dramatically in the last few years. Why? It's probably not that people don't want to be able to watch shows on their own schedule. Instead, people have many more options now than just prerecording shows to watch. For example, a 2013 study shows that 61 percent of cable subscribers have access to video on demand (VOD), with which they can just call up a missed show without doing any recording. They may also have access to a streaming service like Netflix that lets them pick from an enormous library of movies, television shows, and original content.[36] (We'll come back to this at the end of the chapter.)

On Friday, June 12, 2009, the last of the analog television broadcast stations was shut off. That doesn't mean

---

high-definition television (HDTV): A standard for high-quality digital broadcasting that features a high-resolution picture, wide-screen format, and enhanced sound.

standard digital television: A standard for digital broadcasting that allows six channels to fit in the broadcast frequency space occupied by a single analog signal.

Although cable television remains the largest alternative to broadcast programming in the United States, satellite delivery is much more common throughout much of the world, as is illustrated by this block of apartments in the Turkmen city of Türkmenabat.

that everyone started using new digital sets, however. Instead, many people will continue to get their television from a digital cable or satellite box, or get a converter box. On the two days following the shutdown of analog broadcasting, the FCC received approximately 400,000 calls to its hotline, considerably below the 600,000 to 3 million calls it was expecting.[37] There are two distinct digital formats. **High-definition television (HDTV)** is in a wide-screen format (like a theater movie) and features an ultra-clear high-resolution picture with superior sound. The other digital format is **standard digital television**, which makes it possible to broadcast up to six channels on the same frequency space that now carries one channel. (However, the picture is no better than that produced by existing signals.[38]) Using standard digital, a PBS station can choose to put out a single HDTV program or four digital programs at the current resolution, giving children a choice at any given time between *Arthur*, *Barney*, *Sesame Street*, and *Wishbone*.

The development of HDTV began in the 1980s, and on November 1, 1998, the launch of the space shuttle *Discovery* was the first event to be covered in a nationwide broadcast using a digital television signal. The broadcast was viewed by a tiny audience of just a few hundred people in twenty cities, with forty-two stations carrying digital signals.[39] As of March 2014, approximately 77 percent of U.S. homes had at least one HDTV set, and 46 percent of U.S. homes had more than one HDTV. Overall, 59 percent of the televisions in use in the United States in 2014 were HDTVs, up from 34 percent in 2010 and just 18 percent in 2008.[40]

Since all television broadcasting went digital in 2009, HDTVs have become increasingly popular. Viewers need either a cable/satellite connection or a converter box if they want to keep using analog sets.

Richard Levine/Alamy

From Broadcasting to Narrowcasting: The Changing Business of Television

Television got its start with the three networks that dominated the radio industry in the 1940s: NBC, CBS, and ABC. There were some independent stations as well, such as WGN in Chicago and WOR in New York, which had grown out of major independent radio stations, but for the most part, everyone in the country was watching NBC, CBS, or ABC. This would remain the status quo until cable and VCRs exploded in popularity in the 1980s.

Networks and Affiliates

The Big Three **television networks** are the companies that have provided programs to local stations around the country since the start of the television industry. These affiliate stations require a license from the FCC, equipment, and a local staff. The choice of what shows to carry is up to the local station. If a station carries a particular program, the station receives a fee from the network, along with the revenue from selling local commercials during the show. The network makes its money from the national commercials that run during the program. If an individual station decides that it could make more money running a locally produced program, such as a college basketball game, or a program from an independent producer, it can do so. In that case, the station pays for the program but keeps all the advertising revenue. The only exceptions are the dozen or

so stations that each network owns and operates; although they have a certain amount of independence, these stations must please their network owners.[41]

Educational Broadcasting Becomes Public Broadcasting

Noncommercial broadcasting in the United States was conceived as a way of delivering educational programming. Then Congress passed the Public Broadcasting Act of 1967, which established the Corporation for Public Broadcasting to provide funds for a wide range of noncommercial programs, including public service and educational programs. The noncommercial, or public, stations came to share programming through a new network, the **Public Broadcasting Service (PBS)**. This nonprofit broadcast network is funded by government appropriations, private industry underwriting, and support from viewers.[42]

While PBS stations eventually became widely available, they tended to have small audiences except for their daytime children's programming, which included the groundbreaking *Sesame Street*.[43] *Sesame Street*'s creator, Joan Ganz Cooney, says that the goal of the show was to give disadvantaged inner-city children a head start on school: "We argued that it would make all the psychological difference in their success in school if [disadvantaged children] came in with the same kind of skills as a middle-class child."[44] *Sesame Street* was also designed to have a slick, fast-paced, commercial look. It even had "sponsors," such as the number 5 and the letters Q and U.

When the show premiered on November 8, 1969, it immediately grabbed a significant audience, and even now it is among the most watched of all children's shows. But was it a success at helping disadvantaged children develop reading and math skills? That question is difficult to answer. At least one major study found that *Sesame Street* was successful in preparing children for school, but that "advantaged" children gained fully as much from it as disadvantaged students; thus, the show was not closing the gap between the haves and the have-nots.

In the 1990s, PBS started attracting a significant audience with programming such as the Ken Burns documentaries *The Civil War* and *Baseball*. Those larger audiences, in

television network: A company that provides programs to local stations around the country; the local affiliate stations choose which programs to carry.

Public Broadcasting Service (PBS): A nonprofit broadcast network that provides a wide range of public service and educational programs. It is funded by government appropriations, private industry underwriting, and viewer support.

turn, led to support from a number of large corporations that hoped their brief underwriting announcements would reach the upscale audiences who watch PBS. These announcements are not quite commercials, but they do allow corporations to present a short message to viewers. Among recent PBS underwriters are oil giant BP, GMC Trucks, AT&T, and State Farm Insurance. More recently, PBS has been attracting big audiences with British imports such as *Downton Abbey* and *Sherlock*.

The Fox Network

The 1980s brought numerous changes to the broadcasting market. Not only were VCRs and cable becoming popular, but there was also a new broadcast network. Australian newspaper publisher Rupert Murdoch started the Fox broadcast network after buying 20th Century Fox and incorporating it into his mammoth global media empire (see Chapter 3). He put the new network on the air in 1986 by buying stations in six of the top ten television markets. Although companies had tried to set up alternative broadcast networks before, none had really succeeded. Murdoch had an advantage in that during the 1980s people were becoming accustomed to watching cable channels, which meant they were no longer wed to regular network programming.

Fox was able to attract independent stations because it was offering them free programming rather than making them rely on syndicated material, most of which consisted of network reruns. The offerings were initially limited, with a late-night talk show starring Joan Rivers followed by Sunday-evening programming beginning in 1987.

While Fox managed to attract viewers with shows such as *The Simpsons* and *Married With Children,* what put it on the map was stealing NFL football away from the Big Three. NFL football was a show that people were accustomed to watching; now they just had to watch it on a new network. Fox also brought in the under-thirty viewers coveted by advertisers with hit programs such as *The X-Files* and *Melrose Place*.[45] The Big Three broadcast networks were becoming the **Big Four networks**.

More recently, Fox has been attracting large audiences with hit shows such as *American Idol, Family Guy,* and *The Simpsons* (which as of this writing has been on the air more than twenty-five years!).

Defining Ratings

One of the biggest concerns for television networks, whether broadcast or cable, is the size of their audiences.

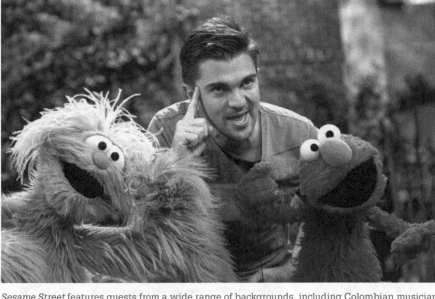

Sesame Street features guests from a wide range of backgrounds, including Colombian musician Juanes, posing here with Muppets Rosita (left) and Elmo (right).

Rates for commercials, which provide all the income for broadcast networks and a substantial portion of the income for cable services, are determined by how many people are viewing a show at a given time.

Measuring television audiences used to be pretty simple, at least in principle. You found out how many people watched a given show at a given time on one of three major networks, and you had your answer. The fact that you depended on a limited sample of people who had to fill out complex diaries or use a set-top "people meter" may have complicated things a bit, but basically it was simple. But now we have four major English-language broadcast networks, the Univsion Spanish-language broadcast network, PBS, several minor broadcast networks, dozens of major cable networks, and hundreds of specialized cable networks. There is also the issue of measuring the alternative methods for viewing these programs, the most important of which is delayed viewing on DVR.

Due to the expansion of viewing choices, the ratings required for a show to be a success have gotten smaller. In 2011, the top-rated singing competition show *American Idol* attracted an average of 29 million viewers per week. In 1996, *ER* was the top-rated drama, and it drew an audience of more than 30 million viewers per week.[46]

Now that DVRs are in more than 47 percent of all homes, the number of people watching shows on a

---

Big Four networks: The broadcast landscape we know today: the Big Three networks plus the Fox network.

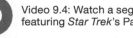 Video 9.4: Watch a segment of *Sesame Street* featuring *Star Trek*'s Patrick Stewart.

Video 9.5: Watch puppets explain how the Nielsen ratings system works.

delayed basis has become more important. Nielsen, which measures television audiences, now considers:

- Live only—People who are watching the program live as it happens.
- Live + SD—People who watch the program the same day as it airs. If you record a program on your DVR and start watching it fifteen minutes after it starts, this is you.
- Live + 3—People who watch the program live or within three days of airing.
- Live + 7—People who watch the program within seven days of its airing. This is the most complete measure of a show's popularity. (It does not, however, account for the episode of the Food Network's competition show *Chopped* that I recorded three months ago but finally watched last night.[47])

The major provider of viewership data, known as *ratings*, is Nielsen Media Research. The company keeps track of the shows watched in 9,000 homes located across the United States. Although the Nielsen families receive a token payment for their participation, they are essentially volunteering to keep track of all their television viewing. Nielsen uses a combination of methods to measure audience size. In the largest urban markets, the company uses a device called the **PeopleMeter**. Viewers push buttons on the machine to record who is watching programs at specific times. In smaller markets, viewers fill out daily diaries, listing what they watched.

While Nielsen tracks overall network viewership throughout the year, the company looks at the audience size of individual stations four times a year (November, February, May, and July) during periods known as **sweeps**. Networks and individual stations often schedule their best—or at least most popular—programming during sweeps periods to attract the highest possible ratings. These higher ratings allow them to charge more for commercials. Nielsen also tracks the ages and sex of audience members, and advertisers are oftentimes as concerned about the demographics of their audience as they are about the absolute size of it.

Nielsen provides networks and stations with several different measurements. The most important of these is the **rating point**, the percentage of the total potential television audience actually watching the show. For example, Nielsen estimated that there were 114.5 million households with televisions in use in 2008. If 1,145,000 homes viewed a particular program, that would produce a rating of 1 (1,145,000 / 114,500,000 = .01, or 1 percent of the total potential audience). A program viewed in 15 million households would have a rating of 13.1.[48]

The second major measurement Nielsen provides is the **share**, the percentage of television sets in use that are tuned to a particular show. Instead of telling producers how many households are watching the show, the share measures how popular a particular show is compared to everything else that is broadcast at the time. Although a show that airs at 1:00 a.m. might have a relatively low rating (say, 3 or 4), it could have a high share (30 or 40) because a large portion of a small audience is watching it.[49]

An Earthquake in Slow Motion

Fox, cable, and the VCR changed everything for the television industry—a set of changes that media writer Ken Auletta has called "an earthquake in slow motion." In 1976, the prime-time viewing audience belonged to the Big Three, with nine out of ten viewers watching network programming. By 1991, the Big Three had lost a third of their viewers. These viewers hadn't stopped watching television; they had just moved to other channels. In 1976, the typical home had a choice of seven broadcast channels; by 1991, it had a choice of thirty-three cable channels.[50] Today, homes with digital cable programming can have access to more than one hundred channels.

Another part of the earthquake was that the original Big Three networks were sold to new owners in 1985. NBC was taken over by General Electric, CBS was purchased by investor Larry Tisch, and ABC was purchased by Capital Cities Communications. Since that time, ABC has been acquired by Disney, CBS has been purchased and spun off by Viacom, and Comcast has bought NBC. The networks are no longer controlled by the people who started them.[51]

©iStockphoto.com/acprints

The earthquake also affected profits. Revenues for the broadcast networks plummeted in the 1990s, whereas cable network revenues grew. Cable channels typically make more profit than the broadcast networks. Cable channels are the most profitable part of Walt Disney Co., NBCUniversal, News Corporation, and Time Warner. ESPN, despite spending more than $5.2 billion on content in 2011, was the most profitable part of Disney.[52]

Despite their lower profitability, the broadcast networks generally have much bigger audiences than cable services. Popular cable shows such as professional wrestling or reality programs such as *Swamp People* typically attract an audience

---

PeopleMeter: An electronic box used by the ratings company Nielsen Media Research to record which television shows people watch.

sweeps: The four times during the year that Nielsen Media Research measures the size of individual television station audiences.

rating point: The percentage of the total potential television audience actually watching a particular show. One rating point indicates an audience of approximately 1.14 million viewers.

share: The percentage of television sets in use that are tuned to a particular show.

of, at most, 5 million viewers, whereas top-rated network shows such as *NCIS* typically attract three to four times as many viewers.

Why, then, are cable channels making more money than the broadcast networks? Traditionally, cable programs have cost less to produce than network programs, but spending on cable shows has been growing rapidly over the last several years. But the biggest difference is that broadcasters have a single source of revenue—advertising—whereas most cable channels have both a subscription fee and advertising revenue. In 2010, cable networks brought in nearly $48 billion in revenue. Of that, $22.3 billion came from advertising revenue, but $25 billion came from fees from cable and satellite operators.[53]

Diversity on Television

Broadcast television and the major cable networks have been roundly criticized for presenting a distorted view of reality. Aside from the issue that people on television comedies and dramas are not only attractive and funny, but they also resolve problems in less than an hour, there are complaints that television presents a world that is overwhelmingly white, male, and middle class.

In 1999, the Big Four networks introduced twenty-six new shows; not one of them featured a nonwhite lead character. This led to protests and threats of boycotts by African American and Latino groups. Ralph Farquhar, an African American television producer, told the *Arizona Republic*,

> I don't believe they're intentionally [excluding minority talent]. But people have to pay attention, you know? The makeup of America . . . has changed radically over the past 20 or 30 years, and yet TV doesn't necessarily reflect the diversity and the composition of the American population.[54]

Scott Sassa, a Japanese American network television executive, recalls being upset as a child when he saw an Anglo playing an Asian character. "I've got to tell you, growing up, seeing David Carradine as a Chinese guy [ticked] you off," Sassa said, referring to the martial arts series *Kung Fu*. Sassa says that the networks will have to reach out to nonwhites in a meaningful way if they want to hold on to their audiences:

> You not only want to see someone that looks like you on TV—you want to see someone that is a role model, someone that you want to aspire to be. That's what we need to do—create role models that are diverse, that make people in these minority groups feel good.[55]

Huffington Post pop culture blogger Meron Mogos notes that most recent shows on television have at least one supporting ethnic character, but few have nonwhites in starring roles. The exception to that is the ABC show *Scandal*, the first show in four decades to have an African American

woman as the lead.[56] The show staring Kerry Washington was created by Shonda Rhimes, who also did *Grey's Anatomy*. Washington's character is based on real-life African American woman Judy Smith, who was a communication director for the George W. Bush White House and then went to work as a crisis management expert.

Washington told CNN in an interview that her character Olivia "is someone who happened to be born female and black and those elements add to who she is as a human being. Do I think another person of another race could play her? Yes. Do I think it would change the story a little bit? Do I think it would change the character a little bit? Yes."[57]

Writer/producer Rhimes told *Entertainment Weekly* that although she has seen progress in casting diversity, she thinks there is room for improvement:

> Do I want to see any more shows where someone has a sassy black friend? No, because I'm nobody's sassy black friend. I just want to see shows in which people get to be people and that look like the world we live in. The world is changing, and television will have to follow.[58]

One channel that manages to have a higher level of diversity is the Food Network. While its hosts are not that different from the rest of television, the contestants in the chef competitions, such as *Chopped* and *Cutthroat Kitchen*, have a wide range of racial and ethnic diversity.

One of the things that cooks on the Food Network need to be good at is telling the story of their food, and people of differing backgrounds generally have interesting stories to tell, whether that of being an immigrant, growing up facing adversity, or simply being a determined young person trying to succeed.

Huffington Post Black Voices blogger Deborah Plummer notes that as of 2012, *Chopped* had nine judges, three of whom were women, one of whom was Ethiopian, one of whom was Mexican, and one of whom was Indian. The shows also feature competitors who are of varying sizes, accents, and sexual orientation.[59]

A major research project at UCLA's Ralph J. Bunche Center for African American Studies found that despite some recent improvements, minorities are still radically underrepresented on television, ranging from one-twelfth to one-half their actual share of the population. Not including sports, minorities appeared at about half the

Video 9.6: Watch Ken Auletta talk about his book *Three Blind Mice*.

The ABC television series *Scandal* staring Kerry Washington is the first show in four decades to have an African American woman as the star of the show.

expected rate on cable TV and reality shows, but on broadcast scripted shows, they were underrepresented by a factor of seven to one.[60]

If you want to make some comparisons on your own, 2010 U.S. Census Bureau estimates break down the current population as follows:

White, not Hispanic—64%

Hispanic—16%

African American—13%

Asian—5%

More Than One Race—3%

American Indian—0.9%

Pacific Islander—0.2%

(These values add up to more than 100 percent because some people overlap in categories.)[61]

Univision and Spanish-Language Broadcasting.

Although Latinos are seriously underrepresented on the Big Four English-language networks, there has been substantial growth in Spanish-language television. As discussed at the beginning of this chapter, Univision, a Spanish-language broadcast network, is actually the fifth-largest network, something it trumpeted in a 2005 full-page ad in the *New York Times*. Univision tends to do particularly well in the highly prized eighteen- to thirty-four-year-old

demographic. The network's popular telenovela *Mañana es para siempre* (*Tomorrow Is Forever*) routinely takes second place in its time slot among the younger demographics.[62] In 2013, Univision got the critical fourth place in the Nielsen February sweeps period among the prized audience demographic of adults aged eighteen to forty-nine. Part of this success came from Univision's growing popularity, and some of it came from NBC having a particularly bad year; but while Univision can't count on holding onto that fourth-place spot in the ratings, it does have a strongly growing audience.[63]

In addition to Univision, the Spanish television market includes the much smaller Telemundo network, along with a host of independent stations. Most markets offer no more than two Spanish-language television stations, but Phoenix, Arizona, has at least five.

The most popular programs on Spanish television are the **telenovelas**, or soap operas, which make up fifteen of the top twenty Spanish programs and are popular in both Latin America and the United States. Produced primarily in Mexico and Brazil, the telenovelas are exceedingly detailed and involved miniseries, with each story lasting six months to a year.[64] In December 2010, Univision drew 7.3 million viewers for the final episode of its six-month-long telenovela *Soy tu dueña* (*Woman of Steel*). The series drew an average audience of 5.4 million viewers per episode—an audience that was often better than those for shows airing against it on Fox or NBC. The only shows to defeat the series finale that night were a rerun of the comedy *Two and a Half Men* and ESPN's *Monday Night Football*.[65]

The telenovelas are at the heart of the criticism of Spanish-language networks. Latino critics say that the networks need to do more than just rerun Latin American programs; they need to make programs about Hispanics living in the United States. (Approximately half of Univision's programming comes from outside the United States.) There have also been complaints that the U.S. networks do not show dark-skinned Hispanics.

In an interesting twist, telenovelas have started making the jump over to English-language television. In the 2006–2007 season, ABC had a big hit with *Ugly Betty*, which is based on the hit Colombian telenovela *Yo soy Betty, la fea*. However, *Ugly Betty*'s ratings faded during the 2009–2010 season.[66]

To address the criticisms, Univision has started producing its own American-based sitcom, and it scored major hits by airing live broadcasts of the FIFA World Cup soccer tournaments.[67] It has taken cues from other American networks and created a game show called *A Millón*, which

Web 9.2: Read about a controversial article from the *New York Times* that calls Rhimes an "angry black woman."

telenovelas: Spanish-language soap operas popular in both Latin America and the United States.

TEST YOUR VISUAL MEDIA LITERACY

Netflix/Photofest

What Does a TV Show Look Like?

Broadcast television has long been criticized for lacking racial and ethnic diversity. But the prison drama *Orange Is the New Black* has a diverse range of characters including a transgender African American woman. Laverne Cox, who plays a transgender prisoner, says that the show is a breakout because of the range of faces in the show. "We don't see enough multidimensional portrayals of trans women and women in jail who are different races, ages, body types. . . . We don't see enough multidimensional portrayals of women in general, that show the diversity of womanhood."[68]

Even with its high level of diversity (which some complain gets talked about too much), the core of the series is based on a memoir by a Piper Kerman, a memoir by a "privileged white woman serving a prison sentence." But, as critic Roxane Gay points out, "Unfortunately, we will never see a similar show about a woman of color as a stranger in a strange land, bewildered by incarceration."[69]

Orange Is the New Black (OITNB), Netflix's cutting-edge drama, is making the news for a wide range of reasons. Perhaps the most noteworthy thing about it is that Netflix is a streaming service, not a broadcast or cable network, so Netflix releases the entire season of the series all at once, so fans who want to can binge watch all the episodes in a single weekend. But the prison drama is also notable for its cast of characters. As you look at this cast photo from 2014, what do you notice about the photo? What would you expect from a show with this cast? ■

WHAT does this photo say?

Orange Is the New Black is the story of a twenty-four-year-old white woman college graduate who was convicted of carrying money for a West African drug lord. She was eventually imprisoned in Danbury, Connecticut.[70] Does the cast photo look like the people you usually see on television? Why or why not?

WHAT do these messages mean?

Does the fact that this show has a racially diverse cast with a range of sexual orientations matter? Does the show represent diversity because it has a transgendered woman in the cast? Does it matter that the portrayal of these characters is sometimes stereotypical?

HOW do you and your classmates respond to these images?

Before you started this exercise, had you noticed how diverse the cast of *OITNB* is? Does that change how you feel about the show? Is it important to have diverse casts on television? Why do you think this way? What other types of diversity (beyond racial and ethnic) should television be concerned about? Why?

Web 9.3: Read about "colorblind casting."

Spanish-language soap operas, known as telenovelas, have been very popular, both on Univision and the much smaller Telemundo. This photo shows members of the cast of *Mi Corazan Insiste* working on the program for Telemundo.

SECRET 3 Aside from the network's success in attracting viewers, BET became profitable because major advertisers such as General Motors were looking for media to reach nonwhite consumers. The *New York Times* says that this is part of an ongoing trend of multicultural marketing aimed at African American, Hispanic, and Asian American consumers, which account for increasing segments of the U.S. population. BET's Louis Carr says that nonwhite consumers have to be taken much more seriously, not as a secondary target but as a primary target. In places like New York, Chicago, Los Angeles, Detroit, and Philadelphia, if you add up the African American population, the Hispanic population, and the Asian population, they're not minorities anymore. They're majorities.[77]

(Another example of Secret Three—Everything from the margin moves to the center.)

follows the same basic format as *Who Wants to Be a Millionaire?* The network has also followed the lead of VH1's *Behind the Music* and produced a series highlighting the downfalls of popular music stars.[71]

In 2005, ABC became the first network to start offering its prime-time programs either dubbed or closed-captioned in Spanish. The translation takes considerable effort to make sure that the jokes still work. Ruben Veloso, who heads the company that translated *Desperate Housewives* and *Lost* for ABC, says that sometimes they have to massage the script to keep it true to the storyline and to keep the innuendos and double entendres in the dialogue.[72]

Black Entertainment Television. Cable television also has networks that attempt to appeal to nonwhite audiences. The most significant is Black Entertainment Television (BET). The twenty-four-hour network reaches 60 million households, including 12.5 million black households.[73] When BET was acquired by media giant Viacom, it was already a $2 billion corporation that included restaurants, magazines, books, music, and cable networks.[74]

Started in 1980 as a local Washington, D.C., channel, BET was the nation's first black-owned cable network.[75] Although BET carries primarily talk shows and music videos, the network has also produced a series of made-for-television movies based on the Arabesque line of African American romance novels.[76]

Audience Members as Programmers: Public Access Cable.

Among the greatest voices for diversity on television are the **public access channels** carried on many cable systems. Such channels air public affairs programming and other locally produced shows; these include community bulletin boards, educational programming, coverage of government meetings, and programs created by members of the community. Public access channels allow people to deliver their ideas directly to the public without going through a gatekeeper such as a journalist or another third party. At its best, public access is a soapbox that goes beyond the town square and all the way into a majority of homes in the community.[78]

More than 15,000 hours of public access programming are produced each year at more than 2,000 locations. Following are some examples of public access programming:

- In Greensboro, North Carolina, several African American churches use the public access channel to bring sermons to house-bound people.
- A public access station in Massachusetts carries a weekly show, *Haiti Tele-Magazine Network*, for Haitian immigrants.
- In Dallas, Texas, a weekly program focuses on the local Iranian community.[79]

Public access television doesn't always live up to the standard of the public good, however. According to Laura Linder, who has studied public access television extensively, most programming on these channels is fairly conventional, but some of it is controversial. Unsuccessful experimental

---

 Video 9.7: Check out which telenovelas are currently popular.

public access channels: Local cable television channels that air public affairs programming and other locally produced shows.

films, exhibitionism, and racist hate speech can find their way onto public access channels. For example, viewers in one community complained about an animated film that they believed promoted drug use. On another controversial program, the host butchered and cooked iguanas. (He was eventually arrested for cruelty to animals.) Controversial programs often lead to calls for eliminating public access channels, but the courts have generally ruled that public access cable is a free-speech forum and therefore is protected as long as nothing illegal is broadcast.

How important are local access cable channels? It depends in large part on local activists. According to independent public access television producer Chris Hill, "If there's good public access, it's a result of grassroots organizing by people who see this as an important public resource."[80]

Linder says that public access programming differs from other forms because it is produced by audience members, not by media professionals. Public access cable is part of the trend toward more interactive media, such as the Internet and local talk radio. It transforms viewers into media producers rather than just audience members.

NBC's hit series *The Blacklist* makes income both from airing on broadcast TV and from being shown on the streaming service Netflix.

■ ■ ■ ■ ■ ■ ■ ■ ■ ■ ■ ■ ■ ■ ■ ■ ■

Television and Society

Few new social institutions have become an integral part of society faster than television did in the late 1940s and early 1950s. In 1948, there were fewer than 100,000 televisions in use; a year later, that number was more than 1 million, and by 1959, there were 50 million sets in use. In less than ten years, television had become a part of everyday life in the United States. Television viewership tended to grow more slowly in the highly regulated European market, something we talk about in depth in Chapter 15.

As television became commonplace, people started to worry about its effects on viewers: How much time were people spending viewing television? What activities would it replace? Why were people watching television? Most important, what effect, if any, would the content of television programs have on viewers? Would it lead to violence and juvenile delinquency? Would it take children into the world of adults too early? Would it transform society?

Television as a Major Social Force

In *Tube of Plenty*, Erik Barnouw argues that television had a revolutionary impact on society:

The advent of television was widely compared, in its impact, with that of the Gutenberg printing press

centuries earlier. Television was beginning to be seen as the more revolutionary innovation. The reasons were so obvious that they had seldom been discussed. Television viewing required no skill beyond normal human functions. Reading, on the other hand, was a skill acquired over years via effort and drilling—and not acquired by everyone. It generally involved the mediation of father, mother, grandfather, grandmother, teacher, priest, and others, a factor favoring social continuity, a transmittal of values. Television short-circuited all this. It could begin in cradle or playpen, and often did. It could bypass father, mother, grandfather, grandmother. It reached the child long before teacher and priest. Their role in the acculturation process had been sharply reduced. They had sporadically, fitfully, sought to recapture a more decisive role by seeking to control the images on the tube—but that control had slipped elsewhere, to the world of business. In a development of historical significance, the television's messages had become dominant social doctrine.[81]

Barnouw is arguing that although television audiences have fragmented with the growth of cable, satellite, and

Questioning the Media

When and why do you watch television? Do you watch specific shows or just whatever is airing? Do you think it's possible to watch "too much" television? Why or why not? What did you watch last night?

Web 9.4: Read the Kaiser Family Foundation study "Generation MC2: Media in the Lives of Eight- to Eighteen-Year-Olds"

Actress Mary Tyler Moore raised havoc with network censors in 1961 when she danced on *The Dick Van Dyke Show* wearing capri pants. Moore defended her outfit, saying, "I'll dress on the show the way I dress in real life."

watching television content. This is despite the fact that they are spending less time in front of a television set. How is this possible? While television sets are still the most popular media device among young people, the TV set is gradually losing ground to video they can watch on their computer screens, tablets, or phones.[84] (For more on these figures, turn back to Chapter 1.)

Television as Competition for Other Activities. Although television viewing is often reported in terms of average amounts of time spent viewing, such figures don't always give a complete picture. The differences between heavy and light television viewers can be significant. A 1990 study found that people who watch a lot of television tend to spend more time home alone than light viewers. The study also showed that light viewers spend more time walking than heavy viewers.

Unfortunately, these studies usually cannot determine why people behave in these ways. Do heavy viewers stay home specifically to watch television, or are they unable to get out of the house for one reason or another? Perhaps busy people who like to walk don't have time to watch television. One finding that is not difficult to interpret was that people who watch sports on television also tend to participate in sports. The study also found that the amount of time people spend reading does not seem to be affected by how much television they watch.[85]

How Do Viewers Use Television?

In addition to examining how much television people are watching, researchers have studied how and why people watch television. These uses and gratifications studies seek to determine what uses people make of television viewing and what gratifications (or benefits) they gain from it. The central premise of these studies is that television (like other media) is not an actor that does things to viewers. Instead, audience members are active participants who select programming to meet particular needs.

What might these needs be? The study *Television in the Lives of Our Children* found that children watch television for many of the same reasons that adults do:

- To be entertained.
- To learn things or gain information. In many cases, this information relates to socialization: how to act like an adult, how to be a better athlete, how other people live.
- For social reasons. The content of TV doesn't matter so much as the fact that they watch it with friends or talk about it at school the next day.

home video, television is still the dominant shared experience in the modern world, reaching more people than schools, families, and churches.

Time Spent Watching Television. One reason social critics have been so concerned about the influence of television is that Americans spend a lot of time watching it. Estimates of the amount vary. Nielsen Media Research says that the average person watches about four hours of television a day.[82] According to another estimate, Americans spend fifteen hours a week actively watching television and have the TV turned on for an additional twenty-one hours a week while doing other things.

Television viewing can also be looked at in terms of how it dominates our free time. A study of the functions of television in everyday life notes that on average Americans spend half of their leisure time watching television. The same study showed that at any given moment in the evening more than one-third of the U.S. population is watching television; in the winter that proportion rises to over 50 percent.[83]

A study by the Kaiser Family Foundation found that children spend an average of four and a half hours a day

The researchers also found that different children watched the same program for different reasons. One child might watch a cartoon show because he was lonely and the show provided company, another might watch it because it made her laugh, and a third might watch it because his friends were watching it.[86]

Standards for Television

In the 1950s and 1960s, networks and advertisers imposed strict controls on what could be shown on television. For example, Mary Tyler Moore and Dick Van Dyke played the married couple Laura and Rob Petrie on *The Dick Van Dyke Show*, which aired from 1961 to 1966. Although married, the Petries had to sleep in separate twin beds. Sponsors also raised their eyebrows when Moore wore jeans and capri pants on the show because these garments might be considered suggestive. Moore fought the sponsors and won, saying, "I'll dress on the show the way I dress in real life."[87] This was the era when comedian Lucille Ball had to use the word *expecting* rather than *pregnant* on her show when she was obviously carrying a child.[88]

What could be shown was determined by each network's own standards and practices department. The goal of these departments, which at one time had as many as sixty people working in them, was to make sure the network did not lose viewers or sponsors because of offensive content. Since the 1980s, they have decreased in size by 50 percent or more. This change is due partly to a loosening of societal standards throughout the 1970s, but it is also a response to the more explicit content of cable television programming.[89]

Alfred Schneider, who served as a censor for ABC television for more than thirty years, observes that the networks feel freer to deal with difficult topics today than in earlier decades:

Sometimes the quality of a particular program allows you to do things that you would not permit in other programs. I once said that in my lifetime there would never be full frontal nudity on network television. I was wrong. I lived to see *War and Remembrance*, where I permitted full frontal nudity in the concentration camp scenes. I finally justified it by saying that this was not nudity, this was death.

As we see the growth of more distribution systems, the growth of independents, my position will have to change. As the populace becomes more

While Janet Jackson's 2004 Super Bowl "wardrobe malfunction" resulted in eight years of legal wrangling and threatened fines, when cable news host Nancy Grace exposed her nipple on *Dancing With the Stars* in 2011, it caused little controversy.

educated, more inquisitive, more concerned about issues, I will be more comfortable taking greater risks knowing that people will seek out their choices.[90]

In 1997, broadcasters fundamentally changed their programming controls; instead of placing an occasional warning before programs considered inappropriate for children, they implemented a two-part rating system modeled after the one used for movies. There is an age-appropriateness rating that closely matches the movie system, with ratings of G, PG, TV-14 (for fourteen-year-olds and older), and TV-MA (for mature audiences). Many networks also provide a content rating of S (sexual content), V (violence), L (crude language), and/or D (adult dialogue).[91] It was also in 1997 that the so-called V-chip, an electronic device allowing parents to block programs with certain content ratings, began to be included in television sets.

Television producers were initially concerned that shows with ratings for violence or sexual content might be harder to market. But rather than restricting television content, broadcasters have used the ratings to warn viewers that material on a program will be explicit. As Robert Thompson, director of Syracuse University's Center for Television and Popular Culture, has noted,

Video 9.8: Watch Mary Tyler Moore dancing in capri pants.

No Sense of Place

Media scholar Joshua Meyrowitz, in his book *No Sense of Place,* argues that the very existence of television is an influence on society because it breaks down the physical barriers that separate people. In the past, he says, people were limited to interacting with those whom they could see and hear face-to-face. Meyrowitz describes how the coming of electronic media, and television in particular, changed this:

> The boundaries marked by walls, doors, and barbed wire, and enforced by laws, guards, and trained dogs, continue to define situations by including and excluding participants. But today such boundaries function to define social situations only to the extent that information can still be restricted by restricting physical access.[1]

These boundaries can be broken at many levels. A child watching television can see people talking about adult topics such as infidelity, pregnancy, or cross-dressing. A teenager in New York City can see the impact of drought on people in Iowa. Young men can listen in on what women say on a "girls' night out." In each of these cases, in the pretelevision era, the viewer would have been isolated because of his or her "place," whether it was geographic location, age, sex, or socioeconomic status. But television gives everyone an equal view into these formerly separate worlds.

This breakdown of place has occurred not just within the United States, but throughout the industrialized world. As we discussed in Chapter 3, the United States is the world's largest supplier of entertainment programming; it is also the largest supplier of imagery to the world. The most important effect of CNN and other satellite-based television news services is that they give people everywhere in the world access to the same information at the same time, whether those people are heads of state, diplomats, soldiers, or citizens. The late Don Hewitt, longtime producer of the CBS newsmagazine *60 Minutes,* has said that this global sharing of information is changing the world:

> When there was a disaster, it used to be that people went to church and all held hands. Then television came along, and there was this wonderful feeling that while you were watching Walter Cronkite, millions of other Americans were sharing the emotional experience with you. Now the minute anything happens they all run to CNN and think, "The whole world is sharing this experience with me."[2]

WHO is the source?

Who is Joshua Meyrowitz? What book has he written?

WHAT is he saying?

According to Meyrowitz, how has television transformed society? What does Meyrowitz mean when he says television and other electronic media break down the barriers of place? What kind of barriers does Meyrowitz suggest are being broken by television?

WHAT evidence is there?

What examples of this process does Meyrowitz provide? When and where does this process take place?

WHAT do you and your classmates think about Meyrowitz's arguments?

List some examples of how television has let you see aspects of everyday life that would normally remain hidden from you. Does television take you "places" you couldn't go to otherwise? If so, list some examples. Do you ever use television to deliberately watch worlds you wouldn't be able to see otherwise?

---

[1] Joshua Meyrowitz, *No Sense of Place* (New York: Oxford University Press, 1985).
[2] William A. Henry III, "History as It Happens; Linking Leaders as Never Before, CNN Has Changed the Way the World Does Its Business," *Time,* January 6, 1992, 24–27.

 Web 9.5: Read an interview with Joshua Meyrowitz.

The people who wanted ratings to put the brakes on this new explosion of raunchy television saw just the opposite happen. Anybody should have seen this coming. If you give producers the opportunity to use a TV-MA rating, it's an invitation to make TV-MA programs.[92]

For the most part, the R-equivalent TV-MA rating has been confined to cable television shows such as Comedy Central's raunchy cartoon *South Park.* The Big Four broadcast networks have rarely aired programs with the TV-MA rating, the most notable exceptions being uncut broadcasts of serious R-rated movies such as *Schindler's List* and *Saving Private Ryan.*

Video 9.9: Watch both the Janet Jackson and Nancy Grace wardrobe malfunctions.

 Web 9.6: Read the latest about the settlement of the Janet Jackson indecency case before the Supreme Court.

The Problem of Decency

The line of what was acceptable on broadcast television was redrawn following the 2004 Super Bowl halftime show on CBS when Justin Timberlake exposed Janet Jackson's breast for nine-sixteenths of a second. The FCC received more than 500,000 complaints.[93] Immediately following the broadcast, the FCC started talking about the problem of indecency on television. References to sexual or bodily functions are considered to be indecent. FCC rules say that broadcast radio and television stations can't air indecent material between 6:00 a.m. and 10:00 p.m., when children are most likely to be watching. This differs from obscene programming (discussed further in Chapter 13), which "describes or shows sexual conduct in a lewd and offensive way" and has no "literary, artistic, political, or scientific value."[94] Obscene material is not protected by the First Amendment. Rules about indecency apply to broadcast materials but not to cable or satellite material. On June 29, 2012, the case regarding CBS finally came to a conclusion with the U.S. Supreme Court declining to review a lower court decision throwing out the fine.[95] As a side note in this case, cable news host Nancy Grace also exposed her nipple on the reality show *Dancing With the Stars*, this time for almost an entire second. But so far the FCC has not acted on any complaints, and it appears unlikely to lead to any fines or other legal action.[96]

There is no single standard for what constitutes broadcast indecency, and this standard clearly changes over time. During the 1990s and early 2000s, bare bottoms became common on shows such as *NYPD Blue*. But since the Janet Jackson fuss, even this minimal nudity has been digitally blurred when shown on broadcast television, and reality programs such as *Survivor* have become careful to digitally blur any hint of nudity that occurs during the programs' competitions as well.

There has been some serious fallout from the Janet Jackson stunt as well. Several CBS affiliates hesitated to rebroadcast the documentary *9/11* because of the rough language used by firefighters in the film.[97] In 2004, sixty-six ABC affiliate stations refused to air the R-rated movie *Saving Private Ryan* for fear they would be fined for the movie's graphic violence and extensive profanity.[98] (Congress raised the fines from $32,500 to $325,000 per "incident" following the Jackson case, which is why smaller stations are cautious about any program that might trigger an FCC response.) Broadcast standards in Europe are far more likely to regulate hate speech, advertising, and materials that are harmful to children than to control nudity.[99]

©iStockphoto.com/Jitalia17

Gene Policinski, executive director of the First Amendment Center, questions whether television can really tell the story of events such as the 9/11 attacks or the invasion of Normandy during World War II within the limits of decency rules:

> War is a bloody hell, and *Private Ryan* brought home the terror and anguish, as well as the heroics and sacrifices, of the heralds of the "greatest generation" who stormed ashore at Normandy in a manner no sanitized depiction had done previously. Who can view any veteran of that invasion in the same manner after seeing that film?[100]

The Future of Television

Whether it is delivered by broadcast, cable, or satellite, television is changing so quickly that it might be unrecognizable to Philo T. Farnsworth. The cable industry, for example, is in the process of replacing copper wire with fiber-optic cable that uses light rather than electricity to send out video and other types of signals. Fiber-optic cable has the advantage of being able to carry much more information than copper wire can, but more importantly, it has the capacity to allow audience members to send signals back to the program providers.[101]

Interactive Television

This new control of television by consumers is available at a number of levels. As the number of available channels increases, cable providers can offer multiple versions of single channels. Cable movie provider HBO offers multiple channels, each of which has movies starting at different times. The same is happening with pay-per-view channels, on which movies start at fifteen-minute intervals.

Consumers themselves can add to their degree of control. As mentioned earlier in the chapter, with DVRs, viewers are able to not only record programs and view them whenever they wish; they can also pause a program to take a phone call or get a snack and restart it when they return. In essence, the digital recorders give viewers the same control over "live" television that they have over prerecorded programs.

Video on Demand. One service that has really taken off in the past several years and has the potential to change the

---

video on demand: Television channels that allow consumers to order movies, news, or other programs at any time over fiber-optic lines.

Web 9.7: What do students mean when they say they are watching television?

Defining Television in the Twenty-first Century

Until the mid-2000s, we had a pretty good idea of what watching television meant. You would sit down in front of your television set, which would receive signals over the air from a cable or satellite service or from some kind of media player, such as a VCR or DVD player.

Then, in 2005, Apple started selling an iPod that could play video, and it offered current television shows the day after they aired for $1.99 an episode through the iTunes store. At first, it was primarily ABC programming, owned by Disney, that was available on iTunes.[102] (Remember, at the time of his death, Apple founder Steve Jobs was a member of the Disney board of directors and the company's biggest single stockholder.) But by 2007, all of the Big Four networks were selling episodes through

iTunes, as were many cable powerhouses. So Apple got broad acceptance of the idea that people would pay cash to download current television shows and that they could use portable devices to view those shows almost anywhere.

That was also the year that DVD rental service Netflix started streaming movies and TV shows over the Internet. Initially, the streaming was just to computers, but it soon expanded to devices such as the Roku box, Blu-ray players, and video game consoles that could play Netflix programming instantly on a television set.

Now Netflix and other streaming services, such as Amazon Instant Video, Hulu, and Hulu Plus, can be accessed on smartphones and tablets.[103] In fact, tablets are now the second-most-popular

way to watch television programming, according to research by media giant Viacom. The company's study showed that as of 2012, 15 percent of American's television viewing is done on tablets.[104]

All of these developments raise the question as to whether people are ready to **cut the cord**—disconnect from a traditional pay video service such as cable or satellite and replace it with content streamed over the Internet. Do you really need a cable or satellite subscription to watch a wide range of television programming anymore? Nielsen estimates that approximately 5 percent of television viewers have cut the cord, going exclusively to broadband delivery of video.[105] Among those who have cut the cord is famed media blogger Jim Romenesko, who writes that he made the change when his cable bill hit $203 a month in February 2011. At that point, he says he sold his three flat-screen TVs and took to doing all of his television viewing on his iPad. He says he has no regrets about making the switch, though he might feel differently if he were a big sports fan.[106]

AP Photo/Damian Dovarganes

Netflix is a major provider of streaming movies and television shows that can be played on a computer, a mobile device, or a television set.

Media Transformations Questions:

- **WHAT** does it mean to say you are "watching television" now?
- **DO** you watch video programming on your computer or mobile device? Why or why not?
- **WHAT** kind of programming do you watch on your computer or mobile device?
- **DO** you pay for it or is it free? If it's free, would you pay for the service if free options went away? Why or why not?
- **HAVE** you cut the cord or considered cutting the cord? Why or why not?

cutting the cord: Replacing traditional paid video services, such as cable or satellite television, with Internet-based streaming video services.

Defining Television in the 21st Century

Netflix recently jumped ahead of HBO with a spike in subscribers due in large part to its new content offerings and the increasing ease of streaming content. Both companies have developed new delivery and content strategies in the race to redefine the business model.

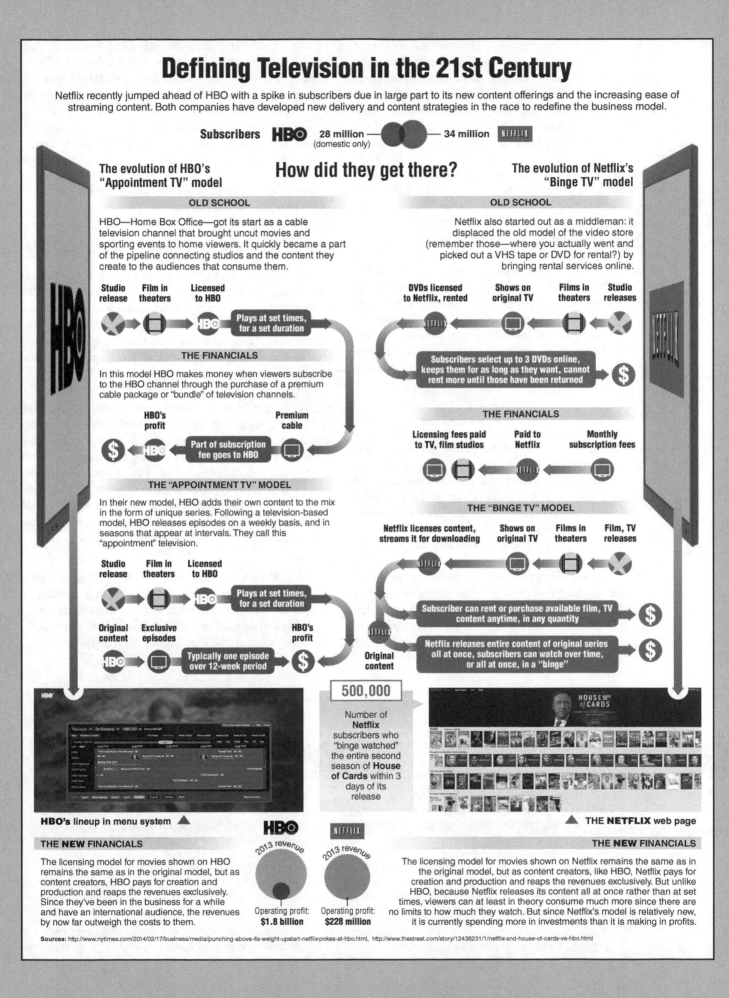

Subscribers **HBO** 28 million — 34 million **NETFLIX** (domestic only)

How did they get there?

The evolution of HBO's "Appointment TV" model

OLD SCHOOL

HBO—Home Box Office—got its start as a cable television channel that brought uncut movies and sporting events to home viewers. It quickly became a part of the pipeline connecting studios and the content they create to the audiences that consume them.

Studio release — Film in theaters — Licensed to HBO — Plays at set times, for a set duration

THE FINANCIALS

In this model HBO makes money when viewers subscribe to the HBO channel through the purchase of a premium cable package or "bundle" of television channels.

HBO's profit — Premium cable — Part of subscription fee goes to HBO

THE "APPOINTMENT TV" MODEL

In their new model, HBO adds their own content to the mix in the form of unique series. Following a television-based model, HBO releases episodes on a weekly basis, and in seasons that appear at intervals. They call this "appointment" television.

Studio release — Film in theaters — Licensed to HBO — Plays at set times, for a set duration

Original content — Exclusive episodes — HBO's profit — Typically one episode over 12-week period

The evolution of Netflix's "Binge TV" model

OLD SCHOOL

Netflix also started out as a middleman: it displaced the old model of the video store (remember those—where you actually went and picked out a VHS tape or DVD for rental?) by bringing rental services online.

DVDs licensed to Netflix, rented — Shows on original TV — Films in theaters — Studio releases

Subscribers select up to 3 DVDs online, keeps them for as long as they want, cannot rent more until those have been returned

THE FINANCIALS

Licensing fees paid to TV, film studios — Paid to Netflix — Monthly subscription fees

THE "BINGE TV" MODEL

Netflix licenses content, streams it for downloading — Shows on original TV — Films in theaters — Film, TV releases

Subscriber can rent or purchase available film, TV content anytime, in any quantity

Netflix releases entire content of original series all at once, subscribers can watch over time, or all at once, in a "binge"

Original content

500,000

Number of **Netflix** subscribers who "binge watched" the entire second season of **House of Cards** within 3 days of its release

HBO's lineup in menu system ▲

THE **NETFLIX** web page ▲

HBO 2013 revenue — Operating profit: **$1.8 billion**

NETFLIX 2013 revenue — Operating profit: **$228 million**

THE NEW FINANCIALS

The licensing model for movies shown on HBO remains the same as in the original model, but as content creators, HBO pays for creation and production and reaps the revenues exclusively. Since they've been in the business for a while and have an international audience, the revenues by now far outweigh the costs to them.

THE NEW FINANCIALS

The licensing model for movies shown on Netflix remains the same as in the original model, but as content creators, like HBO, Netflix pays for creation and production and reaps the revenues exclusively. But unlike HBO, because Netflix releases its content all at once rather than at set times, viewers can at least in theory consume much more since there are no limits to how much they watch. But since Netflix's model is relatively new, it is currently spending more in investments than it is making in profits.

Sources: http://www.nytimes.com/2014/02/17/business/media/punching-above-its-weight-upstart-netflix-pokes-at-hbo.html, http://www.thestreet.com/story/12438231/1/netflix-and-house-of-cards-vs-hbo.html

entire industry is **video on demand**. This service consists of television channels that allow viewers to order movies, news, or other programs that are digitally delivered at any time over fiber-optic lines. Time Warner began experimenting with such a system in 1993 and made its Full Service Network available to subscribers in Orlando, Florida. During the experiment, the company found that people liked having more choices, that they wanted to be able to pause a show and continue it later, and that young people adapted better to new technology than did older people. But the technology Time Warner used in Orlando could not keep up with demand as the number of subscribers increased.[107]

Video on demand has now moved into the mainstream, with more than 60 percent of all cable subscribers having access to it. These systems allow consumers to pick the program they want to watch and to pause, rewind, and fast-forward through the content. But many of these systems also block consumers from fast-forwarding through commercials.[108] Cable and satellite companies are also seeing competition from online services such as Amazon Prime, Hulu, Hulu Plus, and Netflix. We'll talk about that more in a moment.

Interacting With Programs. Interactive television goes beyond giving viewers a chance to select their own programming. It involves making them active participants in the programming. Among the most famous (or infamous) interactive television episodes was one that appeared on *Saturday Night Live*. Comedian Eddie Murphy played a cook who was about to boil Larry the Lobster. Viewers could call in on special phone lines to vote on whether Larry should or should not get cooked at the end of the show. (Compassionate viewers ended up saving Larry that night, though the lobster's final fate remains unknown.) It is not that much of a reach to go from voting on whether to save Larry the Lobster to calling in to vote on which singer to eliminate from the current season of *American Idol*. According to Brian Garden of MTV, "You are growing up with a generation that is almost overly empowered. They aren't satisfied with anything less than full control."[109] John Pavlik of the Center for New Media at Columbia University sees interactivity as becoming a standard part of television:

> When you transform people from couch potatoes into active participants, you turn TV programs into something like a sticky website. They want to keep playing along. Every program can have an interactive component. I think it will become the main way we connect to our televisions.[110]

The Earthquake in Slow Motion Continues

Earlier in this chapter, we discussed Ken Auletta's "earthquake in slow motion"—how the cable and satellite revolution brought about massive changes to the television business in the 1980s and 1990s. This earthquake has continued to shake up television into the twenty-first century due to the growing importance of broadband video and alternative viewing devices.

Convergence of Television and the Internet. Media analysts have been talking for years about convergence in the media industry with audio, video, still images, and text coming together in a single medium. It hasn't happened yet, but computers and television are definitely starting to converge, though not always in the ways that people were expecting. In a 2006 interview, Mike Bloxham of Ball State University told *Media Post* that

> the difference between the TV and the PC is getting less almost by the month. They're kind of morphing, and the only real difference is the size of the screen, where I'm using it, my need state or mind state, and, at the moment, the amount of interactivity.[111]

Chapter SUMMARY

Television was developed in the 1920s and 1930s by independent inventor Philo T. Farnsworth and RCA engineer Vladimir Zworykin. Commercial broadcasting began in the United States in 1939, but its development was put on hold by the outbreak of World War II. By the early 1950s, television was established as the dominant broadcast medium. Color television broadcasts came into widespread use in the 1960s.

Although primitive forms of cable television existed in 1948, cable did not become a significant medium until the early 1980s when satellite distribution of channels became common. Among the early cable channels were a number of networks created by Ted Turner. Viewers gained access to additional choices in the form of VCRs and direct broadcast satellite service. Television broadcasting has switched from analog signals to multiple digital formats, and VCRs have almost completely been replaced by DVRs, DVDs, video on demand, and streaming technology.

Television networks have been criticized for failing to include women and minorities in their programming, but cable channels have delivered more programming that addresses diverse interests. Networks have also been criticized for carrying too much violent and sexually explicit programming. But television has been praised for breaking down geographic and social barriers. Broadcast television is currently going through a cycle in which "indecent" content is being suppressed by the government.

Television is changing rapidly, with audience members getting many new options to control how and when they receive programming. With VCRs, DVRs, interactive television, and broadband video, viewers can choose what they watch and when they watch it. They are also able to interact with the programming through online and mobile resources.

Keep up-to-date with content from the author's blog.

Take the chapter quiz.

Key TERMS

Concept REVIEW

The differences between broadcast television and cable/satellite television

Ted Turner's ideas for repackaging programming for cable and distributing it nationwide

How Hollywood and other content providers have resisted changes in television technology

The impact that digital broadcasting will have on the television industry

Ken Auletta's "earthquake in slow motion"

The changing face of diversity on television

How standards of decency change on television

How audience members are taking control of how they interact with television

Student STUDY SITE

⑤SAGE edge™

Sharpen your skills with SAGE edge at **edge.sagepub.com/hanson5e**

SAGE edge for Students provides a personalized approach to help you accomplish your coursework goals in an easy-to-use learning environment.

The Internet

Interactive and Mobile Media

chapter 10

Fish Plays Pokemon

FishPlaysPokemon playing Pokémon Red/Blue

FPP: 08-12-2014 22:57:30-EST

SELECT · START · RANDOMIZE! · RANDOMIZE!

RECENT PRESSES

Medium

👤 3,195 👁 3,832,789

Follow · Share ▾ · Bookmark ⚙ ▾

In 2014, a pair of technically minded New York college students rigged a motion sensor to allow their fish Grayson to trigger the buttons on a Game Boy emulator playing Pokemon Red and Blue. As of October 2014, Grayson had more than 5 million page views.

As I sit at my computer in the summer of 2014, a fish named Grayson is playing the video games *Pokémon Red and Blue* on a Game Boy emulator using a motion sensor aimed at his fish tank. Each area of the tank is assigned to a different Game Boy button, and as he swims into the area, the button is triggered. That a pair of technically oriented college students in New York would rig some equipment to allow their fish to randomly play a video game is not surprising. It's the kind of hack that might seem reasonable on a late Friday night. The fact that as many as 22,000 people at a time would watch the fish play *Pokémon* using the video game streaming service Twitch is kind of amazing.[1]

Should you join in on the party, you will see a divided screen showing the Pokémon game on the left, the swimming fish with the control grid imposed over it in the center, and a chat session on the right where viewers either try to kibitz the fish or proclaim that he is dead. (The fish's owners point out continually that Grayson isn't dead; he's just sleeping.)

Catherine Moresco and Patrick Facheris, Grayson's owners, were likely inspired by the efforts of an anonymous Australian gamer who rigged the fifteen-year-old Game Boy game *Pokémon Red* to be played by the inhabitants of the stream's chat room. At its peak, as many as 75,000 people at a time were inputting controller commands with text comments. The stream differs from most of the video game viewing that takes place on Twitch because it combines the sport of watching someone play a video game on Twitch.tv with actually participating in the progress of the game.[2]

Streaming video games seems, on the surface, relatively straightforward, but the legal complications are . . . complicated.

After some initial uncertainty, video game manufacturers have gotten on board with their games being streamed and viewed. In fact, the latest consoles from Sony and Xbox (Microsoft) are designed to stream on Twitch. But the music contained within the video games, along with music the player or streamer might be listening to, is not licensed. For example, the music that plays on the radio station in the car within the *Grand Theft Auto* games is licensed for use in the game, but may not be legal for use over streaming video.[3]

LEARNING OBJECTIVES

After studying this chapter, you will be able to:

1. Explain how Internet technology developed.

2. Identify the three levels of communication on the Internet.

3. Describe three defining components of the World Wide Web and the nine principles on which it is based.

4. Describe five characteristics of social media.

5. Explain how legacy media are reacting to the growth of new online media.

6. Describe the four elements of the hacker ethic and how they apply to the contemporary Internet.

7. Discuss conflicts over content, intellectual property, and privacy on the Web.

This problem of unlicensed music leads to the audio for the game recordings being automatically blocked by software looking for violations, in much the same way that content gets blocked on YouTube. The problem is that the same sound blocking that cuts out the music also gets rid of all the video game sounds. Oddly enough, this is only an issue on videos that have been recorded and stored on Twitch's servers, not the music that comes up on live streams. This is also an example of Secret Five—New media are always scary . . . especially to people who own other media.

In May 2014, stories originating in the entertainment press came out saying that Google was preparing to buy video game streaming service Twitch, but in the end, online retail giant Amazon bought the company for $970 million.[4] The streaming service Twitch was founded in 2011 as an outgrowth of the live-streaming video site Justin.tv, and it has more than 50 million users. *Businessweek* reports that the site has 7 million users per day, and more than 1 million people posting or streaming videos from the site.[5] Amazon's purchase of the video game streaming service is part of its larger commitment to gaming. It has an in-house gaming studio, and is one of the largest video game vendors in the world. (Note that while Amazon paid close to $1 billion for Twitch, legacy news provider *The Washington Post* sold for only $250 million to Amazon founder Jeff Bezos.)

Timeline

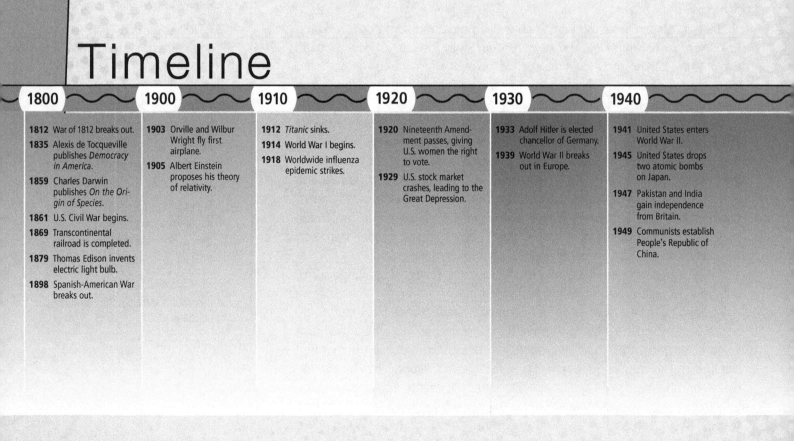

1800	1900	1910	1920	1930	1940
1812 War of 1812 breaks out.	**1903** Orville and Wilbur Wright fly first airplane.	**1912** *Titanic* sinks.	**1920** Nineteenth Amendment passes, giving U.S. women the right to vote.	**1933** Adolf Hitler is elected chancellor of Germany.	**1941** United States enters World War II.
1835 Alexis de Tocqueville publishes *Democracy in America*.	**1905** Albert Einstein proposes his theory of relativity.	**1914** World War I begins.		**1939** World War II breaks out in Europe.	**1945** United States drops two atomic bombs on Japan.
1859 Charles Darwin publishes *On the Origin of Species*.		**1918** Worldwide influenza epidemic strikes.	**1929** U.S. stock market crashes, leading to the Great Depression.		**1947** Pakistan and India gain independence from Britain.
1861 U.S. Civil War begins.					**1949** Communists establish People's Republic of China.
1869 Transcontinental railroad is completed.					
1879 Thomas Edison invents electric light bulb.					
1898 Spanish-American War breaks out.					

The Internet is in the process of establishing itself not just as a new medium of mass communication, but also as one where old types of media can find new ways of content. Not only can you play video games online; you can watch other people play video games, and you can even watch a fish play video games! In this chapter, we look at the origins of the Internet, how it has changed from its original government roots, how it has evolved from a tool for computer sharing into a major new mass medium, and how it has caused social change everywhere from the corporate boardroom to the Middle East. ∎

Video 10.1: Watch fish and fans play *Pokémon* online through Twitch.

> **"Is the fish dead?**
> No, the fish is not dead.
> He just sleeps sometimes
> **I really think the fish is dead.**
> Seriously, it's okay guys.
> *He's just sleeping.* **"**
> —FishPlaysPokemon FAQ

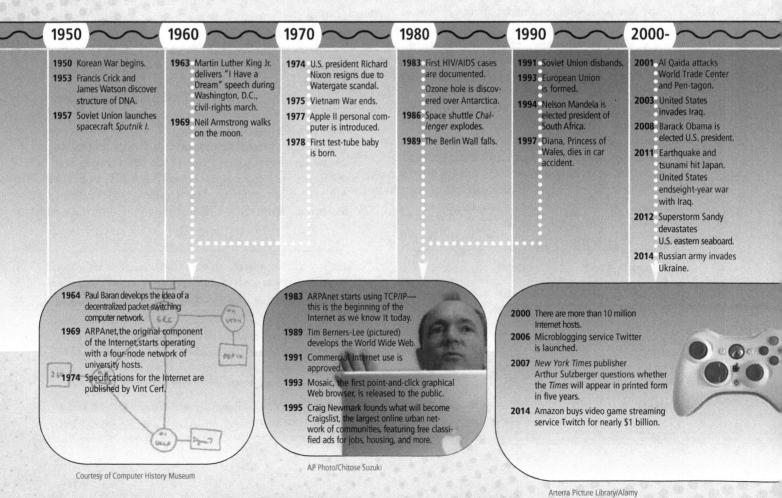

1950	1960	1970	1980	1990	2000-
1950 Korean War begins.	**1963** Martin Luther King Jr. delivers "I Have a Dream" speech during Washington, D.C., civil-rights march.	**1974** U.S. president Richard Nixon resigns due to Watergate scandal.	**1983** First HIV/AIDS cases are documented.	**1991** Soviet Union disbands.	**2001** Al Qaida attacks World Trade Center and Pen-tagon.
1953 Francis Crick and James Watson discover structure of DNA.		**1975** Vietnam War ends.	Ozone hole is discovered over Antarctica.	**1993** European Union is formed.	**2003** United States invades Iraq.
1957 Soviet Union launches spacecraft *Sputnik I*.	**1969** Neil Armstrong walks on the moon.	**1977** Apple II personal computer is introduced.	**1986** Space shuttle *Challenger* explodes.	**1994** Nelson Mandela is elected president of South Africa.	**2008** Barack Obama is elected U.S. president.
		1978 First test-tube baby is born.	**1989** The Berlin Wall falls.	**1997** Diana, Princess of Wales, dies in car accident.	**2011** Earthquake and tsunami hit Japan. United States endseight-year war with Iraq.
					2012 Superstorm Sandy devastates U.S. eastern seaboard.
					2014 Russian army invades Ukraine.

1964 Paul Baran develops the idea of a decentralized packet-switching computer network.

1969 ARPAnet, the original component of the Internet, starts operating with a four-node network of university hosts.

1974 Specifications for the Internet are published by Vint Cerf.

Courtesy of Computer History Museum

1983 ARPAnet starts using TCP/IP—this is the beginning of the Internet as we know it today.

1989 Tim Berners-Lee (pictured) develops the World Wide Web.

1991 Commercial Internet use is approved.

1993 Mosaic, the first point-and-click graphical Web browser, is released to the public.

1995 Craig Newmark founds what will become Craigslist, the largest online urban network of communities, featuring free classified ads for jobs, housing, and more.

AP Photo/Chitose Suzuki

2000 There are more than 10 million Internet hosts.

2006 Microblogging service Twitter is launched.

2007 *New York Times* publisher Arthur Sulzberger questions whether the *Times* will appear in printed form in five years.

2014 Amazon buys video game streaming service Twitch for nearly $1 billion.

Arterra Picture Library/Alamy

The Development of the Internet

The Internet is the most recent of the mass media. It is still rapidly evolving and changing, just as radio did in the 1920s and television did in the 1950s. (Remember Secret Four—Nothing's new: Everything that happened in the past will happen again.) Like radio, the Internet was not conceived initially as a mass medium. Instead, the first wide-area computer networks were designed to enable academics and military researchers to share data. But these early users soon found that the most useful benefit of the network was being able to send electronic mail to one another instantly.

Although the earliest components of the Internet were in use by 1969, the Net was limited largely to interpersonal communication until 1991, when Tim Berners-Lee released the World Wide Web as an easy and uniform way to access material on the Internet. Since then, the Internet has become a medium unlike any other because it is the only one that incorporates elements of interpersonal, group, and mass communications.

So what is the **Internet**? A national panel on the future of the Internet defines it this way: "The Internet is a diverse set of independent networks, interlinked to provide its users with the appearance of a single, uniform network."

The Net starts with the link from your computer to an Internet service provider (ISP). For an ISP, you might choose AOL, a cable company, your telephone company, or possibly a small local company that sells Internet service in one or two counties. The messages then flow from the smaller links into bigger and bigger digital pipelines (the Internet's "backbone") that carry millions of messages across the country.

The backbone was initially a set of high-speed data lines controlled by the National Science Foundation as part of a replacement of its original network, but these lines have since been replaced by high-speed fiber-optic lines run by about a dozen major communication companies.

Packet Switching: Letting Computers Talk to Each Other

Today, people use the Internet to communicate with other people, but the technology was originally developed to let computers talk to one another. In the early 1960s, researchers on both sides of the Atlantic Ocean were working on the problem of how to transfer information stored on one computer to another.

In 1964, engineer Paul Baran was designing a military communication network that could survive a nuclear strike. He sought to design a network in which every computer was connected to several other computers so that if one computer failed, an alternative route using different computers could be established. Baran's second insight was that computers could break large messages into a number of smaller message blocks, or packets, which could be sent independently across the network. **Packet switching**, as Baran's scheme came to be known, cuts messages into little pieces and sends them along the easiest route to their final destination (see Figure 10.1). The receiving computer starts reassembling the messages and asks for any missing packets to be resent.[6]

The U.S. Air Force was initially willing to implement Baran's network, but AT&T, which had a monopoly on long-distance phone service at the time, refused to cooperate, so Baran put his idea on hold.[7] Meanwhile, in England, researcher Donald Davies was working on a proposed public communication network. Davies and Baran, working independently, came up with remarkably similar notions for packet switching.[8]

ARPAnet

Eventually the U.S. military built the first nationwide packet-switching network. However, the network that was built was intended to serve the needs of academic researchers, not to survive nuclear war.

The network was built by a farsighted division of the Pentagon called the Advanced Research Projects Agency (ARPA).[9]

In 1968, the contract to build the network was given to a Boston-based consulting firm on the condition that it be built in under one year. By the fall of 1969, **ARPAnet** connected four different institutions, and the first component of the Internet was running. As the hand-drawn map of ARPAnet in Figure 10.2 shows, the initial nodes were University of California–Los Angeles (UCLA), Stanford Research Institute, University of California–Santa

---

Internet: "A diverse set of independent networks, interlinked to provide its users with the appearance of a single, uniform network"; the Internet is a mass medium like no other, incorporating elements of interpersonal, group, and mass communications.

packet switching: A method for breaking up long messages into small pieces, or packets, and transmitting them independently across a computer network. Once the packets arrive at their destination, the receiving computer reassembles the message into its original form.

ARPAnet: The Advanced Research Projects Agency Network; the first nationwide computer network, which became the first major component of the Internet.

 Web 10.1: Read an interview with Paul Baran.

Web 10.2: Maps of ARPAnet growth.

Figure 10.1 — Packet-Switching Networks

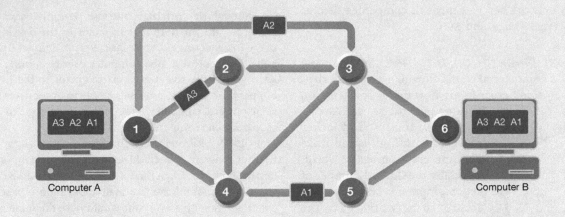

Packet switching is at the core of how wide-area computer networks operate. The sending computer breaks down the message into a number of smaller pieces, or packets, that can be sent separately across the network. These packets each follow their own routes to the destination computer, where they are reassembled into the original message.

Barbara, and University of Utah. ARPAnet came online at about the same time as the first moon landing. Whereas Neil Armstrong's "one small step" was noted throughout the world as one of the great achievements of humanity, no one outside of ARPA was aware that a new, world-changing medium had just been born.[10]

Connecting Incompatible Networks

As ARPAnet expanded to more and more universities, other networks were formed. Each of these small networks worked well in its own limited and defined sphere, but they couldn't communicate with one another. How could they be linked together?

Creating the Internet's Protocols. The answer came from work done by Bob Kahn and Vint Cerf. The pair envisioned a box, or gateway, that would serve as a translator for all the various incompatible networks. The individual networks would talk to the gateways using a common set of rules, or "protocols." Their protocol was known as **TCP/IP**. TCP stands for Transmission Control Protocol, which controls how data are sent out on the Internet. IP stands for Internet Protocol, which provides the address for each computer on the Internet. The term *Internet* was coined in 1973 as an abbreviation for "inter-networking of networks."

TCP/IP: TCP stands for Transmission Control Protocol, which controls how data are sent out on the Internet; IP stands for Internet Protocol, which provides the address for each computer on the Internet. These protocols provided common rules and translations so that incompatible computers could communicate with each other.

Figure 10.2 — Drawing of Four-Node Network

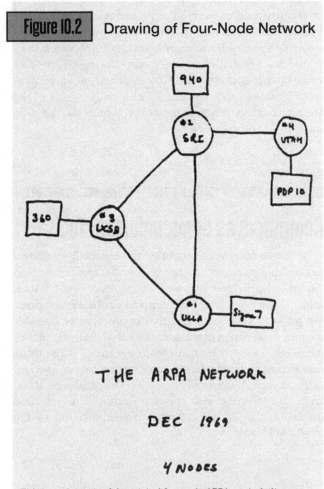

This is a schematic of the original four-node ARPAnet, including University of California–Los Angeles, Stanford Research Institute, University of California–Santa Barbara, and University of Utah.

Source: Courtesy of Computer History Museum.

Commercial Networks. As academics started making personal use of the Internet, nonacademics became interested in computer communication and started buying access to network services through companies such as CompuServe, Prodigy, and AOL.[11]

The Next-Generation Internet. With all the public and commercial traffic flowing on the Internet, next-generation networks are now under construction to serve the same purpose as ARPAnet— to provide academics and other researchers with high-speed links to computers around the world, especially the limited number of supercomputers. These new and improved networks have the potential to move data ten to twenty times faster than the conventional Internet, given ideal conditions. Their primary advantage is that they make possible video and interactive applications that are of much higher quality. For example, students at medical schools in different parts of the country can view an interactive medical simulation simultaneously using the new network, something that would have been impossible with the older, slower lines. In 2009, more than 200 U.S. universities, seventy corporations, forty-five government agencies, and fifty international organizations belonged to the Internet2 consortium, one of the leading next-generation networks, which had an estimated 10 million users.[12]

■ ■ ■ ■ ■ ■ ■ ■ ■ ■ ■ ■ ■ ■ ■ ■ ■ ■ ■

Computers as Communication Tools

With the coming of networks, and especially the inter-networking standards, computers were transformed. Bob Taylor, who helped oversee the creation of ARPAnet, said, "Computers were first born as arithmetic engines, but my own view . . . is that they're much more interesting and powerful as communication devices because they mediate human-to-human communication."[13] The thing that makes computer-based communication so powerful is that it includes virtually every level of communication, from the interpersonal communication of e-mail and instant messaging to the mass communication of the World Wide Web.

Web 10.3: Quotes from Vint Cerf, the "father of the Internet."

Interpersonal Communication: E-mail and Instant Messaging

Although its original purpose was the sharing of resources, the most important factor in the development of the Internet was **electronic mail (e-mail)**, defined simply as a message sent from one computer user to another across a network. Primitive e-mail existed prior to the Internet, but people could send messages only to other users on the same physical computer. There was no way to send a message from one computer to another.

In 1972, ARPAnet's Ray Tomlinson wrote a simple file-transfer program that could send a message from one system to another.[14] When the software that operated ARPAnet was updated, Tomlinson's e-mail application was sent out over the Net so that everyone would have the same materials. Tomlinson also created the form of address using the @ symbol. It was a way of saying, "This is a message for a person 'at' a particular computer." The other reason was that the @ symbol did not appear in users' names or locations. It was the one symbol that meant what Tomlinson wanted it to mean and that was not already in use.[15] Even with all the growth the World Wide Web has undergone throughout the decades, e-mail continues to be the most important Internet application for the largest number of people, even if it isn't as trendy as newer technologies.

Interpersonal communication on the Internet has expanded beyond e-mail through a variety of "chat" services, most notably **instant messaging (IM)** programs, which are e-mail systems that allow users to chat with one another in real time, hold virtual meetings that span multiple cities or even countries, and keep track of which of their "buddies" are currently logged on to the system.[16]

Group Communication: Listservs and Newsgroups

E-mail and instant messaging can act as a vehicle for group as well as individual communication. This occurs through listservs and newsgroups.

Listservs are Internet discussion groups that use e-mail to exchange messages between as few as a dozen people or as many as several thousand. A listserv subscriber sends a message to a central address, where it is duplicated and sent out to all the members of the group.[17] The distinguishing characteristic of a listserv is that users must subscribe to the

electronic mail (e-mail): A message sent from one computer user to another across a network.

instant messaging (IM): E-mail systems that allow two or more users to chat with one another in real time, hold virtual meetings that span multiple cities or even countries, and keep track of which of their "buddies" are currently logged on to the system.

listservs: Internet discussion groups made up of subscribers that use e-mail to exchange messages between as few as a dozen people or as many as several thousand.

group. In some cases, it is limited to people who work in a particular office; in other cases, anyone who is interested in the topic may join.

Newsgroup bulletin boards are the next step. Newsgroups allow people to post and reply to messages from anywhere in the world. They may have a definite list of subscribers or be open to anyone who wants to stop by for a look.[18] Since the birth of the World Wide Web (discussed in the next section), a huge number of Web-based discussion groups have arisen. Frequently associated with media Web sites, these groups often blur the lines between newsgroups and listservs, allowing subscribers to choose between viewing the messages on a central Web site and receiving them via e-mail.

©Wang Lili/xh/Xinhua Press/Corbis

Tim Berners-Lee, the British physicist who created the World Wide Web software, was a part of the opening ceremony of the London 2012 Olympic Games.

Mass Communication: The World Wide Web 🌐

Until 1990, using the Internet for anything more than e-mail was a challenge. Information was scattered about in various places, with no easy way to access it. All that changed with the invention of the World Wide Web by British physicist Tim Berners-Lee. Berners-Lee, who built on the ideas of several Internet pioneers, created the software that allows the Internet to work as a medium of mass communication. He developed a system that is easy to use, allows users to access any type of information, and has a simplified single addressing system for accessing any document located on the Web anywhere in the world.

Predecessors of the Web. The idea of the Web dates back to the 1960s. In 1968, Stanford researcher Doug Engelbart staged a demonstration of his vision of an interactive computer. He used a pair of computer terminals in an "online" session that included word-processing documents, hypertext documents, and live video images (sent over closed-circuit analog lines). Engelbart was ahead of his time and largely ignored, but his work was the first expression of what would come with the Macintosh, Microsoft Windows, and videoconferencing.[19]

Another early vision of the Web, more philosophical than technical, came from Ted Nelson. Nelson described a form of "nonsequential writing" that he called **hypertext**—material formatted to contain links that allow the reader to

move easily from one section to another and from document to document. The most commonly used hypertext documents are Web pages.

Tim Berners-Lee and the Birth of the World Wide Web. When Tim Berners-Lee was a child, his parents owned a Victorian-era advice book called *Enquire Within Upon Everything*. What would it be like, Berners-Lee wondered, if there really was a book that contained everything you might want to know? In 1980, he made his first attempt to create such a resource by writing a program called Enquire to organize documents, lists of people, and projects on his computer. The hypertext program would let him find and connect any of his documents. Although Enquire was limited to Berners-Lee's computer, the young British physicist thought about the possibilities of the program extending beyond his own computer to every computer in the world:

Suppose all the information stored on computers everywhere were linked . . . Suppose I could program my computer to create a space in which anything could be linked to anything? All the bits of information in every computer . . . on the planet would be available to me and to anyone else. There would be a single, global information space.[20]

 Video 10.3: Watch an interview with Tim Berners-Lee.

💻 Web 10.4: Visit the first World Wide Web site.

---

hypertext: Material in a format containing links that allow the reader to move easily from one section to another and from document to document. The most commonly used hypertext documents are Web pages.

Berners-Lee was never asked to create the Web; he simply thought it would be a good idea for researchers to be able to find documents they needed regardless of which computer those documents resided on. In 1989, he returned to his Enquire idea and started writing the software for a system he called the **World Wide Web**, which allows users to view and link documents located anywhere in the world using standard software.

By 1990, the European Organization for Nuclear Research (CERN), where Berners-Lee was working at the time, had the first Web server and a simple browser. (A Web server is a program that makes Web pages available on the Internet. A browser is a program for viewing Web pages.)

The World Wide Web has three major components:

1. The **uniform resource locator (URL)**—the address of content placed on the Web. An example is www.mysite.com.

2. The **hypertext transfer protocol (http)**—the standard set of rules used by Web servers and browsers for sending and receiving text, graphics, or anything else on a Web site. When you type http://, you are telling your Web browser to use this protocol, or set of rules.

3. The **hypertext markup language (HTML)**—the programming language used to create Web pages. It consists of all the tags (brief computer commands) that say how text ought to be presented, where graphics should be placed, and what links should be included.

©iStockphoto.com/ahlobystov

Although the Web has grown immensely in complexity since it was invented, these three basic elements remain central to how it operates.

Berners-Lee released the Web software in the summer of 1991 on several Internet newsgroups. These early users helped him test and debug the program and made suggestions for improvement, and the Web started spreading around the world.

Whereas Berners-Lee developed the Web on a NeXT computer system, the development of browsers for a wide range of computers was done on a volunteer basis by people around the world. These individuals were willing to share their work, but language barriers sometimes posed a problem. One of the early browsers had documentation only in Finnish. (You can read more about Steve Jobs and the NeXT computers at the beginning of Chapter 3.)

The most surprising thing about the World Wide Web may be that it was developed almost entirely as a collaborative, nonprofit venture. "What amazed me during the early days was the enormous amount of free energy that went into developing that technology," says Michael Folk,

one of the early Web developers. "People from all over the world contributed huge amounts of time and ideas in a surprisingly noncompetitive, collaborative way."[21]

A Vision for the Web. Although the World Wide Web has grown far beyond what anyone could have imagined and has changed immeasurably, it is still shaped by the basic vision of Tim Berners-Lee. His goal was to create a completely decentralized system for sharing information that would have no central hub. With no central control, the whole system could scale—that is, grow almost indefinitely—yet still work properly. Berners-Lee was looking for a system in which any computer could link to any other computer: "The power of a hypertext link is that it can link to absolutely anything. That's the fundamental concept."[22]

The success of the World Wide Web illustrates one of the major strengths of the Internet: Although users can buy a Web browser or Web server, the basic technology is free. According to Dave Walden, who worked on the original ARPAnet software,

[Berners-Lee] brought out something, he gave it to a few of his friends, they tried it, they saw that it was good, and he gave it away. It went all over the world. That's how the World Wide Web standard came on the world.[23]

The next time you go surfing on the Web, look for evidence of the principles—openness and accessibility—on which it is based:

- Information of all kinds should be available through the same window, or information space. This means that you don't have to use one program to look up phone numbers and another to find the news.
- All documents on the Web must be equally accessible.
- There must be a single address that will take users to a document.

World Wide Web: A system developed by Tim Berners-Lee that allows users to view and link documents located anywhere in the world using standard software.

uniform resource locator (URL): One of the three major components of the Web; the address of content placed on the Web.

hypertext transfer protocol (http): A method of sending text, graphics, or anything else over the Internet from a server to a Web browser.

hypertext markup language (HTML): The programming language used to create and format Web pages.

- Users should be able to link to any document at any space.
- Users should be able to access any type of material from any type of computer.
- Users should be able to create whatever types of relationships between information that they want to. It should be possible to link a document to any other document.
- The Web should be a tool not just for information, but also for collaboration. It is designed for interaction, as well as publication.
- There is no central control of the Web.
- The Web software should be available free to anyone who wants to use it.

Bringing the Net to the Public

Before 1993, the Internet and the World Wide Web belonged primarily to university and military personnel who had used ARPAnet. But in his history of the Internet, *Nerds 2.0.1*, Stephen Segaller notes that three things happened during the early 1990s to turn the Internet into a significant social force: The World Wide Web code was posted to the Internet, commercial users were allowed onto the Net for the first time, and the first easy-to-use graphical Web browser was written and posted to the Net. With these changes, the Internet outgrew its military and research origins and became a public medium.

Mosaic. Although Berners-Lee had created a browser as part of the original World Wide Web, it was limited in terms of the computers it would run on, and it could not display anything other than text. **Mosaic**, the first easy-to-use graphical Web browser, was created by a group of student programmers led by Marc Andreessen at the University of Illinois at Urbana-Champaign. The developers wanted to create a tool that would make it easier to find things on the Internet and that would provide an incentive to put information on the Web. As with the original Web software, Mosaic was posted on the Internet, free for users to download. More than 1 million users downloaded Mosaic in 1993 (the year it was released), and Andreessen, then twenty-one and a graduate, founded Netscape Communications.[24]

Mosaic: The first easy-to-use graphical Web browser, developed by a group of student programmers at the University of Illinois at Urbana-Champaign.

social media: Web sites that allow users to generate content, comment, tag, and network with friends or other like-minded people.

©Bill Bachmann/Alamy

Mobile devices, such as the iPad being used by these young Cambodian monks, bring Internet access to developing areas without easy access to traditional computers.

■■■■■■■■■■■■■■■■■■■

Social Media: Sharing Our Lives Online

Like so much of the media, social networks (also known as **social media**) are a central part of how we live (Secret One). While time and distance used to be barriers to communication, these can now be crossed with relative ease if you have access to some basic online technology, whether through desktop computers or mobile devices. We think of mobile phones as being a transformational technology, but the social networks we can access through these phones can transform things even further.

What is a social network? According to researchers M. Chethan and Mohan Ramanathan, "Social networks connect individuals or groups over a common platform. Once connected, the human tendency to share information or chat (talk?) trivia becomes the driving force, creating a mind-boggling amount of information and traffic."[25]

What do social media have that makes them social? Chethan and Ramanathan write that there are five basic characteristics that make social media social:

- **User-created generated content**—Social networks aren't Web sites where you go just to consume content; you go there to create it. This content can include written words, photos, podcasts, and streaming audio and video.
- **Comments**—The communication doesn't just flow from one creator to other consumers. Everyone who is active on the social network is commenting on what others are posting. This interaction can range from

Going Mobile

The World Wide Web, which even in the age of mobile apps is still a major part of how we go online, turned twenty-five years old in 2014. And over that time, our access to computers and computer-based media has changed dramatically. If we go back to 1983 in the years before the World Wide Web, a Harris poll found that 10 percent of adults had a home computer and that 14 percent of that small number had a modem to go online using a slow landline phone connection. (If you solve out that story problem, you find that 1.4 percent of American adults

were online that year.) Berners-Lee launched the earliest version of the Web in 1989, and by 1995, 14 percent of American adults had Internet access, primarily using dial-up. But perhaps more significantly, 42 percent of Americans had not even heard of the Internet.[26]

By the year 2000, 37 percent of us were online, but only 3 percent had the fast, always-on broadband connection. **Broadband service**, such as a cable modem from a cable television provider or a digital subscriber line (DSL) from a

phone company, offers connections that are many times faster than dial-up service. But broadband offers more than just increased connection speed. With a broadband connection, subscribers are connected to the Net whenever their computer is turned on. This means that they don't have to download their e-mail;

---

broadband service: A high-speed continuous connection to the Internet using a cable modem from a cable television provider or a digital subscriber line from a phone company.

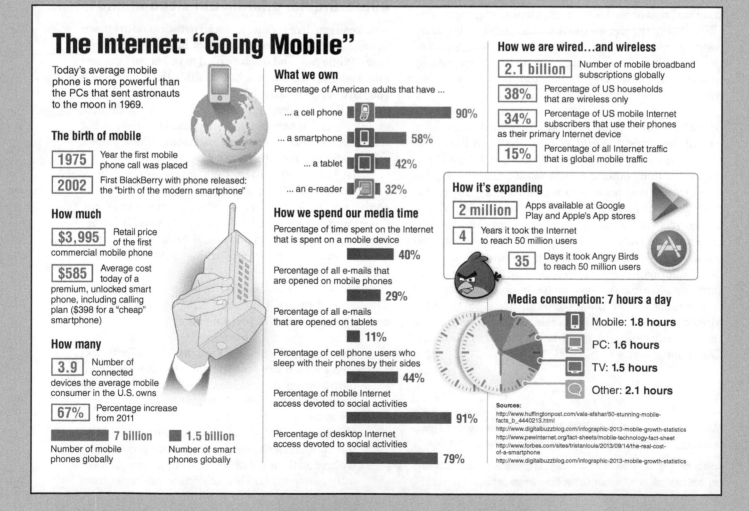

The Internet: "Going Mobile"

Today's average mobile phone is more powerful than the PCs that sent astronauts to the moon in 1969.

The birth of mobile

| 1975 | Year the first mobile phone call was placed |
| 2002 | First BlackBerry with phone released: the "birth of the modern smartphone" |

How much

| $3,995 | Retail price of the first commercial mobile phone |
| $585 | Average cost today of a premium, unlocked smart phone, including calling plan ($398 for a "cheap" smartphone) |

How many

| 3.9 | Number of connected devices the average mobile consumer in the U.S. owns |
| 67% | Percentage increase from 2011 |

7 billion Number of mobile phones globally

1.5 billion Number of smart phones globally

What we own
Percentage of American adults that have ...

... a cell phone — 90%
... a smartphone — 58%
... a tablet — 42%
... an e-reader — 32%

How we spend our media time

Percentage of time spent on the Internet that is spent on a mobile device — 40%

Percentage of all e-mails that are opened on mobile phones — 29%

Percentage of all e-mails that are opened on tablets — 11%

Percentage of cell phone users who sleep with their phones by their sides — 44%

Percentage of mobile Internet access devoted to social activities — 91%

Percentage of desktop Internet access devoted to social activities — 79%

How we are wired...and wireless

2.1 billion	Number of mobile broadband subscriptions globally
38%	Percentage of US households that are wireless only
34%	Percentage of US mobile Internet subscribers that use their phones as their primary Internet device
15%	Percentage of all Internet traffic that is global mobile traffic

How it's expanding

2 million	Apps available at Google Play and Apple's App stores
4	Years it took the Internet to reach 50 million users
35	Days it took Angry Birds to reach 50 million users

Media consumption: 7 hours a day

Mobile: **1.8 hours**
PC: **1.6 hours**
TV: **1.5 hours**
Other: **2.1 hours**

Sources:
http://www.huffingtonpost.com/vala-afshar/50-stunning-mobile-facts_b_4440213.html
http://www.digitalbuzzblog.com/infographic-2013-mobile-growth-statistics
http://www.pewinternet.org/fact-sheets/mobile-technology-fact-sheet
http://www.forbes.com/sites/tristanlouis/2013/09/14/the-real-cost-of-a-smartphone
http://www.digitalbuzzblog.com/infographic-2013-mobile-growth-statistics

it's always there. It means that things such as online radio, instant messaging, and streaming video are easily accessible.

By 2014, the Web's twenty-fifth birthday, 87 percent of American adults were online in one way or another. But it's that "another" that is transformative. More than two-thirds of Americans (68 percent) go online with mobile devices like smartphones or tablets. Beyond that, one-third of all cell phone owners say their mobile device is their primary way of going online. And in its own way, the move to mobile connectivity is just as revolutionary as the move from dial-up to broadband. For while broadband gave us "always on" connections, mobile Internet gives us "anytime-anywhere" access to information.[27]

Media Transformations Questions

- **HOW** many ways do you have to connect to the Internet? What are they?

- **HOW** long can you last without going online?

- **DO** you have a smartphone or tablet? What do you use them for?

- **IF** you do have a mobile device, how is working with it different from using a laptop or desktop computer?

 Web 10.5: Read about how social and mobile technology has transformed our online experience.

---

extensive online debates to things as simple as "liking" a photo on Facebook.

- **Tagging**—People tag, or mark, photos and text in which they are featured. They can also tag ideas or keywords within their posts, such as the "hashtags" in Twitter.

- **Social networking**—People are able to share what they post online with groups of friends or like-minded people. These can be groups of friends on Facebook, "circles" on Google+, or followers on the simple blogging service Tumblr.

- **Customization**—Everyone can make their social network pages unique to them. For example, on your Facebook page you get to choose a small profile photo and a larger "cover" photo. On your Twitter page you get a small "avatar" image, and you can set the colors and background on your Twitter feed page.

Among the most popular social networks are Facebook, the giant of the field; microblogging site Twitter; and pinboard site Pinterest.

While we often think about social media as being primarily for recreational or social purposes, they can also be used by businesses and organizations for collaboration, public relations, and crowdsourcing—a fancy term for getting other people to do your homework.

The big shift in social networking currently is the move to mobile platforms, whether those be smartphones, tablets, or small media devices such as the iPod touch.

Facebook

As anyone who has seen the movie *The Social Network* knows, Mark Zuckerberg created Facebook while he was a student at Harvard back in 2004. As a child, Zuckerberg created a simple messaging program that solved the problem of how his father's front office could announce that a

REUTERS/Robert Galbraith/Landov

Facebook founder Mark Zuckerberg (above) has become a celebrity not only through Facebook but by being portrayed by Jesse Eisenberg in the Oscar-winning film *The Social Network*.

dental patient had arrived. Instead of playing computer games, he created them, according to a profile of him that ran in the *New Yorker*.

While there is controversy as to who developed the idea of Facebook, there can be little doubt that Zuckerberg turned the concept into an incredibly popular tool for

---

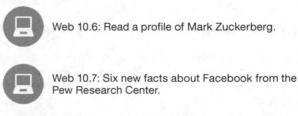

Web 10.6: Read a profile of Mark Zuckerberg.

Web 10.7: Six new facts about Facebook from the Pew Research Center.

Web 10.8: Working with social media.

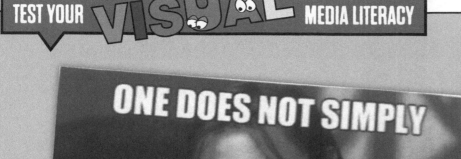

ONE DOES NOT SIMPLY

WALK INTO MORDOR WITH GOOGLY EYES

Dwain Smith

Have you seen this image of actor Sean Bean with the caption that starts "One does not simply . . . "? Where have you seen it? What are some of the versions of it you've seen? Where do this image and quote come from?

One Does Not Simply Create a Meme . . .

What you are looking at is an Internet meme based on the scene in the *Lord of the Rings* trilogy where Prince Boromir tells the group gathered to destroy the ring of power that "One does not simply walk into Mordor." This still from the movie has been repeatedly captioned with a variety of comments, including

- "One does not simply catch all the Pokémon";
- "One does not simply read the terms and conditions";
- "One does not simply leave a Marvel movie before the end of the credits"; and
- a range of topics not suitable for reprinting in your textbook.

The term *meme* was coined by author Richard Dawkins in his book *The Selfish Gene* to describe a "unit of cultural transmission."[1] Memes generally take an established cultural "text" (which can actually be words, video, audio, art, or photography) and use it in repeated ways to make some kind of commentary and create a common bond between those who understand it. Among the most popular memes are the "Hitler Finds Out About" video meme using the bunker scene from the German movie *Downfall*. The meme takes an emotional scene from the movie featuring German dialogue and then adds English subtitles to tell a very different humorous story.

Although the owners of the copyrights on the source materials for memes would often like to prevent the use of their content in such parodies, copyright law generally protects the memes as "fair use," a concept we will talk about more in Chapter 13 on media law.

WHO is the source?

Who came up with the concept of memes? Where do memes come from? Who produces them?

WHAT are they saying?

What is a meme? What do memes tell us about our culture?

WHAT evidence is there?

Follow the video link to the "Hitler Finds Out About" video meme. Watch the original clip from *Downfall* and at least one of the memes based on the clip. How does the meme re-create

and change the meaning of the original clip? How do the creators use the movie about Hitler to comment on contemporary society?

WHAT do you and your friends think about this?

What are your favorite memes? Have you ever taken an established meme and created a new version of it? (For example, your author and this book's multimedia editor created the "One does not simply walk into Mordor with googly eyes" example shown above.) Do you think that memes violate the rights of the

people who created the original text (cultural material) that the meme is based on?

---

[1]Alexia Tsotsis, "What Is a Meme?" November 11, 2010, techcrunch. com/2010/11/11/share-me/.

Video 10.4: Watch the "Hitler Finds Out About" meme.

communicating with friends. He told journalist Jose Antonio Vargas (whom we will talk about further in Chapter 14) that when he was in college, he and his friends would speculate about how people would use the Internet. "We'd say, 'Isn't it obvious that everyone was going to be on the Internet?'" he said. "'Isn't it, like, inevitable that there would be a giant social network of people?' It was something that we expected to happen."[28] As of 2013, more than 70 percent of the American adults who were online were on Facebook, and more than 1.23 billion people were active on Facebook worldwide, making it far and away the biggest social network.[29]

Facebook differs from much of the Web and has more in common with the old AOL than with the Web in general. It is a "walled garden" where people can play games, share articles, and post cute videos of cats. Central to Facebook is the idea that advertisers will be able to reach exactly the consumers that they want to based on information people have shared on Facebook. I can't be certain, but I'm pretty suspicious that the ad offering a good deal on the Blu-ray set of the *Alien* movies was targeted at people like me who are tagged as fans of director Ridley Scott. In any event, the ad worked. I ordered the set.

Twitter

In 2006, three college dropouts developed Twitter, a medium that combines elements of mobile text messaging, online instant messaging, and a good dose of blogging. By 2012, it had more than 182 million people answering the question, "What are you doing?" in 140 characters or less.[30]

Evan Williams, Jack Dorsey, and Biz Stone started the microblogging Twitter service as a project while they were working for the podcasting company Odeo.[31] Twitter is designed to let people communicate with their friends, family, and coworkers using messages no longer than 140 characters. The little messages, known as "tweets," can be delivered to your friends, your acquaintances, or anyone in the world who can be bothered to read them. You can send and receive tweets as e-mails, on Facebook, through a widget on a Web page, or on your cell phone as text messages.

Social networking expert Clay Shirky told NPR's *On the Media* that the 140-character limit of Twitter is essential to its success:

> There's a certain relief . . . in being forced to write in short form. When you're writing an email . . . you can end up agonizing over it and so forth. But if you can only say one thing, if you can only, you know, manage a sentence or even a sentence fragment, it really makes you concentrate on what it is you're wanting to say.[32]

Although much of Twitter's content is made up of reports of ordinary daily activities, it can move beyond the

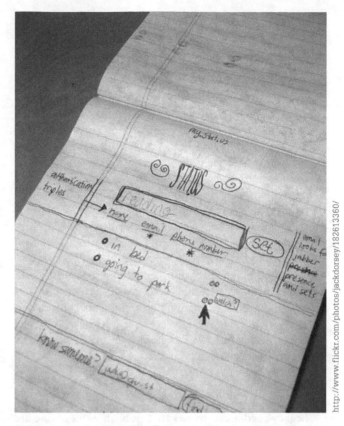

Jack Dorsey's original sketch of what would become Twitter. In this version, he called it stat.us.

mundane. During the 2008 terror attacks in Mumbai, India, much of the news coming out of the country was through social networking tools such as Twitter. For many people, this was their first exposure to Twitter.[33]

Technology consultant Charlene Li told the *Sunday Times* of London that Twitter can be valuable to businesses because they can use it to set up a two-way relationship with their customers, creating a sense of interaction. At a time when many consumers decide not to watch television commercials by fast-forwarding through them using their DVRs, they are still willing to receive messages such as electronic coupons. "Twitter is a great platform to push out those messages," Li said. "I don't mind Starbucks making an announcement on my Twitter page but I don't want them in my inbox."[34]

Questioning the Media

How many different social media accounts do you have? Whom are they with? With whom do you communicate using social media? Do you ever think you share too much through social media? Why or why not?'

Web 10.9: Twitter feeds to follow.

New Media and Online Entertainment

The Internet is evolving rapidly as a mass medium, and the path that it will follow is still uncertain. It will, however, undoubtedly incorporate a range of players. These players include traditional publications and companies, such as the *Washington Post*, CNN, NPR, and the major movie studios. Then there are new media publications and companies, such as the Web magazines *Slate* and *Salon*, which are professionally produced online media that don't have a traditional broadcast or print component. These are often referred to as dot-coms. Most significant are the independent sites—zines, Weblogs, user-generated video, Webcams, and gossip pages—that are operated by anyone who wants to be a publisher and has a Web site, such as the movie gossip site Ain't It Cool News or motorcycle racing news site SuperbikePlanet. Finally, there are aggregator sites, such as Google, YouTube, and Yahoo, which attempt to bring order to the inherently unorganized Web.

Legacy Versus New Media

Legacy media companies that publish news online are sometimes called *click and mortars*. They have larger economic and journalistic resources than do the dot-coms and include existing media companies such as Gannett (publisher of *USA Today*), NBC, and Disney.[35]

Along with reprinting news that is printed or broadcast by traditional media, these sites may include supplementary material that cannot appear in the original publication. For example, the Web version of a profile of author Hunter S. Thompson in *Atlantic Monthly* was accompanied by audio excerpts from the Thompson interview.

News sites from traditional media are particularly effective when there is breaking news. The Web site can provide immediate updates in much the way that television does, but the Web can reach workers at their desks. The other advantage of Internet news is that heavy coverage of a breaking story does not prevent the Web site from covering the rest of the news. Television is more limited because covering one major story prevents stations from devoting time to other stories.[36]

Newspapers have been able to create good Web sites in part because they already have the staff to gather news. In Internet terms, they have a good source of content. In some ways, newspaper Web sites have come to resemble miniature television networks.

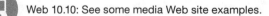

Web 10.10: See some media Web site examples.

Video 10.5: Watch the short film *405*.

Despite the name World Wide Web, one reason newspapers succeed is that they are local. Most people work, buy cars, and rent or buy housing in the city in which they live, making local classified ads an important component of the newspaper. When news Web sites were first launched, they were expected to lose money, but the media conglomerates that control many of the most popular sites now expect to make profits. Whereas banner advertising is the most prominent form of advertising on the Web, employment ads (want ads) and classified ads are the most important source of revenue for newspapers.[37]

The main advantage that online media offer consumers is that they can customize the site to deliver only the news they want. Your sports page leads with the teams you follow, your weather forecast is local, and you don't have to wade through the international news if you aren't interested in it. Cyberpunk author William Gibson likes the idea of being able to control the information coming in to him, but he is also concerned about how such limits will affect him:

> We have access to so much information, the problem is really valving it down and selecting the bits. Eventually we'll all have very specialized software agents that spend their time pre-sorting that stuff for us. That worries me a bit because I know if I had one of those, there are things I would utterly ignore that I should know about. There's something to be said for a certain amount of randomness in your news intake.[38]

Movies, TV, and the Net. The first use of the Internet by the movie industry was to promote films through brochure-like Web pages. Then came *The Blair Witch Project*, which showed how interaction on the Web could draw in viewers. Finally, the Internet started being used as the screening venue for short films. Film sites on the Web have become the minor leagues of the movie and television industry. Aspiring filmmakers first establish themselves with a short, low-cost Internet film in the hope that someone in the industry will notice them.[39] Of course, on user-generated content sites, such as YouTube, the short films can be beyond low budget.

Another thing the Internet can do is air films that may be too avant-garde for conventional media. The Web site UbuWeb, for example, is a repository of a wide range of avant-garde and experimental films, interviews, and e-books. According to Dave Garrett, who broke into Hollywood with an Internet film about elderly women playing Russian roulette,

> The Internet is not the place to look for mainstream fare; that's something you can find on television or at the movies. Our film was perfect for the Internet. You couldn't see it on TV because it had old women shooting themselves.[40]

Among the first big hits on the Internet was *405*, a short film that tells the story of an airliner landing on a highway, which was downloaded more than 2 million times in 2000. The film was created by Bruce Branit and Jeremy Hunt, who worked during the day at the special-effects house Digital Muse. *405* had no budget—allegedly the only significant expense was the traffic ticket the moviemakers got for filming illegally on the highway—though it did make use of Branit and Hunt's special-effects skills and some of the software and equipment to which they had access at work.[41]

As we discussed in Chapter 9, audience members, especially younger ones, are moving away from regarding television sets as the primary way to view video. They can now get both video podcasts and digital downloads of movies and television shows through online services such as iTunes or Amazon.com, or from streaming video services such as Netflix. From there, they can view their video on computers, smartphones, tablets, or other portable video players. Back in 2000, Martin French, who worked for the Internet film site MeTV, put it this way: "Let's be honest, nobody wants to sit in front of the PC and [watch movies]. It's not a comfortable position."[42] Obviously, people *are* willing to view video on their computers, tablets, and even smartphones. It is true that alternative devices have gotten better, but there is an ongoing cultural change on how people view video.

The Internet is also being used as a promotional tool for mainstream media content. We saw this early on with *The Blair Witch Project* Web site, followed by the *Lost Experience* alternate reality game. Consider, too, the online scavenger hunt for the 2007 Nine Inch Nails album *Year Zero*, which featured thumb drives containing downloads of CD tracks located around the country, a mysterious Web site located at iamtryingtobelieve.com, and comments on a blog. Music industry trade magazine *Billboard* suggested that all these elements were not so much a promotional campaign for the album, but rather additional components of "a new entertainment form."[43]

New Media. Competing with the traditional media on the Web are the Web magazines—publications that look a lot like traditional magazines but don't have a print or broadcast counterpart. The two leading Web magazines are *Slate* and *Salon*, which publish articles similar to those in glossy literary magazines such as the *Atlantic* or the *Nation*.[44]

How do these differ from "real" magazines? On the one hand, the Web magazines have low publishing costs and can be updated without the long lead time required for printed magazines. On the other hand, readers expect Web publications to be updated daily, and most of these magazines have no subscription revenue to supplement advertising. Although articles in Web magazines can be of any length, they rarely run longer than 2,000 words, primarily

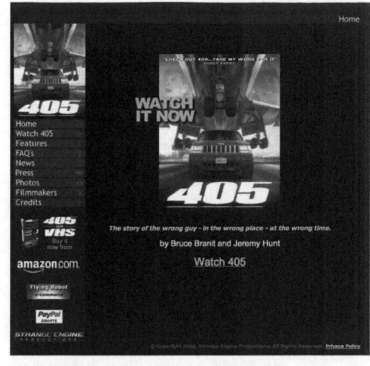

405, created on home computers with specialized video software, was one of the first successful films to be produced for distribution over the Internet.

because that's how much people are willing to read.[45] One thing the Web magazines offer that print and broadcast magazines cannot is the opportunity for readers to respond to articles through a message board.

Aggregator Sites. The biggest challenge facing Web surfers is the enormous amount of content on the Internet. How do people find what they are looking for? An easy first step is to rely on sites produced by traditional media companies. But how do people find specialized information? That's where the aggregator sites come in. Aggregator sites provide surfers with easy access to e-mail, news, online stores, and many other sites. Among the earliest of these was Excite, which started out as a service for litigation-support departments, political campaigns, and public relations agencies. Its product evolved gradually into a navigation aid—something that would help people to find their way around the Internet. Excite co-founder Joe Kraus said, "Basically, we call ourselves Publishing on Steroids. Devoid of print, paper, or ink, we do what a publisher does, or a cable provider does. We aggregate consumers around our programming and then we sell that demographic back to advertisers."[46]

 Web10.11: Check out UbuWeb.

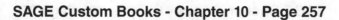 Web 10.12 Who plays video games?

---

aggregator site: An organizing Web site that provides surfers with easy access to e-mail, news, online stores, and many other sites.

With companies such as Google, Yahoo, AOL, and Netscape all providing newspaper- or magazine-like content, the Web has turned into a commercial mass medium supported by advertising, just as television, radio, or magazines might be.

Video Games as Mass Communication. In my own media literacy class, I used to raise the question as to whether video games and video game consoles count as mass communication and whether they are a new mass medium. I think the answer is a definite yes, for a number of reasons[47]:

- Video game consoles are media content delivery devices. The PlayStation 2 was a DVD player as well as a game console, and the PlayStation 3 was among the early Blu-ray players. Microsoft's Xbox One is now pitching itself as a general-purpose media entertainment hub that can be used to stream television programs and movies, play video games, and stream video game play back onto the Internet.[48]
- Video games, like television shows or movies, have stars. They have mascots. The most prominent of these is Super Mario, who has been a force in the gaming world for Nintendo since 1981, but the list also includes characters such as Sonic the Hedgehog for Sega and *Halo*'s Master Chief for the Microsoft Xbox.
- Video games are a new venue for advertising. Just like newspapers, magazines, and Web sites are funded by ad revenue, many game publishers are turning to the advertising world to help manage costs. Companies such as IGA Worldwide are devoted entirely to securing deals for companies to advertise in games, which have a near-perfect saturation in the eighteen-to thirty-four age market. As was mentioned in Chapter 2, Barack Obama advertised in video games during his election campaign—the first presidential candidate ever to do so.[49]
- Video games, now more than ever, are the site of entire communities. One needs only to look to online-specific games, such as *World of Warcraft*, or to online versions of console games, such as the *Halo* or *Call of Duty* series. The concept of online communities has become commonplace today. Now, instead of gathering around the water cooler to discuss the latest news or entertainment item, people are using Bluetooth headsets to talk to friends and family while playing capture the flag or fighting bosses to help their character rise to the next level.[50]
- Video games can be more profitable than the movies. In the summer of 2008, the controversial video game *Grand Theft Auto IV* was released at about the same time as the hit movie *Iron Man*. In its first two weeks of release, *Iron Man* grossed approximately $200 million, whereas *Grand Theft Auto IV* grossed $500 million over the same amount of time.[51]

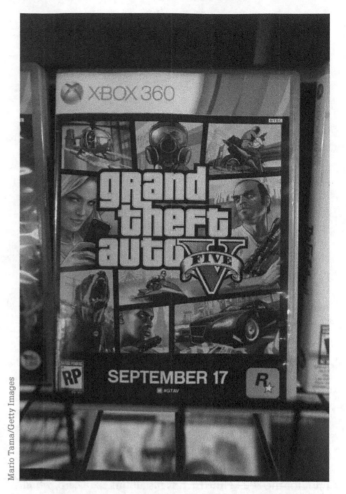

Mario Tama/Getty Images

Video games like *Grand Theft Auto* can cost as much as a major movie to produce, but they also have enormous potential to make money for the publisher. When *Grand Theft Auto V* was released, it racked up more than $800 million the first day it was on sale.

- Video games have become a central part of the synergy used to promote and profit from popular movies, books, and television programs. When the latest *Batman* or *Harry Potter* movie is released, it is almost a given that tie-in video games will be on the shelves, sometimes weeks before the movie comes out, in addition to the expected surge in comic or regular book sales. Even some television shows, such as *Survivor*, have games, and game characters such as Sonic and Mario have had their own Saturday morning cartoon show.[52]

Given all this, it's hard not to see video games as a mass medium or a form of mass communication. According to the Pew Internet and American Life Project, 97 percent of teens aged twelve to seventeen play video games in one form or another, with fully 50 percent reporting having played "yesterday." Of those who play video games, 86 percent play on consoles, 73 percent play on computers, and 60 percent play on portable game systems. As of 2008, the most frequently played games were *Guitar Hero*, *Halo 3*, *Madden NFL*, *Solitaire*, and *Dance Dance Revolution*.[53] Among adults aged eighteen and older, 53 percent play video games, and 21 percent play daily. Computers are the most popular place for older users to play video games; consoles are more common among younger players.[54]

Giving Individuals a Voice

Ultimately the most interesting thing about the Web as a communication medium is that it opens up the world of publishing and broadcasting to anyone who has a computer, an Internet account, and something to say. The line between traditional journalism and newsletter publishing is changing because people no longer need to have a printing press or broadcast station to win national attention for their ideas. If what they write is compelling enough, people will pay attention.

Lawrence K. Grossman, former president of NBC News and PBS, wrote in the *Columbia Journalism Review* that

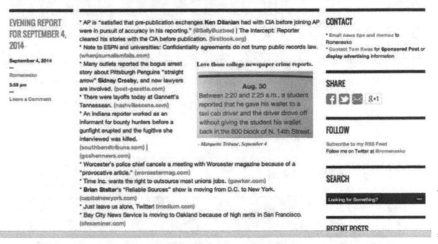

JimRomenesko.com is a leading blog on press and media issues. Romenesko also ran for many years a blog covering gossip about Starbucks coffee (http://starbucksgossip.typepad.com).

> Gutenberg made us all readers. Radio and television made us all first-hand observers. Xerox made us all publishers. The Internet makes us all journalists, broadcasters, columnists, commentators, and critics. To update A. J. Liebling's classic crack about freedom of the press belonging to those who own one: In the next century freedom of the press could belong to everyone, at least everyone who owns a modem.[55]

The Changing Nature of News. There is a vast flood of information of dubious quality on the Web, and distinguishing what is good from what is nonsense can be difficult. As Internet chronicler Stephen Segaller wrote, information on the Internet is "unregulated and uncensored, and its providers are largely unaccountable."[56] The point here is that the information is truly free. Although people with large amounts of money can have a greater presence on the Internet than can poor people, the Net is open to everyone. An example of this can be seen in the online, user-written encyclopedia Wikipedia. Wikipedia was founded in 2001 by Jimmy Wales. Its 1 million articles are among the most viewed pages on the Web. Like the Web as a whole, the entries in this free encyclopedia are of varying quality. A recent *New Yorker* article says that Wikipedia has excellent articles on major topics such as author Franz Kafka or the ships of the U.S. Navy, but it frequently gets bogged down with trivia and political debates.[57]

Because such large amounts of information, accurate and otherwise, are being posted to the Web, the Internet has become a major news source. Many stories start out on the Internet and then creep into the mainstream media. Rumors can start spreading on the Internet and be reprinted without attribution at several sites. Although each version may have the same original source, they can appear to be multiple instances of reporting; thus, the story starts to acquire significance.[58]

When Bill Clinton's White House aide Vince Foster committed suicide, rumors about his death started circulating in politically conservative newsletters. The stories were then discussed on the Internet and spread from there to conservative newspapers and then to more middle-of-the-road media. As media scholar and critic James Fallows says, "Editors in the mainstream press have sometimes acted as if any fact posted on a Web site were . . . part of the public record, ending all arguments about whether to discuss it in newspapers or on the evening news."[59]

Questioning the Media

Before you read this chapter, would you have considered video games to be a form of mass communication? Why or why not? In your mind, what does or does not make video games a mass medium?

Blogs. When Tim Berners-Lee created the World Wide Web, he viewed it not just as a convenient and inexpensive place to access published materials, but also as a forum

 Web 10.13: Read about Wikipedia.

Web 10.14: Read more about Dan Rather and the Pentagon memos.

You can read the full story of Sheldon's visit with Wikipedia at www.sheldoncomics.com/archive/071209.html.

Blogs have exploded in popularity in recent years, allowing anyone with a computer and an Internet connection to publish his or her thoughts on virtually any subject. (This includes the author of this text, at http://ralphehanson.com.)

photos, or commentaries on the news. They often also allow readers to comment on and annotate what the owner has posted.

SECRET 2 ▶ Blogs are in many ways a throwback to the early days of magazine publishing, when authors wrote without expecting to be paid. While there are subsidized blogs, the vast majority are run simply to give the writers a forum.[61]

I made the case earlier in this book that blogs can be almost as mainstream as what we consider to be the mainstream media. (Remember Secret Two—There are no mainstream media.) One test of the importance of a news source is whether it is included in the LexisNexis online news database. LexisNexis is part of a giant subscription service that gives clients access to the full text of major newspapers, magazines, financial reports, and court documents. As of 2006, LexisNexis started including text from selected blogs, including the political gossip site *Wonkette*.

A prominent example of the influence of bloggers came when Dan Rather, on the CBS newsmagazine *60 Minutes II*, reported on a set of memos that seemed to show that President George W. Bush's superior officer had been critical of his service in the Air National Guard. The story ran a couple of months before the 2004 election, and it drew immediate criticism from the conservative blogs *Power Line* and *Little Green Footballs*. The bloggers pointed out inconsistencies in the typefaces used in the memos, suggesting that they looked more like the product of a modern word processor than that of a 1970s vintage typewriter. They also raised questions about the motives and honesty of the source of the documents. Criticisms coming from these and other blogs led to Rather stepping down as the anchor of the *CBS Evening News*.[62]

Blogs have also given readers different perspectives on stories than they might receive otherwise. Army Spc. Colby Buzzell came to national attention when he

where people could interact and create their own materials. "We ought to be able not only to find any kind of document on the Web, but also to create any kind of document, easily," he wrote in his history of the Web. "We should be able not only to follow links, but to create them—between all sorts of media. We should be able not only to interact with other people, but to create with other people."[60]

Berners-Lee's original idea was that every Web browser would also be an editor that ordinary people could use to create content as well as to view it—a vision that the early Web browsers did not support. But the late 1990s brought a new development called the **Weblog** (or **blog** for short), which is a collection of links and commentary in hypertext that can be created and posted on the Internet with relatively little effort. Blogs can be public diaries, collections of

Weblog (blog): A collection of links and commentary in hypertext form on the World Wide Web that can be created and posted on the Internet with relatively little effort. Blogs can be public diaries, collections of photos, or commentaries on the news.

Who Protects Free Speech for Chinese Bloggers?

Chinese journalist and blogger Zhao Jing knew he would likely have trouble from the authorities over the political blog he put online. When he posted an item complaining about the firing of the top editors of a popular Chinese newspaper under the name "Anti," the government filed a complaint with Microsoft, host of the blog, and got it taken down.

According to the *Washington Post*,

> "Anti's Daily Thoughts on Politics and Journalism" tackled a variety of subjects, from public attitudes in Jordan toward the war in Iraq, to the growth of democracy in Taiwan, to the state of Chinese journalism. Zhao generally refrained from topics sure to upset the censors. But his political views were clear.

> "I thought of myself as a salesman, and what I was selling was the concept of democracy," he said. "People think discussing politics is dangerous, but I wanted them to relax, to see it was normal and that it's not so sensitive."

> The December incident sparked outrage among bloggers around the world, and in Washington, members of Congress vowed to scrutinize how U.S. firms are helping the Chinese government censor the Internet. But the reaction inside China's growing community of Internet users was strikingly mixed.

> Many rallied to support Zhao, but some objected to his "Western" views and said he deserved to be silenced. Others, especially those with a financial stake in the industry, said they worried Zhao's writing could lead officials to impose tighter controls on blogging. And a few said they were pleased that Microsoft had been forced to comply with the same censorship rules that its Chinese rivals obey.[1]

Zhao Jing.

WHO is the source?

Who is Zhao Jing? What is his background? What did he do?

WHAT is he saying?

How does Zhao say he was treated by the American companies that hosted his blog? How did the American companies work with the Chinese government to control Zhao's writings?

WHAT evidence is there?

What evidence does Zhao provide to support his critique of the Internet in China? Do the examples he provides support his arguments?

WHAT do you and your friends think about this?

What do you and your classmates think about international Internet controls? Should American Internet companies be willing to do business in countries that censor the Net? Why or why not? Have you ever had to deal with controls or censorship of what you can post or search for online? If so, what kind of problems have you experienced?

---

[1] Philip P. Pan, "Bloggers Who Pursue Change Confront Fear and Mistrust," *Washington Post*, February 21, 2006, www.washingtonpost.com/wp-dyn/content/article/2006/02/20/AR2006022001304.html.

 Web 10.15: Read Zhao Jing's full story.

---

blogged about fighting in a battle at Mosul, Iraq, in August 2004.[63] After he returned home, he published articles in *Esquire* and wrote a book titled *My War*. British writer Julia Darling—poet, playwright, fiction writer, and the winner of the Northern Rock Foundation Writer's Award, one of the United Kingdom's largest literary prizes—blogged about her life as she battled cancer. From 2002 until her death in 2005, Darling wrote about writing, her students, and how cancer can be a "pain in the arse."[64] Dallas Mavericks owner Mark Cuban uses his blog to comment on the news and as a way to respond to his critics and those who report on him. But he also writes about digital music and the RIAA (the Recording Industry Association of America)—not surprisingly, given his background in the high-tech industry.[65] He also uses his blog to speak out on issues as diverse as capital punishment and pay for interns.

Search as a Medium

The question of whether the Internet's search capability is a news medium is significant because various

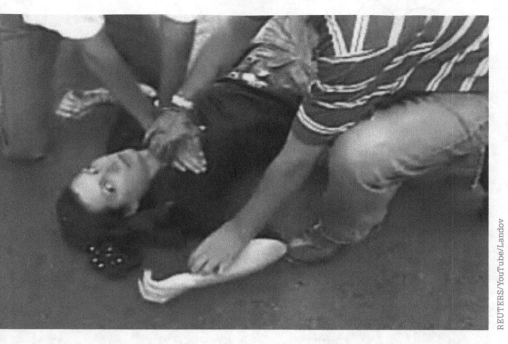

This still image of the murder of Neda Agha-Soltan during the election protests of 2009 in Iran was captured by mobile phone video and distributed worldwide via Facebook and other social media.

REUTERS/YouTube/Landov

such as neighborhood events or elementary school sports. These provide valuable alternatives to stories carried in traditional newspapers or on local television news. But they have more in common with the old-time community newspapers that ran stories about who-had-dinner-with-whom than with cutting-edge journalism.

But news video posted through sites such as YouTube can lead to amateur cell phone video having international implications. Following the disputed elections in Iran during the summer of 2009, a large number of protesters took to the streets. These protests were suppressed by police, who did not allow journalists to cover the events taking place. But that didn't stop people from shooting cell phone video and then posting it to the Internet.

One of the most dramatic examples of this was the news about the murder of Neda Agha-Soltan, a twenty-six-year-old Iranian woman who was studying philosophy and vocal music. Though accurate details about Agha-Soltan are scarce, the *New York Times* reported that she was engaged, valued freedom, and was killed while stopping to get some fresh air after driving home from a singing lesson.[68] When she got out of the car near where protesters were marching, she was shot by a sniper. Her death was captured on cell phone video. The person who captured the video e-mailed it to a friend, who then forwarded it to the Voice of America, the British newspaper the *Guardian*, and several other friends. One of those friends, who lives in the Netherlands, posted the video to Facebook. From there, it moved on to a report on CNN.[69] All of this allowed the person who shot the video to bypass official Iranian censorship efforts to block Internet, cell phone, and text message traffic.[70]

governments around the world want to put limits on Internet searching. And companies such as Google, Microsoft, and Yahoo all seem willing to build limits into their portals as part of the price of doing business in countries that have more restrictions on free speech than the United States. Sometimes the censorship of searches is relatively noncontroversial, such as France's attempts to make Yahoo filter out all references to Nazi paraphernalia.[66] But the collaboration of the search companies with the Chinese government has started to raise major questions in the United States. Yahoo gave up the name of blogger Zhao Jing to the Chinese government after the government required the company to do so. Yahoo defended its actions by saying that it had no choice but to comply with local law.[67] Yahoo also says that the Chinese are better served by a censored Internet than by no Internet at all. Google, which operates with the unofficial motto of "Don't be evil," censors its searches in China, but the company does inform users that it has removed items from their searches.

The Long Tail of Internet News 🌐

The Internet, through blogs, podcasts, and user-video sites such as YouTube, has opened up the options for long-tail news that doesn't get out through legacy (or mainstream) channels. Take the concept of **citizen journalism**. Often when we talk about citizen journalism, we're talking about a newspaper-like blog that posts reports about hyperlocal issues,

■ ■ ■ ■ ■ ■ ■ ■ ■ ■ ■ ■ ■ ■ ■ ■ ■ ■ ■

The Internet and Society

Despite having its roots in the world of military research, the Internet works primarily to permit the independent use of computers. The earliest users of time-sharing computer systems, in which several people on separate terminals could share a single computer, started seeing these large institutional computers as "theirs." Stewart Brand, author of the *Whole Earth Catalog*, said that users soon began to understand how they could use computers for their own purposes:

 Video 10.6: Watch video of Neda Agha-Soltan and read more about her case.

citizen journalism: Journalism created by people other than professional journalists, often distributed over the Internet.

Kennedy had said, "Ask not what your country can do for you. Ask rather what you can do for your country" . . . Basically we were saying, "Ask not what your country can do for you. Do it yourself." You just tried stuff and you did it yourself. You didn't ask permission.[71]

This would become the rallying cry of the Internet: Take control of it for yourself. This attitude sent shock waves throughout the media industry because it transformed the model of mass communication from one in which a minimal number of producers delivered news, entertainment, and culture to a public whose choices were limited. Instead it became one in which consumers can choose for themselves what news they want to learn about, what movies they want to see, what music they will listen to, and when they will do so.

This environment of uncontrolled information is not all bliss, however. Some critics point out that the same giant media companies that dominated the older forms of media produce much of the content available on the Internet. Others complain that information on the Internet is uncontrolled, unreliable, and often unsuitable for young people to view.

Author and journalist Steven Levy laid out the principles of hacker culture in a book he wrote in 1984, *Hackers*, many years before the Internet became a popular mass medium.

Questioning the Media

Do you agree with the hacker ethic that "information wants to be free"? If media content is going to be free, who will pay the content creators? Should the government be stopping people from sharing copyrighted materials? Why or why not?

The Hacker Ethic

As a young man, Steve Jobs saw programming computers as a way of rebelling against and controlling an increasingly technological world. Jobs and Steve Wozniak, the co-founders of Apple, built electronic "blue boxes" that let them place long-distance phone calls for free by bypassing AT&T's control system. Beyond allowing the two to steal phone service and play an occasional prank, the boxes taught Jobs that technology could empower individuals:

What we learned was that we could build something ourselves that could control billions of dollars' worth of infrastructure in the world. . . . We could build a little thing that could control a giant thing. That was an incredible lesson.[72]

Jobs's attitude embodied what is known as the **hacker ethic**. The ethic is summed up in Steven Levy's book *Hackers*, originally published in 1984, before the Internet was a

hacker ethic: A set of values from the early days of interactive computing that holds that users should have absolute control over their computer systems and free access to all information contained on those computers. The hacker ethic shaped much of the development of the Internet.

public medium and before many of the major Internet tools, most notably the World Wide Web, had been developed. (Levy uses the term *hackers* to refer to people who like programming computers and using them to their fullest potential. He prefers using *digital trespassers* to refer to people who break into institutional computers. It appears, however, that many of the "true" hackers are often also digital trespassers.)

SECRET 3 Understanding the hacker ethic is critical to understanding the development of the Internet because its values shaped so many of the new medium's developers. Levy lists four key principles of the hacker ethic[73]:

1. "Access to computers—and anything which might teach you something about the way the world works—should be unlimited and total." Hackers want to obtain programs, data, and computers, and they do not respect rules that keep them from these tools. They believe that they should be able to directly control any computer system they can find; what's more, they believe that they can probably do a better job of running the system than the people who own it.

2. "All information wants to be free." This translates into a disregard for copyright law. Hackers believe that all

information should be available to anyone who wants to make use of it. This was at the heart of file-sharing pioneer Napster and user-video site YouTube. If you have music, photographs, artwork, writings, or programs on your hard drive, why shouldn't you be able to share them? And if those same things exist on other computers, why shouldn't you be able to access them? This idea of universally shared information is at the heart of Berners-Lee's design of the World Wide Web. The problem, as the Napster and YouTube cases show, remains how the creators of these works are going to be paid for the digital copies that users share. Ironically, Steven Levy got a taste of the "information wants to be free" movement in 2001, when he found the entire text of his book *Hackers* posted on a Web site at Stanford University.

3. "Mistrust authority—promote decentralization." The hacker culture distrusts centralized bureaucratic authority. Bureaucracies hide information and make rules controlling who can have access to it. So the best way to keep information free is to keep it out in the open.

4. You should be judged by your skills and not by "bogus criteria such as degrees, age, race, or position." On the Internet, traditional measures of individuals, such as age, education, sex, or income, matter less than they do under most other conditions because people are able to create identities for themselves that may or may not correspond with their actual identities. In essence, this is an extension of the multiple roles and identities people have always had. You can simultaneously be a teacher, a parent, a spouse, and a child. On the Internet, users can further extend their identities, changing their sex, race, and background. On a listserv or newsgroup, people can construct entirely new identities for themselves. When all anyone knows about you is your e-mail address, you are free to be whoever you want to be.

The application of the values of the hacker ethic to the Internet in general provides an example of Secret Three—Everything from the margin moves to the center.

The Notion of Cyberspace

The word *cyberspace* is used extensively to describe the Internet and the interactions that take place there. But the word predates common use of the Internet and the shared culture it has created. The word *cybernetics* (from the Greek *kybernetes*, meaning "pilot" or "governor") has been in use since 1948 to refer to a science of communication and control theory. Science-fiction writer William Gibson is generally credited with coupling the prefix *cyber* to the word *space* in his 1984 novel *Neuromancer*, although the authoritative *Oxford English Dictionary* (see Chapter 4) notes that Gibson originally used the word in a magazine story in 1982. Gibson defines cyberspace in this way: "Cyberspace is where the bank keeps your money. It's where a long-distance telephone call happens. It's this ubiquitous, non-physical place where increasingly a lot of what we think of as our civilization takes place."[74]

Gibson sees cyberspace and the culture of the Internet as an expression of the hippie ideals of freedom and self-expression: "Tired as I am with all the hype about the Internet and the info highway, I suspect that from a future perspective it will be on a par with the invention of the city as a force in human culture."[75]

In addition to coining the word *cyberspace*, Gibson is credited with coming up with the idea of cyberpunk. That word was originally used in the late 1980s to describe the hardboiled style of science fiction that deals with the interface between humans and machines, which Gibson created with *Neuromancer*. In his novels, Gibson paints a picture of the future in which nations are in a decline, international corporations are growing in importance, and the world is dominated by consumerism.[76] The word *cyberpunk* has since been extended to describe movies—most notably the *Matrix* series, *Blade Runner,* and *Total Recall*—that raise questions about the differences between humans and machines. For all his talk about the influence of cyberspace, do not assume that Gibson is enamored of high technology. He wrote *Neuromancer* using a 1927-model portable typewriter. By 1995, he had switched to writing on a computer, but it was a castoff from one of his children.

Community on the Net 🌐

Before the 1900s, it was relatively easy to define community: The community was made up of the people you interacted with every day. But the growth of the mass media led to changes in our understanding of community. People no longer need to be

Do you have any photos up on social media sites such as Facebook that would bring you unwanted attention? How would you feel if your parents or a potential employer saw them?

How Much Privacy Do You Have With Your Social Media Accounts?

The point of having social media accounts such as Facebook, Twitter, Foursquare, and the like is to be able to share aspects of your life with your friends and the rest of the world.

Which is fine when you are going out to dinner with your parents or working on a class project.

But what about when you are sharing pictures of the party you went to last night? The party where you were drinking and you are under age? The party that violated the rules of your athletic scholarship? The photo that shows you passed out as an example of how you acted in college five years ago might be one that an employer wants to look at today.

There's been considerable talk lately about how much privacy you actually have with your social media. Start with the notion that anything that you don't make private is by definition public. So anything that you post to social media that you don't hide can be seen by everyone. Including your parents, your future employers, reporters, and the police.

But what about the things you hide behind a password and privacy settings? Consider the following:

- A Minnesota middle school girl says she was forced to reveal her Facebook password to police and school officials.
- Government agencies and colleges are asking for applicants' Facebook passwords.
- Student athletes are being forced to "friend" coaches if they want to stay on the team.
- Revolutionaries in the Middle East are being forced to give up social media passwords upon arrest.[1]

WHO is the source?

What social media accounts do you have? Are you on Facebook? Twitter? LinkedIn? Foursquare? Pinterest? Any others?

WHAT are they saying?

What do you have posted there? What kind of pictures? Personal information? Comments or status updates?

WHAT evidence is there?

What would your friends be able to see about you? What would someone who is not your "friend" see? If an employer, your parents, the police, a reporter, or a potential date were to look you up online, what would they learn about you? Would letting them "friend" you change what they would find?

WHAT do you and your friends think about this?

1 Do you think that it's an invasion of your privacy to have someone investigate you online without your permission? Why or why not?

2 What would you look for if you were investigating someone online?

3 How would you feel about being asked to let an employer, coach, teacher, or the like into your accounts? Why do you feel that way?

4 Can anything you put online be considered private? Why or why not?

5 What have you done to protect the image of your profile online?

---

[1]Bob Sullivan, "Up Against the Wall! Should District Be Allowed to Demand Middle-Schooler's Facebook Password?" *MSNBC*, March 13, 2012, http://www.nbcrightnow.com/story/17146660/up-against-the-wall-should-district-be-allowed-to-demand-middle-schoolers-facebook-password; Bob Sullivan, "Govt. Agencies, Colleges Demand Applicants' Facebook Passwords," *MSNBC*, March 6, 2012, redtape.msnbc.msn.com/_news/2012/03/06/10585353-govt-agencies-colleges-demand-applicants-facebook-passwords; Kashmir Hill, "Hey Teacher (And Employer), Leave Those Facebook Passwords Alone," Forbes, March 7, 2012, www.forbes.com/sites/kashmirhill/2012/03/07/hey-teacher-and-employer-leave-those-facebook-passwords-alone/; "Watch What You Type: Social Media a Tool for Revolutionaries, and Increasingly, for Security Agencies," *Knowledge @ Wharton*, March 5, 2012, knowledge.wharton.upenn.edu/arabic/article.cfm?articleid=2793&language_id=1.

 Web 10.16: Read articles on social media privacy invasion.

---

face-to-face with each other to interact. Larry Tesler, who helped develop the idea of computer communities at the Xerox PARC research center and at Apple Computer, has said that

> when we were human beings in small tribes hunting and gathering, everybody you had to deal with was somebody you saw every day. We're a species that's based on communication with our entire tribe. As the population grew and people had to split up into smaller tribes and separate, they got to the point where they would never see each other for their whole lives. The Internet is the first technology that lets us have many-to-many communication with anybody on the planet. In a sense, it's brought us back to something we lost thousands of years ago. So one reason I think the Internet's taken off so fast is that we always needed it. And we finally have it.[77]

 Web 10.17: The World Wide Web turned twenty-five in 2014. How well is it aging?

A Kenyan woman checks her cell phone at the Dandora dumpsite, one of the largest and most toxic in Africa. Located near slums in the east of the Kenyan capital Nairobi, the open dump site was created in 1975 and covers 30 acres. People in developing countries in areas like Africa are most likely to go online using mobile devices like phones.

their privacy when they visit certain sites. Finally, it is argued that people spend so much time with their virtual communities and friends that they forget about their real lives.

Controlling Content on the Web. The World Wide Web differs from all other media in that it is essentially an open forum where anyone can publish anything. More importantly, anyone can access anything he or she wants to. Because of this lack of control, unsupervised Web surfing is not particularly suitable for children. As computers and the Internet came to classrooms in the 1990s, parents and teachers became concerned about the possibility of students viewing pornography, hate speech, or even instructions on how to build a homemade bomb.

One solution to this problem is the use of filtering software, which can block access to certain kinds of material. This approach has been successful to a degree, but no filtering scheme can block all offensive material and still allow access to a full range of sites. For example, in 1998, the Loudoun County, Virginia, public libraries installed filtering software. The software successfully blocked pornographic material, but it also blocked sites with information on sex education, breast cancer, and gay rights.[80]

The fundamental problem with trying to control information on the Net is that the network of networks was designed specifically to overcome blocks and breakdowns. Once information is on the Net, it is virtually impossible to stop it from spreading. Net pioneer John Gilmore summed up the issue neatly: "The Net interprets censorship as damage and routes around it."[81]

Is It Really a World Wide Web?

When Tesler claims that the Internet allows people to interact with others anywhere on the planet, he overstates the case. Worldwide, approximately 40 percent of the population has Internet access. In developing countries, that number can average 30 percent, compared to 75 percent of the population in developed nations.[78] But the spread of mobile technology is helping bring change. Africa has the lowest percentage of people online, with only 20 percent having access, but that's up from 2 percent in 2010. This growth is coming because people are now getting access via phones using mobile broadband. And that technology is allowing for the 40 percent growth rate in Africa. Companies like Facebook and Google are putting substantial effort into bringing inexpensive over-the-air Internet services to poorer areas.

The Digital Divide.

Even in the United States, access to a high-quality Internet connection is not universal. Although there are not large systemic differences in access based on race and ethnicity, research by Pew shows that access to high-speed broadband connections go up as people's education levels and income increase. Urban people are also more likely to have broadband than people in rural settings.[79]

Conflicts Over Digital Media

For all the benefits associated with the Web, the new medium has been criticized on a number of fronts. For one thing, a great deal of material on the Web is inappropriate for children. Another criticism is that Web surfers give up

Web 10.18: Read the whole Pew report on home broadband access.

Protecting Intellectual Property on the Web. **SECRET 6** Secret Six tells us that activism and analysis are not the same thing, and that is clearly seen in the discussion over how much control there should be to protect intellectual property online. The year 2012 brought intense debate over two laws before the U.S. Congress: SOPA and PIPA. The Stop Online Piracy Act and the Protect IP (intellectual property) Act were designed to allow the government to shut down Web sites that traffic in unlicensed media content and to prohibit American companies from doing business with Web sites that carry unlicensed media content. Big media companies argued that they need the protection such laws provide to protect them from massive economic losses from online piracy. But many tech companies, including Google, and individuals who make a living selling their own media content online claimed that laws such as SOPA and PIPA would stifle legal online media and hand over complete control of the Web to big media companies. While Congress was debating these laws, numerous Web sites, including online encyclopedia Wikipedia, went dark for the day, blacking out their pages in protest of the proposed controls.[82] Eventually, both laws were withdrawn from consideration.[83]

The advocacy group Public Knowledge has provided suggestions for a more balanced approach that protects the rights of both consumers and producers. These ideas can be reviewed at *Wonkblog*, the policy blog of the *Washington Post*'s Brad Plumer[84]:

- Ways to punish companies that demand material be taken off the Web without any justification need to exist. As the law stands now, any request made that demands that material be taken down for copyright violation must be complied with. The person who posted the offending material can appeal, but in the interim, the content is down.
- Copyright terms need to be shortened. (You can read more about the development of modern copyright law in Chapter 13.)
- "Fair use" law needs to be simplified and have penalties limited to actual damages suffered by the copyright holder.
- Companies need to be stopped from making overreaching copyright claims. Public Knowledge uses as an example the disclaimer that runs before NFL games. It prohibits "any pictures, descriptions, or accounts of the game without the NFL's consent."
- Consumers should be allowed to bypass electronic copy protection for legal uses of the media. As an example, most DVDs and Blu-ray discs have software in place that keeps consumers from making copies of the discs they have purchased. According to copyright law, consumers are allowed to make backup copies of media they own. At the same time, the Digital Millennium Copyright Act makes it illegal to break the copy protection that keeps you from making a legal copy of the media.

Privacy and the Web. A consumer walking into a conventional bookstore can wander from aisle to aisle, picking up titles of interest. After leaving the store, no one knows what books the consumer looked at. But when that same consumer shops at the online bookstore Amazon .com, the store keeps track of everything looked at. The Amazon software will then make recommendations to the

shopper according to previous searches and purchases. Is this a great convenience or a serious loss of privacy?

Web users give up their privacy every time they go online. Each time they fill out a form, join a group, or buy something, information (name, address, interests, etc.) is stored so that the owner of the site will know more about its visitors. Web sites create tiny files called **cookies** to identify Web site visitors and potentially track their actions on the Web. Cookies may identify users so that they don't have to reenter their names and passwords. Or, as Amazon's cookies do, they might keep track of which types of items a visitor likes to look at. Cookies are generally designed to assist users as they visit one particular Web site, but they can also be used to track users' Web-surfing habits or to provide evidence of what sites they have visited.

Web site developers can use cookies to tailor sites to a particular visitor. For example, a news site could use information from a cookie to provide the scores of your favorite teams, quotes for the stocks in your portfolio, or reviews of the style of music you like. This tailoring to individual tastes could take a more sinister cast, however. Web creator Tim Berners-Lee speculates that cookies could even be used to tailor propaganda to match the biases of the viewer:

Imagine an individual visiting the Web page of a political candidate, or a controversial company. With a quick check of that person's record, the politician or company can serve up just the right mix of propaganda that will warm that particular person's heart—and tactfully suppress points he or she might object to.[85]

Convergence of Old and New Media

There is lots of talk these days about convergence and new media, such as why the Web will replace the old dead-tree media (newspapers and magazines), broadcast media, and other formats as the main source for news. New media synergy, we are told, will bring together the depth of text with an abundance of photos, audio, and video. You get all of the advantages of the old media in one package.

There are signs that this is happening. NPR (formerly National Public Radio) launched its new NPR.org Web site in July 2009 with the goal of enabling journalists to present photos, video, audio, and written stories to go with streaming copies and transcripts of all the stories that have aired on NPR since May 2005. The site also makes these resources available on mobile media such as the iPhone and Android.[86]

---

cookies: Tiny files that Web sites create to identify visitors and potentially track their actions on the site and the Web.

 Web 10.19: Read the full post on Public Knowledge's arguments here.

Convergence is also delivering media that wouldn't be available otherwise. As will be discussed in Chapter 15, the Arab news channel Al Jazeera started its English-language service in November 2006, but it had trouble finding any U.S. cable or satellite services willing to carry it. For the time being, Americans who are interested in watching Al Jazeera must do so primarily over the Internet or using a mobile device app, though a few cable services started carrying it following the Arab Spring movement in 2011.

Reverse Synergy SECRET 7 > Sometimes you get reverse synergy—the worst of the old and new media in one new package. A prime example of reverse synergy happened in 2008 when Bloomberg's online financial news service posted a six-year-old news story about United Airlines (UAL) filing for bankruptcy. The story was true—it was just six years out of date. What happened was this: An undated story about UAL's 2002 bankruptcy filing showed up on a Google search on "bankruptcy 2008" done by a

reporter working for *Income Securities Advisor*. The story from the *South Florida Sun-Sentinel* dated back to December 10, 2002, when UAL did file for bankruptcy. The reporter who performed the search posted the story to Bloomberg News. In response to the story, investors started dumping their shares in UAL, dropping the stock from $12.17 a share to approximately $3 a share. Not realizing what had happened, United Airlines was baffled by the tanking of its stock, but it quickly posted an online denial of the story. By the time the market closed, UAL stock was back up to $10.92.[87]

What can we learn from this? Think about Secret Seven—There is no "they." The story that sent the stock price crashing was a single story from a single Web site. Wouldn't you think that if a major corporation had filed for bankruptcy twice in six years the story would be playing on every major news site, not just a single Florida paper that had no local connection to the story? At the risk of oversimplifying things, the story was posted because someone—a "they"—said it was so. This resulted in a huge destruction of wealth, albeit a temporary one, because of a story that had no truth value and apparently was posted completely by accident.

 Web 10.20: Read about another "oops" article republished—this one from 1918 reprinted in 2012 as news.

Chapter SUMMARY

The Internet arose in the late 1960s out of efforts to share expensive computer resources provided by the military to universities across the United States. The initial network, called ARPAnet, went online for the first time in the fall of 1969. The network operated using packet switching, a method of transferring information that breaks down messages into small packets that are transmitted separately across the network and reassembled once they are received. Through e-mail and file sharing, ARPAnet soon became a tool used by academics to collaborate and communicate across the country.

As the number of incompatible networks grew in the 1970s, Bob Kahn and Vint Cerf developed the TCP/IP protocols that allowed the networks to communicate with each other. In 1983, ARPAnet started using the TCP/IP protocols. This is commonly seen as the true beginning of the Internet.

The Internet is unique among the mass media in allowing interpersonal communication through e-mail and instant messaging; group communication through listservs, newsgroups, and discussion boards; and mass communication through the World Wide Web.

The World Wide Web was developed in 1989 by British physicist Tim Berners-Lee while he was working at the European Organization for Nuclear Research in

Switzerland. His goal was to produce a decentralized system for creating and sharing documents anywhere in the world. The Web has three major components: the uniform resource locator (URL), the hypertext transfer protocol (http), and the hypertext markup language (HTML). Berners-Lee published the code for the World Wide Web on the Internet in 1991 for anyone in the world to use at no cost.

The Internet in general and the Web in particular were based on a set of values known as the hacker ethic. This ethic holds that information should be freely distributed and that individuals should have as much control over computers as possible.

The World Wide Web has turned the Internet into a major mass medium that provides news, entertainment, and community interaction. The Web offers a mix of content providers, including traditional media companies, new media companies offering publications available only on the Web, aggregator sites that offer help in navigating the Web, and individuals who have something they want to say.

The Web has been criticized for elevating rumors to the level of news, making inappropriate material available to children, collecting private information about users, and creating a false sense of intimacy and interaction among users.

Over the past several years, users have moved increasingly from slow dial-up connections to high-speed "always on" connections to mobile "access everywhere" connections that have changed how people view and use the Internet. Media are making use of these high-speed and mobile connections to deliver content that includes a rich mix of video, audio, photos, and text.

 Keep up-to-date with content from the author's blog.

Take the chapter quiz.

Key TERMS

Internet   248

packet switching   248

ARPAnet   248

TCP/IP   249

electronic mail (e-mail)   250

instant messaging (IM)   250

listservs   250

hypertext   251

World Wide Web   252

uniform resource locator (URL)   252

hypertext transfer protocol (http)   252

hypertext markup language (HTML)   252

Mosaic   253

social media   253

broadband service   254

aggregator sites   259

Weblog (blog)   262

citizen journalism   264

hacker ethic   265

cookies   269

Concept REVIEW

The merging of the different levels of communication

Tim Berners-Lee's idealistic conception of the World Wide Web

How the Internet gives voice to individuals

The long-term effect of the hacker ethic

How convergence is changing the media industry

Student STUDY SITE

$SAGE edge™

Sharpen your skills with SAGE edge at **edge.sagepub.com/hanson5e**

SAGE edge for Students provides a personalized approach to help you accomplish your coursework goals in an easy-to-use learning environment.

06 COMMUNICATION, CULTURE, AND DIVERSITY

Official GDC

Describe the influence of culture and diversity in the Communication Age.

 Identify the importance of understanding cultural context for effective and ethical communication.

3 Describe the importance of cultural competence for communicating in a globalized world.

4 Discuss different examples of diversity across communication contexts.

5 Examine how to become more aware of and overcome barriers to communication, culture, and diversity.

In August 2014, Anita Sarkeesian was forced from her home after receiving numerous death threats from anonymous people online. Sarkeesian, a communications graduate who runs the website Feminist Frequency, has been an outspoken critic of misogyny and sexism in pop culture, with a special focus on gaming. In 2012, Sarkeesian successfully launched a Kickstarter for her "Tropes vs. Women in Video Games" video series. Since the series aired, Sarkeesian has been regularly harassed, but recently the messages have escalated to threats of sexual assault and death. "Trolls" (a term for Internet harassers) have even created a game called "Beat Up Anita Sarkeesian" and sent Sarkeesian illustrations of her being sexually assaulted (McDonald, 2014). When asked why the backlash to her videos was so intense, Sarkeesian explained:

> The gaming industry has been male-dominated ever since its inception, but over the last several years there has been an increase in women's voices challenging the sexist status quo. We are witnessing a very slow and painful cultural shift. Some male gamers with a deep sense of entitlement are terrified of change. They believe games should continue to cater exclusively to young heterosexual men with ever more extreme virtual power fantasies. So this group is violently resisting any movement in the direction of a more inclusive gaming space. (McDonald, 2014)

Students at U.C. Berkeley hold an "Increase Diversity Bake Sale" to protest legislation that would allow public universities to consider race in admissions decisions. How would you describe the culture and diversity on your campus?

As you begin your study of communication's relationship to culture and diversity, it is important to realize that change does not always come easily. In many cases (such as the previous example) change can be met with belligerence and violence. As you move forward in your professional and social life, be aware that communication and culture are constantly evolving; if you find yourself resisting change to the point of violence, it would probably be a good time to step back and reflect on what side of history you are standing.

Brent has just transferred from a community college in Southern California to a 4-year university in Texas in order to finish his undergraduate degree in computer science. The transfer process and move were exhausting, but he is thrilled with his new campus. He knows that the 4-year university will present a challenge academically. Brent is excited about attending a large university with a big-name sports team as well as getting to know a new diverse student body. He is certain the transition will be easy. After all, it has always been his dream to attend a large school. What could possibly go wrong?

Similar to Brent, the amount of time spent searching for the right college or university will pay off, and the day you have been awaiting will finally arrive. Perhaps you have been working as a professional for a number of years and have decided to return to school. Indeed, the transition to college varies from person to person and across age groups. Regardless of your personal journey, you can finally step off the emotional roller coaster of uncertainty, right? Well, don't get too comfortable quite yet. Making the transition to college or even transferring from one campus to another can be challenging. Will you meet new friends? What is the campus culture going to be like? Will you fit in? Will there be people there with whom you can relate? This chapter explores the importance of communication, culture, and diversity in everyday contexts—the relation of self to others in the Communication Age. As you make the transition in your educational experience, it is critical to get to know not only the campus culture, but also the array of diverse people in your environment. Let's begin by defining culture and diversity.

CULTURE AND DIVERSITY DEFINED

This section defines culture and diversity as connected to your study of communication. Consider your transition to college (e.g., as a first-year student, a working professional returning to school, or a student facing a change in career/life goals) as a reference point in your study of culture and diversity in the Communication Age. As you get more familiar with this topic, think about issues that you associate with culture and diversity.

Culture

From day 1, your parents, your siblings, your relatives, your friends, your teachers, and even strangers have been working to socialize you into the culture(s) that make up their experiences—the rules of living and functioning in a particular society (Jandt, 2010; Samovar, Porter, & McDaniel, 2009; Ting-Toomey & Chung, 2005; Wahl & Scholl, 2014). Communication is key to this socialization into culture. The way you talk, the way you behave, the way you dress, and the way you think have all been shaped by the way others have socialized you into various cultural groups. There are a number of things to consider that will help you to start thinking carefully about culture. For example, Joel is a gay high school student who has recently "come out" to friends and family. He is being bullied at school and is unsure how to share this difficult time with others. An experience like Joel's emphasizes the need for communication competence and sensitivity related to diverse groups of people.

▶ **COMMUNICATION IN ACTION 6.1**

WATCH: Communication, Culture, and Diversity

A failure to pay attention to cultural differences leads to irritation. How could the student have dealt with difference more effectively and sensitively?

Diversity

Diversity is a term used to describe the unique differences in people. These unique differences are based upon a variety of factors such as ethnicity, race, heritage, religion, gender, sexual orientation, age, social class, and the like. When culture and diversity are discussed in the United States, the terms are often understood in relation to co-cultural communication, which refers to the communication among people from a variety of different cultures (Orbe, 1998). Many students describe culture by referencing national borders and language, but a person can be a member of many different cultures, most of which have nothing to do with boundaries or nationalities.

If you take a moment to think about your own college or university campus, there is likely a sense of culture. How would you describe it? Obviously, some groups are more distinct than others. For instance, athletic teams have their own distinct culture: Athletes have a common interest in their sport, they engage in team-specific rituals, they support one another, and they share a sense of community. There might be certain phrases or expressions that people outside of the athletic team do not recognize or understand. Some interesting nonverbal rituals athletic teams practice are butt slaps, body bumps, and high fives, to name a few. Nonverbal behaviors (specifically, various forms of touch) are ways for athletic teams to celebrate winning or to convey "good job" or "nice try." Outside of the team environment, butt slaps and body bumps might be viewed by others as strange or even inappropriate. Clearly, one must be a part of this team culture in order to truly understand it.

As this picture shows, the foundations of culture are learned at a young age.

Consider the experience of Emily, who not only was concerned about adjusting to a new college setting but also wondered if she would be able to establish a network of gay and lesbian friends. When Emily entered college she thought to herself, "Succeeding in college will be no different than succeeding in high school." During her first semester, she

The way sports teams celebrate after a goal might provide a glimpse of team culture.

took a course with Professor Chiles, who also happened to be the faculty sponsor for ALLY, a student organization supporting gay, lesbian, bisexual, and transgendered student issues. Emily felt safe knowing that Professor Chiles was accepting and inclusive of her as a lesbian woman. During office hours Emily visited Professor Chiles and asked, "How would you recommend studying for this exam?" Emily was also able to find out more information about ALLY and ended up joining the organization. In the end, Emily learned a lot about study skills as a new college student, but was also able to explore a student organization she could join that would help her adjust to a new environment.

Cultural Rituals

As a new student you learned cultural rituals—practices, behaviors, celebrations, and traditions common to people, organizations, and institutions. Rituals include things like professors' passing out syllabi on the first day of class and rush for Greek organizations. Graduation is the most important ritual at a college or university and one that you most certainly aspire to be a part of someday. What are some other rituals on your campus? What do they tell you about the culture?

As an entering first-year student, you also had to learn the language of higher education. For example, students trying to get admitted into college learn acronyms like SAT and ACT. Every organization and profession has its own language or jargon that you must learn in order to communicate effectively in your chosen field (Quintanilla & Wahl, 2014). Part of your education will be learning that jargon so you can communicate with other professionals once you graduate. Can you think of any examples of miscommunication that occurred as you were learning the jargon? What is some of the jargon you have learned as part of your major? What jargon is used on your college campus?

Communication scholar Walter Fisher (1984) argues that human beings are all storytelling creatures. Using narratives or stories, we as communicators come to understand the cultural context and one another. Paying attention to stories is central to understanding any cultural context. Many of you have probably used stories to determine which courses to take, and from which professors. All of you

Another aspect of assimilating to college life is meeting others from a variety of cultural and ethnic backgrounds.

have heard the good and bad about various faculty on your campus. In fact, today's high-tech world has taken storytelling to a whole new level, with programs like Pick-a-Prof and RateMyProfessors.com allowing students to hear stories from students they have never met (Edwards, Edwards, Qing, & Wahl, 2007). Listening to what students use as criteria to deem a professor good or bad will tell you a lot about your campus culture. What are the criteria on your campus? What stories helped you learn the culture on your campus? Indeed, the terms *culture, diversity,* and *cultural rituals* are important to your study of the Communication Age. The section that follows focuses on cultural awareness and several other important concepts, such as forms of cultural context and cultural value dimensions.

CULTURAL AWARENESS

The Communication Age is a global age, and cultural awareness is more important than ever before (DeAndrea, Shaw, & Levine, 2010; Wahl & Scholl, 2014). Specifically, being culturally aware improves communication, makes you an educated citizen, and promotes ethical communication across life contexts. Having cultural awareness across communication contexts is important for the following reasons: (1) In order for you to succeed in any personal, social, or professional context, you must be aware of and sensitive to differences between yourself and others, and (2) your ability to communicate effectively when encountering differences of ethnicity, race, language, religion, marital status, or sexual orientation is an essential component to being an educated citizen. In the Communication Age, you will be interacting with people who may present you with differences that you have never encountered before, and your communication choices will shape the experience as positive or negative (Cruikshank, 2010; Quan, 2010). We will now explore a few important concepts related to diversity in the Communication Age. The section that follows explains high- versus low-context cultures.

High-Context Versus Low-Context Cultures

Your study of communication, culture, and diversity is informed by understanding the importance of context (see Figure 6.1). Cultures can generally be described as either high or low in terms of context. In high-context cultures, spoken words are less important than the rest of the context. For instance, as far as relationships are concerned, it may be much more important for people to indicate respect for one another in various verbal and nonverbal ways than it is for them to pay close attention to the exact word spoken (Kittler, Rygl, & MacKinnon, 2011). In countries like China and Iraq, for example, a person's status in society is extremely important (Jandt, 2010). People tend to rely on their history and their relationship to the audience when communicating with one another. For example, in Iraq, it is important to be able to recognize a person's religious perspective or tribe in order to assign meanings to a conversation. Other examples of high-context cultures are Japan, Korea, Native American culture, many Latin American cultures, and both the southern and eastern Mediterranean cultures of Greece and Turkey (Jandt, 2010; Kittler et al., 2011). The background knowledge that individuals gather from their relationships is always relevant to what goes on during any communicative experience. Clear communication is inseparable from the context of relationships including personal status, influence, and knowledge of the other person.

In low-context cultures, people separate their relationships from verbal communication and focus on the information conveyed and logical argumentation (Kittler et al., 2011). Examples

In the TV series *Felicity*, we follow the central character as she adapts to university life in New York. How would you describe the culture at your college or university?

of countries considered to be low-context cultures are Switzerland, Germany, and the United States. Several characteristics of low-context cultures center on the need for information to be provided in very specific formats (normally using verbal communication): Knowledge and competency are important, expert knowledge is valuable, background/contextual information is a preference, and there tends to be less awareness of nonverbal communication.

Cultural Value Dimensions

Expanding upon the concept of high- and low-context cultures, Geert Hofstede, a Dutch social psychologist and anthropologist, added several important terms to the study of communication, culture, and diversity in the Communication Age. Hofstede (2001) based his approach on the idea of people having particular ways of thinking that develop from the time of childhood—he refers to these ways of thinking as cultural value dimensions that are reinforced throughout life. This approach relates to communication because it helps you understand communication choices, various verbal and nonverbal forms of expression, and the expectations you have given the cultural context (Erdur-Baker, 2010; Murthy, 2011; Quan, 2010; Yu, King, & Jun Hye, 2010). Hofstede's research explains the primary ways of thinking along the following five dimensions: (1) individualism versus collectivism, (2) power distance, (3) uncertainty avoidance, (4) masculinity

Communication unplugged
BE AWARE OF SELF-DISCLOSURE IN ONLINE AND OFFLINE CONTEXTS

Recent studies seem to indicate that disclosure of personal information is more frequent in online compared to offline communication. However, this assumption is contested both theoretically and empirically. Researchers Melanie Nguyen, Yu Sun Bin, and Andrew Campbell examined existing research comparing online and offline self-disclosure to determine the evidence for current theories on self-disclosure through mediated or nonmediated contexts. Contrary to expectations, disclosure was not consistently found to be greater in online contexts (Nguyen, Bin, & Campbell, 2012). Factors such as the relationship between communicators, mode of communication, and the context of communication appear to moderate the amount of disclosure between communicators. This indicates that meaningful interactions and degrees of self-disclosure can depend greatly on the environment of communication.

As we continue to discuss communication's relationship with culture and diversity, imagine a scenario where you are communicating with a person from a contrasting culture to your own. Without the use of nonverbal cues and lack of feedback, do you believe you could gain more disclosure from that person

in an offline, face-to-face meeting? Feedback gained in an offline, personal communication context is critical to limiting misunderstandings and gaining effective knowledge about others.

Although the Internet is not inherently a poor communication medium (in some cases, online communication is extremely successful, and sometimes the only avenue for communication), it is important to utilize your offline encounters with cultural others effectively.

WHAT TO DO NEXT
To be more aware of self-disclosure in online and offline contexts, try to:

- Watch nonverbal cues closely to get important feedback.
- Politely communicate your confusion and ask for specific explanations if you have a misunderstanding.
- Minimize distractions (cell phones, other online media).
- Ask for verbal feedback concerning your communication with another.

Low-Context Cultures	High-Context Cultures
Less aware of nonverbal cues	Focus on nonverbal cues
Need for detail	Open/free communication
Emphasis on verbal detail	Emphasis on surroundings/environment
Desire expert knowledge/logic	Little need for explicit information

FIGURE 6.1
HIGH-CONTEXT VERSUS LOW-CONTEXT CULTURES

versus femininity, and (5) long-term versus short-term orientation to time. Let's take a look at each of the five dimensions in more detail.

Individualism Versus Collectivism

In individualistic cultures, there is more emphasis placed on individuals rather than groups. Individualistic culture is also characterized by a focus on self and the immediate family. One example to consider that helps explain individualism can be seen in decision making. Individualistic cultures do not consider exterior groups in the decision-making process. If an important goal needs to be set when planning for the future, individualistic cultures tend to limit the decision to a smaller number of immediate family members. Health care professionals experience communication influenced by individualistic culture when patients and perhaps a few family members request privacy regarding health information or specific expectations about how many family members can visit at one time.

In collectivist cultures, more emphasis is placed on the group rather than the individual to promote group cohesion and loyalty. In collectivist cultures, other groups are consulted during the decision-making process or when planning for the future. Returning to the health care example, professionals experience communication influenced by collectivist cultures when patients and a fairly large number of family members are engaged in treatment plans or specific medical information. The decision-making process about a patient's medical process might rest in the hands of a large number of family members, indicating the influence of a collectivist culture. Individualistic and collectivist cultures illustrate value tendencies that influence the preferences and expectations related to communication across a variety of life contexts. Think about how these values impact your communication choices. Take a moment to complete the communication assessment to see where you stand.

Power Distance

Power distance refers to the perceived equality or inequality felt between people in certain cultural or social contexts. For example, a high level of power distance would be characterized by a society in which slavery is accepted, and where some individuals hold all the power while others have none. That is,

ASSESS YOUR COMMUNICATION

INDIVIDUALISM VERSUS COLLECTIVISM

This measure will allow you to assess your own tendency toward individualism or collectivism.

Directions: The following statements, modified from Shulruf, Hattie, and Dixon's (2007) Auckland Individualism and Collectivism Scale, describe the tendencies some people have toward individualistic and collective value tendencies. Please indicate in the space at the left of each item the degree to which you believe the statement applies to you, using the following 5-point scale:

1 = Not at all true of me; 2 = Mostly not true of me; 3 = Neither true nor untrue of me; undecided; 4 = Mostly true of me; 5 = Very true of me

_____ 1. I discuss job- or study-related problems with my parents.

_____ 2. I consult my family before making an important decision.

_____ 3. Before taking a major trip, I consult with most members of my family.

_____ 4. It is important to consult close friends and get their ideas before making a decision.

_____ 5. Even when I strongly disagree with my group members, I avoid an argument.

_____ 6. I hate to disagree with others in my group.

_____ 7. It is important to make a good impression on one's manager.

_____ 8. In interacting with superiors, I am always polite.

_____ 9. It is important to consider the needs of those who work above me.

_____10. I sacrifice my self-interest for the benefit of my group.

_____11. I consider myself as a unique person separate from others.

_____12. I enjoy being unique and different from others.

_____13. I see myself as "my own person."

_____14. I take responsibility for my own actions.

_____15. It is important for me to act as an independent person.

_____16. Being able to take care of myself is a primary concern for me.

_____17. I prefer to be self-reliant rather than depend on others.

_____18. It is my duty to take care of my family, even when I have to sacrifice what I want.

_____19. When faced with a difficult personal situation, it is better to decide for myself than to follow the advice of others.

_____20. I consult with my supervisor on work-related matters.

How did you score? Items 1–10 reflect your tendency toward collectivism, while 11–20 reflect your tendency toward individualism. Add up your total score for items 1–10 and 11–20. Which score is higher? What surprised you about your score? Do you have an individualistic or a collectivistic value tendency? Be aware of how your individualistic and collectivistic value tendencies influence your communication behaviors across life contexts.

Source: From "Development of a New Tool for Individualism and Collectivism," by B. Shulruf, J. Hattie, and R. Dixon, 2007, in *Journal of Psychoeducational Assessment, 25*(4), pp. 385–401.

inequality is the accepted norm, and there is no opportunity for the "have-nots" to gain power or advancement. In contrast, a low level of power distance would be characterized by less rigid power structures. Instead, a collective of people allows equal opportunities for all.

Uncertainty Avoidance

Uncertainty avoidance deals with the way that a culture handles change and accepts uncertainty within social or cultural contexts. For example, a society or cultural group with a high amount of uncertainty avoidance would not handle the unexpected very well. Thus, a high degree of uncertainty avoidance usually leads to a variety of rules and policies to establish predictability and control. Think about the expectation that exists for U.S. chain restaurants to open and close at scheduled times. If you drive up to a

What it means culturally to be a woman or a man has been established historically in the early years of life.

fast-food restaurant like Taco Bell or Wendy's in the United States, there tends to be an expectation that the business hours will be posted. There is also an expectation that businesses open and close for service as posted. Therefore, cultural groups with a high amount of uncertainty avoidance would not respond well to a drive-through closing before the posted time. In contrast, a society or cultural group with a low amount of uncertainty avoidance would be more flexible and willing to adapt to the unexpected, leading to fewer rules and more of an emphasis on creativity. Therefore, cultural groups with a lower amount of uncertainty would be open to explore other dining options if the drive-through closed before the scheduled time.

Masculinity Versus Femininity

This dimension reflects the cultural values of "masculine" and "feminine" behaviors. Masculinity—what it means culturally to be a man—is described by traits connected to being assertive, competitive, and even aggressive (clear behaviors that display to others that one is "acting like a man"). Put a different way, clear statements and expectations exist in culture about masculinity. From early on, young boys are instructed how to act and behave like men (e.g., tough, strong, heterosexual). Femininity—what it means culturally to be a woman—is explained by being caring or compassionate toward others. In general, femininity is also about being sensitive and relating to others. Perhaps some of the women reading this text recall being told to "act like ladies" at a young age. Just like masculinity, femininity is constructed with cultural expectations about how women should act, talk, behave, dress, and the like. Both masculinity and femininity relate to communication because they drive particular expectations and social norms. Acting like a man or a woman culturally is achieved by particular verbal and nonverbal communication choices. In fact, almost everything about masculinity and femininity is achieved through communication behaviors and choices. Remember that these communication choices and forms of expressing self allow men to be feminine and women to be masculine. Indeed, all individuals have a unique communication style that's part of who they are, so avoid judging others with the expectation for them to act or communicate in a particular way.

Long-Term Versus Short-Term Time Orientation

This next cultural value dimension is about how people use time as well as their expectations of how time is managed. Long-term time orientation emphasizes processes for accomplishing tasks. In other words, long-term time orientation is not focused on a quick end result. Instead, a persistent and focused process is believed to achieve the best outcome. Perhaps more technical processes or those that deal with human safety are illustrative of long-term time orientation. Companies like Boeing and Airbus focusing on the design and manufacturing of large passenger jets sold to airlines across the globe have more of a long-term time orientation due to safety and mechanical testing. In contrast, short-term time orientation is all about efficiency, production, and fast results. The United States, in general, has a short-term time orientation, which might best be illustrated by corporate business practices. A short-term time orientation is illustrated by trying to sell products to a lot of customers in a short amount of time. In fact, fast-food restaurants serve as good examples of intentional design driven by the need for customer turnover and corporate profits (Eaves & Leathers, 1991). The facility's design, seating, colors, lighting, smells, sounds, and temperature are based on short-term time orientation. Put simply, fast-food executives like for people to "eat and run" so there is room for the next group to order.

Now that you have more of an understanding of the importance of cultural awareness, contexts, and value dimensions, the next section emphasizes the need for cultural competence in the Communication Age.

CULTURAL COMPETENCE

In the Communication Age, awareness of diversity across communication contexts is crucial to navigating in a globalized world (Cruikshank, 2010; DeAndrea et al., 2010; Wahl & Scholl, 2014). One way to prepare for the diverse social situations and environments is to improve your cultural competence. Cultural competence refers to the level of knowledge a person has about others who differ in some way in comparison to self. A culturally competent citizen is sensitive to the differences among people and strives to learn more. A person with a high level of cultural competence is usually good at perception checking—the practice of asking others to get a more informed sense of understanding. Remember to pay attention to cultural differences across contexts, make your own interpretation of those differences, and then consider the following direct or indirect approach: (1) Check your interpretation with others to get a different perspective before you draw a conclusion, and (2) use a more direct approach, in which you ask the people you're communicating with about culture. Now that you have explored the connection between cultural competence and perception checking, the next section emphasizes the importance of mutual respect.

Mutual Respect

You develop positive personal and professional relationships with people who are different in terms of race, ethnicity, religion, gender, and sexual orientation by coming to understand those differences. When individuals and groups communicate with the goal of mutual respect—also known as mutual understanding—cultural tensions, misunderstandings, and conflict can be avoided (Christian,

Porter, & Moffit, 2006; Jandt, 2010; Wahl & Scholl, 2014). Mutual respect develops when a person seeks to understand another with an open attitude and dialogue; doing so encourages others to respond in a similar way.

When cultural competence and mutual respect are absent, conflict usually follows. Consider this example: Jovita was in charge of decorating for the annual hospital holiday party. She had been working in health care for 3 years, but this was the first time she'd been able to call the shots. The prior year, Jovita had helped decorate for the annual Christmas play at her church. Since she had paid for the decorations with her own money, she felt comfortable reusing the Christmas play decorations at her work party. This would allow her to save money on decorations and purchase more door prizes. One of her favorite decorations was a large ceramic

In the romantic comedy *The Mindy Project* characters from diverse racial and ethnic backgrounds engage in respectful communication as they juggle their work lives and their personal lives.

scene featuring Baby Jesus. It fit perfectly on the serving table; Jovita just knew that the scene would be a big hit with everyone! As Jovita started to decorate for the party, the department manager called her to the side and informed her that he had received numerous complaints from Muslim and Jewish employees who felt like their religious perspectives were disrespected due to Jovita's emphasis on Christianity. Jovita was asked to completely rethink the party decorations due to a lack of religious sensitivity. She was highly offended and initiated confrontations with several coworkers she perceived to be "nonbelievers." The preceding example illustrates that you need to be aware of problems that can emerge when there is an absence of mutual respect. While mutual respect and cultural competence are important in all facets of life, organizations are implementing training programs to increase cultural sensitivity, tolerance, and appreciation of diversity in the workplace (Burkard, Boticki, & Madson, 2002; Quintanilla & Wahl, 2014). Positive communication cannot happen in a diverse context without cultural competence, perception checking, and mutual respect.

Cultural Imperatives

There are many different reasons to study communication, culture, and diversity. On any given day, you come into contact with other people from different cultures. The foundations of communication, culture, and diversity are located in five imperatives (Martin & Nakayama, 2004). These include peace, economic, technological, self-awareness, and ethical. The sections that follow examine each imperative in more detail and relate them to your study of communication, culture, and diversity.

Peace Imperative

As a global community, people are dependent on one another to maintain peace. As the 9/11 attacks and other acts of war indicate, select countries have the ability to accomplish mass destruction with advanced weapons technology while others pose terrorist threats with car bombs, airline hijackings, mass-transit sabotage, and the like. Many of the tensions seen globally today are brought on by strong cultural differences that evolve into war and acts of terrorism. This is why the peace imperative is essential in understanding the foundations of communication, culture, and diversity. While conflict exists between various cultures, it is a top priority to maintain overall peace.

Economic Imperative

Also connected to communication and culture is an understanding of the economic imperative. Countries are becoming more and more interdependent in shaping a global economy. Importing and exporting is important to countries across the globe. Clearly, communication and culture are associated with the economic needs of all nations concerning trade relations, international business ventures, and the like.

Technological Imperative

The technological imperative continues to gain more importance in today's society as technological advances make the world more easily accessible. Because of the Internet alone, people are able to communicate with others across oceans and beyond mountains, something that was not possible in the past unless long journeys were prepared. In the Communication Age, you can buy something from Japan and receive it in just a few days. You have the ability to drive down to the airport and find yourself on the other side of the planet within 24 hours if desired. Consider your online relationships with friends, classmates, family, and so on. If it were not for the technology, how often would you be able to stay in contact with others? Not only are you able to stay in contact, but you are also more likely to come across people from other cultures with these technological advances.

Self-Awareness Imperative

The self-awareness imperative is particularly significant because it is important for communicators to learn about other cultures. Not only do you learn about other cultures themselves, but by doing so, you learn more about your own culture. People never truly understand their own culture until they compare it to others. Have you ever found yourself in an encounter with a person from a different culture and suddenly realized something new about your own?

iStock

Technological advances like the Internet make communication across the world more accessible.

Ethical Imperative

The ethical imperative is also important to understand. The ethical imperative should guide you in doing what is right versus what is wrong in various communication contexts. It is also important to understand why some other cultures value different things. You may find someone else's cultural norms unusual, but remember that this might be a sign of culture shock.

While all of the cultural imperatives are important in our study of communication and culture, the next section explores specific examples of diversity across contexts to inform your study of the Communication Age.

EXAMPLES OF DIVERSITY ACROSS COMMUNICATION CONTEXTS

The previous sections reviewed some important concepts related to diversity in the Communication Age. This section surveys a number of examples of diversity that you may encounter. Gender, ethnicity and race, language differences, religion, disability, and sexual orientation are just a few examples of the diversity you will experience across communication contexts.

Gender Influences

Like culture, gender influences cannot be avoided in communication. In fact, gender, culture, and communication are all inextricably bound. A great deal of research has examined the communication differences between men and women. Some scholars assert that men and women differ greatly in their relational needs and communication behaviors, while others contend that men and women are more alike than they are different. In general, communication scholars have shifted their focus from communication differences that stem from being born male or female to the ways in which gender socialization (being *raised* as male or female) may create distinctive communication tendencies. So, to begin, let's make an important distinction between sex and gender.

Sex is biological. It's about the chromosomal combinations that produce males, females, and the other possible, but rarer, sexes. Usually, when individuals refer to behaviors associated with a particular sex, what they are really referring to is gender. Gender is social. It's about the culturally constructed norms connected to biological sex. Whereas sex refers to male and female, gender refers to masculinity, femininity, and/or androgyny. Commonly these characteristics are associated with masculinity or the cultural signifiers associated with being a man in a specific culture; femininity, what it means culturally to be a woman; or androgyny, a blend of both feminine and masculine traits (Ivy, 2012; Ivy & Wahl, 2014). For example, you may have heard that "women always have to go to the bathroom together" or "men never want to talk about emotions or relationships." These statements comment on the perceived patterns of social behavior shown by men and women, but not on their biological traits. Rather, these tendencies arise from differences in what a society expects from women and men—differences in how men and women may be taught to speak, act, dress, express themselves, and interact with others. Thus, let's examine the role of *gender* in communication.

There are numerous ways that gender may affect communication, but we will focus on the different *purposes* for which men and women use communication. For many women, talk is used as the primary means to establish closeness and intimacy in a relationship (Riessman, 1990). By self-disclosing personal information and sharing their lives through conversation, women show their relational partners they are trusted and cared for. Communication is a way to spend time together and build the relationship. For that reason, it may not matter to women

▶ **COMMUNICATION IN ACTION 6.2**

WATCH: *Understanding Gender Differences*

Prof. Deborah Borisoff explains nonverbal and verbal communication and the reason why gender communication styles are so distinct.

COMMUNICATIONHOW-TO
REDUCING CULTURE SHOCK

Have you ever experienced culture shock? What was your reaction?

1. Be aware if you find yourself feeling awkward in a new surrounding and try to adjust.

2. Use positive self-talk and nonverbal communication if you find yourself feeling disoriented when outside of your usual setting.

3. If you feel anxious when you find yourself in a new/ unfamiliar cultural environment, realize that the audience probably does not know how you really feel.

4. If you feel challenged when experiencing new cultures, focus on establishing mutual respect and view the situation to learn more about self in relation to others.

5. Use direct and indirect perception checking to reduce uncertainty in a new cultural context.

whether they have discussed "important" issues or accomplished a goal. What matters is keeping the dialogue going. Men do not necessarily view relationships this way. Many men enjoy doing things together to build their relationships. Participating in joint activities creates a sense of belonging with many men, and talk is used in primarily functional ways, like solving problems and accomplishing tasks. According to Deborah Tannen (1991), women engage in a greater degree of rapport talk (cooperative messages used to establish connection), whereas men engage in a greater degree of report talk (information-based messages used to establish status and gain power). These may sound like stereotypes, and they do not necessarily apply to *all* men and *all* women, but do you find these descriptions accurate? Have these differences ever caused misunderstandings in your relationships?

Consider this example: Jake and Kristy have been married for almost a year, and they are very happy. Even though things are going well, Kristy wonders if Jake is committed to keeping their relationship going; he never seems to talk to her about how the relationship is going. He spends time with her, and he makes sure the two of them make time to do things together, but he has never shown interest in sitting down to talk about their marriage. Kristy worries that Jake is keeping things bottled up inside and tries harder to get him to open up. When she does this, Jake is suddenly alarmed that something is wrong between them. Have you ever experienced a misunderstanding like this? Kristy simply wanted to use talk to develop and deepen the relationship, but when she wanted to talk, Jake mistakenly assumed it was because she wanted to solve a problem. Awareness of this culturally constructed difference between men and women may help you in your own communication.

Ethnicity and Race

When you think of diversity in the world, you probably most often think of differences in race or ethnicity. Although the terms *race* and *ethnicity* are often linked, when it comes to communication competence people focus on differences based on ethnicity, not race. Race is the categorization of people based on physical characteristics such as skin color, dimensions of the human face, and hair. The old typology categorized people into one of three races, but those typologies are no longer deemed useful and have been replaced with ethnic identification or classifications. Ethnicity refers to a social group that may be joined together by factors such as shared history, shared identity, shared geography, and shared culture. If you rely on nonverbal cues to detect someone's ethnic background, you do so without taking into account that what you see visually may not always be accurate. In other words, people's physical qualities may lead you to perceive them as being a part of one particular ethnic group, when in fact they identify with a different ethnic group. Unfortunately, people across the globe are categorized, stereotyped, and discriminated against based on physical appearance, specifically on the color of their skin (Bloomfield, 2006; Ivy & Wahl, 2014).

Thus, as you get to know the people around you, it is important to remember that what you see visually through nonverbal dimensions of physical appearance does not always shape accurate perceptions of another person's ethnicity. The same sensitivity and awareness for cultural competency is important in the Communication Age as issues of race, gender, sexuality, health, and more are topics fostered in online and social networking communities (Cruikshank, 2010; DeAndrea et al., 2010; Quan, 2010; Wahl & Scholl, 2014). Now that you have considered the importance of race and ethnicity in your study of the communication, culture, and diversity, the next section explains the importance of language differences.

To what extent do the differences in how men and women bond, as portrayed in these photos, mirror your real-life experiences? To what extent do you believe that women use talk as the centerpiece of relationships, while men use activities?

Language Differences

Globalization will continue to present emerging professionals with the challenge of language differences as presented in a variety of industries and career choices. According to intercultural communication scholars Samovar, Porter, and McDaniel (2009), the impact of globalization is an unstoppable process that will continue to emphasize the need for an international orientation that impacts your personal and professional life. Consider your own future goals and realize the likely impact of diversity and globalization on your academic major and occupation.

Globalization exposes people to new and different accents, dialects, and languages. For example, a person's accent may provide you with clues as to where that person is from. If someone in your class speaks with a German accent, she probably hails from a German-speaking country in Europe. If someone else speaks with an accent as well as different vocabulary and syntax, she has a different dialect. You may encounter a coworker or

▶ COMMUNICATION IN ACTION 6.3

WATCH: What does interracial communication mean?

Prof. Tina Harris talks about her work in interracial communication. How does interracial communication differ from interpersonal communication?

CAREER FRONTIER: MULTICULTURAL, DIVERSE WORKPLACES

iStock

PEOPLE TRANSITIONING INTO a new workplace often face the challenge of successfully socializing into their working communities (Quintanilla & Wahl, 2014). The process through which people integrate into the workplace has traditionally been termed *organizational socialization* (Bauer, Morrison, & Callister, 1998). Throughout this process, newcomers acquire the knowledge and skills that characterize their new working environment. To study this aspect of communication, researchers Bernie Chun Nam Mak and Hin Leung Chui examined the discourse of small talk collected from a new expatriate from the Philippines (Anna) and her new

colleagues in a Hong Kong firm. The study, which specifically examined the "small talk" in which Anna engaged with her new coworkers, indicated that small talk can be both a hurdle and a useful instrument during socialization, an indicator of in/appropriate behavior and un/successful socialization, and a handy tool in the development of rapport (Mak & Chui, 2013). However, the authors warn that small talk is not a universal behavior; attempts in the wrong cultural context can be counterproductive due to cultural differences.

Think about the ways you begin socialization, either at school or in the workplace. Do you enjoy small talk? Do you use it as a tool to socialize yourself with fellow coworkers and students, or do you find it a pointless exercise? Globalization has helped the workplace to become increasingly diverse and asks professionals to be effective communicators across different cultural contexts. As a professional, remember to gauge your communication context appropriately to ensure that you build successful relationships in a multicultural workplace.

ISSUES TO CONSIDER

1. What steps can you take to ensure you communicate effectively with other professionals from different backgrounds?
2. How can Anna's Hong Kong connection be applied to cultural communication in the United States?

---

classmate who speaks an entirely different language. Nevertheless, you still will need to communicate with one another despite a lack of shared language through the use of verbal and nonverbal communication. Clearly, accent, dialect, and lack of a shared language impact communication effectiveness in professional settings, both with coworkers and with customers. Language differences will compound other cultural differences that are sure to exist.

When you experience language barriers, be prepared to ask and answer many questions to ensure a clear understanding. Try to avoid the common mistakes of losing patience and giving up or speaking to other people as if they cannot hear you. Speaking louder or, even worse, yelling at another person when a language barrier is present can often lead to frustration and further misunderstanding.

In addition to language differences, language preferences can create language barriers. For example, all students in one dorm can speak English, but three of the students prefer to speak Spanish. When they are speaking to each other in Spanish, other students in the dorm are unable to understand what is being said and often get annoyed. If the resident assistant (RA) tells the Spanish-speaking students to stop using their language, is she discriminating against them or violating their rights? Think critically about the preceding example. Consider alternatives the RA could use to promote cultural competence. She could also consider asking the English speakers to learn Spanish. As a counterexample, consider English students studying abroad in Italy. What would English students do if their Italian dorm leader told them to stop speaking English to one another outside of class or organized functions? Remember that speaking in one's language is a matter of choice and a fact of life.

Religion and Spirituality

Religion and spirituality are other areas of diversity among people (Driscoll & Wiebe, 2007). Consider how religion or spirituality comes into play with people in your social environment. Remember Brent's experience getting to know his new college campus? One guy Brent really related to in his new dorm was Sawyer. Brent had observed that several of the guys from his floor would get together for poker night once a week, and he thought it would be fun if he and Sawyer joined the group. Brent invited Sawyer out for poker several times, but Sawyer always declined. After the third rejection, Sawyer took the time to explain to Brent that he and his family were members of the Church of Jesus Christ of Latter-Day Saints (LDS). Sawyer further explained that he had moral concerns with playing poker and being around others who choose to drink alcoholic beverages. Think of other ways religion and spirituality impact various communication contexts, and keep world religions (e.g., Buddhism, Judaism, Islam) in mind in addition to Christianity.

People With Disabilities

In addition to religion and spirituality, disability is an example of diversity. The verbal and nonverbal cues of a person living with a disability can lead to disrespectful or insensitive communication (Braithwaite & Braithwaite, 2009; Braithwaite & Thompson, 2000; Ivy & Wahl, 2014). Physical appearance is normally a signal that a person is living with a disability, but remember that some forms of disability are invisible (Ivy & Wahl, 2014). Be aware of the communication challenges that a person with a disability deals with every day (e.g., Tourette's syndrome, deafness). Regardless of the type of disability, people can develop cultural competence in this area and support fair treatment and respect. Communication scholar Dawn Braithwaite (1991) examined how people with disabilities are challenged when it comes to managing private information about their disability, because able-bodied people tend to ask personal, often embarrassing questions (e.g., how a person became injured, how difficult it is to live with a disability).

People with disabilities have a major presence in everyday social settings today, and it is important for you to strive for respectful communication. Thus, keep in mind several of the tips that follow to guide competent communication with and among people with disabilities: (1) Avoid staring at a person with a disability; (2) try not to be overly helpful by calling too much attention to someone's disability; and (3) focus on the person, not the disability.

GIVING PEOPLE WITH DISABILITIES
A NEW COMMUNICATION MEDIUM

Nbanerjee

PEOPLE WHO DO not have the ability of sight face many obstacles in their everyday communication. The invention of Braille, a tactile writing system used by the blind and the visually impaired, greatly expanded the communication mediums available for nonsighted people. With all the breakthroughs we've made in nonsighted communication, however, there are still drawbacks to be considered. With this in mind, one student decided to tackle a serious issue facing Braille users.

Shubham Banerjee, 13, created a Braille printer out of Lego pieces for a school science project, which has now gained financial backing from the tech company Intel Corp. (Grisham, 2015). Shubham came up with the idea while researching Braille online and realizing that printers for the blind can cost $2,000 or more. Using a $350 Lego robotics kit, Shubham built a working model and shared the plan online in an "open source" format so that anyone could build it.

"He's solving a real problem, and he wants to go off and disrupt an existing industry. And that's really what it's all about," Edward Ross, director of Inventor Platforms at Intel, told the Associated Press (Grisham, 2015). Shubham's dedication to improving communication mediums for the blind offers more hope in defeating the obstacles that all disabled people face in professional and social communication.

Sexual Orientation

Mia is a single college student. When her friends ask about her relationship status, she answers, "It's complicated," and tries to change the topic. One of her friends, Margo, goes on to ask questions such as the following: "Are you still talking to that guy in chemistry class?" "So, when are you all going to go out?" "Would you like for me to set you up on a blind date with my friend Joel?" While some people are open about their relationship status and enjoy sharing information about their personal life in everyday situations, it is important to realize that not everyone feels the same way about the disclosure of personal information.

In Mia's case, she wishes to maintain privacy around her relational status and her sexual orientation. Sexual orientation refers to identity based on who people are attracted to sexually. Like Mia, lesbians, gays, bisexuals, transgenders, and people questioning their sexuality (LGBTQ) often find themselves speaking an entirely different language of ambiguous pronouns. Recognize the choice you will have to make regarding being open or private about your sexual orientation. Being "out" is easier for some LGBTQ people than others. Regardless of your own sexuality, it is critical to recognize that LGBTQ communication and culture are present across communication contexts (Eadie, 2009; Wahl & Scholl, 2014). A couple of things to keep in mind related to communication with and among LBGTQ individuals are (1) do not inadvertently "out" someone, and (2) avoid being heterosexist, or having a view or an assumption that everyone is heterosexual.

Heterosexuality	Physical and romantic attraction to people of the opposite sex
Homosexuality	Physical and romantic attraction to people of the same sex
Bisexuality	Physical and romantic attraction to people of both sexes
Transgender	The state of an individual gender identity not matching biological male or female assignment at birth
Questioning	Exploring or questioning one's sexual orientation
Asexuality	Having little, if any, interest in sex
Queer	An umbrella term often used to describe LGBTQ people in general. Used by some as an activist term. Used by others to refer to an identity that does not conform to common labels and terms of sexual orientation and identity.
Cisgender	Identifying as having a gender that corresponds to the sex one has been assigned at birth; not transgender
Pangender	Identifying as belonging to all genders. Someone who identifies as neither male nor female, but instead a third gender.

This section focused on gender, ethnicity and race, language differences, religion, disability, and sexual orientation as examples of diversity across communication contexts. Now that you have studied specific examples, the next section explores the types of common barriers to communication, culture, and diversity.

BARRIERS TO COMMUNICATION, CULTURE, AND DIVERSITY

Dealing with differences may seem like an overwhelming task. However, you can come to understand fellow classmates, friends, and others, even if they have views and practices different from your own, if you practice cultural competence, perception checking, and mutual respect. To finish your study of communication, culture, and diversity, it is important to understand several barriers, including stereotypes, prejudice, discrimination, ethnocentrism, hate speech, and school bullying.

Stereotypes

While the term tends to have a negative connotation, stereotypes are merely popular beliefs about groups of people. These preconceived notions can be positive, neutral, or negative, but when it comes to individuals, each one is an incomplete picture and potentially harmful. For example, gay men are often stereotyped as being feminine and flamboyant while lesbian women are believed to be aggressive and masculine. When developing your skills related to cultural competence, it is important to take a personal inventory. Also, give attention to the communication context. You can do this by researching a culture to increase your understanding of difference. You can also ask questions of the person with whom you are communicating in a particular situation. Often coupled with stereotypes are the terms *prejudice* and *discrimination*. Focus on these concepts to gain a more detailed understanding of barriers to communication, culture, and diversity.

Prejudice and Discrimination

You may have heard of these two terms previously, but do you know the distinction between them? Many confuse the two and think they are one and the same. Prejudice is the dislike or hatred one has toward a particular group. Discrimination, however, refers to the verbal and nonverbal communication behaviors that foster prejudiced attitudes, including the act of excluding or denying people of products, rights, and services based on their race, gender, religion, age, sexual orientation, or disability (Jandt, 2010; Ting-Toomey & Chung, 2005; Wahl & Scholl, 2014). Discrimination can be carried out in the most obvious ways, such as burning a cross in front of someone's yard, or it can be so subtle people may not know it is there unless they are a member of the group being discriminated against. Consider this: *Monica and Jai were planning a singles party or "mixer" for their apartment complex. They had both lived on the property for several years and wanted to try to bring single people together at their apartment complex clubhouse that was open to all residents of the property. As Monica and Jai were creating the invitations, they decided to leave several people off the invite list. They knew of several single gay and lesbian residents and one or two people with disabilities. They didn't want gay and lesbian residents to "hit on" the straight residents. Monica and Jai also agreed that they didn't want wheelchairs taking up too much space at the party.* The previous example illustrates the presence of discrimination, since Monica and Jai excluded or denied inviting particular people to their party based on sexual orientation and disability.

Ethnocentrism

Another barrier to communication, culture, and diversity is ethnocentrism—placing your own cultural beliefs in a superior position, leading to a negative judgment of other cultures (Jandt, 2010). Severe ethnocentrism impedes cultural competence because a person will reject the uniqueness of other cultures. People who view their culture as dominant are unwilling to learn and are not open to the ideas of other cultures.

Hate Speech

Hate speech is another barrier to communication, culture, and diversity that is still a problematic force in society today (Wahl & Scholl, 2014). The term hate speech refers to insulting discourse, phrases, terms, cartoons, or organized campaigns used to humiliate people based on age, gender, race, ethnicity, culture, sexual orientation, social class, and more. Hate speech has been associated historically with—but is not

BECHDEL TEST

Corbis

The Bechdel test asks if a work of fiction features at least two women who talk to each other about something other than a man. Although originally conceived for evaluating films, the Bechdel test is now used as an indicator of gender bias in all forms of fiction. Although this test has been criticized as misleading and unfair in certain contexts, it does serve to point out gender discrepancies in popular media. Author Alexandra Donald examined the 50 highest-grossing films of 2013 to see how they fared on the Bechdel test. She found that 36%, or 17 films, passed with flying colors, with an additional 7 films passing "dubiously" (Donald, 2015). Although this number can seem alarming, it is important to remember that the Bechdel test is not a perfect measurement. The 2013 film *Gravity*, for example, completely fails the test, even though lead actress Sandra Bullock occupies the screen for 87% of the film. Why does the film fail? Bullock is the film's only female character, which makes it ineligible for the Bechdel test.

Although the Bechdel test is an imperfect measure, its results and even the criteria needed to take the test can illustrate the discrepancies in gender equality in modern media. In 2012, the voting membership of the Academy of Motion Picture Arts and Sciences was almost 94% Caucasian and 77% male (Donald, 2015). As you become a more critical consumer of modern media, try to apply the Bechdel test whenever possible, and assess whether what you enjoy can be considered gender equal.

QUESTIONS

1. What movies can you think of that would be considered unethically biased against gender equality?

2. How can institutions like Hollywood improve their record of gender equality in media?

---

limited to—racist groups such as the Ku Klux Klan and other White pride groups that argue that White people are superior to African Americans and other ethnic groups.

Hate speech is clearly persuasive communication used to intimidate and segregate based on gender, sexual orientation, race, and ethnicity. In contrast, the newer forms of hate speech have been revised to focus on "us" (White people) versus "them" (ethnic minorities, gays, and women). New forms of hate speech are more about how the authenticity of being White is somehow reinforced by religiosity. Put simply, hate speech in the Communication Age uses the Internet and new media to disseminate messages of fear and intimidation.

Getty

Hate speech and racism are still alive today.

Corbis

Celebrities like Taylor Swift have spoken out against bullying.

School Bullying

The use of hate speech is also a troubling practice related to school bullying. Hate speech targeting gay and lesbian youth led to a 2008 advertising campaign, Think Before You Speak, sponsored by Ad Council, ThinkB4YouSpeak .com, and Gay, Lesbian, and Straight Education Network (GLSEN) to address the homophobic phrase "That's so gay" popularly used among young Americans. The campaign was designed to discourage use of this slur. Each advertisement features people in various situations stating that something they do not like is "so gay." Then a popular celebrity, such as Wanda Sykes or Hilary Duff, walks out and tells them that they should not use the word *gay* to describe something that they do not like. Each advertisement ends with text and a voiceover saying, "When you say, 'That's so gay,' do you realize what you say? Knock it off." This campaign won the Ad Council's top award for "Best Public Service Advertising Campaign" and received much attention across the nation for taking on the issue of homophobia.

COMMUNICATION, CULTURE, DIVERSITY, AND CONVERGENCE

Remember to connect your study of communication, culture, and diversity to convergence in the Communication Age. As you think back to many of the examples presented in this chapter related to communication, culture, and diversity, consider how social networking and new media could help foster cultural competence and fight against barriers such as discrimination and school bullying. Think about the possibility of communication, culture, and diversity in the Communication Age.

Shiva, a featured character in *Resident Evil 5*, is pictured here. Real human images were used in Shiva's video game character design.

Consider the opportunities you have related to cultural sensitivity regarding new media and convergence. While there are ways to overcome barriers to communication, culture, and diversity using new media (e.g., social networking, blogs, text messages) (Cruikshank, 2010; Erdur-Baker, 2010; Murthy, 2011), realize that barriers still exist in the Communication Age. One troubling example can be found in the realm of video game culture. The qualities of convergence and new media, as covered in this chapter, appear to empower ethnic minorities and offer hope to gay teens facing bullies face to face and online. However, game and culture scholar André Brock (2011) reminds us that the world of new media and video games (i.e., *Resident Evil 5*) in the Communication Age is not always based on inclusion and cultural sensitivity. Consider the concerns Brock raises about Africans being dominated by Whites in the popular game *Resident Evil 5*. Brock (2011) argues that "at no point [in the video game] are Africans allowed to be anything other than savage; they are never seen within familiar Western contexts such as high-rise buildings, shopping centers, or at leisure" (p. 443).

Considering Brock's (2011) view, it appears that work still needs to be done related to communication, culture, and diversity in the Communication Age.

Think about what cultural competency can become as face-to-face communication and new media communities converge to help us foster new possibilities in the Communication Age. What do you see? What issues do you want to engage? What type of community do you want to help create? Do you need to improve your communication in diverse contexts? What have you learned in this chapter that could help you improve? Your study of communication, culture, and diversity in this chapter is applicable to both your face-to-face and your mediated communication experiences in the Communication Age.

Describe the influence of culture and diversity in the Communication Age.

The study of culture and diversity helps initiate a more extended conversation about their influence in the Communication Age. In order for you to succeed in any personal, social, or professional context, you must be aware of and sensitive to differences between yourself and others.

▶ Breaking Down Stereotypes Using Art and Media

🎙 College Campuses Address Diversity

 Identify the importance of understanding cultural context for effective and ethical communication.

Communication and culture are shaped by several important concepts. These include communication competence, high- versus low-context cultures, individualism versus collectivism, and cultural imperatives (peace, economic, technological, self-awareness, and ethical).

▶ Map the World: Hofstede's Five Cultural Dimensions Visualized

💻 LGBTQ Campus Climate

3 **Describe the importance of cultural competence for communicating in a globalized world.**

Positive communication cannot happen in a diverse context without cultural competence, perception checking, and mutual respect. Your ability to communicate

effectively when encountering differences of ethnicity, race, language, religion, marital status, or sexual orientation is an essential component to being an educated citizen.

▶ Women's Rights Movement

💻 Calling for the Redskins to Change Its Name

 Discuss different examples of diversity across communication contexts.

Gender, ethnicity and race, language differences, religion, disability, and sexual orientation exemplify diversity you will experience across communication contexts. You develop positive personal and professional relationships with people who are different than you by coming to understand those differences.

▶ Colleges Looking Beyond Standardized Testing

 Examine how to become more aware of and overcome barriers to communication, culture, and diversity.

Prejudice, discrimination, ethnocentrism, and hate speech all serve as barriers to communication and diversity. You can take on the barriers to communication, culture, and diversity if you practice cultural competence, perception checking, and mutual respect.

🌐 Anti-Gay Hate Crimes

💻 13 Years After 9/11, Anti-Muslim Bigotry Is Worse Than Ever

KEY TERMS

Review key terms with eFlashcards. **edge.sagepub.com/edwards2e**

Androgyny   137
Co-cultural communication   127
Collectivist cultures   131
Cultural competence   134
Cultural rituals   128
Cultural value dimensions   130
Culture   126
Discrimination   144
Diversity   127
Economic imperative   136
Ethical imperative   136
Ethnicity   139
Ethnocentrism   144

Femininity   133
Gender   137
Hate speech   144
Heterosexist   142
High-context cultures   129
Individualistic cultures   131
Long-term time orientation   134
Low-context cultures   129
Masculinity   133
Mutual respect   134
Peace imperative   136
Perception checking   134
Power distance   131

Prejudice   144
Race   139
Rapport talk   138
Report talk   138
Self-awareness imperative   136
Sex   137
Sexual orientation   142
Short-term time orientation   134
Stereotypes   143
Technological imperative   136
Uncertainty avoidance   133

REFLECT

1. In the Communication Age, virtual communities and other forms of social networking media allow people from across spaces, languages, and cultures to connect and engage. In general, do you think social media like Facebook and YouTube bring people together or cast them farther apart, considering made-up names (anonymity) and the vast amount of information people have to keep up with?

2. Take a moment to think about an issue covered in this chapter that resonates with your lived experience relating to communication, culture, and diversity. What helped you adjust the most? In what ways did your communication impact the assimilation?

3. Review the various cultural imperatives covered in this chapter. Which imperative, if any, stands out to you as important? Which imperative connects with an issue important in your life?

4. What examples of diversity resonate with you personally? Have you ever faced an awkward social situation involving religion, sexual orientation, disability, or any other examples of diversity covered in this chapter?

5. Think of an issue or problem that you are passionate about related to the barriers to communication, culture, and diversity. How could you engage in communication activism to advocate against hate speech, racism, or prejudicial language/action?

REVIEW

To check your answers go to **edge.sagepub.com/edwards2e**

1. What is culture?

2. Define co-cultural communication.

3. In_____, spoken words are less important than the rest of the context.

4. In _____, people separate their relationships from verbal communication and focus on the information conveyed and logical argumentation.

5. _____ refers to the practice of asking others to get a more informed sense of understanding.

6. List five cultural imperatives.

7. _____ is the categorization of people based on physical characteristics such as skin color, dimensions of the human face, and hair.

8. _____ refers to a social group that may be joined together by factors such as shared history, shared identity, shared geography, and shared culture.

9. Explain why the study of communication, culture diversity, and convergence is important in the Communication Age.

04 NONVERBAL COMMUNICATION

WHAT YOU'LL LEARN   After studying this chapter, you will be able to:

1 Identify the importance of nonverbal communication in your life.

2 Explain the functions of nonverbal communication as it works with verbal communication.

3 Describe the codes of nonverbal communication.

4 Describe the impact nonverbal communication has in a variety of situations.

5 Examine how nonverbal communication is influenced in the Communication Age.

Health care in the Communication Age is changing and evolving rapidly. As birthrates decline in some parts of the world and baby boomers reach an age that requires more health care assistance, we reach a global dilemma of how to provide adequate health care for older adults. The country of Japan has long been examining how to utilize robots in a health care context. As a result, a Japanese research institute has created Robear, a 308-pound robotic nurse with a cute bear face. Research leader Toshiharu Mukai says of the robot, "The polar cub–like look is aimed at radiating an atmosphere of strength, geniality, and cleanliness at the same time" (Mogg, 2015). This occurs through nonverbal communication.

Robear the robot is able to "exert force in a gentle way" by moving patients around precisely where they need to be (Mogg, 2015). The bright, big eyes and smile on the robotic nurse-bear face were specifically developed to help patients feel at ease through nonverbal communication. As more development occurs, the nonverbal communication characteristics of the robotic nurse-bear will only become more realistic and responsive to the needs of the patient.

Nonverbal communication will be an important part of this convergence if avatars are to be successful. In this chapter, you will learn about nonverbal communication and types of codes that matter in any interaction, whether it is in a face-to-face setting or a computer-mediated setting. As you read the chapter, think about the ways in which nonverbal communication is starting to become more common in a mediated world.

Imagine this: You enter your friend Daniel's house in the middle of August. You see food all over the dirty kitchen walls, and notice that the thermostat reads

How would you respond to a friend's room that looked like the one pictured here?

89 degrees and that there are dirty underwear, trash, and old sushi boxes everywhere. The nonverbal cues you experience in Daniel's house impact your perceptions in a number of ways. As established in Chapter 1, communication is defined as the collaborative process of using messages to create and participate in social reality. In the Communication Age, it is important also to be familiar with nonverbal communication—all the ways we communicate without using words (Ivy & Wahl, 2014). Verbal and nonverbal communication enable us to actualize possibility, realize human potential, and achieve change and growth, both for ourselves and our communities. Have you ever had a conversation in which the other person breaks off talking to answer a text or an e-mail? Think about how nonverbal communication is influenced in the Communication Age. Nonverbal communication can include your clothing, your physical appearance, your gestures, your facial and eye expressions, and more. As you focus on nonverbal communication in this chapter, keep the following questions in mind: How can nonverbal cues be used to communicate important messages to others? What are the specific codes (categories) of nonverbal communication? How do you connect with others nonverbally in the Communication Age? Why does nonverbal communication matter?

WHY DOES NONVERBAL COMMUNICATION MATTER?

Nonverbal messages matter because they communicate feelings and attitudes. With the many tools of mediated communication at our disposal, it is easier than ever to observe examples of nonverbal communication in photos or streaming videos. When looking back at family photo albums, you can usually tell that the people smiling with their arms around each other are comfortable in that particular moment. On the other hand, a photo of a friend or loved one with her arms crossed, not looking into the camera, would suggest that she was not enjoying herself.

Nonverbal messages matter because they are more convincing than verbal messages. Think about situations where someone's facial expressions tell you everything you need to know. These are situations that illustrate the power of nonverbal communication. Perhaps you're working in human resources for a large corporation. Job interviews are being held for a new training and development position, and you are assisting with interview check-in. The first candidate comes to the interview in a tight outfit, sweating, and looking at his watch in frustration. You try to be supportive by asking if he is nervous, and he replies, "No, I'm not nervous at all." In this interview context, the candidate's nonverbal cues would be much more powerful than the verbal message that was given to you. As the saying goes, actions speak louder than words.

As you can learn from the robot and messy room examples that lead off this chapter, nonverbal communication is important in many aspects of life. This chapter explores messages communicated through nonverbal communication. To begin exploring this diverse topic, take a moment to familiarize yourself with the specific functions of nonverbal communication in the section that follows.

FUNCTIONS OF NONVERBAL COMMUNICATION

Nonverbal communication performs a number of functions as it works with verbal communication. Specifically, let's discuss how nonverbal communication helps to repeat, accent, conflict with, complement, regulate, and substitute messages in the communication process.

Repeating

A nonverbal message may "repeat" the verbal message. For example, you may simultaneously say, "Yes" and shake your head up and down. Or you might hold up four fingers while saying, "It's about four blocks south."

Accenting

A nonverbal message may highlight the verbal message by emphasizing or enhancing a certain point. You may stress the word *despise* in "I despise this weather" to emphasize your strong negative feelings.

Conflicting

You may use a nonverbal message to contradict your verbal message. For instance, you might say, "I'm having a great time at this party," while simultaneously shaking your head "no" with eyes wide open. Or you may say, "Of course I'm taking this seriously!" while laughing. The contradiction of verbal and nonverbal messages adds a new dimension to the possible meaning of your message.

Complementing

A nonverbal message can reinforce a verbal message. For instance, you might tell your friend, "I'm listening to you," while making sure to perform the nonverbal behaviors associated with listening. You could lean forward, make eye contact, and avoid engaging in any other tasks.

Regulating

Nonverbal messages often manage the flow of verbal conversation. For example, you may raise your hand to signal that you would like to say something. Or you may make eye

▶ **COMMUNICATION IN ACTION 4.1**

WATCH: Proxemics, Nonverbal Communication Codes

Communication technology and space management convey differing nonverbal messages as two classmates interact. What is your interpretation of these nonverbal actions?

contact with a quiet member of the group to make it clear that you would like him or her to contribute.

Substituting

The use of a nonverbal message can replace a verbal message. Examples include pointing when you're asked where an item is located, shrugging your shoulders when you don't know the answer to a question, or flashing a thumbs-up to indicate that you're doing fine.

Now that you have reviewed the different functions of nonverbal communication, the next section examines the categories or *codes* of nonverbal information researchers have studied: vocalics (voice), kinesics (body movement), proxemics (space), environment, facial expressions, eye behavior, haptics (touch), and physical appearance.

CODES OF NONVERBAL COMMUNICATION

Let's face it—nonverbal communication is complicated. Thus, there is a need for classification to make nonverbal communication easier to study. Although this chapter focuses on these nonverbal communication codes in Western culture, remember that perceptions of or reactions to nonverbal communication can vary in other cultures.

Vocalics

Vocalics refers to the study of the use of voice to express self. Just like the face, the voice plays a major role in sharing our thoughts and emotions. Your voice conveys information about who you are as an individual (not just what someone thinks of you) and, importantly, who you are as a member of a group. Speech accents are an example of this. We also use the vocal channel to modify/change the meaning of our utterances. One example is the use of sarcasm to convey the opposite of what we say in words.

Vocalic cues include tone (quality) of voice, volume, articulation, pitch (highness or lowness), the rate of speech, and use of silence. Imagine that your best friend just got a new haircut and asked you what you thought about it. If you really hated your friend's new haircut, you could say enthusiastically, "It looks awesome!"—which would be either a lie to avoid hurt feelings or an expression of sarcasm. You might also say, "It looks good," in a halfhearted way. It is due to your voice that you're able to express these different reactions.

Your voice reveals your emotions, your thoughts, and the relationships you have with others. It also

Getty

In addition to Idina Menzel (*Frozen*) and Ellen DeGeneres (*Finding Nemo*), pictured here, what other famous voices come to mind?

provides information about your self-confidence and knowledge and influences how you are perceived by others (Hinkle, 2001). Think about the famous voices you hear in movies. Morgan Freeman, Drew Barrymore, and Steve Carell all have very distinct voices that audiences find interesting for different reasons. Morgan Freeman's voice is one that audiences find trustworthy and caring, while Drew Barrymore's voice is pleasing and sympathetic. Steve Carell, on the other hand, is fun to listen to because he can change his voice to create almost any kind of sound.

In the digital world, vocalics encompasses the use of ALL CAPS in text messages, personal e-mails, and social networking. ALL CAPS indicates an increased volume, or that you are shouting. If you text your best friend that you need to speak to her, you might use ALL CAPS to indicate that it is extremely urgent.

Now that you know more about vocalics, or the study of the use of voice, let's move on to the study of body movement, also known as kinesics.

Kinesics

Kinesics is the study of body movement, including both posture and gestures. It's been long known that kinesics provides important information to others. People have a certain walk, posture, and stance, which become their own, by which they are recognized, and which can be impacted by their mood or emotions. Have you ever heard someone make reference to how certain people "carry themselves"? You know you can't physically "carry yourself," so this must mean your posture, stance, and movement. Have you noticed how some people seem to carry themselves in ways that make them unapproachable? Or have you seen a person who walked with confidence and could light up the room? Your posture says a lot about you as a person.

Did your parents ever tell you to "stand up straight"? As annoying as that command may be, posture is indeed important. In many cultures, including the United States, an upright but relaxed body posture is associated with many attractive attributes, such as confidence, positivity, and high self-esteem (Guerrero & Floyd, 2006). People judge others' personalities based on something as subjective as posture, so it's worth considering. Do you pay attention to your posture? How do mood and emotions affect your posture? Posture says a lot about dominance and status. Social psychologist David Johnson (2006) contends that "individuals with high status and power may engage in a dominance display by puffing themselves up to full size, stiffening their backs, tightening their brows, thrusting their chins forward, and leaning toward the challenger in an attempt to convince others of their power" (p. 199). However, dominant nonverbal behaviors aren't always linked to high-status behaviors. Think about the job interview situation. An interviewer is typically much more relaxed than a job applicant, who is typically more tense and nervous.

Gestures

Gestures are the movements you make with your hands and arms. Some people "talk with their hands" in order to complement what they're saying, whereas others might prefer using fewer gestures to avoid distracting from the verbal message.

Giorgos Katidis raises his hand in a Nazi-style salute as he celebrates scoring a goal in a Greek league game.

Ekman and Friesen (1969b) classified movement and gestures according to how they function in human interaction. The five categories of kinesics include emblems, illustrators, affect displays, regulators, and adapters. Let's take a look at each in more detail.

Emblems

Emblems are meanings in specific communication and cultural contexts that substitute for words. Flipping someone off with a specific hand gesture is an emblem because it has a direct translation to the written word. Emblems have widely understood meanings, yet it's important to note that they don't have *universally* understood meanings. There are only a few gestures that have practically the same meaning across cultures. Three gestures that have the widest meaning cross-culturally include the pointing gesture, the "come here" gesture, and the opposite "stay away" gesture. Emblematic gestures should be used with caution because emblems become known or are negotiated within cultures. Our nonverbal behaviors can easily offend whole groups of people and lead to unpleasant consequences. Consider this example: In 2013, Greek soccer player Giorgos Katidis made the "Heil, Hitler" gesture after scoring the game-winning goal for his team, AEK Athens. Katidis took off his shirt after scoring and made the gesture—he later said that he was simply pointing to one of his teammates. The Greek Soccer Association didn't believe his explanation and ended up banning him from the sport for life. In this example, a gesture upset large groups of people, which shows the connection between nonverbal communication and sensitivity.

Illustrators

Gestures that complement, enhance, or substitute for the verbal message are called illustrators. If you were describing the length of the biggest fish you ever caught, you might use your hands to illustrate the size. Or, when you are giving directions, you might point to show which way to go. Sometimes verbal messages are inappropriate or can't be heard, making illustrators a convenient nonverbal choice. For example, you're at a baseball game, and there's too much noise to convey to the pretzel stand workers what you want, so instead of shouting your order, you point at the food and hold up some fingers to indicate how many you want. This is a substitution function of an illustrating gesture.

Affect Displays

Nonverbal gestures, postures, and facial expressions that communicate emotions are called affect displays. Typically, nonverbal cues can be detected before they accompany the verbal message. Therefore, if you're happy, you are more likely to reveal the happiness you feel through your nonverbal cues before you actually express it verbally to someone. The kind of emotion you feel is usually expressed in your face, while how much you feel of the emotion is expressed in your body. If you're excited, for example, your face may show your excitement to others. The movement of your hands, the openness of your posture, and the speed of your movement tell others just how excited you are.

Regulators

Gestures used to control the turn-taking in conversations are known as regulators. For example, you might make a hand motion to encourage someone or raise your own hand to get a turn at speaking. When you're eager to answer a message, you normally make eye contact, raise your eyebrows, open your mouth, take in a breath, and lean forward slightly. You do the opposite if you don't want to answer. Little head nods, vocal expressions (such as "um"), facial expressions, body postures, and eye contact can be seen as connectors that keep the conversation together and make it coherent. When these sorts of nonverbal cues are absent from a conversation, it might trigger a negative reaction, and you could come to believe that your conversational partner isn't listening at all.

Adapters

Gestures we use to release tension are called adapters. Playing with our hands, poking, picking, fidgeting, scratching, and interacting nonverbally with our environment are all adapters that reveal our attempts to regulate situations and to make ourselves feel more at ease and able to function effectively. Adapters can clue us that another person is uncomfortable in some way.

Proxemics

Proxemics refers to the study of how people use space and distance to communicate. There are three reasons why it is important to make the connections between people, space, and distance: (1) Who you are as person can be revealed by your preferred use of distance and space at home and at work, (2) your verbal and nonverbal communication is influenced by distance and space, and (3) you use metaphors of distance and space to talk about and explain your interpersonal relationships.

Have you ever been in a crowded elevator and felt uncomfortable because it seemed like people were invading your personal space? Your rules and norms about space have become so understood that you don't think much about them until they are violated. Violations can be alarming, possibly even threatening. Your relationships with others, your power and status, and your cultural background determine how physically close you get to others and how close you let others get to you (Burgoon & Jones, 1976; Docan-Morgan, 2011).

Considering your own preferences regarding space, does dancing in a crowd like this appeal to you?

Corbis

Barack Obama embraces Burmese opposition politician Aung San Suu Kyi, a culturally inappropriate way of greeting in Burma. What experiences have you had related to nonverbal communication and cultural differences?

What preferences do you have related to space and distance? In U.S. culture, we as communicators tend not to like people "up in our personal business." Edward T. Hall (1963) identified four zones of space in middle-class U.S. culture. First, there is the intimate zone, which is about 0 to 18 inches and usually reserved for our significant others, family members, and closest friends. It is rare that a stranger can enter the intimate zone without making us feel violated. These interactions mostly occur in private and signify a high level of connection, trust, and affection. The personal zone, 18 inches to about 4 feet, is reserved for personal relationships with casual acquaintances and friends. The social zone, 4 to 12 feet, is the distance at which you usually talk to strangers or conduct business. If you went to your professor's office to discuss a grade, for example, you would most likely remain at a distance of 4 to 12 feet. The public zone, over 12 feet, refers to the distance typical of large, formal, public events. In large lecture classrooms, campaign rallies, or public speeches, the distance between speaker and audience is usually over 12 feet. Understanding these spatial zones is important to your everyday nonverbal communication competency.

Just like so many other things, spatial zones vary among cultures. In Arab cultures, for example, it is common to have less personal space. Hall (1966) observed Arab cultures for their use of space and found significant differences between how Arabs and Westerners view public space and conversational distance. Arabs do not seek privacy in public space, preferring to converse intimately in public and viewing less-than-intimate conversations as rude behavior. Therefore, whereas people in the United States appreciate their personal space, other cultures have different ideas about the use of space.

Gender and Sexual Orientation

A person's gender and sexual orientation is another factor that contributes to proxemics. Gender has an immense influence on personal space management, which leads to particular communication patterns (Hamilton, 2007). For example, it is socially accepted and completely natural in U.S. culture for women to sit next to each other, whereas men are more likely to sit facing one another. Of course, men can and do sit side by side, but it's likely to cause some uneasiness or lead them to feel like they have to joke their way through the behavior (Fair, 2011). Have you ever seen a group of men at a movie theater who don't sit directly next to each other but instead insist on having one seat between them to provide more space? One explanation for this behavior is that men simply need more space than do women because they are larger in size. Another possibility is that more space in the movie theater makes it very clear to everyone that these men aren't gay (Solebello & Elliot, 2011). Homophobia is still very prevalent in U.S. culture. And although homosexuality has become more acceptable in our culture in recent years, the primary explanation for men's spatial behavior relates to

"TEACH-IN" HELPS STUDENTS COMMUNICATE ABOUT GENDER, RACE, AND SEXUALITY

THE UNIVERSITY OF Virginia is one of the oldest higher education institutions in the United States. Although the university has a long tradition, UVA Women's Center program director Jaronda Miller feels that student advocacy should change some long-standing institutions at the university. "Some of the things I've tried to do is bring people in the community that work in advocacy to show students what it takes," Miller said.

"[I have tried to show students] how to organize and what strategic steps you take to have an issue and get results" (Griesedieck, 2015).

With this in mind, the university's Women, Gender, and Sexuality Program hosted what is called a "teach-in" to discuss recent events at the university. Teach-ins—which date back to the Vietnam War—are designed as methods of knowledge distribution that take place outside the classroom, and allow both students and teachers to collaborate their class curriculum with current events. Topics included the need for a better wage for the university staff, as well as a need for greater diversity at UVA.

Student involvement in university policy is a much-underutilized resource in many higher learning institutions. Examples, such as the "teach-in" or student government, illustrate how powerful students' voices can be in enacting effective change to university culture. As you move forward in your college career, reflect on methods you and fellow students can use to create a better university life for yourselves, faculty, and future students.

---

homophobia—a fear of being perceived as or labeled gay (Fair, 2011; Solebello & Elliot, 2011). Most women don't have to deal with this perception because acceptance for women's behavior tends to be wider than for men's.

Territoriality

Another concept related to the study of proxemics is territoriality, which is the study of how people use space and objects to communicate occupancy or owner-ship of space (Ivy & Wahl, 2014). You determine your territory and want it to be safe from strangers. Therefore, you will do your best to defend it from intrusion by using verbal and nonverbal means. Let's think about a less obvious example: placing a jacket or a book bag on a chair to let others know that the seat is taken. In this example, it might be nice to have a little territory to engage in conversation. How do you feel about people as territory? It might be a little weird to look at people as territory in the first place, but you most likely know people who view their boyfriend or girlfriend as their own private territory, and they can become seriously forceful when they feel their territory is being invaded. How do people violate our territories? Three types of intrusion are typically viewed as negative: violation, invasion, and contamination (Lyman & Scott, 1967).

iStock

Take a moment to think about your preferences related to seating in movie theaters. Do you like to sit in a particular row? Do you form perceptions of others in movie theaters based on how they sit?

Violation

Violation is entering or using territory without permission. If you've ever had a roommate, you will be able to relate to the story of someone who eats the favorite food that you bought or wears your favorite sweater when you're not in. Taking advantage of your belongings without your knowledge or permission is a violation of your personal territory.

Invasion

Invasion is an intentional intrusion of a specific territory. Perhaps you have experienced a situation in which you were enjoying some quiet solitude at a beach or a restaurant when a rowdy group of people arrived and disrupted the peace and quiet of the space. Fed up with the distraction, you decided to pack up and go home.

Contamination

This type of intrusion, in which someone's territory is marked with noise or pollution, is known as contamination. Contamination is about doing something to a territory to show that you were there, such as leaving your trash in a park after a barbecue with friends.

Clearly, proxemics, or the study of how space influences communication, is an important topic. The next section examines the power of environment as a nonverbal communication category.

Environment

The environment refers to the surroundings that shape the communication context. People are influenced by environmental factors such as architecture, design, doors, windows, color, lighting, smell, seating arrangements, temperature, and cleanliness (Harris & Sachau, 2005; Jackson, 2005). The environment is a component when studying nonverbal communication because it influences the way people act and interact.

You shape your environments to express your own feelings and beliefs to others. Think about the type of art you may put on your walls. What does it say about you? Consider other things in the environment that can serve as nonverbal cues about who you are. It is these environmental factors that you create and control that serve as nonverbal messages to others who enter the space. As one scholar put it, "People cannot be understood outside of their environmental context" (Peterson, 1991, p. 154). Nonverbal actions can be interpreted meaningfully only when context is taken into account.

The environment is important to the study of nonverbal behavior in two ways: (1) The decisions you make about the environments in which you live and work reveal a good deal about who you are, and (2) your nonverbal behavior changes according to the environments in which you communicate. First, the physical environments in which you function can be seen as extensions of your personality. It might not be possible to manipulate all elements of your environment, yet to a certain extent you can "personalize" it. It's natural for you to structure the settings in which you work, study, or live to make them more unique and to make people feel more comfortable. The environments you create for yourself often speak volumes about those relationships you consider most important (Lohmann, Arriaga, & Goodfriend, 2003). Second, your behavior and perceptions are altered by the physical environments in which you find yourself. For example, you are more likely to wear formal clothes and whisper at a religious service than at a sporting event, where you would probably wear comfortable clothes and scream wildly for your favorite team.

What about environments that you don't create personally? Do they influence you? And if so, how? Think about how you would behave at the White House or the Statue of Liberty. Many college campuses have a central building that is connected to student and alumni identity and which serves as a focal or historical point for the campus (Biemiller, 2007). Our verbal and nonverbal communication is impacted by these structures because those buildings communicate something before people even walk in.

Impression Management

Remember in the beginning of this section you were invited to think about your own personal space, how you represent yourself with it, and what it says about you to others? Just as there are environments that you can own and operate, there are also environments that are beyond your control. Picture a situation in which you show up for a job interview and the office you enter is dirty, with food leftovers piled everywhere. What does an office like that tell you about the owner's professionalism, credibility, and organizational skills? An environment like that is all about impression management—the formation of an impression, a perception, or a view of the other (Goffman, 1971). You haven't even met the owner yet, so all you have to go by are nonverbal clues. Would this be a good place to work? People want to communicate in comfortable environments, whether they have thought about it before or not. The environments you create in your homes, offices, and classrooms establish certain communication contexts, comfortable or uncomfortable, that have an influence on your perceptions of safety and comfort, as well as the attitude and character of the people inhabiting the space (Ivy & Wahl, 2014).

Perceptions of Environment

The way you perceive your environment is an important factor related to how you respond to others. Overall, there are six ways by which people distinguish the environment around them: formality, warmth, privacy, familiarity, constraint, and distance (Ivy & Wahl, 2014).

Formality is an understanding that people have of environment that relates to how comfortably they can behave, in light of their expectations. Sometimes it is more about the atmosphere of a certain place rather than the place itself. Imagine you go to a restaurant, and it's too fancy for your taste. You would probably walk right back out because it doesn't have the type of atmosphere you desire and in which you feel comfortable. The second way we can perceive the environment is warmth. Your sense of warmth describes how you see and desire a welcoming context that is part of your past or current experience. Smells, visions, sounds,

CAREER FRONTIER: IMPRESSION MANAGEMENT

THINK ABOUT THE evolution of mediated environments. In the last decade, there has been an explosion in the amount of time people spend online. Whether it's Facebook, Twitter, or a similar medium, social networking sites seem to be a popular way to meet people and communicate. Sites like these create virtual communities. Websites that offer chat rooms and other services give users the opportunity to "escape" from everyday life and communicate anonymously outside of their public and private spaces. Facebook encourages users to create an environment of personhood by providing space to upload pictures, post journals, and list personal interests. All of these elements are used to decorate and personalize computerized space.

Beyond social networking, think about the influence websites such as Facebook and LinkedIn have not only on how you and others view your online persona, but how companies and professions utilize the information you provide. Researchers Rob Heyman and Jo Pierson analyzed how the business models of Facebook and LinkedIn blend mass self-communication with advertising. They found that once personal information has been posted by a user, that person is no longer able to control production, selection, and distribution of his or her personal identifiable information (PII) when it is used in advertising (Heyman & Pierson, 2013). At this point, a person's user-generated content is only relevant if it has economic value. In other words, the impression you want to convey to others online may be distorted by the advertising interests of the social medium. As you express yourself online, remember that your information is available for *everyone* (not just your online friends) to see and use.

In your career, the relationships you build will rely greatly on how you manage your impressions of others, as well as how you create the impressions others have of you. Nowhere is this more critical than the job interview process. Before any further impressions can be made, you must first utilize a résumé and cover letter to form an employer's impression that you are well suited for the job. Research has indicated that résumés serve as contextual metaphors by presenting potential employers with surface-level descriptions of the applicant's professional experience (Lipovsky, 2013). Applicants must then infuse these basic descriptions of their background with evaluative meanings that validate their claims of professional competence and persuade recruiters to agree to a job interview.

Your best resource to understand how to attract potential employers is to speak with people currently employed in your field of choice, preferably people who are recruiters themselves. Whether you know them personally, professionally, or academically, use these resources to help you craft the perfect résumé and cover letter that can set you apart from the other applicants. Also, online forums for specific professions can be a valuable guide to the dos and don'ts of résumé creation.

and lighting in an environment can all contribute to your perception of warmth. Think of a favorite smell or song from your childhood that has always given and still gives you a sense of warmth when thinking about it.

Privacy is another way the environment can be perceived. Do you prefer a crowded and popular restaurant or a quiet one off the beaten path? People all have a sense of privacy. Some of you don't mind being around a lot of people, and some of you do. If you ask someone who works at a restaurant, he or she will tell you that booths typically fill up faster than tables because they offer more privacy.

Another perception you have is familiarity, which refers to how cautiously you react to meeting new people or being in unfamiliar environments. Not knowing where they are and what to expect makes some people feel less comfortable than others. That's why many people tend to return to favorite hangouts or certain restaurants. Most people like knowing what to expect and how to behave in the environment.

Next on the list is constraint. Whenever you feel like your personal space is invaded, you feel constraint. For example, some individuals are more inhibited living with roommates, while others are not. Most of your perceptions of constraint are shaped by the amount of privacy and space available to you.

The final perception of your environment is distance. Your perceptions of distance in an environment pertain to physical arrangements. People like to know how far away the closest door is located or how many people can fit into an elevator. People create distance by avoiding eye contact or taking a longer route in order to avoid saying "hello" to a person they find annoying.

Think about how you perceive the environments in which you live. Did you realize that your perceptions of those environments are influenced by the six ways just discussed? The way you perceive the environments you inhabit says a lot about you and influences how others perceive you.

The characters in the TV show *How I Met Your Mother* frequently spend time together in a local pub. Would you want to hang out in an environment like the one pictured here?

Reactions to Environment

Now that you have some idea about how people perceive the environment, you can look at how people react to it. Remember that while environment serves as a form of nonverbal communication, it also impacts our interactions within it. The drive-through at a fast-food restaurant creates a certain atmosphere. You are expected to quickly order your food, pay, pick up your food, and drive away. This environment does not invite conversation. A coffeehouse, on the other hand, encourages conversation with the arrangement of tables and couches. Let's look at the college classroom again.

Think of a course you're currently taking and the classroom where the course is delivered. What color are the walls? What about the seating arrangement? What can you smell and hear? What's the lighting like? Are there windows? How does all this influence the learning environment? What type of interaction is encouraged by the arrangement of the environment? A well-arranged classroom in which you feel comfortable should encourage you to interact with your classmates and teacher. Environment is communicative because people have perceptions of and reactions to environment. Let us now look at another element that influences the communicative environment—time.

Chronemics

Chronemics is the study of the ways in which time is used to structure interactions (Kalman & Rafaeli, 2011). Have you ever been casually late to a party? In some situations being late is a violation of important cultural norms. Yet, at many parties, the acceptable window of arrival is much larger. U.S. and most of Western European culture is monochronic, in that being on time and maintaining a schedule for events is important. In other cultures, such as South American and Mediterranean cultures, you will find a polychronic time orientation. A polychronic time orientation places less emphasis on keeping a tight schedule and values greater flexibility.

Time can also be used to denote power and role differences. Your boss might keep you waiting while she is talking on the phone because doing so communicates a difference in power, the implication being that her time is more valuable than yours. Indeed, time plays an important role in relation to communication. Think about how time has an influence in your life as well as on your perceptions of others.

Facial Expressions

The next nonverbal code that is important to study is the face. This code encompasses the use of the face to communicate emotion and feelings (see Figure 4.1). The face can be considered a gallery for our emotional displays (Gosselin, Gilles, & Dore, 1995). It is so important in communication that it has become, according to communication scholars Domenici and Littlejohn (2006), "a symbol of close personal interaction" (p. 10). Consider common expressions such as "face-to-face," "face time," "in your face," or "saving face": Your face and your public identity are intimately connected; in fact, your face is the *you* presented to others in everyday encounters. Scholar Erving Goffman (1967) wrote about this presentation of self in everyday life, explaining how face can be "lost," "maintained," "protected," or "enhanced."

It is important to have a basic understanding of how you manage your face in daily interactions. Social norms and communication expectations in our culture set the rules for what kinds of emotional expressions are appropriate in certain situations. Facial management techniques are categories of behavior created by Paul Ekman and Wallace Friesen (1969a, 1969b, 1975) that determine the appropriate facial response for a given situation. The four most common techniques include neutralization, masking, intensification, and deintensification.

The process of controlling facial expressions to erase or numb how you really feel is called neutralization. People who neutralize

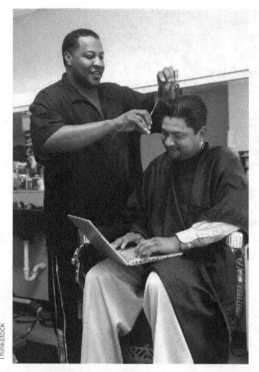

How do you manage time in your own life, and how does that impact your communication?

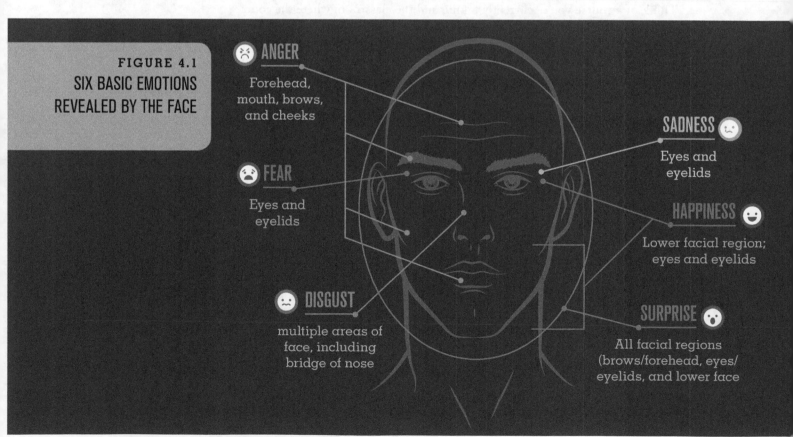

Canstock

Despite the common use of emoticons and emoji, research has shown that the intended impact of emoticons tends to be rather ambiguous, or relatively weak. It almost seems like people use emoticons in a habitual or unconscious way. However, research has indicated that messages such as Facebook postings, while intended to be innocuous, can cause negative emotional reactions based on how nonverbal cues are perceived. Also, the relationship between the sender and receiver can impact how the message is construed (Fleuriet, Cole, & Guerrero, 2014). For example, an emoticon with a winking face sent between your romantic partner and his or her ex-partner is likely to arouse jealousy, even if that was not the intent of the message. Below are some issues to keep in mind when using emoticons on social media:

1. Before making a post or sending a message, step outside your personal frame of reference to a third-person point of view. How would a stranger evaluate the message? If a person could easily misinterpret what you are trying to convey, it might be best to alter your communication.

2. When using emoticons, remember that there is no universal agreement on what they can mean. A winking or blushing face

can seem innocent to many people, but romantic or flirtatious to others.

3. There are significant nonverbal differences in communication across cultures. For example, a common hand gesture at the University of Texas, "Hook 'Em Horns," can mean an insult to marriage fidelity in certain European and Asian cultures.

Images: canstock and istock.

their facial expressions are often referred to as having a poker face. Masking means hiding an expression connected to a felt emotion and replacing it with an expression more appropriate to the situation. If you use an expression that exaggerates how you feel about something, it is called intensification. On the other hand, if you reduce the intensity of your facial expression of a certain emotion, it is called deintensification.

Emoticons and Emoji

The use of emoticons, a textual expression of emotions, and emoji, meaning "picture letter" in Japanese, are how you show your feelings in the digital world (Dresner & Herring, 2010). The use of :-), :-(, or :-D demonstrates your feelings in text. However, the situation should determine their use. In a text message, personal e-mail, or Facebook status line, emoticons and emoji are appropriate; however, steer clear of using them in professional e-mails or memos to your professors, coworkers, or boss. A good rule of thumb is that emoticons and emoji work best when they are used in interactions that once occurred primarily face to face. Using emoticons and

Actor Ben Affleck shows his nonverbal communication skills—that is, his poker face—at a celebrity charity poker tournament.

emoji to add some feeling in a text message to your boyfriend or girlfriend can help replace the expressiveness that may be lost because you are not face to face. In interactions that have long occurred primarily in writing (like office memos, professional reports, and business e-mails), emoticons and emoji may be interpreted as overly casual, irrelevant, and unprofessional.

Eye Behavior

The eyes are said to be the window to the soul. A significant part of facial expressions involves the use of the eyes. Approximately 80% of the information in our everyday surroundings is taken in visually (Morris, 1985). Are you comfortable making eye contact with most people or only with people you know well? If you want to flirt with someone you find attractive, you might stare, get her attention, and then look away. If you are mad at someone, you might stare him down. The eyes have social and cultural importance for communication. In U.S. culture as well as in many other cultures, eye contact is extremely important. People tend to make all kinds of judgments about others—particularly their trustworthiness and sincerity—on the basis of whether they make or avoid eye contact. People tend to trust those who will look them in the eye more and to believe what they are saying.

Think of eye behavior in terms of its influence on the social interactive process. Eye behavior is very powerful, and it can stimulate arousal, which can be a positive or negative reaction in response to another person. Seeing another person will always trigger some degree of arousal. It can be positive if you haven't seen a person for a while and you're excited to see him or her. However, it can also be negative if you see someone you would rather avoid. Eye behavior is crucial in social interaction because what you do with your eyes is more obvious than other actions of the face and body.

Eye behavior also commands involvement or the need to interact with another person even if it's a simple eye acknowledgment or head nod. Ever smiled at a complete stranger while you were passing him or her? Although you don't know the person, you tend to get involved with him or her, even if it's just through a slight smile or a head nod promoted by brief eye contact.

Your eyes also reveal deception cues, or hints that a person is being less than forthright. Consider behaviors you associate with lying: Behaviors like avoiding eye contact, looking down at the floor, fidgeting, clearing the throat, and using lots of filled pauses like "um" and "er" commonly indicate that someone is lying. Breaking or being unable to sustain eye gaze is also commonly believed to indicate deception. Studies have also shown that people tend to decrease eye contact when they lie (Hirsch & Wolf, 2001; Hocking & Leathers, 1980). Other studies, however, found an increase in eye gaze during deceit, possibly because the deceivers want to compensate for their lying by making more eye contact (DePaulo et al., 2003).

Haptics

Haptics is the study of touch. Whether it is a handshake, a punch, or a hug, touch has the potential to communicate a powerful message. The lack of traditional touch in mediated communication led first to XOXO in written correspondence to indicate hugs and kisses, and then to the development of behaviors like "poking" someone on Facebook. Of the five human senses, touch develops first (Montagu, 1978). Of all of the nonverbal codes, touch is the most powerful one. However, it is also the most complicated and misunderstood.

Whether face to face or online, the use of touch and how to interpret it is always contextual. Your might shake a stranger's hand but hug a friend. It would be quite a violation of nonverbal norms to go hug a stranger. In this sense, touch is influenced by relationship, situation, and culture. In some countries, it is normal for men to hold hands to indicate friendship and respect for each other (Fountain, 2005). In the United States you're less likely to see this behavior. A careful touch of the hand while delivering bad news can demonstrate care. A high-five for a job well done communicates excitement and accomplishment. Touch can also show power and role differences between individuals. The president of the United States might approach you to shake your hand, but you would never be allowed to approach the president. A doctor might touch you in a physical examination, but you would not touch the doctor to return the favor.

It is important to understand touch ethics, or people's beliefs about and preferences for touch. This ethic includes your rules about appropriate and inappropriate touch, your expectations as to how people will receive as well as extend touch to you, whether you are a touch-inclined person or not, and how you in reality act regarding touch. Your preference develops early in life and remains fairly constant. However, your relationships and experience might influence your touch preferences during your life span.

Therapeutic Touch

Touch as a nonverbal communication category has been examined in this chapter. However, what value does touch have in everyday life that makes a difference? Touch has been examined from a variety of scholarly perspectives, including affection in parenting, communication with the elderly, touch within marriage, touch as a way to offer comfort, touch related to gender, touch related to sexuality, and more. Beyond the work of nonverbal communication scholars who have spent years classifying and testing touch and its influence on human relationships is an area that points to the intersection of human communication and health. Remember the opening portion of the chapter that highlighted the importance of nonverbal communication in the practice of virtual nurses? Medical professionals like virtual nurses are using technology to communicate empathy and support online as they connect with patients and explain treatment details, medication schedules, and more. In a recent study, Coakley and Duffy (2010) found that Therapeutic Touch (TT), a method used in nursing and medical practice to reduce psychological distress and help patients relax, leads to significantly lower levels of pain as well as other positive health benefits in postoperative patients. This study illustrates an intersection between health and the nonverbal communication category of touch. The findings of this study are significant, but research on TT will only continue to reveal more of the benefits of touch to human health. Indeed, TT illustrates how nonverbal communication can make a difference. For more information about TT and other holistic treatments, visit www.ahna.org (American Holistic Nurses Association).

Why do couples hold hands? What does it do for their relationship?

Types of Touch

Several different systems for categorizing touch have been developed to help us better understand this complex code of nonverbal communication. One of the best means of classifying touch behavior was developed by Richard Heslin (1974).

First, there are *functional/professional* touches, which serve a specific purpose. These touches normally take place within the context of a professional relationship and are low in intimacy. An example would be a doctor giving a patient a physical exam. Second, there are *social/polite* touches. Touches like these are connected to cultural norms, such as handshakes. Once again there is relatively low intimacy within a relationship. Then there are *friendship/warmth* touches, which people use to show their platonic affection and support toward each other. Hugs and kisses on the cheek might be exchanged between two close friends, for example. *Love/intimacy* touches, on the other hand, are highly personal and intimate. People communicate strong feelings of affection toward each other with these kinds of touches. In this case, hugs may last longer and kisses may be on the lips, leading to sexual arousal. These touches are extremely intimate.

Appropriateness of Touch

The appropriateness of touch is a tricky topic because rules about appropriateness or inappropriateness of touch vary among individuals and cultures. The following section focuses on several aspects that can help explore the appropriateness of touch.

Appropriateness of touch depends on the location, meaning both the place on the body where contact is made and the setting within which touch occurs. The first option has a significant impact on whether you believe a touch to be appropriate or inappropriate. You make your own rules about who can touch you, when, where on your body, and in what setting. The second option determines the circumstances in which touch is made. For example, when you meet your boyfriend's or girlfriend's parents for the first time, should you shake hands with them or hug them?

Duration of the touch is the next point on our list of appropriateness. Duration means how long a touch lasts. A doctor's examination is never very pleasant, so if doctors do a good job they will get the exam over with quickly and without unnecessary contact. However, among loved ones, a lingering touch of the hand or embrace is usually expected.

Finally, intensity of touch refers to the power, force, or concentration of bodily contact. The amount of intensity that you put into a touch is influenced by your emotions. Therefore, if you're nervous before a job interview, you might use a firmer handshake than usual.

Culture and Touch

Culture plays an important role when it comes to touch, which means that you should interpret the meaning of a touch only within its appropriate cultural context (Anderson & Taylor, 2011). Hall (1966, 1981) distinguishes between contact cultures, in which people do not shy away from frequent touch, and noncontact cultures, in which individuals tend to be more reserved when it comes to touch. Contact cultures include Latin America, India, France, and Arab countries, whereas noncontact cultures include Germany and Northern European nations, North America, and many Asian countries such as China, Japan, Korea, Indonesia, and Malaysia (Hall, 1966, 1981). Greetings in different cultures are a good way to observe the cultural distinctions. For example, French Canadian greetings involve a handshake for men and brief hugs for women, whereas Puerto Rican women often grasp each other's shoulders and kiss both cheeks when greeting. Saudi Arabian men shake right hands to greet each other, and may also place their left hands on each other's shoulders while kissing both cheeks (Hickson, Stacks, & Moore, 2004).

Touch can indicate intimacy or hostility. It can be greatly misunderstood or incredibly needed. It can violate one's touch ethic as well as provide comfort and warmth (Anderson & Taylor, 2011). Touch is a powerful nonverbal behavior that says a lot about the relationships you're in as well as the person you are.

Physical Appearance

The final nonverbal code is physical appearance, which refers to observable traits of the body and its accessories and extensions. There are two reasons why it's important to make the connection between physical appearance and nonverbal communication: (1) The way you represent yourself and your physical appearance reveals a lot about who you are, and (2) the physical appearance of other people influences your perception of them, how you talk to them, how approachable they are, how attractive or unattractive they are, and so on. The level of physical attractiveness is an important dimension of physical appearance. Physical attractiveness is a perception of beauty derived from cultures. Each culture has a different idea about physical attractiveness. It is formed by features of our appearance such as height, weight, size, shape, and so on. In other words, there's a certain standard of physical appearance that dictates what is and is *not* attractive. Even though people have a limited amount of power to dramatically alter their physical appearances, others treat appearances as if they communicate important information. Teachers tend to judge attractive students as smarter and more social than less attractive students (Ritts, Patterson, & Tubbs, 1992), and attractive people often make more money in their jobs (Judge, Hurst, & Simon, 2009). Similarly, features of appearance like height, weight, and skin color are interpreted as important messages about who you are and what you're like. However, people misjudge one another on the basis of physical appearance so often that it is worth questioning whether you can make correct attributions about other people based on aspects of their appearance. Clothing and other objects you use to represent your identities, interests, and backgrounds are also a part of physical appearance. You may wear glasses, carry handbags, flaunt phones, wear jewelry, or sport tattoos to express who you are or how you would like to be seen. What personal artifacts, if any, are important to your appearance?

Body Type, Shape, and Size

Have you ever avoided interaction with someone because of his or her body shape or size? Generally, size and shape of our bodies communicate something nonverbally.

Luigi Novi

New Jersey governor Chris Christie himself had to experience the judgments and stereotypes that are triggered whenever people don't conform to the "standard" of physical appearance. When Christie deliberated whether to opt in or out of the presidential race in October 2011, the media went crazy over his body weight. He was mocked for his "puffed-up body," and was accused of being undisciplined (Puhl, 2011). Christie's qualifications were completely ignored. Instead, reports consisted of derogatory comments such as fat jokes and weight-related puns "providing a clear example of how socially acceptable weight bias and discrimination against obese persons have become in

our society" (Puhl, 2011). In Christie's case, people just assumed that he couldn't be an effective political leader due to his body weight. Does this surprise you? The sad truth is that discrimination due to physical appearance has become quite common in today's society, in which two thirds of Americans are now overweight or obese (Kaufman, 2011). Weight discrimination in the United States has increased by 66% over the past decade, and research has shown that it is the third most common type of discrimination for women and the fourth most common type for men.

When people negatively judge others on their physical appearance, they are denying them the opportunity to connect and engage with others. Ethical communication occurs when you pay attention to and evaluate the message of another person. You should strive not to let physical appearance characteristics get in the way of hearing others' ideas or thoughts.

QUESTIONS

1. From an ethical perspective, should physical appearance be a factor in voting decisions? What other nonverbal communication codes explained in this chapter do you pay attention to in political figures and leaders?

2. Many people present an altered or idealized version of their physical appearance in the Communication Age. When does altering your physical appearance online cross the line from permissible to unethical?

Scholars have even developed a system called somatyping that classifies people according to their body type (Sheldon, Stevens, & Tucker, 1942).

Shape and size also matter when it comes to judging physical appearance. The perception of body weight varies from culture to culture. Especially in American culture there seems to be an obsession with body weight; however, in other cultures around the world body weight isn't that big of a deal. Many of you probably feel like you have to look as perfect as the models in the commercials on TV, on billboards, in magazines, and so on. Such portrayals in the media make money off of people's weight insecurities. The opposite problem of obesity also has grown to be a real problem in today's society. The detrimental effects obesity can have on health lead Americans to spend a lot of time listening to messages or reading books about weight loss.

Height and status play a huge role in the process of deciding who's attractive and who's not. Tall and handsome men are favored by heterosexual women in American culture. For women the issue seems a little more complicated. Like men, tall women with long legs are seen to be more attractive. Yet women who gained above-average height during their puberty years feel like they are at a disadvantage socially and professionally because they can appear intimidating to men due to their height.

IMPROVING YOUR NONVERBAL COMMUNICATION SKILLS

Connecting with others is an essential component of the Communication Age. How do you nonverbally communicate your connection and engagement with others? Nonverbal immediacy is defined as the use of closeness-inducing nonverbal behavioral cues (Andersen, 1979). These behaviors include touching someone in a nonviolent manner, smiling, orientating your body toward the other person, looking at the person, or using vocal cues in an animated fashion. Many communication scholars have found that nonverbal immediacy helps produce liking (McCroskey & Richmond, 1992). The effects of nonverbal immediacy have been demonstrated in many different contexts. Doctors who are nonverbally immediate have patients who are more satisfied (Conlee & Olvera, 1993). Coaches who utilize nonverbal immediacy behaviors are able to create better groups of athletes (Turman, 2008). In the classroom, teachers who engage in nonverbal immediacy behaviors have students who learn more (Christensen & Menzel, 1998). In other words, the more nonverbally immediate you are, the more others will like you, work with you, and learn from you. Positive nonverbal immediacy behaviors can help you to improve your nonverbal communication skills. To promote the development of your nonverbal communication skills, use the "Assess Your Communication" feature to check your nonverbal immediacy score.

ASSESS YOUR COMMUNICATION

Nonverbal Immediacy Scale-Observer Report (NIS-O)

This measure will allow you to assess your own nonverbal immediacy behaviors.

Directions: The following statements describe the ways some people behave while talking with or to others. Please indicate in the space at the left of each item the degree to which you believe the statement applies to you, using the following 5-point scale:

1 = Never; 2 = Rarely; 3 = Occasionally; 4 = Often; 5 = Very Often

_____ 1. I use my hands and arms to gesture while talking to people.

_____ 2. I touch others on the shoulder or arm while talking to them.

_____ 3. I use a monotone or dull voice while talking to people.

_____ 4. I look over or away from others while talking to them.

_____ 5. I move away from others when they touch me while we are talking.

_____ 6. I have a relaxed body position when I talk to people.

_____ 7. I frown while talking to people.

_____ 8. I avoid eye contact while talking to people.

_____ 9. I have a tense body position while talking to people.

_____ 10. I sit or stand close to people while talking with them.

_____ 11. My voice is monotonous or dull when I talk to people.

_____ 12. I use a variety of vocal expressions when I talk to people.

_____ 13. I gesture when I talk to people.

_____ 14. I am animated when I talk to people.

_____ 15. I have a bland facial expression when I talk to people.

_____ 16. I move closer to people when I talk to them.

_____ 17. I look directly at people while talking to them.

_____ 18. I am stiff when I talk to people.

_____ 19. I have a lot of vocal variety when I talk to people.

_____ 20. I avoid gesturing while I am talking to people.

_____ 21. I lean toward people when I talk to them.

_____ 22. I maintain eye contact with people when I talk to them.

_____ 23. I try not to sit or stand close to people when I talk with them.

_____ 24. I lean away from people when I talk to them.

_____ 25. I smile when I talk to people.

_____ 26. I avoid touching people when I talk to them.

Scoring for NIS-O:

Step 1. Start with a score of 78. Add the scores from the following items:

1, 2, 6, 10, 12, 13, 14, 16, 17, 19, 21, 22, and 25.

Step 2. Add the scores from the following items:

3, 4, 5, 7, 8, 9, 11, 15, 18, 20, 23, 24, and 26.

Total Score = Step 1 minus Step 2

How did you score? What surprised you about your score? You can also try the NIS-O on others. Simply fill out the measure with another person's behaviors in mind. For instance, you might find it interesting to fill out the survey for your least and most favorite professors to determine whether their nonverbal immediacy might play some role in the degree to which you like them. Do you notice differences in their use of nonverbal immediacy behaviors? Have you learned more in one class? What class do you enjoy more?

Source: Richmond, McCroskey, & Johnson (2003).

NONVERBAL COMMUNICATION
AND CONVERGENCE

The study of nonverbal communication is especially important to convergence in the Communication Age (Darics, 2010; Kalman & Rafaeli, 2011; Robinson, 2010). People are now using new media and the latest technology to replace nonverbal messages seen in face-to-face encounters, forcing new kinds of communal bonds and definitions of place (Erickson, 2010; Soukup, 2006). No longer do people need to only meet face to face to send nonverbal messages. How you come across through computer-mediated communication is very similar to how you meet people face to face. Consider the following nonverbal codes and think critically about how you present yourself nonverbally using computer-mediated communication and other forms of new media:

- Physical appearance
- Voice
- Facial and eye expressions
- Gestures
- Touch

How do you present yourself nonverbally using new media?

Scholar Erving Goffman's research on how people present or represent themselves in everyday life is applicable to the Communication Age. Goffman (1959) suggests that "the expressiveness of the individual (and therefore his [*sic*] capacity to give impressions) appears to solve two radically different kinds of sign activity: the expression that he *gives,* and the expression that he *gives off*" (p. 2). What people *give* refers to verbal communication occurring in face-to-face settings. The *giving off* part is nonverbal (e.g., facial expressions, gestures, body movements; Martey & Stromer-Galley, 2007). Common nonverbal cues may be altered in computer-mediated communication, but we as communicators still *give off* these cues to assist in the communication of the verbal message and to connect our self to others online (Li, Jackson, & Trees, 2008).

Reflecting on the sense of play fostered by technology, Sherry Turkle (1995) suggests that "the computer offers us both new models of mind and a new medium on which to project our ideas and fantasies" (p. 1). "Life on the screen," she explains, "makes it very easy to present oneself as other than one is in real life" (p. 228). As we explained in Chapter 2, avatars are ways that computer users express themselves with digital representations. Avatars allow users to visually and nonverbally express human characteristics and emotions (Li et al., 2008). One study examined how participants in the online community known as The Palace used avatars and props to manage space and express themselves (Soukup, 2004). The research determined that the placement and actions of avatars expressed computer users' closeness of relationship to others (proxemics). These embodiments of computer users represent extensions of the self—yet another nonverbal means of expressing oneself in a virtual community. Since many of your daily actions, interactions, and experiences are mediated by technology, it's important to think about how you express yourself and how this form of expression changes your understanding of nonverbal communication and personal identity as face-to-face and mediated experience blend in the Communication Age (Erickson, 2010; Ha & Lennon, 2010; Walther, Loh, & Granka, 2005).

Communication unplugged

TO IMPROVE COMMUNICATION, BALANCE YOUR FACE-TO-FACE INTERACTIONS AND ONLINE PERSONA

It's no secret that many people work hard to craft an online persona that portrays them in the best possible light. However, crafting an online persona (especially regarding Facebook) takes a person out of the more dynamic, immediate setting of face-to-face interaction. As you move forward in your social and professional life, you must still have the ability to communicate yourself to others in nonmediated contexts. Researcher Neil James Henderson identifies the "commodification of the self" on Facebook and its role in "flattening" the available interactivity of the online self (Henderson, 2014). Henderson analyzes the short film *Noah* (2013), wherein an adolescent boy attempts to build relationships strictly through computer-mediated platforms. The story shows the breakdown of a relationship mainly due to vague, computer-mediated nonverbal cues and lack of immediate feedback. The story serves as an example that many intimate relationships can have difficulties when there is not enough face-to-face interaction to complement the online communication.

The online self, while problematic, can still assist certain "face-to-face" interactions; Skype and Chatroulette offer a very close approximation of face-to-face communication in that they both take place in real time, offer video to provide eye contact and body language feedback, and allow for the analysis of vocalics. Furthermore, research has indicated that face-to-face networks have a larger effect of satisfaction than do their Facebook system counterparts (Wright, Rosenberg, Egbert, Ploeger, Bernard, & King, 2013).

WHAT TO DO NEXT
To increase the effectiveness of your face-to-face interactions, try to:

- **Address body language.** This perhaps sets face-to-face communication apart from any other. We express emotions through body language, and the immediacy of face-to-face communication offers valuable insight into a relationship.

- **Make eye contact.** This conveys a great deal about what we are communicating. Eye contact is very important in terms of first impressions.

- **Make sure to listen.** While this may sound obvious, face-to-face interaction does not carry the same luxury as, for example, e-mail. Unlike e-mail, where you can reread the other person's message multiple times before replying, face-to-face communication requires you to be an active listener.

Think critically about how computer-mediated communication and social networking will influence nonverbal communication. The study of nonverbal communication is only going to become more crucial in the Communication Age. It is your job and responsibility to be aware of and understand how nonverbal messages are impacted by convergence in the Communication Age.

1 Identify the importance of nonverbal communication in your life.

Nonverbal communication includes all the ways people communicate without using words. Nonverbal communication can include your clothing, your physical appearance, your gestures, your facial and eye expressions, and more.

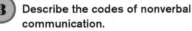 Saying What You Mean: A Children's Book About Communication Skills

2 Explain the functions of nonverbal communication as it works with verbal communication.

Nonverbal communication has different functions. These functions include repeating, accenting, conflicting, complementing, regulating, and substituting.

Decoding Body Language

3 Describe the codes of nonverbal communication.

In order to understand nonverbal communication better, people study the different codes that define nonverbal communication. These codes are vocalic, kinesics, proxemics, environment, facial expressions, eye behavior, haptics, and physical appearance.

The Proxemic Project

How Well Do You Read Other People? A Body Language Quiz

4 Describe the impact nonverbal communication has in a variety of situations.

Emblems, illustrators, affect displays, regulators, and adapters, or the five categories of kinesics, are important to keep in mind when dealing with nonverbal communication in a variety of situations. Be aware of cultural differences. In some cultures these same emblems might have a completely different meaning, and to avoid an uncomfortable situation you need to be culturally sensitive.

Dressing for a Job Interview

Checking Your Tone in E-Mail Messages

5 Examine how nonverbal communication is influenced in the Communication Age.

All nonverbal codes are influenced in the Communication Age with new media. The latest technology to replace nonverbal messages seen in face-to-face encounters promotes new kinds of social connections and understanding of space.

 Using Emojis at Work

KEY TERMS

 Review key terms with eFlashcards. **edge.sagepub.com/edwards2e**

Adapters 83
Affect displays 82
Chronemics 89
Contact culture 95
Contamination 86

Deception cues 92
Deintensification 91
Emblems 82
Emoji 91
Emoticons 91

Environment 86
Gestures 81
Haptics 92
Illustrators 82
Impression management 87

REFLECT

1. How prevalent is nonverbal communication in your life? In what situations is nonverbal communication appropriate, and when should you be more cautious about it?

2. Based on your experience with nonverbal communication, which of the named functions of nonverbal communication is most used in everyday life? How do these functions enhance or maybe even worsen our interactions with others?

3. Which perception of environment can you best relate to, and why? How has the environment shaped your communication interaction before?

4. How does your online nonverbal behavior differ from your face-to-face nonverbal behavior? Do you feel more comfortable in an online or a face-to-face interaction, and why?

REVIEW

To check your answers go to **edge.sagepub.com/edwards2e**

1. What is nonverbal communication?

2. Define kinesics.

3. _____ is a perception of beauty derived from cultures.

4. The process of controlling facial expressions to erase or numb how you really feel is called_____.

5. _____ means hiding an expression connected to a felt emotion and replacing it with an expression more appropriate to the situation.

6. List the different types of touch.

7. Scholars have developed a system called _____, which classifies people according to their body type.

8. _____ is defined as the use of closeness-inducing nonverbal behavioral cues.

9. Explain why the study of nonverbal communication is important to convergence in the Communication Age.